Exam Ref AZ-104 Microsoft Azure Administrator Certification and Beyond
Second Edition

A pragmatic guide to achieving the Azure administration certification

Riaan Lowe

Donovan Kelly

BIRMINGHAM—MUMBAI

Exam Ref AZ-104 Microsoft Azure Administrator Certification and Beyond
Second Edition

Group Product Manager: Rahul Nair

Publishing Product Manager: Niranjan Naikwadi

Senior Editor: Arun Nadar

Content Development Editor: Nihar Kapadia

Technical Editor: Rajat Sharma

Copy Editor: Safis Editing

Project Coordinator: Ajesh Devavaram

Proofreader: Safis Editing

Indexer: Manju Arasan

Production Designer: Shankar Kalbhor

Marketing Coordinator: Nimisha Dua

Senior Marketing Coordinator: Sanjana Gupta

First published: May 2019

Second edition: June 2022

Production reference: 1140622

Published by Packt Publishing Ltd.

Livery Place

35 Livery Street

Birmingham

B3 2PB, UK.

ISBN 978-1-80181-954-1

www.packt.com

First off, I would like to thank God for the opportunities and intellectual blessing in my life. To my loving wife, Michelle, who always supported me through this process and all the late-evening hot chocolate sessions to get through the work. To my parents, Andrew, Marion, Alf, and Erna – thank you for always believing in me. Lastly, I would like to thank my two loving dogs, Max and Teddy, for being part of my stress relief program when things got hectic.

– Riaan Lowe

To my beautiful and loving wife – thank you for all the support and many sacrifices you have endured with me in making the writing of this book possible. To my kids, Tyler and Bella – thank you for your never-ending enthusiasm, energy, and love. You are the fun and joy in my life. I love you all!

– Donovan Kelly

Contributors

About the authors

Riaan Lowe is a cloud security architect and has been in the industry for nearly 10 years. He is a firm believer in *practice what you preach* and, therefore, has attained the following relevant certifications, among others: Microsoft Certified Solutions Expert in Azure, Azure Administrator, Azure Security Engineer, Microsoft Certified Solutions Associate (Server), Microsoft Certified Professional, Microsoft Specialist in Virtualization, and Microsoft Certified Trainer. His passion is cloud and cybersecurity, and he likes to share his hard-gained knowledge based on real-world experiences with customers.

One of his favorite quotes is, *"Find a job you enjoy doing, and you will never have to work a day in your life"* (Mark Twain).

Donovan Kelly is an Azure architect lead with extensive experience in presales, engineering, architecting, and leading teams. He has over 8 years of experience in the public cloud space and over 10 years of experience working in both solution and technical architecture.

Donovan has many Microsoft Azure certifications, including AZ-900, AZ-103, AZ-104, AZ-303, AZ-304, and AZ-500. His passion for training and sharing knowledge with others has culminated in the work on this book, in the hope that those who read it will find value in its pages and learn from the experiences of others that live and breathe this environment daily.

One of his favorite quotes is, *"Two roads diverged in a wood; I took the one less traveled by, and that has made all the difference"* (Robert Frost).

"All glory to my father, God, who has blessed me with my abilities and opportunities; without Him, all this would not be possible.

I am grateful to those who have given me the opportunity to learn and grow. To all the instrumental leaders in my life – thank you for pushing me to be more. Thanks to my parents for teaching me about a life of gratitude and love, and for always being there for me. Special thanks to Riaan for being pivotal in starting my journey as an author."

About the reviewer

Ricardo Cabral, based in Portugal, is a licensed computer engineer. He has several Microsoft certifications, and he also is a **Microsoft Certified Trainer** (**MCT**). He has worked in both administration and development roles, with several years of experience in IT management, development, and projects. He now works as an Azure solution architect and IT trainer. In his free time, he actively participates in, volunteers for, speaks at, and organizes technical community meetings.

"I'd like to thank my family, all my friends, and a special thanks to Eugenia Azevedo, who helped guide me in my decisions and encouraged me in everything that I do. I'd also like to thank Packt Publishing for the opportunity to review this wonderful book."

Table of Contents

3
Creating and Managing Governance

4
Managing Governance and Costs

5

Practice Labs – Managing Azure Identities and Governance

Part 2: Implementing and Managing Storage

6

Understanding and Managing Storage

7

Securing Storage

8

Practice Labs – Implementing and Managing Storage

Part 3: Deploying and Managing Azure Compute Resources

9

Automating VM Deployments Using ARM Templates

10

Configuring Virtual Machines

11

Creating and Configuring Containers

12

Creating and Configuring App Services

13

Practice Labs – Deploying and Managing Azure Compute Resources

Part 4: Configuring and Managing Virtual Networking

14

Implementing and Managing Virtual Networking

15

Securing Access to Virtual Networks

16

Configuring Load Balancing

17
Integrating On-Premises Networks with Azure

18
Monitoring and Troubleshooting Virtual Networking

19
Practice Labs – Configuring and Managing Virtual Networking

Part 5: Monitoring and Backing Up Azure Resources

20

Monitoring Resources with Azure Monitor

21

Implementing Backup and Recovery Solutions

22
Practice Labs – Monitoring and Backing Up Azure Resources

23
Mockup Test Questions and Answers

Index

Other Books You May Enjoy

Preface

In this book, we will take you on a journey to navigate the Azure landscape and become confident in managing Azure like a professional. The skills in this book have been designed to not only enable candidates to pass confidently but also to apply their skills in their daily roles working in Azure. We have taken a pragmatic approach to the delivery of the material to cater to various levels of readers. This book helps cement a good foundation for becoming an Azure master.

Who this book is for

This book is targeted toward cloud administrators, engineers, and architects who are looking to understand Azure better, who want to gain a firm grasp on administrative functions, and who intend to take the Microsoft Azure Administrator (AZ-104) exam.

What this book covers

Chapter 1, *Managing Azure Active Directory Objects*, teaches you how to create and manage users and groups within Azure AD.

Chapter 2, *Managing Role-Based Access Control*, covers role-based access control.

Chapter 3, *Creating and Managing Governance*, looks at establishing governance in Azure and creating the mechanisms for managing it.

Chapter 4, *Managing Governance and Costs*, explores how to manage resources and services available in Azure that support governance objectives.

Chapter 5, *Practice Labs – Managing Azure Identities and Governance*, gives you hands-on experience testing your skills on identities and governance.

Chapter 6, *Understanding and Managing*, delves into understanding, creating, configuring, and managing storage.

Chapter 7, *Securing Storage*, teaches you about securing storage on the Azure platform.

Chapter 8, Practice Labs – Implementing and Managing Storage, gives you hands-on experience testing your skills in implementing and managing storage.

Chapter 9, Automating VM Deployments Using ARM Templates, explores how to read and modify ARM templates and how to deploy resources using ARM templates.

Chapter 10, Configuring Virtual Machines, examines virtual machines and the management of networking, high-availability, and host configurations.

Chapter 11, Creating and Configuring Containers, covers configuring the sizing and scaling of containers, working with Azure container instances, working with **Azure Kubernetes Service** (**AKS**) storage, scaling AKS, and the networking side of AKS.

Chapter 12, Creating and Configuring App Services, teaches you how to create and configure app services in Azure.

Chapter 13, Practice Labs – Deploying and Managing Azure Compute Resources, offers hands-on experience of managing Azure compute resources.

Chapter 14, Implementing and Managing Virtual Networking, shows you how to create and configure virtual networks, peer networks with each other, configure private and public IP addresses, create user-defined network routes, implement subnets, create endpoints on subnets, configure private endpoints, and finally, how to configure Azure DNS, including custom DNS settings and private or public DNS zones.

Chapter 15, Securing Access to Virtual Networks, shows you how to create security rules and associate a **network security group** (**NSG**) with a subnet or network interface. You will also learn how to effectively evaluate security rules and get hands-on deployment on Azure Firewall and Azure Bastion.

Chapter 16, Configuring Load Balancing, delves into Azure load balancing services, including creating and configuring an internal and public load balancer, configuring an Azure Application Gateway, creating health probes for your load balancer, and how to configure load balancing rules. The chapter will end with how to troubleshoot these load balancing services.

Chapter 17, Integrating On-Premises Networks with Azure, teaches you how to integrate your on-premises network with an Azure virtual network. This chapter is about VPN connections from your on-premises environment to Azure, creating an Azure VPN gateway, and how to configure a **Site-to-Site** (**S2S**) VPN using an on-premises server and the Azure VPN gateway. We will also explore Azure Virtual WAN and the capabilities it introduces.

Chapter 18, Monitoring and Troubleshooting Virtual Networking, looks at how to manage your virtual network connectivity and how to monitor and troubleshoot on-premises connectivity as well as use Network Watcher.

Chapter 19, Practice Labs – Configuring and Managing Virtual Networking, offers hands-on experience testing your skills in configuring and managing Azure virtual networking.

Chapter 20, Monitoring Resources with Azure Monitor, shows you how to monitor the rest of your Azure estate. We will explore the Azure Monitor service and explore the various components exposed through the service such as Metrics, Alerts, Log Analytics, and Application Insights.

Chapter 21, Implementing Backup and Recovery Solutions, explores how to configure backup and recovery solutions. This includes how to deploy a recovery services vault, configure backup policies, how restore operations work, and how to perform site-to-site recovery via Azure Site Recovery. The last portion will focus on how to configure backup reports.

Chapter 22, Practice Labs – Monitoring and Backing Up Azure Resources, gives you hands-on experience of monitoring and backing up Azure resources.

Chapter 23, Mockup Test Questions and Answers, lets you practice your skills on a mockup set of exam questions to prepare for taking the exam.

To get the most out of this book

You are expected to have a basic understanding of the Azure platform, but if you are astute, you may comfortably learn all concepts without having worked on the platform before by following all examples in the book. You should also understand the basic concepts of a public cloud and the services that are typically offered.

Software/hardware covered in the book	Operating system requirements
PowerShell 5.1 or later (preferably version 7) (Alternatively Azure Cloud Shell can be used)	Windows, macOS, or Linux
.NET Framework 4.7.2 or later	Windows
AZ PowerShell Module	Windows, macOS, or Linux
Azure subscription	N/A (browser required)

If you are using the digital version of this book, we advise you to type the code yourself or access the code from the book's GitHub repository (a link is available in the next section). Doing so will help you avoid any potential errors related to the copying and pasting of code.

Download the color images

We also provide a PDF file that has color images of the screenshots and diagrams used in this book. You can download it here: https://static.packt-cdn.com/downloads/9781801819541_ColorImages.pdf.

Conventions used

There are a number of text conventions used throughout this book.

Code in text: Indicates code words in text, database table names, folder names, filenames, file extensions, pathnames, dummy URLs, user input, and Twitter handles. Here is an example: "Tags will be applied to the resource named AZ104Storage."

A block of code is set as follows:

```
$tags = @{"Purpose"="Demo"}
$resource = Get-AzResource -Name AZ104Storage -ResourceGroup
AZ104-Chapter3
New-AzTag -ResourceId $resource.id -Tag $tags
```

Bold: Indicates a new term, an important word, or words that you see onscreen. For instance, words in menus or dialog boxes appear in **bold**. Here is an example: "Click on the **Assignments** menu on the left menu pane, then click **Assign policy**."

> **Tips or Important Notes**
> Appear like this.

Get in touch

Feedback from our readers is always welcome.

General feedback: If you have questions about any aspect of this book, email us at customercare@packtpub.com and mention the book title in the subject of your message.

Errata: Although we have taken every care to ensure the accuracy of our content, mistakes do happen. If you have found a mistake in this book, we would be grateful if you would report this to us. Please visit www.packtpub.com/support/errata and fill in the form.

Piracy: If you come across any illegal copies of our works in any form on the internet, we would be grateful if you would provide us with the location address or website name. Please contact us at copyright@packt.com with a link to the material.

If you are interested in becoming an author: If there is a topic that you have expertise in and you are interested in either writing or contributing to a book, please visit authors.packtpub.com.

Share Your Thoughts

Once you've read *Exam Ref AZ-104 Microsoft Azure Administrator Certification and Beyond*, we'd love to hear your thoughts! Scan the QR code below to go straight to the Amazon review page for this book and share your feedback.

https://packt.link/r/1-801-81954-8

Your review is important to us and the tech community and will help us make sure we're delivering excellent quality content.

Part 1: Managing Azure Identities and Governance

This is the first part of the official Microsoft exam objectives and will focus on how to manage identities within Azure, as well as governance.

This part of the book comprises the following chapters:

- *Chapter 1, Managing Azure Active Directory Objects*
- *Chapter 2, Managing Role-Based Access Control*
- *Chapter 3, Creating and Managing Governance*
- *Chapter 4, Managing Governance and Costs*
- *Chapter 5, Practice Labs – Managing Azure Identities and Governance*

1
Managing Azure Active Directory Objects

This first chapter of this book is focused on learning how to manage **Azure Active Directory** (**Azure AD**) objects. In this chapter, you will learn how to create and manage users and groups within Azure AD, including user and group properties. Additionally, we will look at Azure AD's **administrative units** (**AUs**) and discover how to create them alongside managing device settings and performing bulk user updates. You will also learn how to manage guest accounts within Azure AD, configure Azure AD join, and configure **Self-Service Password Reset** (**SSPR**).

In brief, in this chapter, the following topics will be covered:

- Creating Azure AD users and groups
- Creating AUs
- Managing user and group properties
- Managing device settings
- Performing bulk user updates

- Managing guest accounts
- Configuring Azure AD join
- Configuring SSPR

Technical requirements

In order to follow along with the hands-on exercises, you will need access to Azure AD as a global administrator. If you do not have access to this, students can enroll for a free account at https://azure.microsoft.com/en-in/free/.

An Azure AD Premium P1 license is also required for some of the sections. Luckily, there is also a free 1-month trial for students at https://azure.microsoft.com/en-us/trial/get-started-active-directory/.

Creating Azure AD users and groups

Azure AD offers a directory and identity management solution within the cloud. It offers traditional username and password identity management, alongside roles and permissions management. On top of that, it offers more enterprise-grade solutions, such as **Multi-Factor Authentication** (**MFA**) and application monitoring, solution monitoring, and alerting.

Azure AD can easily be integrated with your on-premises Active Directory to create a hybrid infrastructure.

Azure AD offers the following pricing plans:

- **Free**: This offers the most basic features, such as support for **single sign-on** (**SSO**) across Azure, Microsoft 365, and other popular SaaS applications, Azure **Business-to-Business** (**B2B**) for external users, support for Azure AD Connect synchronization, self-service password change, user and group management, and standard security reports.

- **Office 365 Apps**: Specific Office 365 subscriptions also provide some functionality such as user and group management, cloud authentication, including pass-through authentication, password hash synchronization, seamless SSO, and more.

- **Premium P1**: This offers advanced reporting, MFA, Conditional Access, **Mobile Device Management** (**MDM**) auto-enrollment, Azure AD Connect Health, advanced administration such as dynamic groups, self-service group management, and Microsoft Identity Manager.

- **Premium P2**: In addition to the Free and Premium P1 features, the Premium P2 license includes Azure AD Identity Protection, Privileged Identity Management, access reviews, and entitlement management.

> **Note**
>
> For a detailed overview of the different Azure AD licenses and all the features that are offered in each plan, you can refer to `https://www.microsoft.com/nl-nl/security/business/identity-access-management/azure-ad-pricing?rtc=1&market=nl`.

Creating users in Azure AD

We will begin by creating a couple of users in our Azure AD tenant from the Azure portal. To do this, perform the following steps:

1. Navigate to the Azure portal by opening a web browser and browsing to `https://portal.azure.com`.

2. In the left-hand menu, select **Azure Active Directory**.

3. Under the **Manage** blade of Azure AD in the left-hand menu, select **Users | All users**. Then, select the **+ New user** option from the top-level menu, as follows:

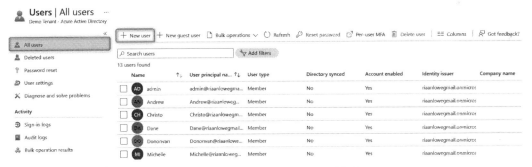

Figure 1.1 – The Azure AD Users blade

4. We are going to create three users. Add these values that are shown in the following screenshot:

-   **Name**: `PacktUser1`.

-   **User name**: The username is the identifier that the user enters to sign in to Azure AD. Select your domain name, which has been configured, and add this to the end of the username. The default is usually an **onmicrosoft.com** domain, but in my case, I have assigned a custom domain name, called **safezone.fun**. In the **First name** section, I have chosen `Packt`, and in the **Last name** section, I have added `User1`. Therefore, the **User name** value, in my case, will be `PacktUser1@ safezone.fun`:

Home > Contoso > Users >

New user   ...
Contoso

♡ Got feedback?

⦿ **Create user**	◯ **Invite user**
Create a new user in your organization. This user will have a user name like alice@m365x164803.onmicrosoft.com. I want to create users in bulk	Invite a new guest user to collaborate with your organization. The user will be emailed an invitation they can accept in order to begin collaborating. I want to invite guest users in bulk

Help me decide

Identity

User name * ⓘ	PacktUser1 ✓ @ safezone.fun ∨ 🗋
	The domain name I need isn't shown here
Name * ⓘ	PacktUser1 ✓
First name	Packt ✓
Last name	User1 ✓

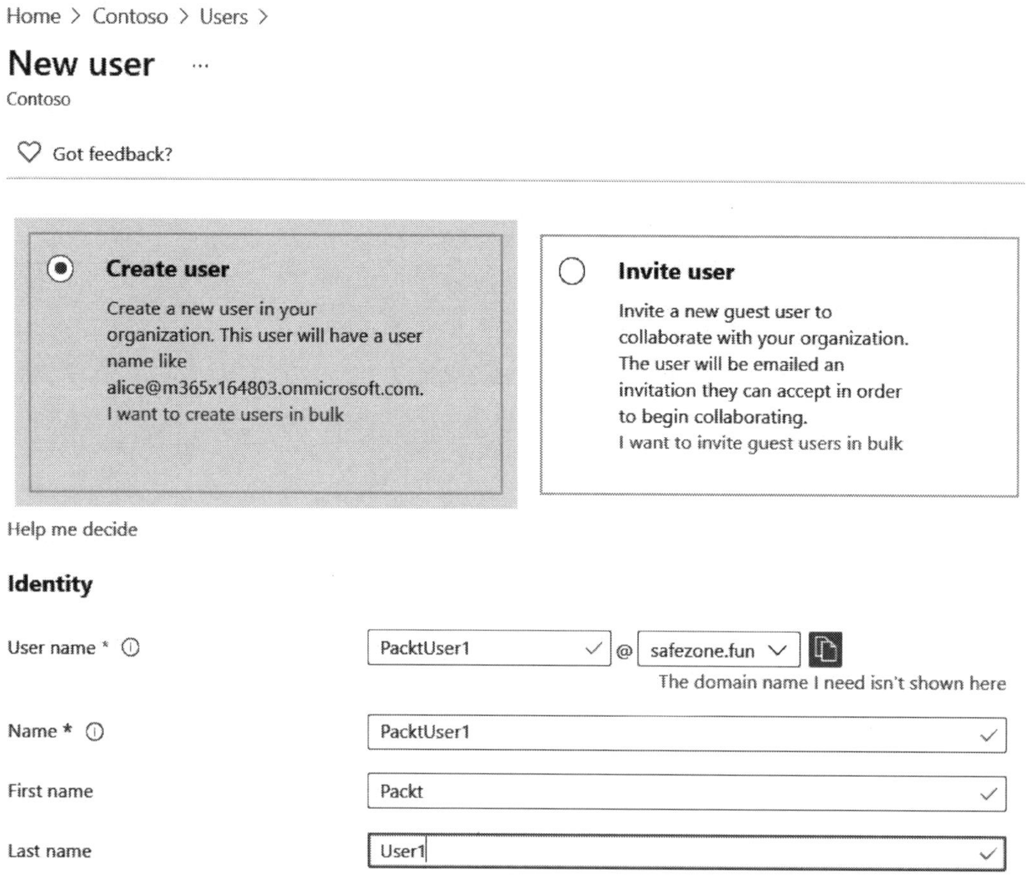

Figure 1.2 – The Azure AD user creation page part 1

5. Leave the sections under **Groups** and **Roles** in their default settings for now.

6. Next, we need to fill in information regarding the following:

- **Block sign in**: **No**
- **Usage location**: **South Africa**
- **Job title**: Azure administrator
- **Department**: IT
- **Company name**: Packt1
- **Manager**: **No manager selected**:

Groups and roles

Groups   0 groups selected

Roles   User

Settings

Block sign in   (Yes   No)

Usage location   South Africa   ∨

Job info

Job title   Azure administrator   ∨

Department   IT   ∨

Company name   Packt1   ∨

Manager   No manager selected

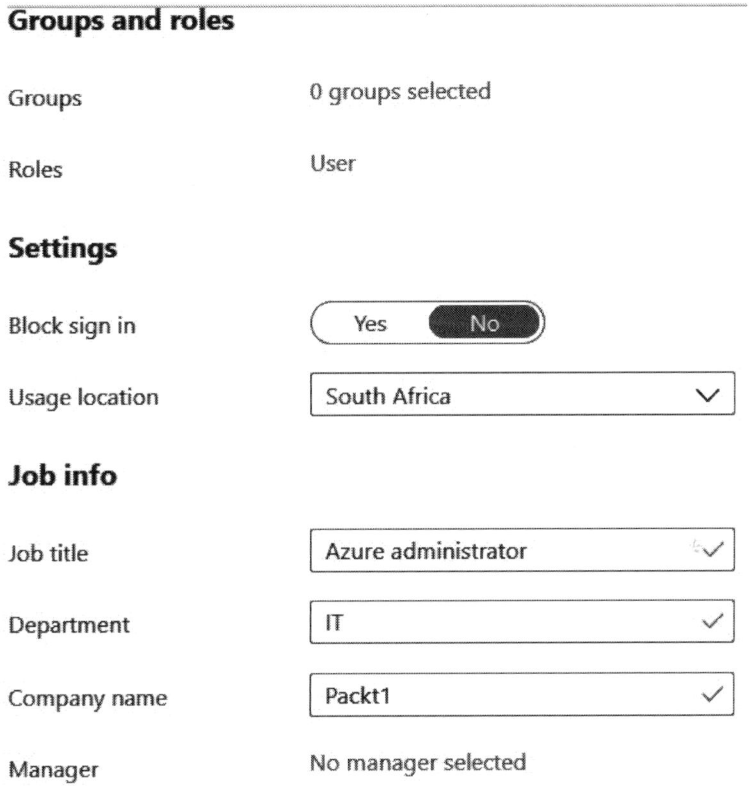

Figure 1.3 – The Azure AD user creation page part 2

7. Click on **Create**.

8. Repeat these steps to create two more users: **PacktUser2** and **PacktUser3**.

Now that we have created users in our Azure AD tenant, we can add them to a group in Azure AD.

Creating groups in Azure AD

There are two main group types, as follows:

- **Security groups**: These groups serve the same function as traditional on-premises groups, which is to secure objects within a directory. In this case, it is to secure objects within Azure AD.

- **Microsoft 365 groups**: These groups are used to provide a group of people access to a collection of shared resources that is not just limited to Azure AD but also includes shared mailboxes, calendars, SharePoint libraries, and other Microsoft 365-related services.

Security groups are used as container units to group users or devices together. There are three main membership types for security groups:

- **Assigned**: This is where you manually assign users to a group.

- **Dynamic user**: This is where you can specify parameters to automatically group users, for example, grouping all users who have the same job title.

- **Dynamic device**: This is where you can specify parameters to automatically group devices, for example, grouping all devices that have the same operating system version.

To create and manage groups from the Azure AD tenant in the Azure portal, you have to perform the following steps:

1. Navigate to the Azure portal by opening a web browser and browsing to `https://portal.azure.com`.

2. In the left-hand menu, select **Azure Active Directory**.

3. Under the **Manage** blade of Azure AD in the left-hand menu, select **Groups | All groups**. Then, select the **+ New group** option from the top-level menu, as follows:

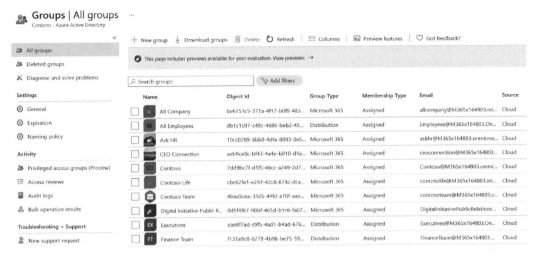

Figure 1.4 – The Azure AD group creation page part 1

4. Add the following values to create the new group:

-   **Group type: Security**

-   **Group name**: Azure Admins

-   **Group description**: Dynamic group for all Azure Admins

-   **Azure AD roles can be assigned to the group**: No

-   **Membership type**: Dynamic User

- **Owners: No owners selected:**

New Group   ...

Group type *   ⓘ

| Security | ⌄ |

Group name *   ⓘ

| Azure Admins | ✓ |

Group description   ⓘ

| Dynamic group for all Azure Admins | ✓ |

Azure AD roles can be assigned to the group (Preview)   ⓘ

(Yes   **No**)

Membership type *   ⓘ

| Dynamic User | ⌄ |

Owners

No owners selected

Dynamic user members *   ⓘ

Add dynamic query

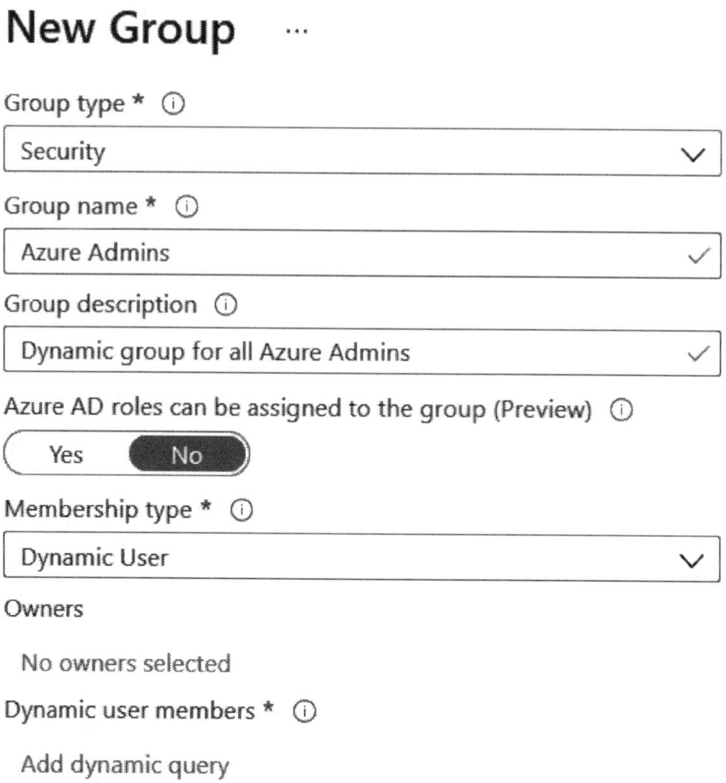

Figure 1.5 – The Azure AD group creation page part 2

5. Refer to the following screenshot to add a dynamic query.

For the **Dynamic Query** rule, the property is jobTitle, the operator is Equals, and the value is Azure administrator, as shown in the following screenshot:

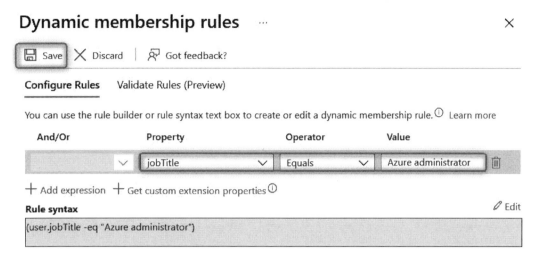

Figure 1.6 – The Azure AD group dynamic query

6.   Click on **Create**.

> **Tip**
> Remember that when using dynamic groups, a Premium P1 license needs to be assigned to the user.

Now that we have created the group, replication takes around 5 minutes. Refresh the Azure web page, and the users will appear as members of the Azure admins group that we just created:

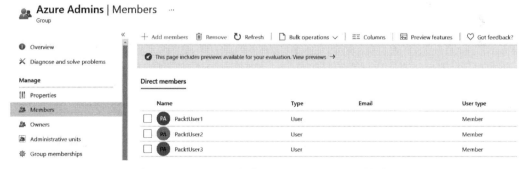

Figure 1.7 – The Azure AD group's dynamic group users added automatically based on the membership rules

In this section, we took a look at Azure AD users and groups and created a few accounts. We also created a dynamic membership group to include users via dynamic membership rules.

We encourage students to read up further by using the following links, which are based on Azure AD fundamentals such as adding users in Azure AD, assigning RBAC roles, creating Azure AD groups, and also creating dynamic groups in Azure AD:

- `https://docs.microsoft.com/en-us/azure/active-directory/fundamentals/add-users-azure-active-directory`

- `https://docs.microsoft.com/en-us/azure/active-directory/fundamentals/add-custom-domain`

- `https://docs.microsoft.com/en-us/azure/active-directory/fundamentals/active-directory-users-profile-azure-portal`

- `https://docs.microsoft.com/en-us/azure/active-directory/fundamentals/active-directory-users-assign-role-azure-portal`

- `https://docs.microsoft.com/en-us/azure/active-directory/enterprise-users/groups-create-rule`

- `https://docs.microsoft.com/en-us/azure/active-directory/enterprise-users/groups-dynamic-membership`

Next, we are going to look at Azure AUs, specifically where they can be used and how to create an AU.

Creating Azure AD AUs

Azure AD AUs are used in scenarios where granular administrative control is required. AUs have the following prerequisites:

- An Azure AD Premium P1 license is required for each AU administrator.
- An Azure AD Free license is required for AU members.
- A privileged role administrator or global administrator is required for configuration.

> **Tip**
> AUs can be created via the Azure portal or PowerShell.

The easiest way to explain AUs is by using a scenario. A company called Contoso is a worldwide organization with users across 11 countries. Contoso has decided that each country is responsible for its own users from an administrative point of view. That is where Azure AD AUs come in handy. With AUs, Contoso can group users per country and assign administrators that only have control over these users and cannot administrate users in other countries.

The following diagram displays a high-level overview of how AUs work in the same tenant across different departments. The following example is based on different regions:

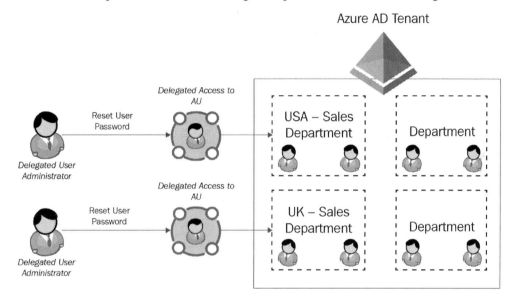

Figure 1.8 – An AU overview displaying the separation of users for US sales and UK sales

The following roles can be assigned within an AU:

- Authentication administrator
- Groups administrator
- Help desk administrator
- License administrator
- Password administrator
- User administrator

> **Important Note**
> Groups can be added to the AU as an object; therefore, any user within the group is not automatically part of the AU.

Now, let's go ahead and create an AU via the Azure portal:

1. Navigate to the Azure portal by opening a web browser and browsing to `https://portal.azure.com`.

2. In the left-hand menu, select **Azure Active Directory**.

3. Under the **Manage** blade of Azure AD in the left-hand menu, select **Administrative units** and click on **+ Add**:

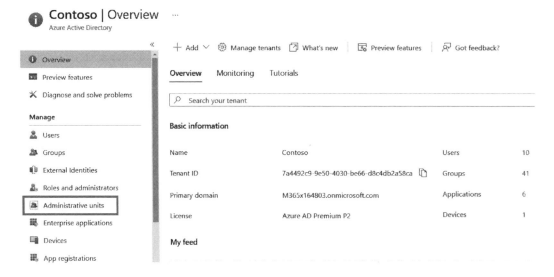

Figure 1.9 – The AU blade within Azure AD

4. Enter a name for the group. I'm using `South Africa Users`. In the **Description** field, it is best practice to add a brief description of what this AU is going to be used for:

Home > Contoso >

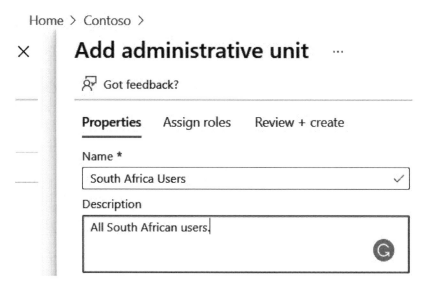

Figure 1.10 – The creation blade for an AU

5.   Next, under **Assign roles**, add the users that you want to be administrators based on the available roles. Then, select **Password administrator** and choose **PacktUser1**.

6.   Click on **Review + create**:

Figure 1.11 – The AU summary page

7. The next step is to add all the users you want **PacktUser1** to manage; in our case, we need to add **PacktUser1**, **PacktUser2**, and **PacktUser3**. On the left-hand side, under **Manage**, click on **Add member** and select the members:

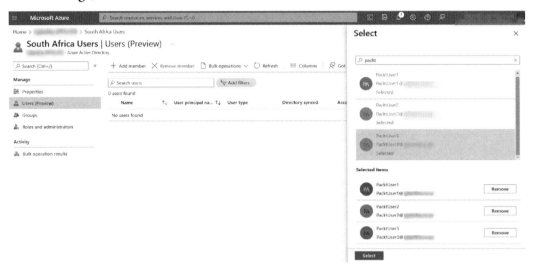

Figure 1.12 – Adding users to the AU

8. Now you will see that all three users have been added to the AU:

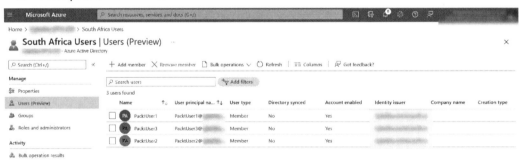

Figure 1.13 – Displaying the users added to the AU

9. You can now log in with **PacktUser1**, and you should be able to reset the password of **PacktUser2**.

> **Important Note**
>
> Remember, you need to assign an Azure AD P1 license to administrators within the AU.

In this section, we explained what an AU is and how it can be used. Additionally, we went through the creation of an AU step by step.

We encourage students to read up further by using the following links, which will provide additional information around AU management:

- `https://docs.microsoft.com/en-us/azure/active-directory/roles/admin-units-manage`
- `https://docs.microsoft.com/en-us/azure/active-directory/roles/admin-units-add-manage-users`

Now, let's move on and take a look at how to manage user and group properties.

Managing user and group properties

Part of an Azure administrator's task is to understand what can be done from a user and group perspective within Azure AD. Let's take a look at what we can configure for an Azure AD user account:

- **Profile**: This is where you can view and update information such as the name, user type, job information, and more.

- **Assigned roles**: This setting is where you can view all of the role assignments for that specific account; assignments can be in the form of eligible, active, or expired assignments.

- **Administrative units**: This setting displays the AUs that the user is part of.

- **Groups**: This setting displays the AD groups that the user is part of.

- **Applications**: This setting displays the application assignments.

- **Licenses**: This setting displays what licenses are currently assigned to the user account.

- **Devices**: This setting shows what devices are associated with the user account, including the join type such as Azure AD joined.

- **Azure role assignments**: This setting displays the resources on a subscription level to which the account has access.

- **Authentication methods**: This setting displays the authentication contact information, such as the phone number and email address for MFA. From here, you can also set the account to reregister for MFA or revoke current MFA sessions.

Now that we have reviewed all the user properties, let's take a look at the group settings.

Azure AD groups have the following settings available:

- **Overview**: This displays the membership type, the source directory, the object ID, the creation date, and more.

- **Properties**: This setting displays the general settings for the group, such as the group name, the description, the group type, and the membership type, which can be changed here.

- **Members**: This setting displays all of the current members of the group; bulk operations can also be performed from here.

- **Owners**: This setting displays the owners of the group who can modify the group and the members within it.

- **Administrative units**: This setting displays the AUs that the group is part of.

- **Group memberships**: This setting displays all of the security groups that the group belongs to (nested grouping).

- **Applications**: This setting displays the application assignments.

- **Licenses**: This setting displays the licenses that are assigned to the group, which group members will inherit automatically.

- **Azure role assignments**: This setting displays the resources of a subscription level to which the group members have access.

- **Dynamic membership rules**: This setting displays the configuration rules; for dynamic groups, this is where you can change the configuration rules, which will affect the members of the group.

And that brings an end to the user and group properties. In this section, we have looked at all of the different settings for Azure AD users and Azure AD groups.

We encourage students to read up further by using the following links, which will provide additional information around managing group settings via the command line and also dive into external user attribute flows:

- `https://docs.microsoft.com/en-us/azure/active-directory/enterprise-users/groups-settings-v2-cmdlets`

- `https://docs.microsoft.com/en-us/azure/active-directory/external-identities/user-flow-add-custom-attributes`

Next, we are going to look at how to manage device settings within Azure.

Managing device settings

Azure AD offers the ability to ensure that users are accessing Azure resources from devices that meet corporate security and compliance standards. Device management is the foundation of device-based conditional access, where you can ensure that access to the resources in your environment is only possible from managed devices.

Device settings can be managed from the Azure portal. To manage your device settings, your device needs to be registered or joined to Azure AD.

To manage the device settings from the Azure portal, you have to perform the following steps:

1. Navigate to the Azure portal by opening `https://portal.azure.com`.

2. In the left-hand menu, select **Azure Active Directory**.

3. In the Azure AD **Overview** blade, under **Manage**, select **Devices**, as follows:

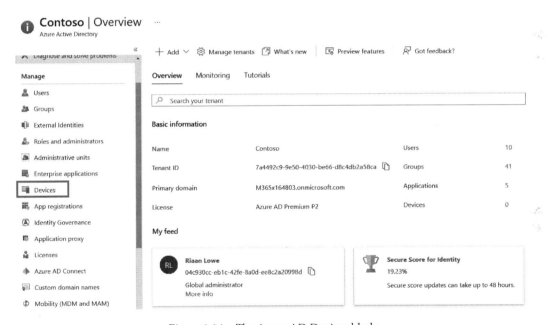

Figure 1.14 – The Azure AD Devices blade

The device management blade will open. Here, you can configure your device management settings, locate your devices, perform device management tasks, and review the device management-related audit logs.

4. To configure the device settings, select **Device settings** from the left-hand menu. From here, you can configure the following settings, which are shown in the following screenshot:

- **Users may join devices to Azure AD**: Here, you can set which users can join their devices to Azure AD. This setting is only applicable to Azure AD join on Windows 10.

- **Users may register their devices with Azure AD**: This setting needs to be configured to allow devices to be registered with Azure AD. There are two options here: **None**, that is, devices are not allowed to register when they are not Azure AD joined or hybrid Azure AD joined, and **All**, that is, all devices are allowed to register. Enrollment with Microsoft Intune or MDM for Office 365 requires registration. If you have configured either of these services, **All** is selected and **None** is not available.

- **Require Multi-Factor Authentication to register or join devices with Azure AD**: Here, you can request that the user is required to perform MFA when registering a device. Before you can enable this setting, MFA needs to be configured for the users who register their devices.

- **Maximum number of devices per user**: This setting allows you to select the maximum number of devices that a user can have in Azure AD.

- **Manage Additional local administrators on all Azure AD joined devices**: This setting allows you to add additional local administrators for Azure AD joined devices.

- **Manage Enterprise State Roaming settings**: This setting provides users with a unified experience across all of their Windows devices and reduces the turnaround time when configuring new devices:

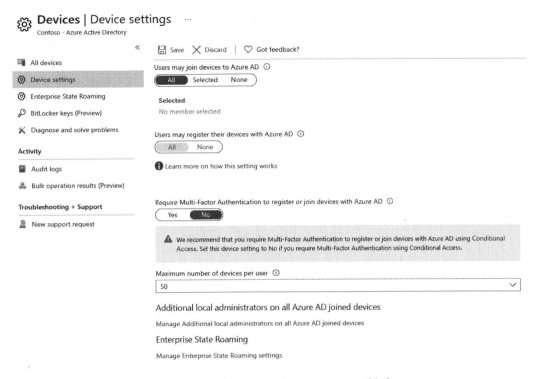

Figure 1.15 – The Azure AD Device settings blade

5. To locate your devices, under **Manage**, select **All devices**. In this overview, you will see all the joined and registered devices, as follows:

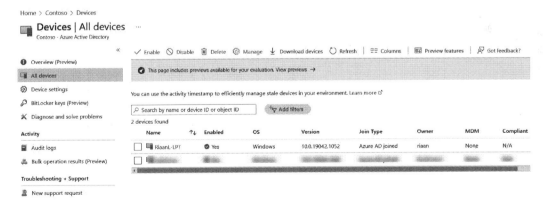

Figure 1.16 – The Azure AD All devices blade displaying all of the devices linked to Azure AD

6. Additionally, you can select the different devices from the list to get more detailed information about the device. From here, global administrators and cloud device administrators can **disable or delete** the device, as follows:

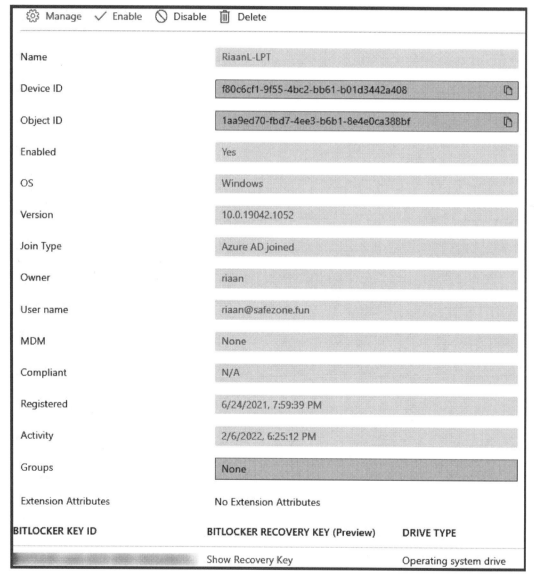

Figure 1.17 – The Azure AD device details for a specific device with the option
to disable or delete the selected device

7. To audit logs, under **Activity**, select **Audit logs**. From here, you can view and download the different log files. Additionally, you can create filters to search through the logs, as follows:

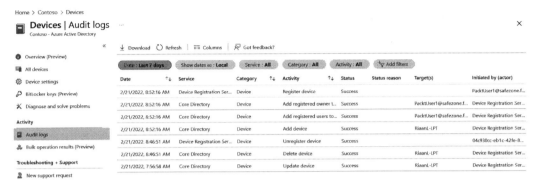

Figure 1.18 – The Azure AD device Audit logs blade

This concludes our section on how to manage your device settings via the Azure portal.

We encourage students to read up further by using the following links:

- https://docs.microsoft.com/en-us/azure/active-directory/devices/device-management-azure-portal
- https://docs.microsoft.com/en-us/microsoft-365/business/manage-windows-devices?view=o365-worldwide

Next, we are going to look at how to perform bulk user updates.

Performing bulk updates

Performing bulk user updates is similar to managing single users (such as internal and guest users). The only property that can't be set for multiple users is resetting the password. This has to be done for a single user.

Azure has also improved its bulk user settings by adding a drop-down menu that enables you to do the following via the downloadable CSV template and then re-uploading it:

- Bulk user creation
- Bulk user invitation
- Bulk user deletion
- Bulk user downloads

To perform a bulk user update, you have to perform the following steps:

1. Navigate to the **Users** overview blade again in Azure AD.

2. Select the **Bulk operations** drop-down menu:

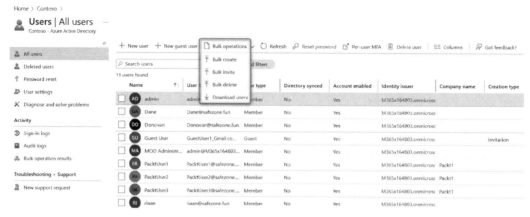

Figure 1.19 – The Azure AD bulk user operations option

3. From the menu, select the action you want to complete; for example, select **Download users**:

Figure 1.20 – The Azure AD bulk user download setting

4. Also, you can update multiple users by selecting them and choosing to delete them or configure MFA for each user:

Figure 1.21 – The alternative Azure AD method for bulk user operations

This concludes our demonstration on how to perform bulk user updates and how it works.

We encourage students to read up further by using the following links, which will look at adding bulk users:

- `https://docs.microsoft.com/en-us/azure/active-directory/`
  `enterprise-users/users-bulk-add`

- `https://docs.microsoft.com/en-us/azure/active-directory/`
  `enterprise-users/groups-bulk-import-members`

In the next section, we are going to cover how you can manage guest accounts.

Managing guest accounts

You can also add guest accounts in Azure AD using Azure AD B2B. Azure AD B2B is a feature on top of Azure AD that allows organizations to work safely with external users. To be added to Azure B2B, external users don't require a Microsoft work or personal account that has been added to an existing Azure AD tenant.

All sorts of accounts can be added to Azure B2B. You don't have to configure anything in the Azure portal to use B2B; this feature is enabled by default for all Azure AD tenants. Let's see how to manage guest accounts by performing the following steps:

1. Adding guest accounts to your Azure AD tenant is similar to adding internal users to your tenant. When you navigate to the **Users** overview blade, you can choose **+ New guest user** from the top-level menu, as follows:

Figure 1.22 – The Azure AD Users blade to add a new guest user

2. Then, you can provide an email address and a personal message, which is sent to the user's inbox. This personal message includes a link to log in to your tenant.

3. Select **Invite user** to add the user to your Azure AD tenant, and send an invitation to the user's inbox:

Figure 1.23 – Azure AD – inviting a guest user

4. To manage external users after creation, you can select them from the **Users** overview blade. They will have a **User type** value, which is named **Guest**. Simply select the user from the list, and you will be able to manage the settings that are displayed in the top-level menu for this user, as follows:

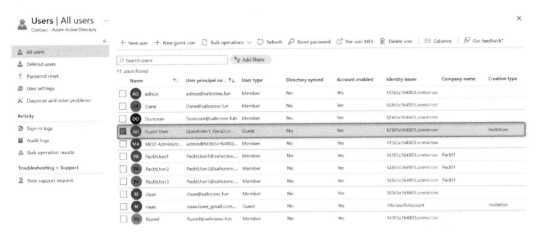

Figure 1.24 – The Azure AD Users blade displaying the account as Guest under User type

And that brings an end to this section. In this short section, we have reviewed guest accounts in Azure AD and learned how to configure them.

We encourage students to read up further by using the following links, which will provide additional information around restricting guest permissions: `https://docs.microsoft.com/en-us/azure/active-directory/enterprise-users/users-restrict-guest-permissions`.

In the next section, we are going to look at what Azure AD join is and how to configure it for Windows 10 devices.

Configuring Azure AD join

With Azure AD join, you are able to join devices directly to Azure AD without the need to join your on-premises Active Directory in a hybrid environment. While hybrid Azure AD join with an on-premises Active Directory might still be preferred for some scenarios, Azure AD join simplifies the process of adding devices and modernizes device management for your organization. This can result in the reduction of device-related IT costs.

Your users are getting access to corporate assets through their devices. To protect these corporate assets, you want to control these devices. This allows your administrators to ensure that your users are accessing resources from devices that meet your standards for security and compliance.

Azure AD join is a good solution when you want to manage devices with a cloud device management solution, modernize your application infrastructure, simplify device provisioning for geographically distributed users, and when your company is adopting Microsoft 365 as the productivity suite for your users.

Azure AD join can be deployed by using any of the following methods:

- **Bulk deployment**: This method is used to join large numbers of new Windows devices to Azure AD and Microsoft Intune.

- **Windows Autopilot**: This is a collection of technologies used to preconfigure Windows 10 devices so that the devices are ready for productive use. Autopilot can also be used to reset, repurpose, and recover devices.

- **Self-service experience**: This is also referred to as a *first-run experience*, which is mainly used to join a new device to Azure AD.

When it comes to joining devices to Azure AD, there are two main ways of managing those devices:

- **MDM only**: This is when the device is managed exclusively by an MDM provider such as Intune.

- **Comanagement**: This is when the device is managed by an MDM provider and **System Center Configuration Manager (SCCM)**.

When joining a Windows 10 device to Azure AD, there are two scenarios that we need to look at:

- Joining a new Windows 10 device via the **Out-of-Box Experience (OOBE)**.

- Joining an already configured Windows 10 device to Azure AD.

Let's take a look at how we can join an existing Windows 10 device to Azure AD:

1. On the Windows 10 device, search for **Settings** and open **Accounts**.

2. Select **Access work or school**, and choose **Connect**:

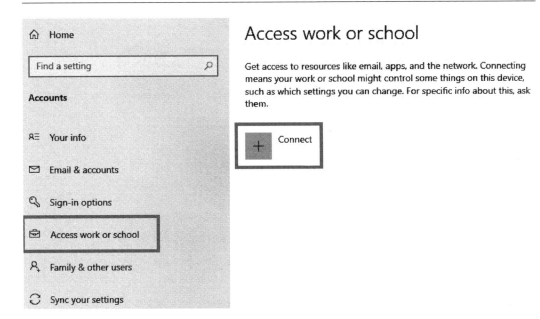

Figure 1.25 – The Windows 10 settings menu to add and connect a device to Azure AD

3. Under **Alternate actions**, choose **Join this device to Azure Active Directory**:

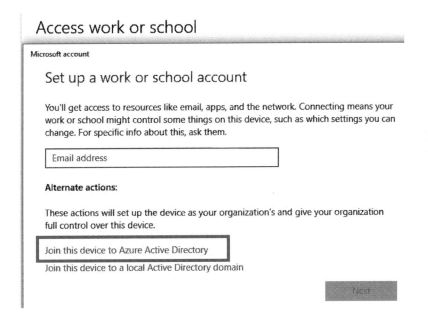

Figure 1.26 – The Windows 10 device with the selected option to join the device to Azure AD

4.   A new window will pop up and ask you to sign in. Sign in with your organization's account. In my case, this will be `PacktUser1@safezone.fun`:

Figure 1.27 – The Windows 10 device requires you to sign in to an
Azure AD account to join it to Azure AD

5. You will be prompted to verify whether you want to join your domain. Proceed by clicking on the **Join** button:

Make sure this is your organization

If you continue, system policies might be turned on or other changes might be made to your PC. Is this the right organization?

Connecting to: safezone.fun
User name: PacktUser1@safezone.fun
User type: Administrator

Figure 1.28 – The Windows 10 device summary page before joining it to Azure AD

And now the Windows 10 device has been successfully joined to Azure AD:

You're all set!

This device is connected to Contoso.

When you're ready to use this new account, select the Start button, select your current account picture, and then select '**Switch account**'. Sign in using your **PacktUser1@safezone.fun** email and password.

Figure 1.29 – The Windows 10 device has successfully been joined to Azure AD

6. As a final step, let's navigate to the Azure portal and under **Manage**, select **Devices**, and our newly Azure AD joined device will show up:

Figure 1.30 – Displaying the recently joined Windows 10 device in Azure AD under the Devices blade

That brings an end to this section. We have learned what Azure AD join is, the methods to enroll, and we have also shown the steps of how to manually join a Windows 10 device to Azure AD.

We encourage students to read up further by using the following links, which will provide additional information around Azure AD join, Windows Autopilot, and bulk device enrollment:

- `https://docs.microsoft.com/en-us/azure/active-directory/devices/concept-azure-ad-join`

- `https://docs.microsoft.com/en-us/mem/autopilot/windows-autopilot`

- `https://docs.microsoft.com/en-us/mem/intune/enrollment/windows-bulk-enroll`

- `https://docs.microsoft.com/en-us/azure/active-directory/devices/azuread-joined-devices-frx`

In the next section, we are going to take a look at SSPR.

Configuring SSPR

By enabling a self-service password for your users, they are able to change their passwords automatically, without calling the help desk. This will significantly eliminate the management overhead.

> **Note**
> The Azure AD free-tier license only supports cloud users for SSPR, and only password change is supported, not password reset.

SSPR can be easily enabled from the Azure portal. To do this, perform the following steps:

1. Navigate to the Azure portal by opening `https://portal.azure.com`.
2. In the left-hand menu, select **Azure Active Directory**.
3. In the Azure AD **Overview** blade, in the left-hand menu, under **Manage**, select **Password reset**, as follows:

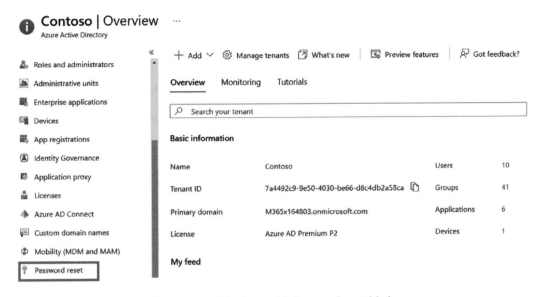

Figure 1.31 – The Azure AD Password reset blade

4. In the **Password reset** overview blade, you can enable SSPR for all your users, by selecting **All**, or for selected users and groups, by selecting **Selected**. For this demonstration, enable it for all users and click on **Save** in the top-level menu, as follows:

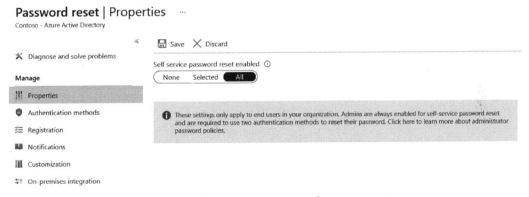

Figure 1.32 – The Azure AD Password reset properties

5. Next, we need to set the different required authentication methods for your users. To do this, under **Manage**, select **Authentication methods**.

6. In the next blade, we can set the number of authentication methods that are required to reset a password and explore what methods are available for your users, as follows:

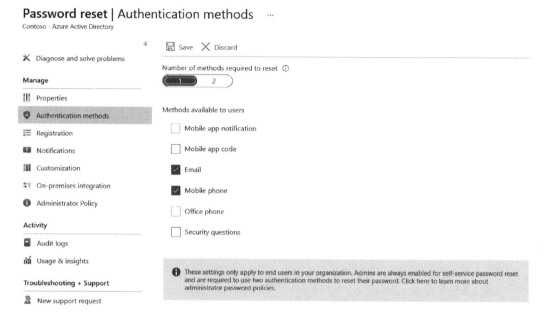

Figure 1.33 – The Azure AD Password reset blade displaying the available authentication methods for users

7. Make a selection and click on **Save**.

> **Important Note**
> If you want to test SSPR after configuration, make sure that you use a user account without administrator privileges.

We encourage students to read up further by using the following links:

- `https://docs.microsoft.com/en-us/azure/active-directory/authentication/concept-sspr-howitworks`

- `https://docs.microsoft.com/en-us/azure/active-directory/authentication/tutorial-enable-sspr`

Summary

In this chapter, we discussed how to create Azure AD users via the Azure portal, how to create a dynamic group, and how to add users to that dynamic group. We addressed user and group properties. Additionally, we discussed the different bulk user operations and how to create a guest account from the Azure portal. Finally, we discussed how to join a Windows 10 device to Azure AD and how to enable the configuration options for SSPR.

In the next chapter, we'll cover **Role-Based Access Control** (**RBAC**) and get hands-on with creating custom RBAC roles. Additionally, we will learn how to interpret role assignments.

2
Managing Role-Based Access Control

This chapter is focused on managing **Role-Based Access Control** (**RBAC**), and you will learn what RBAC is and how to apply it at the different scope levels. This chapter also covers how to create and assign custom RBAC roles and how to interpret RBAC roles within the Azure portal.

In brief, the following topics will be covered in this chapter:

- Creating a custom role
- Providing access to resources by assigning roles at different scopes
- Interpreting access assignments

> **Important Note**
>
> Azure makes use of an additive model when there are overlapping permissions for a specific user: `https://docs.microsoft.com/en-us/azure/role-based-access-control/overview#multiple-role-assignments`.

Technical requirements

In order to follow this chapter hands-on, you will need access to an Azure Active Directory tenant as a global administrator. If you do not have access to one, you can enroll with a free account: `https://azure.microsoft.com/en-in/free/`.

You will also need an Azure subscription of which you have owner permissions with a resource group deployed and a virtual machine of any size that is part of the resource group.

Creating a custom RBAC role

RBAC is a general term used for restricting access to users, based on a role. It works on the **Just Enough Access (JEA)** concept where a specific user/group will be provided minimum access to perform their specific job on a specific resource. Custom roles can only be created and updated by a user who has the following role assigned: `Microsoft.Authorization/roleDefinitions/write permissions`.

When it comes to RBAC, it is very important to understand how and where it is applied. Azure RBAC can be applied to the following security principals:

- User
- Group
- Service principal
- Managed identity

Now that we know what security principals support RBAC, the next step is to have a look at role definitions. A *role definition* is a collection of permissions that can be applied to security principals; however, in Azure, this is referred to as a **role**. A role is what determines what operations are allowed – for example, read access, write access, or the deletion of resources.

The following are some built-in roles within Azure:

- **Owner role**: This is the role that includes all permissions; you can read, add, and remove resources. You also have the capability to add and remove other users to and from resources as owners or other roles.
- **Contributor role**: This role has the same permission as an owner, except you cannot add or remove additional users to and from resources.
- **Reader role**: This role has the ability to view resources, but cannot amend, add, or remove users or resources.

There are multiple built-in roles within Azure, and it is recommended that you have a look at them: `https://docs.microsoft.com/en-us/azure/role-based-access-control/built-in-roles`.

The next part is to understand scope. **Scope** is the target resource that you need to assign a role to. In Azure, there are mainly four scope levels that roles can be assigned to:

- Management group
- Subscription
- Resource group
- Resource

The following diagram displays the main scope levels in Azure:

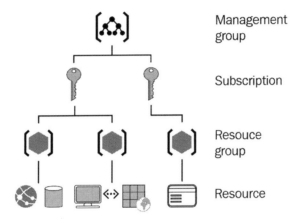

Figure 2.1 – A visual representation of the scope levels in Azure

In summary, RBAC consists of three main sections:

- **Security principal**: Selects who is going to have access
- **Role**: Selects what type of access is going to be assigned to the security principal
- **Scope**: Selects the resource that the user and the role will be applied to

Now that we understand built-in RBAC roles within Azure, let's take a look at custom RBAC roles.

> **Note**
>
> Azure **Active Directory** (**AD**) roles are used to manage the identities within the directory, whereas RBAC in this section is used to define permissions for resources that reside within the relevant subscription or management group.

Custom RBAC roles can be created if the built-in RBAC roles do not meet specific requirements.

> **Tip**
>
> There is a limit of 5,000 custom RBAC roles per Azure directory.

Custom RBAC roles can be created in the following ways:

- The Azure portal
- Azure PowerShell
- The Azure CLI
- The REST API

In this section, we had a look at RBAC in Azure and how it works from a logical perspective.

We encourage you to read further by using the following links, which provide an overview of RBAC and also built-in roles:

- `https://docs.microsoft.com/en-us/azure/role-based-access-control/built-in-roles`
- `https://docs.microsoft.com/en-us/azure/role-based-access-control/overview`

Now, let's see how to create a custom role.

Creating a custom role

Let's go ahead and use the Azure portal to create a custom RBAC role from scratch named `IT Support - Restart VMs only`, which can only restart virtual machines and deny the startup and shutdown of them:

1. Navigate to the Azure portal by opening a web browser and browsing to `https://portal.azure.com`.

2. In the top section search bar, search for and select **Subscriptions**:

Figure 2.2 – The search bar in Azure

3. Select an active subscription; in my case, this will be the **Demo** subscription, as seen in the following screenshot:

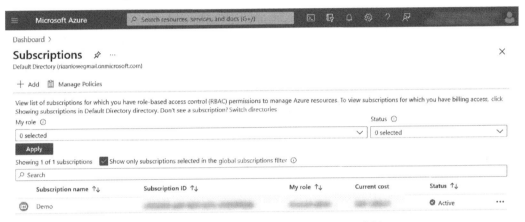

Figure 2.3 – A display of all subscriptions available

4. Select **Access control (IAM)**, click on **Add**, and select **Add custom role**:

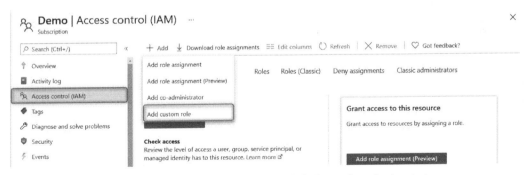

Figure 2.4 – The Access control (IAM) blade for a selected subscription

Next, under the **Basics** tab, enter the custom role name and description and select the **Start from scratch** setting under **Baseline permissions**. Under **Custom role name**, specify IT support - Restart VMs only; it is also best practice to provide a brief description in the **Description** field when creating resources in Azure:

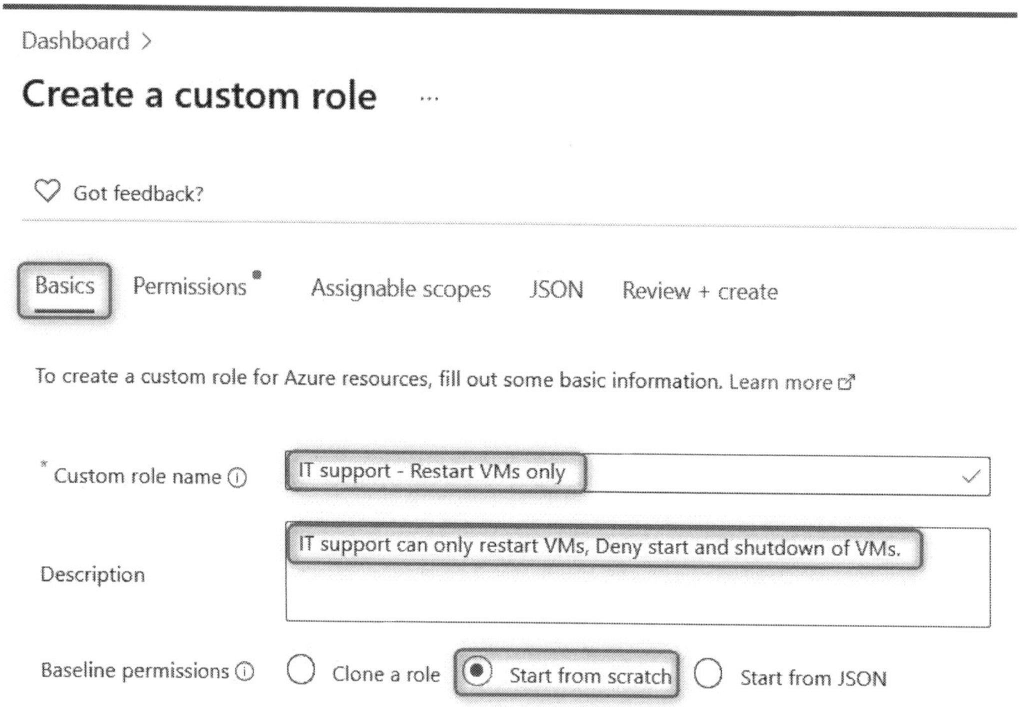

Dashboard >

Create a custom role   ...

♡ Got feedback?

| Basics | Permissions * | Assignable scopes | JSON | Review + create |

To create a custom role for Azure resources, fill out some basic information. Learn more ☐

* Custom role name ⓘ   IT support - Restart VMs only   ✓

Description   IT support can only restart VMs, Deny start and shutdown of VMs.

Baseline permissions ⓘ   ◯ Clone a role   ⦿ Start from scratch   ◯ Start from JSON

Figure 2.5 – The custom role creation blade

5. Next, we need to specify the permissions. Click on the **Add permissions** button, and in the search bar that pops up, search for Virtual machines and select **Microsoft ClassicCompute**:

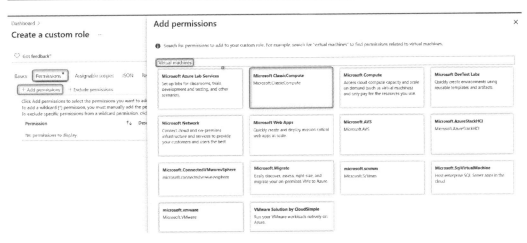

Figure 2.6 – The Permissions blade when creating a custom role

6. A new blade will pop up with all the compute permissions. Scroll all the way down to **Microsoft.Compute/virtualMachines** and select **Read: Get Virtual Machine and Other: Restart Virtual Machine**, and then click **Add**:

Microsoft.Compute permissions

☐ Read : Get Virtual Machine in Scale Set Metric Definitions ⓘ	Reads Virtual Machine in Scale Set Metric Definitions
⌄ Microsoft.Compute/locations/vmSizes	
☐ Read : List Available Virtual Machine Sizes in Location ⓘ	Lists available virtual machine sizes in a location
⌄ Microsoft.Compute/virtualMachines	
☑ Read : Get Virtual Machine ⓘ	Get the properties of a virtual machine
☐ Write : Create or Update Virtual Machine ⓘ	Creates a new virtual machine or updates an existing virtual machine
☐ Delete : Delete Virtual Machine ⓘ	Deletes the virtual machine
☐ Other : Start Virtual Machine ⓘ	Starts the virtual machine
☐ Other : Power Off Virtual Machine ⓘ	Powers off the virtual machine. Note that the virtual machine will continue to be billed.
☐ Other : Reapply a virtual machine's current model ⓘ	Reapplies a virtual machine's current model
☐ Other : Redeploy Virtual Machine ⓘ	Redeploys virtual machine
☑ Other : Restart Virtual Machine ⓘ	Restarts the virtual machine
☐ Other : Retrieve boot diagnostic logs blob URIs ⓘ	Retrieves boot diagnostic logs blob URIs
☐ Other : Deallocate Virtual Machine ⓘ	Powers off the virtual machine and releases the compute resources
☐ Other : Generalize Virtual Machine ⓘ	Sets the virtual machine state to Generalized and prepares the virtual machine for capture
☐ Other : Capture Virtual Machine ⓘ	Captures the virtual machine by copying virtual hard disks and generates a template that can be used to create similar virtual machines
☐ Other : Run Command on Virtual Machine ⓘ	Executes a predefined script on the virtual machine

Add   Cancel

Figure 2.7 – The custom role creation permissions available for Microsoft.Compute

7. Next, we need to exclude this role from starting and shutting down virtual machines. Click on the **Exclude permissions** button and search for `Virtual machines` again, and then select **Microsoft Compute**:

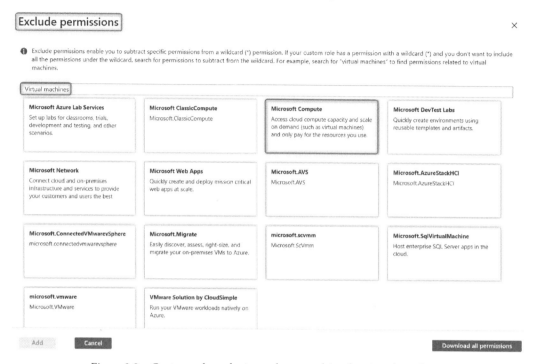

Figure 2.8 – Custom role exclusions when searching for virtual machines

8. Go to **Microsoft.Compute/virtualMachines** and select **Other: Start Virtual Machine** and **Other: Power Off Virtual Machine**, and then click **Add**:

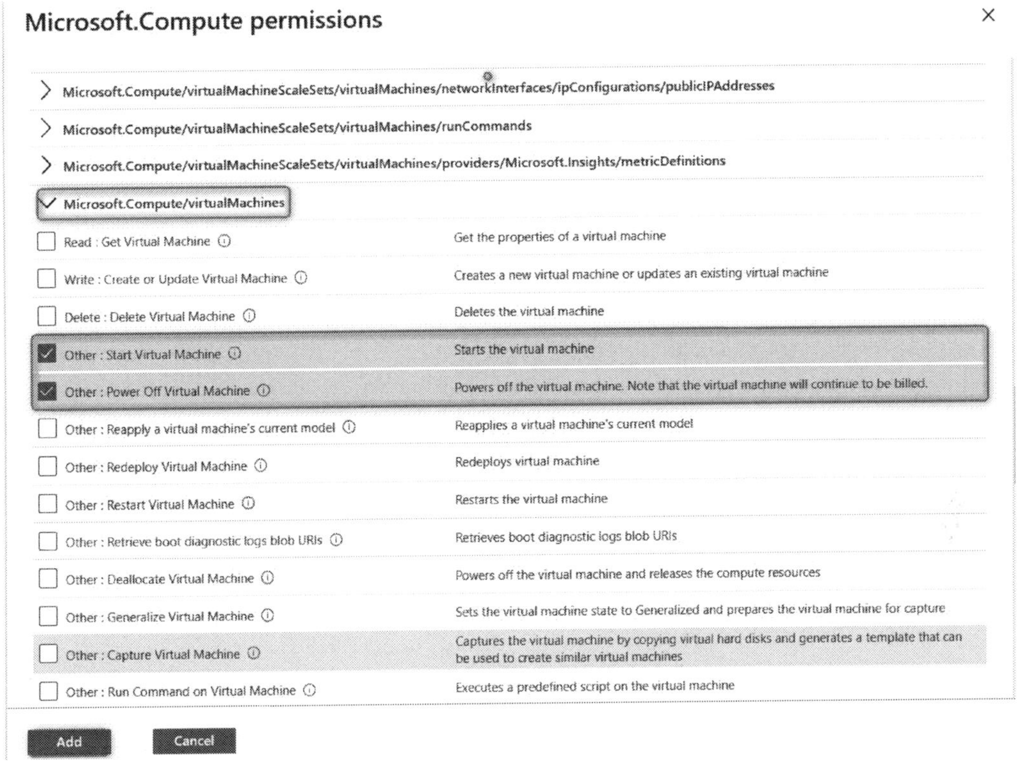

Microsoft.Compute permissions   ✕

> Microsoft.Compute/virtualMachineScaleSets/virtualMachines/networkInterfaces/ipConfigurations/publicIPAddresses

> Microsoft.Compute/virtualMachineScaleSets/virtualMachines/runCommands

> Microsoft.Compute/virtualMachineScaleSets/virtualMachines/providers/Microsoft.Insights/metricDefinitions

☑ Microsoft.Compute/virtualMachines

☐ Read : Get Virtual Machine ⓘ | Get the properties of a virtual machine

☐ Write : Create or Update Virtual Machine ⓘ | Creates a new virtual machine or updates an existing virtual machine

☐ Delete : Delete Virtual Machine ⓘ | Deletes the virtual machine

☑ Other : Start Virtual Machine ⓘ | Starts the virtual machine

☑ Other : Power Off Virtual Machine ⓘ | Powers off the virtual machine. Note that the virtual machine will continue to be billed.

☐ Other : Reapply a virtual machine's current model ⓘ | Reapplies a virtual machine's current model

☐ Other : Redeploy Virtual Machine ⓘ | Redeploys virtual machine

☐ Other : Restart Virtual Machine ⓘ | Restarts the virtual machine

☐ Other : Retrieve boot diagnostic logs blob URIs ⓘ | Retrieves boot diagnostic logs blob URIs

☐ Other : Deallocate Virtual Machine ⓘ | Powers off the virtual machine and releases the compute resources

☐ Other : Generalize Virtual Machine ⓘ | Sets the virtual machine state to Generalized and prepares the virtual machine for capture

☐ Other : Capture Virtual Machine ⓘ | Captures the virtual machine by copying virtual hard disks and generates a template that can be used to create similar virtual machines

☐ Other : Run Command on Virtual Machine ⓘ | Executes a predefined script on the virtual machine

Add   Cancel

Figure 2.9 – The custom role exclusion list for Microsoft.Compute

9.   You will notice that the new role now has the following permission types:

- **Action**: Read the **Virtual Machine (VM)**.

- **Action**: Restart the VM.

- **NotAction**: Start the VM.

- **NotAction**: Shut down the VM.

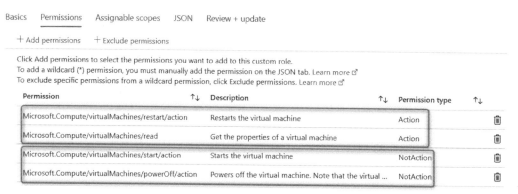

Figure 2.10 – A custom role permissions overview displaying Actions and NotActions

> **Tip**
> **Actions** are permission actions that are allowed; **NotActions** are permission actions that are specifically not allowed.

Click on **Next**.

10.   Next, we have **Assignable scopes**, where we can choose where this custom role will be available for assignment. In this scenario, we are going to leave it at the default subscription level that was automatically added and then click on **Next**:

Dashboard >

Create a custom role ...

♡ Got feedback?

Basics   Permissions   [Assignable scopes]   JSON   Review + create

+ Add assignable scopes

Click Add assignable scopes to select the scopes (management groups, subscriptions, or resource groups) where this role will be available for assignment. Your role must have at least one assignable scope. Learn more ⬚

Assignable scope	↑↓	Type	↑↓
/subscriptions/		Subscription	🗑

Figure 2.11 – The custom role assignable scopes

11. Next, we have the **JSON** tab, which shows the permissions for the new role in JSON format; we also have the ability to download the JSON code. For now, let's click on **Next**:

Basics   Permissions   Assignable scopes   JSON   Review + update

Here is your custom role in JSON format. Learn more ⬚

[Download]   [⧉]   [Edit]

```
 1  {
 2      "properties": {
 3          "roleName": "IT support - Restart VMs only",
 4          "description": "IT support can only restart VMs, Deny start and shutdown of VMs.",
 5          "assignableScopes": [
 6              "/subscriptions/c4353459-a26f-4603-b27e-cfc836f4fddb"
 7          ],
 8          "permissions": [
 9              {
10                  "actions": [
11                      "Microsoft.Compute/virtualMachines/restart/action",
12                      "Microsoft.Compute/virtualMachines/read"
13                  ],
14                  "notActions": [
15                      "Microsoft.Compute/virtualMachines/start/action",
16                      "Microsoft.Compute/virtualMachines/powerOff/action"
17                  ],
18                  "dataActions": [],
19                  "notDataActions": []
20              }
```

[Review + update]   [Previous]   [Next]

Figure 2.12 – The custom role JSON notation

12. The last tab is the **Review + update** tab, which is a summary of our configuration; click on **Create**:

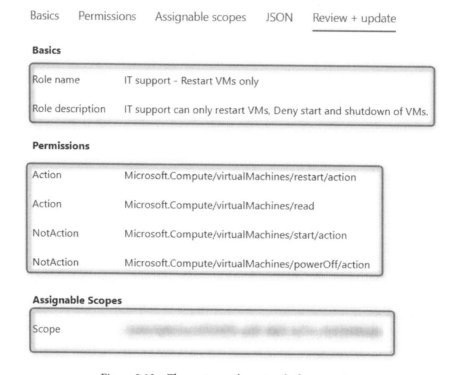

Figure 2.13 – The custom role review before creation

13. A new pop-up window will appear, stating that the new custom role has been created and that we can start assigning the role as soon as replication has taken place, which is usually around 5 minutes or less.

In this section, we have created a custom RBAC role via the Azure portal from scratch, which only allows a VM to be restarted and blocks any start or shutdown attempts on a VM.

We encourage you to read up further by using the following links, which go into detail about Azure AD custom roles:

- https://docs.microsoft.com/en-us/azure/role-based-access-control/custom-roles

- https://docs.microsoft.com/en-us/azure/active-directory/roles/custom-create

> **Important!**
> Students should be comfortable using the JSON format while creating a custom role.

Providing access to resources by assigning the custom RBAC role

The next step is to assign this custom role for a user on a different level. We are going to assign access on the resource group level with an account that has owner permissions on the resource group level:

1. Navigate to the Azure portal by opening a web browser and going to `https://portal.azure.com`.

2. Select **Resource groups** on the left, which will show all the current resource groups:

Figure 2.14 – Selecting Resource groups from the main Azure menu

3. Select one of your resource groups; if you do not have one yet, you need to create one in any region you want and call it `Az-104`. In this scenario, I will use one of my resource groups, also called `Az-104`:

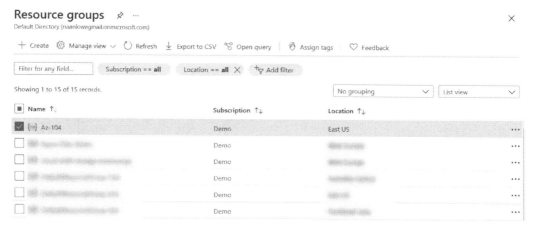

Figure 2.15 – Selecting a resource group

4. Next, go to the **Access control (IAM)** section, click on **Add**, and select **Add role assignment**:

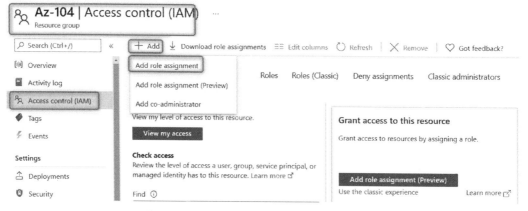

Figure 2.16 – The Access control (IAM) blade for the selected resource group

5. A new blade opens up; under **Role**, search for the custom role we created called `IT support - Restart VMs only`. Under **Assign access to**, leave it as **User, group, or service principal** and select `PacktUser1`, which we created in *Chapter 1*, *Managing Azure Active Directory Objects*, and click on **Save**:

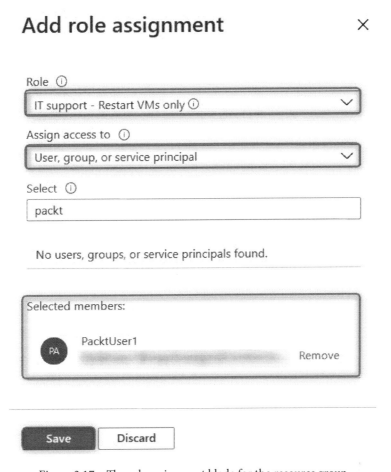

Figure 2.17 – The role assignment blade for the resource group

That's it – we have now successfully created and assigned a custom RBAC role to a user named `PacketUser1`. The final step is to validate the role assignment.

Confirming the role assignment steps

Now that we have assigned a role to a user, let's go ahead and confirm that it's working as expected:

1. Navigate to the Azure portal by opening a web browser and browsing to `https://portal.azure.com` (you will need to sign in as the user that you assigned your custom role to).

2. Select **All resources** on the left, which will show all the current resource groups:

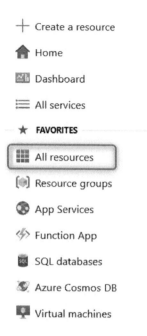

Figure 2.18 – Selecting All resources from the main Azure menu

3. You will be able to see all the VMs listed that are part of the specified resource group:

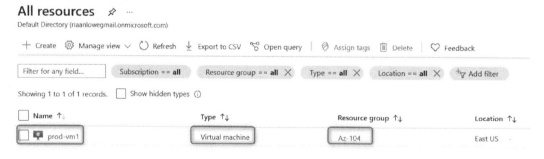

Figure 2.19 – Displaying all resources for the resource group

4. Select a started VM that is available – in my case, this will be prod-vm1 – and see if you can stop the VM:

Figure 2.20 – Stopping the VM

5. A pop-up error message will display **Failed to stop virtual machine**, and that is how we can confirm our custom RBAC role, which denies a user stopping a VM that is working as expected and that only restarting the VM is allowed:

Figure 2.21 – An error message stating the user does not have permissions to stop the virtual machine

In this section, we looked at how to assign a custom RBAC role via the Azure portal and confirmed that the custom role is applied and working as expected.

We encourage you to read further by using the following link, which goes into more detail about assigning roles in Azure: `https://docs.microsoft.com/en-us/azure/role-based-access-control/role-assignments-portal?tabs=current`.

Interpreting access assignments

There are a few tips we can provide when interpreting access assignments. First off, you need to understand the scope of the assignment – that is, is it at the management group, subscription group, resource group, or resource level?

Next, you can have a look at the role rules; in order to do this, you need to do the following:

1. Navigate to the Azure portal by opening a web browser and browsing to `https://portal.azure.com`.

2. Select **Resource groups** on the left, which will show all the current resource groups, and select a resource group in your subscription (in my case, it will be Az-104).

3.   Under **Access control (IAM)**, choose **Role assignments** and select a role you want to have a look at in detail:

Figure 2.22 – The Role assignments section under the Access control (IAM) blade for a resource group

4.   In my case, I'm going to select the **Contributor** role:

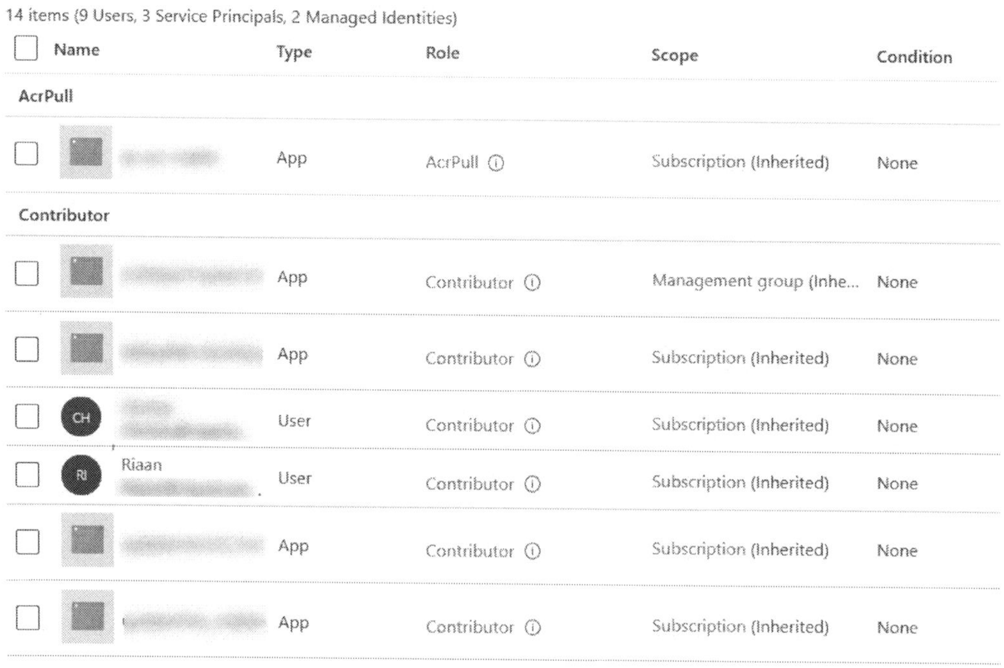

14 items (9 Users, 3 Service Principals, 2 Managed Identities)

Name	Type	Role	Scope	Condition
AcrPull				
App	App	AcrPull ⓘ	Subscription (Inherited)	None
Contributor				
App	App	Contributor ⓘ	Management group (Inhe...	None
App	App	Contributor ⓘ	Subscription (Inherited)	None
CH	User	Contributor ⓘ	Subscription (Inherited)	None
Riaan	User	Contributor ⓘ	Subscription (Inherited)	None
App	App	Contributor ⓘ	Subscription (Inherited)	None
App	App	Contributor ⓘ	Subscription (Inherited)	None

Figure 2.23 – The available role assignments

5.   Click on **JSON**; now, we will be able to view what the role has access to and also what actions are not allowed:

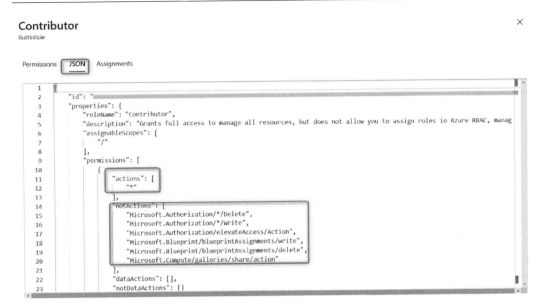

Figure 2.24 – JSON notation of the Contributor role

> **Tip**
> **NotActions** always take preference over **Action** items.

In this section, we discussed how to interpret role assignments by viewing the JSON format for a specific role.

We encourage you to read further by using the following links, which go into more detail about custom RBAC:

- https://docs.microsoft.com/en-us/azure/role-based-access-control/custom-roles-template
- https://docs.microsoft.com/en-us/azure/role-based-access-control/role-assignments-list-portal

Summary

In this chapter, we discussed what custom roles are, how they work within Azure, and the different scope levels to which RBAC can be applied. We also created a custom RBAC role that only allows a user to restart a VM and not stop it. Finally, we went over how to interpret RBAC role assignments within the Azure portal.

In the next chapter, we'll cover managing subscriptions and governance.

3
Creating and Managing Governance

This chapter covers how to establish governance in Azure and create mechanisms for managing it. The topics we will cover will include how to create Azure policies and resource locks and why they exist, as well as applying and managing resource tags. This chapter will assist you in building the skills required to establish a good governance baseline within your organization and understanding the importance of policies and tags in Azure, with practical application of these skills in the examples. Establishing good governance within an organization is an audacious task, but this chapter sets to guide you along the right path in the journey, knowing where to find resources to support you as you apply this within your organization and with your customers.

In this chapter, we are going to cover the following main topics:

- Understanding Azure policies

- Applying and managing tags on resources

Technical requirements

In order to follow along hands-on, you will need the following:

- Access to an Azure subscription with global administrator and billing administrator privileges. If you do not have access to one, students can enroll for a free account at `https://azure.microsoft.com/en-us/free/`.

- PowerShell 5.1 or later installed on a PC from which labs can be practiced. Note that many examples can only be followed from a PC. Alternatively, Cloud Shell may be considered: `https://shell.azure.com`.

- Installation of the **Az module**. This can be performed by running the following command in an administrative PowerShell session:

```
Set-ExecutionPolicy -ExecutionPolicy RemoteSigned -Scope
CurrentUser
Install-Module -Name Az -Scope CurrentUser -Repository
PSGallery -Force
```

Understanding Azure policies

Azure Policy is a mechanism for effecting organizational compliance on the Azure platform. The service allows aggregated views to understand the overall state of an environment, with the ability to view resource-level granularity for compliance. All this can be viewed on the compliance dashboard. Remediation can be applied automatically and through bulk operations.

The following screenshot illustrates an example policy overview for an organization:

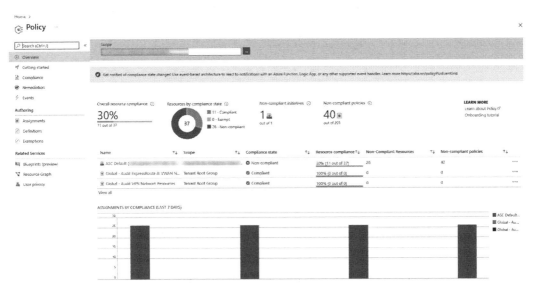

Figure 3.1 – Azure policy example

As you will observe, this is where we will create and manage policies, as well as get an overview of compliance for policies that you have implemented in Azure.

How does Azure Policy work?

Azure Policy assesses compliance by comparing resource properties to business rules defined in a **JavaScript Object Notation (JSON)** format. These are known as **policy definitions**.

A policy initiative is a grouping of definitions that align with business objectives such as the secure configuration of **virtual machines (VMs)**. This could contain a policy to assess antivirus compliance and a policy for assessing disk encryption compliance, as well as other policies.

Azure Policy resides above the subscription and management group layers, and it can therefore be assigned to various scope levels—an individual resource, resource group, subscription, or management group. This is defined as **policy assignment** or **scope**.

Azure Policy versus RBAC

Both Azure Policy and **role-based access control** (**RBAC**) contribute to controlling governance within Azure. While both create methods of controlling access, there is often confusion between the two. We distinguish the difference between them for clarity, as follows:

- **Azure Policy** focuses on resource properties for existing resources and resources being deployed.

- **RBAC** focuses on user actions at different scopes.

Working with Azure Policy

Azure offers predefined built-in policies, as well as an option to create custom policies. The same applies to initiatives, which we will explore in this section.

Some examples of built-in policies include the following:

- **Allowed virtual machine size SKUs**: This policy specifies a set of VM sizes and types that can be deployed in Azure.

- **Allowed locations**: This policy restricts available locations where resources can be deployed.

- **Allowed resource types**: This policy defines a list of resource types that can be deployed. Resource types that are not on the list can't be deployed inside the Azure environment.

- **Not allowed resource types**: This policy prevents certain resource types from being deployed.

- **Require a tag and its value on resources**: Enforces a required tag and its value. Does not apply to resource groups.

If the built-in policies don't meet your desired requirements, you can create a custom policy instead. Custom policies are created in JSON, with the code defining several properties. When creating in the portal, the second part defines policy rules (which are usually just extended in the same JSON file).

The following code is an example of a policy definition:

```
{
    "properties": {
        "displayName": "Deny storage accounts not using only
HTTPS",
        "description": "Deny storage accounts not using only
HTTPS. Checks
the supportsHttpsTrafficOnly property on StorageAccounts.",
        "mode": "all",
        "parameters": {
            "effectType": {
                "type": "string",
                "defaultValue": "Deny",
                "allowedValues": [
                    "Deny",
                    "Disabled"
                ],
                "metadata": {
                    "displayName": "Effect",
                    "description": "Enable or disable the
execution of the policy"
                }
            }
        },
```

In this part of the code, we are looking at the policy rule:

```
    "policyRule": {
    "if": {
            "allOf": [
                {
                    "field": "type",
                    "equals": "Microsoft.Storage/storageAccounts"
                },
                {
                    "field":
"Microsoft.Storage/storageAccounts/supportsHttpsTrafficOnly",
```

```
                      "notEquals": "true"
                }
              ]
          },
          "then": {
              "effect": "[parameters('effectType')]"
          }
      }
  } }
```

As you will notice, the preceding policy assesses Azure storage accounts and identifies if the configuration for **HyperText Transfer Protocol Secure (HTTPS)**-only communication is set to `true`. Where it does not comply, then the configured effect will be enforced based on what is entered for the parameter sections.

Constructing a policy definition

Note that a policy definition is constructed of the following key components:

- **Name**: This is the display name of the policy file.

- **Description**: This is a descriptor field that allows you to add a small write-up on the desired effect and scope of the policy.

- **Effect**: Several effects can be applied to policies. To understand these in deeper detail, please refer to the following Microsoft **Uniform Resource Locator (URL)**: `https://docs.microsoft.com/en-us/azure/governance/policy/concepts/effects`. The different effect types are described here:

  - **Append**: This is used for modifying existing or new resources by adding additional fields or properties to a resource.

  - **Audit**: This is used to flag a resource that is not compliant. It notes the non-compliance but will not restrict the deployment request.

  - **AuditIfNotExists**: This is used to identify resources identified within the policy's (or policies') scope that are missing the required properties for the resource type.

- **Deny**: This is used to disallow the deployment of resources that do not meet the policy definition criteria.

- **DeployIfNotExists**: This is used to perform a template deployment when non-compliance is met, as described in the **AuditIfNotExists** policy criteria.

- **Disabled**: This is used for nullifying the effect of a policy and is typically used for testing scenarios.

- **Modify**: This is used to modify the properties of resources and will apply to new and existing resources that meet the policy criteria. Resources can be remediated through a remediation task.

- **Category**: This defines the category type of your policy.

- **Location**: This defines the location of the policy to be deployed.

- **ID**: This is the definition **identifier (ID)** of the policy that is created and is enumerated based on the policy name.

- **Type**: This defines the policy type to be implemented and can be **Built-in**, **Custom**, or **Static**.

- **Mode**: This is used to define whether a policy is scoped toward a **Resource Provider** or **Azure Resource Manager (ARM)** property.

The following screenshot depicts a sample Azure policy definition:

Figure 3.2 – Policy definition overview example

The screenshot that follows provides an example of a policy defined to look for key-value pairs (Tag Name and Tag Value). As you can see in the following screenshot, when the policy assesses resources, if it identifies the resource does not have the required tag (that is, it is not compliant), it will proceed to reject the creation of a resource due to the *deny effect* in place:

Figure 3.3 – Policy definition example

The definition accepts inputs (identified as parameters) for the template assignment; these will be accepted in the definition. For example, we may want a tag environment with a PROD value. If the assignment doesn't see these tags on a resource, it will reject the creation of the resource. This is specified by the if condition, which reads as follows: if the parameter's tag key (Environment) and tag value (PROD) do not match the resource tag, then deny deployment.

Creating a policy definition

In this section, we will run through the creation of a policy definition. The steps are presented here:

1. Search for `Policy` in the portal main search bar and click **Policy** in the returned list, as illustrated in the following screenshot:

Figure 3.4 – Selecting Azure Policy in search bar

2. Click on the **Definitions** blade then click on the **+ Policy definition** button, as illustrated in the following screenshot:

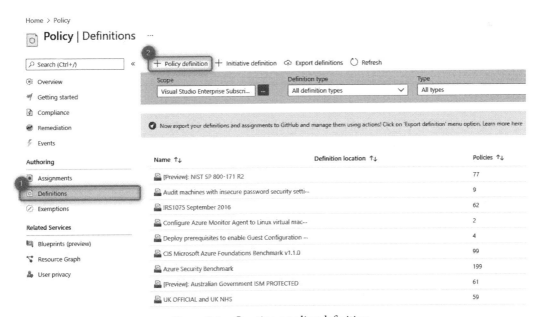

Figure 3.5 – Creating a policy definition

3. On the **New Policy definition** blade, we will populate values for the following:

    -   **Definition location**: This will be the subscription where the policy is to be saved.

    -   **Name**: This is the policy definition name.

    -   **Description**: A brief description of the policy definition to be created.

- **Category**: This will align with a set of predefined service categories in Azure, such as **App Service**, **Azure Active Directory**, **Backup**, and so on, or a custom category can be created; this can be used for future definition grouping too.

- **POLICY RULE**: This will be a rule that determines what the definition will assess, as well as the effect. Policy rules are structured in a JSON format and can be created from scratch or by importing from GitHub.

For this example, we will create a policy definition for allowed locations for resources (this is a predefined definition, therefore the following example is only implemented if additional requirements are needed).

4. Select **Definition location** by clicking the ellipsis button (**…**), as illustrated in the following screenshot:

Figure 3.6 – Selecting Definition location

5. Select **Subscription** from the pane that pops up and click **Select**, as illustrated in the following screenshot:

Figure 3.7 – Selecting Definition location: Subscription

6. Enter the appropriate details for **Name**, **Description**, and **Category**, as illustrated in the following screenshot:

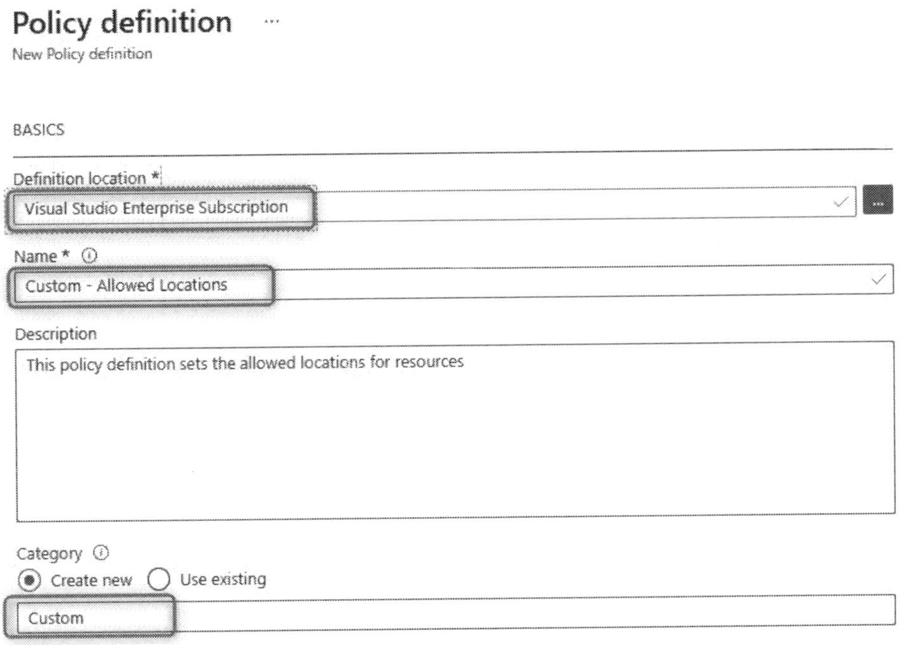

Policy definition ⋯

New Policy definition

BASICS

Definition location *

Visual Studio Enterprise Subscription   ✓ ...

Name * ⓘ

Custom - Allowed Locations   ✓

Description

This policy definition sets the allowed locations for resources

Category ⓘ
◉ Create new   ○ Use existing

Custom

Figure 3.8 – Policy definition

Then, enter the appropriate policy rule JSON code, as follows (the following screenshot is the remaining half of the same **Policy definition** page shown previously):

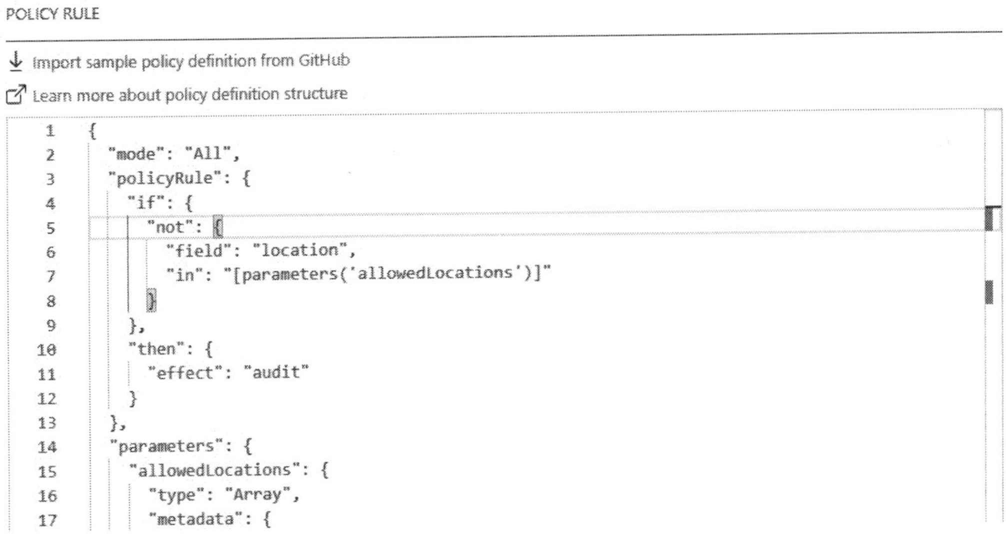

POLICY RULE

↓ Import sample policy definition from GitHub

↗ Learn more about policy definition structure

```
 1  {
 2    "mode": "All",
 3    "policyRule": {
 4      "if": {
 5        "not": {
 6          "field": "location",
 7          "in": "[parameters('allowedLocations')]"
 8        }
 9      },
10      "then": {
11        "effect": "audit"
12      }
13    },
14    "parameters": {
15      "allowedLocations": {
16        "type": "Array",
17        "metadata": {
```

Figure 3.9 – Custom policy definition

7. Click **Save** upon completing the configuration.

    For those that would like to follow along, the JSON code looks like this:

```json
{
    "mode": "All",
    "policyRule": {
      "if": {
        "not": {
          "field": "location",
          "in": "[parameters('allowedLocations')]"
        }
      },
      "then": {
        "effect": "deny"
      }
    },
    "parameters": {
      "allowedLocations": {
        "type": "Array",
        "metadata": {
          "description": "The list of allowed locations for
resources.",
          "displayName": "Allowed locations",
          "strongType": "location"
        }
      }
    }
}
```

8. You will get a notification to signify a policy definition has been created successfully, as illustrated in the following screenshot:

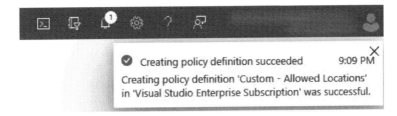

Figure 3.10 – Policy definition success notification

9.   Change the **Category** filter to **Custom** to view the newly created definition, as illustrated in the following screenshot:

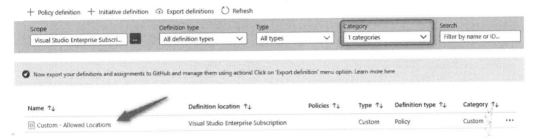

Figure 3.11 – Displaying our custom policy definition

Creating an initiative definition

In this section, you will create an initiative definition that is used for the grouping of policy definitions that align with business objectives, such as the secure configuration of VMs. The initiative that you will be creating is for grouping policies that define resources allowed for the subscription in Azure. Proceed as follows:

1.   To start creating a new policy initiative, in the **Policy | Definitions** menu, select **+ Initiative definition**, as illustrated in the following screenshot:

Figure 3.12 – Creating a new initiative definition

2. Define the fields on the **Basics** tab, as illustrated in the following screenshot, and click **Next** to continue:

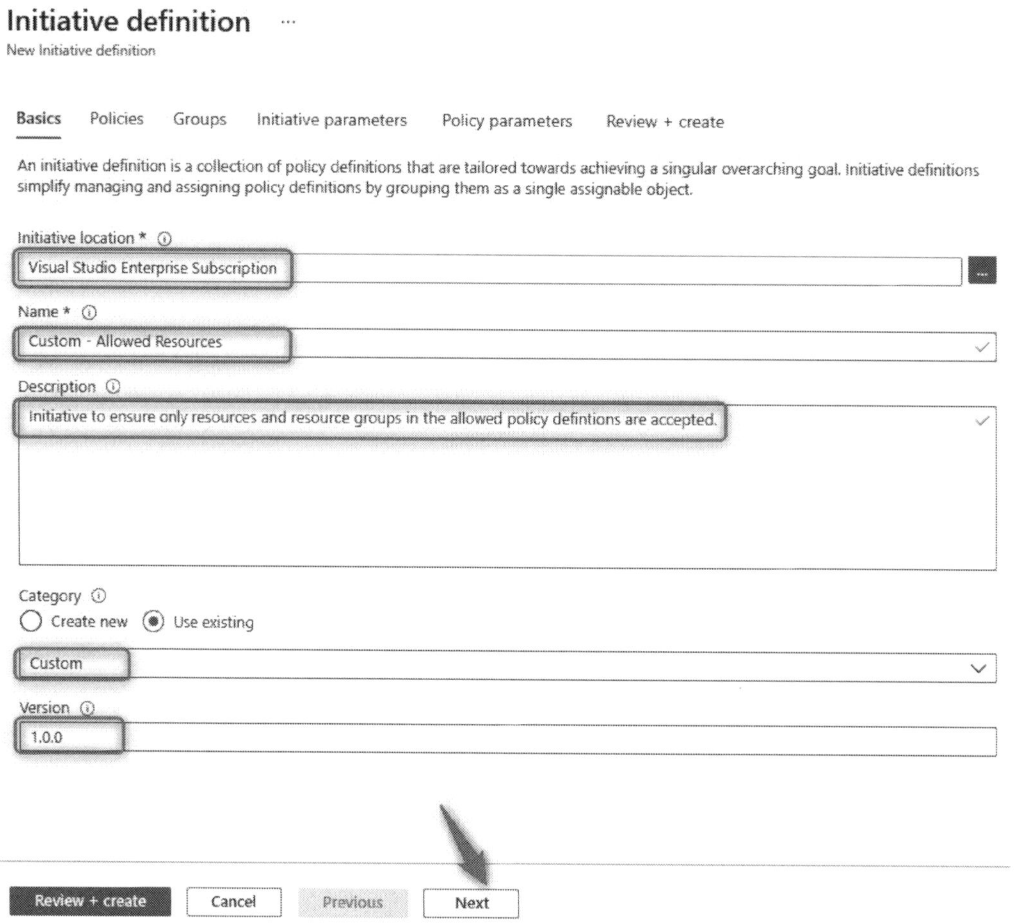

Initiative definition ···

New Initiative definition

Basics   Policies   Groups   Initiative parameters   Policy parameters   Review + create

An initiative definition is a collection of policy definitions that are tailored towards achieving a singular overarching goal. Initiative definitions simplify managing and assigning policy definitions by grouping them as a single assignable object.

Initiative location * ⓘ

Visual Studio Enterprise Subscription

Name * ⓘ

Custom - Allowed Resources

Description ⓘ

Initiative to ensure only resources and resource groups in the allowed policy definitions are accepted.

Category ⓘ
○ Create new   ◉ Use existing

Custom

Version ⓘ

1.0.0

Review + create   Cancel   Previous   Next

Figure 3.13 – Basics tab on Initiative definition screen

3. Select policy definitions to be included in the initiative. The following screenshot shows you how to do this:

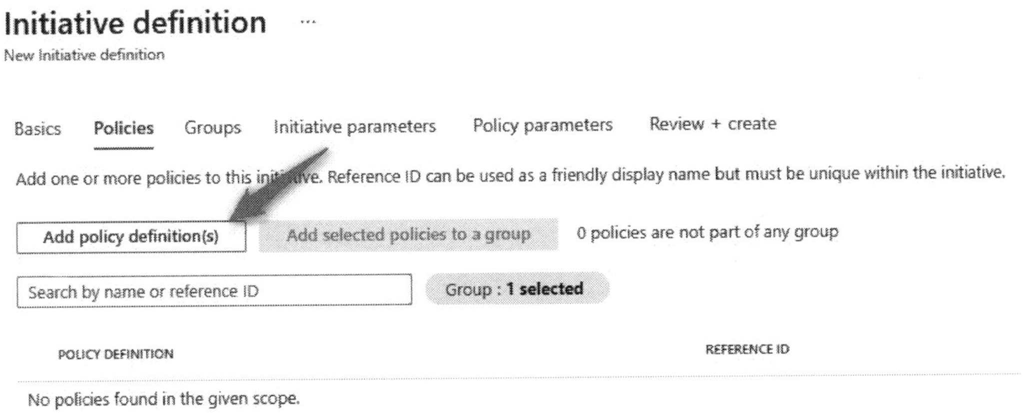

Initiative definition ···
New Initiative definition

Basics   **Policies**   Groups   Initiative parameters   Policy parameters   Review + create

Add one or more policies to this initiative. Reference ID can be used as a friendly display name but must be unique within the initiative.

| Add policy definition(s) | Add selected policies to a group | 0 policies are not part of any group |

| Search by name or reference ID | Group : **1 selected** |

POLICY DEFINITION	REFERENCE ID

No policies found in the given scope.

Figure 3.14 – Policies tab on Initiative definition screen

4. Change the **Type** filter to **Custom** and select policy definition(s), then click **Add**. The process is illustrated in the following screenshot:

Add policy definition(s)   ✕

Automated   Microsoft managed

Select one or more policy definition(s) below to add them to initiative. Policy definitions without parameters that have already been added to the initiative are disabled and can't be added a second time. Only policy definitions with parameters can be added to the initiative more than once.

| Custom | Type : **Custom** |

POLICY NAME	CATEGORY	TYPE
☐ Custom - Allowed Locations	Custom	Custom

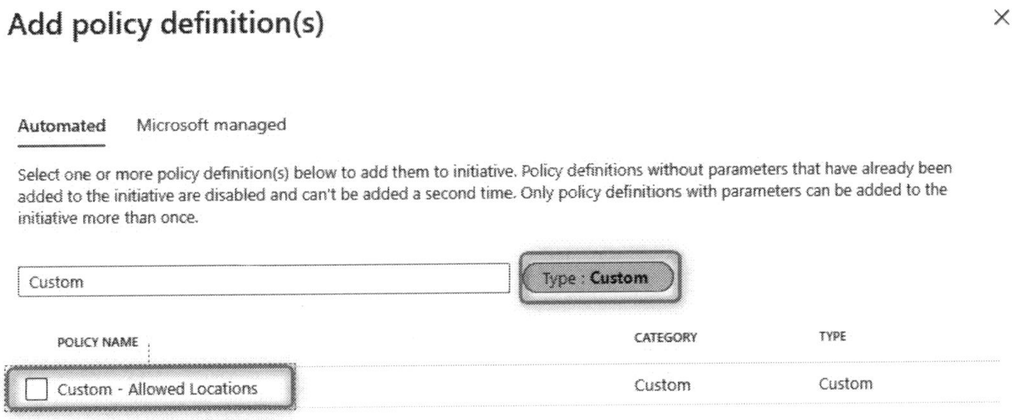

Figure 3.15 – Selecting policies for an initiative definition

5. You may now click **Next** after adding all associated policy definitions. Your screen should now look like this:

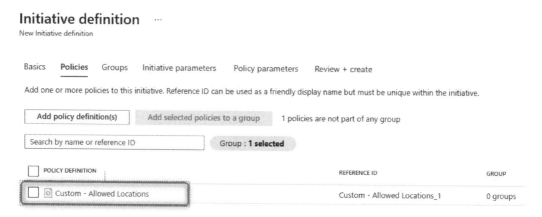

Figure 3.16 – Added policies on Initiative definition screen

6. The **Groups** tab, shown in the following screenshot, allows us to create groups that organize policies within an initiative. Skip this and click **Next**:

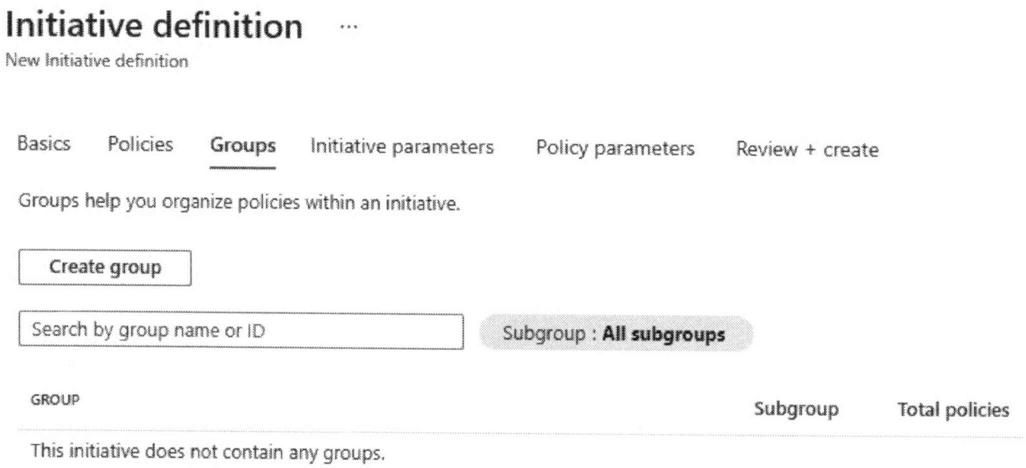

Initiative definition   ...
New Initiative definition

Basics   Policies   **Groups**   Initiative parameters   Policy parameters   Review + create

Groups help you organize policies within an initiative.

    Create group

    Search by group name or ID   Subgroup : **All subgroups**

GROUP   Subgroup   Total policies

This initiative does not contain any groups.

Figure 3.17 – Groups tab on Initiative definition screen

7. Now, we will configure the **Initiative parameters** setting. Initiative parameters are inputs that align with policy definitions. Remember that definitions are a guideline set of rules that are assessed, and parameters are the values to assess for. Click **Create initiative parameter**, as illustrated in the following screenshot:

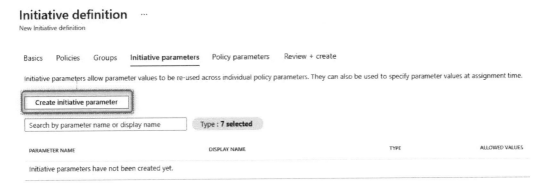

Figure 3.18 – Initiative parameters tab on Initiative definition screen

8. Complete the respective details for **Name**, **Display name**, **Description**, **Type**, **Allowed Values** (*Optional*), and **Default Value**, as illustrated in the following screenshot. This will serve as a placeholder for parameter values to be assigned to policy definitions in the **Policy parameters** section. Click **Next**:

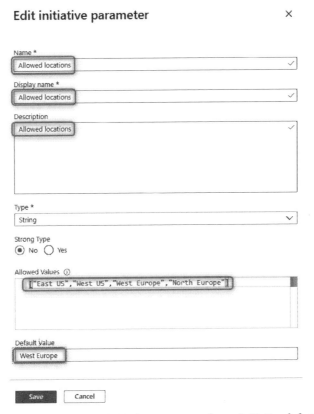

Figure 3.19 – Creating an initiative parameter for an initiative definition

9. For this demonstration, go ahead and delete the initiative parameter again, as illustrated here:

Figure 3.20 – Deleting an initiative parameter on an initiative definition

10. On the **Policy parameters** tab, we have the option to select a value for parameters by choosing predefined values where the value type is set to **Set value**, as illustrated in the following screenshot. Where **Use initiative parameter** is chosen, the values become what was defined previously:

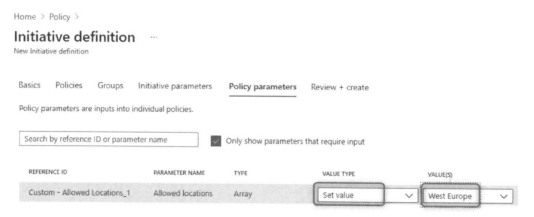

Figure 3.21 – Selecting predefined parameters

11. Click **Review + create**.

12. Click **Create** after reviewing the configuration, as illustrated in the following screenshot:

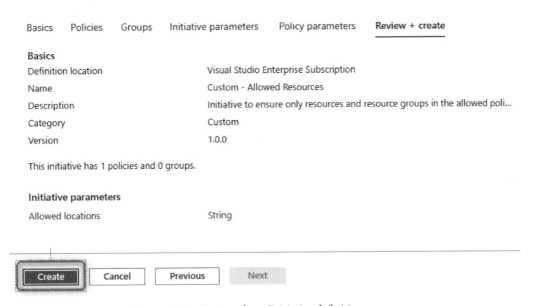

Figure 3.22 – Basics tab on Initiative definition screen

You will be notified of completion and will now have a new initiative definition.

Assigning a policy definition and initiative

Policy definitions or initiatives now need to be applied to take effect; this is where we select the scope. Proceed as follows:

1.   Click the **Assignments** menu on the left menu pane, then click **Assign policy**, as illustrated in the following screenshot:

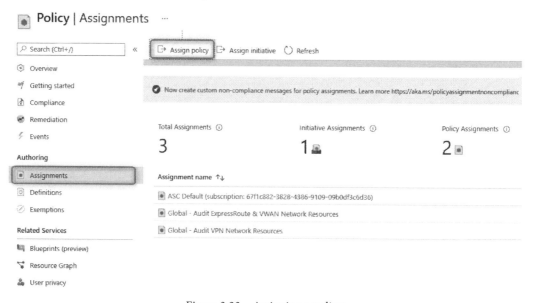

Figure 3.23 – Assigning a policy

2.   On the **Basics** tab, select a policy definition by clicking the ellipsis button (**…**), as illustrated in the following screenshot:

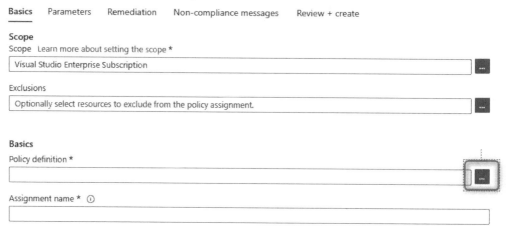

Figure 3.24 – Selecting a policy definition

3. Select the desired definition and click **Select**. In this example, we will select **Custom - Allowed Locations**:

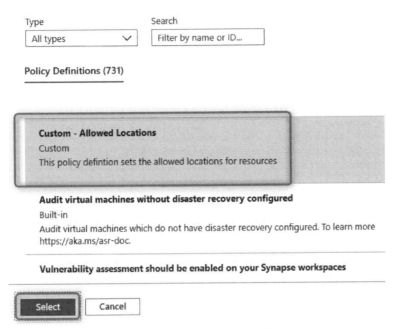

Figure 3.25 – Selecting a policy definition for assignment

4. Click **Next**.

5. On the **Parameters** tab, select a value for **Allowed locations**, as illustrated in the following screenshot. Click **Next**:

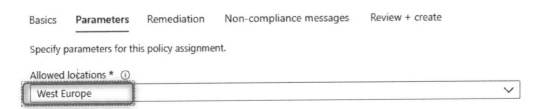

Figure 3.26 – Entering parameters for assigned policies

6.   Remediation can be configured on the next tab for non-compliant resources; this is facilitated through the creation of a managed identity that performs remediation tasks concerned with it. The following screenshot illustrates this in more detail. Click **Next**:

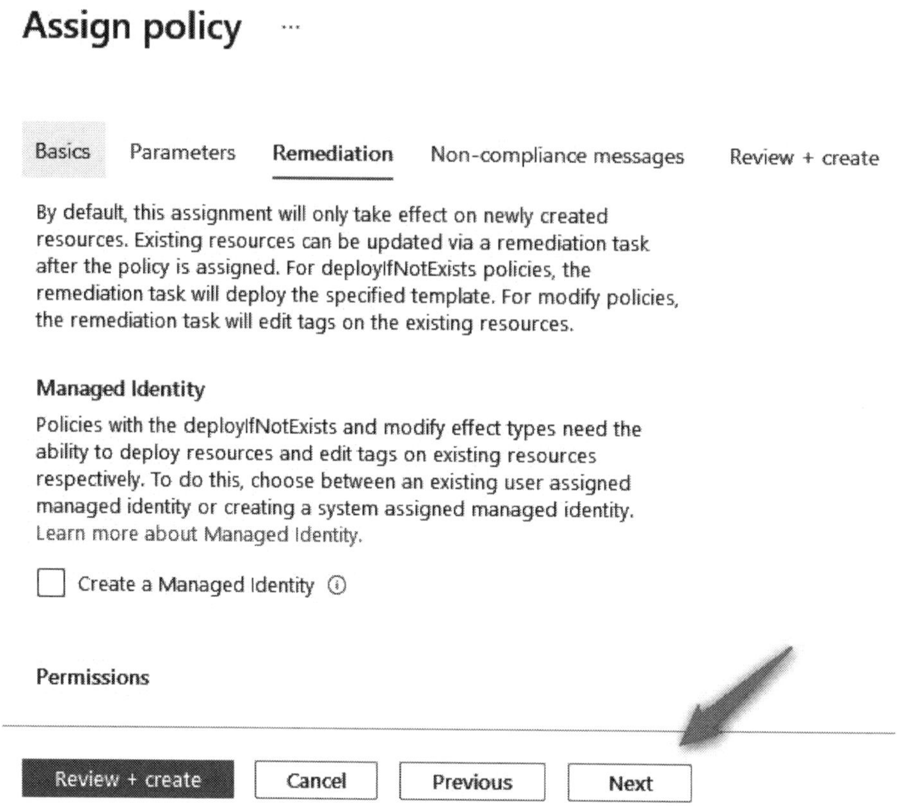

Assign policy   ⋯

Basics   Parameters   **Remediation**   Non-compliance messages   Review + create

By default, this assignment will only take effect on newly created resources. Existing resources can be updated via a remediation task after the policy is assigned. For deployIfNotExists policies, the remediation task will deploy the specified template. For modify policies, the remediation task will edit tags on the existing resources.

Managed Identity

Policies with the deployIfNotExists and modify effect types need the ability to deploy resources and edit tags on existing resources respectively. To do this, choose between an existing user assigned managed identity or creating a system assigned managed identity. Learn more about Managed Identity.

☐   Create a Managed Identity ⓘ

Permissions

[Review + create]   [Cancel]   [Previous]   [Next]

Figure 3.27 – Azure Policy: Remediation

Top Tip

Remediation is only supported for **DeployIfNotExists** and **Modify** effects.

7. Enter a meaningful non-compliance message, as illustrated in the following screenshot, then click **Review + create**:

Figure 3.28 – Non-compliance message

8. Review the configuration and click **Create**. A notification alert will signify a successful operation, as illustrated here:

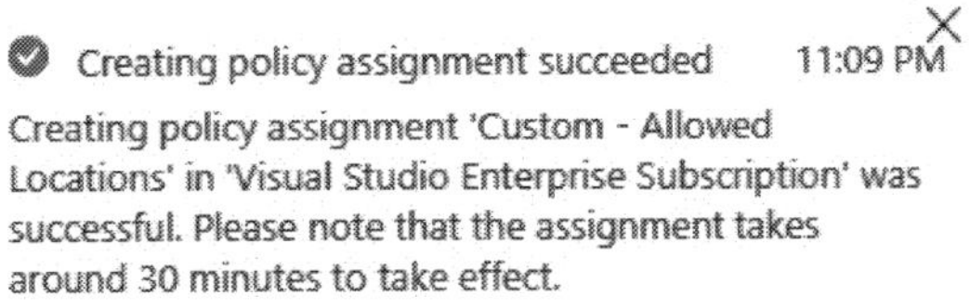

> ✅ Creating policy assignment succeeded   11:09 PM
>
> Creating policy assignment 'Custom - Allowed Locations' in 'Visual Studio Enterprise Subscription' was successful. Please note that the assignment takes around 30 minutes to take effect.

Figure 3.29 – Success notification

9. To confirm our new policy works, we will attempt to deploy a resource that will be denied by the policy. Open any resource group you have and click **Create**, then **Marketplace**, as illustrated in the following screenshot:

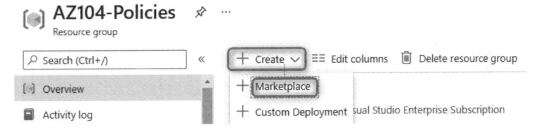

Figure 3.30 – Creating a resource from Marketplace

10. Choose any resource to test; in this example, we will be creating a managed disk. Enter a disk name, choose an unsupported region for the policy, and click **Review + create**. The process is illustrated in the following screenshot:

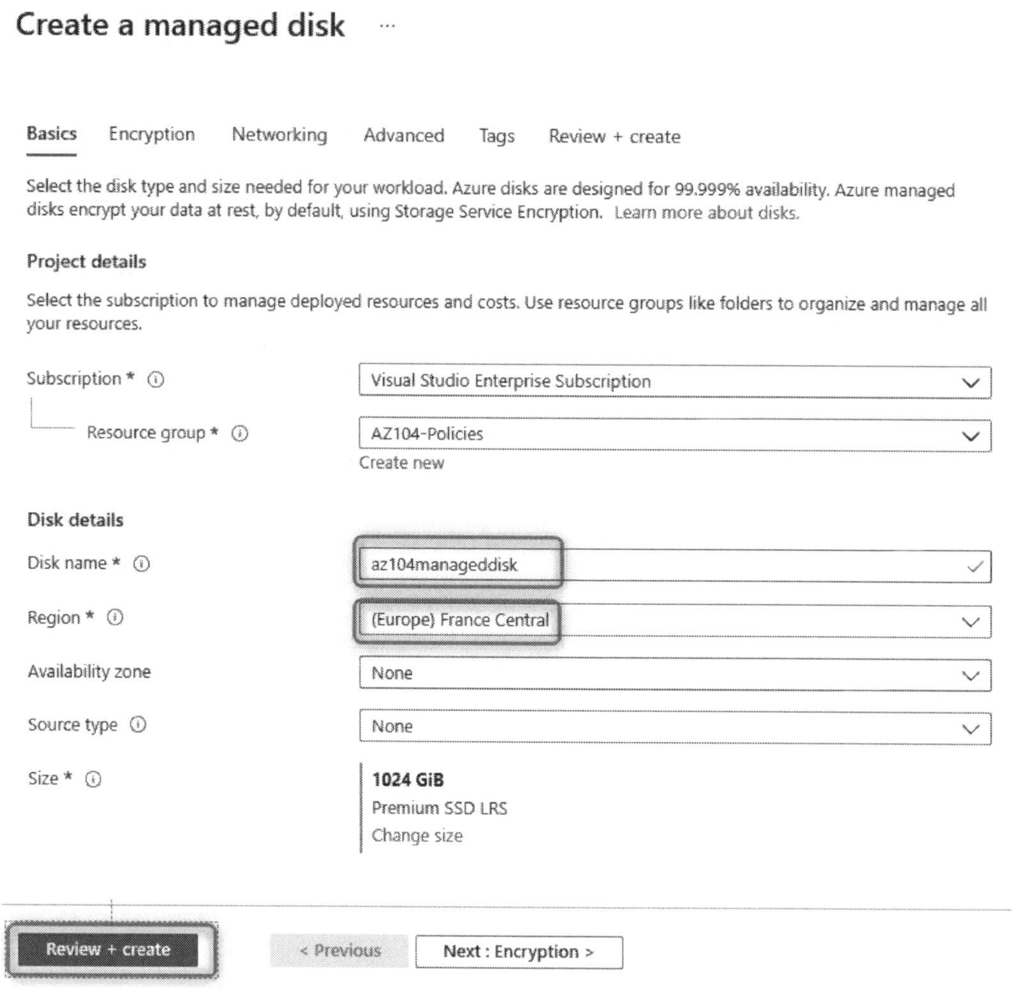

Create a managed disk   ...

Basics   Encryption   Networking   Advanced   Tags   Review + create

Select the disk type and size needed for your workload. Azure disks are designed for 99.999% availability. Azure managed disks encrypt your data at rest, by default, using Storage Service Encryption. Learn more about disks.

Project details

Select the subscription to manage deployed resources and costs. Use resource groups like folders to organize and manage all your resources.

Subscription * ⓘ | Visual Studio Enterprise Subscription   ⌄ |

　　　　Resource group * ⓘ | AZ104-Policies   ⌄ |
                              Create new

Disk details

Disk name * ⓘ | az104manageddisk   ✓ |

Region * ⓘ | (Europe) France Central   ⌄ |

Availability zone | None   ⌄ |

Source type ⓘ | None   ⌄ |

Size * ⓘ | **1024 GiB**
                              Premium SSD LRS
                              Change size

[Review + create]   [< Previous]   [Next : Encryption >]

Figure 3.31 – Creating a managed disk

11. After the validation succeeds, click **Create**. Notice here that the deployment fails due to policy non-conformance:

Figure 3.32 – Non-compliance failure message

Now that we know how to assign policies and initiatives, we will move on to see where we can view compliance for policies and initiatives.

Policy compliance

To view policy compliance status against assigned definitions, you can select the **Compliance** menu on the **Policy** blade and note the compliance on the right-hand side. Compliance is reflected in a percentage (%) form to understand compliance effectiveness. Note that newly applied policies may take several minutes to be applied, as well as for compliance to be reflected. Typically, policies take about 30 minutes to apply, while compliance may take several hours.

The following screenshot provides an example of policy compliance within an Azure estate:

Figure 3.33 – Policy compliance overview

Resource compliance can exist in three different states, as outlined here:

- **Compliant**: A resource conforms to defined policy standards.

- **Non-compliant**: A resource does not conform to the required policy standard.

- **Exempt**: A resource has been identified to be exempted from the policy evaluation. This is explicitly defined for an exemption or can't be evaluated. Exempted resources will still be evaluated in the total compliance rating score.

Diving into any of the line items will provide further details; for this example, we are showing policy compliance for the **ASC Default** initiative:

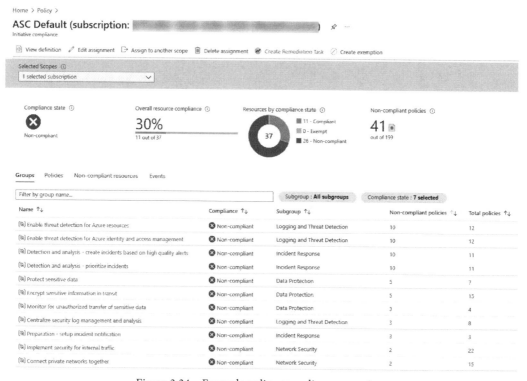

Figure 3.34 – Example policy compliance overview

Now that you understand how to view overall compliance within your subscription, you can begin to apply this in your organization and with your customers.

> **Tip**
> Policies can be used in conjunction with tags to effect compliance in an organization.

Further reading

That brings this section to an end. In this section, we have learned what Azure policies are, why they are necessary, how they work, how to create a policy definition, how to create a policy initiative, and how to manage and apply policies.

We encourage you to read up further by using the following links:

- **Microsoft Azure Policy documentation**: `https://docs.microsoft.com/en-us/azure/governance/policy/`

- **Azure Policy definition structure**: `https://docs.microsoft.com/en-us/azure/governance/policy/concepts/definition-structure`

- **Built-in Azure policy definitions**: `https://github.com/Azure/azure-policy/tree/master/built-in-policies`

Applying and managing tags on resources

Tags are simply name-value pairs and are used to apply taxonomy resources, resource groups, and subscriptions. Tags can assist in several areas for Azure management, primarily in the governance of the platform and cost management. An example of what tags look like on the portal is shown next.

In the following screenshot example, we have these tags:

- **Department**, with a value of `IT`
- **Owner**, with a value of `King`

You can see the tags here:

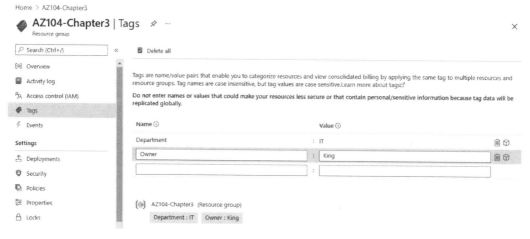

Figure 3.35 – Tag example

> **Tip**
> Tag names are case-insensitive, and tag values are case-sensitive.

Tagging strategy

When implementing a tagging strategy, it's important to consider the requirements for having tags in place. Tags will assist in presenting value to either business or **information technology** (**IT**)-aligned tagging requirements. The key to implementing a defined tag strategy is consistency, in the application of tags as well as the implementation (especially on the casing). Some important common tag patterns are noted here:

- **Functional**: Classification of resources by defining the functionality the resource(s) introduces to the workload environment.

  Application Name: Use this to classify a set of resources for an application.

  Environment: DEV/TEST/UAT/STAGING/PROD/DR.

- **Classification**: This tag can be used to describe data classification pertaining to resources. This is particularly valuable for compliance alignment, such as with the **General Data Protection Regulation** (**GDPR**).

  Confidentiality: Private/Public/Restricted.

- **Accounting**: This set of tags is particularly focused on cost governance and the assignment of resource(s) to a billing unit/entity within the organization.

  Department: `Finance/IT/HR/Marketing/Sales`.

  Region: `West Europe/ Central US`, and so on.

- **Partnership**: This set of tags is used to identify people in the organization who can or should be contacted as they contain relevance to the resource.

  Owner: Identify the product owner for the service.

  Support Email: Identify who to contact when needing support.

  Business Criticality: Define how important the resource is to the business (normally a metric value such as `BC1/BC2/BC3`).

  SLA Objectives: Define a **service-level agreement** (**SLA**) tier that would apply to determine the support required for the service (for example, `SLA Tier 1/SLA Tier 2/SLA Tier 3`).

- **Purpose**: This set of tags is reserved for understanding the key deliverable for the application and is aligned to a business objective.

  Purpose: Describe the application purpose in a single line. This assists later in troubleshooting by creating a basic understanding of what the application is and does.

Applying a resource tag

For this example of applying a resource tag, we will open a resource group on the portal, open the tagging section, and apply a tag. The steps are outlined here:

1. Open the resource group and select **Tags**, as illustrated in the following screenshot:

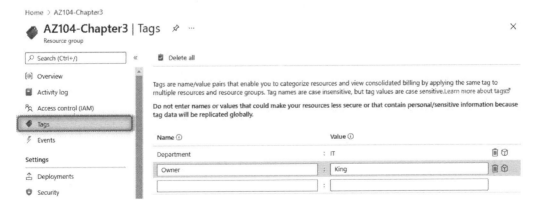

Figure 3.36 – Tag example

2. Apply a tag name and value pair (or multiple pairs), and click **Apply**. We have created a new tag named `Purpose` with a value of `Demo`, as illustrated in the following screenshot:

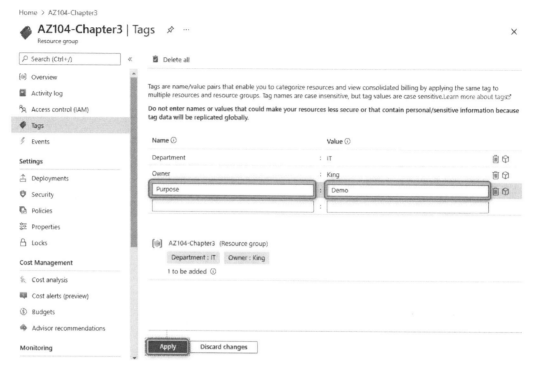

Figure 3.37 – Applying a new tag

3. After being applied, you will get a notification; notice the changes in the section above the **Apply** button. To modify a tag, we simply update the value, as illustrated in the following screenshot, and click **Apply**:

Figure 3.38 – Applied tags overview

Now that you know how to configure and apply tags, you will learn the PowerShell commands to assist with the management of tags.

PowerShell scripts

This section introduces PowerShell scripts that can be used for the automation of tag management, as well as for quicker administration times. Please ensure that the Az module is installed, as per the *Technical requirements* section at the beginning of the chapter.

Applying a tag to a resource group

The following script creates a new tag named `Purpose` with a value of `Demo` in the `AZ104-Chapter3` resource group:

```
$tags = @{"Purpose"="Demo"}
$resourceGroup = Get-AzResourceGroup -Name AZ104-Chapter3
New-AzTag -ResourceId $resourceGroup.ResourceId -tag $tags
```

Applying a tag to a resource

Applying a tag to a resource is very similar; in this instance, we will apply the preceding tag to a storage account resource. Tags will be applied to a resource named `AZ104Storage`. The code is illustrated in the following snippet:

```
$tags = @{"Purpose"="Demo"}
$resource = Get-AzResource -Name AZ104Storage -ResourceGroup
AZ104-Chapter3
New-AzTag -ResourceId $resource.id -Tag $tags
```

Updating tags

`Update-AzTag` is another very useful command; it allows us to update tags to the `$tags` variable that is parsed or to merge tags from the `$tags` variable with existing tags. Merging combines two operations—namely, adding absent tags to the resource or resource group, and updating the value key for existing tags.

In the following example, we will add a new tag named `Tags` with a value of `Merge`. The result will be two tags on the `AZ104-Chapter3` resource group:

```
$tags = @{"Tags"="Merge"}
$resourceGroup = Get-AzResourceGroup -Name AZ104-Chapter3
Update-AzTag -ResourceId $resourceGroup.ResourceId -Tag $tags
-Operation Merge
```

The following example will replace the tags and leave the AZ104-Chapter3 resource group with only the tag for Purpose:

```
$tags = @{"Tags"="Merge"}
$resourceGroup = Get-AzResourceGroup -Name AZ104-Chapter3
Update-AzTag -ResourceId $resourceGroup.ResourceId -Tag $tags
-Operation Replace
```

To run multiple tags in the commands, simply add a ; between tag pairs, as per the following example:

```
$tags = @{"Tag1"="Value1"; "Tag2"="Value2"}
```

> **Tip – AzTag**
>
> The replace command switch will remove tags that are not present in the $tags variable. The merge command will amend tags that are present and add any missing tags defined in the $tags variable.

Further reading

That brings this section to an end. In this section, we have learned what resource locks are, why they are necessary, and how they work.

We encourage students to read up further by using the following links:

- **Microsoft documentation on tags**: https://docs.microsoft.com/en-us/azure/azure-resource-manager/management/tag-resources?tabs=json

- **Resource naming and tagging decision guide**: https://docs.microsoft.com/en-us/azure/cloud-adoption-framework/decision-guides/resource-tagging/?toc=%2Fazure%2Fazure-resource-manager%2Fmanagement%2Ftoc.json

- **Prescriptive guidance for resource tagging**: `https://docs.microsoft.com/en-us/azure/cloud-adoption-framework/govern/guides/complex/prescriptive-guidance#resource-tagging`

- **Applying tags in PowerShell**: `https://docs.microsoft.com/en-us/azure/azure-resource-manager/management/tag-resources?tabs=json#powershell`

Summary

In this chapter, we have established how to create and manage governance in Azure using Azure policies and tags. You have learned how to perform administrative actions through the portal and PowerShell. You also know where to look for information pertaining to managing both policies and tags and how to build a strategy for governance, and have been provided with additional reading sources to improve your application of these new skills. You now have the skills required to implement governance requirements and assist in establishing baselines for governance.

In the next chapter, we will be expanding upon the skills learned in this chapter and investigating how to manage resources and services available in Azure that support governance objectives and costs within Azure.

4
Managing Governance and Costs

This chapter covers how to manage the resources and services available in Azure that support governance objectives, as well as costs. We will cover resource groups, resource locks, subscriptions, costs, and management groups, all of which play a crucial role in maintaining governance within the Azure platform. You will build confidence in this chapter to do just that and understand how to apply what you have learned to your organization.

In this chapter, we are going to cover the following main topics:

- Managing resource groups
- Configuring resource locks
- Managing subscriptions
- Managing costs
- Configuring management groups

Technical requirements

To follow along with the hands-on material, you will need the following:

- Access to an Azure subscription with global administrator and billing administrator privileges. If you do not have access to one, you can enroll for a free account at `https://azure.microsoft.com/en-us/free/`.

- PowerShell 5.1 or later installed on a PC from which labs can be practiced. Note that many examples can only be followed from a PC.

- Installation of the **Az module**. This can be performed by running the following command in an administrative PowerShell session:

```
Set-ExecutionPolicy -ExecutionPolicy RemoteSigned -Scope
CurrentUser
Install-Module -Name Az -Scope CurrentUser -Repository
PSGallery -Force
```

Now, let's understand how to manage resource groups.

Managing resource groups

Resource groups are logical containers for grouping multiple resources together. Resources can be **virtual machines** (**VMs**), databases, virtual networks, web apps, and so forth. A resource group should group all resources that share a similar or same life cycle—for instance, all items that are deployed, updated, or deleted with some form of commonality such as belonging to the same application, service, type, department, or location; in other words, they behave or are viewed as a single entity. Resource groups create a mechanism for logical grouping that enables the order and organization of resources created in Azure.

Some important points to note when defining resource groups are outlined here:

- A resource can only belong in a single resource group at any time.

- Resources can be added and removed from a resource group at any time.

- Resource group metadata (the data describing the resource group and resources) is stored in the region where the resource group is created.

- Resources in a resource group are not bound by the location defined for the resource group and can be deployed into different regions.

- If the resource group's region is temporarily unavailable, then resources in the group cannot be updated since the metadata is unavailable. However, resources deployed in other regions will continue to function as expected, with the caveat that they cannot be updated or managed.

- Access control actions can be associated with resource groups through **role-based access control (RBAC)** roles, Azure Policy, or resource locks.

- Consider a resource group organization strategy when creating resource groups, to identify ownership, billing, location, resource type, department, applications, and access.

Resources can also be moved to a different resource group and subscription; however, there are limitations to this. The following **Uniform Resource Locator (URL)** will assist in considering items before moving: `https://docs.microsoft.com/en-us/azure/azure-resource-manager/management/move-resource-group-and-subscription#checklist-before-moving-resources`. Not all resources support migrations, and the following up-to-date link will provide supported operations by resource type: `https://docs.microsoft.com/en-us/azure/azure-resource-manager/management/move-support-resources`.

Deploying a resource group

In the following section, we are going to run through an exercise of creating a resource group using the Azure portal. Proceed as follows:

1. In the Azure portal, select the hamburger menu icon and click **Resource groups**, as illustrated in the following screenshot:

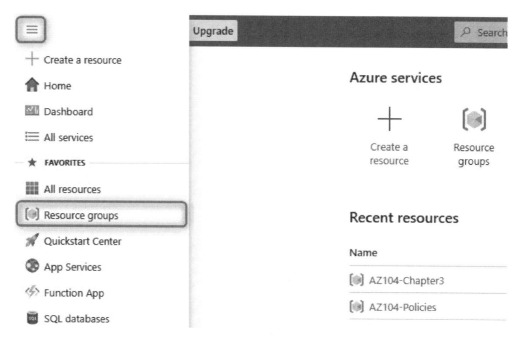

Figure 4.1 – Selecting the Resource groups blade

2. Click **Create**, as illustrated in the following screenshot:

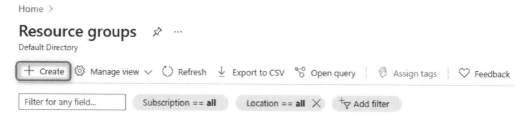

Figure 4.2 – Creating a resource group

3. Enter a resource group name, choose a location, and click **Next: Tags >** if you wish to add tags to the resource group. Alternatively, click **Review + create** to jump to the review pane. In this example, we will click **Review + create**, as illustrated here:

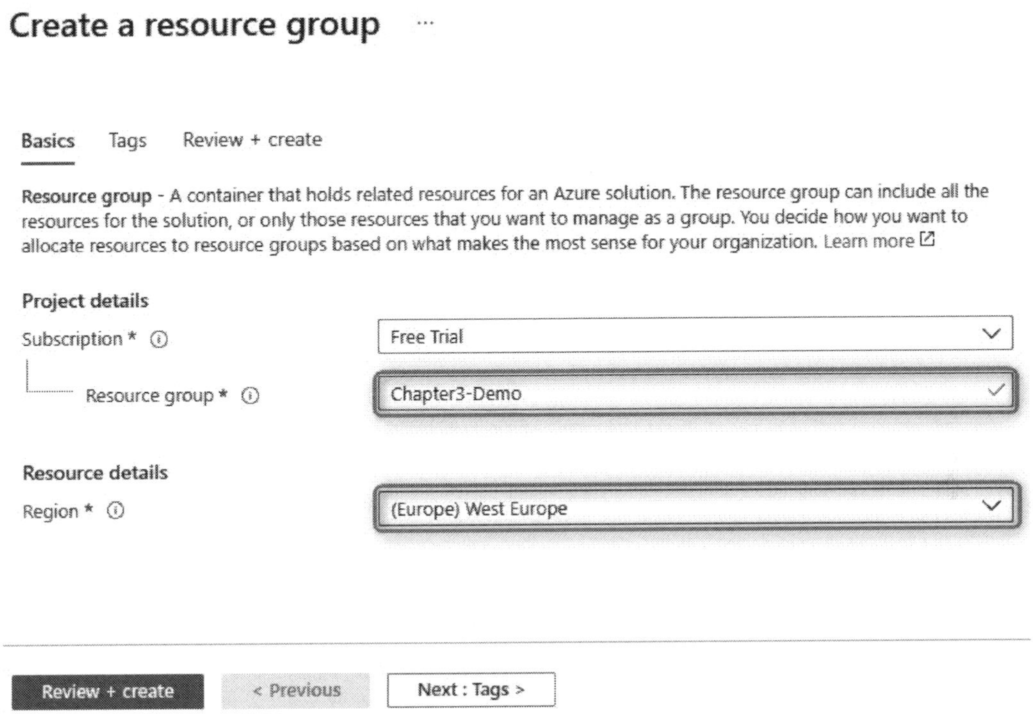

Create a resource group ...

Basics   Tags   Review + create

Resource group - A container that holds related resources for an Azure solution. The resource group can include all the resources for the solution, or only those resources that you want to manage as a group. You decide how you want to allocate resources to resource groups based on what makes the most sense for your organization. Learn more ☑

Project details

Subscription * ⓘ	Free Trial	⌄

Resource group * ⓘ	Chapter3-Demo	✓

Resource details

Region * ⓘ	(Europe) West Europe	⌄

[Review + create]   [< Previous]   [Next : Tags >]

Figure 4.3 – Basics tab: creating a resource group

4.   Upon successful validation, click **Create**, as illustrated in the following screenshot:

Figure 4.4 – Review + create tab: creating a resource group

5.   You will receive a notification to indicate the successful creation of the resource group, as illustrated in the following screenshot:

Figure 4.5 – Resource group overview

You have now learned to deploy a resource group through the Azure portal. In the next section, we will uncover how to view existing resource groups.

> **Top Tip**
> Resource group names must be unique names per subscription.

Listing resource groups

On some occasions, we may want to see which resource groups we have or utilize existing resource groups for future deployments. To do this, we will perform the following steps:

1. On the Azure portal, select the hamburger menu icon and click **Resource groups**, as illustrated in the following screenshot:

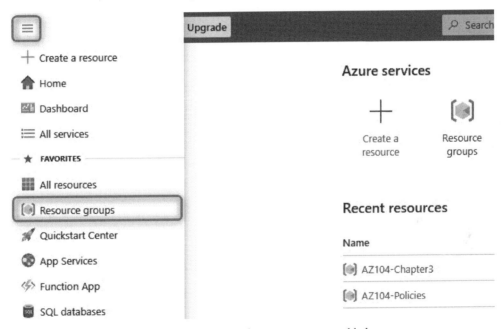

Figure 4.6 – Selecting the Resource groups blade

2. In the following screenshot, notice all the resource groups identified by the **Name**, **Subscription**, and **Location** values:

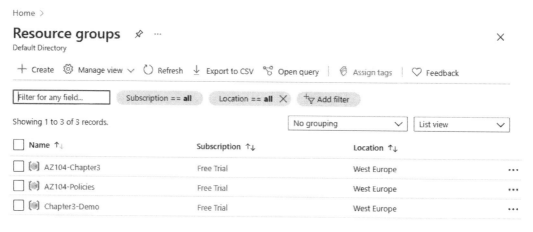

Figure 4.7 – Listing resource groups

You now know how to list resource groups that exist within your subscription. In the next section, we will explore the process behind deleting resource groups.

Deleting a resource group

To delete a resource group, complete the following steps on the portal:

1. On the **Resource groups** blade, select a resource group to be deleted, as illustrated in the following screenshot:

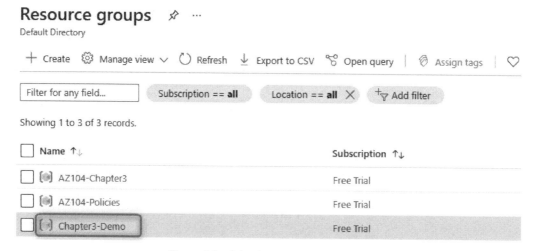

Figure 4.8 – Selecting a resource group

> **Top Tip**
> Deleting a resource group is a quick and easy method of deleting all your resources deployed to that group.

2. On the **Overview** blade, click **Delete resource group** and enter the resource group name in the **TYPE THE RESOURCE GROUP NAME:** dialog box, then click **Delete**. The process is illustrated in the following screenshot:

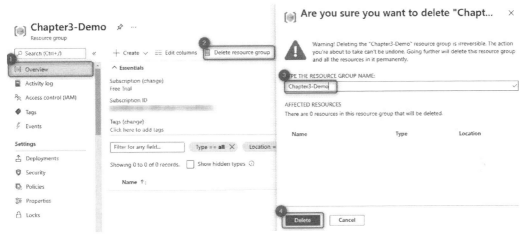

Figure 4.9 – Deleting a resource group

3. You will receive a notification that the resource group has been successfully deleted, as illustrated in the following screenshot:

Figure 4.10 – Resource group deletion notification

You have now learned the process behind deleting resource groups. In the next section, we will look at some PowerShell scripts to accomplish resource group creation tasks.

PowerShell scripts

This section introduces PowerShell scripts that can be used for the automation of resource group management, as well as for quicker administration times. Please ensure that the Az module is installed, as per the *Technical requirements* section at the beginning of the chapter. Then, proceed as follows:

- Create a new empty resource group. Define a location and name for the new resource group to be deployed, as follows:

```
New-AzResourceGroup -Name RG01 -Location "West Europe"
```

- Create a new empty resource group with tags. Define a location, a name, and tags for the resource group, as follows:

```
$tags = @{"Tag1"="Value1"; "Tag2"="Value2"}
New-AzResourceGroup -Name RG01 -Location "West Europe"
-Tag $tags
```

That brings this section to an end. In this section, we have learned about what resource groups are, why they are necessary, the metadata and effects of this, and how to deploy a resource group.

Further reading

We encourage you to read up further by using the following links:

- **Managing resource groups**: https://docs.microsoft.com/en-us/ azure/azure-resource-manager/management/manage-resource- groups-portal

- **Moving resources to other resource groups or another subscription**: https:// docs.microsoft.com/en-us/azure/azure-resource-manager/ management/move-resource-group-and-subscription

Configuring resource locks

You can apply locks to a subscription, resource group, or resource to prevent other administrators from modifying or deleting resources. You can set lock levels to **CanNotDelete** or **ReadOnly** to override permissions that users have, even for administrators. Of the built-in roles, only **Owner** and **User Access Administrator** can create or delete resource locks.

The locks are explained as follows:

- **CanNotDelete** locks deny authorized users from deleting resources but still allow the ability to read and modify resources.

- **ReadOnly** locks grant authorized users the read permissions to resources only. This means that they can't add, delete, or modify resources. The effect is similar to the **Reader** role.

Unlike RBAC, you use management locks to apply a restriction across all users and roles. It is important to note that when applying resource locks the law of inheritance applies, meaning that all resources inherit the lock from the parent scope. The parent scope will be from the highest level of resources in the Azure hierarchy to the resource level, meaning that we can go from subscription down to resource groups down to resources; the parent will be the level at which the lock is applied.

> **Top Tip**
> When applying locks, it's important to understand that the precedence assigned is based on the most restrictive lock that is inherited.

Permissions required for creating or deleting locks

Azure provides very granular control over the delegation of permissions within the platform, but also comes with predefined roles that cater to the deployment and management of resource locks, as with most resources and services. The following roles are required on the platform; either built-in roles or custom roles can be used as per your preference.

Built-in Azure roles

If your preference is to use a predefined Azure role, then either of the following will be suitable:

- **Owner**
- **User Access Administrator**

Custom RBAC roles

If your preference is to define or update a custom role, then the following action permissions are required:

- `Microsoft.Authorization/*`

- `Microsoft.Authorization/locks/*`

Let's move on to add a resource lock.

Adding a resource lock

If you have been following along so far in this book with the previous section and created an `AZ104-Policies` resource group, then please use that for this exercise; alternatively, use any resource group that would suit. We will create a resource group, add a delete lock, add a resource, demonstrate the delete lock effect, remove the lock, and apply a read lock to demonstrate the effect. Your user account will require **Owner** or **User Access Administrator** privileges in order to add the lock. The steps are outlined here:

1. Open the resource group, then on the left menu click on **Locks**, then click **Add**. The process is illustrated in the following screenshot:

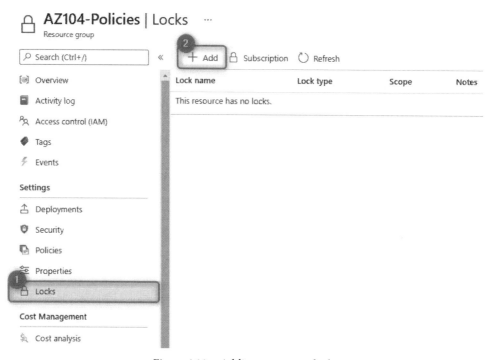

Figure 4.11 – Adding a resource lock

2. Enter the corresponding lock details, such as **Lock name**, **Lock type**, and **Notes** values, as illustrated in the following screenshot:

Add lock

Lock name

| DeleteLock   ✓ |

Lock type

| Delete   ⌄ |

Notes

| Prevents Resource Deletion |

| OK | | Cancel |

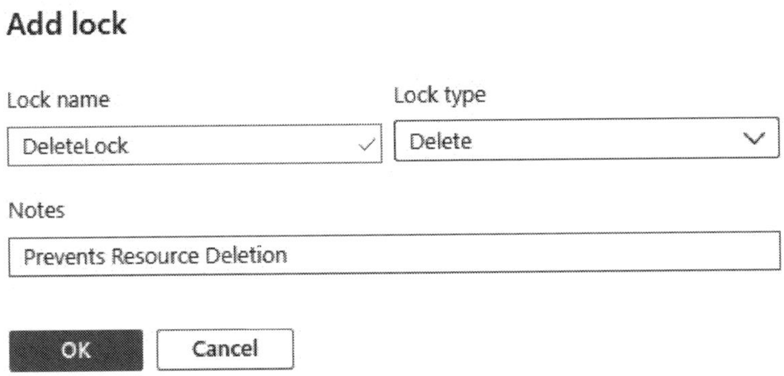

Figure 4.12 – Lock details

3. Open the resource group, then click **Overview** on the left menu, then click **Create**, then **Marketplace**. The process is illustrated in the following screenshot:

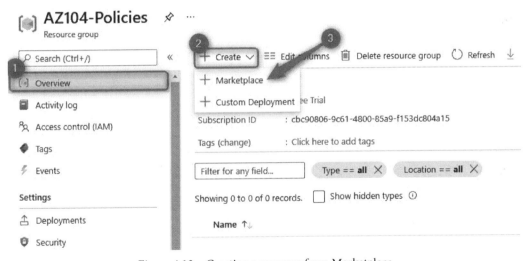

Figure 4.13 – Creating a resource from Marketplace

4.   Create any desired resource; we will create a storage account, as follows. After filling
in the relevant details, click **Review + create**:

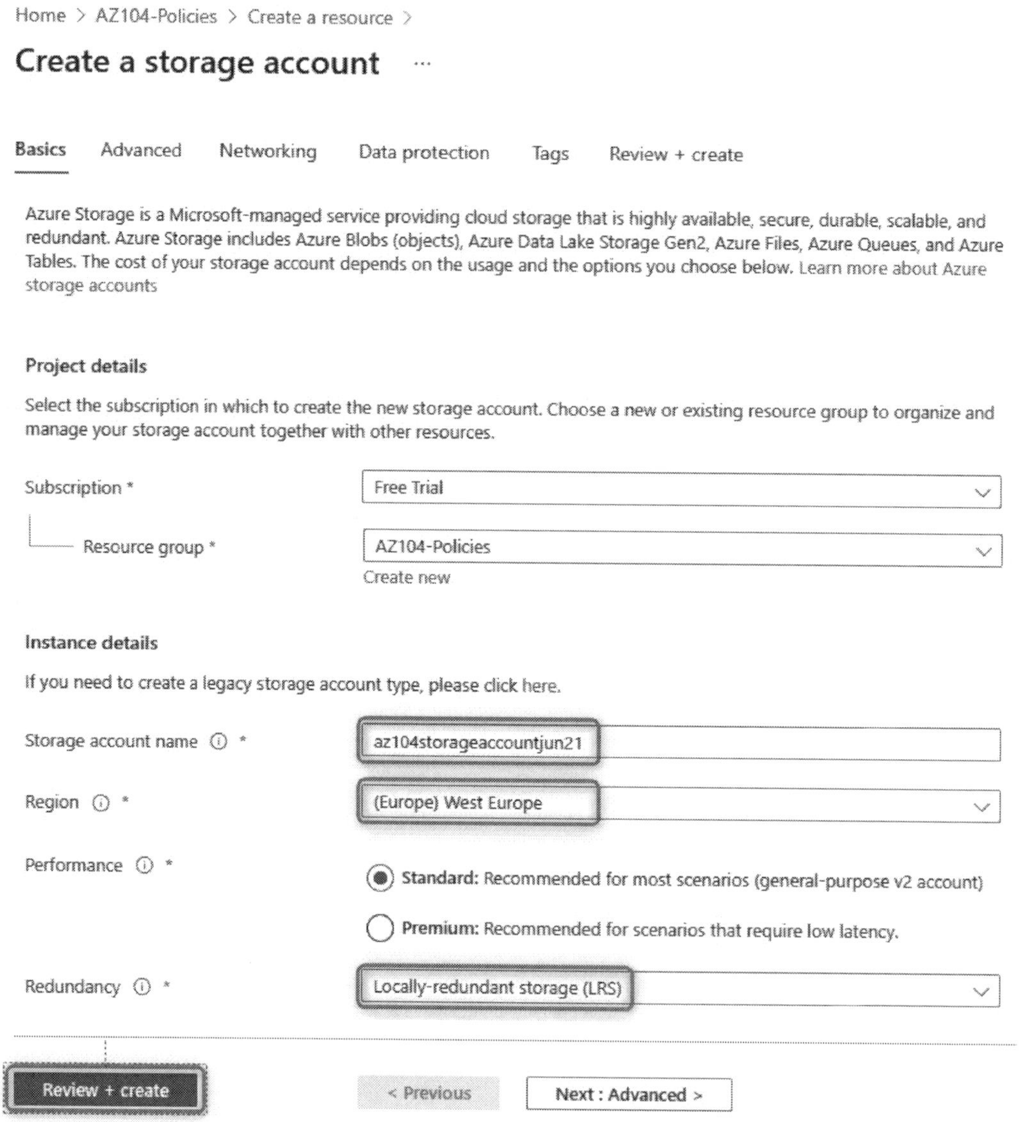

Home > AZ104-Policies > Create a resource >

Create a storage account   ···

Basics   Advanced   Networking   Data protection   Tags   Review + create

Azure Storage is a Microsoft-managed service providing cloud storage that is highly available, secure, durable, scalable, and
redundant. Azure Storage includes Azure Blobs (objects), Azure Data Lake Storage Gen2, Azure Files, Azure Queues, and Azure
Tables. The cost of your storage account depends on the usage and the options you choose below. Learn more about Azure
storage accounts

Project details

Select the subscription in which to create the new storage account. Choose a new or existing resource group to organize and
manage your storage account together with other resources.

Subscription * | Free Trial   ⌄ |

└── Resource group * | AZ104-Policies   ⌄ |
                                         Create new

Instance details

If you need to create a legacy storage account type, please click here.

Storage account name ⓘ * | az104storageaccountjun21 |

Region ⓘ * | (Europe) West Europe   ⌄ |

Performance ⓘ *   (●) **Standard**: Recommended for most scenarios (general-purpose v2 account)

                                      (   ) **Premium**: Recommended for scenarios that require low latency.

Redundancy ⓘ * | Locally-redundant storage (LRS)   ⌄ |

[**Review + create**]   [< Previous]   [Next : Advanced >]

Figure 4.14 – Creating a storage account

5. After validation, click **Create**, as illustrated in the following screenshot:

Figure 4.15 – Deployment screen

6. After the deployment has completed, click **Go to resource**, as illustrated in the following screenshot:

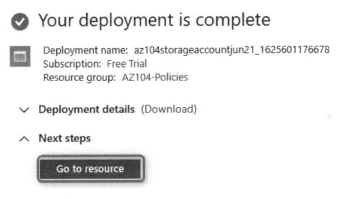

Figure 4.16 – Deployment progress screen

7. Click on **Delete** on the top menu bar, as illustrated in the following screenshot:

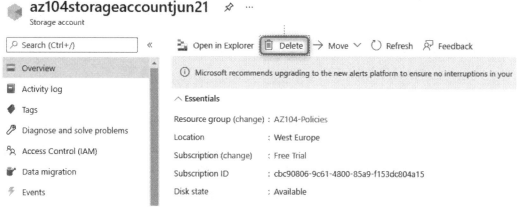

Figure 4.17 – Deleting a storage account

> **Top Tip**
>
> There are times you may want to delete an individual resource, which can be done as per the preceding step, and you will note the process resembles the deletion of a resource group.

8. Notice here the error that follows:

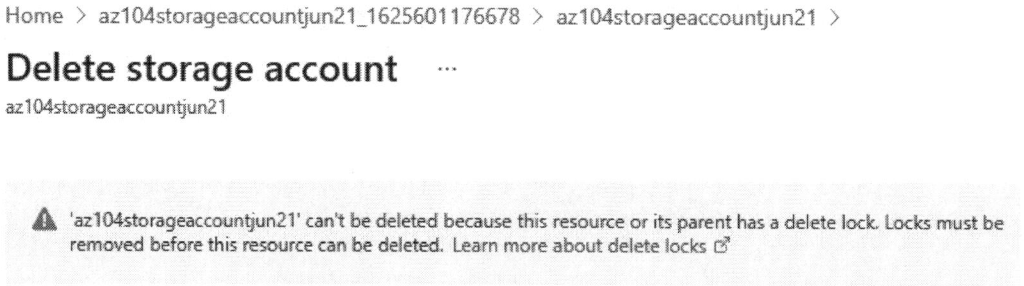

Home > az104storageaccountjun21_1625601176678 > az104storageaccountjun21 >

Delete storage account   ...

az104storageaccountjun21

 'az104storageaccountjun21' can't be deleted because this resource or its parent has a delete lock. Locks must be removed before this resource can be deleted. Learn more about delete locks ⬈

Figure 4.18 – Deletion failure from resource lock

9. Go back to the resource group, select **Locks**, and delete the **DeleteLock** lock, as illustrated in the following screenshot:

Figure 4.19 – Deleting a resource lock

10. Go back to the resource group and attempt a deletion of the resource again. Notice here that we receive a success message this time:

Figure 4.20 – Successful deletion notification

11. Open the resource group, then on the left menu click on **Locks**, then click **Add**. Enter the corresponding lock details, such as **Lock name**, **Lock type**, and **Notes** values, as illustrated in the following screenshot:

Add lock

Lock name

ReadLock

Lock type

Read-only

Notes

Read Lock

OK   Cancel

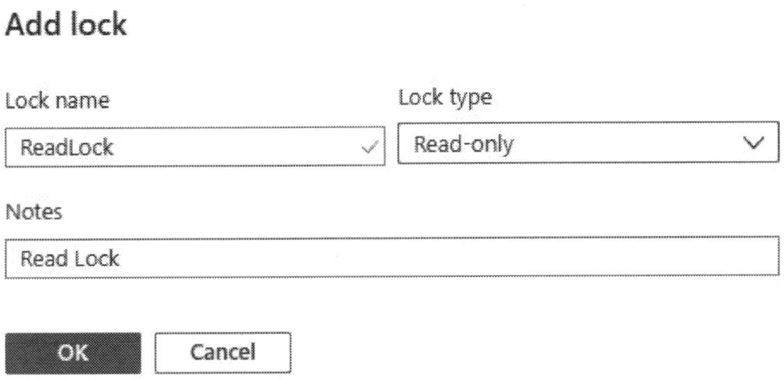

Figure 4.21 – Creating a read-only resource lock

12. Open the resource group, click **Overview** on the left menu, then click **Create**, then **Marketplace**. Attempt to create any resource and notice the validation error, as indicated in the following screenshot:

Figure 4.22 – Failure to create a resource from a lock

You have now learned how to add a resource lock and prove it's working as expected.

PowerShell scripts

This section introduces PowerShell scripts that can be used for the automation of resource lock management, as well as for quicker administration times. Please ensure that the Az module is installed, as per the *Technical requirements* section at the beginning of the chapter.

Applying a resource lock to a resource

To lock a resource, provide the name of the resource, its resource type, and its resource group name for the following script:

```
New-AzResourceLock -LockLevel CanNotDelete -LockName LockSite
-ResourceName examplesite -ResourceType Microsoft.Web/sites
-ResourceGroupName exampleresourcegroup
```

Now, let's try the same for a resource group.

Applying a resource lock to a resource group

To lock a resource group, provide the name of the resource group and the type of lock to be applied using the following script:

```
New-AzResourceLock -LockName LockGroup -LockLevel CanNotDelete
-ResourceGroupName exampleresourcegroup
```

This applies the resource lock to the resource group successfully.

Viewing resource locks in effect

To get information about a lock, use the `Get-AzResourceLock` cmdlet. To get all locks in your subscription, use the following command:

```
Get-AzResourceLock
```

> **Tip**
> Always check restrictions to prevent unexpected behaviors, such as locks preventing backup. See the following URL for more information on this: `https://docs.microsoft.com/en-us/azure/azure-resource-manager/management/lock-resources?tabs=json#considerations-before-applying-locks`.

ARM templates

For automation or simplified administration, we can also make use of **Azure Resource Manager** (**ARM**) templates for the creation of resource locks. This is just another way to achieve the same goal. Here's how to do this:

- When applying to an individual resource, the scope property must be specified.
- When applying to a resource group or subscription, the scope property can be omitted.

  The following example **JavaScript Object Notation** (**JSON**) template code defines a lock at the resource group level:

```
{
    "$schema": "https://schema.management.azure.com/
schemas/2019-04-01/deploymentTemplate.json#",
    "contentVersion": "1.0.0.0",
    "parameters": {
    },
    "resources": [
      {
        "type": "Microsoft.Authorization/locks",
        "apiVersion": "2016-09-01",
        "name": "rgLock",
        "properties": {
```

```
            "level": "CanNotDelete",
            "notes": "Resource group should not be deleted."
        }
      }
   ]
}
```

> **Tip**
> It's advisable to always apply **Delete** locks on resource groups to prevent accidental resource deletion.

Further reading

That brings this section to an end. In this section, we have learned what resource locks are, why they are necessary, and how they work.

We encourage you to read up further by using the following link:

Microsoft documentation for resource locks: `https://docs.microsoft.com/en-us/azure/azure-resource-manager/management/lock-resources?tabs=json`

The following link will provide some references to situations where you might want to apply resource locks within your Azure Blueprints:

Resource locks in Azure Blueprints: `https://docs.microsoft.com/en-us/azure/governance/blueprints/concepts/resource-locking`

Managing subscriptions

Subscriptions are billing units for Azure resources; they are the container where all resources are built and contain resources grouped into resource groups. Inside the Azure subscription, you can create multiple resource groups and resources.

A billing profile will have ownership of an Azure subscription, whereby an Azure subscription will have a trust relationship established with a single **Azure Active Directory** (**Azure AD**) tenant.

Analyzing the hierarchy shown in the following diagram, you will see subscriptions form the bottom layer of an enterprise hierarchy in resource allocation within Azure:

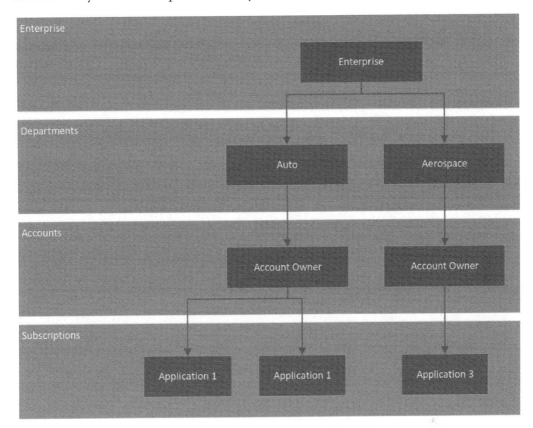

Figure 4.23 – Azure management hierarchy

You will see the hierarchy is divided into four levels, these being **Enterprise**, **Departments**, **Accounts**, and **Subscriptions**. In the following overview, you will get an idea of what these different levels are for:

- **Enterprise**: This is an **identifier** (**ID**) for the organization, normally identified by the Azure AD tenant. The Azure agreement in place is defined at this level, such as Pay-as-you-Go, CSP, and Enterprise Agreement (used for large organizations).

- **Departments**: At the department level, sub-accounts for the different departments in your organization are created. You can also group your departments in a functional way, such as an **information technology** (**IT**) and finance department, or group them in a geographical way, such as North America and Europe, for instance. You can add a department owner here, which will be the person in charge of owning the budget for the department, for instance.

- **Accounts**: This is where different departments can create multiple accounts within their department. They can also add additional owners to manage these accounts. When you create a personal account in Azure, this is the starting point for creating subscriptions. The Microsoft account that you use to log in to the Azure portal is then added to this account as the owner.

- **Subscriptions**: You can create multiple subscriptions in an account. This is the level where the actual billing takes place and where different Azure resources are created. You can add additional subscription owners that can manage subscriptions, create different resources, and assign other users to a subscription. Subscriptions always have a trust relationship with an Azure AD instance.

There are occasions where resource limits might be reached within a subscription, and this may be the criterion for you to create a new one. For resource limits, please refer to the following URL: `https://docs.microsoft.com/en-us/azure/azure-resource-manager/management/azure-subscription-service-limits`.

Relationship between Azure AD and subscriptions

Azure subscriptions have trust relationships associated with Azure AD. Through this trust, a subscription enables Azure AD to authenticate users, services, and devices.

A tenant can have a 1:M relationship with subscriptions (meaning it can be associated with multiple subscriptions), but a subscription can only have a 1:1 relationship with a tenant (meaning a subscription can only be associated with one tenant). You can see an overview of this in the following diagram:

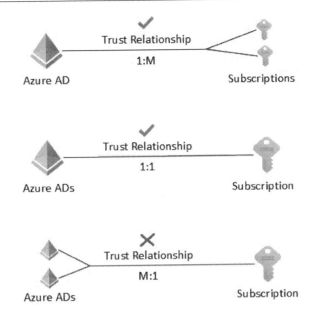

Figure 4.24 – Azure AD and subscription relationship

You have now seen the relationship structure and have an understanding of the management hierarchy.

Why do we have multiple subscriptions in an environment?

This is part of the organizational strategy when defining Azure, and it's important to understand the segregation of data and resources and how this will be managed perpetually by the business. Some motivations to split out resource groups are separating resources by the following:

- Different **business units** (**BUs**) (Finance/IT/Marketing)
- Different environments (Dev/Test/UAT/PROD)
- Geographic (West Europe/Central US)
- Cost centers (could be the same as BUs or a unique code)

> **Tip**
>
> When defining governance around Azure, it's important to define a naming convention that will be applied across multiple layers, including subscriptions. It's recommended to identify a subscription location and purpose in the name—for example, `WE_PROD`.

Further reading

That brings this section to an end. In this section, we have learned about what subscriptions are, why they are necessary, strategic items to consider, and billing ownership associated with subscriptions.

We encourage you to read up further by using the following links:

- **Initial subscription strategy**: `https://docs.microsoft.com/en-us/azure/cloud-adoption-framework/ready/azure-best-practices/initial-subscriptions`

- **Multi-subscription strategy**: `https://docs.microsoft.com/en-us/azure/cloud-adoption-framework/ready/azure-best-practices/scale-subscriptions`

Managing costs

Azure Cost Management + Billing is a suite of tools designed to assist in the analysis, management, and cost optimization of Azure workloads. It assists in the following management tasks relating to costs:

- Billing administration tasks
- Managing billing access
- Reports on cost and usage data
- Configuration of budgets
- Identifying opportunities to optimize costs

Cost Management

Cost Management contains many facets and should be considered in its entirety; this includes costs analysis, governance, and reporting. For the purpose of the exam, we will investigate cost analysis and report scheduling.

Cost analysis

Cost analysis assists in understanding expenditure within Azure. Quick reports are automatically generated to provide insights into current and historical expenditure on the scope chosen. Further to understanding current costs, the utility predicts anticipated forecast expenditure for the month ahead.

In the following screenshot, you will notice expenditure on an **Area** chart on the top portion of the report that shows accumulative expenditure over the course of the current billing period (this is a filter that can be changed), with some charts below that signify costs by **Service name**, **Location**, and **Resource group name** values. It is good to note that Azure also provides insights into the forecasted cost, as you can see for the following subscription. This will be invaluable in predicting your estimated expenditure:

Figure 4.25 – Cost analysis

Additional filters can be added and modified depending on the desired preference for viewing costs. Costs can also be exported for view in **Portable Network Graphics (PNG)**, Excel, and **comma-separated values (CSV)** format by clicking on the **Download** button, as illustrated in the following screenshot:

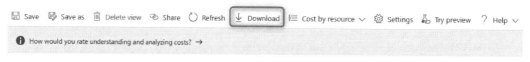

Figure 4.26 – Cost analysis: Download

Select the appropriate download option and click **Download charts**, as illustrated in the following screenshot:

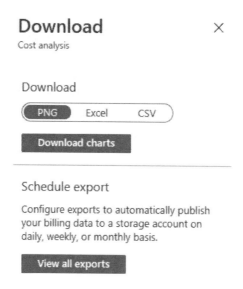

Figure 4.27 – Cost analysis: Download options

Now that you have experienced working with cost analysis data and exporting the data, we will look at how to schedule reports desired from Azure.

Scheduled reports

Depending on requirements, scheduled reports can also be created, as illustrated in the following screenshot:

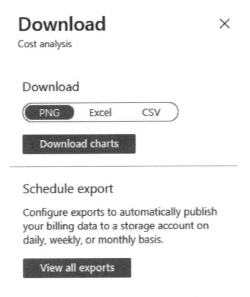

Figure 4.28 – Cost analysis: Download options

Continuing from the previous exercise, clicking the **View all exports** button shown in the preceding screenshot will bring us to the **Exports** blade, where you can click on **Schedule export**. Fill in the relevant details and click **Create**. You will note that a storage account is required for the export. The export-type options consist of daily, weekly, monthly, or one-time exports, as illustrated in the following screenshot:

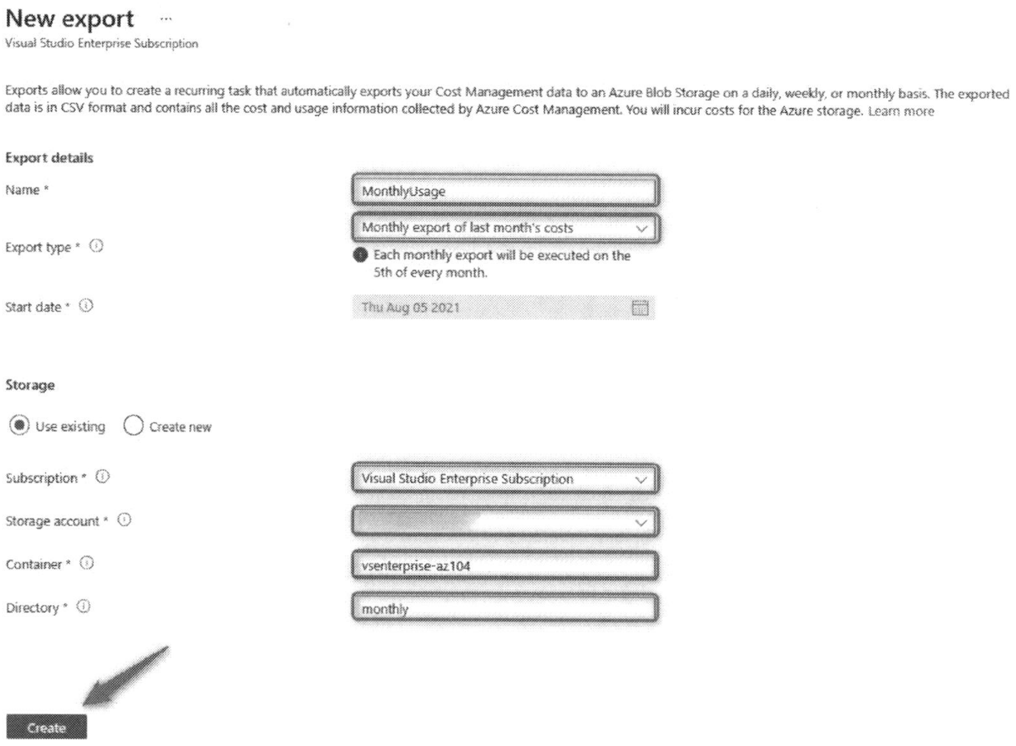

Figure 4.29 – Scheduled report

You have now seen how to analyze costs, export reporting data, and schedule reports. We will now investigate how to create cost alerts in the following section.

Budgets

Budgets create a logical way for a scope defined in Cost Management to manage cost expenditure on resources. Use these to prevent unexpected expenditures such as runaway costs. Here's how to create a budget:

1. Select **Budgets** from the **Cost Management** menu, as illustrated in the following screenshot:

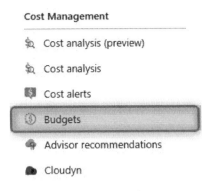

Figure 4.30 – Budgets

2. Click + **Add** and complete the relevant fields, as well as select a scope for the budget. For the **Budget Amount** field, assess the chart information on the right to understand expected costs and predict the budget to be implemented. Click **Next >**. You will note in the following screenshot that the currency is reflected as **ZAR**, which is the national currency of South Africa. This will change depending on the region you billed in:

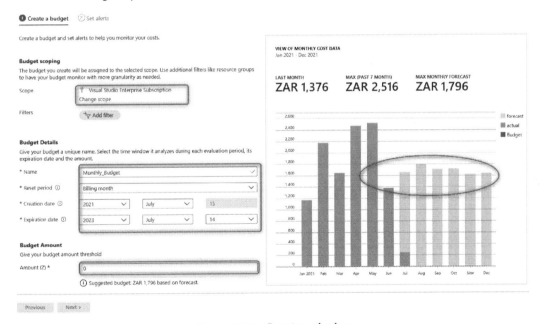

Figure 4.31 – Creating a budget

3. Next, we will need to define conditions for an alert to be triggered; for instance, 85 % of the defined budget. We can select an action group for notifications (more intelligent notification management can include emails, **Short Message Service (SMS)**, Azure Functions, and Azure Logic Apps), and we can specify an *email* notification. Select a *language* for the notification to be delivered in and click **Create**. The following screenshot provides an overview of the process:

Figure 4.32 – Creating a budget: alerts

You have now learned how to define and apply budgets in Azure. In the next section, we will explore Azure Advisor and the recommendations it offers.

Cost alerts

Cost alerts enable notifications for identified alert trigger points that are configured for an environment; we can create these for resources or resource groups that exceed an expected expenditure or when we are getting close to a threshold. To view implemented alerts, select **Cost alerts** from the **Cost Management** menu, as illustrated in the following screenshot:

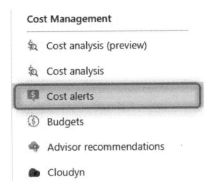

Figure 4.33 – Cost alerts

Any alerts derived from defined budgets will appear here:

Figure 4.34 – Cost alerts: preview

As you can see from the preceding screenshot, we have a single budget alert in our subscription from the budget creation. The following steps will guide you through creating an alert:

1. To create a budget, select **Cost alerts** from the **Cost Management** menu.

2. You will be presented with the same setup window as the previous exercise where you are prompted to create a budget, followed by an alert.

To modify a cost alert, perform the following steps:

1. To create a budget, select **Budgets** from the **Cost Management** menu.

2. Click on your budget, and on the following pane, click **Edit budget**, as illustrated in the following screenshot:

Figure 4.35 – Edit budget

3. On the top of the pane window, click **Set alerts**, as illustrated in the following screenshot:

Configure alert conditions and send email notifications based on your spend.

* Alert conditions

Type	% of budget	Amount (ZAR)	Action group
Actual	45	45.00	None
Select type	Enter %	-	None

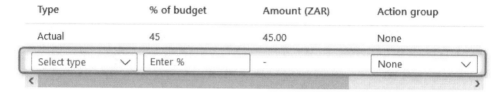

Figure 4.36 – Set alerts

4. Modify the **Alert conditions** values and click **Save**.

You have now learned how to create cost alerts; we encourage this to be implemented as part of your cost management and governance strategy.

Advisor recommendations

Advisor automatically detects cost optimizations that can be implemented within the tenant. While the recommendations are particularly good and will absolutely lead to cost savings, review each item and confirm where costs can be further reduced through an understanding of resources within the Azure environment. Right-sizing is critical for managing costs and is highly advised as the first exercise to be conducted before considering reserved instances and capacity. You can see some example Advisor recommendations in the following screenshot:

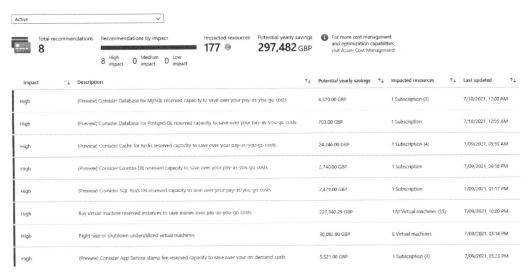

Figure 4.37 – Azure Advisor recommendations

It is recommended to consult Azure Advisor regularly to gain insights into the valuable information shared by the platform, especially when considering costs. In later sections, we visit how this can be used to expose security, performance, and reliability insights too.

Reservations

Reservations are a mechanism for saving money on Azure by committing to 1-year or 3-year plans for resources. Through this, you receive a significant discount from Microsoft, up to 72% compared to pay-as-you-go prices. Reservations must be carefully planned as they are long-term investments and are applied at **stock-keeping unit (SKU)**, scope, and sometimes region levels. Reservations do offer some form of flexibility—especially when applied to VMs—but are limited in nature, particularly on the same family of VMs where a ratio will be applied when the applicable SKU is not found.

> **Tip**
> If the organization you are working with has subscribed to an Enterprise Agreement with Microsoft and has subscribed to Software Assurance, cost-saving can be leveraged on VMs by enabling Azure hybrid benefit on the VM properties page.

Further reading

That brings this section to an end. In this section, we have learned about what subscriptions are, why they are necessary, strategic items to consider, and billing ownership associated with subscriptions.

We encourage you to read up further by using the following links:

- **Transfer billing ownership of a subscription**: `https://docs.microsoft.com/en-us/azure/cost-management-billing/manage/billing-subscription-transfer`

- **Cost Management overview**: `https://docs.microsoft.com/en-gb/azure/cost-management-billing/cost-management-billing-overview`

- **Cost Management best practices**: `https://docs.microsoft.com/en-gb/azure/cost-management-billing/costs/cost-mgt-best-practices`

- **Azure reservations**: `https://docs.microsoft.com/en-us/azure/cost-management-billing/reservations/save-compute-costs-reservations`

Configuring management groups

Azure management groups help you organize your resources and subscriptions and sit above the subscription layer, which allows for global governance of the Azure platform.

Subscriptions are organized into containers called **management groups** that allow a transitive flow of common conditions through subscription layers, such as Azure policies and RBAC permissions. This structure should always dictate a form of logical hierarchy structure that should be constructed to allow for a flow of permissions or policies as required by the organization.

The scope of management within Azure is defined as per the following diagram:

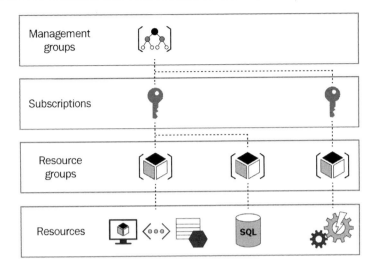

Figure 4.38 – Resource management scope

Generally, aligning to a company organogram can help determine structures to be implemented by discerning the desired outcomes from the management group structure, bearing in mind that this may be policy, permission, and/or governance. To support this decision, logical breakdowns should identify the overall hierarchy to be developed in Azure relating to the management and reporting of services. This is usually defined to be either through functional/business divisions or geographical divisions, and a combination of these can be derived based on the desired outcomes.

An example management group structure is presented here:

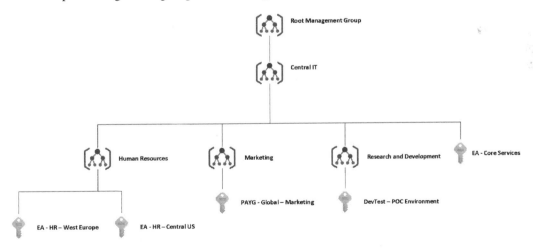

Figure 4.39 – Example management group structure

Now that you understand the structure of management groups, we will create one.

Creating a management group

In the following example, we will create a management group named **IT** and associate our subscription with this group. Here's what we'll do:

1. We will search for `management groups` in the search bar at the top of the Azure portal and click **Management groups** when the service is identified, as illustrated in the following screenshot:

Figure 4.40 – Searching for management groups

2. Since we do not have any management groups yet, we will need to enable the feature. Click **Start using management groups**, as illustrated in the following screenshot:

No management groups to display

Organize your subscriptions into groups called "management groups" to help you manage access, policy and compliance across your subscriptions. Management groups give you enterprise-grade management at a large scale no matter what type of subscriptions you might have. Learn more

Figure 4.41 – Enabling management groups

3. Enter a **Management group ID** and **Management group display name** value and click **Submit**, as illustrated in the following screenshot:

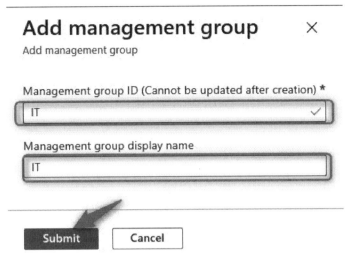

Figure 4.42 – Creating a management group

4. A notification will indicate the successful creation of a management group, and we will be presented with the management group overview. Note the **Tenant Root Group** entity in the following screenshot—this is enabled by default on all environments and sits above all management groups and subscriptions:

Figure 4.43 – Management groups overview

> **Top Tip**
>
> The first management group in Azure is the tenant root group—this is created by default and is the top parent group; all subsequent management groups will fall as child management groups under the root group. Also, the root group cannot be deleted.

You have now created your first management group, and this can be used for better governance and management of Azure.

Further reading

That brings this section to an end. In this section, we have learned what management groups are, how they contribute to organizational structure and management within Azure, and how to create a management group.

We encourage you to read up further by using the following links:

- **Organizing subscriptions**: `https://docs.microsoft.com/en-us/azure/cloud-adoption-framework/ready/azure-best-practices/organize-subscriptions`

- **Management groups documentation**: `https://docs.microsoft.com/en-us/azure/governance/management-groups/`

Summary

In this chapter, we covered resource group management, resource locks, subscription management, costs, and management groups. You have acquired several skills to assist you in driving governance within the organization for Azure resources, as well as understanding costs for effective management of the platform. Resource locks, tagging in Azure, resource groups, subscriptions, **Cost Management + Billing**, and management groups were all covered.

In the next chapter, we will go through some labs relating to this entire first section on managing Azure identities and governance.

5
Practice Labs – Managing Azure Identities and Governance

The best way to become efficient with Azure is to get hands-on experience to test your skill set. This chapter will test the skills you acquired in the first four chapters. The labs in this chapter are referencing the official Microsoft Learning labs on GitHub.

In brief, the following lab sections are required to be completed:

- Managing Azure Active Directory identities
- Managing subscriptions and RBAC
- Managing governance via Azure Policy

Technical requirements

To follow this chapter hands-on, you will need access to an Azure **Active Directory** (**AD**) tenant as a global administrator. If you do not have access to one, students can enroll with a free account: `https://azure.microsoft.com/en-in/free/`.

An Azure subscription is also required; you can either register with your own credit card or enroll for the free $200 one-off credit by using the following link: `https://azure.microsoft.com/en-us/free/`.

An Azure AD Premium P1 license is also required for some of the sections; luckily, there is also a free trial for one month: `https://azure.microsoft.com/en-us/trial/get-started-active-directory/`.

> **Important Note**
> Even though the labs are in GitHub, no GitHub account is required to access the labs.

Managing Azure AD objects

The following is the link to the official Microsoft Learning GitHub labs, which will guide you through each task step by step for managing Azure AD objects:

```
https://microsoftlearning.github.io/AZ-104-
MicrosoftAzureAdministrator/Instructions/Labs/LAB_01-Manage_
Azure_AD_Identities.html
```

Lab scenario one

You are the administrator of an organization and have been instructed to provision users and groups within Azure AD.

This lab scenario consists of four different lab tasks with an estimated time of 30 minutes to complete, and are as follows:

1. **Task one**: Create and configure Azure AD users.
2. **Task two**: Create Azure AD groups with assigned and dynamic memberships.
3. **Task three**: Create an Azure AD tenant.
4. **Task four**: Manage Azure AD guest users.

After you have completed the labs, you can remove the resources created.

> **Note**
> It is best practice to remove unused resources to ensure that there are no unexpected costs, even though the resources created in this lab do not incur additional costs.

Now that we have practically learned how to create users and groups within Azure AD, let's next have a look at how to implement **Role-Based Access Control** (**RBAC**).

Managing RBAC

The following is the link to the official Microsoft Learning GitHub labs, which will guide you through each task step by step for managing RBAC:

```
https://microsoftlearning.github.io/AZ-104-
MicrosoftAzureAdministrator/Instructions/Labs/LAB_02a_Manage_
Subscriptions_and_RBAC.html
```

Lab scenario two

You are the administrator of an organization and have been instructed to improve the management of Azure resources; you need to implement the following:

- Creating a management group that includes all Azure subscriptions
- Granting permissions to submit support requests for all subscriptions in the management group to a specific Azure AD user

This lab scenario consists of three different lab tasks with an estimated time of 30 minutes to complete:

1. **Task one**: Implement management groups.
2. **Task two**: Create custom RBAC roles.
3. **Task three**: Assign RBAC roles.

After you have completed the labs, you can remove the resources created.

> **Important Note**
> It is best practice to remove unused resources to ensure that there are no unexpected costs, even though resources created in this lab do not incur additional costs.

Now that we have practically learned how to create a custom RBAC role and assign the role, let's have a look next at how to configure resource tags.

The following is the link to the official Microsoft Learning GitHub labs, which will guide you through each task step by step for managing subscriptions and governance:

```
https://microsoftlearning.github.io/AZ-104-
MicrosoftAzureAdministrator/Instructions/Labs/LAB_02b-Manage_
Governance_via_Azure_Policy.html
```

Lab scenario three

You are the administrator of an organization and have been instructed to improve the management of Azure resources; you need to implement the following:

- The tagging of resource groups for infrastructure resources
- Ensuring that only tagged resources can be added to infrastructure resource groups
- Remediating any non-compliant resources

This lab scenario consists of three different lab tasks with an estimated time of 30 minutes to complete:

1. **Task one**: Create and assign tags via the Azure portal.
2. **Task two**: Enforce tagging via Azure Policy.
3. **Task three**: Apply tagging via Azure Policy.

After you have completed the labs, you can remove the resources created.

> **Note**
>
> It is best practice to remove unused resources to ensure that there are no unexpected costs, even though the resources created in this lab do not incur additional costs.

After completing the preceding tasks, you have learned hands-on how to assign and even enforce resource tags within the Azure portal.

Summary

In this chapter, we had a look at scenario-based labs, which tested our skills in the following areas: creating users and groups, implementing management groups, creating and assigning custom RBAC roles, creating and assigning tags to resources, and enforcing tags on resources via Azure Policy.

In the next section, we'll cover implementing and managing storage in Azure after looking at how to configure network access to storage accounts.

Part 2: Implementing and Managing Storage

This is the second part of the official Microsoft exam objectives and will focus on how to implement as well as manage storage within Azure.

This part of the book comprises the following chapters:

- *Chapter 6, Understanding and Managing Storage*
- *Chapter 7, Securing Storage*
- *Chapter 8, Practice Labs – Implementing and Managing Storage*

6
Understanding and Managing Storage

In this chapter, we will explore the different types of storage accounts available to Azure, the different access tiers, disk storage, and the varying redundancy options. We will create a storage account, set up file shares and blob storage, and use Azure Storage Explorer to manage storage accounts. We will also explore how to import and export data from Azure. By the end of the chapter, you will have the skills required to implement and configure storage in Azure, as well as be able to identify the appropriate management tool needed.

In this chapter, we are going to cover the following main topics:

- Understanding Azure storage accounts
- Creating and configuring storage accounts
- Using Azure Import/Export
- Installing and using Azure Storage Explorer
- Configuring Azure Files and Azure Blob storage

Technical requirements

To follow along with the hands-on material, you will need the following:

- Access to an Azure subscription with owner or contributor privileges. If you do not have access to one, students can enroll for a free account at `https://azure.microsoft.com/en-us/free/`.

- PowerShell 5.1 or later installed on a PC from which labs can be practiced. Note that many examples can only be followed from a PC. Alternatively, Cloud Shell may be considered: `https://shell.azure.com`.

- Installation of the `Az` module can be performed by running the following command in an administrative PowerShell session:

```
Set-ExecutionPolicy -ExecutionPolicy RemoteSigned -Scope
CurrentUser
Install-Module -Name Az -Scope CurrentUser -Repository
PSGallery -Force
```

Understanding Azure storage accounts

Azure offers a variety of services that can be utilized for storage; these can vary from database options to messaging systems, to files. Azure has identified four core types of services and integrated these into a single service named Azure Storage. These are identified as **Azure Blobs**, **Azure Files**, **Azure Queues**, and **Azure Tables** under an Azure storage account. A storage account may contain several data services in a combination of the ones described previously and stored collectively in a grouped service. Various types of data—such as files, documents, datasets, blobs, and **virtual hard disks (VHDs)**—can be stored in the storage account, and most will be accommodated by the defined structure. The following screenshot illustrates the different storage services associated with a storage account:

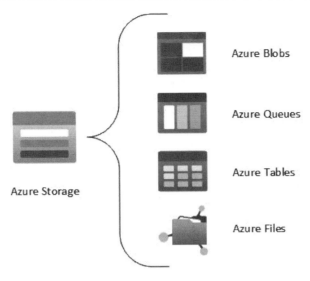

Figure 6.1 – Azure storage account services

Now that you have seen how storage services are provided within a storage account, we will explore the different types of storage accounts available to Azure.

Types of storage accounts

Azure Storage currently offers several different types of storage accounts, as detailed in this section. There are various components to consider when choosing the correct type of account, these being the following:

- Type of storage account (consider the service required)
- Redundancy
- Intended usage
- Performance
- Replication
- Security
- Limitations

Let's now explore the different types of storage accounts.

General-purpose version 1 (legacy)

A **general-purpose version 1 (GPv1)** storage account is the oldest type of storage account. It offers storage for page blobs, block blobs, files, queues, and tables, but it is not always the most cost-effective storage account type. It is the only storage account type that can be used for the classic deployment model but does not support the latest features, such as access tiers. This account type is no longer recommended by Microsoft. It is still generally considered the cheapest of storage options but is highly restricted compared to **general-purpose version 2 (GPv2)** storage. Although legacy, these accounts can be upgraded to GPv2 storage. However, you should also consider storage costs as these might increase as a result of the change.

GPv2

This is a standard storage account and supports blobs, queues, tables, and file shares. This is the storage account type recommended for most scenarios. It supports **locally redundant storage (LRS)**, **geo-redundant storage (GRS)**, **read-access GRS (RA-GRS)**, **zone-redundant storage (ZRS)**, **geo-ZRS (GZRS)**, and **read-access GZRS (RA-GZRS)** redundancy options.

> **Top Tip**
>
> v1 storage accounts can easily be upgraded to v2; however, be aware that an upgrade is permanent and cannot be rolled back. Follow this article for more information: `https://docs.microsoft.com/en-us/azure/` `storage/common/storage-account-upgrade?tabs=azure-` `portal`.

Standard blob storage

Azure Blob storage offers unstructured data storage in the cloud. It can store all kinds of data, such as documents, VHDs, images, and audio files. There are three types of blobs that you can create. This type of storage is also considered a legacy storage account type and consists of various types of blobs, as outlined here:

- **Page blobs**: Blobs that are used for the storage of disks. These blobs are optimized for read and write operations and stored in 512-byte pages. So, when you have a VHD that needs to be stored and attached to your **virtual machine (VM)**, you will have to create a page blob. The maximum size of a page blob is 8 **tebibytes (TiB)**.

- **Block blobs**: Basically, these cover all the other types of data that you can store in Azure, such as files and documents. The maximum size of a block is 4,000 **mebibytes (MiB)** and the maximum size for a blob is 190.7 TiB.

- **Append blobs**: These blobs are optimized for append operations, basically meaning that data (blocks) is added to the end of a blob. Each block can be of different sizes, up to a maximum of 50,000 blocks. Updating or deleting existing blocks written to the blob is unsupported.

The standard blob storage account offers all the features of StorageV2 accounts, except that it only supports block blobs (and append blobs). **Page blobs are not supported**. It offers access tiers that consist of hot, cool, and archive storage, and these will be covered later in this chapter. Microsoft recommends using GPv2 storage instead of standard page blobs as this is supported without the requirement for limitations. It supports LRS, GRS, and RA-GRS redundancy options.

Example workload types include the following:

- Backup and archiving functionality
- **Disaster recovery (DR)** datasets
- Media or unstructured data content

Premium block blob storage

Premium storage is used for situations requiring **lower latency** and **higher performance**. This is enabled through high-performance hardware associated with the presentation of storage within Azure, such as through **solid-state drives (SSDs)**, and provides faster throughput and **input/output operations per second (IOPS)** compared to standard storage, which is backed by hard disks (spinning disks). This storage is typically used for block blobs and append blobs. It supports LRS and ZRS redundancy options.

Example workload types include the following:

- Workloads requiring fast access and functionality, such as e-commerce applications
- Large datasets that are constantly added, manipulated, and analyzed, such as **internet of things (IoT)** applications
- **Artificial intelligence (AI)** or **machine learning (ML)** applications
- Data transformation workloads

> **Top Tip**
>
> Storage is measured in binary units; when translating back to the decimal number system, this does not always reflect as 1 to 1 and depends on the terminology or unit used. For instance, we know that 1 **megabyte** (**MB**) is technically equal to 1,024 **kilobytes** (**KB**); however, we often write 1 MB as 1,000 KB. Therefore, to reflect the correct measurement, we would write this as 1 MiB to reflect we mean 1,024 KiB.

Azure file storage

With Azure Files, you can create file shares in the cloud. You can access your files using the **Server Message Block** (**SMB**) protocol, which is an industry standard that can be used on Linux, Windows, and macOS devices. Azure files can also be mounted as if they were a local drive on these same devices as well, and they can be cached for fast access on Windows Server using **Azure File Sync**. File shares can be used across multiple machines, which makes them suitable for storing files or data that is accessed from multiple machines, such as tools for development machines, configuration files, or log data. Azure Files is part of the Azure Storage client libraries and offers an Azure Storage **Representational State Transfer application programming interface** (**REST API**) that can be leveraged by developers in their solutions.

Premium file shares storage

Premium storage is used for situations requiring **lower latency** and **higher performance**. Premium file shares are typically used for workloads requiring enterprise-scale or high-performance applications. The service presents storage in the form of SMB or **Network File System** (**NFS**) storage. SMB is typically used for Microsoft Windows-type environments such as Windows Server, whereas NFS is typically used for Linux-based environments. NFS can only be enabled on premium file shares. Some differences worth noting when choosing your file-share storage service are IOPS and provisioned storage limitations. GPv2-backed file shares have a limit of 20,000 IOPS and 5 **pebibytes** (**PiB**) of provisioned storage, while premium file shares storage offers 100,000 IOPS but only 100 TiB provisioned storage.

> **Top Tip**
>
> Blob storage has a flat-file hierarchy, meaning that it does not work as a filesystem, as we are traditionally used to working with on servers and workstations. While containers may appear as folders, they are only logical structures to emulate a filesystem. Bearing this in mind, blob storage is not meant to be consumed directly as a shared storage system such as SMB or NFS, but through technologies such as blobfuse, direct storage into a blob can be achieved.

The next chapter will explore more about blob management and will include sections such as blob life cycle management, replication, the Azure File Sync service, versioning, and data protection.

Storage access tiers

Blob storage accounts use access tiers to determine how frequently data is accessed. Based on this access tier, you will get billed. Azure offers three storage access tiers: **Hot, Cool**, and **Archive**. Azure also offers configuration options for blob life cycle management, which we will explore more of in the next chapter.

Hot

The hot access tier is most suitable for storing data that is accessed frequently and data that is in active use. For instance, you would store images and style sheets for a website inside the hot access tier. The storage costs for this tier are higher than for the other access tiers, but you pay less for accessing files. This is the default access tier for storage.

Cool

The cool access tier is the most suitable for storing data that is not accessed frequently (less than once in 30 days). Compared with the hot access tier, the cool tier has lower storage costs, but you pay more for accessing files. This tier is suitable for storing backups and older content that is not viewed often.

Archive

The archive storage tier is set on the blob level and not on the storage level. It has the lowest costs for storing data and the highest cost for accessing data compared to the hot and cool access tiers. This tier is for data that will remain in the archive for at least 180 days, and it will take several hours of latency before it can be accessed. This tier is most suitable for long-term backups or compliance and archive data. A blob in the archive tier is offline and cannot be read (except for the metadata), copied, overwritten, or modified. Although the blob data remains unreadable in the archive tier, its metadata remains readable.

Service-level agreement for storage accounts

It is worth considering the **service-level agreement (SLA)** for all services when designing and deploying to Azure. The great news with storage accounts is that you are assured of 99% availability of services.

Choosing a cool tier infers a lower SLA from Microsoft, whereas the hot tier allows better SLAs up to 99.99%.

> **Top Tip**
>
> Data tiers can be changed between hot and cool; doing so will charge the full premium at the conversion of the existing storage tier. This charge does not apply to blob storage accounts. Costs are incurred as write operation charges when converting from the hot to the cool tier and as read and data retrieval operations when converting from the cold to the hot tier.

Azure disk storage

Disks that are used for VMs are stored in Azure Blob storage as page blobs. Azure stores two disks for each VM: the actual operating system (VHD) of the VM, and a temporary disk that is used for short-term storage. This data is erased when the VM is turned off or rebooted. There are two different performance tiers that Azure offers: **standard disk storage** and **premium disk storage**.

Standard disk storage

Standard disk storage offers a **hard disk drive** (**HDD**) to store data on, and it is the most cost-effective storage tier that you can choose. It can only use LRS or GRS to support **high availability** (**HA**) for your data and applications.

Premium disk storage

With premium disk storage, your data is stored on SSDs. Not all Azure VM series can use this type of storage. It can only be used with DS, DSv2, GS, LS, or FS series Azure VMs. It offers high performance and low-latency disk support.

Unmanaged versus managed disks

Managed disks are the default disk type in Azure and automatically handle storage account creation for you. With unmanaged disks, which are the traditional legacy disks used for VMs, you need to create a storage account manually, and then select that storage account when you create a VM. When you deploy unmanaged disks, you need to ensure that you cater to limits on the storage account (such as a maximum of 40 disks per standard storage account) before incurring throttling limitations. With managed disks, this burden is handled for you by Azure. Performance is predictable and more reliable, disks are secure by default, and you have better SLAs. When deploying, you select the disk type and the performance tier (standard or premium), and a managed disk is created. It also handles scaling automatically for you and removes limitations such as IOPS and disk count limits placed on storage accounts through throttling for unmanaged disks. Managed disks are recommended by Microsoft over unmanaged disks.

Redundancy

Redundancy refers to the number of copies of data that are available at any time; this supports the failure of copies and ensures continuity of services dependent on the redundancy option chosen. Regardless of the option, data is replicated three times in a storage account for the primary region.

LRS

This is storage that is copied three times within a single physical location in a chosen region. Data is copied synchronously within the location, typically within the same data center. This is the cheapest replication option that can be chosen and is not intended for business-critical workloads that require HA or resiliency. Protection is provided against server rack and drive failures. The following screenshot illustrates replication for LRS:

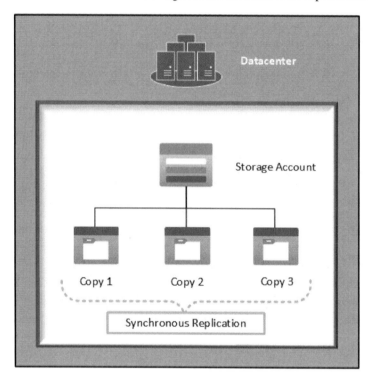

Figure 6.2 – LRS replication

Now that you understand what LRS storage replication is, we will explore ZRS replication.

ZRS

Three copies of data are copied asynchronously across three Azure **Availability Zones** (**AZs**) for the selected region; this protects against failure at a data center layer. This redundancy option is recommended for HA within a single region. If a zone becomes unavailable, your data is still accessible both for read and write operations. This option may also be chosen where data residency requirements apply, such as through a compliance standard that the organization aligns to. The following screenshot illustrates replication for ZRS:

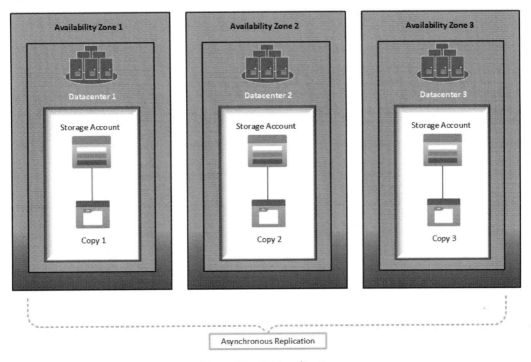

Figure 6.3 – ZRS replication

Now that you understand what ZRS storage replication is, we will explore GRS replication.

GRS

This option is chosen to protect against a region failure while also offering protection within a single data center for each region. Effectively, you get six copies of data (three in each region). Data is copied asynchronously across regions but synchronously within the data center. The following screenshot illustrates replication for GRS:

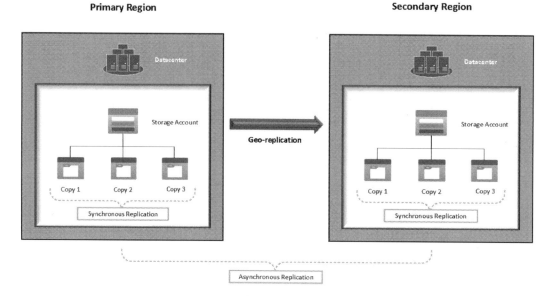

Figure 6.4 – GRS replication

Now that you understand what GRS storage replication is, we will explore GZRS replication.

GZRS

This option is chosen to protect against a region failure while also offering HA and protection within each region. Effectively, you get six copies of data (three in the primary region distributed across AZs, and three distributed within a data center in the secondary region). Data is copied asynchronously across regions but synchronously within the region and data center. The following screenshot illustrates replication for GZRS/RA-GZRS:

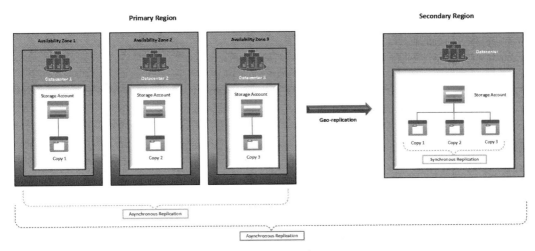

Figure 6.5 – GZRS replication

Now that you understand what GZRS storage replication is, we can conclude this section on storage redundancy types. In the next section, we provide additional reading material to learn more about storage.

> **Top Tip**
> The archive tier of storage does not support ZRS, GZRS, and RA-GZRS redundancy options.

Further reading

That brings this section to an end. In this section, we have learned what **storage accounts** are, why they are necessary, and how they work.

We encourage you to read up further by using the following links:

- **Storage accounts**: https://docs.microsoft.com/en-us/azure/storage/common/storage-account-overview

- **Azure Blob storage**: https://docs.microsoft.com/en-us/azure/storage/blobs/storage-blobs-introduction

- **Blob access tiers**: https://docs.microsoft.com/en-us/azure/storage/blobs/access-tiers-overview

- **Understanding block blobs, append blobs, and page blobs**: `https://docs.microsoft.com/en-us/rest/api/storageservices/understanding-block-blobs--append-blobs--and-page-blobs`

- **blobfuse**: `https://github.com/Azure/azure-storage-fuse`

- **Rehydrating blob data from Archive tier**: `https://docs.microsoft.com/en-us/azure/storage/blobs/storage-blob-rehydration?tabs=azure-portal`

- **Storage account SLA**: `https://azure.microsoft.com/en-us/support/legal/sla/storage/v1_5/`

- **Storage redundancy**: `https://docs.microsoft.com/en-us/azure/storage/common/storage-redundancy`

Creating and configuring storage accounts

Now that we understand more about storage accounts and what to be aware of, we are going to create a storage account in Azure. A storage account needs to be in place before you can upload any data or files to Azure.

Creating a storage account

For this demonstration, we will first proceed with creating a storage account using the portal and then provide the equivalent PowerShell code to create this using the Az module. Proceed as follows:

1. Sign in to the Azure portal at `https://portal.azure.com`.

2. Open the resource group you will be using for this exercise, click **Overview** on the left menu, and then click **Create**.

3. Enter `Storage account` in the search bar and click the **Storage account** search result that pops up, as illustrated in the following screenshot:

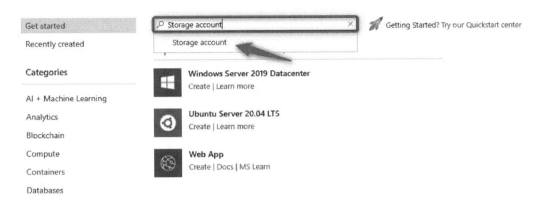

Figure 6.6 – Searching for Storage account in Marketplace

4. On the **Create a resource** blade, click **Create**, as illustrated in the following screenshot:

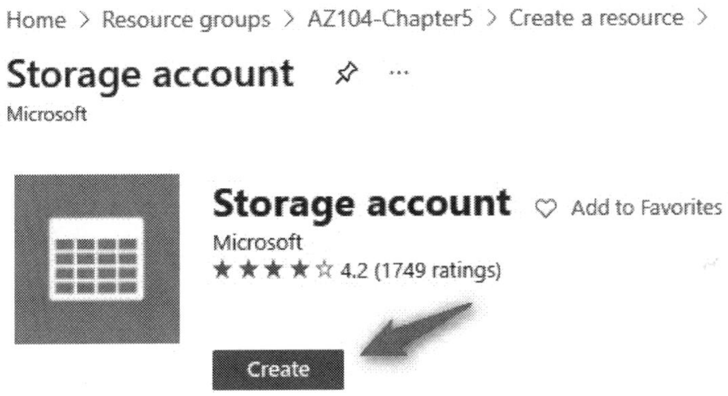

Home > Resource groups > AZ104-Chapter5 > Create a resource >

Storage account

Microsoft

Storage account ♡ Add to Favorites
Microsoft
★ ★ ★ ★ ☆ 4.2 (1749 ratings)

Create

Figure 6.7 – Creating a storage account

5. On the following screen, select a resource group where the storage account must be created, enter a globally unique storage account name (limited to a maximum of 24 characters, consisting only of lowercase letters and numbers), select a region, select a performance tier, and select the desired redundancy for the account. The process is illustrated in the following screenshot:

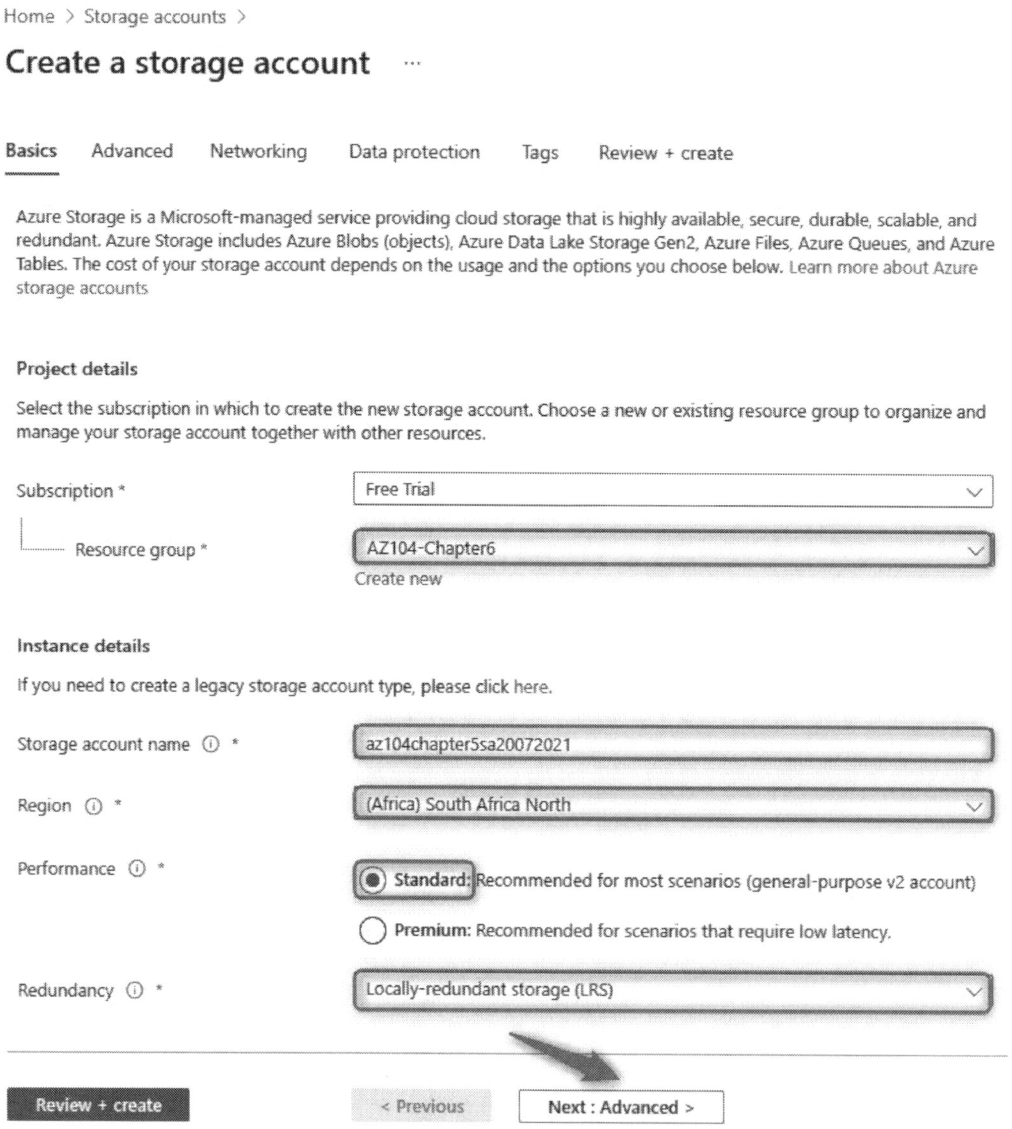

Home > Storage accounts >

Create a storage account   ...

Basics   Advanced   Networking   Data protection   Tags   Review + create

Azure Storage is a Microsoft-managed service providing cloud storage that is highly available, secure, durable, scalable, and redundant. Azure Storage includes Azure Blobs (objects), Azure Data Lake Storage Gen2, Azure Files, Azure Queues, and Azure Tables. The cost of your storage account depends on the usage and the options you choose below. Learn more about Azure storage accounts

Project details

Select the subscription in which to create the new storage account. Choose a new or existing resource group to organize and manage your storage account together with other resources.

Subscription *	Free Trial

Resource group *	AZ104-Chapter6

Create new

Instance details

If you need to create a legacy storage account type, please click here.

Storage account name ⓘ *	az104chapter5sa20072021

Region ⓘ *	(Africa) South Africa North

Performance ⓘ *   ● **Standard:** Recommended for most scenarios (general-purpose v2 account)

                        ○ **Premium:** Recommended for scenarios that require low latency.

Redundancy ⓘ *	Locally-redundant storage (LRS)

[Review + create]   [< Previous]   [Next : Advanced >]

Figure 6.8 – Creating a storage account: Basics tab

6. Notice the different redundancy options available. For this exercise, we are going to choose **Locally-redundant storage (LRS)**, as illustrated in the following screenshot. Click **Next: Advanced >**:

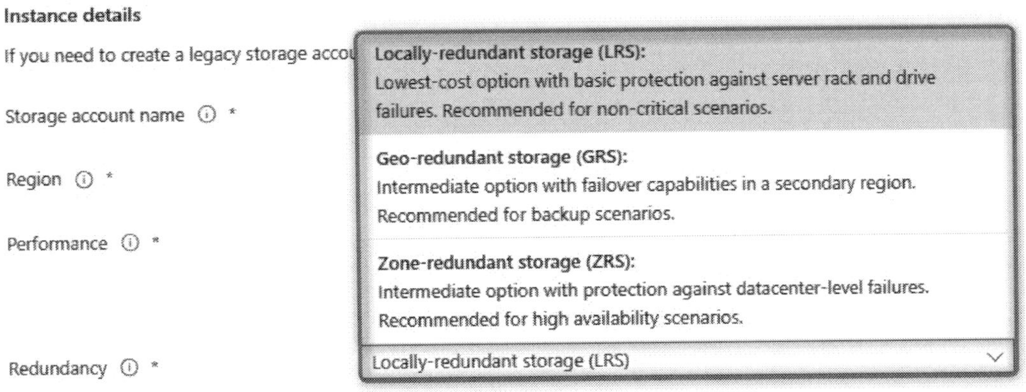

Instance details

If you need to create a legacy storage accou

Storage account name ⓘ *

Region ⓘ *

Performance ⓘ *

Redundancy ⓘ *

Locally-redundant storage (LRS):
Lowest-cost option with basic protection against server rack and drive failures. Recommended for non-critical scenarios.

Geo-redundant storage (GRS):
Intermediate option with failover capabilities in a secondary region. Recommended for backup scenarios.

Zone-redundant storage (ZRS):
Intermediate option with protection against datacenter-level failures. Recommended for high availability scenarios.

Locally-redundant storage (LRS)   ⌄

Figure 6.9 – Storage redundancy options

7. For the **Advanced** tab, we will leave the default options enabled. Note the settings on this tab as we will explore security further in the next chapter. Click **Next : Networking** >, as illustrated in the following screenshot:

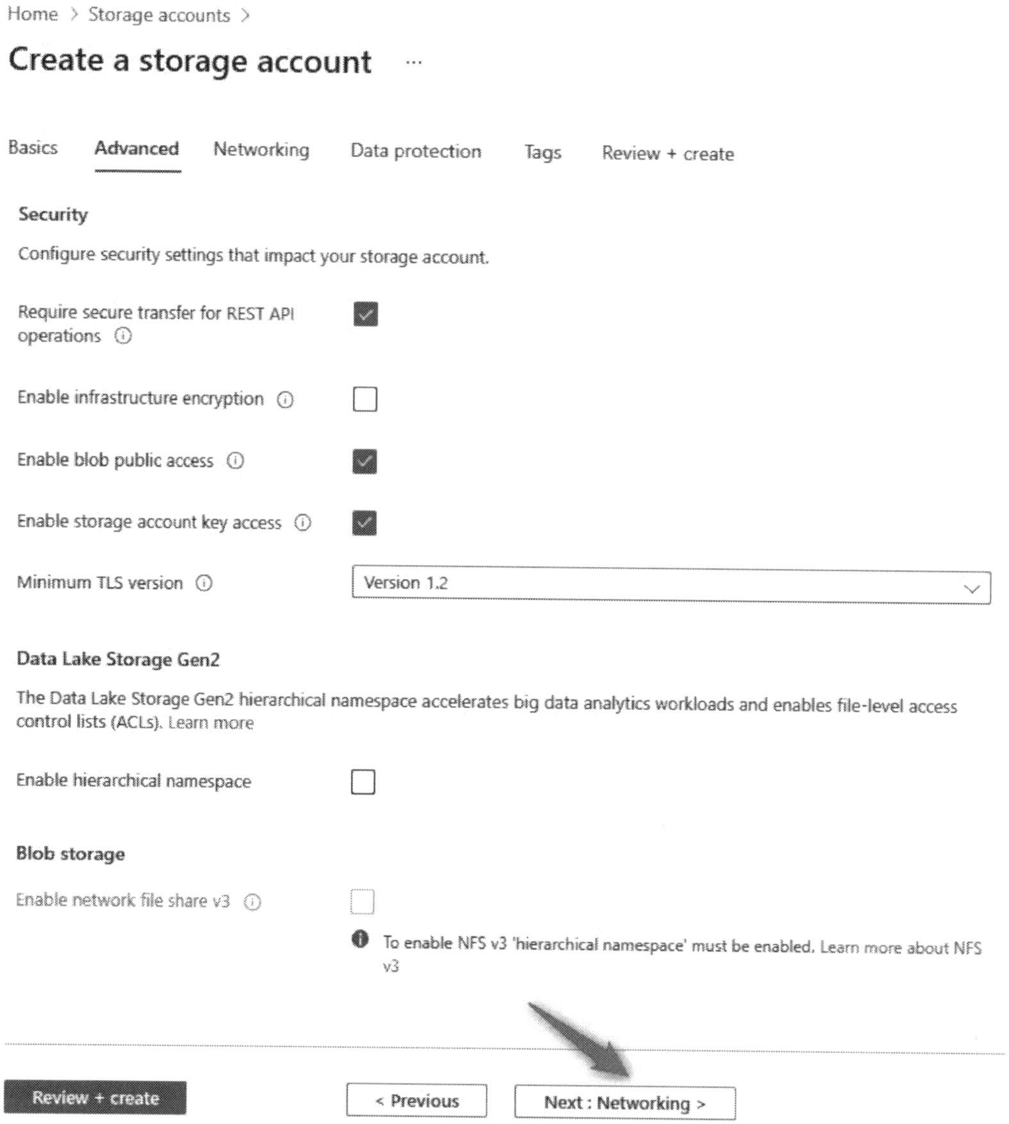

Home > Storage accounts >

Create a storage account   ...

Basics   **Advanced**   Networking   Data protection   Tags   Review + create

Security

Configure security settings that impact your storage account.

Require secure transfer for REST API operations ⓘ   ☑

Enable infrastructure encryption ⓘ   ☐

Enable blob public access ⓘ   ☑

Enable storage account key access ⓘ   ☑

Minimum TLS version ⓘ | Version 1.2   ⌄ |

Data Lake Storage Gen2

The Data Lake Storage Gen2 hierarchical namespace accelerates big data analytics workloads and enables file-level access control lists (ACLs). Learn more

Enable hierarchical namespace   ☐

Blob storage

Enable network file share v3 ⓘ   ☐

ⓘ To enable NFS v3 'hierarchical namespace' must be enabled. Learn more about NFS v3

| Review + create | | < Previous | Next : Networking > |

Figure 6.10 – Creating a storage account: Advanced tab

8. The configurations on the **Networking** tab will also be addressed in the next chapter, but note that the service can be integrated with a **virtual network** (**VNet**) using both the public interface on the storage account and the private interface (private endpoint). Leave the default options and click **Next : Data protection** >, as illustrated in the following screenshot:

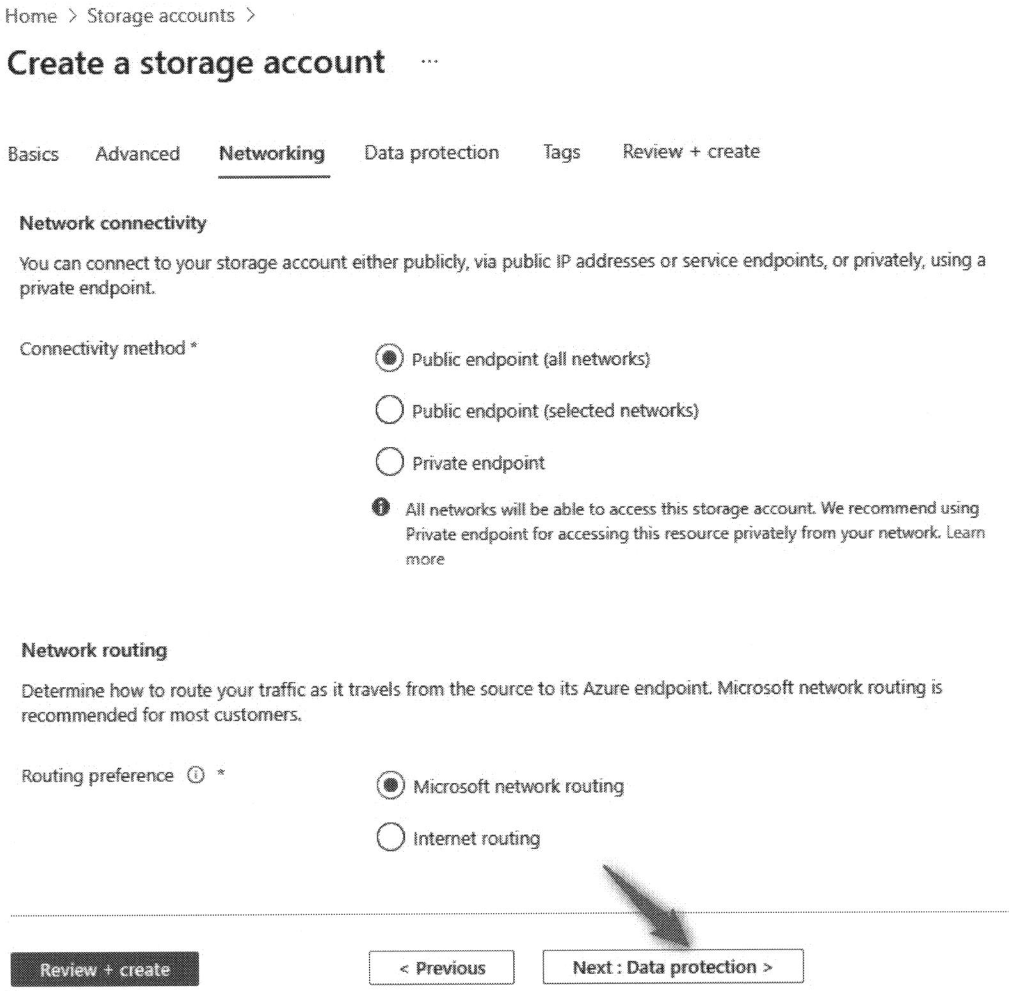

Home > Storage accounts >

Create a storage account   ...

Basics   Advanced   **Networking**   Data protection   Tags   Review + create

Network connectivity

You can connect to your storage account either publicly, via public IP addresses or service endpoints, or privately, using a private endpoint.

Connectivity method *

          ⦿ Public endpoint (all networks)

          ◯ Public endpoint (selected networks)

          ◯ Private endpoint

          ⓘ All networks will be able to access this storage account. We recommend using Private endpoint for accessing this resource privately from your network. Learn more

Network routing

Determine how to route your traffic as it travels from the source to its Azure endpoint. Microsoft network routing is recommended for most customers.

Routing preference ⓘ *

          ⦿ Microsoft network routing

          ◯ Internet routing

Review + create   < Previous   Next : Data protection >

Figure 6.11 – Creating a storage account: Networking tab

9. The **Data protection** tab exposes controls available to you for the recovery of data. Soft delete acts as a *recycle bin* for data on the storage account and allows retrieval of deleted files for a specified period, pertaining to the configuration for each of the storage services in the storage account. **Point-in-time** restoration refers to the ability to restore files based on a moment in time within a defined restore point interval; this is defined in days. Leave the default configurations on this page and click **Review + create**, as illustrated in the following screenshot:

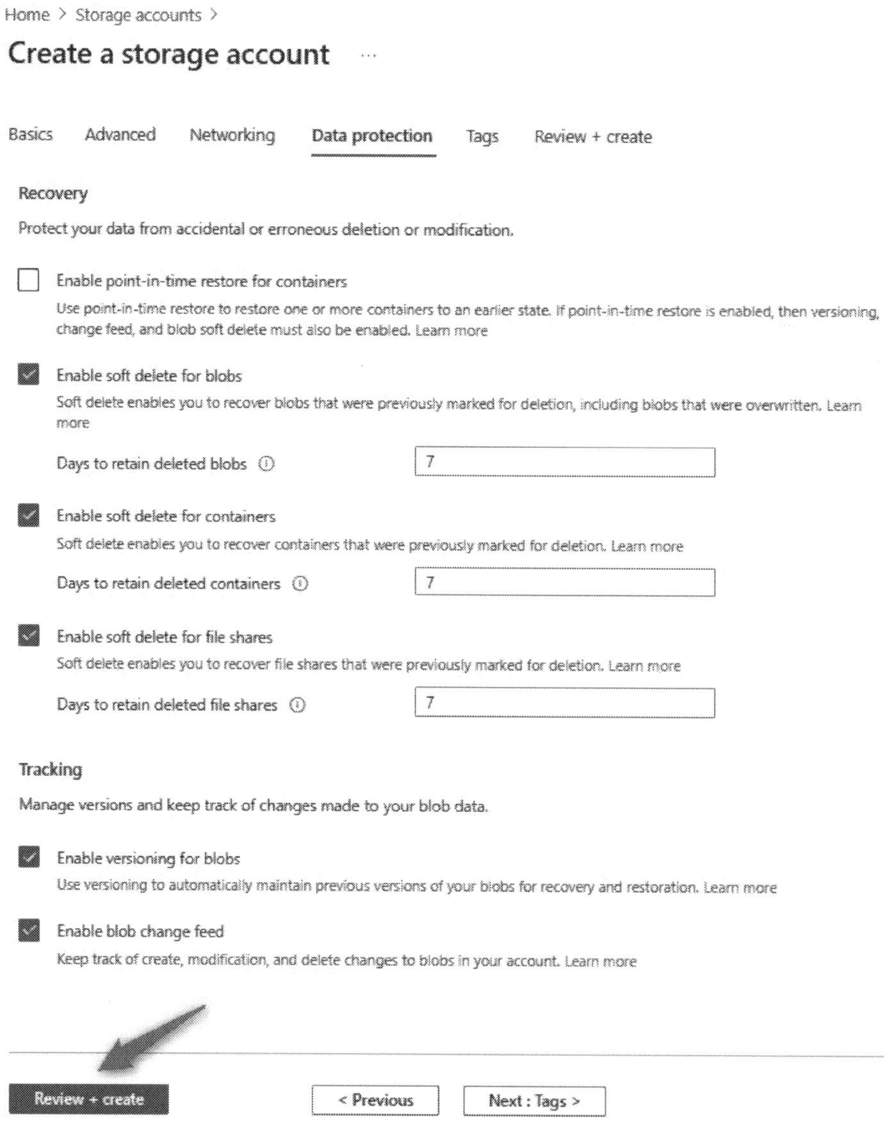

Figure 6.12 – Creating a storage account: Data protection tab

> **Top Tip**
>
> Note that the **point-in-time restoration** option is limited to blob storage only. If a container is deleted, data cannot be restored from this operation. Instead, delete individual blobs to prevent complications if you intend to restore them later using this operation.

10. Review the options and click **Create**, as illustrated in the following screenshot:

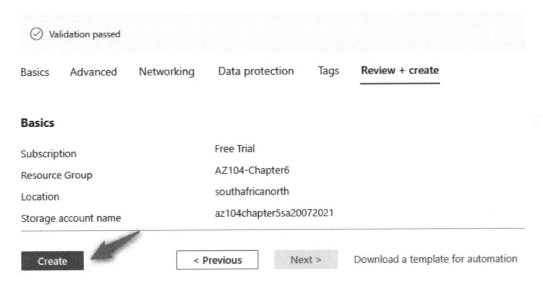

Figure 6.13 – Creating a storage account: Review + create tab

You have now completed the deployment of a storage account.

PowerShell scripts

Please ensure that the Az module is installed, as per the *Technical requirements* section at the beginning of the chapter.

The following script will create a new storage account (*change the parameters to suit your requirements*):

```
# First connect your Azure account credentials
Connect-AzAccount


# Parameters
$ResourceGroup = "AZ104-Chapter6"
$Location = "WestEurope"
$StorageAccountName = "az104chap6acc220072021"
$SkuName = "Standard_LRS"


# Create the Storage Account
New-AzStorageAccount -Name $StorageAccountName
-ResourceGroupName $ResourceGroup -Location $Location -SkuName
$SkuName
```

Further reading

That brings this section to an end. In this section, we have learned how storage accounts can be created using the Azure portal or Azure PowerShell.

We encourage you to read up further by using the following links:

- **Point-in-time restoration for blob storage**: https://docs.microsoft.com/en-gb/azure/storage/blobs/point-in-time-restore-overview
- **Soft delete for blob storage**: https://docs.microsoft.com/en-gb/azure/storage/blobs/soft-delete-blob-overview
- **Data protection overview**: https://docs.microsoft.com/en-gb/azure/storage/blobs/data-protection-overview

Using Azure Import/Export

Azure Import/Export is a service that allows you to import and export data quickly and securely to and from an Azure data center. Data imported is stored either in Azure Blob storage or Azure Files. The value of the services is for managing large amounts of data into or out of Azure where time to get data out is of importance, or costs associated with the transfer of data in and out of Azure are too prohibitive.

The disk drives that are going to be shipped to the Azure data center need to be prepared before shipment. BitLocker encryption needs to be enabled, and once the volume is encrypted, you can copy data to it. After encryption, a disk needs to be prepared using the `WAImportExport.exe` tool. By running this tool, a journal file is automatically created in the same folder that you ran the tool. There are two other files created as well—an `.xml` file and a `drive-manifest.xml` file. You need these files later for creating an import/export job. The disk is now ready to be shipped to Azure. Follow this Microsoft article for more details: `https://docs.microsoft.com/en-us/azure/import-export/storage-import-export-data-to-files?tabs=azure-portal-preview`.

> **Top Tip**
>
> You may come across Azure Data Box Disk in your studies and find its offering looks similar to Azure Import/Export. The key difference is that Azure Data Box Disk is a service where you import Microsoft-owned devices as part of Azure Data Box, whereas Azure Import/Export supports your own disks as long as they conform to requirements.

Importing into an Azure job

After disks are shipped to Azure, you can create an import or export job from the Azure portal. The import process flow for Azure import/export looks like this:

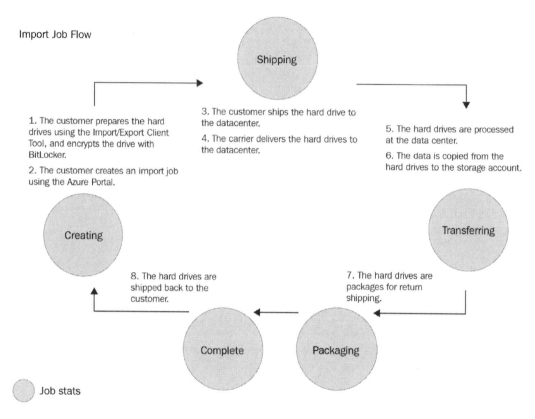

Figure 6.14 – Import process flow

Therefore, you have to take the following steps:

1. Navigate to the Azure portal by opening `https://portal.azure.com`.

2. Enter `import` in the search bar at the top of the portal and click **Import/export jobs**, as illustrated in the following screenshot:

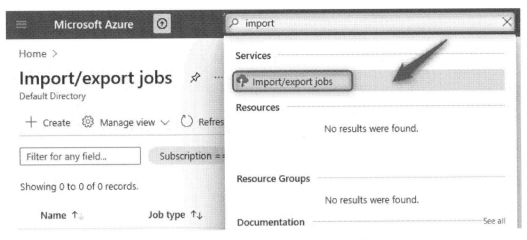

Figure 6.15 – Searching Import/export jobs

3.   Click **Create import/export job**, as illustrated in the following screenshot:

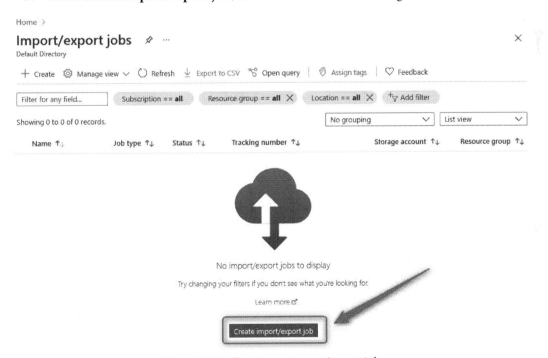

Figure 6.16 – Creating an import/export job

4. In the next blade, select **Subscription** and **Resource group** values and enter a **Name** value for the import/export job (we will use `az104labimport`). Set **Type** to **Import into Azure**, and select a **Destination Azure region** value. Then, click **Next : Job details >**. The process is illustrated in the following screenshot:

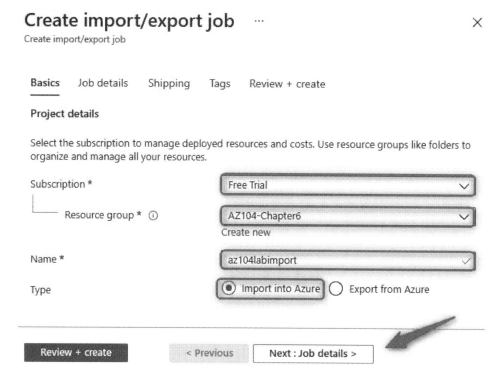

Figure 6.17 – Creating an import job

5. Complete the details as per the following screenshot, selecting your journal file. Click **Next : Shipping >**:

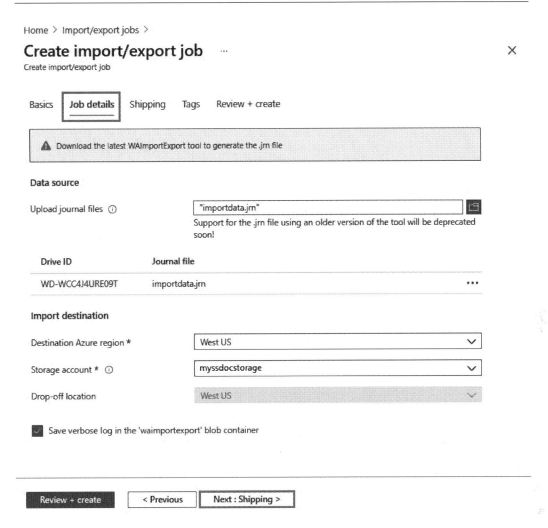

Figure 6.18 – Creating an import/export job: Job details tab

6. Enter your shipping details and click **Review + create**.

7. Once validation has passed, click the **I acknowledge that all the information provided is correct and agree to the terms and conditions above** checkbox, and then click **Create**.

You have completed the import job process, so we will now review the process for performing an export job from Azure.

Exporting from an Azure job

There are two other files created as well—an .xml file and a drive-manifest.xml file. You need these files later for creating an import/export job. The disk is now ready to be shipped to Azure. After the disks are shipped to Azure, you can create an import or export job from the Azure portal.

The export process flow for Azure import/export looks like this:

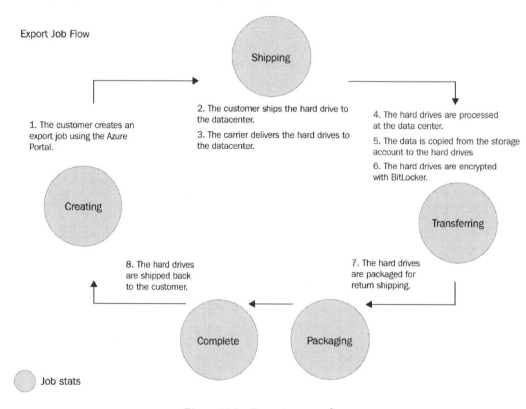

Figure 6.19 – Export process flow

Therefore, you have to take the following steps:

1. Navigate to the Azure portal by opening https://portal.azure.com.

2. Enter import in the search bar at the top of the portal and click **Import/export jobs**.

3. Click **Create import/export job**.

4. In the next blade, select **Subscription** and **Resource group** values and enter a **Name** value for the import/export job (we will use `az104labexport`). Set **Type** to **Export from Azure** and then click **Next : Job details >**.

5. Select **Source Azure region**, **Storage account**, and **Blobs to export** options, and then click **Next : Shipping >**. The process is illustrated in the following screenshot:

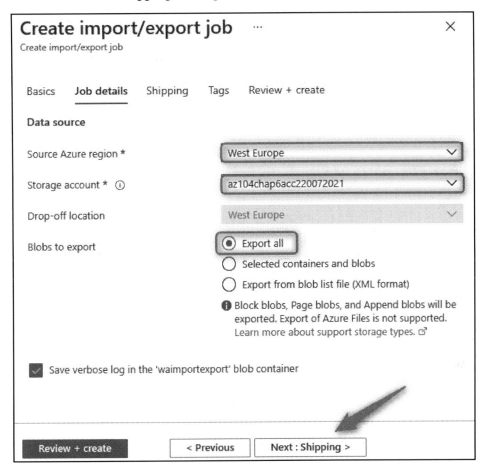

Figure 6.20 – Creating an export job

6. Enter your shipping details and click **Review + create**.

7. Once validation has passed, click the **I acknowledge that all the information provided is correct and agree to the terms and conditions above** checkbox, and then click **Create**.

Further reading

We encourage you to read up further by using the following links:

- **Importing data to blobs**: `https://docs.microsoft.com/en-us/azure/import-export/storage-import-export-data-to-blobs?tabs=azure-portal`

- **Importing data to files**: `https://docs.microsoft.com/en-us/azure/import-export/storage-import-export-data-to-files?tabs=azure-portal`

- **Exporting data from blobs**: `https://docs.microsoft.com/en-us/azure/import-export/storage-import-export-data-from-blobs?tabs=azure-portal`

Installing and using Azure Storage Explorer

Azure Storage Explorer is a standalone application that can be used to easily work with different types of data stored in an Azure storage account. There is also an implementation in preview in the Azure portal that allows integrated access to storage accounts. You can upload, download, and manage files, queues, tables, blobs, data lake storage, and Cosmos DB entities using Azure Storage Explorer. Aside from that, you can also use the application to configure and manage **cross-origin resource sharing** (**CORS**) rules for your storage accounts. This application can be used on Windows, Linux, and macOS devices.

> **Top Tip**
>
> CORS is a mechanism that allows the loading of resources from origins dissimilar to the pattern origin. The feature tells a browser whether it should permit the loading of resources when it detects a CORS pattern. This is a frequently used feature of web design and something to be cognizant of.

Installation

To install the application, you have to perform the following steps:

1. Navigate to `https://azure.microsoft.com/en-us/features/storage-explorer/` to download the application.

2. Once it has been downloaded, install the application.

3. When the application is installed, open the application. Upon first connection, you will be prompted to choose the type of Azure resource you want to connect to. There are several options to choose from, these being **Subscription**, **Storage account or service**, **Blob container**, **ADLS Gen2 container or directory**, **File share**, **Queue**, **Table**, or **Local storage emulator**.

4. For this demonstration, you will connect Storage Explorer to the subscription level of Azure, as illustrated in the following screenshot. This will run under the context (meaning the permissions) for the user credentials you enter. Click **Subscription**:

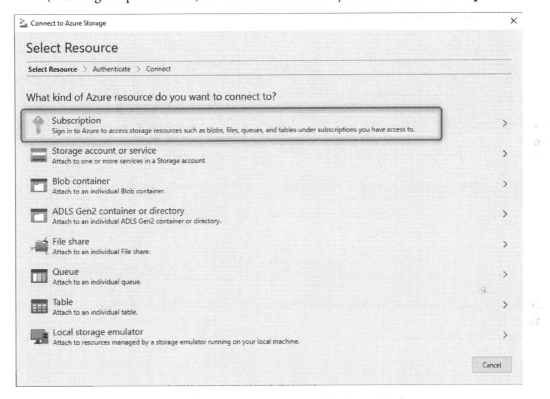

Figure 6.21 – Selecting an Azure resource for Storage Explorer

5. You will notice several environments available to choose from; unless you are working in one of the special Azure regions such as China, Germany, or the **United States (US)** government, you can select **Azure**, as shown in the following screenshot. Azure is the default environment for most Azure users. Click **Next**:

Figure 6.22 – Selecting an Azure environment for Storage Explorer

6. You will be prompted to sign in on the Azure portal, so sign in and click **Next**, as illustrated in the following screenshot:

Figure 6.23 – Signing in to Azure

7. You will be directed to the **ACCOUNT MANAGEMENT** page, as illustrated in the following screenshot. Click **Open Explorer** at the bottom of the screen to view your storage information:

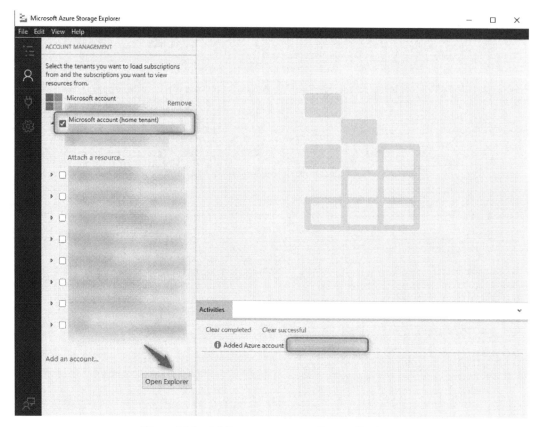

Figure 6.24 – Adding an account to Storage Explorer

> **Top Tip**
>
> Azure Storage Explorer uses your default browser to authenticate you. If you wish to change this and instead sign in with the relevant credentials, you can go to the **Settings** menu, scroll down to **Sign-in**, and change the **Sign in with:** drop-down box to **Integrated Sign-in**.

8. On the **EXPLORER** menu, take some time to familiarize yourself with the different storage options presented. Expand the subscription you have, then expand **Storage Accounts**, and expand any account you have to view its storage options available. Notice in the following screenshot the storage types, as discussed earlier in the chapter:

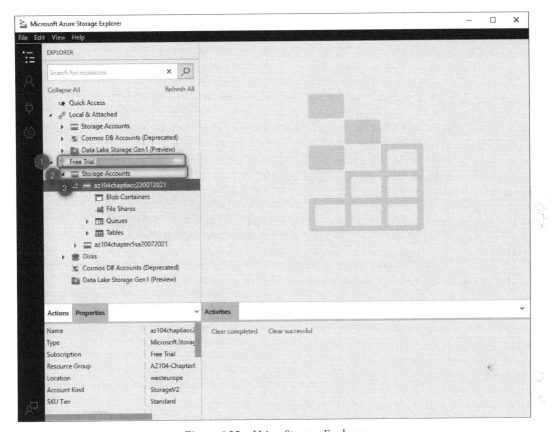

Figure 6.25 – Using Storage Explorer

You have now connected to Azure Storage using Storage Explorer. In the subsequent sections, we will explore storage management using both the Azure Storage Explorer application and the Azure portal.

Configuring Azure Files and Azure Blob storage

In the following section, we will work through an example of how we can create file shares and blob storage on a storage account.

Creating an Azure file share

In the following exercise, we will create a file share named `test` and demonstrate connectivity to this on a Windows system. Proceed as follows:

1. On our **EXPLORER** screen in Azure Storage Explorer, right-click **File Shares** and click **Create File Share**, as illustrated in the following screenshot:

Figure 6.26 – Using Storage Explorer: Create File Share

2. A folder icon will be propagated at the bottom of **File Shares**; you can type in the name `test`, as illustrated in the following screenshot, and press the *Enter* button on your keyboard:

Figure 6.27 – Creating a file share

Top Tip

Creating a file share on Azure will prompt for a **quota** size. A quota is a limit on the amount of storage that can be consumed. You should always configure this.

---

3. You now have your folder in **File Shares**. We will upload something to this folder now. Click the **Upload** button and click **Upload Files…**, as illustrated in the following screenshot:

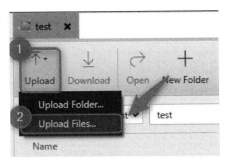

Figure 6.28 – Upload Files… option

4. Select a file by clicking the ellipsis icon (**…**) and click **Upload**, as illustrated in the following screenshot:

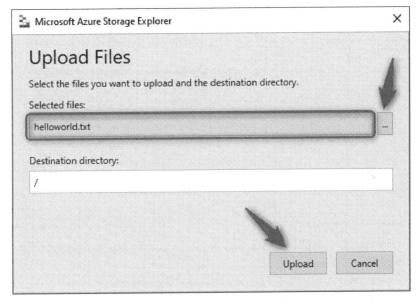

Figure 6.29 – Upload Files: Upload button

5. You will see a success message indicating the file is uploaded successfully. You will now navigate to the Azure portal and select your storage account. Click the **File shares** option on the left menu and click `test`, as illustrated in the following screenshot:

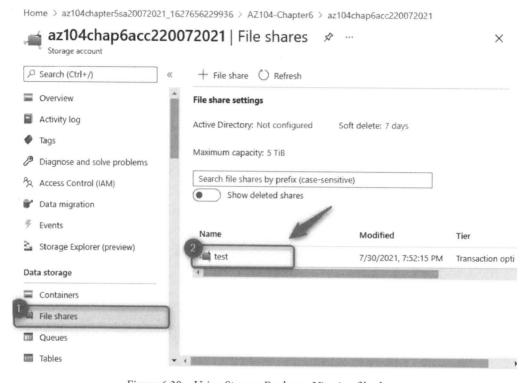

Figure 6.30 – Using Storage Explorer: Viewing file share

6. Notice the file you uploaded through Azure Storage Explorer; this is another method to navigate files. Click on the menu option highlighted on the top-screen breadcrumb navigation to go back to the storage account blade, as illustrated in the following screenshot:

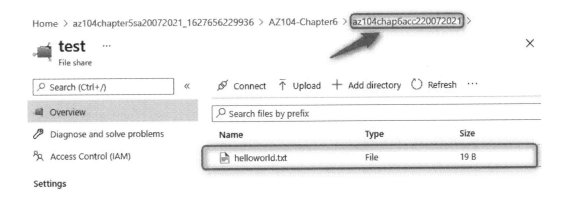

Figure 6.31 – File share: Viewing files

7. Now that you have learned how to create a file share and upload data to it using Storage Explorer, let's move on to connect an SMB share to a Windows machine. On the far right of the `test` folder, you can click the ellipsis icon (**…**) and click **Connect**, as illustrated in the following screenshot:

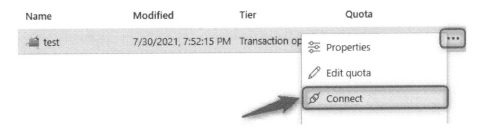

Figure 6.32 – Connecting to Azure File shares

8. Select a **Drive letter** value and copy the code in the gray box below the **Authentication method** option, as indicated in the following screenshot. Paste this into PowerShell and press *Enter*. Note that this is for the Windows operating system:

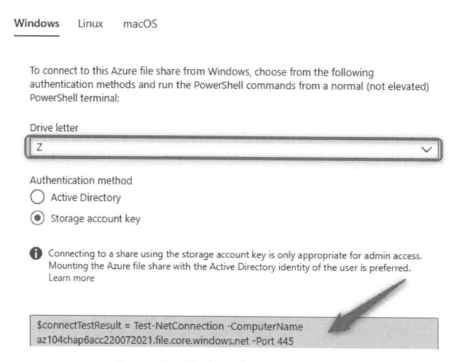

Figure 6.33 – File share: choosing drive letter

9. Notice the success message and the new drive mapping—in the following example, Z:

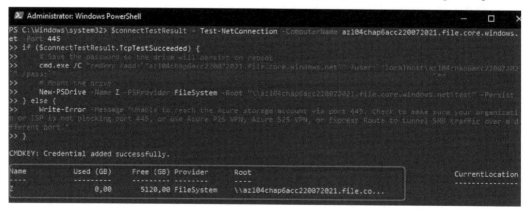

Figure 6.34 – File share: mapping in PowerShell

Notice in the preceding screenshot that there is a -Persist switch used in the command, and this will persist storage to your operating system, meaning that storage is accessible after reboot.

10. Navigate to the Z:\ drive, and notice here that we are now connected and seeing our uploaded file:

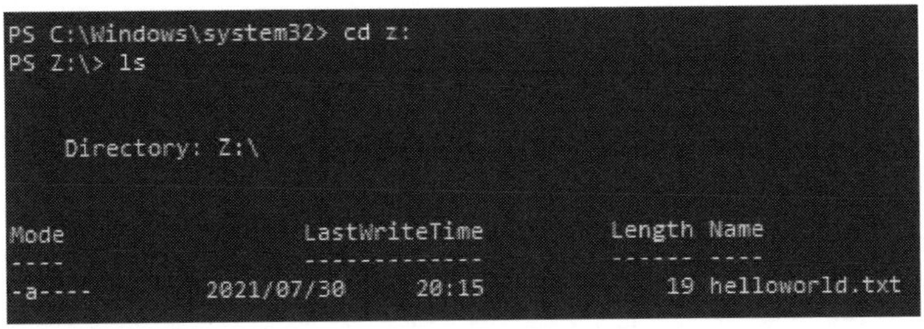

```
PS C:\Windows\system32> cd z:
PS Z:\> ls


    Directory: Z:\


Mode                 LastWriteTime         Length Name
----                 -------------         ------ ----
-a----        2021/07/30     20:15             19 helloworld.txt
```

Figure 6.35 – File share: viewing files in PowerShell

11. Proceed back to Azure Storage Explorer, right-click on the share, and click **Delete**, as illustrated in the following screenshot. Click **Yes** on the following prompt, and your folder is now deleted:

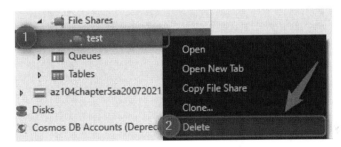

Figure 6.36 – Deleting a file share

You have now learned how to create an Azure file share, map a share, upload and download data, and delete a share.

Top Tip

You may want to mark your file shares as persistent, meaning that after a restart, they will still be there. To achieve this, add the -persist switch to your New-PSDrive command, as illustrated in *Figure 6.34* as part of *Step 9*.

Configuring Azure Blob storage

Thanks to Azure Storage Explorer, working with blobs on a storage account is very similar and just as easy as working on a file share. For this exercise, we will use the storage explorer built into the Azure portal. Since blob storage has no filesystem, it maintains a flat structure; Azure implements logical folders to emulate a filesystem similar to that of file shares to make blobs easier to work with. For this exercise, you will create a blob container and upload a file using the portal. Proceed as follows:

1. Navigate to the Azure portal and select a storage account resource you will use for the exercise. On the left menu, select **Storage Explorer (preview)** and right-click on **BLOB CONTAINERS** on the right menu, then click **Create blob container**. The process is illustrated in the following screenshot:

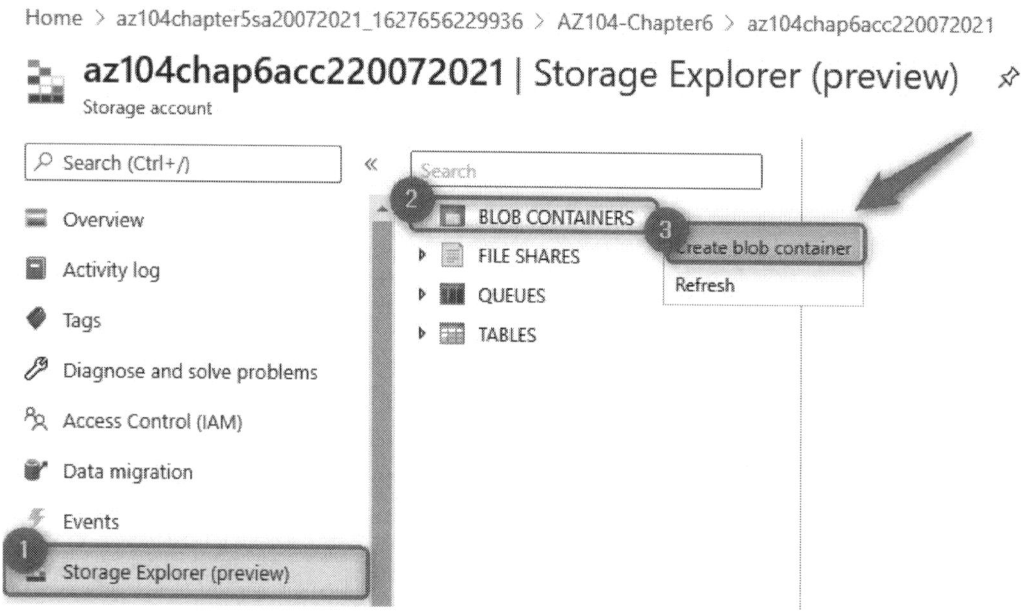

Figure 6.37 – Creating a blob container

2. Name it `test` and click **Create**, as illustrated in the following screenshot:

Figure 6.38 – New container

3. Notice in the following screenshot the new container you just created. Click on the new container, click **Upload**, then select a file and click **Upload**:

Figure 6.39 – Uploading to blob

4.   You have now successfully completed an upload, as we can see here:

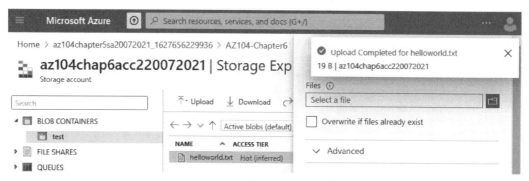

Figure 6.40 – Blob upload success

Now that you have successfully configured Azure blob storage, you will now learn how to configure storage tiers.

Configuring storage tiers

As described earlier in the chapter, there are three storage tiers available for Azure Blob storage—namely, **hot**, **cool**, and the **archive** tier, which can only be set at a blob level. The storage tier can be configured both on the creation of a storage account—for which settings apply for the entire account as a default value (these will reflect as inferred)—and at a blob level. Changing blob storage tiers allows for more granular control of the performance and reliability characteristics required of each blob, such as in backup-type solutions or for DR scenarios. The ability to change between tiers at any stage is available; however, bear in mind that tier changes result in pricing considerations, as the operations incur charges in the changing of tiers. For changes from hot to cool or archive, and from cool to archive, write charges will be incurred (operation and access charges). For archive to cool or hot, and from cool to hot, read charges will be incurred (operation and access charges).

We will now demonstrate the change of storage from hot to cool tier in the following activity:

1.   Open any storage account on the Azure portal.

2.   Upload a file to continue on your blob storage. For this exercise, we can use the container we created in the previous section.

3.   Navigate to your container and select the ellipsis icon (**…**) on the **Overview** section and click **Change tier** on the pop-up menu, as illustrated in the following screenshot:

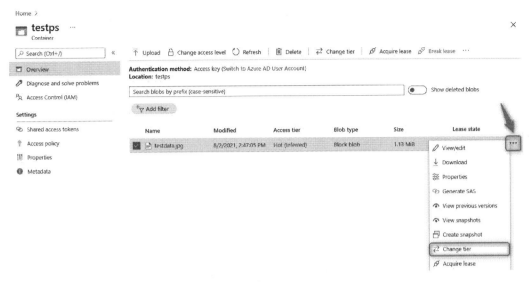

Figure 6.41 – Changing storage tier

4. Select the desired **Access tier** value and click **Save**, as illustrated in the
    following screenshot:

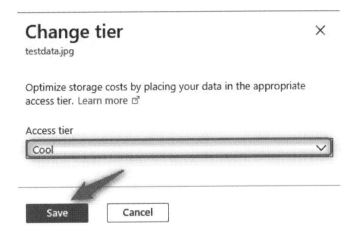

Figure 6.42 – Changing storage tier: Save

5. Note in the following screenshot the change of access tier now applied to your blob, as well as the removal of (**Inferred**) from the tier:

Name	Modified	Access tier	Blob type	Size	Lease state
☐ 🖼 testdata.jpg	8/2/2021, 2:47:05 PM	Cool	Block blob	1.13 MiB	Available

Figure 6.43 – Changing storage tier: blob view

You have completed a storage-tier change in this activity. The same process can be applied to the archive tier, with the difference being that recovery from the archive tier requires storage to be rehydrated into cool or hot to be accessible.

We will now perform an exercise for changing storage to the archive tier and restoring the data, as follows:

1. Select the blob from the previous exercise and proceed to change the storage tier again. This time, select **Archive** and click **Save**, as illustrated in the following screenshot:

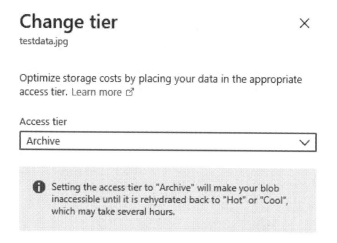

Change tier   ✕

testdata.jpg

Optimize storage costs by placing your data in the appropriate access tier. Learn more ☐

Access tier

Archive   ⌄

ⓘ Setting the access tier to "Archive" will make your blob inaccessible until it is rehydrated back to "Hot" or "Cool", which may take several hours.

Figure 6.44 – Changing storage tier: Archive tier

2. Notice that if you attempt to open the blob, you get an informational message noting that the blob is archived. Click **X** to go to the previous screen, as indicated in the following screenshot:

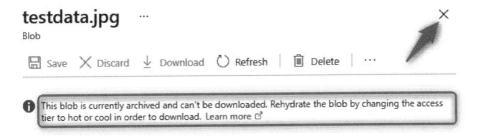

Figure 6.45 – Changing storage tier: informational message

3. Click **Change tier**, select the **Access tier** value on the pop-up menu, and select a **Rehydrate priority** type. Note that changing the priority from **Standard** to **High** will incur additional charges and is only required for critical recovery tasks. Click **Save**. The process is illustrated in the following screenshot:

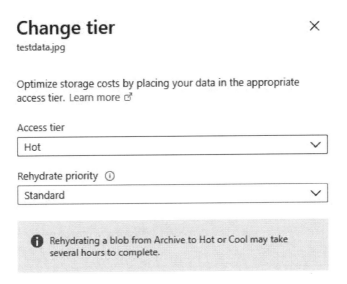

Figure 6.46 – Changing storage tier: rehydrating storage

4. You will need to give this a few hours to rehydrate; Microsoft notes that data can take up to several hours to restore. Once the operation is complete, you will notice the **Access tier** type has changed to the desired tier, as indicated in the following screenshot:

Figure 6.47 – Changing storage tier: rehydrated blob

You have completed the archive tier change as well as rehydrated data. This marks the end of the section on storage tiers, and you now understand how to manage tiering on blob storage within Azure. As part of the exam objectives, in the next section, you will learn about the **Uniform Resource Locator** (**URL**) construct for storage endpoints.

Azure URL paths for storage

Microsoft will expect you to know the construct for all storage endpoints in the exam. Here is a summary of each endpoint by service type:

- **File service**: `https://[storageAccountName].file.core.windows.net`

- **Blob service**: `https://[storageAccountName].blob.core.windows.net`

- **Queue service**: `https://[storageAccountName].queue.core.windows.net`

- **Table service**: `https://[storageAccountName].table.core.windows.net`

- **Data lake storage**: `https://[storageAccountName].dfs.core.windows.net`

- **Static website**: `https://[storageAccountName].web.core.windows.net`

This can also be found on the **Endpoints** menu when browsing the storage account on the portal. Now that you have learned about URL endpoints for storage accounts, we will next list PowerShell scripts that can assist in storage management.

PowerShell scripts

Please ensure that the Az module is installed, as per the *Technical requirements* section at the beginning of the chapter.

The following script will create a blob container in an existing storage account (*change the parameters to suit your requirements*):

```
# First connect your Azure account credentials
Connect-AzAccount

# Parameters
$ResourceGroup = "AZ104-Chapter6"
```

```
$StorageAccountName = "az104chap6acc220072021"
$ContainerName = "testps"


$Context = (Get-AzStorageAccount -ResourceGroupName
$ResourceGroup -AccountName $StorageAccountName).Context;
New-AzStorageContainer -Name $ContainerName -Context $Context
-Permission Blob
```

The following script will create a file share in an existing storage account (*change the parameters to suit your requirements*):

```
# First connect your Azure account credentials
Connect-AzAccount


# Parameters
$ResourceGroup = "AZ104-Chapter6"
$StorageAccountName = "az104chap6acc220072021"
$ShareName= "testfileshare"


$Context = (Get-AzStorageAccount -ResourceGroupName
$ResourceGroup -AccountName $StorageAccountName).Context;
New-AzStorageShare -Name $ShareName -Context $Context
```

You now have some PowerShell scripts to assist you in the daily management of your storage. The next section provides you with additional reading material to learn more about the topics for this section.

Further reading

That brings this section to an end. In this section, we have learned how to create and configure file shares and blob storage in Azure, as well as change tiers within blob storage.

We encourage you to read up further by using the following links:

- **Storage documentation**: https://docs.microsoft.com/en-us/azure/storage/common/storage-introduction

- **Storage API information**: https://docs.microsoft.com/en-us/rest/api/storageservices/

- **Storage rehydration**: https://docs.microsoft.com/en-gb/azure/storage/blobs/archive-rehydrate-overview?tabs=azure-portal

- **Storage access tiers**: `https://docs.microsoft.com/en-us/azure/ storage/blobs/storage-blob-storage-tiers#pricing-and- billing`

- **Deploying Azure File Sync**: `https://docs.microsoft.com/ en-us/azure/storage/file-sync/file-sync-deployment- guide?tabs=azure-portal%2Cproactive-portal`

Summary

In this chapter, we have established the different types of storage accounts available to Azure, the different access tiers, disk storage options, and the various redundancy options. We have explored creating a storage account, setting up file shares and blob storage, and using Azure Storage Explorer to manage storage accounts. We have also explored how to import and export data from Azure. You now have the skills required to implement and configure storage in Azure as well as identify the appropriate management tool needed.

In the next chapter, we will expand upon this knowledge and investigate how to secure storage within Azure, as well as replication and life cycle options for storage.

7
Securing Storage

This chapter focuses on one of the most common concepts when it comes to Azure and that is securing storage on the Azure platform. The focus here will be on implementing and managing storage from a security point of view, such as generating **Shared Access Signature (SAS)** tokens, managing access keys, configuring Azure **Active Directory (AD)** integration, and configuring access to Azure files. We will also explore the storage replication options available to us in Azure and understand the management of a blob's life cycle.

In this chapter, we are going to cover the following main topics:

- Configuring network access to storage accounts
- Storage access keys
- Working with SAS tokens
- Configuring access and authentication
- Copying data by using AzCopy
- Configuring storage replication and life cycle

Technical requirements

To follow along with the hands-on material, you will need the following:

- Access to an Azure subscription with owner or contributor privileges. If you do not have access to one, students can enroll for a free account: `https://azure.microsoft.com/en-us/free/`.

- PowerShell **5.1** or later installed on a PC where labs can be practiced from. Note that many examples can only be followed on a PC.

- Installation of the Az module. This can be performed by running the following in an administrative PowerShell session:

```
Set-ExecutionPolicy -ExecutionPolicy RemoteSigned -Scope
CurrentUser
```

Also run the following:

```
Install-Module -Name Az -Scope CurrentUser -Repository
PSGallery -Force
```

- Storage Explorer.

Configuring network access to storage accounts

You can secure your storage account to a specific set of supported networks which are granted access by configuring network rules so that only applications that request data over the specific set of networks can access the storage account. When these network rules are effective, the application needs to use proper authorization on the request. This authorization can be provided by Azure AD credentials for blobs and queues, with a SAS token or a valid account access key.

Public endpoint and Azure Virtual Network (VNet) integration

By default, storage accounts are provisioned with a public endpoint, and thanks to the enhanced control Azure offers, network traffic can be limited to those trusted IP addresses and networks to which you have granted access on Azure. For good security practice, all public access to storage accounts should be set to deny for the public endpoint by default. The network rules defined for the storage account will apply across all protocols, including SMB and REST; therefore, to allow access, an explicit rule will need to be defined. There are additional **exceptions** that can be configured that give you the ability to allow access to Azure services on the trusted services list to the storage account, as well as configuring logging and metric access for any networks (such as for Log Analytics).

> **Top Tip**
>
> When integrating a resource with an Azure VNet, your VNet needs to exist within the same region as your resource.

In the following demonstration, we are going to configure network access to the storage account that we created in the previous chapter to restrict network access to a specific network in Azure, as well as allowing our public IP to communicate:

1. Navigate to the Azure portal by opening `https://portal.azure.com`.

2. Go to the storage account we created in the previous chapter.

3. On the **Storage account** blade, select **Networking** from the left menu under **Security + networking**.

4. Click **Selected networks** under **Allow access from** and then click **Add new virtual network**. Notice that we can create a new network or choose an existing one.

Figure 7.1 – Storage accounts – Adding a VNet

5. Enter a name and address space, select a subscription, resource group, and location, and then leave all other settings on their default values and click **Create**. You will note that the VNet can be created in a different resource group; it can even be in a different subscription.

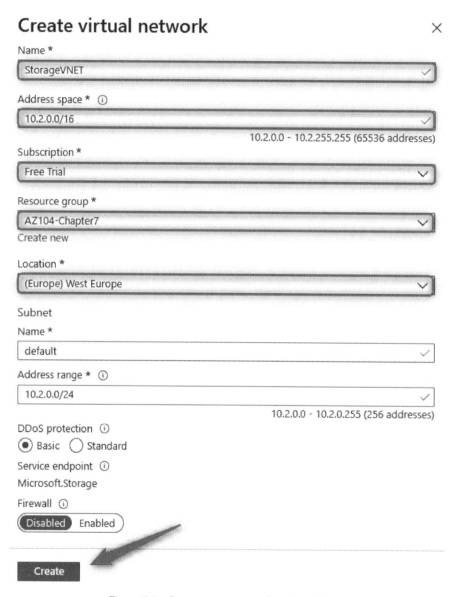

Figure 7.2 – Storage accounts – Creating a VNet

6. Now, click the **Add your client IP address** checkbox and then click **Save**.

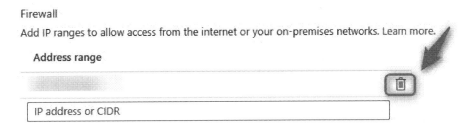

Firewalls and virtual networks   Private endpoint connections   Custom domain

Save   ✕ Discard   ↻ Refresh

ⓘ Firewall settings allowing access to storage services will remain in effect for up to a minute after saving updated settings restricting access.

Allow access from
○ All networks ⦿ Selected networks

ⓘ Configure network security for your storage accounts. Learn more ↗

Virtual networks

+ Add existing virtual network   + Add new virtual network

Virtual Network	Subnet	Address range
⟩ StorageVNET	1	

Firewall
Add IP ranges to allow access from the internet or your on-premises networks. Learn more.

☑ Add your client IP address (   ) ⓘ

Address range

IP address or CIDR

Figure 7.3 – Storage accounts – Configuring the firewall and VNets

7. You have now locked down access to the specified network and your public IP address. Open **Storage Explorer (preview)** on the left menu.

8. Open **FILE SHARES**, click on any of your folders, and note that it is accessible. You can confirm its functionality by uploading a file to the service.

9. To demonstrate the effect of IP restriction from the firewall configuration, navigate back to the **Networking** blade by clicking **Networking** on the left menu. In the **Firewall** context section, click the trash can icon to delete your IP and click **Save**.

Firewall

Add IP ranges to allow access from the internet or your on-premises networks. Learn more.

Address range

IP address or CIDR

Figure 7.4 – Storage accounts – Deleting a public IP

10. Now, navigate back to **Storage Explorer (preview)**, click **FILE SHARES** once more, and open the share you used previously. Note that you are denied access now. Click **OK**.

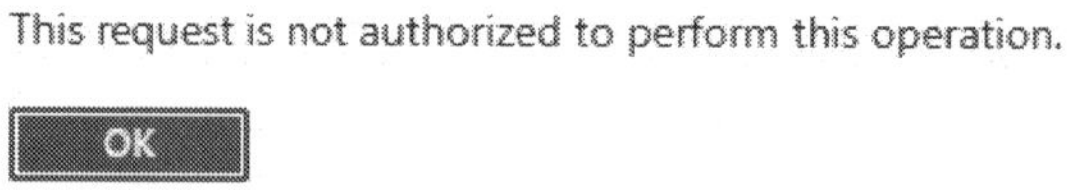

This request is not authorized to perform this operation.

OK

Figure 7.5 – Storage accounts – Authorization failure

You have now completed this section on network restrictions on public endpoints. Should you wish to test connectivity with this, you can deploy a VM in the same VNet as the storage account and connect to the storage account from inside the VM. In the next section, we will discuss private endpoints.

Private endpoints

Private endpoints provide a mechanism for Azure Storage accounts to have a private interface for a storage account and can be used to eliminate public access. They provide enhanced security over a public endpoint because they prevent unauthorized access by not being exposed publicly. When implementing a private endpoint, a **Network Interface Card (NIC)** is associated with the storage account and will be placed in a VNet. The traffic for the storage account will traverse the VNet to which it is associated. Private endpoints are provided through a service called **Private Link**.

> **Top Tip**
>
> For scenarios requiring advanced security, you should disable all public access to the storage account and enable a private endpoint. All traffic should be directed through a firewall for integration and a **Network Security Group (NSG)** should be implemented on the subnet layer to restrict unauthorized access further.

In the following demonstration, we will attach a private endpoint to a storage account:

1. Navigate to the Azure portal by opening `https://portal.azure.com`.

2. Go to the storage account we created in the previous chapter.

3. On the **Storage account** blade, select **Networking** from the left menu under the **Security + networking** context.

4. On the tab menu bar, select the **Private endpoint connections** tab and click +
    Private endpoint.

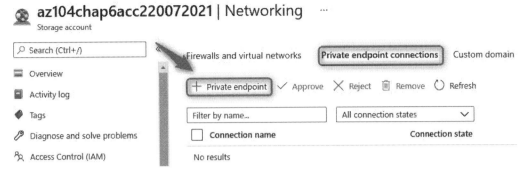

Figure 7.6 – Storage accounts – Private endpoint connections

5. In the **Basics** tab, select the subscription, resource group, and region, then enter
    a name for the instance. For this demo, we will use `az104privateendpoint`.
    Click **Next : Resource >**.

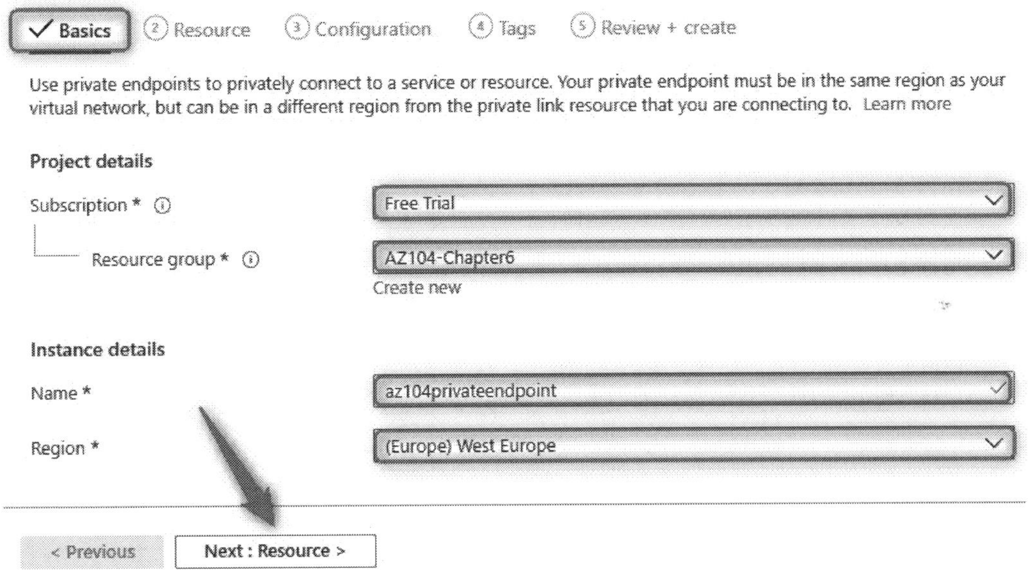

Figure 7.7 – Private endpoint connections – Basics tab

6. On the **Resource** tab, select the target sub-resource. This will be the type of storage being consumed from the storage account. Select **file**. Click **Next : Configuration >**.

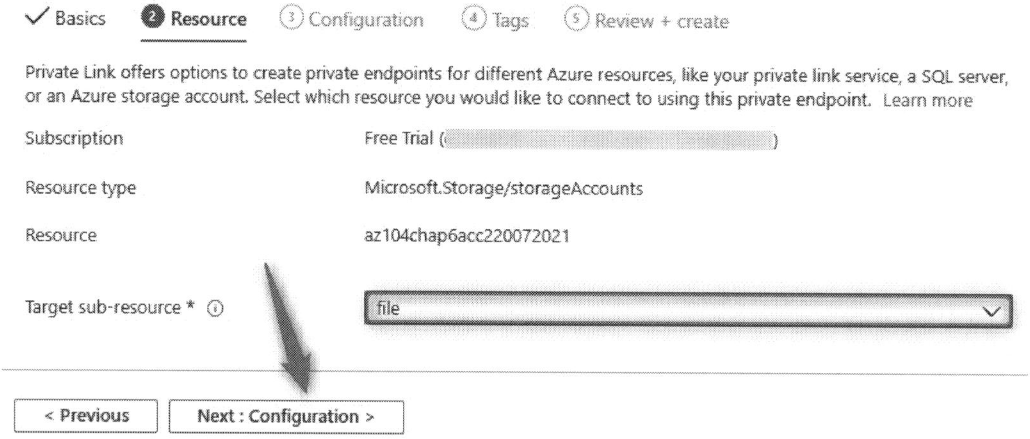

Figure 7.8 – Private endpoint connections – Resource tab

7. On the **Configuration** tab, enter all the networking configurations for the private endpoint. Select your VNet and subnet. For the **Integrate with private DNS zone** option, select **No**. Private DNS allows you to create a DNS entry for the private endpoint you are using on the service. This will be hosted within the private DNS zone you provision in Azure. Private DNS in Azure provides a mechanism for managing your own DNS entries hosted by Azure. We will discuss this in *Chapter 14, Implementing and Managing Virtual Networking*. Click **Review + create**.

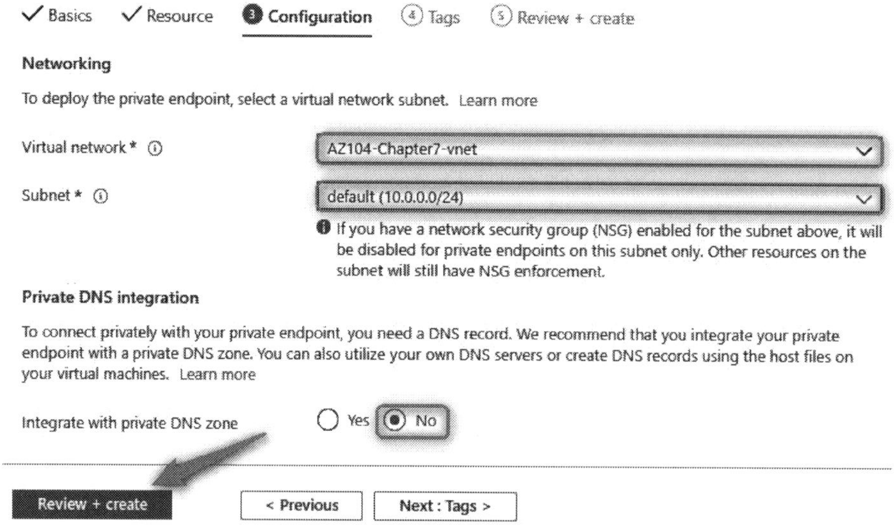

Figure 7.9 – Private endpoint connections – Configuration tab

8. Once validation has passed, click **Create**.

You have now successfully deployed a private endpoint. That brings us to the end of this section. We encourage you to play with this more in the next chapter, where you can follow along with a lab deployment. We will now discuss network routing on a storage account.

> **Top Tip**
> Take note that a private endpoint can also be provisioned on the creation of a storage account.

Network routing from storage accounts

The default network routing preference option chosen for storage accounts and most Azure services will be for the Microsoft network. This is a high-performance, low-latency global connection to all services within Azure and serves as the fastest delivery service to any consuming service or user. This is due to Microsoft configuring several points of presence within their global network. The closest endpoint to a client is always chosen. This option costs slightly more than traversing the internet. If you select **Internet routing**, then traffic will be routed in and out of the storage account outside the Microsoft network.

The following screenshot shows the setting under the **Firewall and virtual networks** tab on the **Networking** blade for your storage account:

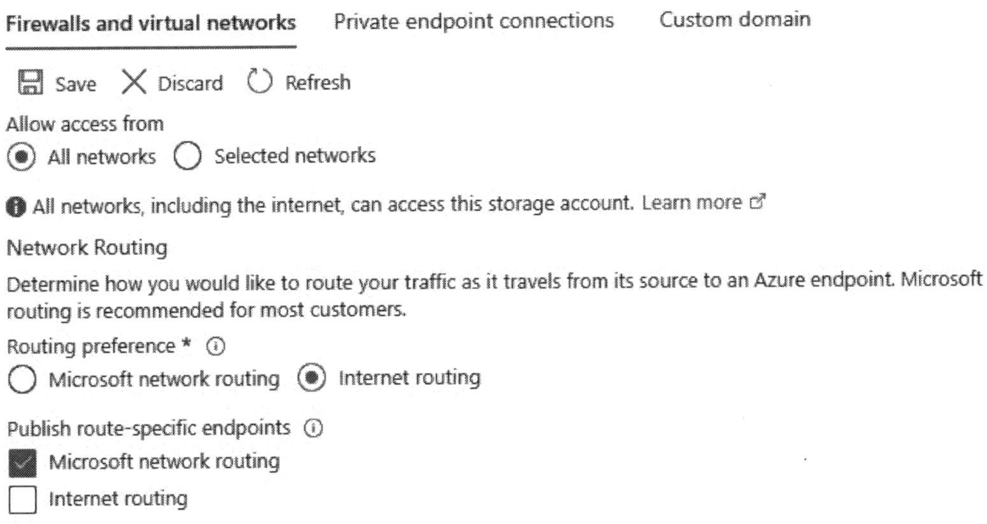

Firewalls and virtual networks   Private endpoint connections   Custom domain

🖫 Save   ✕ Discard   ⟳ Refresh

Allow access from
⦿ All networks   ◯ Selected networks

ⓘ All networks, including the internet, can access this storage account. Learn more ☐

Network Routing

Determine how you would like to route your traffic as it travels from its source to an Azure endpoint. Microsoft routing is recommended for most customers.

Routing preference * ⓘ
◯ Microsoft network routing   ⦿ Internet routing

Publish route-specific endpoints ⓘ
☑ Microsoft network routing
☐ Internet routing

Figure 7.10 – Storage account routing configuration

You will note there is also an option to publish route-specific endpoints for the storage account. This can be used in scenarios where you might want the default network routing option to be configured for the Microsoft network, while providing internet endpoints or vice versa. These endpoints can be found in the **Endpoints** section of your storage account, as shown in the following screenshot:

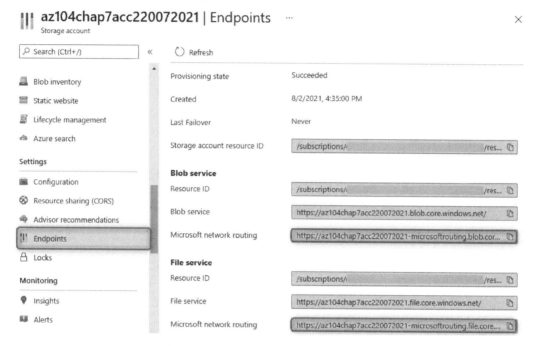

Figure 7.11 – Storage account – Endpoints

From this list, you may copy the endpoints that are required. Now that we have briefly observed the configuration options available for network routing on storage accounts, in the next section, we will explore a PowerShell script for configuring a private endpoint on a storage account.

PowerShell scripts

The following script creates a new private endpoint that is associated with an existing storage account. It is linked to the defined VNet and links to the first subnet within that VNet:

```
$storageAccount = Get-AzStorageAccount -ResourceGroupName
"AZ104-Chapter7" -Name "az104xxxxxxxx"
$privateEndpointConnection = New-AzPrivateLinkServiceConnection
-Name 'myConnection' -PrivateLinkServiceId ($storageAccount.Id)
```

```
-GroupId 'file';
$vnet = Get-AzVirtualNetwork -ResourceGroupName "AZ104-
Chapter7" -Name "StorageVNET"
## Disable private endpoint network policy ##
$vnet.Subnets[0].PrivateEndpointNetworkPolicies="Disabled"
$vnet | Set-AzVirtualNetwork
## Create private endpoint
New-AzPrivateEndpoint -ResourceGroupName "AZ104-
Chapter7" -Name "myPrivateEndpoint" -Location "westeurope"
 -Subnet ($vnet.Subnets[0]) -PrivateLinkServiceConnection
$privateEndpointConnection
```

Once this code has been run, you will have successfully created a private endpoint for your storage account. It will be linked to the VNet and subnet you defined. You can navigate to the private endpoint to discover its private IP address, which will be used for internal communication to the service going forward.

Further reading

That brings an end to this section. We have learned about VNet integration for the storage accounts and the different options available. In the next section, we will explore managing access keys.

We encourage you to read up on this topic further by using the following links:

- **Configuring firewalls and VNets**: https://docs.microsoft.com/en-us/azure/storage/common/storage-network-security?tabs=azure-portal#change-the-default-network-access-rule

- **Private endpoints for your storage accounts**: https://docs.microsoft.com/en-us/azure/storage/common/storage-private-endpoints

- **Private Link resources**: https://docs.microsoft.com/en-us/azure/private-link/private-endpoint-overview#private-link-resource

Storage access keys

Storage access keys are like passwords for your storage account and Azure generates two of these when you provision your account, being a primary and secondary key. Just like passwords, they need to be changed from time to time to ensure you are not compromised. This practice is referred to as key rotation. In the following section, we will run through an example of how to access your keys and how to renew them.

Managing access keys

In this demonstration, we will explore how to view access keys as well as how to renew them:

1. Navigate to the Azure portal by opening `https://portal.azure.com`.

2. Go to a storage account.

3. On the left menu for the storage account, click **Access keys** under the **Security + networking** context. You will notice **key1** and **key2**, as well as the last rotated date for each specified.

4. To copy the access keys, a two-step process will be performed. First, click on **Show keys**.

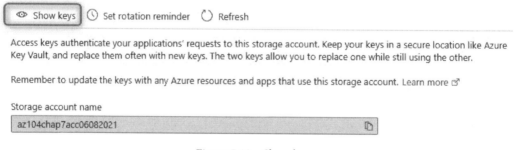

Figure 7.12 – Show keys

5. Then, copy the corresponding key for the storage account by clicking the clipboard icon.

Figure 7.13 – Copying an access key

Now that you know how to access the storage access keys, we will look at how to rotate keys in the following exercise:

1. Navigate to the Azure portal by opening `https://portal.azure.com`.

2. Go to a storage account.

3. On the left menu for the storage account, click **Access keys** under the **Security + networking** context. Click **Rotate key** in the **key2** section.

Figure 7.14 – Rotate key option

4. A notification will come up to confirm that you want to regenerate the key. Click **Yes**.

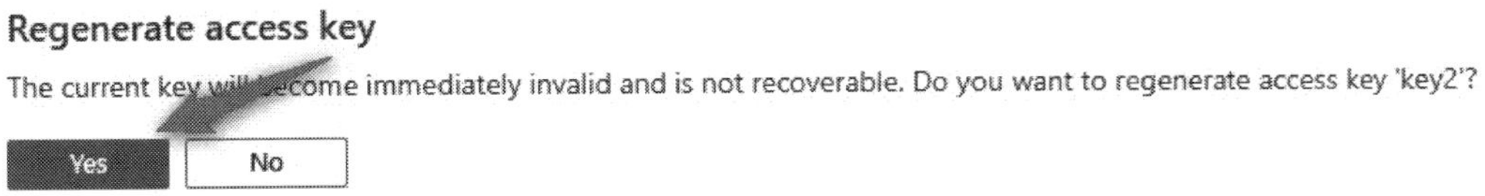

Regenerate access key

The current key will become immediately invalid and is not recoverable. Do you want to regenerate access key 'key2'?

| Yes | No |

Figure 7.15 – Regenerate access key

5. Repeat the process for **key1**.

You have now completed a key rotation for a storage account. This ensures unauthorized access is prevented on the storage keys and it is best practice to rotate these keys every 90 days. As a recommendation, **key2** should be rotated first and updated for any relevant applications and services, then followed by **key1**. This process ensures that the primary key (**key1**) is not directly impacting all business-critical services and causing unnecessary downtime. The rotation process should still be properly planned and maintained through an appropriate change control process within your organization.

Top Tip

As a best practice, keys should be rotated every 90 days to prevent unauthorized exposure to the account. This will also limit the potential attack window for compromised SAS tokens.

In the next section, we will explore SAS tokens.

Working with SAS tokens

SAS tokens are secure access tokens that provide delegated access to resources on your storage account. The storage service confirms the SAS token is valid in order to grant access. The construct of a SAS token includes the permissions granted on the token, the date validity, and the signing key for the storage account. When creating a SAS token, several items need to be considered that govern the granular level of access granted, which are as follows:

- Resource types that the client might use
- Permissions on the resource types that are required
- The period the SAS key should function for

Types of SAS

There are three types of SAS supported by Azure Storage:

- **User-delegated SAS**: This is a SAS token that is secured by AD credentials.
- **Account SAS**: An account SAS is created and secured using a storage key. The permissions granted can span several services (blob, file, queue, and table), as well as accessing permissions for the chosen services.

- **Service SAS**: A service SAS is identical to an account SAS except that it is limited to a single service. There are limitations to some read, write, and delete operations for a service SAS that the account SAS has higher privileges to allow.

Forms of SAS

SAS tokens can take two forms, as detailed here:

- **Ad hoc SAS**: This SAS token is created as needed where permissions are chosen along with accessible services in alignment with the type of SAS used. The configuration is specified in the SAS URI. This is generally used for scenarios where quick access is required for a temporary period. SAS tokens cannot be managed after being issued. User-delegated SAS and account SAS can only be provisioned as an ad hoc SAS.

- **Service SAS with stored access policy**: This form of SAS token is more secure and enhances the functionality that an ad hoc SAS token delivers. SAS tokens can be managed after being issued and are manufactured to comply with policies configured in the stored access policy. SAS tokens can be modified and deleted using a stored access policy.

> **Top Tip**
> Microsoft advises a best security practice is to use Azure AD credentials whenever possible.

Now that you have an understanding of the core components of a SAS, we will explore some exercises for creating and managing these.

Generating SAS tokens

In this demonstration, you will learn how to create a SAS token for sharing access to a storage account:

1. Navigate to the Azure portal by opening `https://portal.azure.com`.
2. Go to a storage account.

3. On the left menu for the storage account, click **Shared access signature** under the **Security + networking** context. Create a new SAS key by selecting the **Container** and **Service** options on the **Allowed resource types** options list. Change the **Allowed services** option list as desired.

Figure 7.16 – SAS permissions

4. Set the time for start to 5 minutes from your current time and click **Generate SAS and connection string**. Copy the connection string – you are only ever presented with this once.

5. Open Azure Storage Explorer, then click the **Open Connect Dialog** button.

Figure 7.17 – Open Connect Dialog

6. Click **Storage account or service**, and select **Connection string** as your connection method, then click **Next**.

7. Paste the connection string copied earlier into the **Connection string** dialog. Change the desired **Display name** text if desired. Click **Next**.

8. You will be presented with a summary page noting all endpoints and other details. Click **Connect**.

9. You will get a success message as follows:

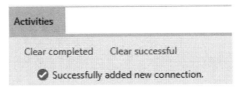

Figure 7.18 – Storage Explorer – Success message

10. Navigate through the hamburger menu to the **Storage Accounts** section, click the arrow to open all accounts, and notice your storage account connection.

Figure 7.19 – Storage Accounts

You now know how to generate a SAS token and connect to a storage account using the token. In the next section, we will explore storage access policies and how these enhance the concept of SAS tokens.

> **Top Tip**
>
> Allowed protocols should be limited to HTTPS on the SAS creation for enhanced security. The SAS start and end time should be limited as far as possible to the necessary time required for access.

Storage access policies

A storage access policy provides an additional layer of control over SAS by introducing policies for managing the SAS token. SAS tokens can now be configured for a start and expiry time with the ability to revoke access after they have been issued. The following steps demonstrate the process for creating a storage access policy on a container:

1. Navigate to the Azure portal by opening `https://portal.azure.com`.

2. Navigate to your storage account, click **Containers** on the left-hand menu, and click on a container.

3. Click **Access policy**, then on the right-hand pane, click **+ Add policy** under **Stored access policies**.

4. Enter an identifier and select permissions. For this exercise, you may select **read** and **list** permissions. Enter the desired start/stop date. Click **OK**.

You have now learned how to create a storage access policy. You will learn how to edit an existing policy in place through the following steps:

1. Navigate to the Azure portal by opening `https://portal.azure.com`.

2. Navigate to your storage account, click **Containers** on the left-hand menu, and click on a container.

3. Click **Access policy**, then click the ellipsis (...) icon of the identifier that matches the name given in the previous step. Click **Edit**.

4. You may modify the **Identifier**, **Start time**, **Permissions**, and **Expiry time**. Click **OK**.

You have now learned how to modify an existing policy. Let's follow the given steps to remove an existing access policy:

1. Navigate to the Azure portal by opening `https://portal.azure.com`.

2. Navigate to your storage account, click **Containers** on the left-hand menu, and click on a container.

3. Click **Access policy**, then click the ellipsis (...) icon of the identifier that matches the name given in the previous step. Click **Delete**.

You have just learned how to delete an access policy. That concludes this section, where we have learned what SAS tokens are and how they work. We have also explored storage access policies as well as how these enhance the management of SAS tokens. In the next section, we have provided additional reading material for you to learn more if desired.

Further reading

We encourage you to read up on the topic further by using the following links:

- **Managing storage account access keys**: `https://docs.microsoft.com/en-us/azure/storage/common/storage-account-keys-manage?tabs=azure-portal`

- **Automation of storage access key rotation**: `https://docs.microsoft.com/en-us/azure/key-vault/secrets/tutorial-rotation-dual?tabs=azure-cli`

Configuring access and authentication

Storage accounts can provide identity-based authentication through either Active Directory (on-premises) or **Azure Active Directory Domain Services (AADDS)**. Both offer the ability to utilize Kerberos authentication offered by Active Directory. The join is limited to a single forest, whereas multiple forest connections will require the configuration of domain trusts.

For the file share to provide authentication capabilities, it will join the respective directory service as a computer account object. There are three primary permissions (authorization) on the SMB share that you should be cognizant of:

- **Storage File Data SMB Share Reader**: This permission grants read access to the SMB share files and directories.

- **Storage File Data SMB Share Contributor**: This grants read, write, list, and delete access to the SMB share files and directories.

- **Storage File Data SMB Elevated Contributor**: This grants contributor access as well as the ability to assign permissions (modify **Access Control Lists (ACLs)**) to other SMB share files and directories.

In the following sections, we will investigate the steps involved in configuring Active Directory domain-joined Azure file shares and the allocation of permissions to these shares.

Configuring Azure AD authentication for a storage account

To authenticate through either directory service, several requirements are needed. The following diagram illustrates the requirements for an Active Directory integration:

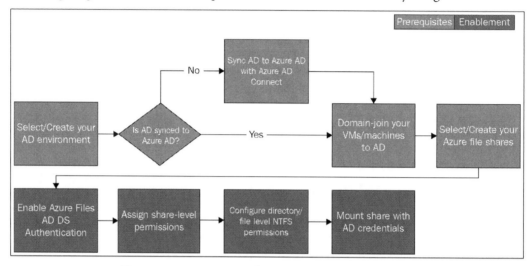

Figure 7.20 – Azure AD authentication enablement process

We will now follow the process for configuring AD authentication on an Azure file share. In the section that follows this, we will explore configuring access to the file share and then mounting the file share. Finally, we will explore how to configure permissions on the share:

1. Create an AD environment. You can run the following quick-start template, which will deploy an Active Directory server in Azure: `https://azure.microsoft.com/en-gb/resources/templates/create-ad-forest-with-subdomain/`.

2. Set up Azure AD Connect and Sync AD with Azure AD.

3. Deploy a test VM.

4. Domain-join your VM to AD.

5. Set up an Azure Storage account (limit the account name to 15 characters) and set up an Azure file share.

6. Download the following module for configuring AADDS authentication: `https://github.com/Azure-Samples/azure-files-samples/releases/tag/v0.2.3`.

7. Enable AADDS authentication on the file share by running the following PowerShell script and change the domain name to what you configured on Active Directory. This must be run on an AD-joined machine. You can use the test VM:

```
Import-Module -name AZFilesHybrid;
Join-AzStorageAccountForAuth -ResourceGroupName
"AZ104-Chapter7" -StorageAccountName "storagename01"
-Domain "domainname.com" -OrganizationalUnitName
"OU=AzureShares,OU=Az104_Resources,DC=domainname,DC=com"
```

Your Azure file share should now be joined to your on-premises AD domain.

> **Top Tip**
>
> Should you receive an error for updating any module, such as the `PowerShellGet` module, you can run the following command to force an update. The module name can be changed accordingly:
>
> ```
> get-module | Where-Object{$_.name -like
> "*PowerShellGet*"} | Update-module
> ```

In the next section, we will explore assigning share-level and file-level permissions, as well as mounting an SMB share on a Windows machine.

Configuring access to Azure files

In the following section, we will explore assigning share and file permissions on the AD-joined storage from the previous exercise, as well as mounting the share and exploring how to validate the security.

Assigning share-level permissions

In this section, we will look at the steps involved to assign share-level permissions:

1. Navigate to the Azure portal by opening `https://portal.azure.com`.
2. Go to the storage account from the previous exercise.
3. Click on **File shares** on the left menu under the **Data storage** context.
4. Create a file share and name it `shared`.

5. Click the new share you just created, and then on the left menu, click **Access Control (IAM)**. Click **+ Add** and then **Add role assignment**.

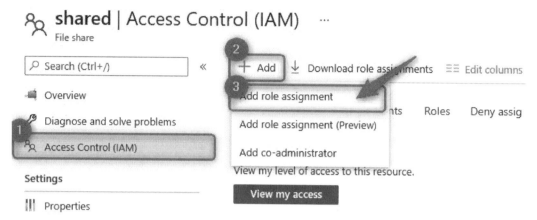

Figure 7.21 – Adding SMB permissions

6. Select **Storage File Data SMB Share Contributor** for **Role** and search for the appropriate user account you created on AD, then click **Save**.

You have just added contributor permissions for a user to your SMB share on Azure. This same process can be applied to the other SMB roles if desired. We will look at assigning file-level permission in the next section.

Mounting the file share

In this section, we will look at the steps involved to mount an Azure file share on the test VM with AD credentials. It should be noted that port 445 will need to be open on the Windows server and SMB 3.x enabled (these should be open by default):

1. Navigate to the Azure portal by opening `https://portal.azure.com`.

2. Go to the storage account from the previous exercise.

3. Click on **File shares** on the left menu under the **Data storage** context.

4. Click the share you used in the previous exercise, and on the left menu, click **Overview**, then click **Connect** on the top menu of the overview blade.

5. Select a drive letter and set **Authentication method** to **Active Directory**. Copy the generated script at the bottom of the page.

6. Navigate to your test VM and log in with the user account you added to the SMB share (this must be an on-premises account). Open PowerShell, then paste your script into the PowerShell window and hit *Enter*. This will map the share as a PSDrive.

7. To have this mapped in Windows File Explorer, you could also map the network path you have from the share as `\\storagename.file.core.windows.net\shared`.

8. Log on to your Active Directory server and attempt the same connection under your administrator account. Note that you get an **Access is denied** message. This is because you haven't assigned SMB permissions to this user.

You have now successfully mounted the SMB share for your Azure files storage and also seen the effect placed on the share using permissions. In the next section, we will explore the effects of file-level permissions.

Configuring file-level permissions

In this section, we will look at the steps involved to assign share-level permissions:

1. Create a new user on AD and assign this user **Storage File Data SMB Share Contributor** permissions for the share from the previous exercise. The synchronization can take some time to replicate to Azure.

2. Navigate to your test VM and paste some files in there. Notice that you have permission to do so. Right-click one of the files and click **Properties**. On the window that pops up, click **Security**.

3. Click **edit**. Notice that your user has full permission. Click **Add...**, type in the new username, click the **Check Names** button, and then click **OK**. Click **Apply**. You get an error stating that you don't have permission. This is because you need to assign the **Storage File Data SMB Share Elevated Contributor** role to this user account to modify ACL permissions. Repeat the operation after assigning this to the new user account and you will now complete the operation.

4. Navigate to the AD server and mount the SMB share using the new user credentials. Note that you may need to wait for synchronization to complete before this works as expected.

5. You can play around with changing settings and completely removing read permissions on the files and confirming the other users indeed cannot read this.

You have now learned how to configure file-level ACLs for Azure Storage shares. This concludes the section for Azure AD authentication and integration for access to Azure file shares. In the next section, we provide additional reading material should you wish to learn more.

Further reading

We encourage you to read up on this topic further by using the following links:

- **Enabling AADDS authentication**: https://docs.microsoft.com/en-us/azure/storage/files/storage-files-identity-auth-active-directory-enable

- **Automation of storage access key rotation**: https://docs.microsoft.com/en-us/azure/key-vault/secrets/tutorial-rotation-dual?tabs=azure-cli

- **How to mount an SMB file share on Windows**: https://docs.microsoft.com/en-us/azure/storage/files/storage-how-to-use-files-windows

- **Configuring file-level permissions**: https://docs.microsoft.com/en-us/azure/storage/files/storage-files-identity-ad-ds-configure-permissions

Copying data by using AzCopy

AzCopy is a utility that can be used for copying files to and from Azure Storage accounts. Authentication can be conducted using either an Active Directory account or a SAS token from storage. AzCopy provides many different functions, but the primary function is for file copying and is structured as `azcopy copy [source] [destination] [flags]`.

Downloading and installing

You can download AzCopy from here: https://docs.microsoft.com/en-us/azure/storage/common/storage-use-azcopy-v10.

In this exercise, you will copy data to your Azure blob using a SAS token:

1. Download and install the relevant AzCopy installer from the preceding link.

2. Extract the files from the archive you downloaded and place them in a location that suits you, such as `C:\AzCopy`.

3. Launch PowerShell, navigate to the folder using the `cd` command, and press *Enter*.

```
PS C:\Azcopy> cd c:\Azcopy
PS C:\Azcopy>
```

Figure 7.22 – Changing directory in PowerShell

You now have a copy of AzCopy on your machine ready to work with.

Copying data by using AzCopy

In this demonstration, we will copy data using the AzCopy utility and SAS tokens. This exercise can also be conducted using Azure AD credentials. Follow these steps to complete the exercise:

1. Identify a file you would like to copy to the Azure Storage account and note the path. For simplification, we will place it in the same path as AzCopy.

2. Navigate to the Azure portal by opening `https://portal.azure.com`.

3. Select a storage account and create two containers on the storage account, one named `azcopysource` and the other `azcopydestination`. These can be any name you choose in later implementations.

4. On the left menu for the storage account, click **Shared access signature** the **Security + networking**. Create a new SAS key by selecting the **Container** option on the **Allowed resource types** options list.

Figure 7.23 – SAS permissions

5. Set the time for **Start** to 5 minutes from your current time and click **Generate SAS and connection string**. Copy the SAS token – you are only ever presented with this once.

6. We will copy the filename for the file identified in *step 1* and insert this name in the following script. The following script will copy the file you enter in **SourceFilePath** to the blob container you specified with **StorageAccountName** and **ContainerName**:

```
# Change all Variables Below
$SourceFilePath = "C:\AzCopy\file1.txt"
$StorageAccountName = "az104chap7acc06082021"
$ContainerName = "azcopydestination"
$SASToken = "?sv=xxxxxxxxxxxxxxxxxxxxxxxxxxxxxxxxxxxxxxxxx
xxxxxxxx%3D"
```

```
# Run AzCopy Command
./azcopy.exe copy "$SourceFilePath"
"https://$StorageAccountName.blob.core.windows.
net/$($ContainerName)?$SASToken"
```

7. The script can either be saved as a PowerShell script file (*.ps1) and called in PowerShell or you can copy and paste your edited script code into PowerShell and press *Enter* for it to run.

Now that you have seen AzCopy in action, you will complete the same task copying files from a source container on a storage account to a destination container on the same storage account.

Copying data between containers using AzCopy

We will now demonstrate a similar copy task to the previous section except this time, you will be copying data from a source container on a storage account to a destination container on the same storage account. Note that this technique can also be used across storage accounts as the principle is the same. Follow these steps:

1. Navigate to the Azure portal by opening `https://portal.azure.com`.

2. Select a storage account and create two containers on the storage account, one named `azcopysource` and the other `azcopydestination`. These can be any name you choose should you want to implement this again later for other environments, just remember to update these names in your copy script.

3. On the left menu for the storage account, click **Containers** under the **Data storage** context, then click on the **azcopysource** container. Click **Shared access tokens** under the **Settings** context on the left menu. Create a new SAS key by setting **Permissions** to **Read** and **List**, setting **time for Start** to 5 minutes from your current time, and then clicking **Generate SAS token and URL**. Copy the SAS token – you are only ever presented with this once. Perform the same operation for the destination container. This time, set the **Shared access tokens** permissions to **Read, Add, Create, Write, Delete**, and **List**.

4. The following script will copy the files from the **source** container, **azcopysource** to the destination container, **azcopydestination**. Note the extra switches (flags) used by the following script. -overwrite=ifsourcenewer performs the operation of overwriting files on the destination if the source files are newer. The --recursive flag recursively copies data from the source container and subsequent folders on any filesystem you copy from, essentially copying all the files and folders it finds:

```
Change all Variables Below
$StorageAccountName = "az104chap7acc06082021"
$SrcContainerName = "azcopysource"
$DestContainerName = "azcopydestination"
$SourceSASToken = "sp=rxxxxxxxxxxxxxxxxxxxxxxxxxxxxxxxx%3D"
$DestSASToken = "sp=rxxxxxxxxxxxxxxxxxxxxxxxxxxxxxxxx%3D"


# Run AzCopy Command
./azcopy.exe copy "https://$StorageAccountName.blob.
core.windows.net/$($SrcContainerName)?$SourceSASToken"
"https://$StorageAccountName.blob.core.windows.
net/$($DestContainerName)?$DestSASToken"
--overwrite=ifsourcenewer --recursive
```

5. After running the preceding script, you will notice text such as this appear indicating that a file copy operation has been completed:

```
Job                          bd11da94f45 has started
Log file is located at:
bd11da94f45.log

0.0 %, 0 Done, 0 Failed, 1 Pending, 0 Skipped, 1 Total,

Job                          bd11da94f45 summary
Elapsed Time (Minutes): 0.0334
Number of File Transfers: 1
Number of Folder Property Transfers: 0
Total Number of Transfers: 1
Number of Transfers Completed: 1
Number of Transfers Failed: 0
Number of Transfers Skipped: 0
TotalBytesTransferred: 15317
Final Job Status: Completed
```

Figure 7.24 – AzCopy script run

You have just learned how to copy data between containers using AzCopy, which brings us to the end of this section, where we have learned what AzCopy is, how to download it, how it works, and also how to copy data between different containers. In the next section, we have provided additional reading material for you to learn more if desired.

Further reading

That brings an end to this section, where we have learned how to use AzCopy to copy files to Azure Storage. In the next section, we will discuss storage replication and life cycle management.

We encourage you to read up on the topic further by using the following links:

- **AzCopy documentation**: `https://docs.microsoft.com/en-us/azure/storage/common/storage-use-azcopy-v10`

- **Authorizing to AzCopy using Azure AD**: `https://docs.microsoft.com/en-us/azure/storage/common/storage-use-azcopy-authorize-azure-active-directory`

Configuring storage replication and life cycle

In the following section, we will explore the various storage replication and life cycle management features available to us in Azure. First, we will describe some key services and configurations you should be aware of.

Storage replication and management services

The following section will explore the various storage replication services available for Azure Storage.

Azure File Sync service

Azure File Sync is a service that can synchronize the data from on-premises file shares with Azure Files. This way, you can keep the flexibility, compatibility, and performance of an on-premises file server, but also store a copy of all the data on the file share in Azure. You can use any protocol that's available on Windows Server to access your data locally, including **Server Message Block (SMB)**, **Network File System (NFS)**, and **File Transfer Protocol** over TLS (**FTPS**).

Blob object replication

Blob object replication provides the capability within Azure to replicate blob objects based on replication rules. The copy will run asynchronously between source and destination containers across two different storage accounts. Several rules can be configured for your desired outcome. Note that for replication to be enabled, blob versioning needs to be enabled.

Blob life cycle management

This is a capability available for GPv2 storage accounts, blob storage accounts, and Azure Data Lake Storage. It allows the management of the blob life cycle through rule-based policies. Data can be automatically transitioned between tiers using this functionality, as well as expired. The following actions can be applied to blobs based on the requirements, automated data tiering, blob snapshots, blob versioning, and blob deletion. Multiple rules can be created and can also be applied to a subset of blobs and containers through filters such as name prefixes. Pricing for blob life cycle management is based upon tier operational charges, as discussed in the previous chapter, but the service itself is free, and the delete operations are also free. It should be noted that this is a great feature to assist in the optimization of your overall storage account costs by automatically transitioning between tiers.

Blob data protection

Blob data protection is a mechanism that assists with the recovery of data in the event of data deletion or being overwritten. The implementation of data protection is a proactive stance to securing data before an incident occurs. Azure Storage provides the capability of protecting data from being deleted or modified, as well as the restoration of data that has been deleted or modified. **Soft delete for containers or blobs** enables the preceding capability to restore data based on the period chosen to retain deleted data, where the default configuration is 7 days. When you restore a container, the blobs, as well as the versions and snapshots, are restored.

Blob versioning

Blob versioning enables a blob to maintain several versions of the object, which can be used for restoring blob data as the version captures the current state of the blob upon being created or modified. This operation is run automatically when blob versioning is enabled.

Immutable storage

Immutable storage, often referred to as **Write Once, Read Many (WORM)**, can be configured on blob storage. This is often used to protect data from accidental deletion or overwrites. Many times, there are legal requirements to manage data in this manner. It is always advised to understand your organization's governance requirements regarding data to ensure you comply with the governance standards required and in place.

Immutable storage can be configured with two types of policies:

- **Time-based retention policies**: Data objects are managed against a time policy, for the duration that the active policy data follows WORM, but after the expiration of this, data may be deleted but not overwritten.

- **Legal hold policies**: Data is held in WORM state until the legal hold policy is explicitly cleared. This is often for litigation requirements.

> **Top Tip**
>
> Container soft delete can only restore the entire container with all the contents, not individual blobs. To achieve blob-level recovery capability, soft delete for blobs should be enabled.

Storage account deletion

There are circumstances where you may delete a storage account and identify that you need to recover the data. There are instances where the storage account can be recovered provided the account was deleted in less than 14 days. The following requirements would also need to be adhered to:

- The storage account was created using the ARM model.

- A storage account with the same name was not provisioned since the deletion of the storage account in question.

- The user performing the recovery has the appropriate permissions.

You can read more about this here: `https://docs.microsoft.com/en-us/azure/storage/common/storage-account-recover`.

Next, we will look at the creation and configuration of the Azure File Sync service.

Creating and configuring the Azure File Sync service

In the next demonstration, we are going to configure Azure File Sync. You will need the following to be in place to follow this demonstration:

- **Windows Server**: You may use Windows Server 2012 R2, 2016, or 2019. Make sure that you enable **Remote Desktop (RDP)** on the server.

- **A storage account**: This storage account needs to be created in one of the supported regions for Azure File Sync. You can refer to the following website for the available regions: `https://azure.microsoft.com/en-gb/global-infrastructure/services/?products=storage`.

- **An Azure file share**: This must be provisioned in the preceding storage account.

> **Top Tip**
> Opening the RDP port for a VM during creation is covered later in the book. This can be configured on VM creation in Azure.

Once the preceding resources are created, we can start with the creation of the Azure File Sync service in Azure and the installation of Azure File Sync on the Windows Server.

First, we will create the Azure File Sync service in Azure. Therefore, take the following steps:

1. Navigate to the Azure portal by opening `https://portal.azure.com`.

2. In the left menu, click **+ Create a resource**, and in the search box, type `Azure File Sync`. Click **Azure File Sync** in the search results. On the following screen, click **Create**.

Figure 7.25 – Searching Azure File Sync

3. Choose a Storage Sync Service name and the resource group that has the storage account you have deployed for this, and then select the same region as the storage account. After entering the values, click **Review + Create**. Click **Create**.

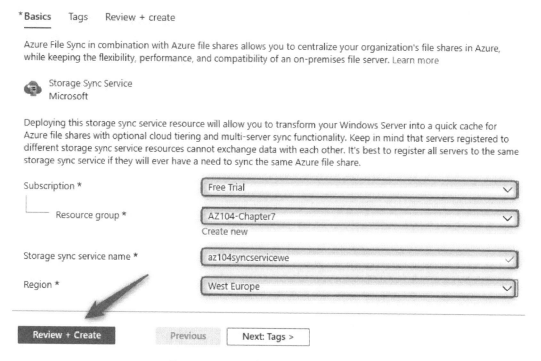

Figure 7.26 – Deploying Azure File Sync

4. After deployment, open the Storage Sync Service and click **+ Sync group** in the top menu.

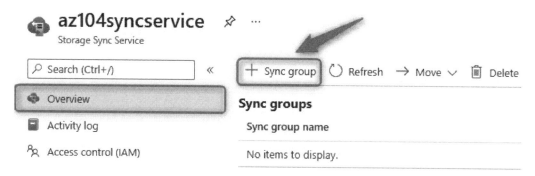

Figure 7.27 – Creating an Azure File Sync group

5. Enter a sync group name, choose a subscription, select your storage account, and choose the Azure file share you created at the beginning of this section. Click **Create**.

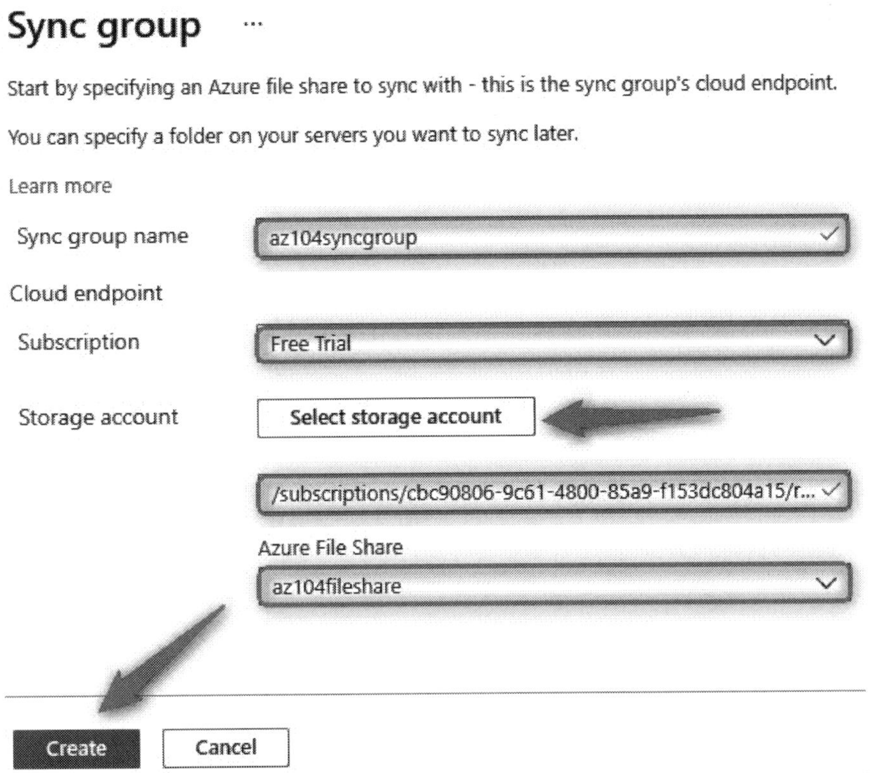

Sync group   ...

Start by specifying an Azure file share to sync with - this is the sync group's cloud endpoint.

You can specify a folder on your servers you want to sync later.

Learn more

Sync group name

| az104syncgroup | ✓ |

Cloud endpoint

Subscription

| Free Trial | ∨ |

Storage account

| Select storage account | ⬅

| /subscriptions/cbc90806-9c61-4800-85a9-f153dc804a15/r... | ✓ |

Azure File Share

| az104fileshare | ∨ |

| Create | | Cancel |

Figure 7.28 – Deploying an Azure file sync group

6. RDP to Windows Server and log in. You should first disable **Internet Explorer Enhanced Security Configuration**. Open **Server Manager**, select **Local Server**, disable it for administrators, then click **OK**.

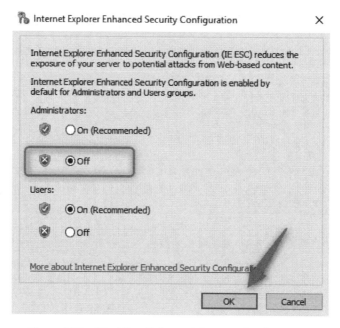

Figure 7.29 – Disabling Enhanced Security Configuration

7. Download the Azure File Sync agent from the following website and select the appropriate downloader: https://www.microsoft.com/en-us/download/details.aspx?id=57159.

8. Install the agent on the server. Keep the default path to install the agent. On the next screen, enable **Use the existing proxy settings configured on the server**.

9. Click **Next**.

10. Select **Use Microsoft Update** and click **Next**. On the following screen, click **Install**.

11. The ServerRegistration tool will start to run. This is where we can register the server. You need to sign in by clicking the **Sign in** button (leave the Azure environment as **AzureCloud**).

12. Choose the Azure subscription, resource group, and Storage Sync Service, then click **Register**.

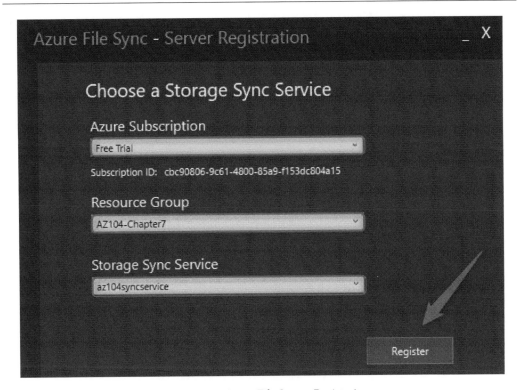

Figure 7.30 – Azure File Sync – Registering

13. After the registration is successful, there is a trust relationship established between the on-premises server and the Storage Sync Service in Azure. Click **OK**.

14. Now, you need to go back to the Azure portal. Go to the Storage Sync Service again and select the sync group that you created earlier. In the sync group settings blade, select **Add server endpoint** in the top menu.

Figure 7.31 – Azure File Sync – Adding a server endpoint

15. Select the registered server and provide the path: D:\Data. Keep **Cloud Tiering** as **Disabled** and leave **Initial Sync** configured as the merge option, with the **Initial download** configuration set to **Download the namespace first**. Click **Create**.

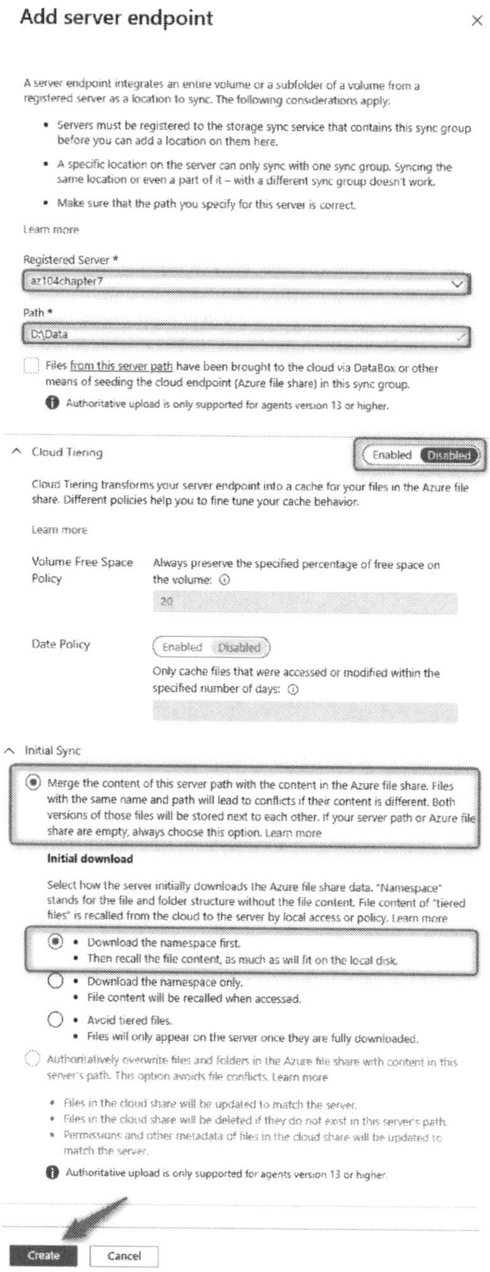

Figure 7.32 – Azure File Sync – Adding a server endpoint

16. If you now go back to the VM where we installed the sync agent and open the D: drive, you will see that there is a folder added called Data. You can copy files to it, as shown in the following screenshot:

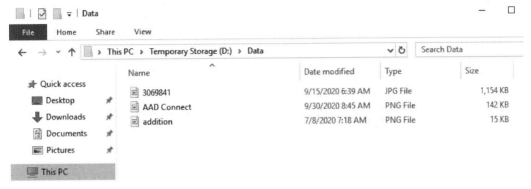

Figure 7.33 – Azure File Sync – Images stored in the Data folder

17. When you switch back to the file share in Azure, you will see that all the files are synced to the storage account in Azure, as shown in the following screenshot:

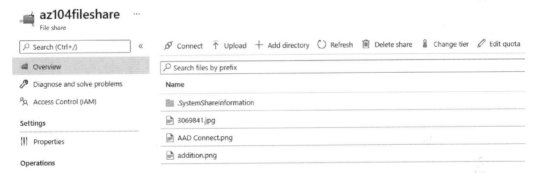

Figure 7.34 – Azure File Sync – Synced files in Azure file storage

This concludes the section about Azure file storage and the Azure File Sync service. In the next section, we are going to look at Azure Storage replication.

Implement Azure Storage replication

In the previous chapter, we uncovered the different replication options available to us in Azure, including **Locally-redundant storage (LRS)**, **Zone-redundant storage (ZRS)**, **Geo-redundant storage (GRS)**, and **Geo-zone-redundant storage (GZRS)**. In this section, we will explore changing the replication chosen for a deployed storage account. Follow the given steps to implement Azure storage replication:

1. Navigate to the Azure portal by opening `https://portal.azure.com`.

2. Select a storage account to configure.

3. On the **Storage account** blade, navigate to the left menu, then under **Settings**, click on **Configuration**. Note the various options available.

4. Click on the **Replication** drop-down menu, then select the appropriate option and click **Save**.

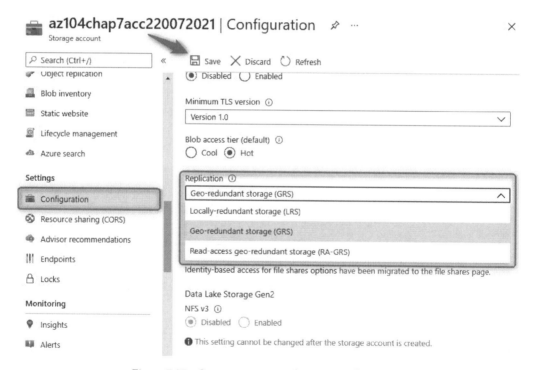

Figure 7.35 – Storage account replication configuration

You have now completed the configuration of the replication type for a storage account.

> **Top Tip**
>
> For enhanced security, it is advised that the **Secure transfer required** and **Allow Blob public access** options in the **Configuration** blade for a storage account are configured to **Enabled**.

Configuring blob object replication

In the following demonstration, you will learn how to configure blob object replication. To follow along, you will require two storage accounts:

1. Navigate to the Azure portal by opening `https://portal.azure.com`.

2. Go to a storage account, then on the left menu, under **Data management**, click **Object replication**. Click **+ Set up replication rules** on the top menu.

Figure 7.36 – Storage account – Object replication

3. Select the destination storage account, then choose a *source* and *destination* container in the lower section.

4. Click **add** under **Filters**, then on the following screen that pops up, enter `Azure` for **Prefix match** and click **Save**. This will be used to filter all items, such as folders and blobs, that match the entered prefix entered.

Figure 7.37 – Object replication – Filters

5. Under the **Copy over** context, click **change**. On the subsequent screen, select **Everything**. Click **Save**.

Figure 7.38 – Object replication – Copy over rules

6. Click **Save and apply**.

7. Navigate to your source container. Upload some items that you name starting with Azure. You can even make some files up, such as a text file.

8. Wait 5 minutes then navigate to your destination container and notice that the files copied across are now in your destination container too, matching the implemented rule(s).

You have now completed the configuration of blob object replication and have seen it in action. In the next section, we will explore blob life cycle management.

> **Top Tip**
>
> While it may be tempting to see object replication as a backup mechanism, this is not something to rely on the same as a backup service, there is a difference in SLAs for instance and errors will be replicated too. Also remember that data is copied asynchronously, meaning there is a delay in the destination copy.

Configuring blob life cycle management

The following exercise will demonstrate the configuration of blob life cycle management:

1. Navigate to the Azure portal by opening `https://portal.azure.com`.

2. Go to a storage account and create a container named `demo`.

3. On the left menu, under **Data management**, click **Lifecycle Management**. Click + **Add a rule** on the top menu.

4. Enter `CoolToHotTiering` as the rule name, and change **Rule scope** to **Limit blobs with filters**. You can leave **Blob type** as **Block blobs** and **Blob subtype** as **Base blobs**. Click **Next**.

5. You will note that the **Base blobs** tab will present a conditional statement (if.. then) for the blobs. Based on a time interval, an automated action can be performed. For the **More than (days ago)** field, enter 1. For the **Then** field, change the drop-down option to **Move to cool storage**. Note that to apply multiple actions for a rule, you can click **+ Add conditions**. Please click this now. The condition you have just configured basically applies as follows: for blobs that are more than 1 day old, automatically move them to cool storage.

6. For the next conditional block, enter 1 in the **More than (days ago)** field, and select **Delete the blob** for the **Then** dropdown. Click **Next**. Click **Next** again. The condition you have just configured basically applies as follows: for blobs that are more than 1 day old, you then automatically delete the blob. The way it will work is that blobs more than 1 day old in the preceding step move to cold storage, and blobs that are a further 1 day old in cold storage are deleted.

7. The **Filter set** tab allows you to define a blob prefix for filtering a subset of blobs. In the **Blob prefix** field, enter demo/pic. Click **Add**.

You have now created your first life cycle management rule. Next, we will explore how to implement a life cycle management policy using JSON code.

Life cycle management policy deployed as code

At times, it may be desired to implement your policy as code, especially where the reuse of policies is applicable. This approach drives better consistency and reduces the likelihood of errors:

1. Navigate to the Azure portal by opening https://portal.azure.com.

2. Go to a storage account and create a container named demo.

3. On the left menu, under **Data management**, click **Lifecycle Management**. Click **Code View**.

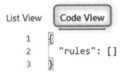

Figure 7.39 – Code View

4. Modify the following JSON code to suit your deployment. The current file code reads as *move any blob to cool tier if the period since the last modification is greater than 1 day*. It will match this to the files container:

```json
{
    "rules": [
        {
            "enabled": true,
            "name": "move-to-cool",
            "type": "Lifecycle",
            "definition": {
                "actions": {
                    "baseBlob": {
                        "tierToCool": {
                            "daysAfterModificationGreaterThan": 1
                        }
                    }
                },
                "filters": {
                    "blobTypes": [
                        "blockBlob"
                    ],
                    "prefixMatch": [
                        "files/log"
                    ]
                }
            }
        }
    ]
}
```

5. Copy the modified code in the preceding code block into the **Code View** section on the Azure portal and click **Save**.

```
🖫 Save   ⟲ Discard   ↓ Download   ◯ Refresh
```

Lifecycle management offers a rich, rule-based policy for general purpose v2 and blob storage new or updated policy may take up to 48 hours to complete. Learn more

List View   Code View

```
 1  {
 2      "rules": [
 3          {
 4              "enabled": true,
 5              "name": "move-to-cool",
 6              "type": "Lifecycle",
 7              "definition": {
 8                  "actions": {
 9                      "baseBlob": {
10                          "tierToCool": {
11                              "daysAfterModificationGreaterThan": 1
12                          }
13                      }
14                  },
15                  "filters": {
16                      "blobTypes": [
17                          "blockBlob"
18                      ],
19                      "prefixMatch": [
20                          "files/log"
21                      ]
22                  }
23              }
24          }
25      ]
26  }
```

Figure 7.40 – Blob life cycle management – Code View

You know how to configure the life cycle management policy using JSON code. In the next section, we will explore the ability to disable and delete the rule.

Deleting a life cycle management rule

You may want to delete a life cycle management rule. The following steps will guide you through the process of doing so:

1. Open a storage account with a life cycle management rule configured and click the **Lifecycle management** button on the storage menu.

2. Hover over the rule you would like to modify and note a checkbox appears to the left of it. Click this.

Figure 7.41 – Selecting a rule

3. Note the top menu bar now provides the option to disable or delete the rule. Disabling will stop the rule from applying until enabled again and deleting will remove the rule permanently. Click **Delete**.

Figure 7.42 – Deleting a rule

That brings us to the end of the blob life cycle management section. In the next section, we will explore blob data protection.

> **Top Tip**
>
> Automated data tiering moves blobs to cooler tiers or deletes them. Associated actions within a single rule must follow a transitive implementation from hotter tiers to cooler tiers.

Configuring blob data protection

In the following exercise, you will explore configuring soft delete options as part of the data protection options available to you:

1. Navigate to the Azure portal by opening `https://portal.azure.com`.

2. Go to a storage account. On the left menu, under the **Data management** context, click **Data protection**. Select the options under the **Recovery** context for **Enable soft delete for blobs** and **Enable soft delete for containers**. Set both periods to 7 days and click **Save**.

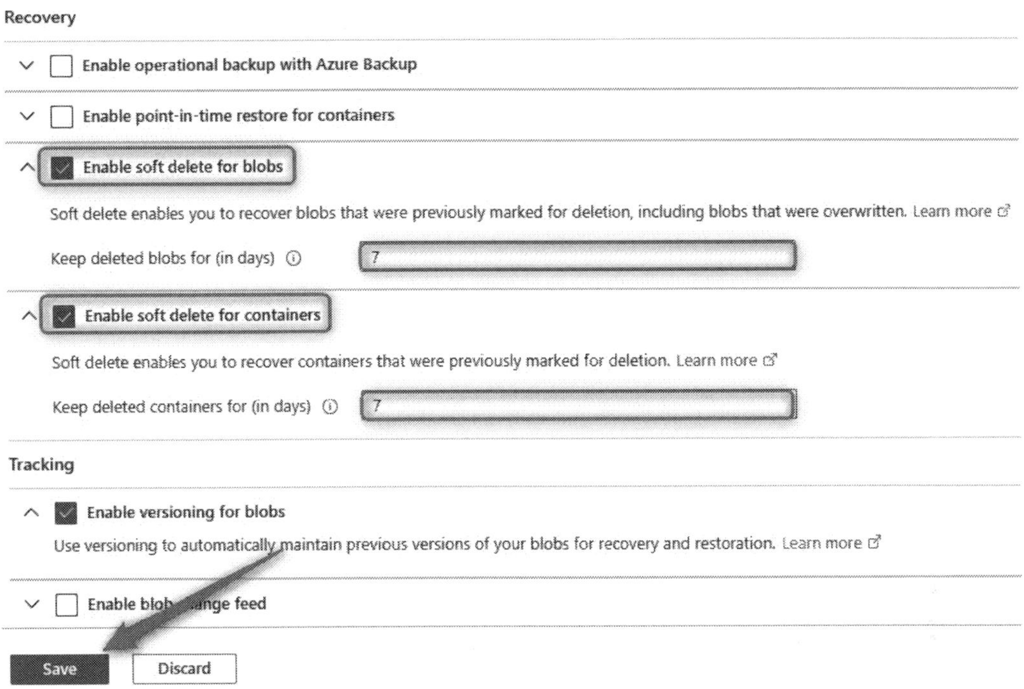

Figure 7.43 – Blob data protection

3. You will receive a success notification indicating that the setting has taken effect.

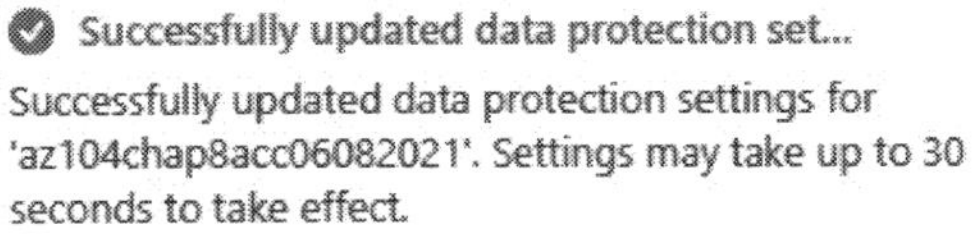

Figure 7.44 – Success notification

You now know how to configure blob data protection settings on your storage accounts. In the next section, we have provided additional reading material for the configuration of storage replication and life cycle management.

Further reading

That brings an end to this section. We have learned about storage replication and life cycle management.

We encourage you to read up on the topic further by using the following links:

- **Azure File Sync services**: `https://docs.microsoft.com/en-us/azure/storage/file-sync/file-sync-introduction`
- **Configuring object replication**: `https://docs.microsoft.com/en-gb/azure/storage/blobs/object-replication-configure?tabs=portal`
- **Blob versioning**: `https://docs.microsoft.com/en-gb/azure/storage/blobs/versioning-overview`
- **Blob life cycle management**: `https://docs.microsoft.com/en-us/azure/storage/blobs/storage-lifecycle-management-concepts?tabs=azure-portal`
- **Blob data protection overview**: `https://docs.microsoft.com/en-us/azure/storage/blobs/data-protection-overview`

Summary

In this chapter, we covered how to manage the security of storage within Azure by integrating storage with VNets, using private endpoints, working with SAS tokens, and configuring access and authentication. You also learned how to configure storage replication and blob life cycle management. You now have the skills to secure and manage Azure Storage.

In the next chapter, we will work through some labs to enhance your new skills for storage management and work through practical applications of storage.

8

Practice Labs – Implementing and Managing Storage

The best way to become efficient with Azure is to get hands-on experience to test your skill set. This chapter will test the skills you acquired in *Chapters 6, Managing Storage*, and *Chapter 7, Securing Storage*. The labs in this chapter reference the official Microsoft learning labs on GitHub as well as some additional labs to enhance your understanding and experience working with storage.

In this chapter, we are going to cover the following topics:

- Managing the Azure Storage lab
- The Azure Functions AzCopy lab
- Connecting storage using a private link endpoint lab

Technical requirements

To execute the labs in this chapter, you will need the following:

- Access to an Azure subscription with owner or contributor privileges. If you do not have access to one, students can enroll for a free account: `https://azure.microsoft.com/en-in/free/`.

- **PowerShell 5.1** or later installed on a PC where the labs can be practiced from; note that many examples can only be followed from a PC or `https://shell.azure.com` (PowerShell 7.0.6 LTS or later is recommended).

> **Top Tip**
>
> Either the AZ module or AzureRM module should be installed; you cannot have both. Installation will fail should you try to run both.

- Installation of the AZ module can be performed by running the following in an administrative PowerShell session:

```
Set-ExecutionPolicy -ExecutionPolicy RemoteSigned -Scope
CurrentUser
Install-Module -Name Az -Scope CurrentUser -Repository
PSGallery -Force
```

> **Note**
>
> Even though the labs are on GitHub, no GitHub account is required to access the labs.

Managing the Azure Storage lab

- This lab will guide you through creating a storage account and configuring the Blob storage, authentication and authorization. Finally, you will create a file share where you restrict network access for the storage account:

- **Estimated time**: 45 minutes.

- **Lab method**: PowerShell and the Azure portal.

- **Lab scenario**: In this lab, you play the role of an administrator evaluating the utility and functionality provided by Azure. You need to determine whether it is fit for purpose and will conduct some basic tests. You need to explore the different mechanisms available to you for storage and whether they can meet any security objectives your organization may have.

- Visit the given link (**Lab URL**) to the official Microsoft learning GitHub labs, where you will be guided through each task step by step to achieve the following objectives.

  Lab objectives:

  I.   **Task one**: Provision the resource groups for the lab.

  II. **Task two**: Create and configure the lab storage accounts.

  III. **Task three**: Create a blob container and upload data.

  IV. **Task four**: Configure the storage account authentication and authorization.

  V.   **Task five**: Create and configure an Azure Files share.

  VI. **Task six**: Configure firewall network access for the storage account.

- **Lab URL**: `https://microsoftlearning.github.io/AZ-104-MicrosoftAzureAdministrator/Instructions/Labs/LAB_07-Manage_Azure_Storage.html`.

- **Lab architecture diagram**:

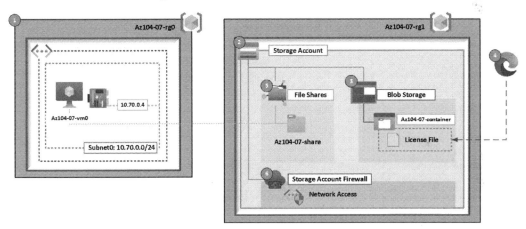

Figure 8.1 – The lab architecture diagram

Let's now proceed to the next lab exercise.

The Azure Functions AzCopy lab

This lab will guide you through creating a storage account, configuring the Blob storage and containers, creating an Azure function, configuring the code for replication, and finally, testing whether replication occurs automatically:

- **Estimated time**: 45 minutes.

- **Lab method**: PowerShell and the Azure portal.

- **Lab scenario**: In this lab, you play the role of an administrator evaluating the utility and functionality provided by AzCopy. You need to determine whether it can be used to replicate data from a source container to another destination container. You need to run AzCopy whenever a file is added to a predetermined share or container.

    Lab objectives:

    I.   **Task one**: Provision the resource groups for the lab.

    II. **Task two**: Create and configure the lab storage accounts.

    III. **Task three**: Create and configure the Azure Files shares.

    IV. **Task four**: Create the blob containers.

    V.   **Task five**: Create and configure an Azure function.

    VI. **Task six**: Upload some data to the source blob container.

    VII. **Task seven**: Confirm replication has occurred.

- **Lab URL**: Not applicable.

- **Lab architecture diagram**:

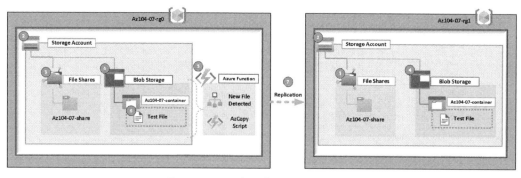

Figure 8.2 – Lab architecture diagram

Let's now proceed to the step-by-step execution of the lab.

Lab steps

The following PowerShell script has been broken into smaller sections to explain what is created at each point.

Prerequisites

The following PowerShell code runs to add the modules required and specifies the location to be used:

```
# Modules
# confirm the required modules are installed
try{Import-Module Az;}
catch{Write-Host "Installing AZ Module..." -NoNewline;
Install-Module AZ -Force -AllowClobber; Write-Host "done"
-ForegroundColor Green;}
try{Import-Module Az.Functions;}
catch{Write-Host "Installing AZ.Functions Module..."
-NoNewline; Install-Module AZ.Functions -Force -AllowClobber;
Write-Host "done" -ForegroundColor Green;}
#? Variables that apply to the whole script
$Location = "Westeurope";
# Authenticate to Azure
Connect-AzAccount
$SubscriptionId = "xxxxxxx";
Select-AzSubscription -SubscriptionId $SubscriptionId
```

Task one: Provision the resource groups for the lab.

The following PowerShell code creates the resource groups for the lab environment:

```
# Resource Group 1
$resourceGroup1 = "Az104-07-rg0";
New-AzResourceGroup -Name $resourceGroup1 -Location $Location;
# Resource Group 2
$resourceGroup2 = "Az104-07-rg1";
New-AzResourceGroup -Name $resourceGroup2 -Location $Location;
```

Task two: Create and configure the lab storage accounts.

The following PowerShell code creates and configures the storage accounts for this lab:

```
# Common Paramters / Variables
$date = Get-date -Format "yyMMddhhmm";
$SkuName = "Standard_LRS";
# Storage Account 1
$storageAccountName1 = "$($resourceGroup1.ToLower() -replace("-
"))$date";
New-AzStorageAccount -Name $storageAccountName1
-ResourceGroupName $resourceGroup1 -Location $Location -SkuName
$SkuName;
# Storage Account 2
$storageAccountName2 = "$($resourceGroup2.ToLower() -replace("-
"))$date";
New-AzStorageAccount -Name $storageAccountName2
-ResourceGroupName $resourceGroup2 -Location $Location -SkuName
$SkuName;
```

Task three: Create and configure the Azure Files shares.

The following PowerShell code creates and configures the Azure file shares:

```
# Common Paramters / Variables
$ShareName= "az104-07-share";
# Storage Account 1
$Context1 = (Get-AzStorageAccount -ResourceGroupName
$ResourceGroup1 -AccountName $StorageAccountName1).Context;
New-AzStorageShare -Name $ShareName -Context $Context1
# Storage Account 2
$Context2= (Get-AzStorageAccount -ResourceGroupName
$ResourceGroup2 -AccountName $StorageAccountName2).Context;
New-AzStorageShare -Name $ShareName -Context $Context2
```

Task four: Create the blob containers.

The following PowerShell code creates the blob containers:

```
# Common Paramters / Variables
$ContainerName = "az104-07-container"
# Storage Account 1
New-AzStorageContainer -Name $ContainerName -Context $Context1
```

```
-Permission Blob
# Storage Account 2
New-AzStorageContainer -Name $ContainerName -Context $Context2
-Permission Blob
```

Task five: Create and configure an Azure function.

The following PowerShell code creates and configures the Azure function:

```
# Create an app service plan, then a function app then
$appServicePlanName = "az104-07-appsp-$date";
$azureFunctionApp = "az10407function-$date";
New-AzAppServicePlan -ResourceGroupName $resourceGroup1
-Name $appServicePlanName -Location $Location -Tier "Basic"
-NumberofWorkers 1 -WorkerSize "Small"
New-AzFunctionApp -Name "$azureFunctionApp" -ResourceGroupName
"$resourceGroup1" -PlanName $appServicePlanName
-StorageAccountName $storageAccountName1 -Runtime PowerShell
```

> **Important Note**
>
> It should be noted that the service plan required must be with a Windows
> operating system; it is for this reason that the deployed service plan will be for
> Windows.

The following screenshot shows the **Windows** operating system selected as part of
the service plan; you can view this from the **Overview** section of the App Service plan
we created:

Figure 8.3 – App Service plan – the Windows operating system

Log in to Azure, navigate to the Azure function that we've created, and click **Functions** on the left menu. Click **+ Create**, and then on the **Create function** blade, leave **Development environment** as **Develop in portal** and select the **Azure Blob Storage trigger** template. Change the **New Function** name to Blobcopy, set the path to az104-07-container/{name}, select **AzureWebJobsStorage** as **Storage account connection**, and click **Create**:

> **Top Tip**
> The App Service plan that is created can be equated to a server environment that will host the function. This can also be used for hosting web applications.

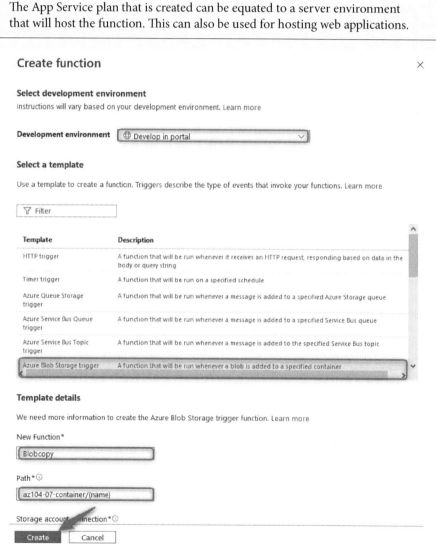

Figure 8.4 – Create function

Generate **Secure Access Tokens (SAS tokens)** for both storage accounts and note them. Now that your function has been created, click **Code + Test** on the left menu and paste the following code, replacing the **$SrcSASToken** text with the SAS token from the storage account in the **Az104-07-rg0** resource group, and replacing the **$DstSASToken** text with the SAS token from the storage account in the **Az104-07-rg1** resource group. Also, replace **StorageAccountName1** with the name of the storage account in the **Az104-07-rg0** resource group, and replace **StorageAccountName2** with the name of the storage account in the **Az104-07-rg1** resource group. Click **Save** once the code is modified:

```
# Input bindings are passed in via param block.
param([byte[]] $InputBlob, $TriggerMetadata)
# Define variables
$SrcStgAccURI = "https://StorageAccountName1.blob.core.windows.
net/"
$SrcBlobContainer = "az104-07-container"
$SrcSASToken = "YourSASToken"
$SrcFullPath =
"$($SrcStgAccURI)$($SrcBlobContainer)/$($SrcSASToken)"
$DstStgAccURI = "https://StorageAccountName2.blob.core.windows.
net/"
$DstBlobContainer = "az104-07-container"
$DstSASToken = "YourSASToken"
$DstFullPath =
"$($DstStgAccURI)$($DstBlobContainer)/$($DstSASToken)"
# Test if AzCopy.exe exists in current folder
$WantFile = "azcopy.exe"
$AzCopyExists = Test-Path $WantFile
# Download AzCopy if it doesn't exist
If ($AzCopyExists -eq $False) {
    Write-Host "AzCopy not found. Downloading...";
    Invoke-WebRequest -Uri "https://aka.ms/downloadazcopy-v10-
windows" -OutFile AzCopy.zip -UseBasicParsing
    Expand-Archive ./AzCopy.zip ./AzCopy -Force
    # Copy AzCopy to current dir
    Get-ChildItem ./AzCopy/*/azcopy.exe | Copy-Item
-Destination "./AzCopy.exe"
}
else { Write-Host "AzCopy found, skipping download." }
# Run AzCopy from source blob to destination file share
```

```
Write-Host "Backing up storage account..."
$env:AZCOPY_JOB_PLAN_LOCATION = $env:temp+'\.azcopy'
$env:AZCOPY_LOG_LOCATION=$env:temp+'\.azcopy'
./azcopy.exe copy $SrcFullPath $DstFullPath
--overwrite=ifsourcenewer --recursive
```

> **Top Tip**
>
> The following lines of code change the plan and log file paths for the AzCopy application. This prevents errors from occurring when running the application in the function, as they cannot write to the default folder locations:
>
> ```
> $env:AZCOPY_JOB_PLAN_LOCATION = $env:temp+'\.
> azcopy'
> ```
>
> ```
> $env:AZCOPY_LOG_LOCATION=$env:temp+'\.azcopy'
> ```

Task six: Upload some data to the source blob container.

We will now upload some data to the source blob container.

Navigate to the storage account in the **Az104-07-rg0** resource group, click on **Containers** on the left menu, click **az104-07-container**, and click **Upload** to upload a file to the container:

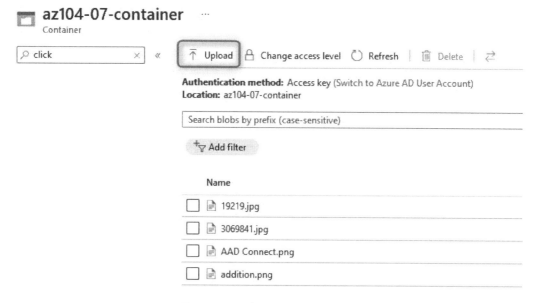

Figure 8.5 – The source container

Let's now proceed to the last task.

Task seven: Confirm replication has occurred.

We will now confirm the replication script is working as expected.

Navigate to the storage account in the **Az104-07-rg1** resource group, click on **Containers** on the left menu, click **az104-07-container**, and note the files in the destination container. These should now emulate the source container, thereby confirming working replication:

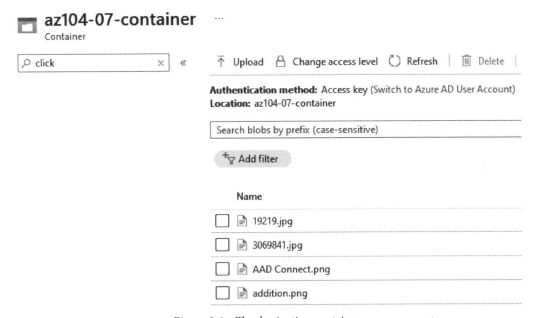

Figure 8.6 – The destination container

You have now demonstrated the replication of data using Azure Functions and AzCopy to replicate data between two different storage accounts and blob containers triggered through an upload operation. Based on the operation's success, you have determined that AzCopy can be utilized through functions to meet your company requirements. You will now need to build a replication strategy to align with business requirements before implementing a production solution.

The lab is completed; you can now remove all the associated resources for the lab.

> **Top Tip**
>
> While performing this exercise, you may have noticed the option on a storage account to configure replication. This replication option replicates all transactions and creates what is known as a mirror of the storage on the source in the destination storage account. Using the AzCopy exercise, you can create your own governance mechanisms on functions to ensure that data is copied as it's initially loaded and never deleted or modified by using AzCopy.

Connecting storage using a private endpoint lab

This lab will guide you through connecting an Azure private endpoint to a storage account, which will connect to a virtual machine in the same VNet. You will then prove connectivity to the storage account through the private endpoint:

- **Estimated time**: 45 minutes.

- **Lab method**: PowerShell.

- **Lab scenario**: In this lab, you play the role of an administrator seeking to employ a secure method to communicate with an Azure Storage account. You have identified an Azure private endpoint as being a mechanism to control traffic over a local endpoint and want to prove its functionality before implementing it within your organization's environment. This lab will guide you through each task step by step to achieve the following objectives.

    Lab objectives:

    I.   **Task one**: Provision the resource groups for the lab.

    II.   **Task two**: Create and configure an Azure Storage account.

    III. **Task three**: Create and configure the Azure Files shares.

    IV.   **Task four**: Provision a vNET.

    V.   **Task five**: Provision a **Virtual Machine (VM)**.

    VI.   **Task six**: Deploy a private endpoint to the storage account.

    VII. **Task seven**: Test connectivity from the server to the file share over the local IP.

- **Lab URL**: Not applicable.

- **Lab architecture diagram**:

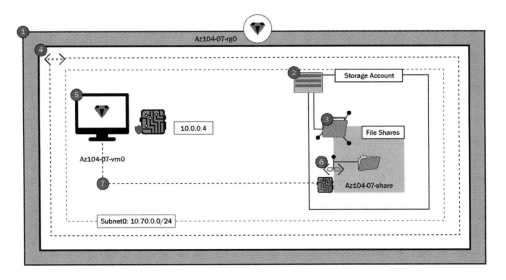

Figure 8.7 – Lab architecture diagram

Let's now proceed toward the step-by-step execution of the lab.

Lab steps

In the following demonstration, we will attach a private endpoint to a storage account:

Task one: Provision the resource groups for the lab.

The following PowerShell code creates the resource groups for the lab environment:

```
#? TASK 1 - Provision the resource groups for the lab
#? //////////////////////////////////////////////////////////
# Resource Group 1
$resourceGroup1 = "Az104-07-rg0";
New-AzResourceGroup -Name $resourceGroup1 -Location $Location;
```

Task two: Create and configure an Azure Storage account.

The following PowerShell code creates and configures the storage accounts for this lab:

```
#? TASK 2 - Create and configure the lab storage accounts
#? //////////////////////////////////////////////////////////
# Common Paramters / Variables
$date = Get-date -Format "yyMMddhhmm";
$SkuName = "Standard_LRS";
```

```
# Storage Account 1
$storageAccountName1 = "$($resourceGroup1.ToLower() -replace("-
"))$date";
New-AzStorageAccount -Name $storageAccountName1
-ResourceGroupName $resourceGroup1 -Location $Location -SkuName
$SkuName;
```

Task three: Create and configure the Azure Files shares.

The following PowerShell code creates and configures the Azure file shares:

```
# Common Paramters / Variables
$ShareName= "az104-07-share";
# Storage Account 1
$Context1 = (Get-AzStorageAccount -ResourceGroupName
$ResourceGroup1 -AccountName $StorageAccountName1).Context;
New-AzStorageShare -Name $ShareName -Context $Context1
```

Task four: Provision a vNET.

The following PowerShell code creates and configures the Azure vNET:

```
## Create backend subnet config. ##
$subnetConfig = New-AzVirtualNetworkSubnetConfig -Name
myBackendSubnet -AddressPrefix 10.0.0.0/24
## Create the virtual network. ##
$parameters1 = @{
    Name = 'MyVNet'
    ResourceGroupName = "$ResourceGroup1"
    Location = "$Location"
    AddressPrefix = '10.0.0.0/16'
    Subnet = $subnetConfig
}
$vnet = New-AzVirtualNetwork @parameters1
```

Task 5: Provision a VM.

The following PowerShell code creates and configures the Azure VM. It will also create an **Network Security Group** (**NSG**) associated with the VM network interface and allow **remote desktop** (**RDP**) access:

```powershell
## Set credentials for server admin and password. ##
$adminUsername = 'Student'
$adminPassword = 'Pa55w.rd1234'
$adminCreds = New-Object PSCredential $adminUsername,
($adminPassword | ConvertTo-SecureString -AsPlainText -Force)
$OperatingSystemParameters = @{
    PublisherName = 'MicrosoftWindowsServer'
    Offer = 'WindowsServer'
    Skus = '2019-Datacenter'
    Version = 'latest'
}
$vmName = "myVM"
$vmSize = "Standard_DS1_v2"
$NSGName = "$vmName-nsg"
$subnetid = (Get-AzVirtualNetworkSubnetConfig -Name
'myBackendSubnet' -VirtualNetwork $vnet).Id
$nsg = New-AzNetworkSecurityGroup -ResourceGroupName
"$ResourceGroup1" -Location "$Location" -Name "$NSGName"
$nsgParams = @{
    'Name'                     = 'allowRDP'
    'NetworkSecurityGroup'     = $NSG
    'Protocol'                 = 'TCP'
    'Direction'                = 'Inbound'
    'Priority'                 = 200
    'SourceAddressPrefix'      = '*'
    'SourcePortRange'          = '*'
    'DestinationAddressPrefix' = '*'
    'DestinationPortRange'     = 3389
    'Access'                   = 'Allow'
}
Add-AzNetworkSecurityRuleConfig @nsgParams | Set-
AzNetworkSecurityGroup
$pip = New-AzPublicIpAddress -Name "$vmName-ip"
-ResourceGroupName "$ResourceGroup1" -Location "$Location"
```

```
-AllocationMethod Dynamic
$nic = New-AzNetworkInterface -Name "$($vmName)$(Get-
Random)" -ResourceGroupName "$ResourceGroup1" -Location
"$Location" -SubnetId $subnetid -PublicIpAddressId $pip.Id
-NetworkSecurityGroupId $nsg.Id


$vmConfig = New-AzVMConfig -VMName $vmName -VMSize $vmSize
Add-AzVMNetworkInterface -VM $vmConfig -Id $nic.Id
Set-AzVMOperatingSystem -VM $vmConfig -Windows -ComputerName
$vmName -Credential $adminCreds
Set-AzVMSourceImage -VM $vmConfig @OperatingSystemParameters
Set-AzVMOSDisk -VM $vmConfig -Name "$($vmName)_OsDisk_1_$(Get-
Random)" -CreateOption fromImage
Set-AzVMBootDiagnostic -VM $vmConfig -Disable


## Create the virtual machine ##
New-AzVM -ResourceGroupName "$ResourceGroup1" -Location
"$Location" -VM $vmConfig
```

Task six: Deploy a private endpoint to the storage account.

The following PowerShell code creates a private endpoint and associates this with the storage account we created earlier:

```
$storageAccount = Get-AzStorageAccount -ResourceGroupName
$resourceGroup1 -Name $storageAccountName1
$privateEndpointConnection = New-AzPrivateLinkServiceConnection
-Name 'myConnection' -PrivateLinkServiceId ($storageAccount.Id)
-GroupId 'file';
## Disable private endpoint network policy ##
$vnet.Subnets[0].PrivateEndpointNetworkPolicies="Disabled"
$vnet | Set-AzVirtualNetwork
## Create private endpoint
New-AzPrivateEndpoint -ResourceGroupName "$resourceGroup1"
-Name "myPrivateEndpoint" -Location "$Location" -Subnet
($vnet.Subnets[0]) -PrivateLinkServiceConnection
$privateEndpointConnection
```

Task seven: Test connectivity from the server to the file share over the local IP address.

Follow the following steps to check connectivity to the file share:

1. Log in to the server we created in *task five* using the credentials you specified. In the Azure portal, navigate to the VM and click **Connect**, and then click **RDP**. Click **Download RDP file** on the screen that follows:

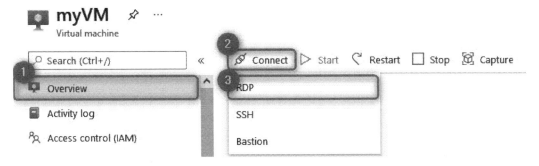

Figure 8.8 – Connect to a VM

Enter the credentials for the VM.

2. Open the file explorer and click **This PC** on the left navigation menu. Click **Computer** on the top menu bar and then click **Map network drive**:

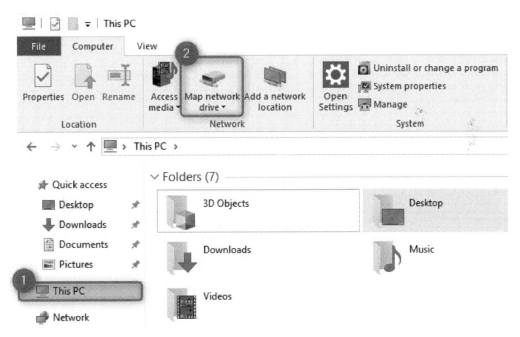

Figure 8.9 – Mapping the network drive

3. Choose a **Drive** letter and enter the IP address and share (10.0.0.5 if following along as per the lab) in the **Folder** input, such as **10.0.0.5\az104-07-share**, click on **Connect using different credentials**, and then click **Finish**:

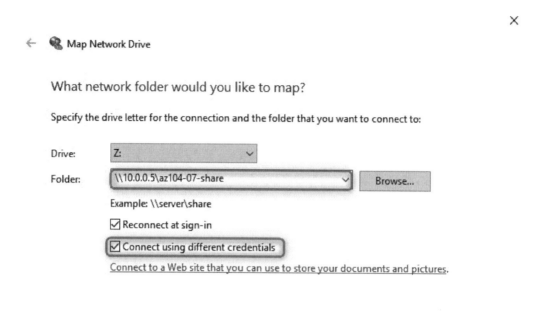

Figure 8.10 – Selecting the folder path

4. For the credentials, enter the storage account name as the username, and then you will need to navigate to the storage account in Azure and use the storage account key as the password. Click **Remember my credentials** and then **OK**:

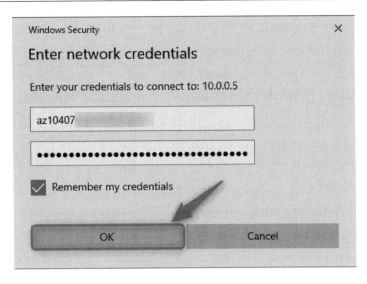

Figure 8.11 – Enter storage account credentials

You have now mapped the network share. This has been connected over the private endpoint. You can test whether it is functional by uploading a file.

The lab is completed; you can now remove all the associated resources for the lab.

> **Note**
> It is best practice to remove unused resources to ensure that there are no unexpected costs, even though resources created in this lab do not incur additional costs.

This brings us to the end of labs for *Chapter 6, Understanding and Managing Storage*, and *Chapter 7, Securing Storage*.

Summary

In this chapter, we had a look at scenario-based labs, which tested our skills in the following areas: managing Azure storage, creating an Azure function with AzCopy for replication, connecting storage to a private endpoint, and proving our deployments and configurations.

In the next part of the book, we'll cover the deployment and management of Azure compute resources. We will explore VMs, automation of VM deployments using **Azure Resource Manager** (**ARM**) templates, containers, and app services.

Part 3: Deploying and Managing Azure Compute Resources

This is the third part of the official Microsoft exam objectives and will focus on compute resources, specifically deploying and managing them.

This part of the book comprises the following chapters:

- *Chapter 9, Automating VM Deployments Using ARM Templates*
- *Chapter 10, Configuring Virtual Machines*
- *Chapter 11, Creating and Configuring Containers*
- *Chapter 12, Creating and Configuring App Services*
- *Chapter 13, Practice Labs – Deploying and Managing Azure Compute Resources*

9

Automating VM Deployments Using ARM Templates

This chapter focuses on how to automate deployments via **Azure Resource Manager (ARM)** templates. You will learn how to read and modify ARM templates. This includes how to deploy resources via ARM templates including the deployment of **virtual machine (VM)** extensions via ARM. One of the main reasons why automating deployments is important is because a lot of organizations are now moving towards **Infrastructure-as-Code (IaC)**, which is a very valuable skill set to have going forward.

In this chapter, we will cover the following topics:

- Modifying an ARM template
- Saving a deployment as an ARM template
- Deploying VM extensions

Technical requirements

To follow along with the hands-on lessons, you will need access to **Azure Active Directory** (**Azure AD**) as a global administrator. If you do not have access, you can enroll for a free account at `https://azure.microsoft.com/en-in/free/`.

An Azure subscription is also required; you can either register with your own credit card or enroll for the free $200 once-off credit if you use the following link: `https://azure.microsoft.com/en-us/free/`.

Modifying an ARM template

ARM templates are used to define infrastructure that needs to be deployed in Azure, which is also often referred to as IaC. One of the benefits of ARM templates is the ability to deploy resources rapidly via code with a level of consistency as opposed to an Azure engineer needing to deploy resources via the Azure portal, which might introduce misconfigurations when repeating tasks. It is also useful to view deployment history.

ARM templates make use of the **JavaScript Object Notation** (**JSON**) format to define the resources. To deploy ARM templates, there are two JSON files of importance:

- **Template file**: This is the main file and has sections to define parameters, variables, user-defined functions, resources, and outputs.

- **Parameters file**: This file can be on its own and linked to the template file, which is usually done when there are many parameters used in complex deployments.

The following is how the ARM template schema looks when empty:

```
{
    "$schema":"http://schema.management.azure.com/
schemas/2019-04-01/deploymentTemplate.json#",
    "contentVersion": "",
    "parameters": {},
    "variables": {},
    "functions": [],
    "resources": [],
    "outputs": {}
}
```

Microsoft also has a range of predefined ARM templates that can be downloaded from GitHub and can be used in deployments directly or can be modified to suit the organizational requirements before deployment.

> **Tip**
> You can download Microsoft's Visual Studio Code application and the ARM tools required for free to view and edit ARM templates.

Now that we understand at a high-level what ARM templates are used for, let's go ahead and start modifying an ARM template. We are going to modify an existing ARM template that is used to create a resource group. Our goal is to modify the template to deploy the resource group in North Europe instead of West Europe.

First, let's have a look at the template file. Under the **resources** section we have the following:

- **Type**: This is where we specify the resource type; in this instance, it is going to be a resource group.

- **ApiVersion**: This is the **application programmable interface (API)** version of the resource.

- **Location**: This is where the resource group and resources will be located and it is specified under the name parameter in the `parameters` file.

- **Name**: This is the name of the resource; this is specified under the name parameter in the `parameters` file.

- **Copy**: This is a `copy` loop that can be used to create multiple instances, but for our example, we are going to deploy only one resource group for now, which includes the name and count variables.

- **Properties**: None specified.

- **Tags**: This is where we reference the resource tags from the `parameters` file.

```
{} ResourceGroups.json 1 ×    {} resourcegroups.parameters.json

E: > Coachable G Drive > AZ-104 > Chapter 8 (9) > {} ResourceGroups.json > [ ] resources > {} 0
  1    {
  2        "$schema": "https://schema.management.azure.com/schemas/2019-04-01/subscriptionDeploymentTemplate.json#",
  3        "contentVersion": "1.0.0.0",
  4        "parameters": {
  5          "resourceGroups": {
  6            "type": "array",
  7            "metadata": {
  8              "description": "Name, location"
  9            }
 10          },
 11          "resourceTags": {
 12              "type": "object",
 13              "metadata": {
 14                  "description": "Tags to be applied"
 15              }
 16          }
 17        },
 18        "variables": {},
 19        "resources": [
 20            {
 21              "type": "Microsoft.Resources/resourceGroups",
 22              "apiVersion": "2020-10-01",
 23              "location": "[parameters('resourceGroups')[copyIndex('rgCopy')].location]",
 24              "name": "[parameters('resourceGroups')[copyIndex('rgCopy')].name]",
 25              "copy": {
 26                "name": "rgCopy",
 27                "count": "[length(parameters('resourceGroups'))]"
 28              },
 29              "properties": {},
 30              "tags": "[parameters('resourceTags')]"
 31            }
 32        ],
 33        "outputs": {}
 34    }
```

Figure 9.1 – Resource group ARM template

Next, let's look at the `parameters` file. We have the following configuration under the `parameters` section:

- `resourceGroups`: This is where we provide additional information regarding the resource group itself. This is where we specify the name of the resource group and the location.

- `resourceTags`: This is where we specify the resource tags for the resource group; in this example, we are going to create three values, `Environment`, `Managed By`, and `Deployed By`.

```
 1  {
 2      "$schema": "https://schema.management.azure.com/schemas/2019-04-01/deploymentParameters.json#",
 3      "contentVersion": "1.0.0.0",
 4      "parameters": {
 5          "resourceGroups": {
 6              "value": [
 7                  {
 8                      "name": "Production_RG",
 9                      "location": "westeurope"
10                  }
11              ]
12          },
13          "resourceTags": {
14              "value": {
15                  "Environment": "Production",
16                  "Managed By": "Azure Support L3",
17                  "Deployed By": "Riaan Lowe"
18              }
19
20          }
21      }
22  }
```

Figure 9.2 – Resource group parameters file

Now that we understand the two templates in more detail, we will only need to change the parameters file to change the deployment region. To do this, we will modify the parameters ARM template and change the location from westeurope to northeurope.

The following screenshot shows the change made under the location parameter:

```
    "$schema": "https://schema.management.azure.com/schemas/2019-04-01/deploymentParameters.json#",
    "contentVersion": "1.0.0.0",
    "parameters": {
        "resourceGroups": {
            "value": [
                {
                    "name": "Production_RG",
                    "location": "northeurope"
                }
            ]
        },
        "resourceTags": {
            "value": {
                "Environment": "Production",
                "Managed By": "Azure Support L3",
                "Deployed By": "Riaan Lowe"
            }

        }
    }
}
```

Figure 9.3 – Changed location from westeurope to northeurope

Now that we have understood how ARM templates work and how to modify a template, let's go ahead and configure a **virtual hard disk** (**VHD**) via an ARM template.

In this section, we had a look at the ARM template structure and how to change the resource location via the ARM template.

We encourage you to read up further by using the following links based on Azure ARM templates:

- `https://docs.microsoft.com/en-us/azure/azure-resource-manager/templates/overview`

- `https://docs.microsoft.com/en-us/azure/azure-resource-manager/templates/deployment-tutorial-local-template?tabs=azure-powershell`

Configure a VHD template

Seeing that the exam objective is to automate the deployment of VMs, we are going to deploy a few resources that will include VHDs, both an **operating system** (**OS**) VHD and a data disk VHD.

We are going to deploy the following resources with our ARM template:

- Windows Server 2019

- Virtual network

- **Network security group** (**NSG**)

> **Important Note**
>
> Microsoft has several ARM templates available on GitHub to help get you started: `https://github.com/Azure/azure-quickstart-templates`.

The following ARM template can be used to deploy the resources. The script is quite long and, therefore, has been split up into sections to explain what the ARM code does. To use the following script, all of the code sections need to be copied into a JSON format template:

The following code section indicates the schema version and relevant details:

```
{

  "$schema": "https://schema.management.azure.com/
schemas/2019-04-01/deploymentTemplate.json#",

  "contentVersion": "1.0.0.0",
```

```
"metadata": {
  "_generator": {
    "name": "bicep",
    "version": "0.4.1.14562",
    "templateHash": "8381960602397537918"
  }
}
```

The following code section indicates the start of the parameters section within the main template file, which will reference the parameters file that can be found in the following snippet. This includes the admin username for the VM as well as the password that is required in secure string format:

```
},
"parameters": {
  "adminUsername": {
    "type": "string",
    "metadata": {
      "description": "Username for the Virtual Machine."
    }
  },
  "adminPassword": {
    "type": "secureString",
    "minLength": 12,
    "metadata": {
      "description": "Password for the Virtual Machine."
    }
  },
```

The following code section indicates the DNS name for the public IP address of the VM as well as the definition of the public IP address:

```
"dnsLabelPrefix": {
  "type": "string",
  "defaultValue": "[toLower(format('{0}-{1}',
parameters('vmName'), uniqueString(resourceGroup().id,
parameters('vmName'))))]",
  "metadata": {
    "description": "Unique DNS Name for the Public IP used
to access the Virtual Machine."
```

```
      }
    },
    "publicIpName": {
      "type": "string",
      "defaultValue": "myPublicIP",
      "metadata": {
        "description": "Name for the Public IP used to access
the Virtual Machine."
      }
```

The following code section indicates that the public IP address is going to use the dynamic type, which means it will change when the VM is restarted:

```
    },
    "publicIPAllocationMethod": {
      "type": "string",
      "defaultValue": "Dynamic",
      "allowedValues": [
        "Dynamic",
        "Static"
      ],
      "metadata": {
        "description": "Allocation method for the Public IP
used to access the Virtual Machine."
      }
```

The following code section indicates that the public IP address is going to make use of the basic SKU; the basic SKU is selected if the user doesn't provide a value:

```
    },
    "publicIpSku": {
      "type": "string",
      "defaultValue": "Basic",
      "allowedValues": [
        "Basic",
        "Standard"
      ],
      "metadata": {
```

```
        "description": "SKU for the Public IP used to access
the Virtual Machine."
    }
```

The following code section indicates the different allowed values to choose from when choosing an OS; this will be in the form of a drop-down list within the Azure portal:

```
    },
    "OSVersion": {
      "type": "string",
      "defaultValue": "2019-Datacenter",
      "allowedValues": [
        "2008-R2-SP1",
        "2012-Datacenter",
        "2012-R2-Datacenter",
        "2016-Nano-Server",
        "2016-Datacenter-with-Containers",
        "2016-Datacenter",
        "2019-Datacenter",
        "2019-Datacenter-Core",
        "2019-Datacenter-Core-smalldisk",
        "2019-Datacenter-Core-with-Containers",
        "2019-Datacenter-Core-with-Containers-smalldisk",
        "2019-Datacenter-smalldisk",
        "2019-Datacenter-with-Containers",
        "2019-Datacenter-with-Containers-smalldisk"
      ],
```

The following code section indicates the VM SKU, which will, in this case, be a Standard_D2_V3 VM with the name of simple-vm:

```
      "metadata": {
        "description": "The Windows version for the VM. This
will pick a fully patched image of this given Windows version."
      }
    },
    "vmSize": {
      "type": "string",
```

```
    "defaultValue": "Standard_D2_v3",
    "metadata": {
      "description": "Size of the virtual machine."
    }
  },
  "location": {
    "type": "string",
    "defaultValue": "[resourceGroup().location]",
    "metadata": {
      "description": "Location for all resources."
    }
  },
  "vmName": {
    "type": "string",
    "defaultValue": "simple-vm",
    "metadata": {
      "description": "Name of the virtual machine."
    }
  }
}
```

The following code section indicates the variables for the virtual network called MyVNET with an address range of 10.0.0.0/16, a subnet with a range of 10.0.0.0/24, and a default NSG:

```
  },
  "functions": [],
  "variables": {
    "storageAccountName": "[format('bootdiags{0}',
uniqueString(resourceGroup().id))]",
    "nicName": "myVMNic",
    "addressPrefix": "10.0.0.0/16",
    "subnetName": "Subnet",
    "subnetPrefix": "10.0.0.0/24",
    "virtualNetworkName": "MyVNET",
    "networkSecurityGroupName": "default-NSG"
  },
```

The following code section indicates the creation of a `Standard_LRS` storage account where the public IP address will reside:

```
"resources": [
  {
    "type": "Microsoft.Storage/storageAccounts",
    "apiVersion": "2021-04-01",
    "name": "[variables('storageAccountName')]",
    "location": "[parameters('location')]",
    "sku": {
      "name": "Standard_LRS"
    },
    "kind": "Storage"
  },
  {
    "type": "Microsoft.Network/publicIPAddresses",
    "apiVersion": "2021-02-01",
    "name": "[parameters('publicIpName')]",
    "location": "[parameters('location')]",
    "sku": {
      "name": "[parameters('publicIpSku')]"
    },
```

The following code section indicates the creation of the NSG with a basic inbound rule that will allow the remote desktop protocol on port 3389 from any source address. It is a security risk to do this with production VMs; it is recommended to rather use VPN access and local IP ranges instead:

```
    "properties": {
      "publicIPAllocationMethod":
"[parameters('publicIPAllocationMethod')]",
      "dnsSettings": {
        "domainNameLabel": "[parameters('dnsLabelPrefix')]"
      }
    }
  },
  {
    "type": "Microsoft.Network/networkSecurityGroups",
```

```json
    "apiVersion": "2021-02-01",
    "name": "[variables('networkSecurityGroupName')]",
    "location": "[parameters('location')]",
    "properties": {
      "securityRules": [
        {
          "name": "default-allow-3389",
          "properties": {
            "priority": 1000,
            "access": "Allow",
            "direction": "Inbound",
            "destinationPortRange": "3389",
            "protocol": "Tcp",
            "sourcePortRange": "*",
            "sourceAddressPrefix": "*",
            "destinationAddressPrefix": "*"
          }
        }
      ]
    }
```

The following code section indicates the creation of the virtual network based on the variables. It is important to note that there is a dependsOn field, which means that to create the resources, it requires another resource to be created first, in this case, the NSG:

```json
    },
    {
      "type": "Microsoft.Network/virtualNetworks",
      "apiVersion": "2021-02-01",
      "name": "[variables('virtualNetworkName')]",
      "location": "[parameters('location')]",
      "properties": {
        "addressSpace": {
          "addressPrefixes": [
            "[variables('addressPrefix')]"
          ]
        }
```

```
        }
    },
    {
        "type": "Microsoft.Network/virtualNetworks/subnets",
        "apiVersion": "2021-02-01",
        "name": "[format('{0}/{1}',
variables('virtualNetworkName'), variables('subnetName'))]",
        "properties": {
            "addressPrefix": "[variables('subnetPrefix')]",
            "networkSecurityGroup": {
                "id": "[resourceId('Microsoft.
Network/networkSecurityGroups',
variables('networkSecurityGroupName'))]"
            }
        },
        "dependsOn": [
            "[resourceId('Microsoft.Network/networkSecurityGroups',
variables('networkSecurityGroupName'))]",
            "[resourceId('Microsoft.Network/virtualNetworks',
variables('virtualNetworkName'))]"
        ]
    },
```

The following code section indicates the creation of the VM **network interface card** (**NIC**) with the variable values:

```
    {
        "type": "Microsoft.Network/networkInterfaces",
        "apiVersion": "2021-02-01",
        "name": "[variables('nicName')]",
        "location": "[parameters('location')]",
        "properties": {
            "ipConfigurations": [
                {
                    "name": "ipconfig1",
                    "properties": {
                        "privateIPAllocationMethod": "Dynamic",
                        "publicIPAddress": {
```

```
                "id": "[resourceId('Microsoft.Network/
publicIPAddresses', parameters('publicIpName'))]"
            },
            "subnet": {
            "id": "[resourceId('Microsoft.Network/
virtualNetworks/subnets', variables('virtualNetworkName'),
variables('subnetName'))]"
            }
          }
        }
      ]
    },
```

The following code section indicates the creation of the VM based on the variables declared in this script, which include vmSize, computerName, adminUsername, and adminPassword:

```
    "dependsOn": [
      "[resourceId('Microsoft.Network/publicIPAddresses',
parameters('publicIpName'))]",
      "[resourceId('Microsoft.Network/virtualNetworks/
subnets', variables('virtualNetworkName'),
variables('subnetName'))]"
    ]
  },
  {
    "type": "Microsoft.Compute/virtualMachines",
    "apiVersion": "2021-03-01",
    "name": "[parameters('vmName')]",
    "location": "[parameters('location')]",
    "properties": {
      "hardwareProfile": {
        "vmSize": "[parameters('vmSize')]"
      },
      "osProfile": {
        "computerName": "[parameters('vmName')]",
        "adminUsername": "[parameters('adminUsername')]",
        "adminPassword": "[parameters('adminPassword')]"
```

```
        },
        "storageProfile": {
          "imageReference": {
            "publisher": "MicrosoftWindowsServer",
            "offer": "WindowsServer",
            "sku": "[parameters('OSVersion')]",
            "version": "latest"
          },
```

The following code section indicates the creation of the VM and specifies the OS type for the OS disk along with a secondary disk size of 1023 GB:

```
        "osDisk": {
          "createOption": "FromImage",
          "managedDisk": {
            "storageAccountType": "StandardSSD_LRS"
          }
        },
        "dataDisks": [
          {
            "diskSizeGB": 1023,
            "lun": 0,
            "createOption": "Empty"
          }
        ]
        },
```

The following code section indicates the virtual network that the VM is going to be a part of based on the variables declared. To do this, the VM is dependent on the NIC being created along with a storage account:

```
        "networkProfile": {
          "networkInterfaces": [
            {
              "id": "[resourceId('Microsoft.Network/
networkInterfaces', variables('nicName'))]"
            }
          ]
```

```
        },
        "diagnosticsProfile": {
          "bootDiagnostics": {
            "enabled": true,
            "storageUri": "[reference(resourceId('Microsoft.
Storage/storageAccounts', variables('storageAccountName'))).
primaryEndpoints.blob]"
          }
        }
      },
      "dependsOn": [
        "[resourceId('Microsoft.Network/networkInterfaces',
variables('nicName'))]",
        "[resourceId('Microsoft.Storage/storageAccounts',
variables('storageAccountName'))]"
      ]
    }
```

The following code section indicates the variables such as the admin username, password, and DNS label:

```
  ],
  "outputs": {
    "hostname": {
      "type": "string",
      "value": "[reference(resourceId('Microsoft.Network/
publicIPAddresses', parameters('publicIpName'))).dnsSettings.
fqdn]"
    }
  }
}
```

The following is the accompanying `parameters` file for the ARM template:

```
{
    "$schema": "https://schema.management.azure.com/
schemas/2019-04-01/deploymentParameters.json#",
    "contentVersion": "1.0.0.0",
    "parameters": {
```

```
        "adminUsername": {
            "value": "administrator"
        },
        "adminPassword": {
            "value": "MyPasswordIslong!"
        },
        "dnsLabelPrefix": {
            "value": "packt-demo-server"
        },
```

The following code section indicates the variables such as the public IP address type and SKU, OS version, VM size and name, and also the location of resources to be deployed:

```
        "publicIpName": {
            "value": "myPublicIP"
        },
        "publicIPAllocationMethod": {
            "value": "Dynamic"
        },
        "publicIpSku": {
            "value": "Basic"
        },
        "OSVersion": {
            "value": "2019-Datacenter"
        },
        "vmSize": {
            "value": "Standard_D2_v3"
        },
        "location": {
            "value": "northeurope"
        },
        "vmName": {
            "value": "demo-server"
        }
    }
}
```

Next, let's focus on the VHD section from the main template file. The screenshot in *Figure 9.4* represents information such as the following:

- osDisk: This is where we specify the OS disk; we have chosen to create the OS disk from an image within the Azure gallery and store it as a managed disk.

- dataDisks: This is where we specify the additional storage disk, which will be 1 TB in size and will be empty (formatted drive).

```
"osDisk": {
  "createOption": "FromImage",
  "managedDisk": {
    "storageAccountType": "StandardSSD_LRS"
  }
},
"dataDisks": [
  {
    "diskSizeGB": 1023,
    "lun": 0,
    "createOption": "Empty"
  }
]
},
```

Figure 9.4 – VHD ARM template

In this section, we had a look at the ARM template, which showed how to configure several resources including a virtual hard disk for the OS and an additional VHD. We encourage you to read up further by using the following links based on Azure ARM templates:

- https://docs.microsoft.com/en-us/learn/modules/deploy-vms-from-vhd-templates/

- https://docs.microsoft.com/en-us/azure/virtual-machines/using-managed-disks-template-deployments

Next, we are going to look at how to deploy from an ARM template via the Azure portal.

Deploy from a template

In the previous section, we had a look at the ARM template, which will configure several resources. Now that we have both of the ARM templates (the main template and the `parameters` file), let's go ahead and see how to deploy this template.

We will begin by deploying the ARM templates via the Azure portal through the following steps:

1. Navigate to the Azure portal by opening a web browser and going to `https://portal.azure.com`.

2. In the left menu, select **Resource groups**:

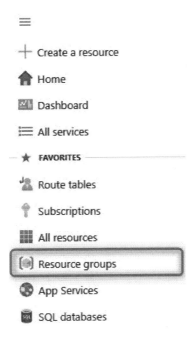

Figure 9.5 – Azure resource groups

3.   Next, choose the resource group you want to deploy the ARM template to:

Dashboard >

Resource groups ⚲ ···
Demo Tenant

＋ Create   ⚙ Manage view ∨   ◯ Refresh   ↓

| Filter for any field... | Subscription == **all** |

Showing 1 to 17 of 17 records.

☐	Name ↑↓
☐	[◉]
☐	[◉]
☐	[◉]
☐	[◉]
☐	[◉]
☐	[◉]
☐	[◉]
☐	[◉]
☐	[◉]
☐	[◉]
☐	[◉]
☐	[◉]
☐	[◉]
☐	[◉] Production_RG

Figure 9.6 – Selecting a specific resource group

4. Click on **Create**:

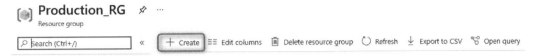

Figure 9.7 – Selecting Create on the resource group

5. In the search bar, type in `template` and choose **Template deployment (deploy using custom** and click on **Create** on the next page:

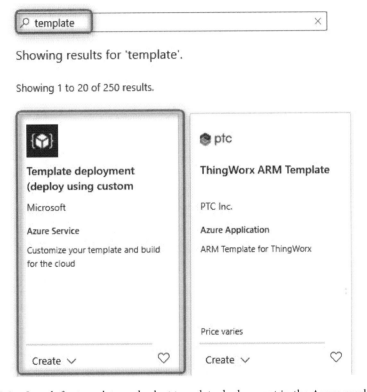

Figure 9.8 – Search for template and select template deployment in the Azure marketplace

6.   Select **Build your own template in the editor**:

Custom deployment   ⋯

Deploy from a custom template

Select a template   Basics   Review + create

Automate deploying resources with Azure Resource Manager templates in a single, coordinated operation. Create or select a template below to get started. Learn more about template deployment ⧉

> ✎   Build your own template in the editor

Common templates

🖥   Create a Linux virtual machine

🖥   Create a Windows virtual machine

⚙   Create a web app

🗄   Create a SQL database

▨   Azure landing zone

Start with a quickstart template or template spec

Template source ⓘ   ⦿ Quickstart template

                                    ◯ Template spec

Quickstart template (disclaimer) ⓘ   [⌄]

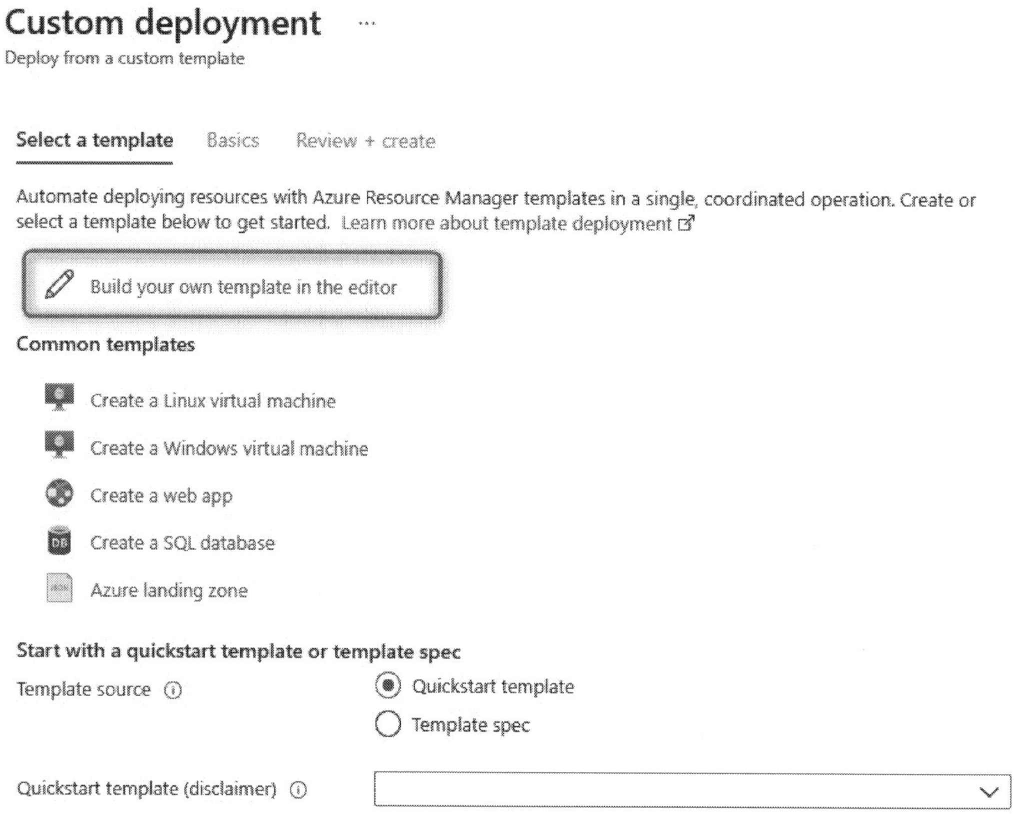

Figure 9.9 – Choosing to build our own ARM template

7. Copy all the text from the VHD template from the previous section and overwrite the existing configuration and click on the **Save** button at the bottom of the page:

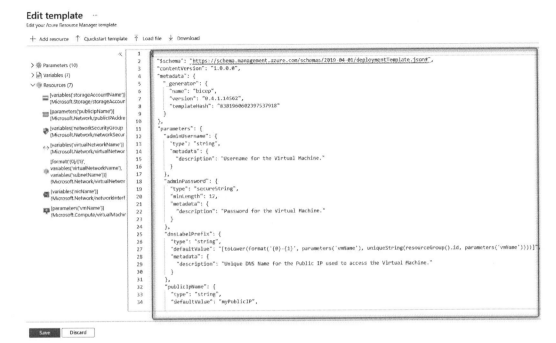

Figure 9.10 – ARM template main file

8. Next, click on **Edit parameters** and copy the parameters script from the previous
    VHD section, overwrite the existing configuration, and click on **Save**:

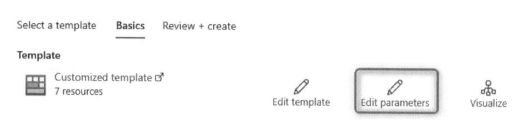

Custom deployment ⋯

Deploy from a custom template

Select a template   **Basics**   Review + create

Template

Customized template ◻
7 resources

Edit template   Edit parameters   Visualize

Figure 9.11 – Selecting to edit parameters

Edit parameters ⋯

↑ Load file   ↓ Download

```
 1
 2    "$schema": "https://schema.management.azure.com/schemas/2019-04-01/deploymentParameters.json#",
 3    "contentVersion": "1.0.0.0",
 4    "parameters": {
 5      "adminUsername": {
 6        "value": "administrator"
 7      },
 8      "adminPassword": {
 9        "value": "MyPasswordIslong!"
10      },
11      "dnsLabelPrefix": {
12        "value": "packt-demo-server"
13      },
14      "publicIpName": {
15        "value": "myPublicIP"
16      },
17      "publicIPAllocationMethod": {
18        "value": "Dynamic"
19      },
20      "publicIpSku": {
21        "value": "Basic"
22      },
23      "OSVersion": {
24        "value": "2019-Datacenter"
25      },
26      "vmSize": {
27        "value": "Standard_D2_v3"
28      },
29      "location": {
30        "value": "northeurope"
31      },
32      "vmName": {
33        "value": "demo-server"
34      }
35    }
```

Save   Discard

Figure 9.12 – ARM template parameters file

You will notice that all the required parameters have been inserted into the `parameters` file. We are now ready to click on **Review + create**. After passing the validation, you can click on **Create** and the resources will be created by the custom ARM template:

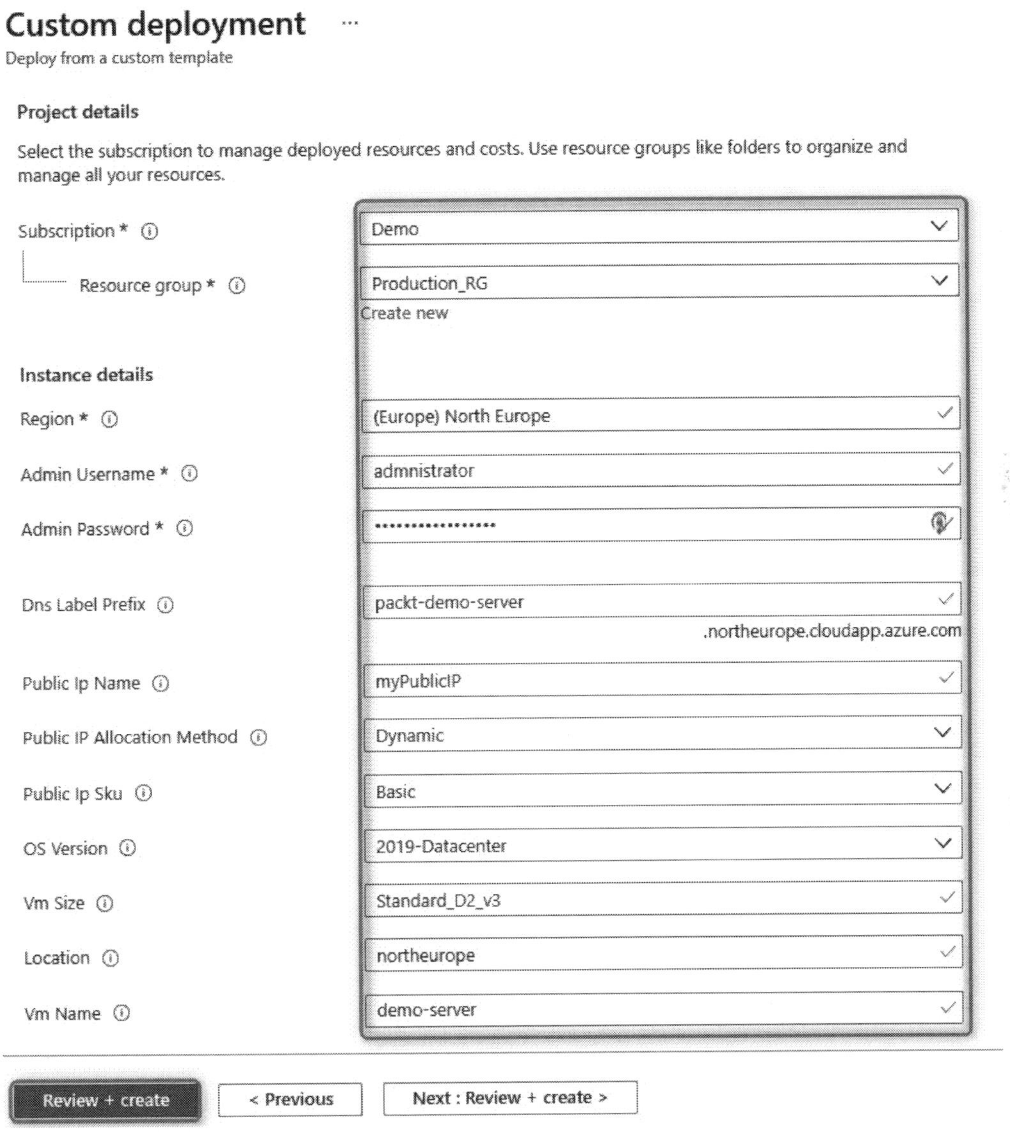

Custom deployment   ...
Deploy from a custom template

Project details

Select the subscription to manage deployed resources and costs. Use resource groups like folders to organize and manage all your resources.

Subscription * ⓘ	Demo ⌄
Resource group * ⓘ	Production_RG ⌄
	Create new

Instance details

Region * ⓘ	(Europe) North Europe ✓
Admin Username * ⓘ	admnistrator ✓
Admin Password * ⓘ	•••••••••••••••• ⌕
Dns Label Prefix ⓘ	packt-demo-server ✓
	.northeurope.cloudapp.azure.com
Public Ip Name ⓘ	myPublicIP ✓
Public IP Allocation Method ⓘ	Dynamic ⌄
Public Ip Sku ⓘ	Basic ⌄
OS Version ⓘ	2019-Datacenter ⌄
Vm Size ⓘ	Standard_D2_v3 ✓
Location ⓘ	northeurope ✓
Vm Name ⓘ	demo-server ✓

[Review + create]   [< Previous]   [Next : Review + create >]

Figure 9.13 – Overview of resources to be deployed via ARM template

9.   After the deployment has succeeded, you can view the resources under the specified resource group:

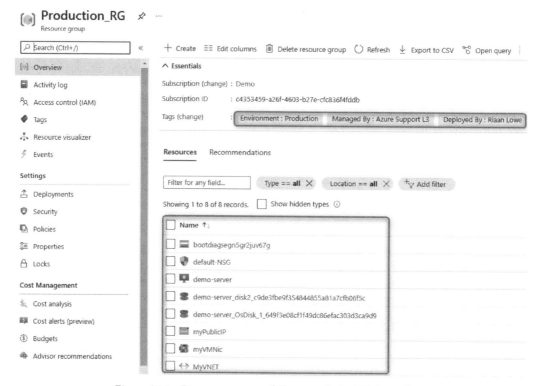

Figure 9.14 – Resources successfully created via ARM template

We have successfully deployed a custom ARM template with a `parameters` file via the Azure portal. In the next section, we are going to look at how to save a deployment in ARM template format to automate future deployments.

Saving a deployment as an ARM template

Now that we know how to deploy resources from custom RBAC templates, let's see how to save an existing deployment to an ARM template via the Azure portal:

1.   Navigate to the Azure portal by opening a web browser and going to `https://portal.azure.com`.

2.   In the left menu, select **Resource groups** and select your resource group. In my scenario, I'm going to use the **Production_RG** resource group:

Figure 9.15 – Azure resource groups

3. On the **Automation** tab of the resource group, select **Export template**:

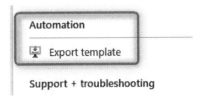

Figure 9.16 – Exporting resources as an ARM template

4. Next, select **Download**, and the ARM template will download, which can then be used to redeploy resources, and amended to create custom resources:

Figure 9.17 – Downloading the ARM templates for existing resources

In this section, we had a look at how to export all existing resources within a resource group to an ARM template via the Azure portal.

We encourage you to read up further by using the following links based on Azure ARM templates:

- `https://docs.microsoft.com/en-us/azure/azure-resource-manager/templates/export-template-portal`

- `https://docs.microsoft.com/en-us/azure/azure-resource-manager/templates/export-template-cli`

- `https://docs.microsoft.com/en-us/azure/azure-resource-manager/templates/export-template-powershell`

In the next section, we are going to have a look at how to deploy VM extensions.

> **Tip**
> You can save a deployment from a resource group or a single resource to an ARM template.

Deploying VM extensions

VM extensions are applications that we can install as part of the script or post-deployment. An example of this would be adding antimalware applications to a VM. VM extensions can be configured for existing and future deployments.

Let's look at how to configure the **Microsoft Antimalware** extension to an existing Windows VM:

1. Navigate to the Azure portal by opening a web browser and going to `https://portal.azure.com`.

2. In the left menu, select **Virtual machines** and select your VM that we deployed with our script in the *Deploy from a template* section of this chapter:

Figure 9.18 – Selecting a VM

3. Under the **Settings** tab, select **Extensions** and click on **add** on the next page:

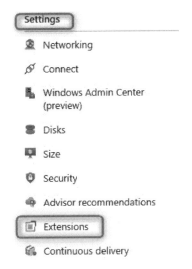

Figure 9.19 – Selecting the Extensions tab

4. Now, scroll down and select the **Microsoft Antimalware** extension and click on **Create**:

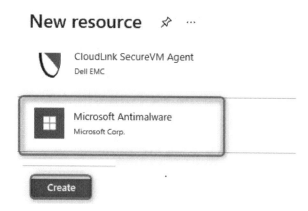

Figure 9.20 – Creating the Microsoft Antimalware extension for the selected VM

5. Next, we can choose the antimalware settings; for this scenario, we are going to leave it at the default settings, and click **OK**:

Figure 9.21 – Extension configuration options

6. Once the extension has successfully been deployed, it will show along with other extensions configured for the VM:

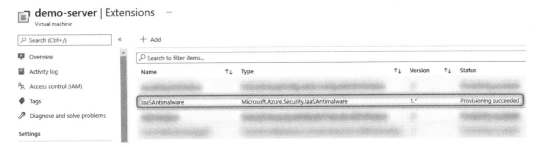

Figure 9.22 – Successfully deployed Microsoft Antimalware extension

In this section, we had a look at how to deploy VM extensions via the Azure portal.

We encourage you to read up further by using the following link based on Azure VM extensions: `https://docs.microsoft.com/en-us/azure/virtual-machines/extensions/overview`.

> **Important Note**
> You can only add VM extensions if the VM is running.

Summary

In this chapter, we discussed how to modify ARM templates and how to configure an ARM template with a VHD. We addressed how to deploy from an ARM template via the Azure portal. Lastly, we addressed how to configure VM extensions. After reading this chapter and following along with the hands-on demos, you should now be able to deploy IaC via ARM templates and work with Azure infrastructure deployments.

In the next chapter, we'll cover how to configure VMs with hands-on examples.

10
Configuring Virtual Machines

In the previous chapter, we covered how to automate VM deployments using ARM templates, which are a good way to standardize and simplify deployments.

In this chapter, we are going to explore Azure virtual machines in more depth: networking, high-availability configurations, and changing the **virtual machine (VM)** host. As part of this topic, we uncover the various types of Azure disks that exist, how they can be added to a VM, and how we can encrypt the disks. VM infrastructure is the base of most common infrastructure platforms these days and a crucial part of your learning. VMs are the cornerstone of running applications and subsequent application offerings such as web apps stem from these. Each section has its own instructions and guidance on how to apply the skills you have learned.

In this chapter, we are going to cover the following main topics:

- Understanding Azure disks
- Understanding Azure VMs
- Deploying a VM in Azure
- VM management tasks

- Azure disk encryption

- Automating configuration management

Technical requirements

This chapter uses the following tools for the examples:

- Access to an Azure subscription with owner or contributor privileges. If you do not have access to one, you can enroll for a free account: `https://azure.microsoft.com/en-in/free/`.

- PowerShell 5.1 or later installed on a PC where labs can be practiced. Note that many examples can only be followed from a PC or `https://shell.azure.com` (PowerShell 7.0.6 LTS or above is recommended).

- Installation of the Az module.

Understanding Azure disks

Azure disks are block storage primarily intended for virtual machines. They present varying levels of performance on Azure depending on your requirements and choice of **stock keeping unit (SKU)**.

Disk management options

Azure disks come with two management options:

- **Managed disks**: Azure takes care of the management of the disks for you. The platform automatically manages where the disk is stored, how it scales, and that it delivers at the intended performance. Managed disks also come with higher **Service Level Agreement (SLAs)** than unmanaged disks. Disk costs are calculated at the size of the provisioned disk regardless of the data consumed. Managed disks are recommended by Microsoft over unmanaged disks.

- **Unmanaged disks**: These disks are managed by you. This requires the allocation of the disk to a storage account. The management of the allocation of disks to storage accounts is vital to ensure the reliability of the disks. Factors such as storage space available on the storage account, and storage account type are pivotal for managing these disk types. Disk costs are calculated based on consumed data on the disk.

Disk performance

When selecting the correct disk for your application's purpose, consider the reliability and performance requirements. Factors that should be considered include the following:

- **IOPS**: IOPS (input/output operations per second) refers to a performance measurement for storage that describes the count of operations performed per second.

- **Throughput**: Disk throughput describes the speed at which data can be transferred through a disk. Throughput is calculated as *IOPS x I/O Size = Disk Throughput*.

- **Reliability**: Azure offers better SLAs based on the disk type chosen in conjunction with a VM.

- **Latency**: Latency refers to the length of time it takes for a disk to process a request received and send a response. It will limit the effective performance of disks and therefore it's pertinent to use disks with lower latency for high-performance workloads. The effect of latency on a disk can be expressed through the following example. If a disk can offer 2,500 IOPs as the maximum performance but has 10 ms latency, it will only be able to deliver 250 IOPs, which will potentially be highly restrictive.

- Premium storage provides consistently lower latency than other Azure storage and is advised when considering high-performance workloads.

> **Top Tip**
> Azure VM SLAs on a single instance that have premium SSD disks attached go up to 99.9% compared to 99.5% for a standard SSD and 95% for a standard HDD. Because of this, it is advised to utilize premium SSD disks on production or critical virtual machines in Azure.

Now that you understand the various factors that impact disk performance, we will now learn about disk caching and its effect on performance.

Disk caching

Caching refers to temporary storage utilized in a specialized fashion to provide faster read and write performance than traditional permanent storage. It does this by loading disk components that are read or written frequently (therefore representing repeatable patterns) to the cache storage. As such, the data needs to be predictable to benefit from caching. Data is loaded into the cache once it has been read or written at least once before from the disk.

Write caching is used to speed up data writes by persisting storage in a lazy write fashion. This means data written is stored on the cache and the app considers this data to be saved to the persistent disk, but the cache in fact waits for an opportunity to write the data to the disk as it becomes available. This leaves an opportunity for risk if the system is shut down prior to the data write completing as expected.

Host caching can be enabled on your VMs and can be configured per disk (both OS and data disks). The default configuration for the OS disk sets this to **Read/write**. The default setting for data disks is **Read-only** mode:

Figure 10.1 – Disk cache configuration on a VM

The following caching modes can be selected depending on your requirement:

- **Read-only**: When you expect workloads to predominantly perform repeatable read operations. Data retrieval performance is enhanced where data is read from the cache.

- **Read/write**: When you have workloads where you expect to perform a balance of repeatable or predictable read and write operations.

- **None**: If your workload doesn't follow either of these patterns, then it's best to set host caching to **none**.

> **Top Tip**
>
> Caching provides little or no value for random I/O, and where data is dispersed across the disk it can even reduce performance and therefore needs to be considered carefully before being enabled.

You now understand the different types of caching available. We will now explore how to calculate the impact on performance by implementing the different caches available.

Calculating expected caching performance

When configuring your VM to take advantage of disk caching, you should consider the type of operations, as mentioned in the preceding sections, and whether your workloads will benefit from caching. Set the disks that will provide caching to the appropriate caching option. Each VM SKU has its unique limit on the performance cap applied to the VM. One of the advantages to the disk performance on the VM is that by enabling caching and setting some disks to not be cached, you can potentially exceed the performance limits of VM storage.

An example would be: imagine you have a **Standard_D16as_v4** VM SKU provisioned with 8 data disks. This VM has the following performance limits:

- Cached IOPS: 32,000

- Uncached IOPS: 25,600

- 8 x P40 data disks that can achieve 7,500 IOPS each

Some items to note are the following:

- 4 of the P40 data disks are attached in **Read-only** cache mode and the others are set to **None**.

- Although the VM SKU is capable of having 32 data disks, only 8 data disks were used and attached for the example.

An application that is installed makes a request for 65,000 IOPS to the VM, 5,000 to the OS disk, and 30,000 to each of the data disk arrays. The following transactions occur on the disks:

- The OS disk offers 2,000 IOPS

- The 4 data disks that are cached offer a collective 30,000 IOPS

- The 4 data disks that are not cached offer a collective 30,000 IOPS

Since the VM limit imposes an uncached limit of 25,600 IOPS, this is the maximum delivered by the uncached disks. The cached disks are combined with the performance of the OS disk for a collective total of 32,000 IOPS. Since this is the limit imposed on the SKU, this performance metric is maxed out too. Using the cache effectively in this example, the VM was able to achieve a total of 57,600 IOPS, which far exceeds either of the single limits imposed on the VM. This is illustrated in the following diagram:

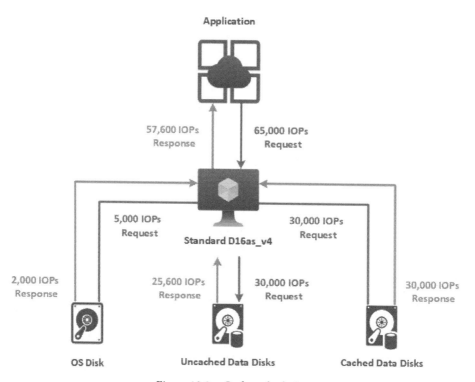

Figure 10.2 – Cache calculations

As you can see from the preceding diagram, by carefully analyzing disk caching, significant performance improvements can be achieved.

> **Top Tip**
>
> Take note that changing the cache setting on the disks will cause an interruption to the disk on the VM. In the event the cache setting is modified on a data disk, it is detached and reattached again, but when the setting is modified for the OS disk, it will cause the VM to be restarted.

Now that you understand the impact of caching on disks and VMs, we will explore the different types/SKUs of disks available to us within Azure.

Disk types

Azure currently offers four disk types to meet specific customer scenarios:

- Ultra disk
- Premium SSD
- Standard SSD
- Standard HDD

Ultra disk

Azure's high-performance SSD storage option is ideal for scenarios where you need fast access to your data such as I/O-intensive or high-throughput workloads. Ultra disks offer flexibility in dynamically changing the throughput and IOPS performance of your disks without requiring a restart of your VM. Examples of workloads where you might want high I/O are SAP HANA and forensic applications. If you have highly transactional SQL workloads that require more performance than premium SSD disks, this is a good option. These can only be used as data disks. The maximum throughput of ultra disks is 4,000 MBps per disk and is provisioned at 256 KiB/s per provisioned IOP. Maximum IOPS performance per disk is limited to 160,000 (160K) IOPS per disk, and 300 IOPS per GiB provisioned storage. The maximum size of disk that can be deployed is 65,536 GiB (64 TiB). These disks are designed to achieve sub-millisecond latencies. There are several limitations as of the time of writing, such as **locally-redundant storage** (**LRS**) replication only, and these should be reviewed prior to utilizing them for your workloads.

> **Top Tip**
> Ultra-disk resize operations can take up to an hour to take effect, and a maximum of 4 resize operations can be performed during a 24-hour period.

Premium SSD

Premium SSD is Azure's high-performance storage option for Azure Virtual Machines and Azure Files. This storage is best suited for production workloads. It is backed by SSD storage offering low latency and high performance at a better price point than ultra disks. If you are looking to offer the best SLAs for your virtual machines, this is the storage type you should select. This is also best for SQL-based workloads. Premium SSDs are available only to Azure VMs that are compatible with premium storage (generally VM SKUs ending with an "s") and can be attached as either OS or data disks.

Standard SSD

Azure standard SSDs provide a cost-effective solution for workloads that need consistent performance at lower IOPS levels. This is one of the best choices for non-production workloads such as Dev/Test workloads. This is best suited for web servers, low IOPS application servers, lightly used or under-used enterprise applications, and Dev/Test workloads. Standard SSDs provide better availability, consistency, reliability, and latency than regular **hard disk drives** (**HDDs**), although the performance is remarkably similar. Standard SSDs are available on all Azure VMs and can be attached as either OS or data disks.

Standard HDD

The Azure standard HDD storage option offers excellent value and consistent performance at a more affordable price point than the other three types of Azure disks. It can only use **locally-redundant storage** (**LRS**) for your data and applications.

Disk summary table

The following table displays key differences between the disk types available to you:

	Standard HDD	Standard SSD	Premium SSD	Ultra disk
Backing Disk Tech	HDD	SSD	SSD	SSD
Max Disk Size	32 TiB	32 TiB	32 TiB	64 TiB
Max Throughput	500 MBps	750 MBps	900 MBps	4,000 MBps
Max IOPS	2,000 IOPS	6,000 IOPS	20,000 IOPS	160,000 IOPS

In the next part, we will explore what disk redundancy is and what options we have.

Disk redundancy options

Redundancy refers to the number of copies of data that are available at any time. This supports the failure of copies and ensures the continuity of services depending on the redundancy option chosen. Regardless of the option, data is replicated three times in a storage account for the primary region.

In *Chapter 6, Understanding and Managing Storage*, we discussed the various redundancy options available in Azure, and the way replication occurs between data centers. You are encouraged to go over this material again.

Azure offers both LRS and **zone-redundant storage** (**ZRS**) for managed disks, with ZRS naturally providing higher availability than LRS. ZRS is only supported for premium SSD disks and standard SSD disks. It is also only available for limited regions (currently West US 2, West Europe, North Europe, and France Central). ZRS also cannot be used with Azure Backup or Azure Site Recovery.

Understanding Azure VMs

A VM is a logical configuration of resources to emulate a machine that runs in a similar fashion to a normal computer. The difference is that you can leverage a set of pooled resources, such as memory, CPU, and storage, to create customized VMs. Typically, a physical machine is limited by its physical specifications and is designed to run a single machine. Through virtualization, though, we can carve up the resources to create several machines in accordance with the limits of our physical resources. Being able to leverage a hyperscale hypervisor such as Azure, you benefit from being able to leverage the nearly unlimited resources that Microsoft builds into its data centers to allow massive scale. You basically need to identify the number and size of resources you need and select an appropriate VM that matches your requirements.

You can run both Windows VMs as well as Linux VMs in Azure. VMs come in all sorts of sizes and a variety of prices, ranging from VMs with a small amount of memory and processing power for general purposes to large VMs that can be used for **Graphics Processing Unit** (**GPU**)-intensive and high-performance computing workloads. To create a VM, you can choose from several predefined images. There are images available for operating systems such as Windows Server or Linux, as well as predefined applications, such as SQL Server images and complete farms, which consist of multiple VMs that can be deployed at once. An example of a farm is a three-tier SharePoint farm. VMs can be created and managed either from the Azure portal, PowerShell, or the CLI, and they come in the following series and sizes.

VM sizes

At the time of writing this book, the following VM series and sizes are available:

Type	Series	Description
General-purpose	B, Dsv3, Dv3, Dasv4, Dav4, DSv2, Dv2, Av2, DC, DCv2, Dv4, Dsv4, Ddv4, Ddsv4, Dv5, Dsv5, Ddv5, Ddsv5, Dasv5, Dadsv5	These VMs are best suited to small and medium-size workloads, typically databases and web servers with low to medium traffic. They have a balanced CPU-to-memory ratio and are ideal for testing and development scenarios too. Typically, the ratio of CPU to memory is 1:4 or 1:3.5.
Compute-optimized	F, Fs, Fsv2, FX	These VMs are best suited to CPU-intensive workloads such as application servers, web servers with medium traffic, and network appliances for nodes in batch processing. They have a high CPU-to-memory ratio. Typically, the ratio of CPU to memory is 1:2.
Memory-optimized	Esv3, Ev3, Easv4, Eav4, Ebdsv5, Ebsv5, Ev4, Esv4, Edv4, Edsv4, Ev5, Esv5, Edv5, Edsv5, Easv5, Eadsv5, Mv2, M, DSv2, Dv2	These VMs are best suited to deployments requiring more memory, such as relational database servers, medium to large caches, and in-memory analytics. They have a high memory-to-CPU ratio. Typically, the ratio of CPU to memory is 1:8.
Storage-optimized	Lsv2	These VMs are best suited to high storage requirement scenarios or high-performance storage. They have high disk throughput and I/O and are suitable for big data, SQL, and NoSQL databases.
GPU	NC, NCv2, NCv3, NCasT4_v3, ND, NDv2, NV, NVv3, NVv4, NDasrA100_v4, NDm_A100_v4	These VMs are best suited to graphically demanding deployments such as heavy graphic rendering and video editing, deep learning applications, and machine learning model training. These VMs are available with single or multiple GPUs.
High-performance compute	HB, HBv2, HBv3, HC, H	These VMs are best suited to batch processing or high-compute, demanding deployments. They are the fastest VMs available and offer the most powerful CPU with optional high-throughput network interfaces (**Remote Direct Memory Access (RDMA)**).

VM series are updated constantly. New series, types, and sizes are added and removed frequently. To stay up to date with these changes, you can refer to the following site: `https://docs.microsoft.com/en-us/azure/virtual-machines/sizes`.

Azure Spot Virtual Machines

Azure offers the ability to buy unused compute capacity for significantly reduced costs. This provides a great mechanism for test or development workloads that can handle interruptions at a very low cost. The limitation is that when Azure needs the capacity again, it will evict the Azure Spot Virtual Machines. The sizes available are completely dependent on the current capacity used within Azure. They will be influenced by factors such as region and the time of day.

When configuring spot instances, you define an **eviction policy** based on **capacity** and the **maximum price** you are willing to pay for the VM. You will also select the action to be taken upon eviction being either to **deallocate** or to **delete**.

When the VM is deployed, the following rules will apply:

- **Max price is set to >= the current price**: The VM will be deployed if capacity and quota are available.

- **Max price is set to <= the current price**: The VM will be evicted and you will be given 30 seconds' notice.

- **The max price option is set to -1**: The VM will not be evicted due to pricing reasons. You will pay up the amount of the standard VM charges and it will not exceed those costs.

- **Changing the max price**: Before you can change the max price on a VM, the VM will need to be deallocated and you will need to define your new max price to apply.

There are limitations that apply on spot instances, such as VMs can't be migrated, there are no offered SLAs, and there are no high availability guarantees.

The following subscription types support spot instances: **Enterprise Agreement (EA)**, Pay-as-you-go (003P), Sponsored (0036P and 0136P), and **Cloud Service Provider (CSP)**.

Networking

VMs on Azure have a plethora of networking options available to them, as you will see further in the chapter when we deploy a VM. The virtual network and subnet can be created on the creation of a VM. Alternatively, we can join an existing subnet on a VNet we have created. Networking can be controlled through a basic five-tuple network firewalling service named a network security group.

Network security groups

Network security groups (**NSGs**) act as a basic five-tuple firewall service for network-connected resources. These can be either applied at a subnet layer or a **network interface card** (**NIC**) layer in Azure. NICs are typically associated directly with VMs but could also be from services that have a private endpoint attached. NSG rules are defined by the following components: **source**, **destination**, **port**, **protocol**, and **action** (deny or allow). Each rule is given a priority and the lower the priority, the higher the precedence. The first rule matched on the traffic will be the rule that is chosen and followed. We use NSGs to restrict who can access services, from what source (such as IP address), and to what hosts (normally the destination). You can choose to associate a single NSG with a NIC and/or subnet. The same NSG can be applied several times and associated with several NICs and subnets. For VM deployments, you will likely open port 3389 (RDP – Windows) or 22 (SSH – Linux) for management of the VM, but carefully consider the source addresses you allow.

Fault domain versus update domain

When you place your VMs in an availability set, Azure guarantees to spread them across fault and update domains. By default, Azure will assign three fault domains and five update domains (which can be increased to a maximum of 20) to the availability set.

When spreading your VMs over fault domains, your VMs sit over three different racks in the Azure data center. So, in the case of an event or failure of the underlying platform, only one rack gets affected and the other VMs remain accessible, as depicted in the following diagram:

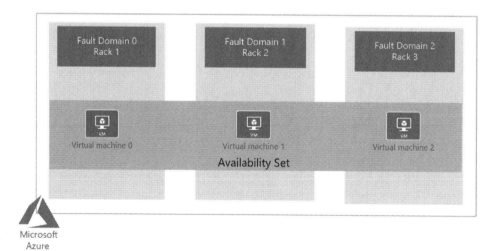

Figure 10.3 – VMs spread across fault domains

Update domains are useful in the case of an OS or host update. When you spread your VMs across multiple update domains, one domain will be updated and rebooted while the others remain accessible, as depicted in the following diagram:

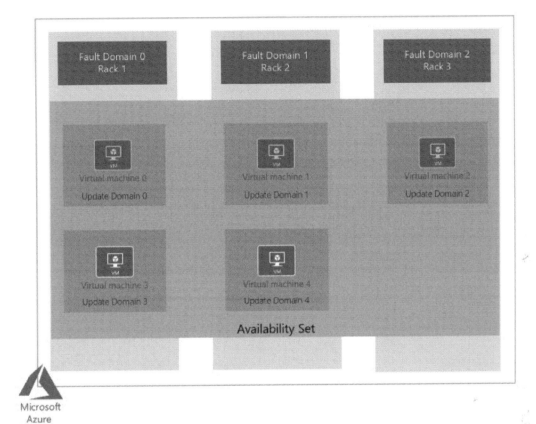

Figure 10.4 – VMs spread across update domains and fault domains

In the next section, we are going to discuss scale sets and the role they play in creating scalable infrastructure.

Scale sets

VM scale sets are used for deploying multiple VMs at once without the need for manual actions or using scripts. You can then manage them all at once from a single place. VM scale sets are typically used to build large-scale infrastructures, where keeping all your VMs in sync is key. The maintenance of VMs, including keeping them in sync, is handled by Azure. VM scale sets use availability sets under the hood. VMs inside a scale set are automatically spread over the fault and update domains by the underlying platform. VM scale sets use **Azure Autoscale** by default. You can, however, add or remove instances yourself instead of using Autoscale.

When creating a scale set, a couple of artifacts are created for you automatically. As well as the number of VMs you specified being added to the set, **Azure Load Balancer** and Azure Autoscale are added, along with a virtual network and a public IP address, as shown in the following screenshot:

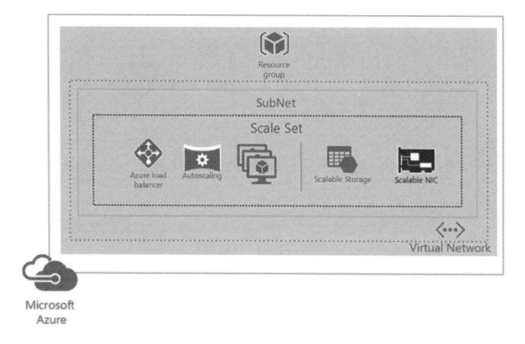

Figure 10.5 – VM scale sets

Now that you understand the role of scale sets, we will explore availability sets in the next section.

Availability sets

To create a reliable infrastructure, adding your VMs to an availability set is key. There are several scenarios that can have an impact on the availability of your Azure VMs. These are as follows:

- **Unplanned hardware maintenance event**: When hardware is about to fail, Azure fires an unplanned hardware maintenance event. **Live migration** technology is used, which predicts the failure and then moves the VM, the network connections, memory, and storage to different physical machines, without disconnecting the client. When your VM is moved, the performance is reduced for a short time because the VM is paused for 30 seconds. Network connections, memory, and open files are still preserved.

- **Unexpected downtime**: The VM is down when this event occurs because Azure needs to heal your VM inside the same data center. A hardware or physical infrastructure failure often causes this event to happen.

- **Planned hardware maintenance event**: This type of event is a periodic update from Microsoft in Azure to improve the platform. Most of these updates don't have a significant impact on the uptime of VMs, but some of them may require a reboot or restart.

To provide redundancy during these types of events, you can group two or more VMs in an availability set. By leveraging availability sets, VMs are distributed across multiple isolated hardware nodes in a cluster within a single region. This way, Azure can ensure that during an event or failure, only a subset of your VMs is impacted and your overall solution will remain operational and available. To meet the 99.95% Azure **Service-Level Agreement** (**SLA**) during outages and other failures, Microsoft advises that two or more VMs are deployed within an availability set. There are no costs associated with availability sets.

> **Top Tip**
> VMs can only be assigned to an availability set during initial deployment.

You have just learned about the various factors to be considered that comprise VM configurations, such as **availability sets** and **scale sets**. Next, we will explore the steps involved in deploying a VM in Azure.

Deploying a VM in Azure

In the previous chapter, we explored the deployment of a VM through ARM templates. In this section, we will briefly explore the manual deployment of a VM using the Azure portal. To do this, follow the given steps:

1. Sign in to the Azure portal: `https://portal.azure.com`.

2. Open the resource group you will be using for this exercise, click **Overview** on the left menu, then click **Create**.

3. Click **Compute** on the left menu under **Categories**, then click **Virtual machine** on the right-hand side:

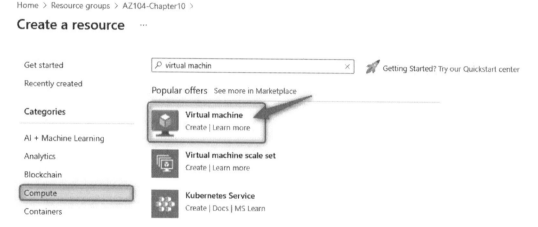

Figure 10.6 – Creating a resource

4. On the **Basics** tab, make a selection for **Subscription** and **Resource group**. Enter a name in the **Virtual machine name** field – this is limited to 15 characters. Choose a region from the **Region** dropdown, leave **Availability options** as **No infrastructure redundancy required**, and for **Image**, select **Windows Server 2016 Datacenter – Gen 1**. Set **Size** to **Standard_D2ds_v4**. Then, fill in the **Username** and **Password** fields, click **Allow selected ports** for the **Public inbound ports** option, choose **RDP (3389)** for the **Select inbound ports** dropdown, and then click on **Next : Disks >**:

Create a virtual machine

Basics   Disks   Networking   Management   Advanced   Tags   Review + create

Create a virtual machine that runs Linux or Windows. Select an image from Azure marketplace or use your own customized image. Complete the Basics tab then Review + create to provision a virtual machine with default parameters or review each tab for full customization. Learn more ⬈

Project details

Select the subscription to manage deployed resources and costs. Use resource groups like folders to organize and manage all your resources.

Subscription * ⓘ	AzureTraining ⌄
└─ Resource group * ⓘ	A2104-Chapter10 ⌄
	Create new

Instance details

Virtual machine name * ⓘ	demovm01 ✓
Region * ⓘ	(Europe) West Europe ⌄
Availability options ⓘ	No infrastructure redundancy required ⌄
Security type ⓘ	Standard ⌄
Image * ⓘ	⊞ Windows Server 2016 Datacenter - Gen1 ⌄
	See all images	Configure VM generation
Azure Spot instance ⓘ	☐
Size * ⓘ	Standard_D2ds_v4 - 2 vcpus, 8 GiB memory (ZAR 2,566.50/month) ⌄
	See all sizes

Administrator account

Username * ⓘ	demovmadmin ✓
Password * ⓘ	•••••••••••••• ✓
Confirm password * ⓘ	•••••••••••••• ✓

Inbound port rules

Select which virtual machine network ports are accessible from the public internet. You can specify more limited or granular network access on the Networking tab.

Public inbound ports * ⓘ	◯ None
	⦿ Allow selected ports
Select inbound ports *	RDP (3389) ⌄

⚠ **This will allow all IP addresses to access your virtual machine.** This is only recommended for testing. Use the Advanced controls in the Networking tab to create rules to limit inbound traffic to known IP addresses.

Licensing

Save up to 49% with a license you already own using Azure Hybrid Benefit. Learn more ⬈

Would you like to use an existing   ☐
Windows Server license? * ⓘ

Review Azure hybrid benefit compliance

Review + create   < Previous   Next : Disks >

Figure 10.7 – Creating a VM

5. For the **OS disk type** option, select **Premium SSD (locally-redundant storage)**, and for **Encryption type**, leave the default selection. Click the **Advanced** drop-down menu and enable **Use managed disks**. Click **Next : Networking >**:

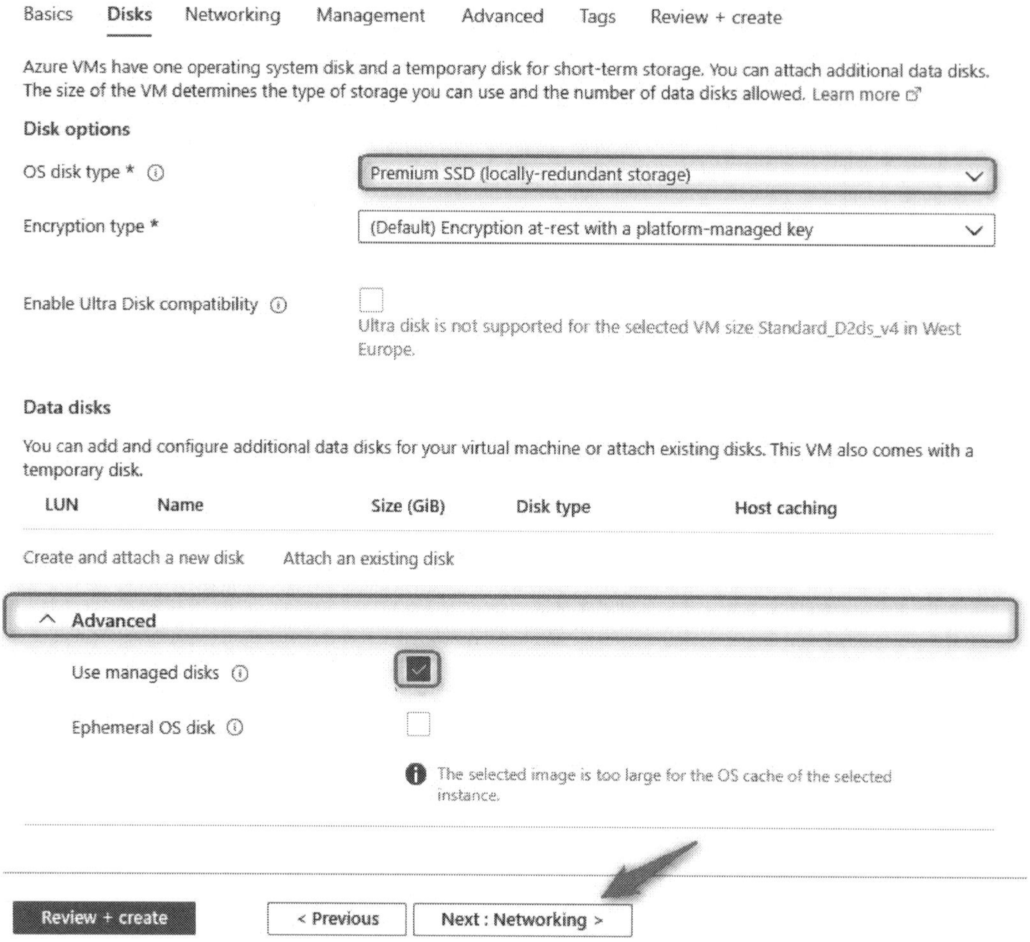

Basics   **Disks**   Networking   Management   Advanced   Tags   Review + create

Azure VMs have one operating system disk and a temporary disk for short-term storage. You can attach additional data disks. The size of the VM determines the type of storage you can use and the number of data disks allowed. Learn more ⃞

Disk options

OS disk type * ⓘ

| Premium SSD (locally-redundant storage) | ⌄ |

Encryption type *

| (Default) Encryption at-rest with a platform-managed key | ⌄ |

Enable Ultra Disk compatibility ⓘ   ☐

Ultra disk is not supported for the selected VM size Standard_D2ds_v4 in West Europe.

Data disks

You can add and configure additional data disks for your virtual machine or attach existing disks. This VM also comes with a temporary disk.

LUN	Name	Size (GiB)	Disk type	Host caching

Create and attach a new disk   Attach an existing disk

∧ **Advanced**

Use managed disks ⓘ   ☑

Ephemeral OS disk ⓘ   ☐

ⓘ The selected image is too large for the OS cache of the selected instance.

Review + create   < Previous   Next : Networking >

Figure 10.8 – Creating a VM – Disks

6. Note that you have the option to create a new network and subnet (the default option) or to join an existing network and subnet. A public IP is not required but leave the default where it will create one for this demonstration. Note that you see the inbound ports selected are set to **RDP (3389)** as you configured on the **Basics** tab. Click **Next : Management >**.

7. On this tab, you can enable **Boot diagnostics**. Set this to **Enable with managed storage account (recommended)**. Leave all other settings as the default configuration and click **Next : Advanced >**.

8. Note that you can configure **custom extensions** as well as select a dedicated host group and proximity placement group. Click on **Review + create**.

9. After validation has been completed and passed, click **Create**.

You have completed the deployment of a VM on Azure. You will have noticed there are several different configurations for a VM that you can deploy. Spend some time reviewing these further to become more comfortable. In the next section, we will explore managing VM sizes.

PowerShell scripts

Please ensure that the Az module is installed as per the *Technical requirements* section at the beginning of the chapter.

In the next demonstration, we are going to create two Windows Server VMs from PowerShell and place them in an Availability Set. To do so, you will perform the following steps:

Note: Change the parameters to suit your requirements.

```
# First connect your Azure account using your credentials
Connect-AzAccount

# Parameters
$ResourceGroup = "AZ104-Chapter10"
$Location = "WestEurope"
$SubscriptionId = "xxxxxxx"
$AvailabilitySetName = "PacktVMAvailabilitySet"
$VirtualNetworkName = "PacktVnet"
$SubnetName = "PacktSubnet"

# If necessary, select the right subscription as follows
Select-AzSubscription -SubscriptionId $SubscriptionId

# Create a resource group for the Availability Set as follows
New-AzResourceGroup -Name "$ResourceGroup" -Location
"$Location"
```

```
# Create an Availability Set for the VMs
New-AzAvailabilitySet `
-Location "$Location" `
-Name "$AvailabilitySetName" `
-ResourceGroupName "$ResourceGroup" `
-Sku aligned `
-PlatformFaultDomainCount 2 `
-PlatformUpdateDomainCount 2

# Setup Your VM Admin Credentials
$adminUsername = 'Student'
$adminPassword = 'Pa55w.rd1234'
$adminCreds = New-Object PSCredential $adminUsername,
($adminPassword | ConvertTo-SecureString -AsPlainText -Force)
# Deploy 2 VMs Inside the Availability Set
for ($vmNum=1; $vmNum -le 2; $vmNum++)
{
    New-AzVm `
    -ResourceGroupName "$ResourceGroup" `
    -Name "PacktVM$vmNum" `
    -Location "$Location" `
    -VirtualNetworkName "$VirtualNetworkName" `
    -SubnetName "$SubnetName" `
    -SecurityGroupName "PacktNetworkSecurityGroup" `
    -PublicIpAddressName "PacktPublicIpAddress$vmNum" `
    -AvailabilitySetName "$AvailabilitySetName" `
    -Credential $adminCreds
}
```

In these last two demonstrations, you have created a VM using the Azure portal and deployed two VMs inside an Availability Set using PowerShell. In the next section, we are going to cover deploying scale sets.

Deploying and configuring scale sets

To create a VM scale set from the Azure portal, take the following steps:

1. Navigate to the Azure portal by opening `https://portal.azure.com/home`.

2. Click on **Create a resource** and type in `Scale Set` in the search bar. Select **Virtual machine scale set**.

3. On the next screen, click on **Create** and add the following settings to create the scale set:

    - **Subscription**: Select a subscription

    - **Resource group**: `PacktVMGroup`

    - **Virtual machine scale set name**: `PacktScaleSet`

    - **Region**: `East US`

    - **Availability zone**: `None`

    - **Orchestration mode**: `Uniform`

    - **Security type**: `Standard`

    - **Image**: `Windows Server 2016 Datacenter - Gen 2`

    - **Size**: `Standard_DS2_v2`

    - **Username**: `SCPacktUser`

    - **Password**: Add a password

- **Licensing**: Unchecked

Create a virtual machine scale set   ···

all your resources.

Subscription *	AzureTraining ∨
Resource group *	AZ104-Chapter10 ∨
	Create new

Scale set details

Virtual machine scale set name *	PacktScaleSet ✓
Region *	(Africa) South Africa North ∨
Availability zone ⓘ	None ∨

Orchestration

A scale set has a "scale set model" that defines the attributes of virtual machine instances (size, number of data disks, etc).
As the number of instances in the scale set changes, new instances are added based on the scale set model.
Learn more about the scale set model ⬀

Orchestration mode * ⓘ

◉ **Uniform:** optimized for large scale stateless workloads with identical instances

◯ **Flexible:** achieve high availability at scale with identical or multiple virtual machine types

Security type ⓘ	Standard ∨

Instance details

Image * ⓘ	⊞ Windows Server 2016 Datacenter - Gen2 ∨
	See all images | Configure VM generation
Azure Spot instance ⓘ	☐
Size * ⓘ	Standard_DS2_v2 - 2 vcpus, 7 GiB memory (ZAR 2,757.87/month) ∨
	See all sizes

Administrator account

Username * ⓘ	SCPacktUser ✓
Password * ⓘ	•••••••••••• ✓

Review + create	< Previous	Next : Disks >

Figure 10.9 – Creating a scale set

4. If you click the **Scaling** tab, you can configure the autoscale settings. You can configure **Initial instance count**, **Scaling policy**, and **Scale-in policy**:

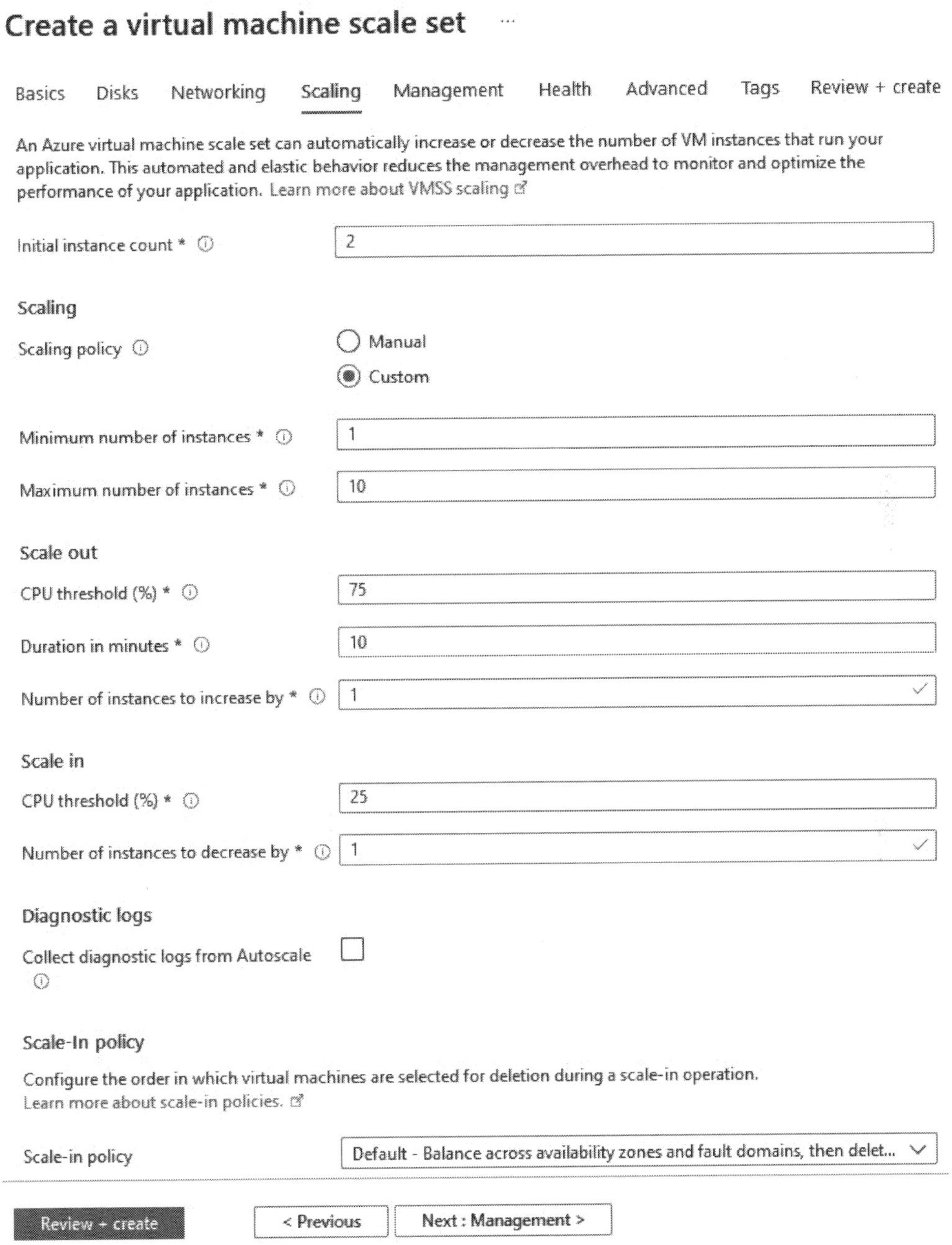

Create a virtual machine scale set   ...

Basics   Disks   Networking   **Scaling**   Management   Health   Advanced   Tags   Review + create

An Azure virtual machine scale set can automatically increase or decrease the number of VM instances that run your application. This automated and elastic behavior reduces the management overhead to monitor and optimize the performance of your application. Learn more about VMSS scaling

| Initial instance count * ⓘ | 2 |

Scaling

Scaling policy ⓘ

◯ Manual
◉ Custom

| Minimum number of instances * ⓘ | 1 |
| Maximum number of instances * ⓘ | 10 |

Scale out

CPU threshold (%) * ⓘ	75
Duration in minutes * ⓘ	10
Number of instances to increase by * ⓘ	1 ✓

Scale in

| CPU threshold (%) * ⓘ | 25 |
| Number of instances to decrease by * ⓘ | 1 ✓ |

Diagnostic logs

Collect diagnostic logs from Autoscale ☐
ⓘ

Scale-In policy

Configure the order in which virtual machines are selected for deletion during a scale-in operation. Learn more about scale-in policies.

| Scale-in policy | Default - Balance across availability zones and fault domains, then delet... ∨ |

Review + create   < Previous   Next : Management >

Figure 10.10 – Configuring a scale set

5. Click **Review + create**, then click **Create**. The scale set with the number of provided VMs in it is now deployed.

You have now covered how to deploy a VM scale set. In the next section, we will explore the various VM management tasks that we need to be aware of.

VM management tasks

In this section, we are going to look at some management capabilities for virtual machines. We will explore items such as VM sizing, data disks, networking, moving VMs, redeploying VMs, disk encryption, availability sets and zones, scales sets, and configuration management automation.

Managing VM sizes

After creating your VM, you can manage and change (vertically scale) the sizes of Windows and Linux VMs from the Azure portal, PowerShell, and the CLI. **Vertical scaling**, also known as scale-up and scale-down, means increasing or decreasing VM sizes in response to different workloads.

In the following demonstration, we will explore how to change the VM size of your VM:

1. Sign in to the Azure portal: `https://portal.azure.com/home`.

2. Navigate to the VM you created in the previous exercise. On the left menu, under the **Settings** context, you will see a **Size** button – click this:

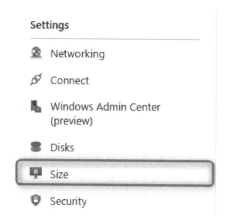

Figure 10.11 – VM Size setting

3.   Note that you are presented with several virtual machine options to choose from. You also will note there is a filter bar above the VMs that allows the viewing of VMs against the configuration you choose. Click **vCPUs : All**, select **2**, and click **OK**. You will see the options for VMs change:

Figure 10.12 – VM Size filter

4.   Click the **Cost/month** filter button. You will notice this changes the sorting for the list. The default sorting is smallest to largest. Clicking this button again will reverse the order:

Figure 10.13 – VM Size selection

5.   Click **D2s_v3** and click **Resize**.

You have successfully resized your VM. You now know how to manage VM size as needed. In the next section, we will explore the process behind adding data disks.

Top Tip

VM sizes that contain an "s" at the end of the size component typically support premium SSD storage; for example, D2s_v3.

Now that you have seen how to resize a VM using the Azure portal, we will explore how to perform this action through the CLI.

Resizing a VM using the CLI

You can also resize your VM using the CLI. You can run CLI scripts from Azure Cloud Shell or from your local filesystem. You can use Azure Cloud Shell for PowerShell scripts and commands as well. We are going to resize the VM from Azure Cloud Shell using the CLI in this demonstration.

To resize a VM using the CLI, you will perform the following steps:

1. Navigate to the Azure portal by opening `https://portal.azure.com/home`.

2. Open Azure Cloud Shell by clicking the following menu item in the top-right menu in the Azure portal:

Figure 10.14 – Opening Azure Cloud Shell

3. Make sure that the Bash shell is selected.

4. Add the following line of code to list the different available machine sizes for your region:

```
az vm list-vm-resize-options --resource-group
PacktVMResourceGroup --name myVM1 --output table
```

5. To resize your VM to a different size, add the following line of code. If the size is not available, you can replace the required VM size with one that is available for your subscription or region:

```
az vm resize --resource-group PacktVMResourceGroup --name
myVM1 --size Standard_DS3_v2
```

We have now resized our VM using the Azure portal and the CLI. In the next section, we are going to work on adding data disks to a VM.

Adding data disks

In the following exercise, we will explore adding data disks to a VM in Azure:

1. Sign in to the Azure portal: `https://portal.azure.com/home`.

2. Create a new managed disk in Azure, set the resource group to the one you used in the previous chapter, name the disk `demovm1_datadisk2`, change **Storage type** to **Standard HDD**, and change **Size** to **32 GiB**. For **Encryption**, you can leave this as **(Default) Encryption at-rest with a platform-managed key**. The following is a screenshot of the configuration at the **Review + create** stage. Click **Create**:

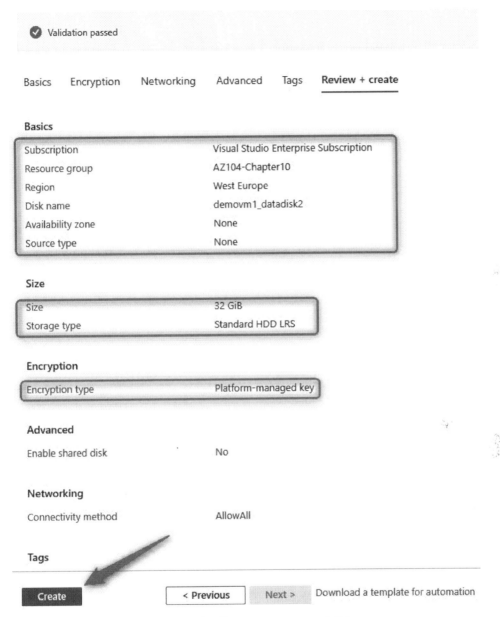

Create a managed disk   ···

Validation passed

Basics   Encryption   Networking   Advanced   Tags   **Review + create**

Basics

Subscription	Visual Studio Enterprise Subscription
Resource group	AZ104-Chapter10
Region	West Europe
Disk name	demovm1_datadisk2
Availability zone	None
Source type	None

Size

Size	32 GiB
Storage type	Standard HDD LRS

Encryption

Encryption type	Platform-managed key

Advanced

Enable shared disk	No

Networking

Connectivity method	AllowAll

Tags

Create   < Previous   Next >   Download a template for automation

Figure 10.15 – Create a new managed disk

3. Navigate to the VM you created in the previous exercise. On the left menu, under **Settings**, click the **Disks** button.

4. This page will display all disks attached to the VM. Notice the OS disk deployed and attached to the VM. In the **Data disks** section, you will see the options to create a new disk or attach existing storage. Click **Create and attach a new disk**:

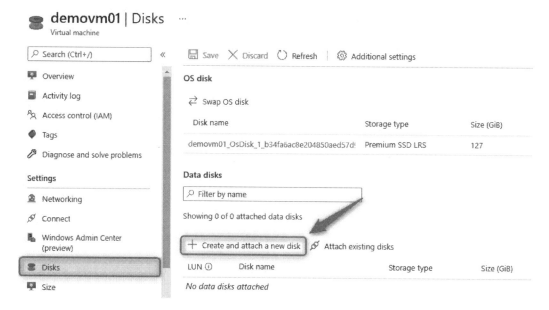

Figure 10.16 – VM – Create and attach a new disk

5. Leave **LUN** as **0** and name the disk demovm1_datadisk1. Change **Storage type** to **Standard HDD** and change **Size (GiB)** to **32**. For **Encryption**, you can leave this as **Platform-managed key** and **Host caching** can be left as **None**:

Figure 10.17 – VM – Creating a data disk

6. Click **Attach existing disks** now and select the disk you made in *step 2*:

Figure 10.18 – VM – Attaching a data disk

7. At the top of the blade, click the **Save** button.

Figure 10.19 – Save

You have just learned how to create and attach a data disk to a VM, as well as how to attach an existing data disk. In the next section, we will explore the network options available for Azure.

Configuring networking

In the following sections, we will assess the connectivity of two VMs within a network, we will join two VMs onto the same subnet within a VNET, and we will prove they can communicate. We will then configure an NSG on both the NIC and subnet layers and demonstrate the net effect, and finally, connect the VMs to another subnet and demonstrate communication between the VMs.

1. Sign in to the Azure portal: `https://portal.azure.com`.

2. Navigate to the VM you created in the previous exercise. On the left menu, under **Settings**, click **Networking**.

3. Note the name and subnet assigned to the NIC. Also note the private IP:

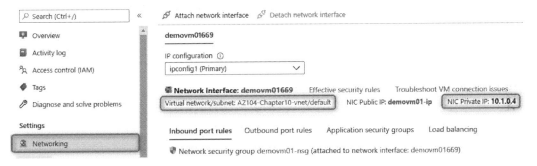

Figure 10.20 – VM networking

4. Create a new VM and store this in the same resource group as your previous VM.
    On the **Networking** tab, click the dropdown for **Virtual network** and select the
    same network as your previous VM. Do the same on the subnet:

Basics	Disks	**Networking**	Management	Advanced	Tags	Review + create

Define network connectivity for your virtual machine by configuring network interface card (NIC) settings. You can control
ports, inbound and outbound connectivity with security group rules, or place behind an existing load balancing solution.
Learn more ☐

Network interface

When creating a virtual machine, a network interface will be created for you.

Virtual network * ⓘ

    AZ104-Chapter10-vnet   ⌄
    Create new

Subnet * ⓘ

    default (10.1.0.0/24)   ⌄
    Manage subnet configuration

Public IP ⓘ

    (new) demovm02-ip   ⌄
    Create new

NIC network security group ⓘ

    ○ None
    ◉ Basic
    ○ Advanced

Public inbound ports * ⓘ

    ○ None
    ◉ Allow selected ports

Select inbound ports *

    RDP (3389)   ⌄

    ⚠ **This will allow all IP addresses to access your virtual machine.** This is only
    recommended for testing. Use the Advanced controls in the Networking tab
    to create rules to limit inbound traffic to known IP addresses.

Accelerated networking ⓘ

    ☑

Review + create		< Previous	Next : Management >

Figure 10.21 – Create a new VM store

5. Navigate to the new VM you just created. On the **Overview** pane, click **Connect**:

demovm02
Virtual machine
Search (Ctrl+/)
Overview
Connect
Start
Restart
Stop
Capture
Delete
Refresh
Open in mobile
Essentials

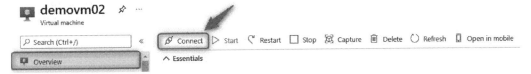

Figure 10.22 – New VM

6. Click **RDP** on the drop-down menu:

Connect
Start
RDP
SSH
Bastion

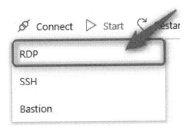

Figure 10.23 – Select RDP

7. Click the **Download RDP File** button on the screen. Open the file that downloads:

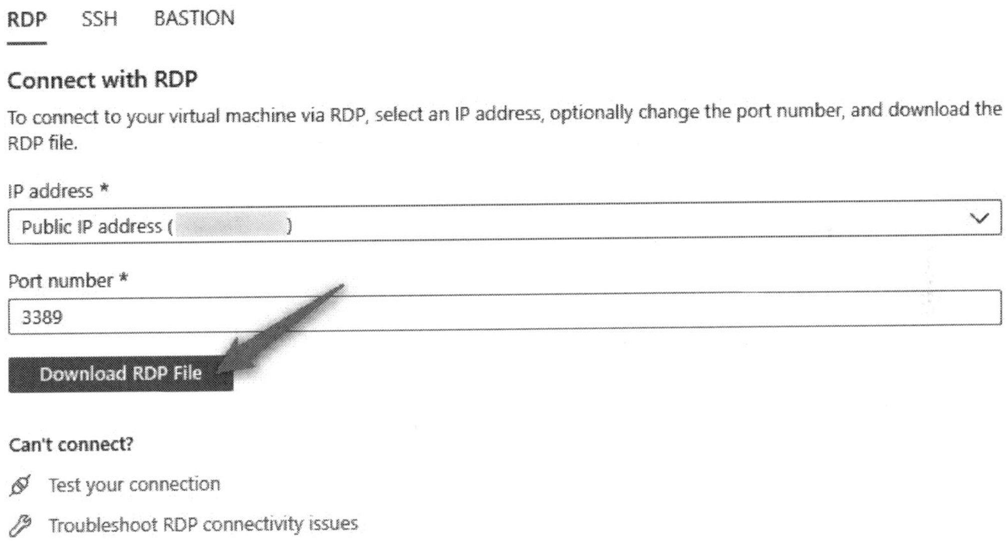

RDP
SSH
BASTION
Connect with RDP
To connect to your virtual machine via RDP, select an IP address, optionally change the port number, and download the RDP file.
IP address *
Public IP address ( )
Port number *
3389
Download RDP File
Can't connect?
Test your connection
Troubleshoot RDP connectivity issues

Figure 10.24 – Click Download RDP File

8. On the screen that shows up, click **More choices** to change the username. Click on **Use a different account**:

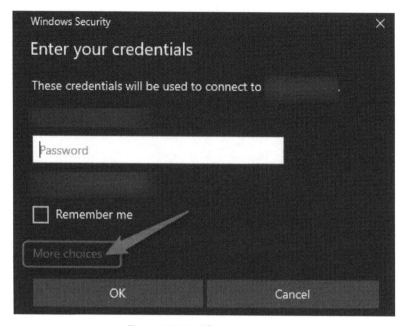

Figure 10.25 – Change account

9. Enter the username and password you created when creating your VM. Click **OK**:

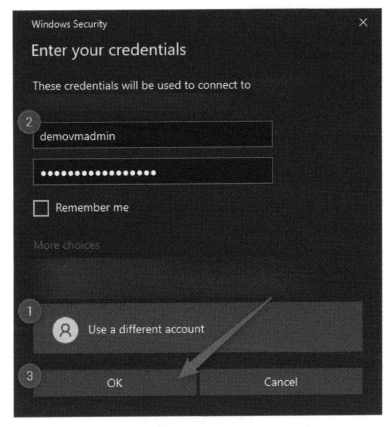

Figure 10.26 – Enter username and password

10. You have just created a remote desktop connection to your VM.

11. Click the **Start** button and type `PowerShell`. Click the **PowerShell** option that comes up on the search pane. In PowerShell, enter the following command, adjusting the private IP address to match the IP you noted in *step 3*:

```
test-netconnection 10.1.0.4 -Port 3389
```

12. Note the successful connection.

> **Top Tip**
>
> Management ports, port 22 – SSH (Linux) and port 3389 – RDP (Windows), should always be restricted and preferably not exposed to the internet. If exposed to the internet, access should be restricted to specific known IP addresses.

Moving VMs from one resource group to another

In this section, we will perform the migration of a VM from one resource group to another. We will validate readiness for the migration and then work through the process:

1. Open the Azure portal and navigate to the resource group where your VM is saved.

2. Select the **Overview** option on the left menu and select each resource to be moved that is associated with the VM, then click **Move**:

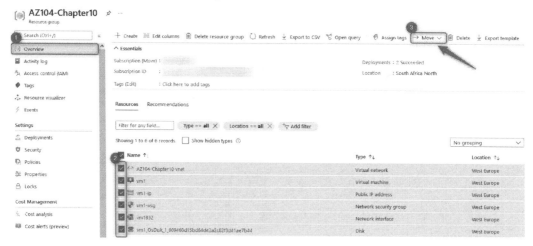

Figure 10.27 – Selecting Azure VM resources

3. Select the **Move to another resource group** option:

Figure 10.28 – Move to another resource group

4. Select the target resource group and click **Next**:

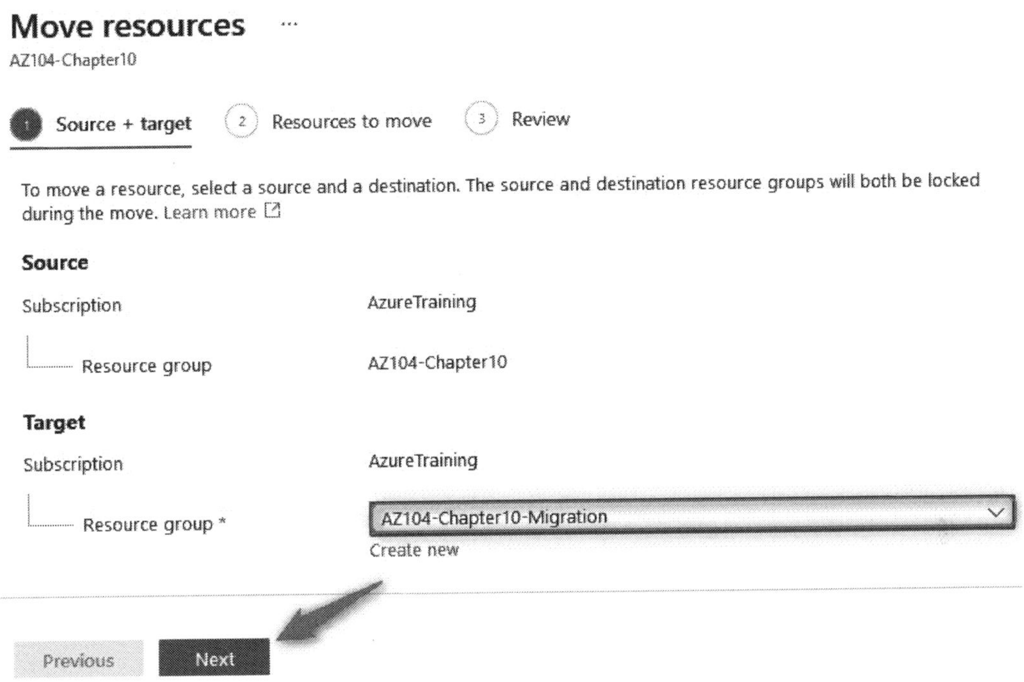

Move resources   ...
AZ104-Chapter10

① **Source + target**   ② Resources to move   ③ Review

To move a resource, select a source and a destination. The source and destination resource groups will both be locked during the move. Learn more ☐

Source

Subscription   AzureTraining

└───── Resource group   AZ104-Chapter10

Target

Subscription   AzureTraining

└───── Resource group * | AZ104-Chapter10-Migration   ∨ |
                                    Create new

| Previous | Next |

Figure 10.29 – Moving Azure resources – Source and Target

5. Wait for the validation to complete that confirms the resources can be migrated:

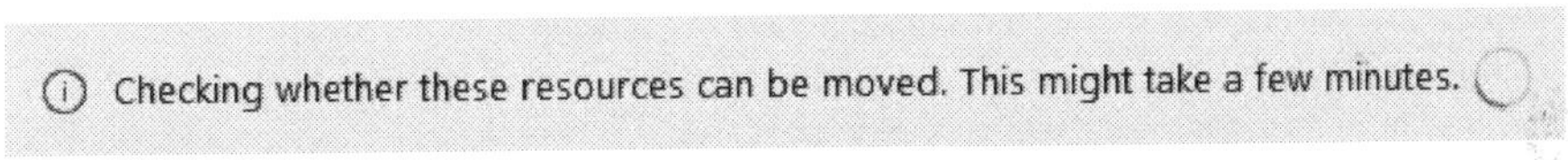

ⓘ Checking whether these resources can be moved. This might take a few minutes. ◯

Figure 10.30 – Resource migration validation message

6. Once validation has been completed successfully, click **Next**:

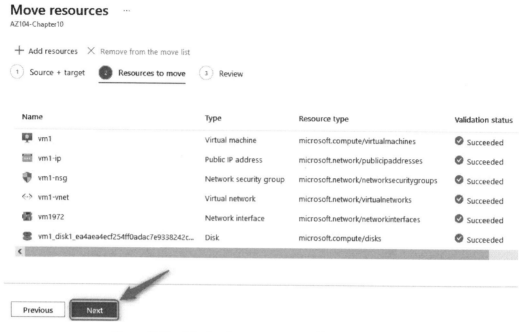

Figure 10.31 – Moving Azure resources – Resources to move

7. Click the checkbox and click **Move**:

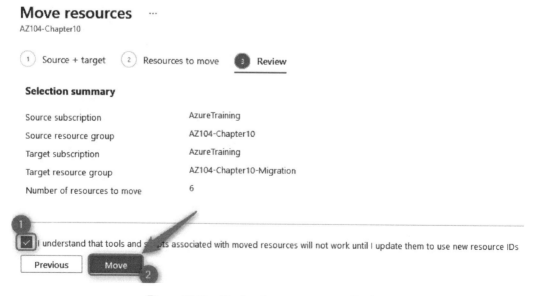

Figure 10.32 – Moving Azure resources – Review

8. The move will take several minutes to complete. Once complete, you will receive a notification informing you of the success status:

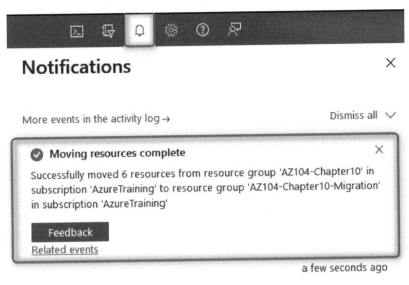

Figure 10.33 – Move success notification

> **Top Tip**
>
> You may be tempted to think that migrating a resource from one resource group to another would change its location, but this is not the case. You will remember that resources can reside in a different location to the resource group. Further, a resource location cannot, at the time of writing, be changed and will require redeployment for the desired location.

You have completed the migration of resources across resource groups. This process is almost identical in behavior when performing a migration across subscriptions. In the next section, we discuss redeploying VMs.

Redeploying VMs

There are occasions when you may experience some difficulties in working with VMs and identify that certain services aren't functioning as expected, such as **remote desktop connections** using the **Remote Desktop Protocol** (**RDP**) or other types of services. In these circumstances, you may find that redeploying a VM will help. The redeployment will result in your VM moving to a new node within the Azure infrastructure. This will obviously also result in the VM shutting down during the move and restarting on the new node. All your configurations and associated resources will still be retained.

Top Tip

When you redeploy a VM, take note that the dynamic IP assigned to your VM will be updated, and your temporary disk data will be lost.

---

1. Navigate to the VM that you wish to deploy. On the left menu pane, near the bottom, click on the **Redeploy + reapply** option:

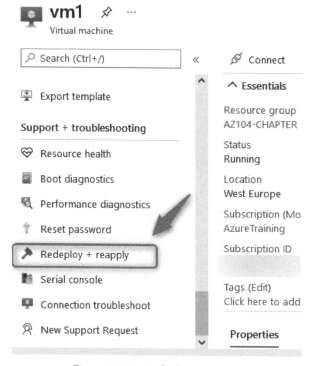

Figure 10.34 – Redeploy + reapply

2. Click the **Redeploy** button:

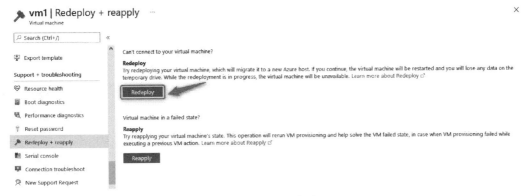

Figure 10.35 – Redeploy

3. You will see a notification that the process has started:

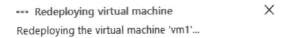

Figure 10.36 – Redeploy notification

4. You will receive a success message signifying successful reallocation for the server:

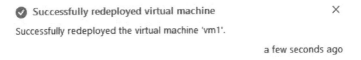

Figure 10.37 – Redeploy success notification

Now that you have redeployed a VM using the Azure portal, we will explore redeploying a VM using PowerShell.

Redeploying a VM from PowerShell

To redeploy a VM from PowerShell, you will perform the following steps:

1. Navigate to the Azure portal by opening `https://portal.azure.com`.

2. Open Azure Cloud Shell again by clicking the following menu item in the top-right menu in the Azure portal:

Figure 10.38 – Top navigation bar

3. Make sure that, this time, PowerShell is selected.

4. Add the following line of code to redeploy the VM:

```
Set-AzVM -Redeploy -ResourceGroupName
"PacktVMResourceGroup" -Name "myVM1"
```

That brings us to the end of the VM redeployment topic. Next, we will explore what Azure disk encryption is and how to configure it.

Disk encryption in Azure

Encrypting Azure disks ensures that unattended and unauthorized access to the disks will be prevented by encrypting the data. This can be done at both an infrastructure level, through **server-side encryption (SSE)**, and at an **operating system (OS)** level too, through **Azure disk encryption (ADE)**.

SSE is the encryption of data stored on Azure managed disks when persisting to the cloud.

ADE provides a mechanism to safeguard and protect your data. It is zone resilient just like Azure VMs. In Windows, the encryption is done through **BitLocker** in the Windows OS with the option to store the encrypting key in Key Vault. The same is true for Linux with the utility for encryption being **DM-Crypt**.

In the following exercise, we are going to explore how to encrypt an Azure Windows VM.

Configuring ADE

We will now walk through the steps involved in performing ADE. This will be performed on a Windows VM:

1. Navigate to your VM in the Azure portal and select the **Disks** option on the left-hand menu. Click on **Additional settings**:

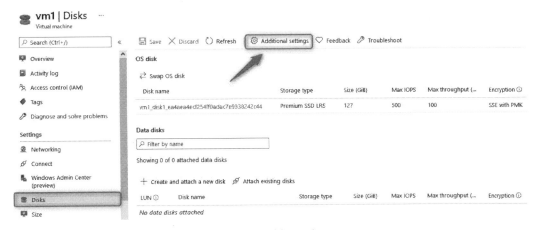

Figure 10.39 – Additional settings

2. Configure for **OS and data disks** and click **Create new** in the **Key Vault** section:

Disk settings   ⋯
vm1

Ultra disk

Enable Ultra disk compatibility ⓘ

- ◯ Yes
- ◉ No

Ultra disk is available only for Availability Zones in westeurope.

Encryption settings

Azure Disk Encryption (ADE) provides volume encryption for the OS and data disks. Learn more about Azure Disk Encryption.

Disks to encrypt ⓘ

OS and data disks   ⌄

Azure Disk Encryption is integrated with Azure Key Vault to help manage encryption keys. As a prerequisite, you need to have an existing key vault with encryption permissions set. For additional security, you can create or choose an optional key encryption key to protect the secret.

Key Vault * ⓘ

Select a key vault   ⌄
Create new

Key ⓘ

Select a key   ⌄

Version ⓘ

Select a key version   ⌄

[Save] [Cancel]

Figure 10.40 – Encryption disk settings

3. Enter a name in the **Key vault name** field and click **Next : Access policy** >:

Create key vault   ⋯

Basics   Access policy   Networking   Tags   Review + create

Azure Key Vault is a cloud service used to manage keys, secrets, and certificates. Key Vault eliminates the need for developers to store security information in their code. It allows you to centralize the storage of your application secrets which greatly reduces the chances that secrets may be leaked. Key Vault also allows you to securely store secrets and keys backed by Hardware Security Modules or HSMs. The HSMs used are Federal Information Processing Standards (FIPS) 140-2 Level 2 validated. In addition, key vault provides logs of all access and usage attempts of your secrets so you have a complete audit trail for compliance.

Project details

Select the subscription to manage deployed resources and costs. Use resource groups like folders to organize and manage all your resources.

Subscription	AzureTraining	⌄
└── Resource group *	AZ104-Chapter10-Migration	⌄
	Create new	

Instance details

Key vault name * ⓘ	keyvault27102021	⌄
Region	West Europe	⌄
Pricing tier * ⓘ	Standard	⌄

Recovery options

Soft delete protection will automatically be enabled on this key vault. This feature allows you to recover or permanently delete a key vault and secrets for the duration of the retention period. This protection applies to the key vault and the secrets stored within the key vault.

To enforce a mandatory retention period and prevent the permanent deletion of key vaults or secrets prior to the retention period elapsing, you can turn on purge protection. When purge protection is enabled, secrets cannot be purged by users or by Microsoft.

Review + create		< Previous	Next : Access policy >

Figure 10.41 – Create key vault – Basics

4. Select the checkboxes next to both the **Azure Virtual Machines for deployment** and **Azure Disk Encryption for volume encryption** options. Click **Review + create**:

Figure 10.42 – Create key vault – Access policy

5. Click **Create**.

6.   Note that your disk is now encrypted:

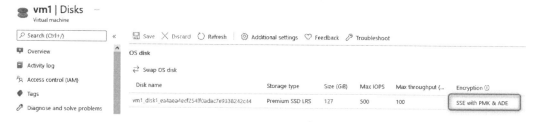

Figure 10.43 – Disks pane

You have completed the disk encryption exercise and now understand how to perform this operation within Azure. In the next section, we will discuss the reliability and availability options available to us in Azure.

Automating configuration management

There are various ways in Azure to automate the creation and configuration of your infrastructure. You can use ARM templates to deploy your infrastructure as code or use Azure Automation, PowerShell scripts, and more. When different Azure resources are deployed, there are some tools that you can use to manage the configuration of the resources. For example, when you want to automate the configuration of your VMs, Azure provides the following tools:

- **Chef**: Chef is a third-party solution that offers a DevOps automation platform for Linux, Windows, and macOS devices. It can be used for virtual and physical server configurations. It requires an agent to be installed on the virtual machines or servers, which connects to the Chef server to check whether there are available updates and other configurations for the machines. You can use the Chef Automate platform to package and deploy applications as well.

- **Puppet**: Puppet is a third-party solution as well, and it has similar capabilities to Chef. You can enable support for Puppet when you create a virtual machine from the Azure portal automatically. You can add it as an extension when you create a new virtual machine that installs the Puppet agent and connects to the master server. Although the Puppet agent supports Windows and Linux, the Puppet VM extension on Azure is supported on the Linux operating system only.

- **Desired State Configuration (DSC)**: DSC is the process of forcing a configuration on a system. It uses configuration files that consist of PowerShell scripts. These scripts are responsible for doing the required configurations for the system and for ensuring that these systems stay in sync. So, for example, when you have created a DSC file to configure IIS on a Windows server and it is removed by an administrator, the DSC file will reinstall and configure IIS again. This can be used in conjunction with Azure Automation for enhanced reporting.

- **Custom Script Extensions**: You can configure software installation tasks and various post-deployment, configuration, and management tasks using Custom Script Extensions. Scripts can be downloaded from Azure Storage or GitHub, or provided to the Azure portal at extension runtime, and are executed on the VMs. You can integrate Custom Script Extensions with ARM templates, and you can run them using PowerShell, the CLI, the VM REST API, and the Azure portal.

Summary

In this chapter, we covered Azure VMs, how to configure them, and the various management functions, including components such as networking, high-availability configurations, and changing the VM host. As part of this topic, we unpacked the various types of Azure disks that exist, how these can be added to a VM, and how we can encrypt the disks.

You have now attained the skills required for the management of VMs within the Azure environment and should be able to confidently provision, scale, and manage these going forward. You have also learned different methods of deployment to assist you with consistent delivery on the platform while ensuring fewer mistakes and faster deployment times than doing this manually, using PowerShell or the Cloud CLI. Alongside these skills, you also know the various storage options available, how to best scope the storage required, and how to implement this as needed.

In the next chapter, we will cover Azure containers and how to configure and manage them.

11
Creating and Configuring Containers

This chapter focuses on the creation and configuration of containers. Some topics to look forward to include the following: configuring the sizing and scaling of containers, working with **Azure Container Instances** (**ACI**), working with **Azure Kubernetes Service** (**AKS**) storage, scaling AKS, and the networking side of AKS. You will explore what containers are and the difference between containers and **virtual machines** (**VMs**), you'll understand use cases for containers, and you'll also learn how to manage and orchestrate container deployments within Azure. By the end of this chapter, you should feel confident in working with containers and being able to administer them on Azure.

In this chapter, we are going to cover the following main topics:

- Introduction to containers
- Containers versus VMs
- **Azure Container Instances** (**ACI**)
- Container groups
- Docker platform

- AKS

- Creating an Azure container registry

- Deploying your first Azure container instance

- Configuring container groups for Azure container instances

- Configuring sizing and scaling for Azure container instances

- Deploying AKS

- Configuring storage for AKS

- Configuring scaling for AKS

- Configuring network connections for AKS

- Upgrading an AKS cluster

Technical requirements

This chapter uses the following tools for our examples:

- Access to an Azure subscription with owner or contributor privileges. If you do not have access to one, students can enroll for a free account at `https://azure.microsoft.com/en-in/free/`.

- **PowerShell 5.1** or later installed on a PC from which labs can be practiced. Note that many examples can only be followed from a PC or `https://shell.azure.com` (PowerShell 7.0.6 **Long-Term Support** (**LTS**) or above is recommended).

For this exercise, we are going to configure Docker so that you can see your first container in action. Follow the given steps to configure Docker:

1. Sign up on Docker Hub at the following **URL**: `https://hub.docker.com/signup?redirectTo=/subscription%3Fplan%3Dfree`.

2. Next, proceed to download the Docker application, as follows:

   - For Windows, use the following link: `https://desktop.docker.com/win/stable/amd64/Docker%20Desktop%20Installer.exe`.

   - For Linux, use the following link: `https://hub.docker.com/search?q=&type=edition&offering=community&operating_system=linux`.

   - For macOS, use the following link: `https://hub.docker.com/editions/community/docker-ce-desktop-mac`.

Introduction to containers

Businesses are constantly looking for newer and quicker ways to deploy applications and keep businesses running. These requirements lead to software development and support teams to find solutions for saving money and time. Adopting an approach of using containers for rapid deployments leaves more time for software deployment and reduces time spent on creating and configuring environments.

Containers are specialized packages of software that bundle application software with associated configuration files, libraries, and dependencies that are required to enable an application to run. Containers also contain the kernel for an **operating system (OS)** and don't require the whole OS in itself, which allows for larger-scale deployments than what VMs could achieve using the same resources. The reason for this is that the OS consumes resources, such as storage, memory, and processing power. In the previous chapter, you learned about VMs and how they work by logically creating a machine using resources; we say that VMs abstract the hardware layer. Containers, by association, abstract the OS layer. When deploying a VM, you will still need to specify the type of OS you require—this is typically Windows or Linux. The exact kernel version won't be required to make it work as the kernel will be packaged in your container, and you just need to concern yourself with the application code, libraries, and dependencies to get your application to work. Using this approach allows for easy scaling, and only a single OS is consumed on the host of all the containers for the OS type, such as Windows or Linux. Being more lightweight, containers become easier to manage and much faster to deploy and scale. They introduce a standardized and repeatable mechanism for packaging, managing, and deploying applications.

Prior to containers, the challenge was writing applications for various systems with different versions of dependencies that the developers couldn't control. This leads to several issues that make solutions very difficult to manage. With containers, you can standardize the deployment with dependencies and enable a consistent experience for all users.

Azure container instances allow you to run containers in Azure without the requirement to deploy your own container host or VM.

> **Top Tip**
> Windows container hosts can run both Windows and Linux containers; conversely, Linux can only run Linux containers to date. Running Linux containers on Windows will require Hyper-V services and using a system called LinuxKit (essentially a Linux VM). When deploying to ACI, however, it is important to select the correct OS for your requirement, as Linux containers run on the Linux OS and Windows containers run on the Windows OS.

Containers versus VMs

Hardware virtualization has enabled the possibility of running multiple isolated OS instances at the same time on physical hardware. As containers abstract the OS by virtualizing it, this enables several applications to be run using the same OS while still being isolated from each other. VMs, on the other hand, contain the full OS and files and essentially only abstract the hardware layer, whereas containers abstract the OS layer and contain your application files as well as configuration files and dependencies. Containers are much smaller in size and utilize fewer resources.

A hypervisor is the software, firmware, and hardware that enables VMs to be created and run. It is the layer that resides between the physical hardware and the software-implemented VM. New machines have virtualization instruction sets built into the processes and specialized hardware to enable VMs to run just as well as physical hardware and leverage physical hardware resources as native services.

The following diagram depicts the relationship between VMs and containers:

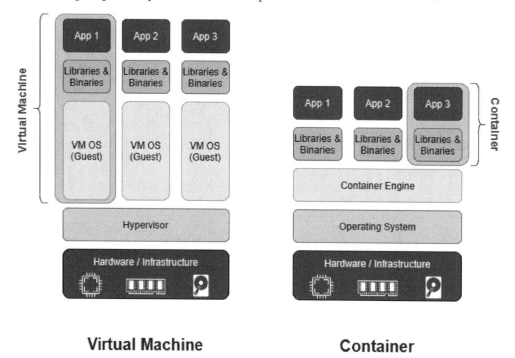

Figure 11.1 – VMs versus containers

It should be noted that hypervisors are formed at different levels of integration from systems. As you will note from the preceding diagram, there is a hypervisor layer present just above the hardware/infrastructure layer—this is referred to as a type 1 hypervisor (also known as a bare-metal hypervisor) as it has direct access to hardware. There is another type of hypervisor referred to as type 2 (also known as a host OS hypervisor); this runs much like an application within the OS, and this is the technology that Docker uses.

It can become confusing to distinguish between containers and VMs, so to help you better understand their differences, we have identified some key concepts to be aware of, as outlined next.

Isolation

VMs provide the most complete and secure isolation solution to isolate all other VMs and even the host OS from each other. This is the best mechanism for security when you have shared infrastructure and are looking to isolate applications or services from competing companies that are on the same server or cluster.

Containers, in comparison to VMs, provide a much lighter-weight isolation mechanism. They don't provide as strong a security boundary from the host and other containers as a VM does.

> **Takeaway**
> When choosing a solution that requires the most secure method of isolation, it is best to go with VMs.

OS

VMs run the entire OS, including the kernel. This will obviously be a more resource-intensive approach as the OS requires system resources such as memory, **central processing unit** (**CPU**), and storage.

Containers, by comparison, require far fewer system resources to run applications. They do this by only running the customized user-mode portion of OSs that contain only services that are essential for running your application.

> **Takeaway**
> When choosing a solution that requires better utilization of system resources, you can't go wrong with containers. In fact, your resources will go much further than with a VM.

Deployment

VMs are deployed using some form of a hypervisor. With Windows systems, they can be deployed and managed by **Windows Admin Center**, **Hyper-V Manager**, and **System Center Virtual Machine Manager (SCVMM)**. PowerShell can also be used with the relevant Hyper-V modules enabled.

Containers, in comparison to VMs, are deployed using Docker through the command line for single instances, and for multiple containers, it is advised that an orchestrator service such as AKS is used.

> Takeaway
>
> Understand the tools for each deployment type, knowing that on Azure, we predominantly use Docker containers and AKS for container orchestration.

Storage persistence

VM storage is very easy to scale and maintain in Azure. We simply add or scale up disks as required, as you experienced in the previous chapter. This storage is persistent as it doesn't disappear if disconnected or if the VM shuts down. Another mechanism of providing persistent storage is through **Server Message Block (SMB)** shares.

Containers, in comparison, have the option of leveraging Azure disks for local storage on a single-node deployment and configuring SMB shares for multiple nodes or servers.

> Takeaway
>
> Identify whether storage requires persistence and find the mechanism that best suits your requirements. For shared storage, SMB shares make a lot of sense, but there are several other mechanisms that can be used to achieve the same result. These are beyond the scope of this book, however, but you are still encouraged to explore and find what works for you.

Fault tolerance

VMs can fail over to another server in a cluster when configured for fault tolerance. The resultant effect, however, is that the VM's OS will be restarted on the new hosting server, which can add potentially significant time to restore services.

Containers, in comparison, have the ability to quickly recover instances. The orchestrator recreates the container on another cluster node when it detects a failed cluster node.

> **Takeaway**
>
> Catering to fault tolerance is always advised, especially when dealing with production workloads. You need to understand the caveats of each system and be able to plan accordingly. Containers, being more lightweight, are more resistant to failures and more readily restored.

Having understood the preceding key comparative areas, it is important to highlight the several advantages containers hold over VMs and physical machines, as follows:

- Due to better resource utilization, containers can achieve better workload density.

- They standardize deployments and simplify the application testing process.

- Application deployment is quicker and more streamlined. It is also more standardized, making it more consistent and reliable.

- Improved speed and flexibility in developing application code, as well as sharing.

You should now understand the key differences between containers and VMs, as well as be able to identify scenarios that best suit either deployment. In the next section, we will explore ACI and how this allows easy deployment of containers to the Azure platform.

ACI

ACI is a container hosting service that provides a fast and easy method for running containers in Azure. Using this solution will enable you to deploy containers without needing to manage any VMs or utilize any higher-level services. Azure container instances provide a great solution for applications that can run in isolated containers. There are several benefits to working with container instances on Azure, as outlined here:

- **Fast startup times**: Azure containers are designed to be able to start in seconds.

- **Public connectivity**: Azure containers have been designed to enable direct exposure to the internet by associating with a public **Internet Protocol (IP)** address that also allows the association of a **fully qualified domain name (FQDN)** (public **Domain Name System (DNS)** name associated with the public IP).

- **Security**: Azure container applications apply hypervisor-level security that enables container applications to be isolated as they would be in a VM.

- **Custom sizes**: Azure container nodes are designed to be dynamically scaled to meet the resource demands required for an application.

- **Storage persistence**: Azure containers enable storage persistence through Azure File Shares by allowing them to be directly mounted. Without this, storage is only ephemeral.

- **Various OSs**: Azure container instances can schedule containers for both Windows and Linux systems. Simply select the OS type you need when you create your container groups.

- **Co-scheduled groups**: Azure container instances are designed to support the sharing of host machine resources through multi-container groups on the same host.

- **Virtual network (VNet) deployment**: Azure container instances have been designed to allow integration into Azure VNets.

Now that you understand what Azure container instances are and the several benefits they can offer, we will start to understand how container groups fit into the structure. You will learn what container groups are and what to consider when designing and deploying these.

Container groups

Container groups contain a set of containers that share their life cycle, resources, network configuration, and storage resources, essentially grouping them together. Containers within a container group are scheduled together on the same host (the server on which these run) and in ACI, which is the top-level resource. Container groups can consist of one or more containers. The following diagram is an example container group that contains two containers scheduled on the same host. The container group exposes port 80 on a single public IP (an IP accessible from the internet) and has a public DNS label associated with it. The container group also contains two different storage accounts, each of which is associated with one of the containers. Of the two containers, one container exposes port 80 while the other exposes port 1433. On private ports, as illustrated in the following diagram, private refers to ports, IP, or DNS being restricted to access within the local network only:

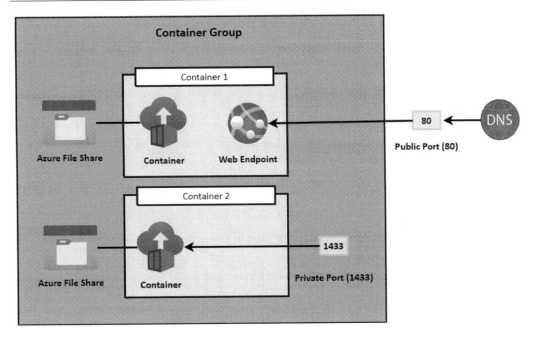

Figure 11.2 – Example container group

You now have a basic understanding of what a container group is, so next, we will explore some common scenarios for using multi-container groups.

Common scenarios

There are several scenarios where multi-container groups prove beneficial, such as when you define a frontend and backend for your container groups. Tasks may be divided into an application container and a logging or monitoring container; they perform two separate functions but are both complementary to the end service delivery of the application. Images can be deployed and managed by different teams within your organization.

Some other scenarios include the following:

- An application container and a database container. The application container(s) may deliver the end application, while the database container commits data to a service location.

- A web application service deployed to a container within the group and another container for managing source control.

Resources

Container groups are allocated resources by ACI by adding resource requests for all instances in a container group, such as CPUs, memory, and even **graphics processing units (GPUs)**. For example, if you have two container instances in a container group and each instance requires two CPUs and 4 **gigabytes (GB)** of memory, the container group will then be allocated four CPUs and 8 GB of memory, as depicted in the following diagram:

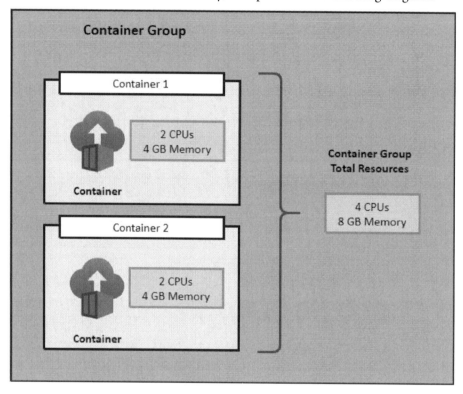

Figure 11.3 – Container group resource allocation

You now understand how resources are allocated for container groups. Next, we will explore the networking components of the Azure Container Instance service.

Networking

Containers within a container group can share a public-facing IP address with an associated DNS label. This label is referred to as an FQDN, which is a user-friendly name for finding an IP associated with your web application. The container group exposes ports on the public IP address to enable external clients to reach a container. The exposed public ports must also be enabled on the container level, which doesn't always need to be publicly accessible but can be limited internally too. When the container group is deleted, then the associated public IP and FQDN will be released too. A note on containers within the group is that all containers within the group share a port namespace, and because of this, port mapping isn't supported.

An example to help you understand the concept better is provided here: imagine you have a container group deployment that contains one frontend server and one backend server. The frontend server requires access over port 443 (**HyperText Transfer Protocol Secure**, or **HTTPS**) on a public IP, while the backend server communicates over port 8080 and will be limited to local communication. You can see a depiction of this in the following diagram:

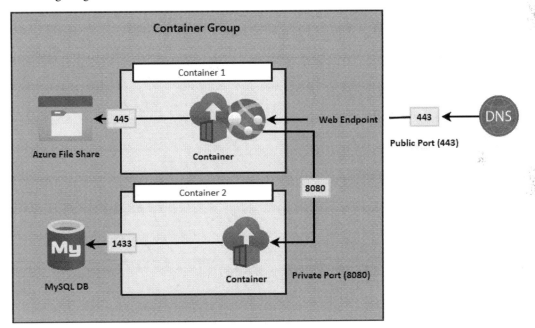

Figure 11.4 – Example container group frontend and backend

You now understand more about how some networking components work for container groups, so next, we will explore how we run deployments.

Deployment

There are two primary methods of deployment for a multi-container group: an **Azure Resource Manager** (**ARM**) template or a **YAML Ain't Markup Language** (**YAML**) file. In *Chapter 9*, *Automating VM Deployments Using ARM Templates*, we explored the deployment of VM resources using ARM templates; this serves as an extension of that prior knowledge. The beauty of ARM deployment is that it allows for additional resources to be deployed alongside container instances, such as Azure File Shares. YAML files, on the other hand, are designed for supporting container instance deployments within a container group only. These are designed as an alternative to ARM templates for container deployments due to them being more concise in their nature and structure.

Now that you understand more about container groups, in the next section, we will explore Docker, which is one of the platforms that enable containerization. Docker is one of the most popular platforms and is well integrated into Azure.

Docker platform

Docker is one of the most popular platforms that enable developers to host their applications within containers. It can be run on either the Windows, Linux, or macOS and ensures a standardized software deployment. The beauty of the system is that it allows local development on a container platform (such as Docker) and can be easily redeployed into the Azure cloud for sharing and distribution. The package will run as expected since all the package components are bundled into the Docker image you deploy. Docker acts as the container host as well as a tool for building containers. When containers are deployed through ACI, the service allows them to be scaled easily.

Docker terminology

When working with Docker and container instances, you should understand the following terminology. This will help you become comfortable working with containers and performing actions such as creating, building, and testing containers:

- **Container**: This refers to an instance of one of your Docker images. As we discussed, containers are specialized packages of software that bundle application software with associated configuration files, libraries, and dependencies that are required to enable an application to run. In Docker, this consists of the Docker image, the execution environment, and your standard set of instructions. The platform enables you to create multiple instances of a container using the same image, which is important to remember when you want to scale your application.

- **Container image**: This refers to all the dependencies and information packaged together that are required to create a container. These include frameworks, as well configurations for deployment and executions that a container runtime uses. An image is typically created from multiple base images stacked on top of each other to form the container's filesystem. An image is immutable once it has been created.

- **Docker Registry**: This is the repository provided by the Docker platform for storing various image files. Azure has another solution, however— **Azure Container Registry**, which is the solution we will use.

- **Build**: This is the action of building your container. The build will be based on the container image and will be constructed based on the information provided by the Dockerfile. The build also includes any other necessary files.

- **Pull**: This refers to the action of downloading a container image from one of your container registries.

- **Push**: This refers to the action of uploading a container image to one of your container registries.

- **Dockerfile**: This defines instructions for building your image. It is stored as a text file. The first line in a Dockerfile structure is used to identify the base image needed, while the rest of the file contains the associated build actions for your image.

The Docker platform is structured as per the following diagram. You will notice the container registry comprises Azure Container Registry, Docker Hub, or another container registry, the Docker Engine components, and the containers. The following diagram will help you understand the relationship between these components:

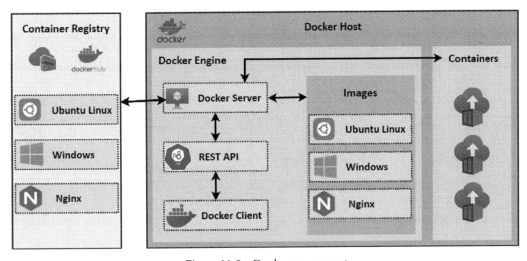

Figure 11.5 – Docker components

You now understand more about the Docker platform, and you are now aware of the various components that work together to enable your solution. Next, we will explore how to set up Docker.

Setting up Docker

For this exercise, we are going to configure Docker so that you can see your first container in action. Proceed as follows:

1. Sign up on Docker Hub at the following URL: `https://hub.docker.com/signup?redirectTo=/subscription%3Fplan%3Dfree`.

2. Next, proceed to download the Docker application and install it. For the remainder of the exercise, it will be assumed you are running from a Windows machine. After installing the Docker application, you may be required to restart your machine.

    For Windows, use the following link: `https://desktop.docker.com/win/stable/amd64/Docker%20Desktop%20Installer.exe`.

    For Linux, use the following link: `https://hub.docker.com/search?q=&type=edition&offering=community&operating_system=linux`.

    For Mac, use the following link: `https://hub.docker.com/editions/community/docker-ce-desktop-mac`.

3. After installation on Windows, you will want to update the **Windows Subsystem for Linux 2 (WSL 2)** package. Run the following link and restart your machine: `https://wslstorestorage.blob.core.windows.net/wslblob/wsl_update_x64.msi`.

4. Once Docker is set up, run the following command for your first Docker image. Launch an administrative PowerShell session for this and add the following command, then press *Enter*:

```
docker run -d -p 80:80 docker/getting-started
```

The following screenshot shows the output of the preceding command:

```
PS C:\Program Files\Docker\Docker> docker run -d -p 80:80 docker/getting-started
Unable to find image 'docker/getting-started:latest' locally
latest: Pulling from docker/getting-started
97518928ae5f: Pull complete
a4e156412037: Pull complete
e0bae2ade5ec: Pull complete
8f3577460f48: Pull complete
e362c27513c3: Pull complete
a2402c2da473: Pull complete
eb65930377cd: Pull complete
69465e074227: Pull complete
Digest: sha256:86093b75a06bf74e3d2125edb77689c8eecf8ed0cb3946573a24a6f71e88cf80
Status: Downloaded newer image for docker/getting-started:latest
9325aab9d7a90f05ae2f8b4be9dabd9330230f23fc4e59ecdbc953923a4c725a
```

Figure 11.6 – First Docker container

Note that this command runs a `pull` command for a `docker/getting-started` image.

> **Top Tip**
>
> If you are one of the users that face an issue when running the previous command, try running the following command to fix Docker: `cd "C:\ Program Files\Docker\Docker`. Then, press *Enter* and add the following code: `./DockerCli.exe -SwitchDaemon`. Following this, press *Enter*.

After running this command, you may open the Docker Desktop application, and if you click **Containers / Apps** on the left menu, you will notice an image on the right, as illustrated in the following screenshot. A name is randomly generated each time you create a container unless you specify otherwise:

Figure 11.7 – First Docker container: Docker Desktop

You will note that this is running on port 80, which means the application is accessible as a web application locally. To access this, launch a browser and navigate to the following URL: http://127.0.0.1. You will see a success message, along with guidance on other exercises you can follow, as illustrated in the following screenshot. We encourage you to carry this out and learn more:

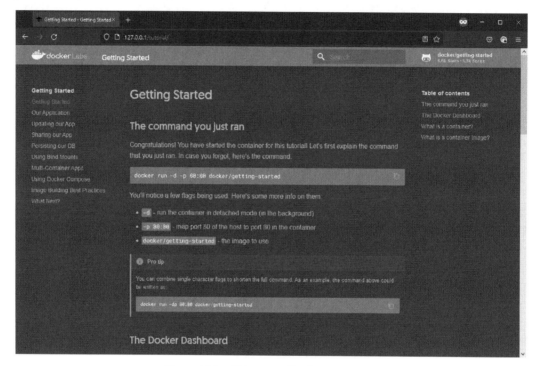

Figure 11.8 – Using your Docker container

Now that you have successfully installed Docker and run your first container from a precompiled image, we will explore the creation of your first image and publish it to Docker Hub.

Creating our first Docker image

For this exercise, you will need to first sign in to Docker Hub. Then, follow the next steps:

1. Once signed in, click on the **Repositories** button on the top menu bar, as illustrated in the following screenshot:

Figure 11.9 – Repositories button

2. Enter a name and description for this repository, then click **Create**. Note that you may select whether your repository is **Public** or **Private** too. For this repository, I'll leave it as **Public**, as illustrated in the following screenshot:

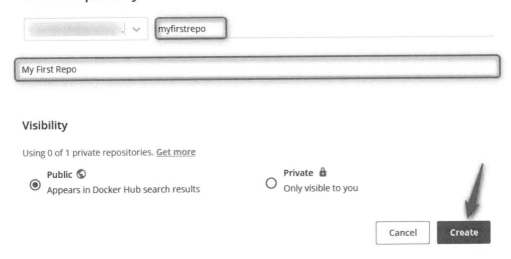

Create Repository

myfirstrepo

My First Repo

Visibility

Using 0 of 1 private repositories. Get more

Public 🌐
Appears in Docker Hub search results

Private 🔒
Only visible to you

Cancel   Create

Figure 11.10 – Creating your repository

3. Return to your PowerShell window and paste the following command into it:

```
docker pull mcr.microsoft.com/azuredocs/aci-helloworld
```

For our demonstration, we will be using the following image to demonstrate how we upload an image to Docker as well as to use this later in ACI:

```
PS C:\Program Files\Docker\Docker> docker pull mcr.microsoft.com/azuredocs/aci-helloworld
Using default tag: latest
latest: Pulling from azuredocs/aci-helloworld
6d987f6f4279: Pull complete
a1b9769c94cd: Downloading [=====================>                             ]  8.059MB/19.19MB
ea13ff2dbf08: Download complete
3be0618266da: Download complete
9e232827e52f: Download complete
b53c152f538f: Waiting
```

Figure 11.11 – Pull of the aci-helloworld image

4. Now that your image is downloaded, run `docker images`, as illustrated in the following screenshot, and press *Enter*:

```
PS C:\Program Files\Docker\Docker> docker images
REPOSITORY                                      TAG       IMAGE ID       CREATED       SIZE
docker/getting-started                          latest    26d80cd96d69   10 days ago   28.5MB
mcr.microsoft.com/azuredocs/aci-helloworld      latest    7367f3256b41   4 years ago   67.6MB
```

Figure 11.12 – Listing all local Docker images

This command lists all images on your local system. Now, you will list all running containers on your system using the following command: `docker ps`. Then, press *Enter*.

5. You will notice the container you ran from earlier in the PowerShell window. Note the name and proceed by running the following command: `docker stop [container name]`. Then, press *Enter*. To confirm the container has been stopped run `docker ps`, then press *Enter*. The process is illustrated in the following screenshot:

Figure 11.13 – Using PowerShell to manage Docker containers

6. Let's start our downloaded image; we will run it on the local port `80`, and expose port `80` for connecting back to the container. Note your image name from earlier; you can run `docker images` to confirm, as illustrated in the following screenshot:

```
PS C:\Program Files\Docker\Docker> docker images
REPOSITORY                                    TAG       IMAGE ID       CREATED        SIZE
docker/getting-started                        latest    26d80cd96d69   10 days ago    28.5MB
mcr.microsoft.com/azuredocs/aci-helloworld    latest    7367f3256b41   4 years ago    67.6MB
```

Figure 11.14 – Listing Docker images

7. The command will be constructed as follows, after which you can run `docker ps` again:

```
docker run -d -p 80:80 mcr.microsoft.com/azuredocs/
aci-helloworld
```

The following screenshot shows the output of the preceding command:

```
PS C:\Program Files\Docker\Docker> docker run -d -p 80:80 mcr.microsoft.com/azuredocs/aci-helloworld
779ada96ae161de188da7966bcb9897a97172c19647e76cb0d102a0707cf3523
PS C:\Program Files\Docker\Docker> docker ps
CONTAINER ID   IMAGE                                        COMMAND               CREATED         STATUS         PORTS                  NAMES
779ada96ae16   mcr.microsoft.com/azuredocs/aci-helloworld   "/bin/sh -c 'node /u…" 13 seconds ago  Up 11 seconds  0.0.0.0:80->80/tcp     thirsty_stonebraker
```

Figure 11.15 – Our second container

8. To access this container, launch a browser and navigate to the following URL: `http://127.0.0.1`. You will see a welcome message, as illustrated in the following screenshot, and will then know that the application is working:

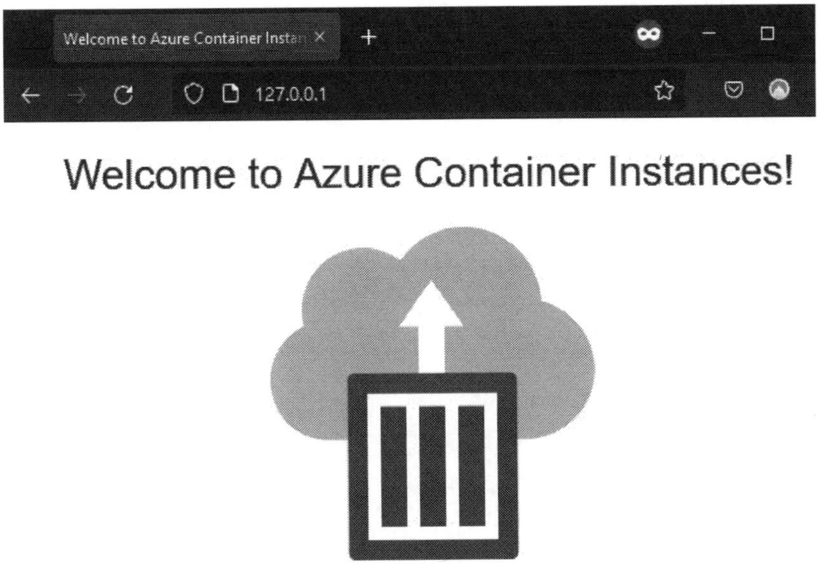

Figure 11.16 – Our second container running

9. You will now push the image to your repository based on the repository name you gave earlier. You will first need to tag your image for Docker to understand which image file to push. Run the following command in PowerShell and press *Enter*:

```
docker tag mcr.microsoft.com/azuredocs/aci-helloworld
[docker hub username]/myfirstrepo
```

The following screenshot shows the output of the preceding command:

```
docker tag mcr.microsoft.com/azuredocs/aci-helloworld                    admin/myfirstrepo
```

Figure 11.17 – Pushing the Docker image

10. Run docker images and note in the following screenshot our newly tagged image:

```
PS C:\Program Files\Docker\Docker> docker images
REPOSITORY                                   TAG       IMAGE ID       CREATED        SIZE
docker/getting-started                       latest    26d80cd96d69   10 days ago    28.5MB
          admin/myfirstrepo                  latest    7367f3256b41   4 years ago    67.6MB
mcr.microsoft.com/azuredocs/aci-helloworld   latest    7367f3256b41   4 years ago    67.6MB
```

Figure 11.18 – Tagging the Docker image

11. Now, log in to Docker using the `docker login` command. We will now proceed to push an image to your Docker repository. The easiest way to push is to follow this command on the page where we created our repository earlier:

Figure 11.19 – The docker push command

12. Run this command in PowerShell:

```
docker push [docker hub username]/myfirstrepo
```

Here is the output of the preceding command:

```
PS C:\Program Files\Docker\Docker> docker push                    admin/myfirstrepo
Using default tag: latest
The push refers to repository [docker.io/              admin/myfirstrepo]
31ba1ebd9cf5: Pushing [>                                          ]  29.7kB/2.948MB
cd07853fe8be: Pushing [=========================================>]  7.168kB
73f25249687f: Pushing  3.072kB
d8fbd47558a8: Pushing [>                                          ]  47.02kB/3.915MB
44ab46125c35: Preparing
5bef08742407: Waiting
```

Figure 11.20 – Pushing your first image

You have now successfully pulled and pushed an image from and to Docker Hub. In the next section, we will explore deploying an Azure container instance and using Azure as the host instead of Docker for your images.

AKS

Kubernetes is designed as a management and orchestration service to assist with managing containers and creating a mechanism for scale. AKS is a serverless implementation of the Kubernetes service, which minimizes the management of the Kubernetes cluster for us. The service is designed so that you just take care of the agent nodes. Azure builds upon Kubernetes by enhancing some of its default implementations to enable functions, such as the following:

- **Identity and Access Management (IAM)**: Identity is integrated into **Azure Active Directory (Azure AD)** and managed or the system identity can be used on the service.

- **Azure VNet integration**: Enable private networking natively to Azure networks, **network security groups (NSGs)**, and even network policies.

- **Persistent storage**: Azure overcomes the ephemeral-based storage native to containers by enabling easy integration of persistent storage mechanisms such as Azure File Shares.

- **Autoscaling**: This function enables the autoscaling of Pods and clusters.

AKS also enables health monitoring for the service and the coordination of upgrades. As part of the service, master nodes are not billed for and are included for free, but all agent nodes are billed for. The service constitutes master nodes, node pools, Pods, networks, and storage. It's important to understand how all these components function together. The **control plane** component of the service contains all the functions that allow you to administer your containers within AKS as well as the master node, which is the orchestrator service within AKS. Node pools are essentially your VM infrastructure and are used to provide resources for your Pods and, by association, containers for the service. Then, Pods are your collections of containers within AKS where containers are grouped into their respective functions or applications. The following diagram illustrates the relationship between these various components:

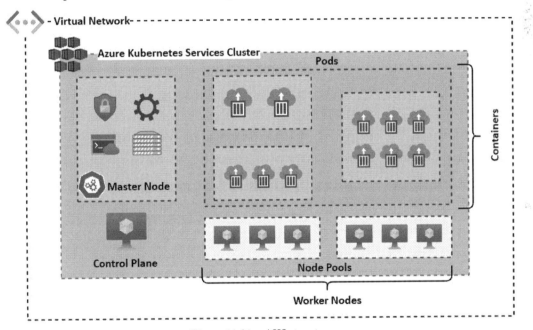

Figure 11.21 – AKS structure

Now that you are more familiar with containers and the orchestration tools that we can use such as AKS, let's dive into some exercises to give you some hands-on experience of working with these services.

Creating an Azure container registry

For this exercise, we are going to create a registry in Azure Container Registry. As mentioned previously, this is very similar to Docker Hub but is native to Azure. Proceed as follows:

1. Sign in to the Azure portal at `https://portal.azure.com`.

2. Open the resource group you will be using for this exercise, click **Overview** on the left menu, then click **Create**.

3. On the top search bar, type `container registry`, and click the **Container Registry** option that appears. Then, click **Create**, as illustrated in the following screenshot:

Figure 11.22 – Creating a container registry

4. Ensure that you have selected the right resource group, give it a unique **Registry name** entry, and select the appropriate **Location** entry. Then, we will leave the **SKU** value as **Standard** for this exercise. Click **Review + create**. The process is illustrated in the following screenshot:

Create container registry   ···

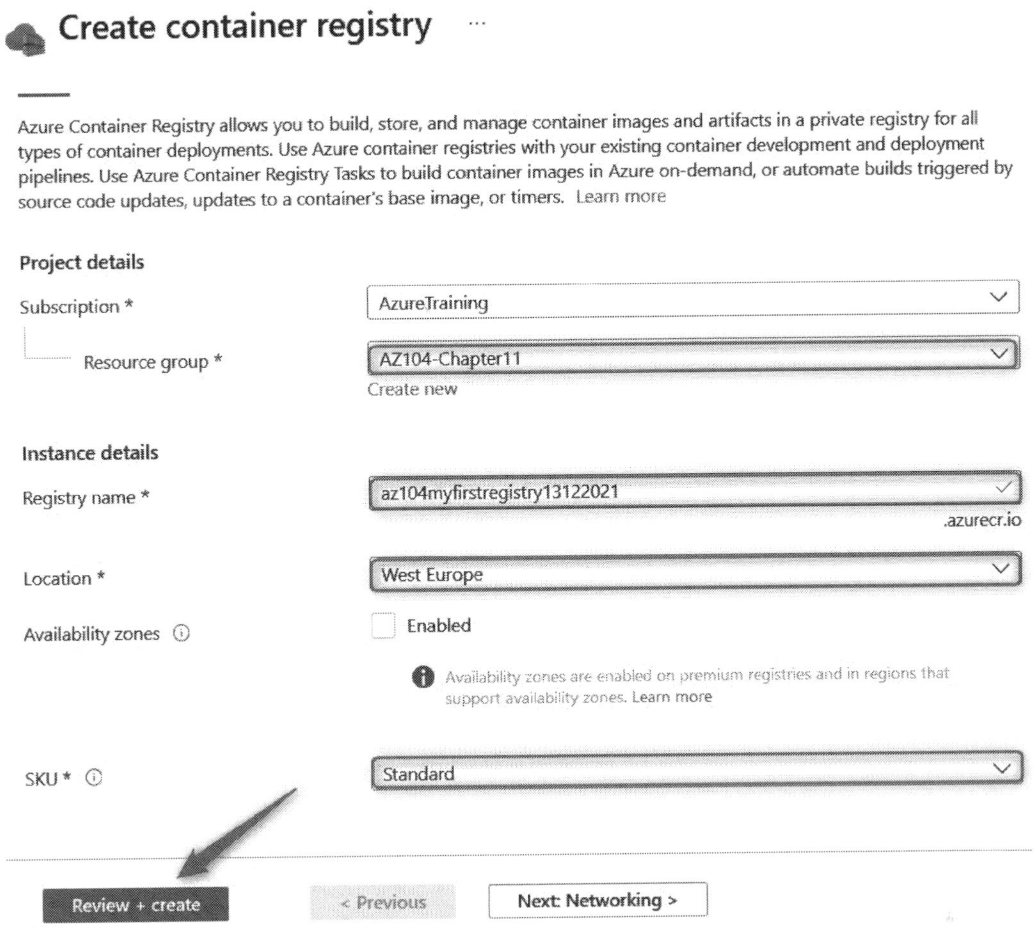

Azure Container Registry allows you to build, store, and manage container images and artifacts in a private registry for all types of container deployments. Use Azure container registries with your existing container development and deployment pipelines. Use Azure Container Registry Tasks to build container images in Azure on-demand, or automate builds triggered by source code updates, updates to a container's base image, or timers. Learn more

Project details

Subscription *   AzureTraining   ⌄

       Resource group *   AZ104-Chapter11   ⌄
                              Create new

Instance details

Registry name *   az104myfirstregistry13122021   ⌄
                                                         .azurecr.io

Location *   West Europe   ⌄

Availability zones ⓘ   ☐ Enabled

                    ⓘ Availability zones are enabled on premium registries and in regions that
                       support availability zones. Learn more

SKU * ⓘ   Standard   ⌄

[Review + create]   [< Previous]   [Next: Networking >]

Figure 11.23 – Creating an Azure container registry

5.   Click **Create**.

6. After the deployment has succeeded, navigate to the resource. Click on **Access keys** on the left-hand menu. Then, on the right screen, click the toggle button next to **Admin user**, and note your username and passwords. This will enable you to connect to the registry using Docker. The process is illustrated in the following screenshot:

Figure 11.24 – Container registry access keys

7. In PowerShell, type the following command and press *Enter*:

```
docker login [yourregistryname].azurecr.io
```

For your username and password, enter the username and password you just copied from the portal, as illustrated in the following screenshot:

```
PS C:\Program Files\Docker\Docker> docker login az104myfirstregistry13122021.azurecr.io
Username: az104myfirstregistry13122021
Password:
Login Succeeded
```

Figure 11.25 – The docker login command

8. You will now tag the image we used previously for Azure Container Registry using the following command:

```
docker tag mcr.microsoft.com/azuredocs/aci-helloworld
[your registry name].azurecr.io/myimages/
containerdemo:latest
```

9. You will then run the following push command to push your container to the registry:

```
docker push[your registry name].azurecr.io/myimages/
containerdemo:latest
```

The output of the preceding command is shown in the following screenshot:

```
PS C:\Program Files\Docker\Docker> docker push az104myfirstregistry13122021.azurecr.io/myimages/containerdemo:latest
The push refers to repository [az104myfirstregistry13122021.azurecr.io/myimages/containerdemo]
61ba1ebd9cf5: Pushing [=======================================>]    3.78MB
cd07853fe8be: Pushing [=======================================>]    7.168kB
73f25249687f: Pushing   3.072kB
48fbd47558a8: Pushing [=======================================>]    3.949MB
44ab46125c35: Pushing [=========>                              ]    9.994MB/56.78MB
6bef08742407: Waiting
```

Figure 11.26 – Pushing your image to Docker

10. On the Azure portal, if you navigate to **Repositories** on the left menu, you will now notice that your image has been uploaded to the registry, as illustrated in the following screenshot:

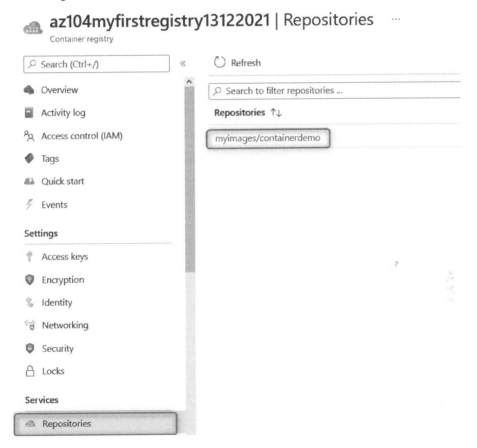

Figure 11.27 – Listing Azure container images

You have successfully uploaded your first Docker image to Azure Container Registry. Now that you have the basics under your belt, we will explore deploying your first container instance in the next section.

Deploying your first Azure container instance

For this exercise, you will create a container group and then deploy a container instance to the group with the following steps:

1. Sign in to the Azure portal at `https://portal.azure.com`.

2. Open the resource group you will be using for this exercise, click **Overview** on the left menu, then click **Create**.

    On the left menu bar, click **Containers**, then click **Container Instances**, as illustrated in the following screenshot:

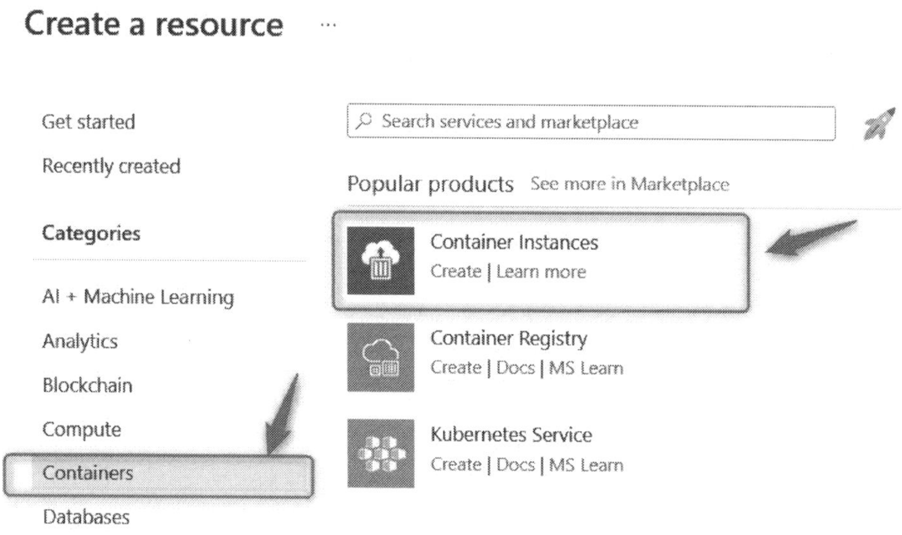

Figure 11.28 – ACI

3. Enter your **Resource group** type, then give your container a name (in this case, I have used `myfirstcontainer`), and then select your **Region** value. Now, for **Image source**, we will use our previously uploaded image, but you will note that you have a choice to connect to **Docker Hub** and other registries too. You will also have the choice to start with some **Quickstart images**, which are sample images created to enable you to set up your container faster. Select **Azure Container Registry** and select the **Registry** type we created in the previous exercise; the **Image** type will also be the one we created previously, and the **Image tag** value will be the latest one. Leave the **Size** field as the default setting. A note on sizing is that you can change this to select between **one and four CPUs** and **0.5 to 14 GB memory** for your instance. Click **Next: Networking >**. The process is illustrated in the following screenshot:

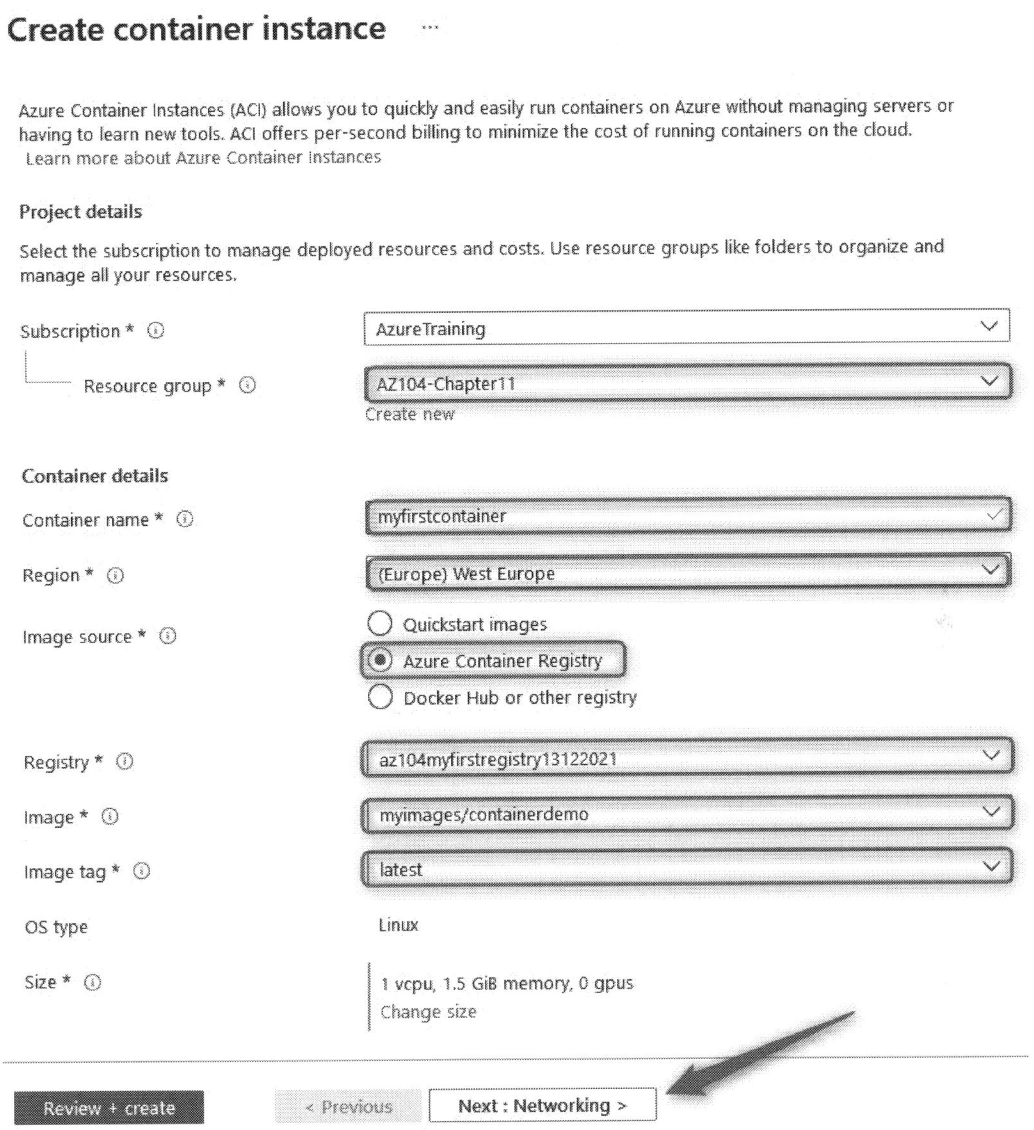

Create container instance   ...

Azure Container Instances (ACI) allows you to quickly and easily run containers on Azure without managing servers or having to learn new tools. ACI offers per-second billing to minimize the cost of running containers on the cloud.
Learn more about Azure Container Instances

Project details

Select the subscription to manage deployed resources and costs. Use resource groups like folders to organize and manage all your resources.

Subscription * ⓘ

> AzureTraining ⌄

└── Resource group * ⓘ

> AZ104-Chapter11 ⌄
Create new

Container details

Container name * ⓘ

> myfirstcontainer ⌄

Region * ⓘ

> (Europe) West Europe ⌄

Image source * ⓘ

⭘ Quickstart images
◉ Azure Container Registry
⭘ Docker Hub or other registry

Registry * ⓘ

> az104myfirstregistry13122021 ⌄

Image * ⓘ

> myimages/containerdemo ⌄

Image tag * ⓘ

> latest ⌄

OS type

Linux

Size * ⓘ

1 vcpu, 1.5 GiB memory, 0 gpus
Change size

[Review + create]   [< Previous]   [Next : Networking >]

Figure 11.29 – Creating a container instance

4. For this exercise, select **Public** as your **Networking type** value, and create a unique **DNS name label** value for your container, then leave the **Ports** configuration as it is. Just note that we are exposing port 80 (HTTP) traffic to the internet for access to this container. Click **Next: Advanced >**. The process is illustrated in the following screenshot:

Create container instance   ⋯

Basics   **Networking**   Advanced   Tags   Review + create

Choose between three networking options for your container instance:

- **'Public'** will create a public IP address for your container instance.
- **'Private'** will allow you to choose a new or existing virtual network for your container instance. This is not yet available for Windows containers.
- **'None'** will not create either a public IP or virtual network. You will still be able to access your container logs using the command line.

Networking type   (●) Public   ( ) Private   ( ) None

DNS name label ⓘ   myfirstcontainer

                                            .westeurope.azurecontainer.io

Ports ⓘ

Ports	Ports protocol	
80	TCP	🗑
		⌄

Review + create   < Previous   Next : Advanced >

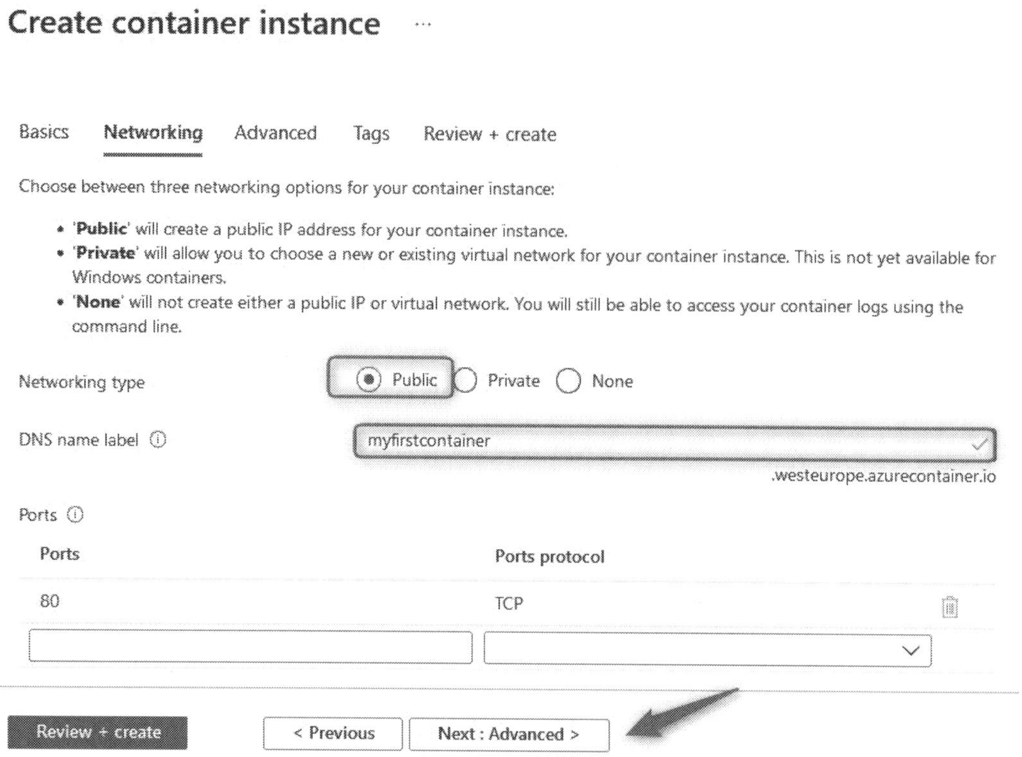

Figure 11.30 – Creating your container instance: Networking tab

5. On the **Advanced** tab, we can configure the **Restart policy** field for your container. The default option is **On failure**, and we will leave ours as it is. You also can configure **Environment variables** values. Click **Review + create**, then click **Create**. The process is illustrated in the following screenshot:

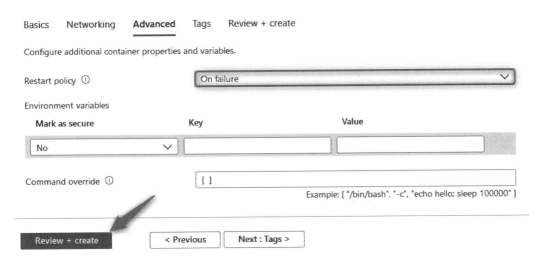

Figure 11.31 – Creating your container instance: Advanced tab

6. Once your resource has been deployed, you can now connect to it on the DNS name label you configured previously.

You now know how to deploy a container instance within Azure and are ready to start your journey on containers. In the next exercise, you will explore creating your first container group.

Configuring container groups for Azure container instances

For this exercise, we are going to configure an Azure container group using an ARM template and Azure Cloud Shell using the following steps:

1. Sign in to the Azure portal at `https://portal.azure.com`.

2. On the top menu bar, click the *Cloud Shell* icon, as illustrated in the following screenshot:

Figure 11.32 – Azure icons

3. Type `code azuredeploy.json` and press *Enter*. You may resize the screen on the highlighted points shown in the following screenshot:

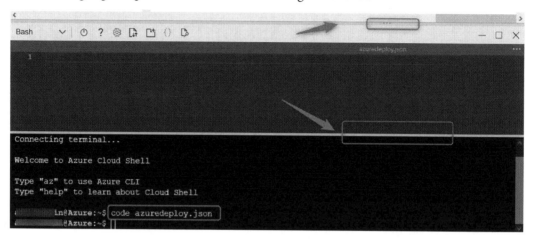

Figure 11.33 – Azure Cloud Shell

Alternatively, you could also select **Open a new session**, which will open a shell in a new browser tab. You can see the icon for this in the following screenshot:

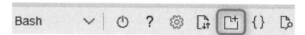

Figure 11.34 – Azure Cloud Shell: Open a new session icon

4. In the top section of the window, paste the following code and then click the ellipsis (…) on the top right and click **Save**:

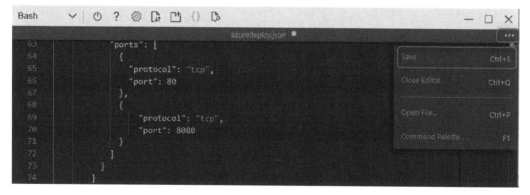

Figure 11.35 – Azure Cloud Shell: Visual Studio Code (VS Code)

The following code snippet contains the ARM template code for deploying your container instances:

```json
{
    "$schema": "https://schema.management.azure.com/
schemas/2019-04-01/deploymentTemplate.json#",
    "contentVersion": "1.0.0.0",
    "parameters": {
      "containerGroupName": {
        "type": "string",
        "defaultValue": "myfirstcontainergroup",
        "metadata": {
          "description": "My First Container Group"
        }
      }
    },
    "variables": {
      "container1name": "aci-tutorial-app",
      "container1image": "mcr.microsoft.com/azuredocs/
aci-helloworld:latest",
      "container2name": "aci-tutorial-sidecar",
      "container2image": "mcr.microsoft.com/azuredocs/
aci-tutorial-sidecar"
    },
    "resources": [
      {
        "name": "[parameters('containerGroupName')]",
        "type": "Microsoft.ContainerInstance/
containerGroups",
        "apiVersion": "2019-12-01",
        "location": "[resourceGroup().location]",
        "properties": {
          "containers": [
            {
              "name": "[variables('container1name')]",
              "properties": {
                "image": "[variables('container1image')]",
                "resources": {
```

```
              "requests": {
                "cpu": 1,
                "memoryInGb": 1.5
              }
            },
            "ports": [
              {
                "port": 80
              },
              {
                "port": 8080
              }
            ]
          }
        },
        {
          "name": "[variables('container2name')]",
          "properties": {
            "image": "[variables('container2image')]",
            "resources": {
              "requests": {
                "cpu": 1,
                "memoryInGb": 1.5
              }
            }
          }
        }
      ],
      "osType": "Linux",
      "ipAddress": {
        "type": "Public",
        "ports": [
          {
            "protocol": "tcp",
            "port": 80
          },
```

```
            {
                "protocol": "tcp",
                "port": 8080
            }
         ]
       }
     }
    }
  ],
  "outputs": {
    "containerIPv4Address": {
       "type": "string",
       "value": "[reference(resourceId('Microsoft.
ContainerInstance/containerGroups/',
parameters('containerGroupName'))).ipAddress.ip]"
     }
   }
 }
```

5. Now, type in the following code to deploy the ARM template:

```
az deployment group create --resource-group AZ104-
Chapter11 --template-file azuredeploy.json
```

Press *Enter*. This will take a few minutes to run and will show the following output:

```
az104admin@Azure:~$ az deployment group create --resource-group AZ104-Chapter11 --template-file azuredeploy.json
[\] Running ..
```

Figure 11.36 – ARM template deployment

6. Once your deployment has completed, you can close the Cloud Shell window by clicking the cross on the top-right bar, as illustrated in the following screenshot:

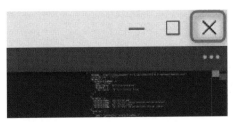

Figure 11.37 – Closing VS Code

Navigate to the resource group where you deployed your container group. Open the container group resource by clicking on it. On the **Overview** pane, note the public IP address and that you have two containers. Copy the IP address to your browser, and note that you can connect to the site where your container group is functional, as illustrated in the following screenshot:

Figure 11.38 – Container group public IP

7. Click on the **Containers** menu option on the left pane and note your two containers are deployed to the container group, as illustrated in the following screenshot:

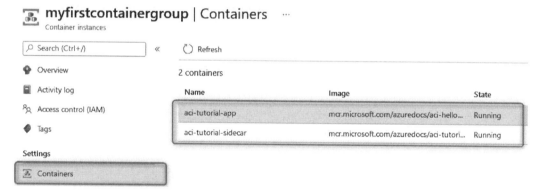

Figure 11.39 – Container group: Containers

You have just successfully deployed your first container group in Azure. In the next section, we will explore how to manage the sizing and scaling of your deployed container instances.

Configuring sizing and scaling for Azure container instances

Azure container instances cannot be resized after deployment; you will notice there are no options to do so in the Azure portal. The only way to resize a container instance is to redeploy the solution with the required size. If you are looking to scale horizontally (multiple instances), you can achieve this through the container group or by deploying several instances. To configure sizing for your container instance, you will recall that on the instance setup, there is a **Change size** sizing option, as illustrated in the following screenshot:

Figure 11.40 – ACI: Size

The following screen will pop up for you to configure the desired size for your container instance:

Change container ...   ✕

Configure the resource requirements for your container. The available values are based on region, OS type, and networking options. Learn more about resource requirements in ACI ⧉

Number of CPU cores * ⓘ

| 1 | ✓ |

1-4

Memory (GiB) * ⓘ

| 1.5 | ✓ |

1-16

GPU type (Preview) * ⓘ

| None | ⌄ |

Ok   Discard

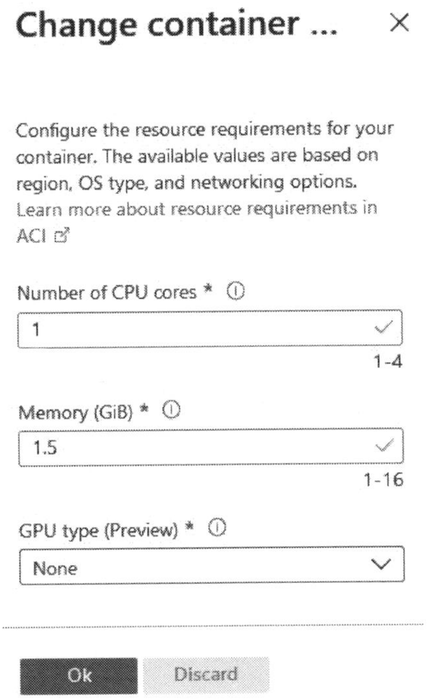

Figure 11.41 – ACI: Size options

For **Number of CPU cores**, you can select a value between 1 and 4. You can select from between 1 and 16 for **Memory (GiB)**. Where you have GPU-based applications or requirements, you will note that you can change your GPU type. Note that GPUs are only available to some regions, and at the time of writing, this is still a preview feature. The options available are K80, P100, or V100. The GPU selected enables further options for selecting the number of GPUs you would like, 1, 2, or 4, as shown in the following screenshot:

Figure 11.42 – ACI: GPU options

> **Top Tip**
>
> 1 **gibibyte (GiB)** = 1,024 **mebibyte (MiB)** where GB = 1,000 **megabytes (MB)**. Most people refer to MB or GB, and due to easy conversions and the internet industry, the conversion is often defined as 1,000 MB in 1 GB, where computers work on a binary-based number system, meaning that all numbers are calculated from a base of 2. Therefore, GiB is defined as 2^10 MiB, which is 1,024.

You now know about the sizing available to container instances, so in the next section, we will explore how Kubernetes can assist in the management of our containers.

Deploying AKS

This exercise is to help you gain familiarity with AKS. We will deploy our first AKS instance, and then with the corresponding exercises, we will explore the different management components for this. Proceed as follows:

1. Sign in to the Azure portal at `https://portal.azure.com`.

2. Open the resource group you will be using for this exercise, click **Overview** on the left menu, then click **Create**.

3. On the left **Category** menu, select **Containers**, then click **Create** under **Kubernetes Service**, as illustrated in the following screenshot:

Figure 11.43 – Creating an Azure Kubernetes service

4. Select your **Resource group** type, enter your **Kubernetes cluster name** value, select your **Region** type, and then leave all the other settings on their default configuration and click **Next: Node pools >**. The process is illustrated in the following screenshot:

Create Kubernetes cluster   ···

Basics   Node pools   Authentication   Networking   Integrations   Tags   Review + create

Azure Kubernetes Service (AKS) manages your hosted Kubernetes environment, making it quick and easy to deploy and manage containerized applications without container orchestration expertise. It also eliminates the burden of ongoing operations and maintenance by provisioning, upgrading, and scaling resources on demand, without taking your applications offline. Learn more about Azure Kubernetes Service

Project details

Select a subscription to manage deployed resources and costs. Use resource groups like folders to organize and manage all your resources.

Subscription * ⓘ	AzureTraining ∨
Resource group * ⓘ	AZ104-Chapter11 ∨
	Create new

Cluster details

Cluster preset configuration	**Standard ($$)**
	Quickly customize your cluster by choosing the preset configuration applicable to your scenario. Depending on the selection, values of certain fields might change in different tabs. You can modify these values at any time.
	View all preset configurations
Kubernetes cluster name * ⓘ	myfirstakscluster ∨
Region * ⓘ	(Africa) South Africa North ∨
Availability zones ⓘ	Zones 1,2,3 ∨
	🔆 High availability is recommended for standard configuration.
Kubernetes version * ⓘ	1.20.9 (default) ∨

Primary node pool

Review + create		< Previous	Next : Node pools >

Figure 11.44 – Creating a Kubernetes cluster

5. Scroll down the page, and note that we can change the **Node size** value. Changing this option allows you to choose a size very similar to what you saw in the previous chapter with VMs. Next, you can select how you would like to manage scaling; this can be either **Manual** or **Autoscale**. **Manual** means that you would like to modify the scale count yourself whenever you would like to change the count of nodes for your pool, whereas **Autoscale** will allow you to scale automatically based on a scaling rule. For this option, you select a range being the minimum number of nodes you want and the maximum you would like to scale it up to. As you can see, there is a lot of room for scaling with this service. Click **Next: Node pools >**. The process is illustrated in the following screenshot:

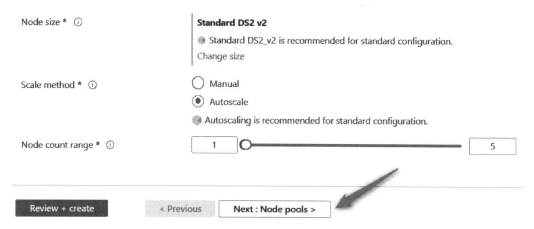

Primary node pool

The number and size of nodes in the primary node pool in your cluster. For production workloads, at least 3 nodes are recommended for resiliency. For development or test workloads, only one node is required. If you would like to add additional node pools or to see additional configuration options for this node pool, go to the 'Node pools' tab above. You will be able to add additional node pools after creating your cluster. Learn more about node pools in Azure Kubernetes Service

Node size * ⓘ	**Standard DS2 v2**
	Standard DS2_v2 is recommended for standard configuration.
	Change size
Scale method * ⓘ	◯ Manual
	◉ Autoscale
	Autoscaling is recommended for standard configuration.
Node count range * ⓘ	1 ──O────── 5

Review + create   < Previous   Next : Node pools >

Figure 11.45 – Primary node pool sizing

6. On the **Node pools** tab, you will note the ability to add additional pools that can also be configured to scale in the same fashion as the **Primary node pool** type we configured in the previous step. You also have the **Enable virtual nodes** option, which enables you to scale your containers beyond your VM specified in the previous steps, and scale to use ACI as additional nodes when AKS needs to scale out. The final option available is **Enable virtual machine scale sets**. You will note that it is already checked for our deployment, the reason being that it's required to support the **Availability zones** configuration we have from *Step 4*. Scale sets enable us to have a scaling VM supporting the container service; this allows better scaling of resources when it's required since a single VM will be limited in the number of containers it can host. This also enables dynamic scaling (no downtime) due to horizontal scaling ability. Having to change the size vertically (such as more or fewer resources—essentially, the **stock-keeping unit** (**SKU**)) would result in losing access to the resource temporarily while it's resized and restarted. This is a more static type of scaling. Next, click **Next: Authentication >**. The process is illustrated in the following screenshot:

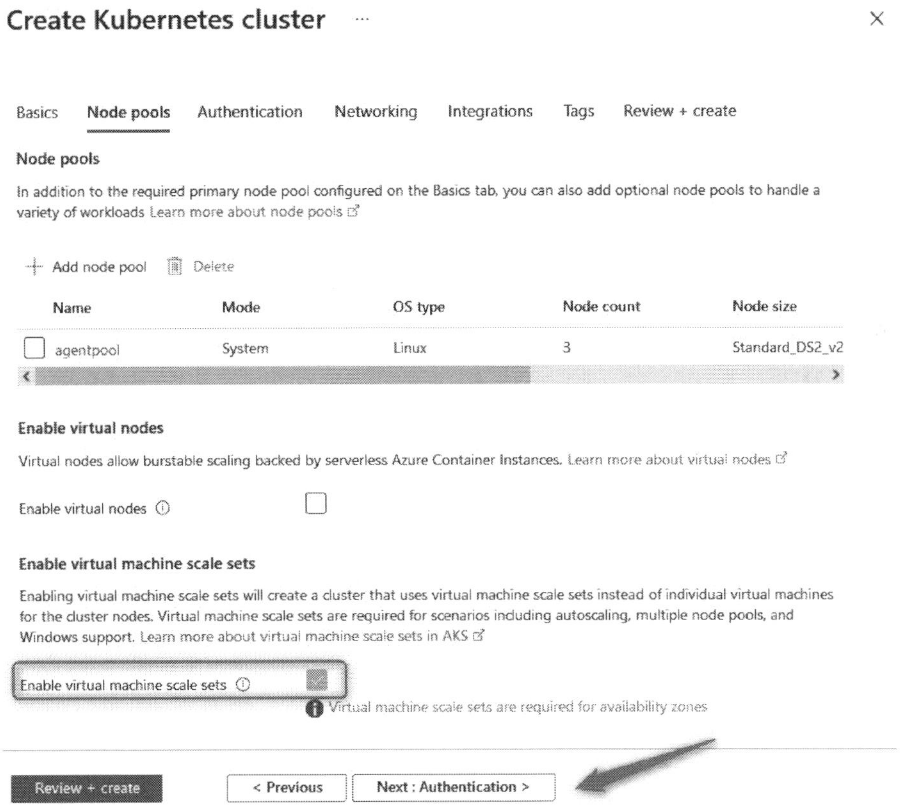

Figure 11.46 – Creating a Kubernetes cluster: Node pools tab

7. Next, we have the **Authentication** tab; here, you will note we can modify the setting for the **Authentication method** type to either **Service principal** or **System-assigned managed identity**. This will be used by AKS for managing the infrastructure related to the service. For this exercise, we will leave this at its default setting. Then, you have the **Role-based access control (RBAC)** option. By default, this is set to **Enabled**; this is the best option to manage the service as it allows fine-grained access control over the resource; leave this as **Enabled**. You will also have the choice to enable **AKS-managed Azure Active Directory**. Checking this will enable you to manage permissions for users on the service based on their group membership within Azure AD. Note that once this function has been enabled, it can't be disabled again, so **leave this unchecked** for this exercise. Finally, you have the option of the **Encryption type** value you want. For this exercise, leave it as the default setting. Click **Next: Networking >**. The process is illustrated in the following screenshot:

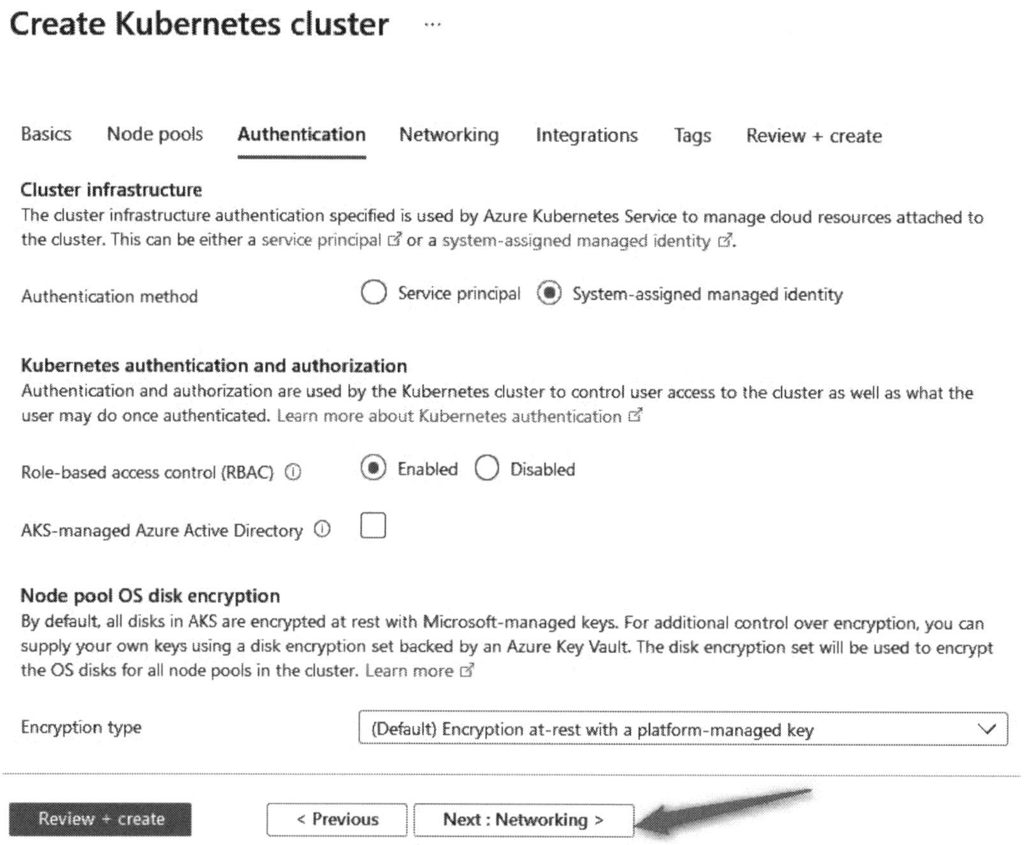

Create Kubernetes cluster   ...

Basics   Node pools   **Authentication**   Networking   Integrations   Tags   Review + create

Cluster infrastructure

The cluster infrastructure authentication specified is used by Azure Kubernetes Service to manage cloud resources attached to the cluster. This can be either a service principal ☐ or a system-assigned managed identity ☐.

Authentication method   ◯ Service principal ⦿ System-assigned managed identity

Kubernetes authentication and authorization

Authentication and authorization are used by the Kubernetes cluster to control user access to the cluster as well as what the user may do once authenticated. Learn more about Kubernetes authentication ☐

Role-based access control (RBAC) ⓘ   ⦿ Enabled ◯ Disabled

AKS-managed Azure Active Directory ⓘ   ☐

Node pool OS disk encryption

By default, all disks in AKS are encrypted at rest with Microsoft-managed keys. For additional control over encryption, you can supply your own keys using a disk encryption set backed by an Azure Key Vault. The disk encryption set will be used to encrypt the OS disks for all node pools in the cluster. Learn more ☐

Encryption type   [(Default) Encryption at-rest with a platform-managed key   ⌄]

[Review + create]   [< Previous]   [Next : Networking >]

Figure 11.47 – Creating a Kubernetes cluster: Authentication tab

8. For the **Networking** section, we will leave most of the settings as their default configuration. Note that for **Network configurations** we have two options here, one for **Kubenet** and another for **Azure CNI**. kubenet is a new VNet for the cluster whereby Pods are allocated an IP address and containers have **network address translation (NAT)** connections over the shared Pod IP. **Azure Container Networking Interface (Azure CNI)** enables Pods to be directly connected to a VNet. In association, this allows containers to have an IP mapped to them directly, removing the need for NAT connection. Next, we have the **DNS name prefix** field, which will form the first part of your FQDN for the service. You will then notice **Traffic routing** options available to us for the service—we will discuss this more in one of the next exercises, as well as the **Security** options available to us. Select **Calico** under **Network policy**. Click **Next: Integrations >**. The process is illustrated in the following screenshot:

Create Kubernetes cluster   ···

Basics	Node pools	Authentication	**Networking**	Integrations	Tags	Review + create

You can change networking settings for your cluster, including enabling HTTP application routing and configuring your network using either the 'Kubenet' or 'Azure CNI' options:

- The **kubenet** networking plug-in creates a new VNet for your cluster using default values.
- The **Azure CNI** networking plug-in allows clusters to use a new or existing VNet with customizable addresses. Application pods are connected directly to the VNet, which allows for native integration with VNet features.

Learn more about networking in Azure Kubernetes Service

Network configuration ⓘ
  ◉ Kubenet
  ◯ Azure CNI

DNS name prefix * ⓘ
  myfirstakscluster-dns   ✓

Traffic routing

Load balancer ⓘ   Standard

Enable HTTP application routing ⓘ   ☐

Security

Enable private cluster ⓘ   ☐

Set authorized IP ranges ⓘ   ☐

Network policy ⓘ
  ◯ None
  ◉ Calico
  ◯ Azure
  ❶ The Azure network policy is not compatible with kubenet networking.

| Review + create | | < Previous | Next : Integrations > |

Figure 11.48 – Creating a Kubernetes cluster: Networking tab

9. On the **Integrations** tab, you will note the option to select a container registry. We will select the registry that we previously deployed. You will also note you have the option to deploy a new registry directly from this creation dialog. Next, we have the option to deploy container monitoring into the solution on creation. We will leave the default setting here, but monitoring will not be covered under the scope of this chapter. Finally, you have the option of applying Azure Policy directly to the solution; this is recommended where you want to enhance and standardize your deployments. This solution enables you to deliver consistently and control your deployments on AKS more effectively. Click **Review + create**, then click **Create**. The process is illustrated in the following screenshot:

Create Kubernetes cluster ...

Connect your AKS cluster with additional services.

Azure Container Registry
Connect your cluster to an Azure Container Registry to enable seamless deployments from a private image registry. You can create a new registry or choose one you already have. Learn more about Azure Container Registry ☐

Container registry	az104myfirstregistry13122021 ⌄
	Create new

Azure Monitor
In addition to the CPU and memory metrics included in AKS by default, you can enable Container Insights for more comprehensive data on the overall performance and health of your cluster. Billing is based on data ingestion and retention settings.
Learn more about container performance and health monitoring
Learn more about pricing

Container monitoring	◉ Enabled ◯ Disabled
	🖼 Azure monitor is recommended for standard configuration.
Log Analytics workspace ⓘ	DefaultWorkspace-cbc90806-9c61-4800-85a9-f153dc804a15-WEU ⌄
	Create new

Azure Policy
Apply at-scale enforcements and safeguards for AKS clusters in a centralized, consistent manner through Azure Policy.
Learn more about Azure Policy for AKS ☐

Azure Policy	◯ Enabled ◉ Disabled

Review + create		< Previous	Next : Tags >

Figure 11.49 – Creating a Kubernetes cluster: deployment

You have just successfully deployed your first Kubernetes cluster; you now know how to deploy and manage containers at scale and in a standardized way. Next, we will look at how we configure storage for Kubernetes and make persistent storage available to our solution.

Configuring storage for AKS

AKS enables different storage options available for containers; you can leverage either local (non-persistent) storage or shared storage (persistent storage) for your containers through AKS. For persistent storage options, you can leverage Azure Managed Disks, which is primarily focused on premium storage solutions, such as for fast **input/output (I/O)** operations, as we discussed in *Chapter 6, Understanding and Managing Storage*. Azure File Shares is another option available and the default storage mechanism for enabling persistent storage on containers. This is typically cheaper to deploy and provides decent levels of performance for most workloads. For better performance, premium file shares can be used. Azure File Shares is also great for sharing data between containers and other services, whereas a managed disk will be restricted to a single Pod but is easier to deploy.

The following diagram illustrates the different storage options available:

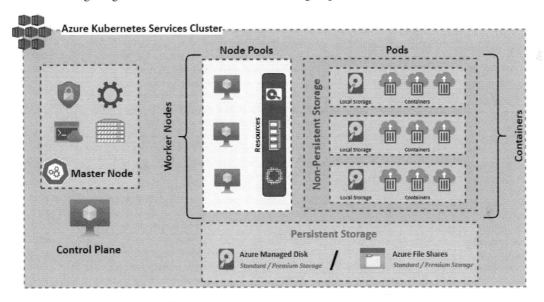

Figure 11.50 – Kubernetes: Storage layers

In this exercise, we will configure shared storage using Azure File Shares in your AKS cluster. Proceed as follows:

1. Sign in to the Azure portal at `https://portal.azure.com`.

2. Create a storage account and a file share named `fileshare01`. Once created, note the primary storage account key.

3. Launch Azure Cloud Shell and run the following commands. Replace the resource group name with your name and the AKS cluster name for the **Name** field:

```
Az login
Install-AzAksKubectl
Import-AzAksCredential -ResourceGroupName AZ104-Chapter11
-Name myfirstakscluster
```

4. Modify the following script with your storage account name and storage account key, then paste it into Cloud Shell and press *Enter*:

```
kubectl create secret generic azure-secret --from-literal
=azurestorageaccountname=storageaccountname --from-litera
l=azurestorageaccountkey=storageaccountkey
```

5. Navigate to the AKS cluster you created in the previous section. Click on **Storage** on the left menu, then ensure you are on the **Persistent volume claims** tab, and click **Add**, as illustrated in the following screenshot:

Figure 11.51 – Adding a persistent volume claim

6. Click **Add with YAML**, as illustrated in the following screenshot:

Figure 11.52 – Add with YAML

7. Paste or type the following YAML document into the window:

```
apiVersion: v1
kind: PersistentVolume
```

```
metadata:
  name: azurefile
spec:
  capacity:
    storage: 5Gi
  accessModes:
    - ReadWriteMany
  azureFile:
    secretName: azure-secret
    shareName: fileshare01
    readOnly: false
  mountOptions:
  - dir_mode=0777
  - file_mode=0777
  - uid=1000
  - gid=1000
  - mfsymlinks
  - nobrl
```

Then, click **Add**, as illustrated in the following screenshot. This will create your **persistent volume**:

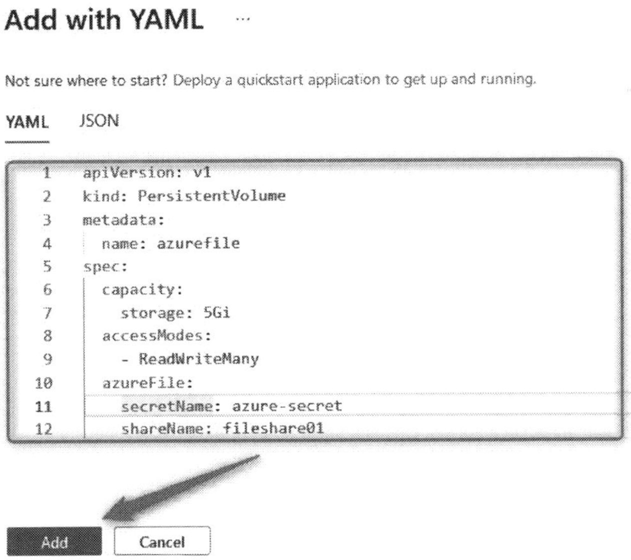

Figure 11.53 – Adding a persistent volume using YAML

8. Now, to create a **persistent volume claim**, click **Add** again, and paste the following YAML. Click **Add**:

```
apiVersion: v1
kind: PersistentVolumeClaim
metadata:
  name: azurefile
spec:
  accessModes:
    - ReadWriteMany
  storageClassName: ""
  resources:
    requests:
      storage: 5Gi
```

9. You now have a persistent volume claim. Click on the **Persistent volume claims** tab, as illustrated in the following screenshot:

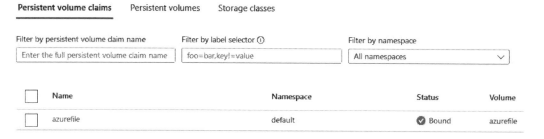

Figure 11.54 – Persistent volume claims tab

10. Note your persistent volumes by clicking on the **Persistent volumes** tab, as illustrated in the following screenshot:

Name	Capacity	Access modes	Reclaim policy	Status
azurefile	5Gi	ReadWriteMany	Retain	✔ Bound

Figure 11.55 – Persistent volumes tab

You have successfully added persistent storage to your AKS cluster. You now know the tasks involved to achieve this goal. In the next section, we will explore AKS scaling.

Configuring scaling for AKS

You will note that from our previous exercises, there was no option to automatically scale and resize containers. The only way to change this was to redeploy our container instances and groups. With Kubernetes, this dynamic changes as you can change the scale settings before and after your deployment, and they can be configured to scale manually or automatically. For this exercise, we will run through changing the auto-scale settings of our AKS cluster. Proceed as follows:

1. Sign in to the Azure portal at `https://portal.azure.com`.

2. Navigate to the AKS cluster you created in the previous section. On the left menu, select the **Node pools** option and click on your deployed `agentpool` node pool, as illustrated in the following screenshot:

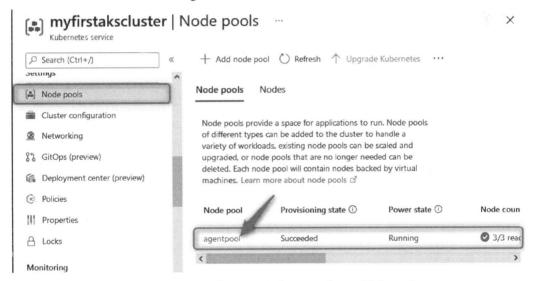

Figure 11.56 – Configuring a Kubernetes cluster: Node pools

3. Selecting either the **Overview** or **Configuration** pane will present you with the option to change your pool scale settings. Click **Scale node pool**, as illustrated in the following screenshot:

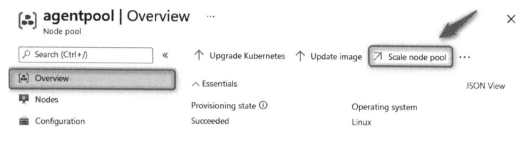

Figure 11.57 – Configuring a Kubernetes cluster: Overview

4. To change the automatic scale option, set the **Scale method** type to **Autoscale**, enter a value for your **Min** and **Max** node count, then click **Apply**. The process is illustrated in the following screenshot:

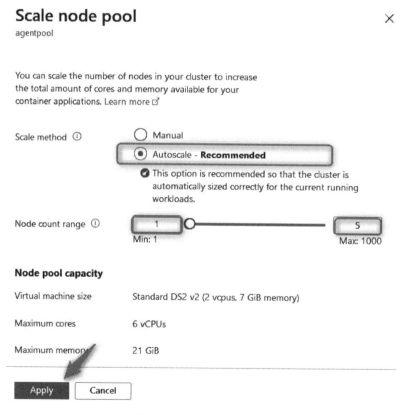

Figure 11.58 – Configuring a Kubernetes cluster: Scale node pool

5. For the manual scale option, set the **Scale method** type to **Manual**, enter a **Node count** value (this will be the number of nodes you want to run), and click **Apply**. The process is illustrated in the following screenshot:

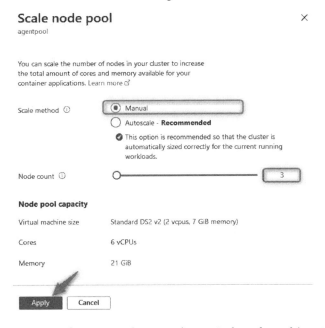

Figure 11.59 – Configuring a Kubernetes cluster: Scale node pool (continued)

6. After applying the settings, you will notice your agent pool goes into an **Updating** state, as illustrated in the following screenshot:

Figure 11.60 – Configuring a Kubernetes cluster: Updating

You now know how to scale your agent pools within AKS and can feel confident about managing this aspect. If you would like to change the VM size for the agent pool, you will need to redeploy the pool. In the next section, we will look at managing network configurations on your AKS cluster.

Configuring network connections for AKS

We have covered AKS cluster deployment in one of the previous exercises. In this section, we will elaborate on some networking configurations to give you a better understanding of the options available to you.

Network configuration

The first component in your network configuration is the different types of networks that are available for you to deploy.

kubenet

This is the most basic networking service for AKS. With kubenet, an IP address is allocated from an Azure VNet to the nodes for a Pod. The Pods receive an IP address from an internal network that is deployed in a logically different address space from the VNet. Connections to these Pods are then performed through NAT connections that allow Pods to communicate to resources on the Azure VNet. This approach reduces the number of IP addresses required for your solution but disables the ability to directly connect to your containers.

Azure CNI

This is a more advanced implementation networking service for AKS. Azure CNI enables Pods to be directly connected to an Azure VNet, and therefore every Pod is allocated an IP address on the VNet. Without careful planning, you may exhaust your IP allocation on the subnet you are connecting to.

Regardless of the solution you choose, external traffic is still conducted over a NAT connection to nodes within AKS from a public IP interface.

Traffic routing

Traffic routing comprises the load balancing and application routing configurations available to your AKS cluster.

Load balancer

The AKS cluster can be deployed using both a **standard SKU** and a **basic SKU**. A standard SKU enforces traffic securely, restricts traffic by default, and requires explicit allow rules to enable traffic flow. The default option is **Standard** and is the recommended choice unless there is a specific reason for **Basic**, such as your organization only allowing private IP access. **Basic** can only be deployed using the Azure **command-line interface** (**CLI**), PowerShell, or an ARM template.

Enabling HTTP application routing

Please note before enabling this feature that it is currently not designed or ready for production environments and is something I would advise being cautious about enabling until Microsoft's documentation reflects that this is ready for production use.

The solution deploys two components, one being an **External-DNS controller** component, which creates DNS host A records for the cluster DNS zone, and the second resource being an **ingress controller** component, which is responsible for routing ingress traffic to application endpoints.

Security

When configuring your network for AKS, you should consider the security components that also impact your design and management decisions. There are several items to consider (which we discuss in the following sections) that can improve the security of your containers.

Enabling a private cluster

For enhanced security, you can enable a private cluster. This ensures that traffic between your **application programming interface (API)** server and node pools is conducted over private network paths only. When configured, the control plane (API server) is run within the AKS-managed Azure subscription while your AKS cluster runs in your own subscription. This separation is key. Communication will then occur over a private endpoint (private link) from your AKS cluster to the private link service for the AKS VNet.

Setting authorized IP ranges

These are ranges that you will limit to accessing your AKS cluster. This can be specified as a single IP, as a list of IP addresses, or as a range of IP addresses in **classless inter-domain routing (CIDR)** notation.

The following screenshot is an example of setting authorized IP addresses:

Figure 11.61 – Authorized IP addresses

You now understand the role that authorized IP ranges play in your AKS deployment. Next, we will explore the impact that network policy has on deployments.

Network policy

This is used to manage traffic flow between Pods in an AKS cluster. By default, all traffic is allowed, and by utilizing network policy, you enable the mechanism to manage this traffic using Linux iptables. Two implementations can be followed: **Calico** and **Azure Network Policies**. Calico is an open source solution provided by Tigera, whereas Azure has its own implementation of the same type of technology. Both services are fully compliant with the Kubernetes specification. The choice of network policy provider can only be chosen on the creation of the AKS cluster and can't be changed, so it's pivotal that you understand the differences between the solutions prior to making your choice.

The key differences between the solutions are presented here:

Supported systems	Calico supports both Linux and Windows Server 2019 (in preview), whereas Azure's service only supports Linux.
Supported networking options	Calico supports both Azure CNI and kubenet, whereas Azure's service only supports Azure CNI.
Support options	Calico is supported by the Calico community and not Azure, whereas the Azure service is fully supported by the Azure support and engineering teams.

Upgrading an AKS cluster

You have the choice to automatically upgrade your AKS clusters or to manually manage upgrades yourself. As part of your upgrade decisions, you can decide if you would like to upgrade both the node pools and control plane or the control plane only. Automatic upgrades have the option of choosing different channels that best apply to your requirements; these are listed as follows:

- **None**: Used for disabling auto upgrading.

- **Patch**: The cluster is automatically updated to the latest support patch version.

- **Stable**: The cluster is automatically updated to the latest stable version.

- **Rapid**: The cluster is automatically updated to the latest N-2 minor version.

- **Node-image**: The cluster is automatically updated to the latest version available.

> **Top Tip**
>
> It's important to note that when upgrading your AKS clusters, you will upgrade to a supported patch version for your cluster, one version at a time where more than one version upgrade exists.

We will now perform the exercise of upgrading your cluster with the following steps:

1. Sign in to the Azure portal at `https://portal.azure.com`.

2. Navigate to the AKS cluster you created in the previous section. On the left menu, select the **Cluster configuration** option and click **Upgrade version** on the right, as illustrated in the following screenshot:

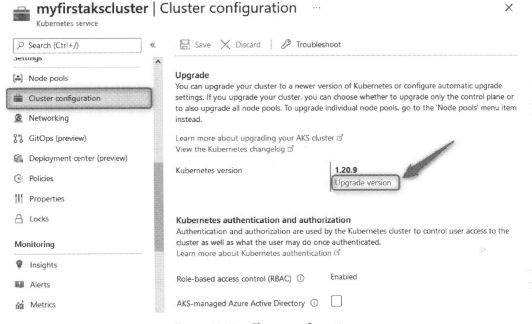

Figure 11.62 – Cluster configuration

3. Select your desired Kubernetes version and select an **Upgrade scope** type, then click **Save**. The process is illustrated in the following screenshot:

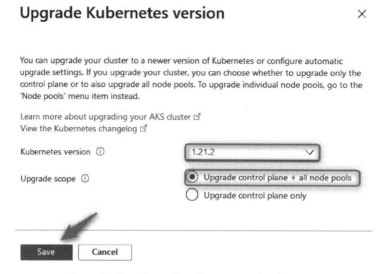

Figure 11.63 – Upgrading the version of Kubernetes

You have just successfully upgraded your Kubernetes version and understood the various automated options also available to do this. Next, we will run through the chapter summary and all that we have covered in this chapter.

Summary

In this chapter, we discovered what containers are and how we deploy and manage them, we learned about Docker, the limitations of Docker, and container deployments, and finally, we found out how we can extend default container services through orchestration tools such as Kubernetes that greatly enhance the way we manage and scale containers. As part of your learning, you have discovered how to work with ACI Instances and learned how to also attach persistent storage to containers using AKS, how to enhance the security around containers, and about the various networking options available to you as part of AKS. You also experienced working with deployments and administrative tasks such as creating an Azure container registry, deploying Azure container instances, and creating and configuring Azure container groups.

You should now feel confident about the administration of containers within Azure, the methods of deployment, and how to orchestrate and manage these.

In the next chapter, we will explore Azure App Service, what this is, how to configure and deploy it, and becoming confident in how to use this on Azure.

12
Creating and Configuring App Services

This chapter focuses on how to create and configure app services in Azure. We will explore what app services are, the relevance they have, and why you should consider using them. You will also learn about the administrative functions you will need to perform concerning app services, such as configurations, scaling, backups, and networking integrations. After reading this chapter, you should be confident in how to administer these services and how to present solutions when needed.

In this chapter, we are going to cover the following main topics:

- Understanding App Service plans and App Service
- Creating an App Service plan
- Creating an app service
- Configuring the scaling settings of an App Service plan
- Securing an app service
- Configuring custom domain names

- Configuring a backup for an app service
- Configuring network settings
- Configuring deployment settings

Technical requirements

For this chapter, you will need the following:

- Access to an Azure subscription with owner or contributor privileges. If you do not have access to one, you can enroll for a free account: `https://azure.microsoft.com/en-in/free/`.

- **PowerShell 5.1** or later must be installed on a PC where this chapter's labs can be practiced. Note that many of this chapter's examples can only be followed from a PC or by going to `https://shell.azure.com` (PowerShell 7.0.6 LTS or above is recommended).

- The Az PowerShell module must be installed.

Understanding App Service plans and App Service

When discussing Azure app services and understanding what they are, compared to traditional servers, it's important to understand the relationship between **Infrastructure as a Service (IaaS)**, **Platform as a Service (PaaS)**, **Software as a Service (SaaS)**, and serverless (such as **Function as a service (FaaS)**). As you move through the different service offerings, you have different layers of responsibility that you manage. This is also the easiest way of understanding the differences between the services. IaaS, PaaS, SaaS, and serverless are cloud-based services and fit well into the Azure platform since Microsoft has developed some great ways to manage the services you deploy. This also allows you to choose the level of control you would like to adopt. There are limitations to each model, which is a much deeper topic, but understanding these limitations at a core level will help you succeed in your Azure journey. The following diagram illustrates the management relationships between the cloud-based services:

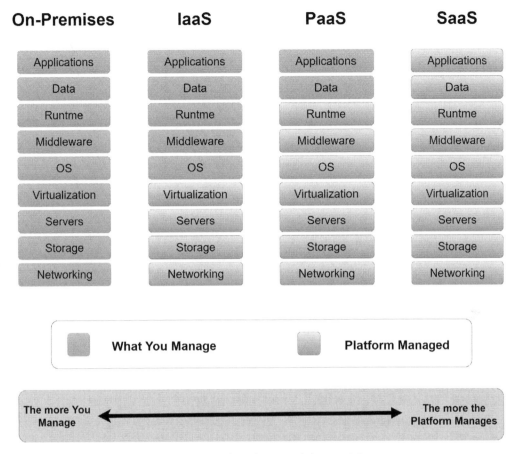

Figure 12.1 – Shared responsibility model

As you can see, the closer you approach SaaS, the fewer components you are required to manage and, subsequently, can manage. Finally, the serverless component can be a little confusing as it falls between the PaaS and SaaS layers; you can only manage your code and, ideally, split your code into single repeatable components called functions. Serverless components are also classified as **microservices** since the services are broken down into their most basic forms. Here, you define the functions you need to run your code; you can deploy the code and forget about which server it runs on. This approach does lead to more in-depth and complex discussions that are beyond the scope of this book; you just need to understand that this exists and that in Azure, we often refer to it as FaaS. Now that you understand the relationship between these services and what you manage, we can classify Azure app services. They fall into the PaaS category; therefore, you only have to worry about how you manage your application and its data. You also have the choice to secure your application using controls that have been exposed to Azure. The rest is taken care of by the platform itself.

App Service plans

To run your applications, you must deploy and configure your server infrastructure appropriately to suit your applications. For example, your applications may require the Windows operating system and the .NET Framework. To accommodate these configurations, Azure has App Service plans. This is a server that's related to your application deployments, where you can choose an operating system, the number of nodes in your cluster, server-related security configurations, and operations. It also allows you to run several applications against a server with the chosen specifications for memory and CPU resources and only scales as per your requirements or budget.

> **Top Tip**
>
> Although Azure Functions falls into the serverless category, when assigned to an App Service plan, it becomes a PaaS service since it is linked to a server. This increases what you can manage on the service and allows better control over, for example, security features.

Now that you understand more about Azure App Service and App Service plans, let's dive into some exercises where we will work with these later. In the next section, we will deploy an App Service plan and dive into the available configuration options.

Creating an App Service plan

In this exercise, you will be creating an App Service plan for Azure. This will act as the server configuration for hosting your Azure web applications and function applications. Follow these steps to do so:

1. Sign in to the Azure portal at `https://portal.azure.com`.

2. Open the resource group you will be using for this exercise, click **Overview** via the left menu, and click **Create**.

3. Type `app service plan` in the search bar and click **App Service Plan**:

Figure 12.2 – App Service Plan

4. On the next screen, click **Create**:

Figure 12.3 – App Service Plan – Create

5. Enter the name of your **Resource Group**, then enter a name for your App Service plan. Here, we have used myappserviceplan. Next, choose an **Operating System**. For this demo, we will deploy a **Windows** App Service plan. Finally, select your **Region** and **SKU and size**; we will select **Standard S1**. Click **Review + create**, then **Create**:

Create App Service Plan   ⋯

Basics   Tags   Review + create

App Service plans give you the flexibility to allocate specific apps to a given set of resources and further optimize your Azure resource utilization. This way, if you want to save money on your testing environment you can share a plan across multiple apps. Learn more ⧉

Project Details

Select a subscription to manage deployed resources and costs. Use resource groups like folders to organize and manage all your resources.

Subscription * ⓘ	AzureTraining ⌄
└ Resource Group * ⓘ	AZ104-Chapter12 ⌄
	Create new

App Service Plan details

Name *	myappserviceplan ⌄
Operating System *	○ Linux ⦿ Windows
Region *	West Europe ⌄

Pricing Tier

App Service plan pricing tier determines the location, features, cost and compute resources associated with your app. Learn more ⧉

Sku and size *	**Standard S1**
	100 total ACU, 1.75 GB memory
	Change size

Review + create   < Previous   Next : Tags >

Figure 12.4 – Create App Service Plan

With that, you have configured your first App Service plan and are ready to host your first application on the service. In the next section, you will learn how to create an App Service in your newly deployed App Service plan.

Creating an app service

In this exercise, you will deploy your first web application in Azure using the Azure Web Apps service. Follow these steps:

1. Sign in to the Azure portal at `https://portal.azure.com`.

2. Open the resource group you will be using for this exercise, click **Overview** via the left menu, and click **Create**.

3. From the left menu bar, click **Web**, then click **Create** under **Web App**:

Figure 12.5 – Web App

4. Enter the name of your **Resource Group**, then enter a name for your web app. Here, we have used `myfirstwebapp221221`. Next, choose the type of deployment you would like. We will select **Code**. Note that you could also select a **Docker Container**. Then, select a **Runtime stack** – this will support the code you are deploying. Now, choose an **Operating System**. For this demo, we will deploy a **Windows** web app; we did this for the App Service plan we deployed previously. Select your **Region**, this will also be the same as what you selected for your App Service plan:

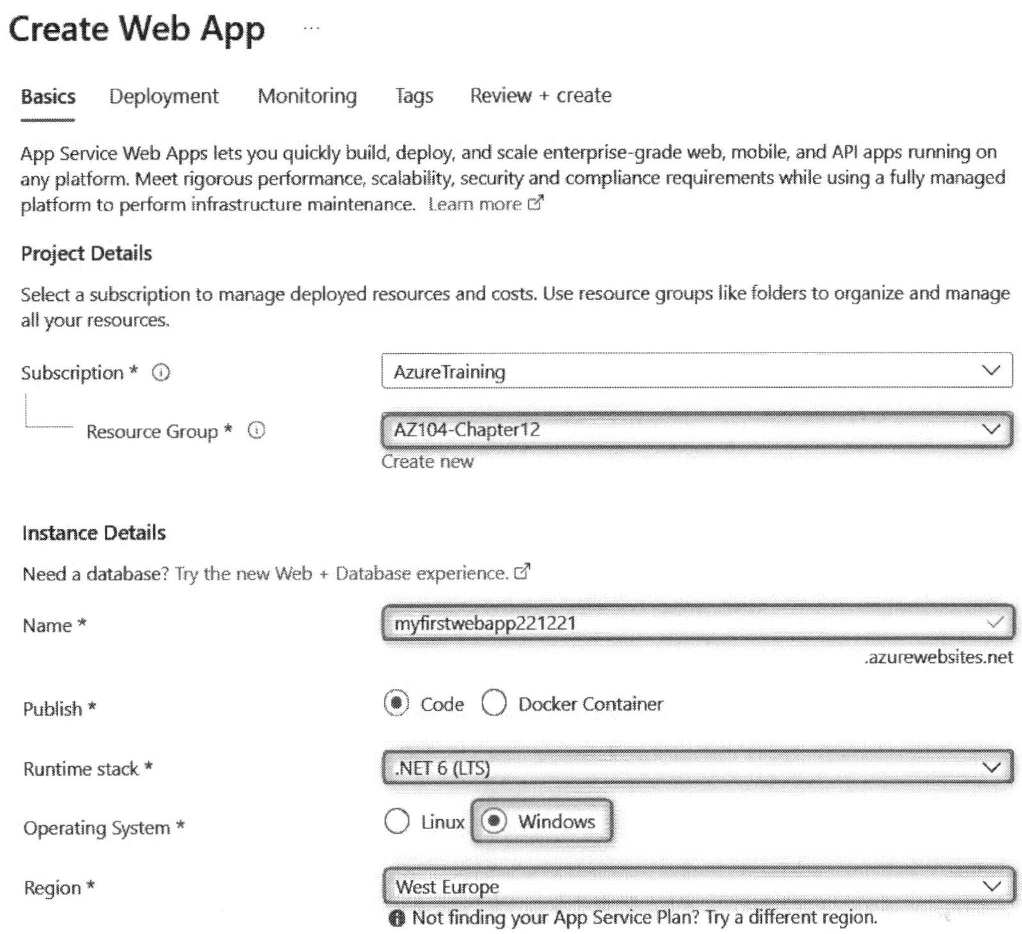

Create Web App   ...

Basics   Deployment   Monitoring   Tags   Review + create

App Service Web Apps lets you quickly build, deploy, and scale enterprise-grade web, mobile, and API apps running on any platform. Meet rigorous performance, scalability, security and compliance requirements while using a fully managed platform to perform infrastructure maintenance. Learn more ☐'

Project Details

Select a subscription to manage deployed resources and costs. Use resource groups like folders to organize and manage all your resources.

Subscription * ⓘ | AzureTraining | ⌄

Resource Group * ⓘ | AZ104-Chapter12 | ⌄
Create new

Instance Details

Need a database? Try the new Web + Database experience. ☐'

Name * | myfirstwebapp221221 | ✓
.azurewebsites.net

Publish * | ⦿ Code ◯ Docker Container

Runtime stack * | .NET 6 (LTS) | ⌄

Operating System * | ◯ Linux ⦿ Windows

Region * | West Europe | ⌄
ⓘ Not finding your App Service Plan? Try a different region.

Figure 12.6 – Create Web App – Basics

Finally, select a **Windows Plan** – this is the App Service plan you created previously. Note that when you select this, it automatically configures your **SKU and size**, which will match what you chose for your App Service plan. Also, note that you have the option to create your App Service plan directly in the **Deployment** menu. Click **Next : Deployment** >:

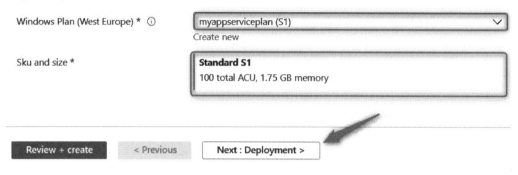

App Service Plan

App Service plan pricing tier determines the location, features, cost and compute resources associated with your app. Learn more ⅽ

Windows Plan (West Europe) * ⓘ   [myappserviceplan (S1)   ⌄]
                                   Create new

Sku and size *   [**Standard S1**
                                     100 total ACU, 1.75 GB memory   ]

[Review + create]   [< Previous]   [Next : Deployment >]

Figure 12.7 – Create Web App – Basics 2

5. Here, you have the option to do a **Continuous deployment**. We won't be configuring this in this exercise. Click **Next : Monitoring** >:

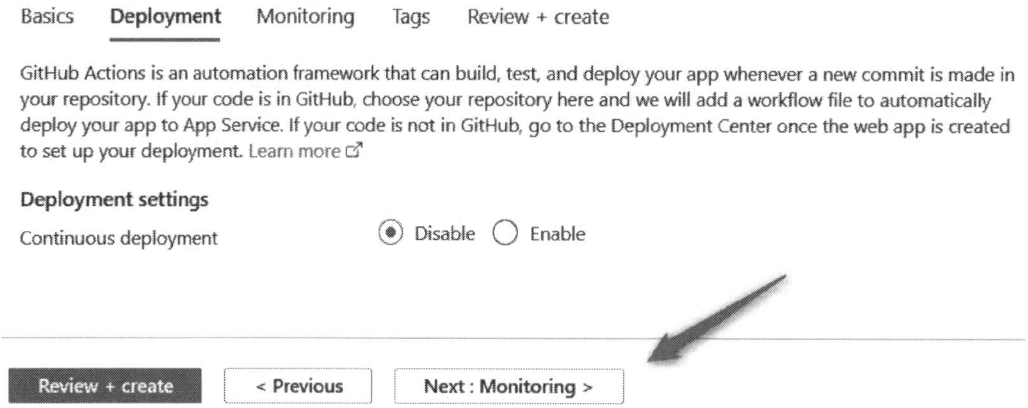

Basics   **Deployment**   Monitoring   Tags   Review + create

GitHub Actions is an automation framework that can build, test, and deploy your app whenever a new commit is made in your repository. If your code is in GitHub, choose your repository here and we will add a workflow file to automatically deploy your app to App Service. If your code is not in GitHub, go to the Deployment Center once the web app is created to set up your deployment. Learn more ⅽ

Deployment settings

Continuous deployment   (●) Disable   ◯ Enable

[Review + create]   [< Previous]   [Next : Monitoring >]

Figure 12.8 – Create Web App – Deployment

6. On the **Monitoring** tab, you will have the option to deploy **Application Insights** for your application. Note that you can either create a new Application Insights deployment through this blade or create it as part of the deployment. For this exercise, we will select **No** for **Enable Application Insights**. Click **Review + create**, then **Create**:

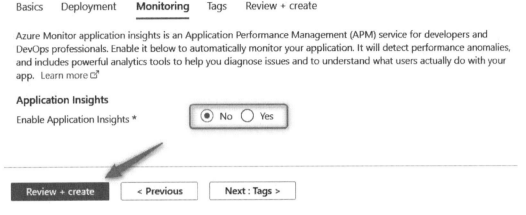

Figure 12.9 – Create Web App – Monitoring

7. Navigate to your application, click on **Overview** via the left-hand menu, and note your **URL** for your application. This blue text is clickable; you can either click on this or copy it into your browser to navigate to your application to confirm that it's working:

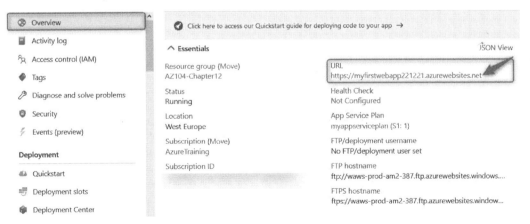

Figure 12.10 – Web App – Overview

You will be presented with a screen similar to the following for your application. Congratulations – you have successfully deployed your application using the Azure portal!

Figure 12.11 – Web App – running in your browser

Now that you know how to deploy a web application using the Azure portal, let's learn how to do the same using PowerShell. This time, we will create a Linux service plan.

PowerShell scripts

Please ensure that the Az module is installed, as per the *Technical requirements* section at the beginning of this chapter.

Here, we are going to create an App Service plan and Web Apps service via PowerShell. To do so, follow these steps:

Note: Change the parameters to suit your requirements

```
# First connect your Azure account using your credentials
Connect-AzAccount

# Parameters
$ResourceGroup = "AZ104-Chapter12"
$Location = "WestEurope"
$SubscriptionId = "xxxxxxx"
$WebAppName = "mysecondwebapp10101"
$AppServicePlanName = "mylinuxappserviceplan10101"
```

```
# If necessary, select the right subscription as follows
Select-AzSubscription -SubscriptionId $SubscriptionId

# Create a resource group for the Availability Set as follows
New-AzResourceGroup -Name "$ResourceGroup" -Location
"$Location"

# Create an App Service Plan for Linux
New-AzAppServicePlan -Name $AppServicePlanName -Tier Standard
-Location $Location -Linux -NumberofWorkers 1 -WorkerSize Small
-ResourceGroupName $ResourceGroup

# Create a Web App
New-AzWebApp -Name $WebAppName -ResourceGroupName
$ResourceGroup -Location $Location -AppServicePlan
$AppServicePlanName
```

Just as you did previously, you can browse to the web application's URL and see the same screen you did prior. With that, you have just completed your first few web application deployments to Azure using the Web Apps service. You should now feel confident in deploying web applications when required in Azure, either through the portal or through PowerShell. Next, you will learn how to scale your applications.

Configuring the scaling settings of an App Service plan

In this exercise, you will configure the scaling settings for the App Service plan you created previously. Recall that we mentioned that there are two different types of scaling options you can choose from. Horizontal scaling (**Scale out** in the application menu) refers to the number of app services that have been deployed, while vertical scaling (**Scale up** in the application menu) refers to the size of the VM hosting the web app service. The VM refers to the App Service plan. As you may recall, we have the option to choose an SKU and size when we deploy that refers to the specifications for the App Service plan that we would like to have. First, we will explore **Scale up**:

1. Navigate to the App Service plan you worked on in the previous exercise.
2. From the left menu blade, under **Settings**, click **Scale up (App Service plan)**.

3. You will be presented with a screen containing different SKU sizes that you can
    choose from. The top bar represents the category that identifies the SKUs that
    are suitable for the type of workloads you will be deploying, such as dev/test
    and production.

    The **Isolated** environment is a more secure environment that deploys a set of
    resources that are isolated from the shared server environment you typically
    consume from; this will cost more to deploy as you will be the only one utilizing
    the server resources you are looking to consume for the applications in your service
    plan. Select **Dev / Test** and then select **B1** as the SKU size. Note that the bottom part
    of the screen will display the features and hardware that are included related to the
    SKU you've selected. Also, note that under the SKUs, you have the option to **See
    additional options**. Click **Apply**:

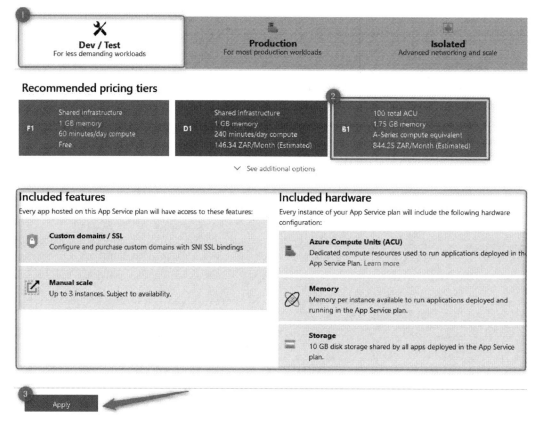

Figure 12.12 – Scale up

Here, you scaled down your application from the S1 SKU to the B1 SKU, which shows how easy it is to change its size. Note that the *application will restart upon being resized.* You will need to resize the application so that it's a production SKU for the next exercise. When changing its size, select **Production** and click **See additional options**. Click **S1** and then **Apply**:

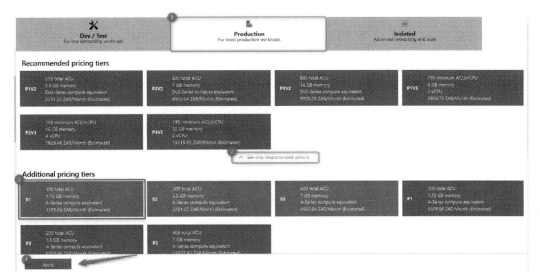

Figure 12.13 – Scaling up to S1

Now, let's learn how to scale out horizontally:

1. Navigate to the App Service plan you worked on in the previous exercise.

2. From the left menu blade, under the **Settings** context, click **Scale out (App Service plan)**.

3. Note that you can choose either **Manual scale** or **Custom autoscale**. Here, it would be best to manually scale since you are working on **Dev / Test** workloads, but for production workloads, you should choose **Custom autoscale**. Change **Instance count** to **2** and click **Save**:

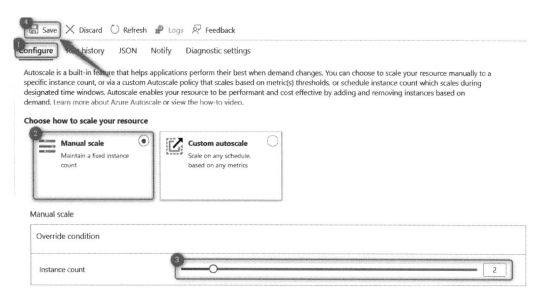

Figure 12.14 – Manual scale

4. Now, change the setting to **Custom autoscale**. Enter a name for your **Autoscale setting name** and select your **Resource group**:

Choose how to scale your resource

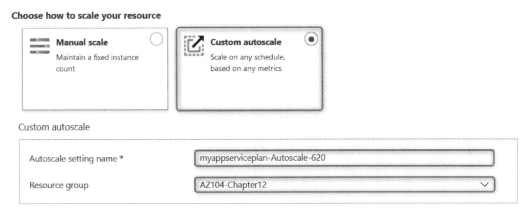

Figure 12.15 – Custom autoscale

For our **Default** scale condition, we will create the first one using **Scale based on a metric** for **Scale mode**, and we will set **Instance limits** to **1** for **Minimum**, **2** for **Maximum**, and **1** for **Default**. Then, click **Add a rule**:

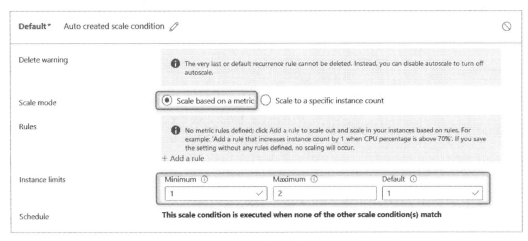

Figure 12.16 – Scale condition setup

5. For the **Criteria** section, set **Time aggregation** to **Average**, **Metric namespace** to
    App Service plans standard metrics, and **Metric name** to **CPU Percentage**. Set
    Operator to = and **Dimension Values** to **All values** (this means any web app).
    Note the timeline chart at the bottom of the screen, which indicates the average
    CPU percentage that you have experienced over time, with the average also written
    below it. In this case, it is **3.78 %**:

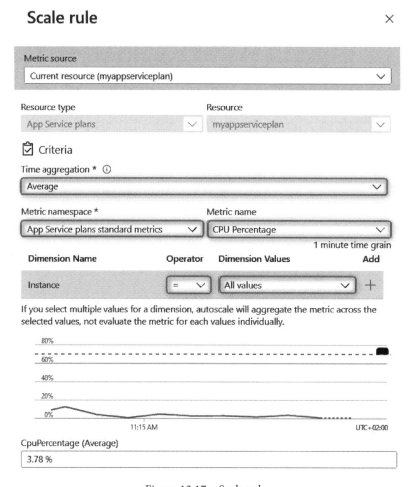

Figure 12.17 – Scale rule

6. Below the **CPUPercentage (Average)** section, you will notice some other
    configuration options. Set **Operator** to **Greater than** and **Metric threshold**
    to trigger scale action to **70**. Then, set **Duration (minutes)** to **10** and **Time**
    grain statistic to **Average**. This will define a rule that states that when the CPU
    average percentage reaches greater than 70% usage over 10 minutes, it will trigger
    an **Action**.

7. For the **Action** section, set **Operation** to **Increase count by**, **Cool down (minutes)** to **5**, and **Instance count** to **1**. This will increase the instance count of the running web applications by 1 when the criteria that we configured in *step 7* have been identified. Once triggered, a cooldown period will occur, where no further actions can be performed until the cooldown window has elapsed. In this case, it is **5** minutes. If the criteria for scaling are observed again after this cooldown period, then the action will be triggered again. Click **Add**:

Operator *

| Greater than ∨ |

Metric threshold to trigger scale action * ⓘ

| 70 ✓ |

%

Duration (minutes) * ⓘ

| 10 |

Time grain (minutes) ⓘ

| 1 |

Time grain statistic * ⓘ

| Average ∨ |

♟ Action

Operation *

| Increase count by ∨ |

Cool down (minutes) * ⓘ

| 5 |

Instance count *

| 1 ✓ |

Add

Figure 12.18 – Configuring a scale rule – Thresholds

8. You have just configured a rule for scaling your application up in terms of its instance count, but what if you would like the application to scale back down when you don't need as many instances anymore? You would need to configure a new scale condition to trigger a scale-down action you would like to perform. Click **+ Add a rule** below the **Scale out** rule you just created:

Rules

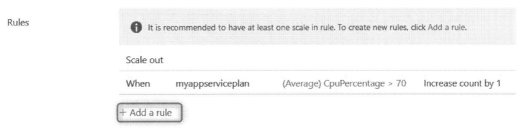

Figure 12.19 – Add a rule

9. For the **Criteria** section, set **Time aggregation** to **Average**, **Metric namespace** to **App Service plans standard metrics**, and **Metric name** to **CPU Percentage**. Set **Operator** to = and **Dimension Values** to **All values** (this means any web app). Note that the timeline chart at the bottom of the screen indicates the CPU percentage average that you have experienced over time, with the average also written below it. In this case, it is **2.55 %**:

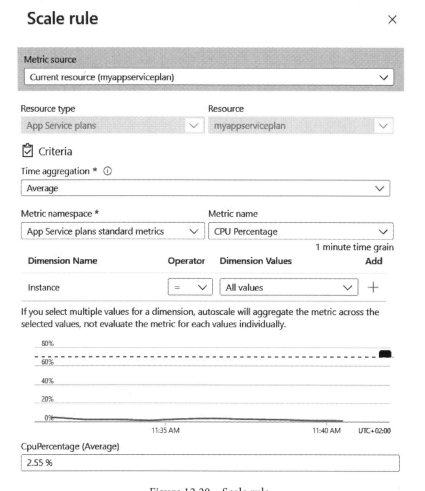

Figure 12.20 – Scale rule

10. Below the **CPUPercentage (Average)** section, you will notice some other configuration options. Set **Operator** to **Less than** and **Metric threshold to trigger scale action** to **30**. Then, set **Duration (minutes)** to **10** and **Time grain statistic** to **Average**. This will define a rule that states that when the CPU average percentage reaches less than 30% usage over 10 minutes, it will trigger an **Action**.

11. For the **Action** section, set **Operation** to **Decrease count by**, **Cool down (minutes)** to **5**, and **Instance count** to **1**. This will decrease the instance count of the running web applications by 1 when the criteria that we configured in *Step 11* have been identified. Once triggered, there will be a cooldown period where no further actions can be performed until the cooldown window has elapsed. In this case, it is **5** minutes. If the criteria for scaling are observed again after this cooldown period, then the action will be triggered again. Click **Add**:

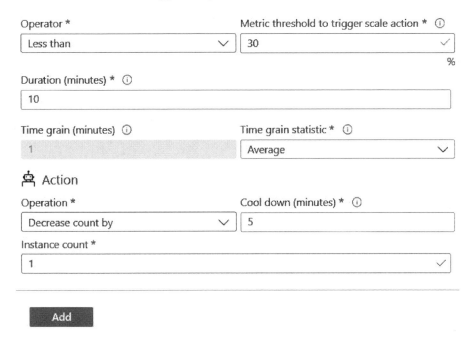

Figure 12.21 – Scale rule – Threshold and Action sections

12. Click **Save**.

Now that you have configured your autoscale rules using the Azure portal, let's learn how to use PowerShell to do the same.

PowerShell scripts

Please ensure that the Az module is installed, as per the *Technical requirements* section at the beginning of the chapter.

Here, we are going to create an App Service plan and Web Apps service via PowerShell. To do so, follow these steps.

Note: Change the parameters to suit your requirements.

```
# Parameters
$ResourceGroup = "AZ104-Chapter12"
$Location = "WestEurope"
$SubscriptionId = "xxxxxxx"
$WebAppName = "mysecondwebapp10101"
$AppServicePlanName = "mylinuxappserviceplan10101"


# If necessary, select the right subscription as follows
Select-AzSubscription -SubscriptionId $SubscriptionId


# Create an App Service Plan for Linux
$AppServicePlan = Get-AzAppServicePlan -Name
$AppServicePlanName -ResourceGroupName $ResourceGroup


# Create an Autoscale Rule
$AutoScaleRule = New-AzAutoscaleRule -MetricName
"CpuPercentage" -Operator "GreaterThan" -MetricStatistic
"Average" -Threshold 70 -TimeAggregationOperator
"Average" -TimeGrain "00:01:00" -TimeWindow "00:10:00"
-MetricResourceId $AppServicePlan.Id -ScaleActionCooldown
00:10:00 -ScaleActionDirection Increase -ScaleActionScaleType
ChangeCount -ScaleActionValue 1


# Create an Autoscale Profile
$AutoScaleProfile = New-AzAutoscaleProfile -Name "Default"
-DefaultCapacity 1 -MaximumCapacity 2 -MinimumCapacity 1 -Rule
$AutoScaleRule


# Assign the Autoscale Profile to the App
Add-AzAutoscaleSetting -Location $Location -Name "Auto Scale
Setting" -ResourceGroupName $ResourceGroup -TargetResourceId
$AppservicePlan.Id -AutoscaleProfile $AutoScaleProfile
```

You should now understand how to scale your applications via Azure App Service. You have learned how to perform manual scaling, as well as autoscaling, using the Azure portal and PowerShell. Autoscaling allows you to manage your applications and accommodate varying workload requirements. Next, you will learn about the security configurations that you can use to secure your application.

Securing an app service

There are several mechanisms you can use to enhance the security of your application on Azure. As part of the AZ-104 exam, we will explore the configuration options that are native to the web application directly. However, note that for real-world implementations, you should investigate additional measures for enhancing the security of your applications, such as employing a firewall – especially a web application firewall – for your web-based applications. These services provide traffic that's in line with your application and scan for disallowed or heuristic behavior.

In this exercise, we will look at various native application configurations that can be used to increase the security level of your app services:

1. Navigate to the App Service plan you worked on in the previous exercise.

2. From the left menu blade, under the **Settings** context, click **Configuration**. The first tab you will be greeted with is called **Application settings**. Application settings are variables that are presented securely to your application, but they can be configured externally from the application code. This enhances security by obfuscating the password from code and prevents developers that don't have RBAC permissions on the Azure portal for the App Service resource from seeing sensitive data, such as secrets that may be stored under **Application settings**. The other item that can be configured is **Connection strings**:

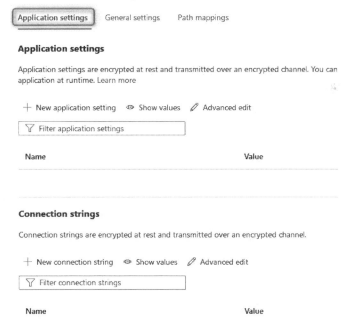

Figure 12.22 – Application settings

3. The next tab is **General settings**. Here, you will want to ensure **File Transfer Protocol (FTP)** traffic is conducted securely if it's allowed by your organizational policies. FTP is a technology that enables file transfer operations for your systems. It is commonly used by developers to upload code to the system; an alternative, as we explored in the previous chapter, is to use a source code repository such as Git. The most secure option is to disallow all FTP-based traffic as prevention is better than a cure. However, since many applications require developers to be able to upload their code, changing the FTP transfer protocol that's being used is the next best option. Setting traffic to FTPS only ensures that the FTP traffic is conducted over an HTTPS tunnel, meaning that all the data is encrypted. So, even if it is intercepted, it is less likely to be compromised. Set this to **FTPS only** for this exercise:

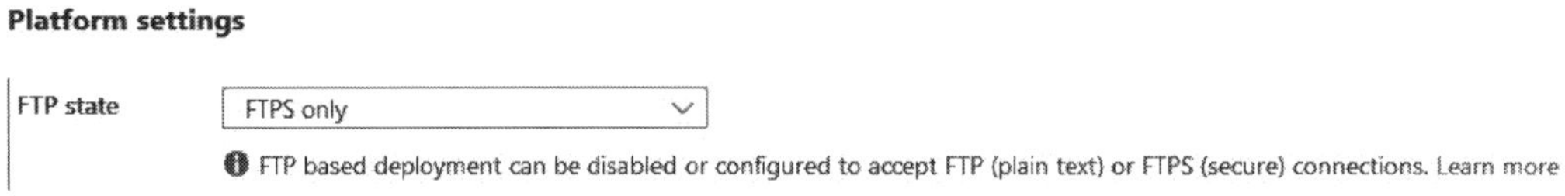

Platform settings

FTP state   FTPS only   ⌄

     ❶ FTP based deployment can be disabled or configured to accept FTP (plain text) or FTPS (secure) connections. Learn more

Figure 12.23 – FTP state

4. Click **Save** at the top of the screen:

Figure 12.24 – Options menu

Note that after clicking **Save**, you will be warned that the application needs to be restarted.

5. The last tab that can be configured in the **General settings** menu is **Path mappings**. We won't explore this here.

6. From the left menu pane, click **Authentication**. This blade contains the configuration settings related to authentication, the type of identity provider service that's being used, and the authentication flow. To explore the available configurations, click **Add identity provider**:

Add an identity provider

Choose an identity provider to manage the user identities and authentication flow for your application. Providers include Microsoft, Facebook, Google, and Twitter.

Learn more about identity providers ☐

Figure 12.25 – Add identity provider

7. At the time of writing, you can choose from several identity providers – that is, Microsoft, Facebook, Google, Twitter, and OpenID Connect. Click **Microsoft**:

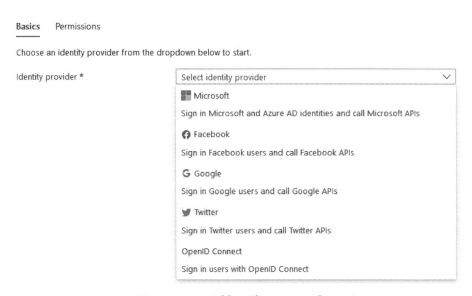

Figure 12.26 – Add an identity provider

8. You will see a screen with additional configuration settings. The first item to configure is the application registration. This can be used to assign permissions and will configure a service principal account in Azure AD called an app registration. For this exercise, select **Create new app registration** and assign a name. Next, select the option for supported account types for your application. Depending on how and where your application is used, this will dictate the configuration that best suits your security requirements. For instance, if you are looking to deliver an internal application such as something that lists the mobile numbers of employees within your organization so that you can contact someone urgently (where sharing this information is disallowed publicly), then you would want to restrict public access (that is, anyone external to your organization).

Using your identity provider will help you determine if they have an account with your organization or not. In such cases, you can select **Current tenant – Single tenant**. **Any Azure AD direction – Multi-tenant** will allow you to accept user logins from any other Azure AD directory. The next option, **Any Azure AD directory & personal Microsoft accounts**, opens access to public accounts too, where personal accounts can be used. Finally, **Personal Microsoft accounts only** removes access from other Azure accounts and limit this to personal Microsoft accounts. This is typically used for gaming services, where you want to allow friends to connect but you also want to restrict business accounts from accessing the service. As you can see, the most secure option is **Current tenant – Single tenant**. You can also configure **Restrict access**, where you can force authentication to be conducted before access is granted to your application. **Unauthenticated access** allows users to log in anonymously. Choose **Require authentication** since this is the most secure option. Finally, you can choose what kind of error handling you would like to deliver upon detection, such as delivering an **HTTP 401 Unauthorized** error message. **Select HTTP 302 Found redirect**. Then, click **Next : Permissions >**:

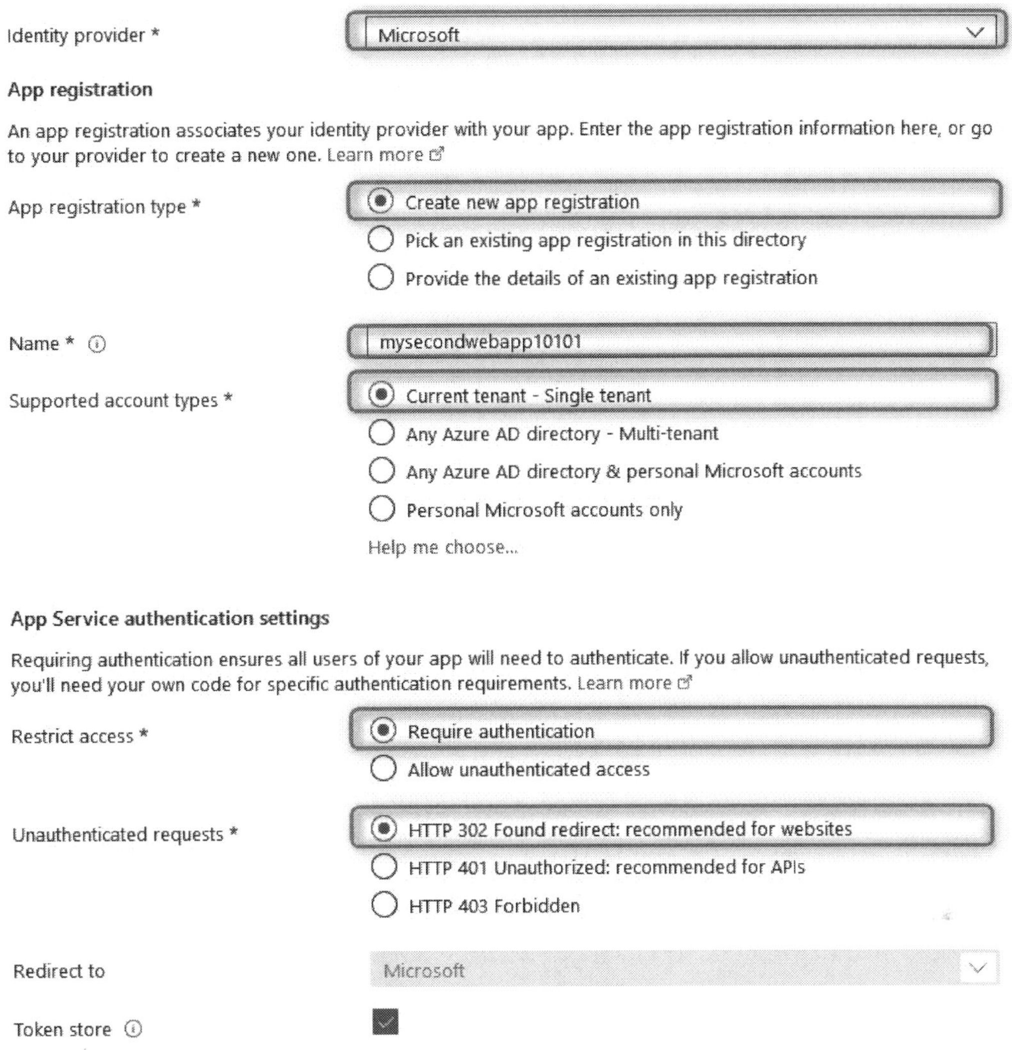

Identity provider *   [Microsoft   ∨]

App registration

An app registration associates your identity provider with your app. Enter the app registration information here, or go to your provider to create a new one. Learn more ☐

App registration type *
- (●) Create new app registration
- ( ) Pick an existing app registration in this directory
- ( ) Provide the details of an existing app registration

Name * ⓘ   [mysecondwebapp10101   ]

Supported account types *
- (●) Current tenant - Single tenant
- ( ) Any Azure AD directory - Multi-tenant
- ( ) Any Azure AD directory & personal Microsoft accounts
- ( ) Personal Microsoft accounts only

Help me choose...

App Service authentication settings

Requiring authentication ensures all users of your app will need to authenticate. If you allow unauthenticated requests, you'll need your own code for specific authentication requirements. Learn more ☐

Restrict access *
- (●) Require authentication
- ( ) Allow unauthenticated access

Unauthenticated requests *
- (●) HTTP 302 Found redirect: recommended for websites
- ( ) HTTP 401 Unauthorized: recommended for APIs
- ( ) HTTP 403 Forbidden

Redirect to   [Microsoft   ∨]

Token store ⓘ   [✓]

Figure 12.27 – Identity provider configuration

9. The next blade relates to the **Permissions** options you would like to grant. The default option is **User.Read**, which allows the application to read the user's profile. These permissions can be modified as needed to deliver the required information to your application. These permissions will be prompted by the user when they access the application and are being authenticated. They will need to consent to this permission request if they wish to access the application. Click **Add**:

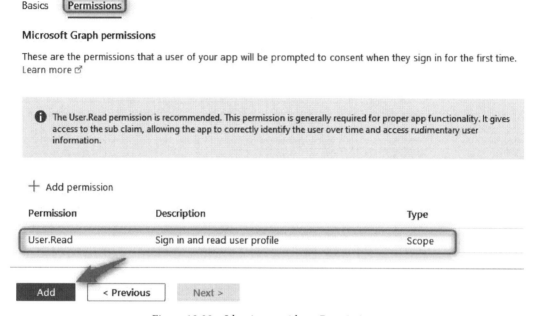

Figure 12.28 – Identity provider – Permissions

10. Click **Identity** from the left menu pane for the application. You will be presented with two tabs – **System assigned** and **User assigned**. Here, you can choose which deployment configuration you would like to use. **System assigned** allows you to create a managed identity whose life cycle is controlled and managed by Azure. A managed identity allows you to grant RBAC permissions to the application as if it were a user, which gives them better control over resources and prevents user management issues such as abuse of privileges or mistakes being made. Enabling this setting increases the security of your application and prevents credentials from being injected directly into code, which would allow account and system compromise to occur. **User assigned** is managed manually but can be configured more granularly for control over the specific RBAC permissions you would like to grant to the application. On the **System assigned** tab, click **On** under the **Status** option, then click **Save**:

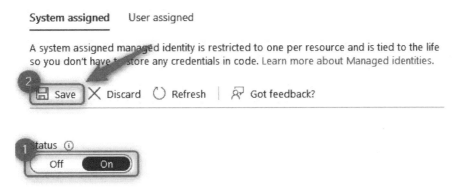

Figure 12.29 – System assigned

11. After clicking **Save**, you will see a new configuration option, where you can configure the Azure RBAC permissions for your application:

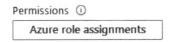

Figure 12.30 – Adding a role assignment

12. You can also consider using backups and **disaster recovery** (**DR**) for your applications. But why? If your application becomes compromised and you need to perform restoration tasks, without backups, you would potentially lose all your critical data. Therefore, anything that could cause the application to go offline or become inaccessible would compromise the security of the application. The same is true for DR; if you can't restore an active instance of the application, its security is compromised as potential usage of the application will be restricted, which could lead to several other issues for an organization and a loss of revenue.

13. The next menu you should click through is **TLS/SSL settings**. On this blade, select the **Bindings** tab and ensure that **HTTPS Only** is set to **On**. This ensures that all your traffic is encrypted and secured to the application, where HTTP traffic allows compromises to occur and should always be configured to forward all HTTP requests to HTTPS. HTTP communicates in clear text, so any credentials or sensitive information that's sent would be visible to anyone that could intercept the traffic, which is highly insecure. HTTPS requires a certificate, which can be configured within the same blade. Azure offers one free certificate per web application for a single domain:

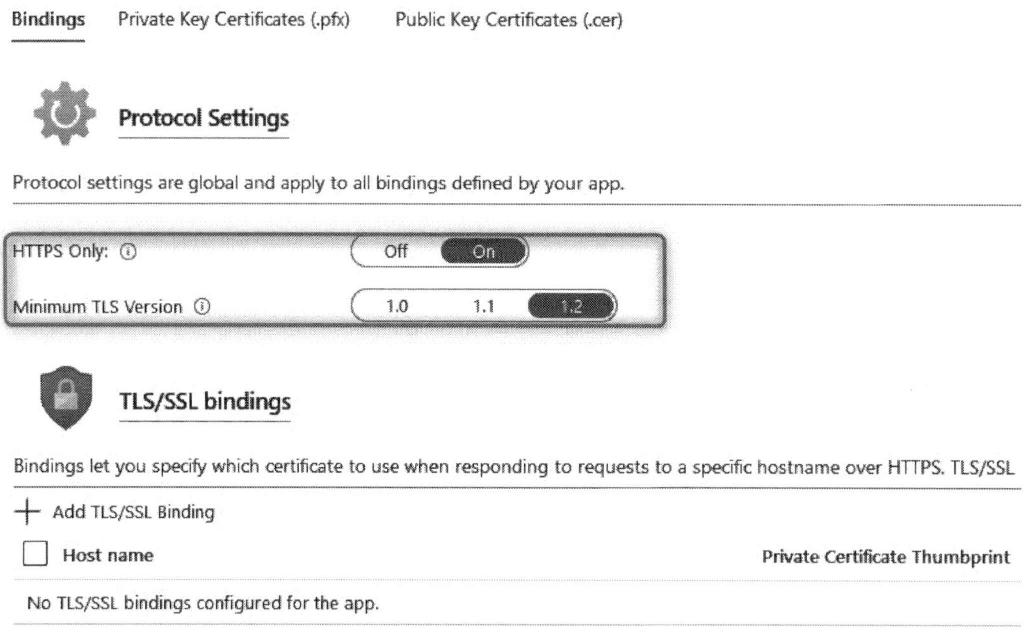

Bindings   Private Key Certificates (.pfx)   Public Key Certificates (.cer)

Protocol Settings

Protocol settings are global and apply to all bindings defined by your app.

HTTPS Only: ⓘ	Off ⬤ On
Minimum TLS Version ⓘ	1.0 1.1 ⬤ 1.2

TLS/SSL bindings

Bindings let you specify which certificate to use when responding to requests to a specific hostname over HTTPS. TLS/SSL

+ Add TLS/SSL Binding

☐ Host name	**Private Certificate Thumbprint**

No TLS/SSL bindings configured for the app.

Figure 12.31 – Protocol Settings – TLS/SSL bindings

14. Next, click on the **Networking** option from the left menu of the application. Networking is an interesting topic for your applications and can result in many sleepless nights if it's not planned and managed correctly. The rule of thumb for hardening your network is to secure your perimeters and isolate traffic via perimeters, as well as by adopting the **Zero Trust model** (where you don't trust any application or service that doesn't intend to communicate with the application). It should only be public-facing if your application requires public access. You will also want to consider a **Web Application Firewall** (**WAF**) and **firewall** service for public traffic, as well as something internal. Azure provides several options for privatizing traffic for your application and it's important to understand your traffic flow when you're considering your implementation. The first item you must configure here is **Access restriction**, which applies to inbound traffic. This will act as a whitelist or blacklist for your traffic, depending on how you configure your rules. To configure this, click **Access restriction**:

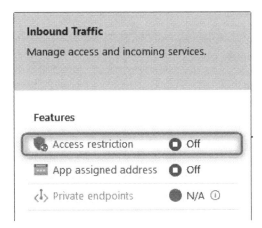

Figure 12.32 – Network settings – Inbound Traffic 1

15. As the most secure option, you should restrict all traffic except for your allowed rules. You will notice that you can configure your restriction rules for two different endpoints. The first is the public endpoint for your application, while the second has a suffix starting with **scm**, which is used for the Kudu console and web deployments. To see the available configuration options, click **+ Add rule**:

Figure 12.33 – Network settings – Access Restrictions

16. On the **Add Restriction** pane that appears, you can set a **Name**; enter something meaningful. Next, you must decide on an **Action**, which can be either **Allow** or **Deny**; click **Allow**. You can also enter a **Priority** and, optionally, a **Description**. The next option, **Type**, is very important as it is used to determine the type of restriction that's being implemented and how the rule is invoked. The default configuration is IPv4, which is limited to a known IPv4 address or range (usually a public address or range) and is added to the **IP Address Block** text box. When entering a range, you can enter it in CIDR notation, with a single IP being /32 for the CIDR. Enter an IP address. IPv6 works in the same fashion except for IPv6 addresses or ranges. The **Virtual Network** source option allows you to select a network that you have configured previously to allow traffic through. The final option is **Service Tag**. Click **Add rule**:

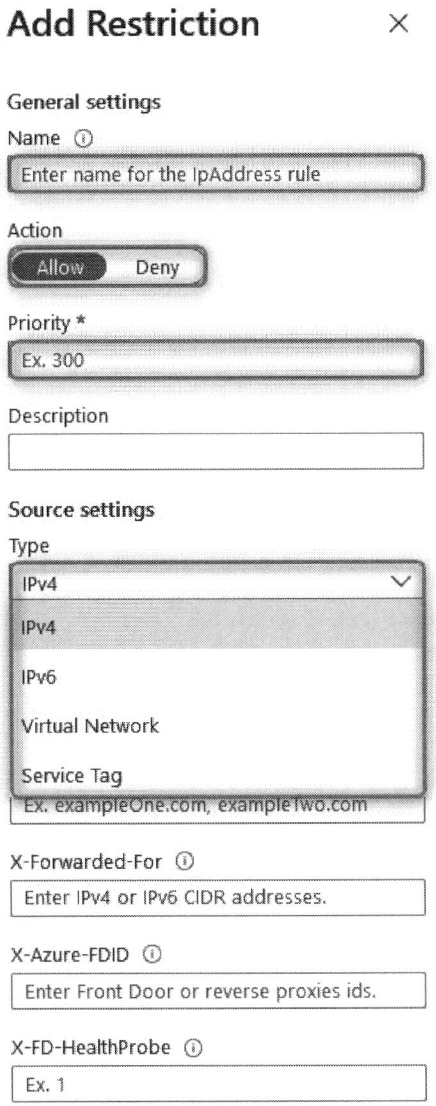

Add Restriction   ✕

General settings

Name ⓘ

Enter name for the IpAddress rule

Action

Allow   Deny

Priority *

Ex. 300

Description

Source settings

Type

IPv4   ⌄

IPv4

IPv6

Virtual Network

Service Tag

Ex. exampleOne.com, exampleTwo.com

X-Forwarded-For ⓘ

Enter IPv4 or IPv6 CIDR addresses.

X-Azure-FDID ⓘ

Enter Front Door or reverse proxies ids.

X-FD-HealthProbe ⓘ

Ex. 1

Figure 12.34 – Add Restriction

17. The next configuration for inbound traffic is **App assigned address**. Clicking this option will take you to the **TLS/SSL settings** blade. This is used to determine your **Custom Domain**, which we will configure in the next section. This is another method of enhancing security as the domain can be configured to something that is trusted by your organization or users. It will confirm that you are using certificate delivery to enhance the security of your application:

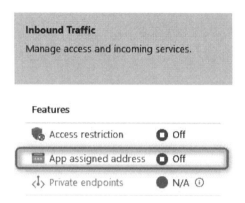

Figure 12.35 – Network settings – Inbound Traffic 2

18. The last inbound configuration option is **Private endpoints**. Selecting this allows you to completely remove all public access to your application. Your application will be assigned an NIC with a private IP from the associated VNet and subnet you connect it to. To enable public access for this configuration, you would need some form of **network address translation (NAT)** configuration to reach your application. This can be achieved by deploying an Application Gateway or using Azure Front Door, or by using your firewall service to translate traffic from one of its public IP addresses to your application over the private endpoint. This is a great way to secure traffic to your application, but as you can see, it can quickly cause complications. This setting will force you to consider how other components of your application communicate with each other and the outside world.

19. For outbound communication, you can perform VNet integration, which will associate your application with a designated subnet. Note that to assign a web app to a subnet, it will need to assume delegated access for the subnet. This means that it can manage the DHCP deployment for the subnet and will be responsible for IP assignment on the subnet. Furthermore, it restricts what can access the subnet and limits you to which subnet can be used for what service as only a single service can have delegated administration. Note that this is for outbound communication only and will not protect inbound communication. The subnet should also be allowed to communicate with the relevant services within Azure. Click **VNet integration**:

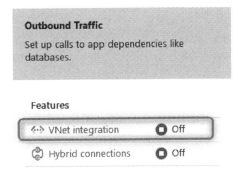

Figure 12.36 – Network settings – Outbound Traffic 1

20. Click **+ Add VNet**:

Figure 12.37 – VNet Configuration

21. You can also select an appropriate **Virtual Network**, which will give you the option to either create a new subnet or use an existing one. Use whichever best suits this demo and click **OK**:

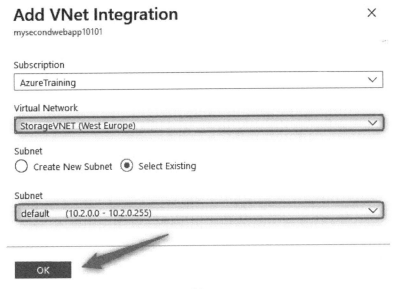

Figure 12.38 – Add VNet Integration

Note that your application is now connected to the VNet and subnet you selected. Note the address details as well. Traffic from your application can now be controlled for outbound traffic using **user-defined routes (UDRs)** on the network:

Figure 12.39 – VNet Configuration

22. The last configuration item for outbound traffic is **Hybrid connections**. This feature is a service that enables endpoint connectivity for your application and provides a connection solution where you don't have direct access paths to your on-premises environments or other environments from Azure. It enables a mechanism for TCP communication that's mapped to a port number for that corresponding system or service. Each hybrid connection is associated with a single host and port that enhances security as it's easier to manage and correlate the traffic:

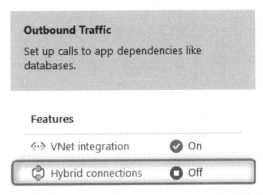

Figure 12.40 – Network settings – Outbound Traffic 2

The final security configuration item to be aware of is the **CORS** option under **API context** on the left menu pane. CORS should be disabled unless it's required as it exposes more vulnerabilities to your application, especially when it's not managed correctly:

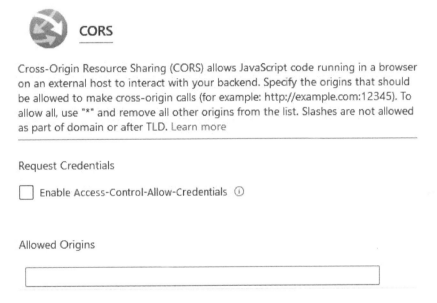

Figure 12.41 – Network settings – CORS

Now that you have reviewed the different security settings, you should feel more familiar with the controls that are available and when to use them. It's especially important to understand the configurations that are relative to traffic flow. In the next section, you will learn how to configure custom domain names.

Configuring custom domain names

Custom domains allow you to connect to your web application using the public DNS name that you have chosen for your application. To do this, you need to own the respective domain and prove that you have authority over it. Your custom domain could be, for example, www.yourapp.com. There are several providers for purchasing a domain, though this is outside the scope of this book. For suggestions on getting started, you could buy directly from Microsoft, which also leverages GoDaddy. To configure a custom domain, follow these steps:

1. Navigate to the App Service plan you worked on in the previous exercises.

2. From the left menu blade, the **Settings**, click **Custom domains**. From the blade that appears, click + **Add custom domain**.

3. Enter a **Custom domain** name of your choice, such as www.yourapp.com (this must be for a domain that you own). Click **Validate**:

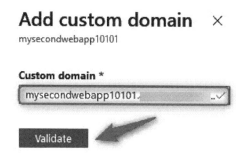

Figure 12.42 – Add custom domain

4. You will be presented with a screen that gives you a **Custom Domain Verification ID**:

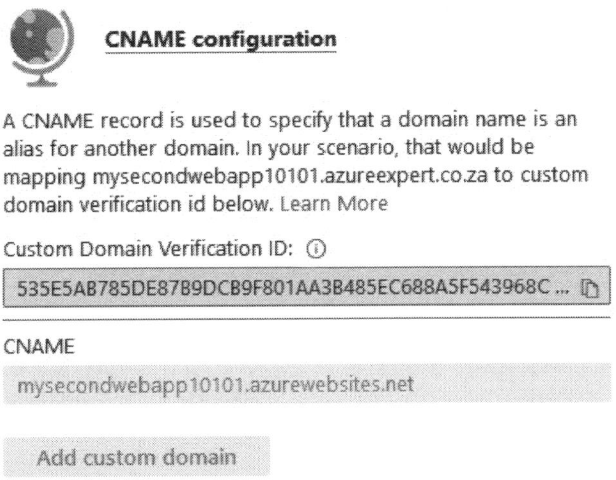

 CNAME configuration

A CNAME record is used to specify that a domain name is an alias for another domain. In your scenario, that would be mapping mysecondwebapp10101.azureexpert.co.za to custom domain verification id below. Learn More

Custom Domain Verification ID: ⓘ

535E5AB785DE87B9DCB9F801AA3B485EC688A5F543968C ... 🗋

CNAME

mysecondwebapp10101.azurewebsites.net

Add custom domain

Figure 12.43 – CName configuration

Copy this ID and create a new **CName** and **TXT** record for your domain, as follows. These values will be used to determine that you have authority over the domain you have specified:

Type	Host	Value
CName	[sub domain] or [sub domain].[sub domain] Eg: **www** or **www.[sub domain]**	Azure app service FQDN Eg: **[appName].azurewebsites.net**
TXT	Asuid.[sub domain]. Or Asuid.www.[sub domain] Eg: **asuid.www** or **asuid. www.[sub domain]**	Custom Domain Verification ID from *Figure 12.43.*

Top Tip

You can also map custom domains using **A** records or a wildcard (*) **CNAME** record. Go to `https://docs.microsoft.com/en-us/azure/app-service/app-service-web-tutorial-custom-domain?tabs=a%2Cazurecli#dns-record-types` for more details.

5. Once completed, click the **Validate** button again.

6. The following screenshot shows an example of the **TXT and CName records** that you may have created with your domain host (all the providers have slightly different configurations):

Figure 12.44 – TXT and CName records

7. You will get two successful messages after clicking the **Validate** button. Now, click **Add custom domain**:

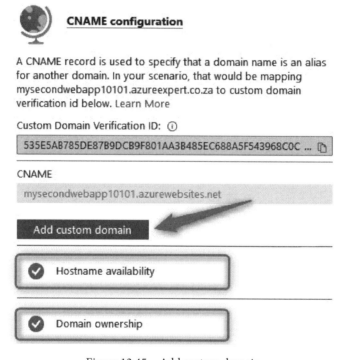

Figure 12.45 – Add custom domain

8. With that, your custom domain has been added. However, you now have an entry on your screen that shows that this endpoint is not secure. You will need to add a certificate to make it secure. Click **TLS/SSL settings** from the left menu:

Figure 12.46 – Insecure custom domain

9. Click the **Private Key Certificates (.pfx)** tab. Then, click **+ Create App Service Managed Certificate**:

Figure 12.47 – Private Key Certificate

10. Once Azure has analyzed the eligibility of the hostname, click **Create**. Azure allows one certificate per web app to be generated by the platform for your custom domain. This can save you a lot of money as, typically, you will need to procure a certificate from a third-party vendor. Your certificate will be valid for 6 months once it's been created.

11. DNS propagation can take up to 48 hours to occur, though sometimes, this can happen within minutes, depending on whether your DNS was used and the **Time to Live** (**TTL**) setting has been configured. You should now be able to browse your web app using the custom domain you configured. Note that you can connect using HTTPS and get a valid certificate check:

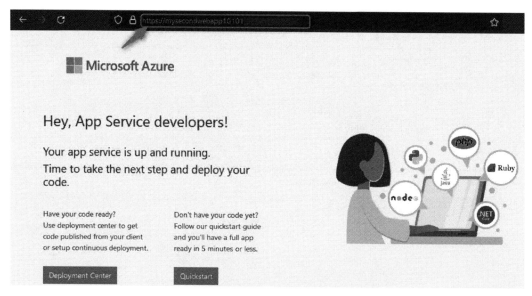

Figure 12.48 – Browsing to your custom domain

You now know how to configure a custom domain for your web app within Azure, as well as how to generate a valid certificate using the platform for a certified secure HTTPS connection. Typically, this can be done for production-based applications that are exposed to the internet and it is a common administrative duty for those that work in organizations that utilize many web applications. In the next section, you will learn how to configure backups for your applications.

Configuring a backup for an app service

Your application is running well, but you're concerned that if something should fail or data is lost, you can't restore your application. You decide that backing it up is a good idea and start to explore different ways to back up your application. Thankfully, Azure makes this a simple process, where you just need to think about what your backup strategy needs to look like and then configure the service accordingly. Remember that using a backup is different from performing DR in that DR restores operational services, whereas backups enable point-in-time restorations of data to recover from loss or accidental deletion. Follow these steps to configure a backup for your application:

1. Navigate to the App Service plan you worked on in the previous exercises.

2. From the left menu blade, under **Settings**, click **Backups**. From the blade that appears, click **Configure** at the top of the screen. The **Backup Configuration** blade will appear.

3. You will need a storage account to store your backups. Since we haven't pre-created an account, we will create it as part of this exercise. Click the **Storage Settings** button:

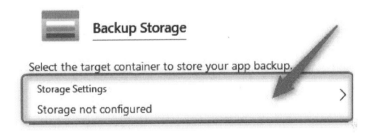

Figure 12.49 – Storage Settings

4. Create your storage account and click **OK**. Next, you will be prompted for a container. Currently, this doesn't exist since we created a new storage account. Click + **Container**, name the container backups, and click **Create**. Click the new container and click **Select**.

5. For backups, you have the option to decide if you would like an automated schedule or if you would like to manually back up as and when needed. Preferably, you would like an automated schedule that prevents mistakes from occurring, such as forgetting to back up. Enable **Scheduled backup**. Configure your backup so that it runs every day at a set time from the date you would like this to start. In this example, we have set this to 28/12/2021 at 7:05:38 pm. Set your **Retention** period (in days) and set **Keep at least one backup** to **Yes**:

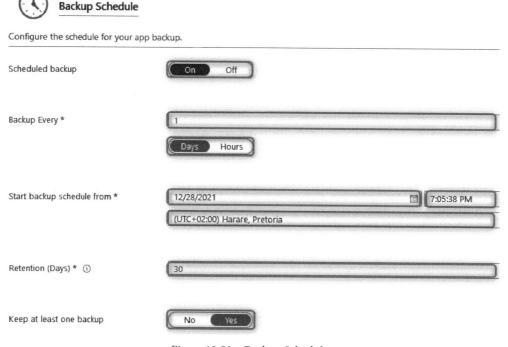

Figure 12.50 – Backup Schedule

6. Note that you also have the option to configure a backup for your database. We won't configure this for this exercise. Click **Save**:

Figure 12.51 – Backup Database

7. You will see that your first backup is currently in progress and that the light blue box reflects the configuration for your backup schedule. You will also see two other blue buttons; the first, **Backup**, is for manually initiating a backup to be performed, while the other, **Restore**, allows you to recover data when required:

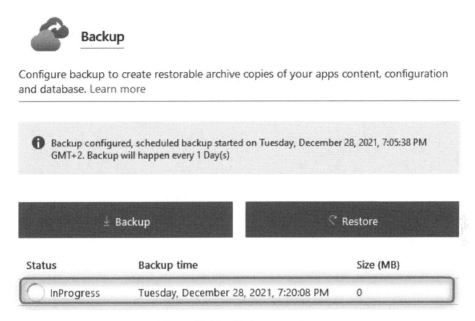

Figure 12.52 – Backup overview

You now understand how to back up your Azure App Service and should feel confident in configuring this going forward. In the next section, you will learn about the various network settings. Since we covered some of the available networking configurations in the previous sections, we will focus predominantly on how to configure a private endpoint.

Configuring networking settings

You learned how to perform VNet integration in the *Securing an app service* section. In this section, you will learn how to configure behind a private endpoint:

1. Navigate to the App Service plan you worked on in the previous exercises.

2. From the left menu blade, under **Settings**, click **Scale up (App Service plan)**. On the blade that appears, ensure that you have chosen the **Premium V2**, **Premium V3**, or **Elastic Premium** SKU to continue with this exercise. Click **Apply**.

3. From the left menu blade, under **Settings**, click **Networking**. From the blade that appears, click **Private endpoints** in the **Inbound Traffic** section:

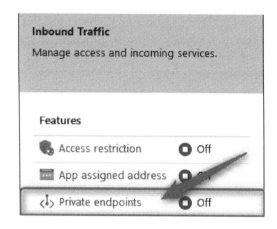

Figure 12.53 – Private endpoints

4. Click **Add**:

Figure 12.54 – Private Endpoint connections – Add

5. Enter a **Name**, ensure that you have the right **Subscription** selected, and select the correct **Virtual network** your private endpoint will be connecting to. Then, select a **Subnet** you would like to connect to. Finally, select **Yes** for **Integrate with private DNS zone**. This feature allows Azure to create a **Fully Qualified Domain Name** (**FQDN**) for your private endpoint that can be reached by your resources. If you select **No**, then you will need to ensure that your DNS zone is maintained by another DNS service, such as Active Directory (on-premises version), and configured on your VNet for DNS lookup queries to forward to your DNS server(s):

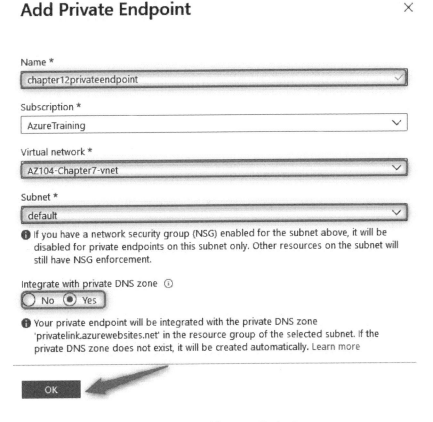

Figure 12.55 – Add Private Endpoint

6. On the **Private Endpoint connections** screen, which you will see after deploying your resource, click on the new endpoint you have created. Click the name of your **Private endpoint** (where the text is highlighted in blue) to open the **Private endpoint** blade:

Figure 12.56 – Backup overview

7. From the left menu blade, under the **Settings** context, click **Networking**. From the blade that appears, scroll down to **Customer Visible FQDNs** and note the FQDN names associated with your service. Note that these are now associated with a private IP that belongs to the subnet you selected previously:

Customer Visible FQDNs

DNS records visible to the customer

Network Interface	IP addresses	FQDN
∨ 🖥 chapter12privateendp...		
∨	10.0.0.5	
		mysecondwebapp10101.azurewebsites.net
		mysecondwebapp10101.
		mysecondwebapp10101.scm.azurewebsites.net

Figure 12.57 – Customer Visible FQDNs

8. Scrolling down further, you will see **Custom DNS records**. Note that the **FQDN** variable that's been assigned is very much the same as the website FQDN you have for `azurewebsites.net`, except it also contains **privatelink** as a prefix. So, you now have an FQDN of `[app name].privatelink.azurewebsites.net`. This is also associated with the private IP we saw previously. Note that if you performed an NSLookup on the preceding FQDNs, you will get a public IP address for your service:

Custom DNS records

To be configured correctly, the following FQDNs are required in your private DNS setup. Learn more

FQDN	IP addresses
mysecondwebapp10101.azureexpert.co.za	10.0.0.5

Configuration name	FQDN	IP address	Subscription
∨ privatelink-azurewebsites-net			AzureTraining
∨	mysecondwebapp10101.privatelink.azurewebsites.net		
		10.0.0.5	
∨	mysecondwebapp10101.scm.privatelink.azurewebsit...		
		10.0.0.5	

Figure 12.58 – Custom DNS records

9. Attempting to access your site now will deliver a **403-Forbidden** error since public access is now revoked:

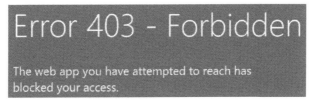

Figure 12.59 – Error 403 – Forbidden

> **Top Tip**
>
> If you have applied DNS to the VNet you are associating with and have configured a private DNS zone, you will need to ensure that your DNS servers have been configured to forward lookup to Azure for the private endpoint namespace related to your service.

With that, you have just configured a private endpoint and should feel confident in how to deploy one. You are also aware of some of the DNS complexities you should look out for to ensure you can resolve the host correctly by your resources.

Configuring deployment settings

There are several deployment settings related to your app service that you should be aware of. These allow you to upload your code or manage source control and deployment slots.

Deployment slots are logical segmentations of your application that can pertain to different environments and versions. Let's say you have an application that is running in production mode (meaning it's live and operational), and you want to work on some new code updates to introduce new features to the next version of your application. Typically, you would work on this in a test environment and deploy it accordingly to the production environment, once you felt that adequate testing had been performed before deploying anything to production.

Well, deployment slots provide a solution that allows you to deploy code to these slots to test the different functions and features of your applications, as well as code updates. You can run your primary deployment slot as the native application and deploy additional slots, such as TEST, that can be used for your new code. You have the option to swap deployment slots and revert at any time. The transition period is quick and enables a different paradigm in app management. You can, for instance, switch to the TEST slot and find that your application is not connecting to the required services and is slow. In this case, you can quickly flip back to the original code you had before any changes were made.

Let's look at a brief configuration of a deployment slot before proceeding to the next part of this section:

1. Navigate to the App Service plan you worked on in the previous exercises.

2. From the left menu blade, under **Deployment**, click **Deployment slots**.

3. From the top of the blade, click **+ Add Slot**. Enter a **Name** – in this case, TEST – and leave **Clone settings from** set to **Do no clone settings**. Click **Add**, then **Close**:

Add a slot   ✕

Name

TEST

mysecondwebapp10101-TEST.azurewebsites.net

Clone settings from:

Do not clone settings   ∨

Figure 12.60 – Add a slot

4. The name you chose previously will form part of the FQDN for the deployment slot so that it can be accessed as a normal application, as shown in the preceding screenshot.

5. Click **Swap** and set your **Source** as the new deployment slot you just created, and **Target** as the current slot. Click **Swap**, then **Close**:

Figure 12.61 – Swap

Now that you know about deployment slots, let's explore the Deployment Center:

1. Navigate to the App Service plan you worked on in the previous exercises.

2. From the left menu blade, under **Deployment**, click **Deployment Center**. Click the **Settings** tab.

3. Here, you have the option to deploy code from a **Continuous Integration/ Continuous Deployment (CI/CD)** tool. At the time of writing, the available options are **GitHub**, **Bitbucket**, and **Local Git**. Once you have chosen your **Source** CI/CD tool, you must **Authorize** your account and click **Save**:

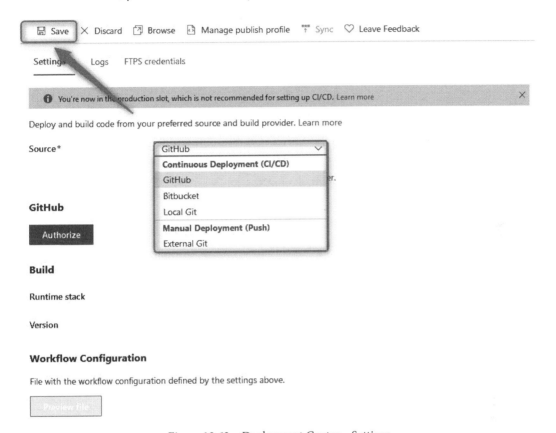

Figure 12.62 – Deployment Center – Settings

4. Click the **FTPS credentials** tab and note **FTPS endpoint**. **Application scope** is an automatically generated **Username** and **Password** that's limited to your application and deployment slot. You can use this to connect to your **FTPS endpoint**. You can also define a **User scope** and create a username and password:

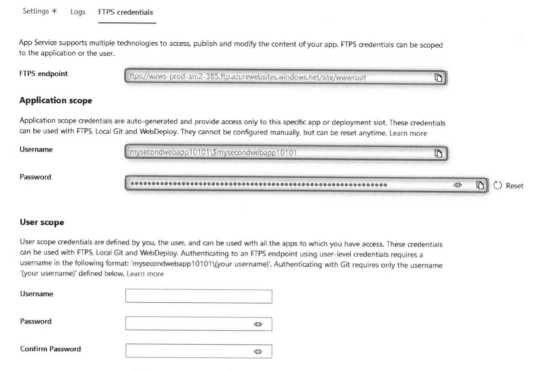

Figure 12.63 – Deployment Center – FTPS credentials

With that, you have learned about the deployment settings that are available to you for your app services. You should now feel comfortable navigating this component of Azure App Service as you know where to integrate CI/CD and where to find your FTPS credentials so that you can modify your application code. Next, we will summarize what we covered in this chapter.

Summary

In this chapter, we covered what an App Service is within Azure, the role of App Service plans and why they are essential to your App Service, and how to deploy an application, including how to manage its settings and configurations and how to secure it. Then, we explored and discussed various networking configurations for your application and the considerations you need to have when configuring these settings. You should now feel confident working with applications on Azure using App Service.

In the next chapter, we will cover some examples of deploying and managing compute services within Azure. There will be a VM lab, a container lab, and an App Service lab. After following these examples, you will feel more comfortable working with Azure compute services.

13
Practice Labs – Deploying and Managing Azure Compute Resources

The best way to become efficient with Azure is to get hands-on experience to test your skill set. This chapter will test the skills you acquired in *Chapter 9, Automating VM Deployments Using ARM Templates*, *Chapter 10, Configuring Virtual Machines*, *Chapter 11, Creating and Configuring Containers*, and *Chapter 12, Creating and Configuring App Services*. The labs in this chapter reference the official Microsoft Learning labs on GitHub.

In this chapter, we are going to cover the following labs:

- Managing virtual machines lab
- Deploying an Azure Container Instances lab
- Deploying Azure Kubernetes Service lab
- Deploying a Web App service lab

Technical requirements

The following are the technical requirements for this chapter:

- Access to an Azure subscription with Global Administrator and Billing Administrator privileges. If you do not have access to one, students can enroll for a free account: `https://azure.microsoft.com/en-in/free/`.

- PowerShell 3.6.1 or later installed on a PC from where labs can be practiced (note that many examples can only be followed from a PC) or `https://shell.azure.com`.

- Installation of the AZ PowerShell module, which can be performed by running the following in an administrative PowerShell session:

```
Set-ExecutionPolicy -ExecutionPolicy RemoteSigned -Scope
CurrentUser
Install-Module -Name Az -Scope CurrentUser -Repository
PSGallery -Force
```

> **Important Note**
>
> Even though the labs are on GitHub, no GitHub account is required to access the labs.

Downloading and extracting files for labs

Follow these steps to download and extract the required files:

1. Navigate to the following URL and download the archive folder (`.zip`): `https://github.com/MicrosoftLearning/AZ-104-MicrosoftAzureAdministrator/archive/master.zip`.

2. Depending on the browser you are using, you will likely be presented with different versions of the following dialog. Click **Save File** and **OK** at the bottom of the screen:

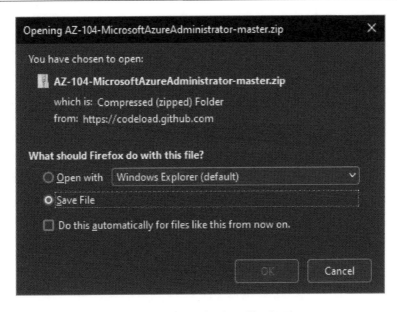

Figure 13.1 – Downloading files (ZIP)

3. Right-click the ZIP file you downloaded and click **Extract All...**
    (on Windows systems):

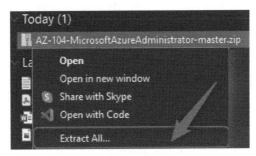

Figure 13.2 – Extract All... (ZIP)

4. Navigate to your downloaded folder and follow instructions from labs when
    needing files that will be in that folder.

You have now downloaded all the files you need for performing the labs later in
the chapter.

Managing virtual machines lab

This lab will guide you through creating standalone **Virtual Machines** (**VMs**) and VMs as a scale set, as well as exploring storage for these different deployments and how both solutions can be scaled. Furthermore, you will explore how VM custom script extension can be assigned and use to automatically configuring your VMs.

Estimated time: 50 minutes.

Lab method: PowerShell, ARM templates, and the Azure portal.

Lab scenario: In this lab, you play the role of an administrator evaluating different methods for deploying VMs for scale and resiliency. You are also exploring how VMs manage storage to support your scale. You need to determine whether standalone VMs or VMs deployed as a scale set are best suited to your deployments and understand the differences between them to ascertain when to use the different deployment types. As part of your exploration task, you want to see whether there is any mechanism that can assist you in reducing the administrative effort involved in deploying your VMs or automatically completing configuration tasks. You have heard that a custom script extension can assist with this, and you want to see how this will guide you to achieve your expected result.

Visit the following link (**Lab URL**) to the official Microsoft Learning GitHub labs, where you will be guided through each task step by step to achieve the following objectives.

Lab objectives:

I.   **Task one**: Deploy two VMs in two different zones for resiliency.

II. **Task two**: Use VM extensions to configure your VMs.

III. **Task three**: Configure and attach data disks to your VMs.

IV. **Task four**: Register the required resource providers for your subscription.

V.   **Task five**: Deploy your VM scale sets.

VI. **Task six**: Use VM extensions to configure your scale set.

VII. **Task seven**: Configure autoscale for your scale set and attach data disks.

Lab URL: `https://microsoftlearning.github.io/AZ-104-MicrosoftAzureAdministrator/Instructions/Labs/LAB_08-Manage_Virtual_Machines.html`.

Lab architecture diagram: The following diagram illustrates the different steps and deployment components involved in the exercise. The tasks are numbered **1** to **7** to correlate with the steps in the exercise:

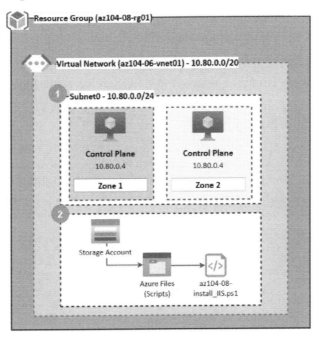

Figure 13.3 – Managing VMs – architecture diagrams

You have now experienced working with VMs both as individual resources and scale sets and should feel confident in working with these in your environments. It's best practice to delete your resources from the lab to prevent unnecessary spending.

Deploying an Azure Container Instances lab

This lab will guide you through creating a container group using Azure Container Instances using a Docker image and testing connectivity to your deployed containers.

Estimated time: 20 minutes.

Lab method: PowerShell and the Azure portal.

Lab scenario: In this lab, you play the role of an administrator who is looking to reduce their container management activities. Your organization, Contoso, has several virtualized workloads, and you want to explore whether these can be run from Azure Container Instances using Docker images.

Visit the following URL to the official Microsoft Learning GitHub labs, where you will be guided through each task step by step to achieve the following objectives.

Lab objectives:

   I. **Task one**: Use Azure Container Instances to host your container.
   II. **Task two**: Confirm connectivity to your container and functionality.

Lab URL: `https://microsoftlearning.github.io/AZ-104-MicrosoftAzureAdministrator/Instructions/Labs/LAB_09b-Implement_Azure_Container_Instances.html`.

Lab architecture diagram:

The following diagram illustrates the different steps involved in the exercise:

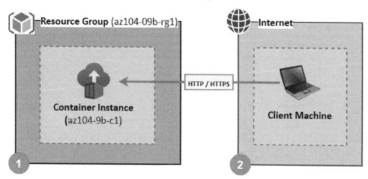

Figure 13.4 – Deploying an Azure container instance – architecture diagram

After running through this lab, you should now feel confident to deploy container instances to Azure. The next lab will take you through using Azure Kubernetes Service for the orchestration of your container instance deployments.

Deploying an Azure Kubernetes Service lab

This lab will guide you through setting up an Azure Kubernetes Service instance and deploying an NGINX pod for your multi-tier applications. You will implement node scaling as part of the exercise and learn to leverage Kubernetes as an orchestration service in Azure.

Estimated time: 40 minutes.

Lab method: PowerShell and the Azure portal.

Lab scenario: In this lab, you play the role of an administrator who is looking to reduce container management activities and implement container orchestration services. Your organization, Contoso, has several multi-tier applications that are not suitable for Azure Container Instances. You want to explore running these through Kubernetes, and since Azure has **Azure Kubernetes Service** (**AKS**), you want to leverage this to minimize administrative effort and complexity in deploying your solution.

Visit the following URL to the official Microsoft Learning GitHub labs, where you will be guided through each task step by step to achieve the following objectives.

Lab objectives:

    I. **Task one**: Register the required resource providers for your subscription.

    II. **Task two**: Deploy AKS.

    III. **Task three**: Deploy your AKS pods.

    IV. **Task four**: Configure scaling for your AKS cluster.

Lab URL: `https://microsoftlearning.github.io/AZ-104-MicrosoftAzureAdministrator/Instructions/Labs/LAB_09c-Implement_Azure_Kubernetes_Service.html`

Lab architecture diagram:

The following diagram illustrates the different steps involved in the exercise:

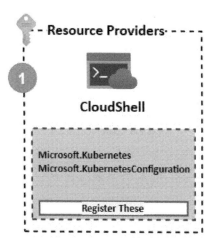

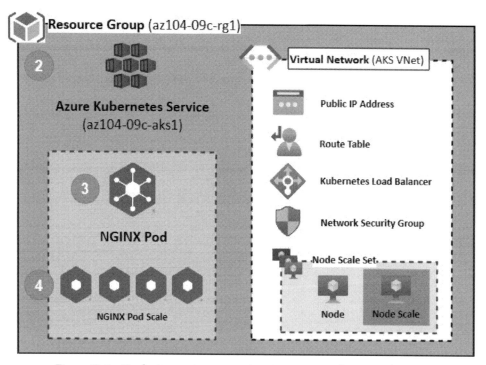

Figure 13.5 – Deploying an Azure container instance – architecture diagram

After working through these previous labs, you should feel confident working with containers on Azure. You are also familiar with some aspects of the Kubernetes service, which can be used for the orchestration of your container instances. You've also experienced managing scale using these tools and will be prepared for performing this aspect of your role going forward. The next lab will explore working with Web App service on Azure.

Deploying Web App service lab

In this lab, you will be guided through the deployment of an Azure container instance with using a Docker image as the source. Finally, you will test connectivity to your containers to prove a successful deployment.

Estimated time: 30 minutes.

Lab method: PowerShell and the Azure portal.

Lab scenario: In this lab, you play the role of an administrator who is looking to utilize Azure App Services for hosting your company's web applications. Your organization, Contoso, has several websites running in on-premises data centers on servers using a PHP runtime stack. Furthermore, you are looking to start using DevOps practices within your organization and want to use app deployment slots to improve your deployment strategy.

Visit the following URL to the official Microsoft Learning GitHub labs, where you will be guided through each task step by step to achieve the following objectives.

Lab objectives:

   I.   **Task one**: Deploy your Web App and Service plan.

   II. **Task two**: Create a staging deployment slot for your web app.

   III. **Task three**: Configure deployment settings for the local Git.

   IV. **Task four**: Deploy your staging code.

   V.   **Task five**: Swap the staging and production deployment slots.

   VI. **Task six**: Configure autoscaling and test your web app.

Lab URL: `https://microsoftlearning.github.io/AZ-104-MicrosoftAzureAdministrator/Instructions/Labs/LAB_09a-Implement_Web_Apps.html`.

Lab architecture diagram: The following diagram illustrates the different steps involved in the exercise:

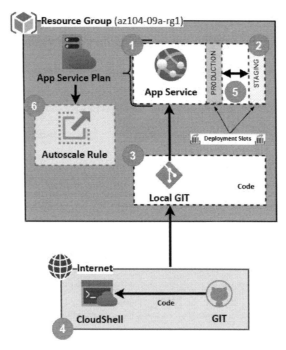

Figure 13.6 – Deploying an Azure web app – architecture diagram

You have now experienced working with Azure web apps on the Azure portal as well as configuring autoscale rules. You should now feel confident in using this service within your daily role. It is best practice to remove unused resources to ensure that there are no unexpected costs.

Summary

In this chapter, we looked at several compute infrastructure type deployments. We explored the deployments of app services, Azure Container Instances, Azure Kubernetes Service, and VM deployments. We also looked at how to scale and manage these systems through a practical demonstration. You should now feel confident in managing Azure compute resources and working with these on Azure.

In the next part of the book, we'll cover the deployment and configuration of network-related services and components. We will explore the management of Azure virtual networks and securing services. We will then explore the load balancing services available to us, and finally, how to monitor and troubleshoot network-related issues.

Part 4: Configuring and Managing Virtual Networking

Configuring and managing virtual networking is one of the main exam objectives, with a total of 25-30% of the AZ-104 exam.

This part of the book comprises the following chapters:

14
Implementing and Managing Virtual Networking

This chapter is the start of the exam objective called *configure and manage virtual networking*, which has an exam weighting of 20–30% of the overall exam.

In this chapter, we are going to look at implementing and managing virtual networking. This includes how to create and configure virtual networks, peer networks with each other, configure private and public IP addresses, create user-defined network routes, implement subnets, create endpoints on subnets, configure private endpoints, and finally, configure Azure DNS, including custom DNS settings and private or public DNS zones. This chapter is very important, as networking is often referred to as the cornerstone of **Infrastructure as a Service (IaaS)**.

In brief, the following topics will be covered in this chapter:

- Creating and configuring virtual networks, including peering
- Configure private and public IP addresses
- Configure user-defined network routes
- Implement subnets

- Configure endpoints on subnets
- Configure private endpoints
- Configure Azure DNS, including custom DNS settings and private or public DNS zones

Technical requirements

To follow along with the hands-on lessons, you will need access to an Azure Active Directory as a global administrator. If you do not have access to one, students can enroll for a free account at `https://azure.microsoft.com/en-in/free/`.

An Azure subscription is also required; you can either register with your own credit card or enroll for the free $200 once-off credit if you use the following link: `https://azure.microsoft.com/en-us/free/`.

PowerShell will be used for some of the lab sections. For more details on how to configure PowerShell, visit `https://docs.microsoft.com/en-us/powershell/azure/install-az-ps?view=azps-1.8.0`.

Creating and configuring virtual networks, including peering

In this section, we are going to look at how to create and configure **Virtual Networks** (**VNets**) and peering. Let's start with an overview of VNets and IP addressing and how it works within Azure.

A VNet overview

Before we dive into how to configure VNets, let's take a moment to understand what VNets are and what their purpose is. A VNet in Azure is a representation of your network in the cloud that is used to connect resources such as virtual machines and other services to each other.

Unlike traditional networks, which make use of physical cables, switches, and routers to connect resources, VNets are completely software-based. VNets have isolated IP ranges, and resources placed inside a VNet do not talk to the resources in other VNets by default. To allow resources in two different VNets to talk to each other, you would need to connect the VNets using VNet peering.

> **Important Note**
> All resources deployed to a VNet must reside in the same region.

An IP addressing overview

Azure supports both private and public IP addresses. Private IP addresses are assigned within the VNet in order to communicate with other resources within it and cannot be accessed via the internet by design. Public IP addresses are internet-facing by design and can be assigned to a **virtual machine** (**VM**) or other resources, such as VPN gateways.

Both private and public IP addresses can be configured to be dynamic or static. Dynamic IP addresses change when the host or resource is restarted, whereas static IP addresses do not change even if the resources are restarted.

Dynamic IP addresses are automatically assigned by Azure based on the subnet range. When a VM is deallocated (stopped), the dynamic IP address goes back into the pool of IP addresses that can be assigned to other resources again. By default, private IP addresses are dynamic but can be changed to static via the Azure portal when needed.

Static public IP addresses are random public IP addresses that do not change after being assigned to a resource. Unlike a dynamic IP address that changes when a resource is restarted, the static IP address is persisted. Public IPs are usually assigned to internet-facing resources such as VPN gateways and, in some instances, VMs.

Now that we have covered the basic networking components, let's go ahead and configure a VNet via PowerShell:

1. First, we need to connect to our Azure tenant by using the following PowerShell command:

    ```
    Connect-AzAccount
    ```

    The output appears as shown in the following screenshot:

    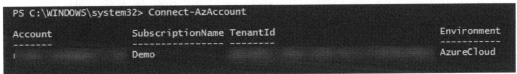

    Figure 14.1 – Connecting to the Azure tenant via PowerShell

2. If you have multiple Azure subscriptions, you can use the following PowerShell command to select a specific subscription:

    ```
    Select-AzSubscription -SubscriptionId "your-
    subscription-id"
    ```

3. Now that we have selected our Azure tenant and subscription, let's go ahead and create a new **Resource Group** (**RG**):

```
New-AzResourceGroup -Name VNet_Demo_ResourceGroup
-Location WestEurope
```

The following screenshot shows the output of the command:

```
PS C:\WINDOWS\system32> New-AzResourceGroup -Name VNet_Demo_ResourceGroup -Location WestEurope


ResourceGroupName : VNet_Demo_ResourceGroup
Location          : westeurope
ProvisioningState : Succeeded
Tags              :
ResourceId        : /subscriptions/(                                    /resourceGroups/VNet_Demo_ResourceGroup
```

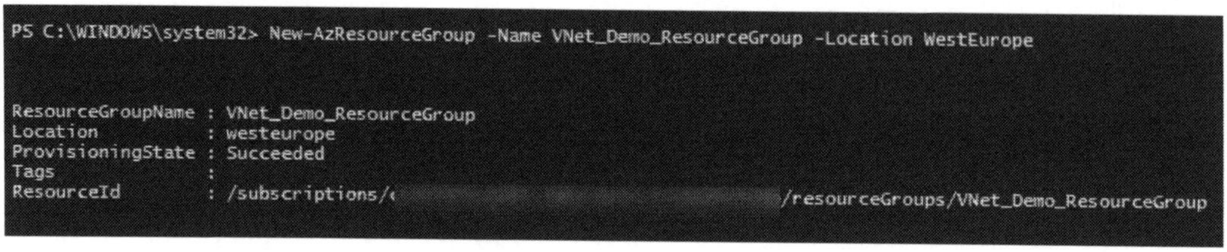

Figure 14.2 – A new RG is created

4. Next, let's create the VNet:

```
$vnet = @{
        Name = 'DemoVNet'
        ResourceGroupName = 'VNet_Demo_ResourceGroup'
        Location = 'WestEurope'
        AddressPrefix = '10.0.0.0/16'
}
$virtualNetwork = New-AzVirtualNetwork @vnet
```

The following screenshot shows the output of the command:

```
PS C:\WINDOWS\system32> $vnet = @{
        Name = 'DemoVNet'
        ResourceGroupName = 'VNet_Demo_ResourceGroup'
        Location = 'WestEurope'
        AddressPrefix = '10.0.0.0/16'
}
$virtualNetwork = New-AzVirtualNetwork @vnet

PS C:\WINDOWS\system32>
```

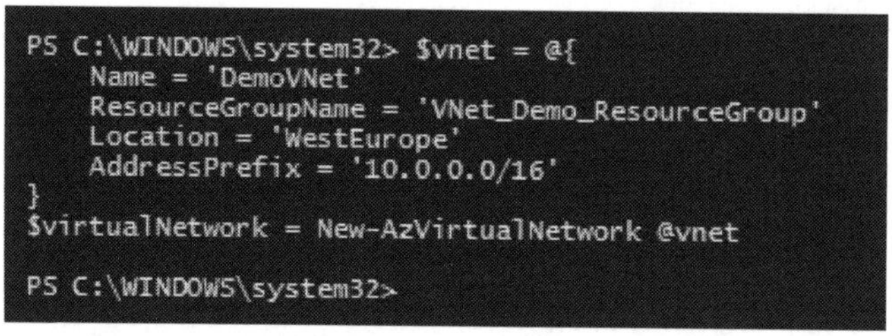

Figure 14.3 – A new VNet is created

5. Next, we need to configure a subnet range within the VNet:

```
$subnet = @{
    Name = 'Demo_Subnet'
    VirtualNetwork = $virtualNetwork
    AddressPrefix = '10.0.0.0/24'
```

```
}
$subnetConfig = Add-AzVirtualNetworkSubnetConfig @subnet
```

6. Lastly, we need to associate the newly created subnet to the VNet with the help of the following command:

```
$virtualNetwork | Set-AzVirtualNetwork
```

7. Verify in the Azure portal that the new VNet and subnet have been created:

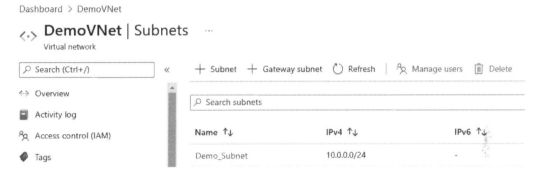

Figure 14.4 – The VNet and subnet showing in the Azure portal

> **Hint**
> If you are getting an error stating that scripts are disabled on your system, you can use the following PowerShell command to resolve it: `set-executionpolicy unrestricted -Scope CurrentUser`.

One of the exam objectives for this chapter is to gain the ability to configure VNet peering. VNet peering is when two or more VNets are linked with each other so that traffic can be sent from one network to another. There are two types of VNet peering:

- **VNet peering**: Connects VNets with the same region. There is also a cost associated with inbound and outbound data transfers for VNet peering.

- **Global VNet peering**: Connects VNets across different regions. This is more costly than VNet peering within the same region.

When using the Azure portal to configure VNet peering, there are a few settings that you should be aware of:

- **Traffic to a remote VNet**: Allows communication between two VNets, as this allows the remote VNet address space to be included as a part of the virtual-network tags.

- **Traffic forwarded from a remote VNet**: Allows traffic forwarded by a VNet appliance in a VNet that did not originate from the original VNet to flow via VNet peering to the other VNet.

- **Virtual network gateway or Route Server**: This is relevant when a VNet gateway is deployed to the VNet and needs traffic from the peered VNet to flow through the gateway.

- **Virtual network deployment model**: Select which deployment model you want with the peered VNet. This will either be classic or the standard resource manager method.

Let's go ahead and configure VNet peering. To do this, we need to create another VNet first using these steps:

1. In PowerShell, use the following command:

```
Connect-AzAccount
```

2. Next, the following command will create another VNet, which will include a subnet that links to the VNet in the same RG that we created earlier in this chapter:

```
$vnet = @{
    Name = 'DemoVNet_2'
    ResourceGroupName = 'VNet_Demo_ResourceGroup'
    Location = 'WestEurope'
    AddressPrefix = '192.168.0.0/24'
}
$virtualNetwork = New-AzVirtualNetwork @vnet
$subnet = @{
    Name = 'Main_Subnet'
    VirtualNetwork = $virtualNetwork
    AddressPrefix = '192.168.0.0/24'
}
$subnetConfig = Add-AzVirtualNetworkSubnetConfig @subnet
$virtualNetwork | Set-AzVirtualNetwork
```

3. Sign in to the Azure portal by visiting `https://portal.azure.com` and navigating to the RG:

Figure 14.5 – Both VNets showing in the Azure portal

4. Next, select **DemoVNet**, and under **Peerings**, select **Add**:

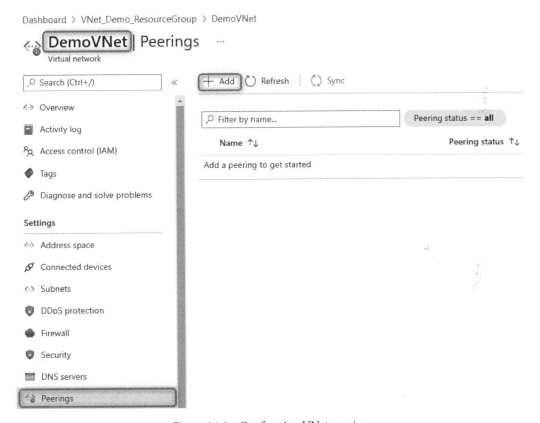

Figure 14.6 – Configuring VNet peering

5. Next, configure the peering link name, as shown in *Figure 14.7*, and set the following fields as **Allow (default)**:

   I.   **Traffic to remove virtual network**

   II. **Traffic forwarded from remote virtual network**

   III. **Virtual network gateway or Route Server**:

Add peering ...

DemoVNet

> ℹ️ For peering to work, two peering links must be created. By selecting remote virtual network, Azure will create both peering links.

This virtual network

Peering link name *

| VNet_Peering | ✓ |

Traffic to remote virtual network ⓘ
- ◉ Allow (default)
- ◯ Block all traffic to the remote virtual network

Traffic forwarded from remote virtual network ⓘ
- ◉ Allow (default)
- ◯ Block traffic that originates from outside this virtual network

Virtual network gateway or Route Server ⓘ
- ◯ Use this virtual network's gateway or Route Server
- ◯ Use the remote virtual network's gateway or Route Server
- ◉ None (default)

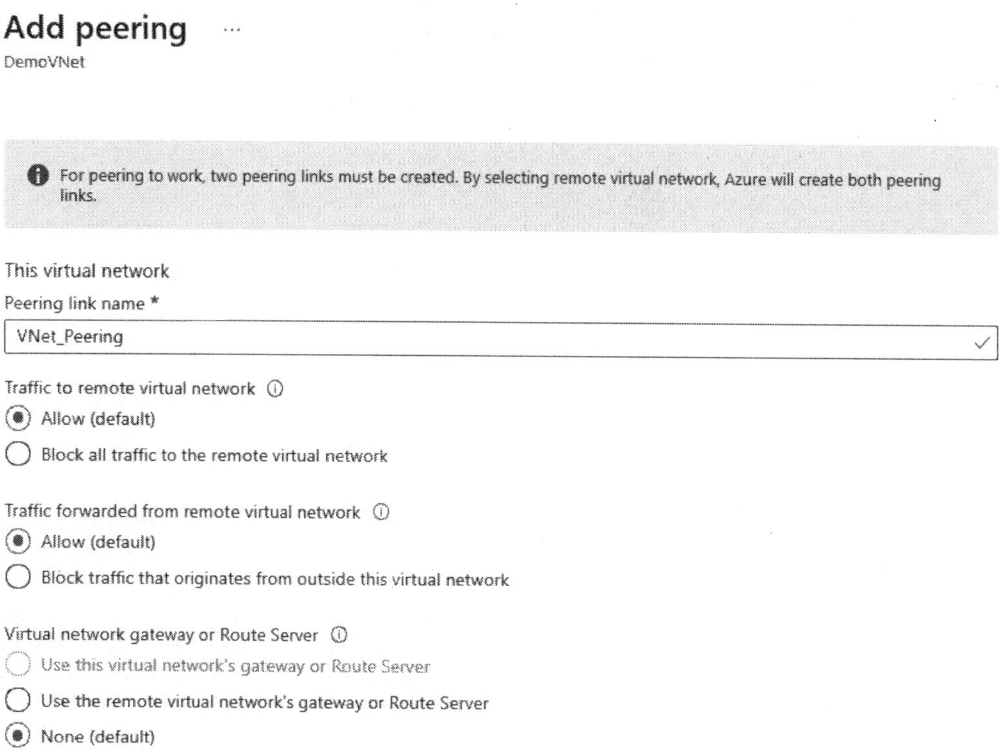

Figure 14.7 – Configuring VNet peering for DemoVNet

6. Next, give the remote peering link a name of `VNet_Peering`, select the VNet, and configure the following fields as **Allow (default)**:

   I.   **Traffic to remove virtual network**

   II. **Traffic forwarded from remote virtual network**

   III. **Virtual network gateway or Route Server**

   Next, click on **Add**:

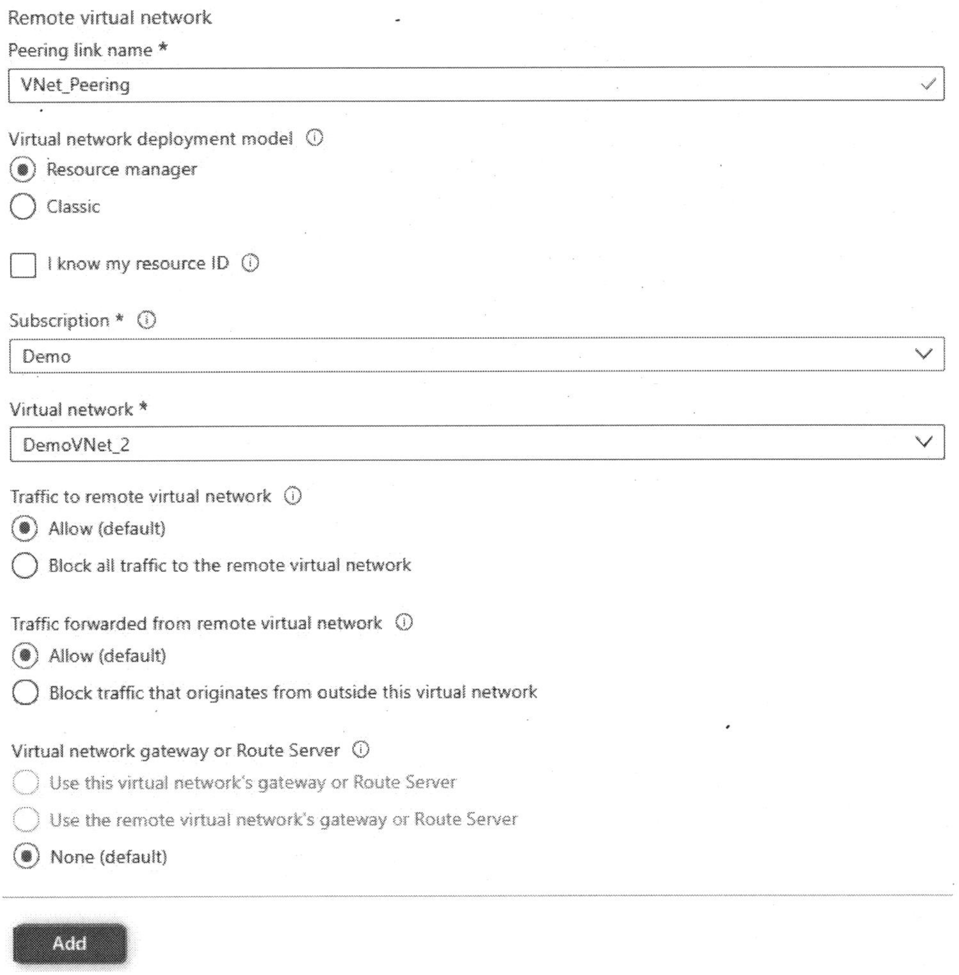

Remote virtual network

Peering link name *

VNet_Peering   ✓

Virtual network deployment model ⓘ

(●) Resource manager

( ) Classic

[ ] I know my resource ID ⓘ

Subscription * ⓘ

Demo   ∨

Virtual network *

DemoVNet_2   ∨

Traffic to remote virtual network ⓘ

(●) Allow (default)

( ) Block all traffic to the remote virtual network

Traffic forwarded from remote virtual network ⓘ

(●) Allow (default)

( ) Block traffic that originates from outside this virtual network

Virtual network gateway or Route Server ⓘ

( ) Use this virtual network's gateway or Route Server

( ) Use the remote virtual network's gateway or Route Server

(●) None (default)

Add

Figure 14.8 – Configuring VNet peering for DemoVNet_2

7.   Give the peering status a few minutes to enforce the peering. The final peering
     status will be **Connected**:

Figure 14.9 – Successfully configured peering between VNets

In this section, we had a look at how virtual networking works in Azure as well as how to create a VNet and subnet via PowerShell. We also had a look at how to configure VNet peering between two VNets.

We encourage you to read up on Azure virtual networking and VNet peering further by using the following links:

- `https://docs.microsoft.com/en-us/azure/virtual-network/quick-create-powershell`

- `https://docs.microsoft.com/en-us/azure/virtual-network/manage-virtual-network`

- `https://docs.microsoft.com/en-us/azure/virtual-network/virtual-network-peering-overview`

Create private and public IP addresses

In the previous section, we had a brief look at IP addressing, such as public and private IP addressing and also static and dynamic IP addresses. This section focuses on how to configure private and public IP addresses.

Let's first look at how to configure a private IP address for a VM from dynamic to static via the Azure portal. In order to do this, we are going to reference a VM we created earlier in this book:

1. Navigate to the Azure portal by opening a web browser and navigating to `https://portal.azure.com`.

2. In the left menu, select **Resource groups** and choose an RG with a VM. In this case, we're going to select the **Az-104** RG:

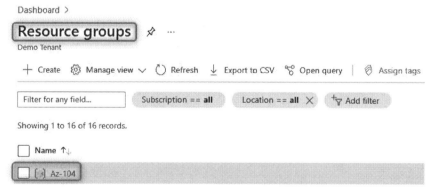

Figure 14.10 – Selecting a previously deployed RG that has a VM

3. Next, select the VM:

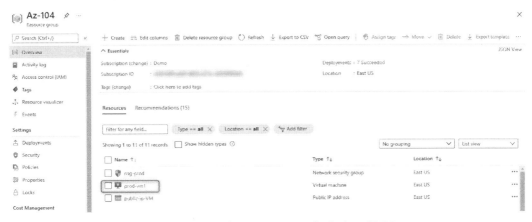

Figure 14.11 – Selecting a previously deployed VM

4. Under the **Settings** tab, select **Networking** and click on the **Network Interface Card** (**NIC**) associated with the VM:

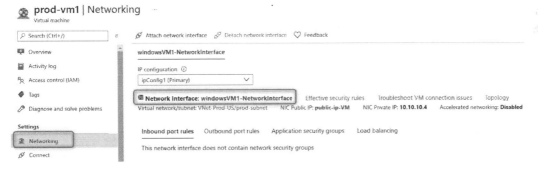

Figure 14.12 – Select the NIC for the VM

5. Next, click on **IP configurations** and select **Private IP address**:

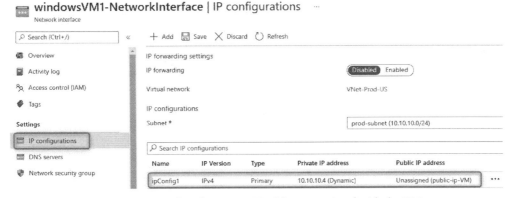

Figure 14.13 – Select the private IP address associated with the VM

6. Finally, under **Assignment**, select **Static** instead of **Dynamic**, and click **Save**:

Figure 14.14 – Select Static and save the configuration

That is how we configure private IP addresses to be static instead of dynamic.

Next, we are going to look at how to create a public IP address via PowerShell:

1. In PowerShell, use the following command to connect to our Azure tenant:

```
Connect-AzAccount
```

The following screenshot shows the output of the command:

Figure 14.15 – Authenticating to the Azure tenant via PowerShell

2. Next, the following code will create a new static public IP address in the West Europe region as a standard SKU:

```
$ip = @{
    Name = 'myStandardPublicIP'
```

```
        ResourceGroupName = 'VNet_Demo_ResourceGroup'
        Location = 'WestEurope'
        Sku = 'Standard'
        AllocationMethod = 'Static'
        IpAddressVersion = 'IPv4'
        Zone = 1,2,3
}
New-AzPublicIpAddress @ip
```

The following screenshot shows the output of the command:

Figure 14.16 – Creating a new public IP address via PowerShell code

3.   Finally, verify that the public IP address has been created in the Azure portal:

Name ↑↓	Type ↑↓	Location ↑↓
⟨·⟩ DemoVNet	Virtual network	West Europe
⟨·⟩ DemoVNet_2	Virtual network	West Europe
▦ myStandardPublicIP	Public IP address	West Europe

Figure 14.17 – Verifying the new public IP address in the Azure portal

It is that simple to create a public IP address via PowerShell. Once the IP address has been created, it is now ready to be assigned to a resource such as a VM or other types of resources that support pre-created public IP addresses.

Next, we are going to look at user-defined routing.

User-defined routing

By default, Azure automatically creates system routes and assigns them to the different subnets within a VNet. These routes can't be removed but can be overridden by custom routes known as **User-Defined Routes** (**UDRs**). These routes have a *next hop* setting that points to the next interface from a routing perspective so that traffic can be sent to the correct destination.

There are three main next hop types for system routes:

- **VNet**: This routes traffic between address ranges within the address space of a VNet.

- **Internet**: This routes traffic specified by the address prefix to the internet; the default route is 0.0.0.0/0, which means anything by default is routed to the internet.

- **None**: Traffic routed to a next hop type as *none* is dropped.

UDRs create a route table if you want to create custom routes. When working with UDRs, it is important to note that they support the preceding routing types as well as the following:

- **VNet gateway**: This is used to route traffic to a VNet gateway.

- **Virtual appliance**: A virtual appliance is a VM that usually acts as a firewall.

Let's go ahead and create a UDR via the Azure portal to forward all traffic to a VNet gateway:

1. Navigate to the Azure portal by opening a web browser and navigating to https://portal.azure.com.

2. Select **Create a resource**. Search for Route table and click on **Create**:

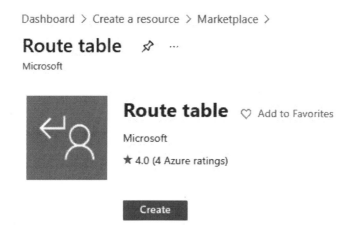

Figure 14.18 – Creating a new route table via the Azure portal

3. Next, select the subscription and RG that the route table needs to be deployed to. Enter the region and name and set **Propagate gateway routes** to **Yes**:

Create Route table ...

Basics   Tags   Review + create

Project details

Select the subscription to manage deployed resources and costs. Use resource groups like folders to organize and manage all your resources.

Subscription * ⓘ	Demo	⌄
Resource group * ⓘ	VNet_Demo_ResourceGroup	⌄
	Create new	

Instance details

Region * ⓘ	West Europe	⌄
Name * ⓘ	Demo-UDR	✓
Propagate gateway routes * ⓘ	⦿ Yes	
	◯ No	

Figure 14.19 – The route table creation configuration settings

4. Now that the route table has been created, you can select it, and under **Settings**, select **Routes**, and then click on **Add**:

Figure 14.20 – Adding a new route on the newly created route table

5. Next, enter the route name as `VPN-Traffic` and the address prefix as `0.0.0.0/0` (which indicates all traffic), set **Next hop type** to **Virtual network gateway**, and click **OK**:

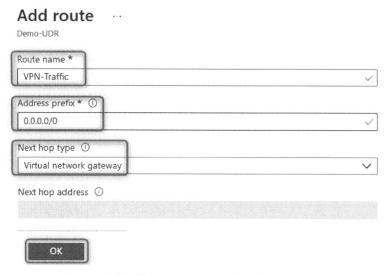

Figure 14.21 – The new route configuration settings

6. Finally, we'll have to verify whether the route is showing up under **Routes**:

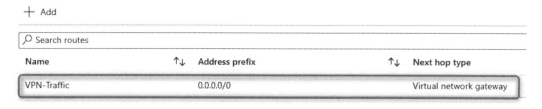

Figure 14.22 – The newly configured route successfully created

We encourage students to read up further on Azure **user-defined routing** (**UDRs**) by visiting the following link: `https://docs.microsoft.com/en-us/azure/virtual-network/virtual-networks-udr-overview`.

In this section, we created a route table with a custom route to route all traffic via the VPN gateway. Next, we are going to look at implementing subnets.

Implementing subnets

Inside a VNet, subnets allow you to segment your IP address ranges in which to place your resources. Resources in a single subnet get an IP address from the subnet IP address range. Resources in subnets within the same VNet can talk to each other. A VNet can have one or more subnets. Traffic can be filtered between subnets either via **Network Security Groups** (**NSGs**) or UDRs. It is also important to know that Azure reserves five IP addresses within each subnet that cannot be used. The reason for this is that these IPs are reserved for the network address, the Azure default gateway, Azure DNS, and the network broadcast address. An example of this would be the following:

Let's say there is a `10.1.1.0/24` subnet; the following addresses are reserved:

- `10.1.1.0`: This is reserved for the network address.
- `10.1.1.1`: This is reserved for the default gateway.
- `10.1.1.2` and `10.1.1.3`: These are reserved by Azure to map DNS IPs to the VNet space.
- `10.1.1.255`: This is reserved for broadcast traffic.

> **Important Note**
> Subnets can be added, removed, or modified.

Subnets within a VNet can be managed via the following methods:

- **The Azure portal**: This is done by signing into the Azure portal.
- **PowerShell**: This is done by authenticating to your Azure tenant and making changes via the **Command-Line Interface** (**CLI**).
- **The Azure CLI**: This is done by authenticating to your Azure tenant and making changes via the CLI.
- **A REST API**: This is done by authenticating to your Azure tenant and using the `PUT` command.

> **Important Note**
> Subnets' address spaces cannot overlap one another.

Let's go ahead and add a subnet to an existing VNet via the Azure portal using the following steps:

1. Navigate to the Azure portal by opening a web browser and navigating to `https://portal.azure.com`.

2. Browse to an RG that has a VNet. In our instance, this is the **VNet_Demo_ResourceGroup**. Select **DemoVNet** and then **Subnets** under the **Settings** blade:

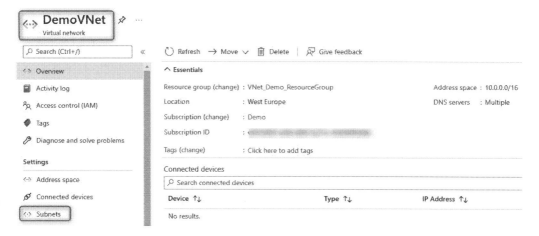

Figure 14.23 – The subnet selection section for a VNet

3. Next, click on add **Subnet**:

Figure 14.24 – Adding a subnet

4. Provide a name in the **Name** field and choose a subnet address range that is available based on the VNet range. Set the following fields to **None**:

    I.   **NAT gateway**

    II. **Network security group**

    III. **Route table**

    IV. **SUBNET DELEGATION**

Important Note

In the real world, the preceding changes may be configured instead of being set to **None**, depending on the requirements.

Set the **Services** fields to **0 selected**, and click on **Save**:

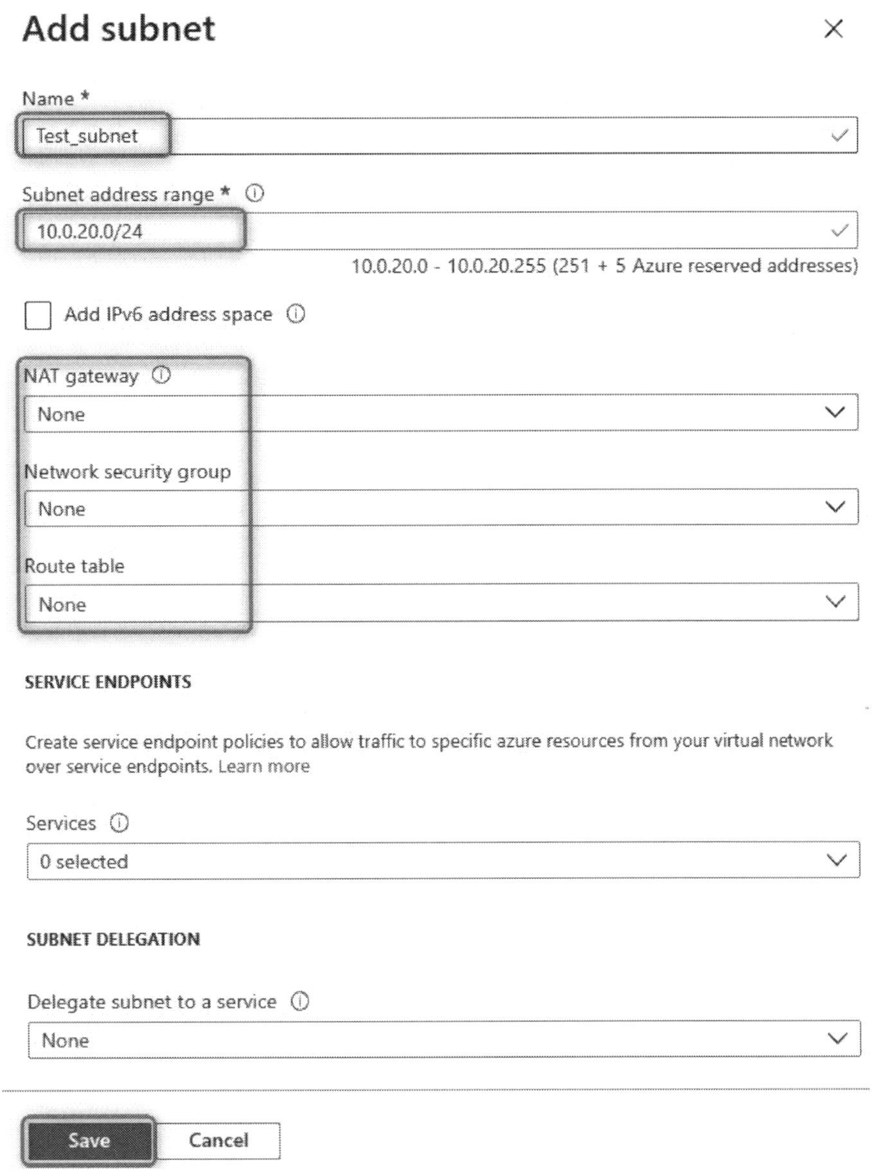

Add subnet   ✕

Name *

| Test_subnet | ✓ |

Subnet address range * ⓘ

| 10.0.20.0/24 | ✓ |

10.0.20.0 - 10.0.20.255 (251 + 5 Azure reserved addresses)

☐ Add IPv6 address space ⓘ

NAT gateway ⓘ

| None | ⌄ |

Network security group

| None | ⌄ |

Route table

| None | ⌄ |

SERVICE ENDPOINTS

Create service endpoint policies to allow traffic to specific azure resources from your virtual network over service endpoints. Learn more

Services ⓘ

| 0 selected | ⌄ |

SUBNET DELEGATION

Delegate subnet to a service ⓘ

| None | ⌄ |

| Save | Cancel |

Figure 14.25 – Configuring the new subnet

5. The new subnet will show up under the **Subnets** section once created:

Figure 14.26 – A new subnet created successfully

In this short section, we had a look at subnetting in Azure and learned how to create additional subnets via the Azure portal. In the next section, we are going to look at configuring endpoints on subnets.

Configuring endpoints on subnets

Endpoints, also referred to as **service endpoints**, allow secure and direct connectivity to Azure services over the Azure backbone network. Endpoints allow you to secure the traffic between your VNets, including subnets, and critical Azure resources such as Key Vault and SQL databases. Service endpoints allow private IP addresses in a VNet to be routed over the Azure backbone without requiring a dedicated public IP address.

Service endpoints are only supported on a limited number of Azure services.

Here are some of the key benefits of using service endpoints:

- **Improved security for Azure service resources**: Routing of traffic to Azure services *to* and *from* the VNet. Subnets are routed through the Azure network without the need to make use of dedicated public IP addresses.

- **Optimal routing for Azure service traffic from your VNet**: Optimized routing and keeps traffic on the Azure backbone network, allowing you to still audit and monitor outbound internet-facing traffic.

- **Ease of configuration and management**: Less work is required as there are no more public IP addresses required to manage via the firewall and also no **Network Address Translation** (**NAT**) or gateway devices to configure and manage.

Let's go ahead and configure a SQL service endpoint on a subnet via the Azure portal using the following steps:

1. Navigate to the Azure portal by opening a web browser and entering the following URL: `https://portal.azure.com`.

2. Browse to an RG that has a VNet and Azure SQL deployed. In our case, this will be **AZ-104SQL**. Select the VNet, which in our case will be **VNet_Demo_SQL**, and then select **Subnets** in the **Settings** blade. Next, choose a subnet:

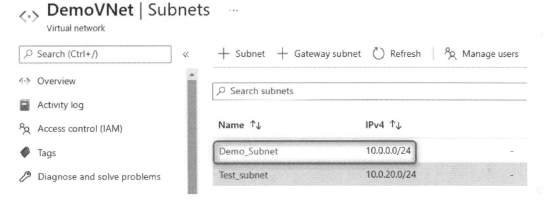

Figure 14.27 – Selecting a subnet to configure service endpoints

3. Next, under **SERVICE ENDPOINTS**, click on the drop-down menu for **Services**, and select **Microsoft.Sql**. Next, click on **Save**:

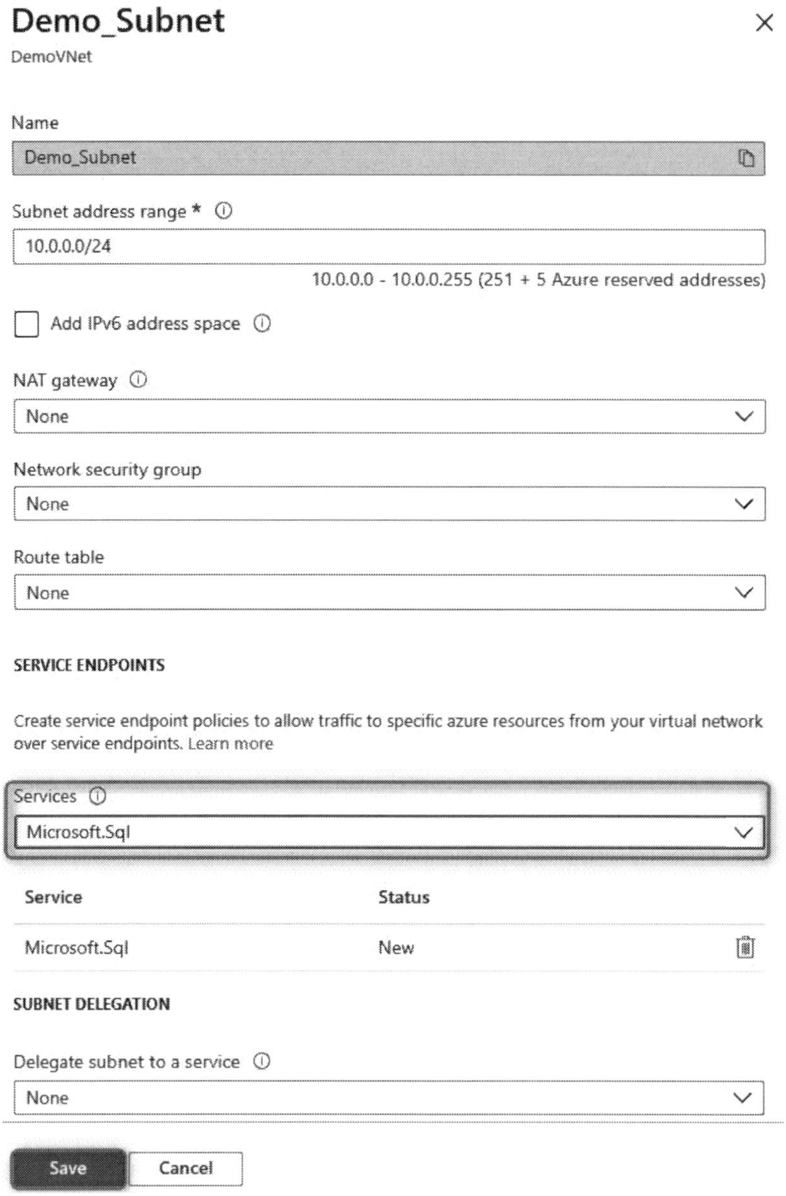

Demo_Subnet   ✕

DemoVNet

Name

| Demo_Subnet | 🗐 |

Subnet address range * ⓘ

| 10.0.0.0/24 |

10.0.0.0 - 10.0.0.255 (251 + 5 Azure reserved addresses)

☐ Add IPv6 address space ⓘ

NAT gateway ⓘ

| None | ⌄ |

Network security group

| None | ⌄ |

Route table

| None | ⌄ |

SERVICE ENDPOINTS

Create service endpoint policies to allow traffic to specific azure resources from your virtual network over service endpoints. Learn more

Services ⓘ

| Microsoft.Sql | ⌄ |

Service	Status	
Microsoft.Sql	New	🗑

SUBNET DELEGATION

Delegate subnet to a service ⓘ

| None | ⌄ |

[Save] [Cancel]

Figure 14.28 – Selecting the SQL service under SERVICE ENDPOINTS

4. Next, navigate to the SQL server instance, and under **Security**, select **Firewalls and virtual networks**:

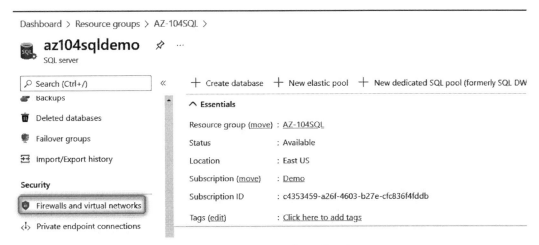

Figure 14.29 – Selecting the SQL firewall and VNet option

5. Select **Add existing virtual network** in the **Virtual networks** section:

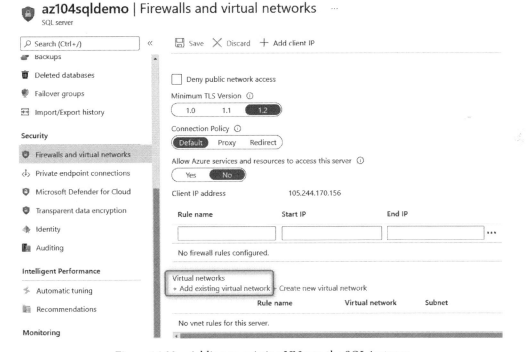

Figure 14.30 – Adding an existing VNet to the SQL instance

Following are the settings to create the network rule:

- **Name**: `SQLTrafficRule`
- **Subscription**: **Demo** (choose your own subscription here)
- **Virtual network**: **VNet_Demo_SQL**
- **Subnet name / Address prefix**: **SQL / 10.50.0.0/24**

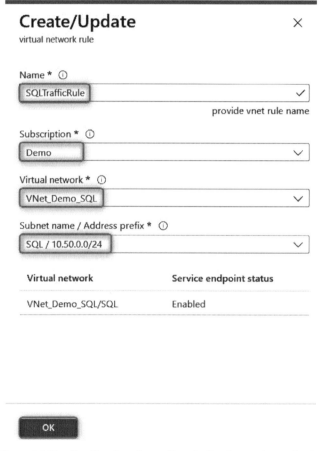

Figure 14.31 – Configuring the traffic rule for the service endpoint

In this section, we had a look at what service endpoints are and learned how to configure them for an SQL service with a specific subnet.

We encourage you to read up on Azure service endpoints further by visiting the following link: `https://docs.microsoft.com/en-us/azure/virtual-network/virtual-network-service-endpoints-overview`.

Configuring private endpoints

Azure Private Link enables you to access **Platform as a Service (PaaS)** services such as Azure Storage and SQL databases, and Azure-hosted services over a *private endpoint* in your own VNet.

Much like service endpoints, private endpoints allow traffic between a VNet and a service to travel through the Microsoft backbone network. This way, exposing your service over the internet is no longer required.

A key difference between service endpoints and private endpoints is that service endpoints connect to Azure/Microsoft services over their backbone while the PaaS resources are still outside of the VNet and, thus, need to be routed as such, whereas private endpoints bring the resources directly into your VNet. It is important to understand that private endpoints keep all the traffic within your VNet:

1. Let's go ahead and configure a Key Vault private endpoint via the Azure portal using the following steps:

2. Navigate to the Azure portal by opening a web browser and visiting the following URL: `https://portal.azure.com`.

3. Under **Create a resource**, search for `private link` and click on **Create**.

4. Next, click on **Create private endpoint**:

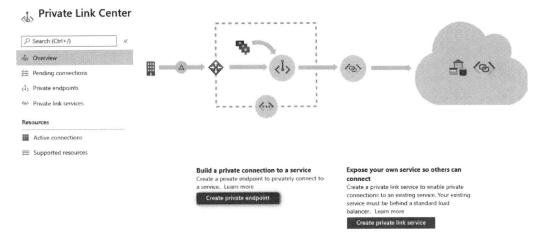

Figure 14.32 – Creating a private endpoint

5. Next, choose a subscription, RG, name, and region:

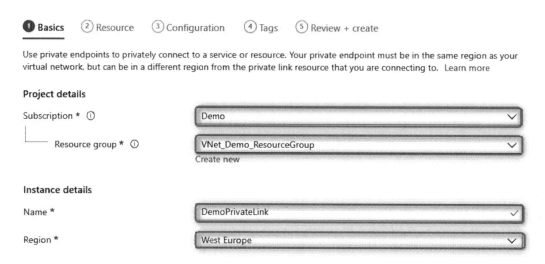

Figure 14.33 – Page one of creating a private endpoint

6. Next, we choose a subscription from the drop-down list, select **Resource type** as **Microsoft.KeyVault/vaults**, and choose the name for the existing resource, and the target sub-resource:

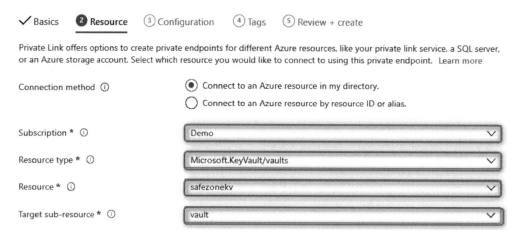

Figure 14.34 – Page two of creating a private endpoint

7. Next, select the VNet that you want the Key Vault service to be added to, as well as the **Subnet** name. Set **Private DNS integration** to **No**:

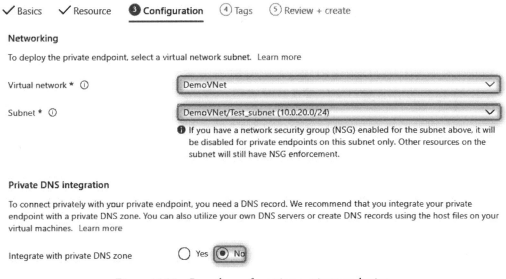

Figure 14.35 – Page three of creating a private endpoint

8. Next, it is optional to provide a name and value as a resource tag. In our case, we're going to skip this for now.

9. On the **Review and create** tab, click **Create**.

10. Finally, once the private endpoint has been created successfully, you can verify it by navigating to the resource and confirming that **Connection status** is **Approved**:

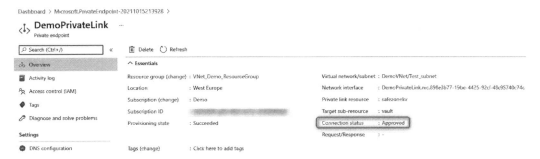

Figure 14.36 – Verifying that the private endpoint has been created successfully

In this section, we had a look at what private endpoints are and how they differ from service endpoints, and learned how to configure private endpoints for an existing key vault and VNet.

We encourage you to read up further on Azure private endpoints by visiting the following links:

- https://docs.microsoft.com/en-us/azure/private-link/private-link-overview

- https://docs.microsoft.com/en-us/azure/private-link/create-private-endpoint-portal

- https://docs.microsoft.com/en-us/azure/private-link/private-endpoint-dns

Configuring Azure DNS

Azure DNS is a hosting service for DNS domains where the name resolution is done via the Microsoft Azure infrastructure. It is important to note that you cannot buy domains via Azure DNS. However, you can delegate permissions to Azure DNS for record management.

There is also a feature called Azure Private DNS that provides a reliable and secure DNS service for VNets. When using private DNS zones, you can use a custom domain name instead of using the default domain names provided by Azure. One of the main reasons for using Azure Private DNS is that the domain names in the VNet will be resolved without having to configure custom DNS on the VNet.

The following is a high-level overview of how Azure Private DNS works:

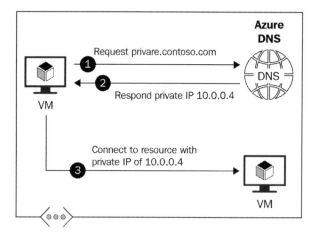

Figure 14.37 – Azure Private DNS

> **Important Note**
> Azure DNS does not support **Domain Name Security Extensions** (**DNSSEC**).

The following are some of the benefits of using Azure Private DNS:

- **Removes the need for custom DNS solutions**: DNS zones can be managed via native Azure infrastructure, which simplifies DNS configuration, since complex custom DNS solutions are no longer required.

- **Supports common DNS record types**: Azure DNS supports the following records – A, AAAA, CNAME, NX, PTR, SOA, SRV, and TXT.

- **Automatic hostname record management**: Azure automatically maintains hostname records for VMs within VNet.

- **Hostname resolution between VNets**

- **Familiar tools and user experience**: You can use the following to update DNS records – the Azure portal, PowerShell, the Azure CLI, ARM templates, and a REST API.

- **Split-horizon DNS support**: The creation of DNS zones with the same name that resolve to different IPs within a VNet and the internet.

- **Availability**: DNS private zones are available across all Azure regions and the Azure public cloud.

Let's go ahead and configure Azure Private DNS via PowerShell using the following steps:

1. In PowerShell, use the following command to connect to our Azure tenant:

```
Connect-AzAccount
```

2. Next, we will need to install the Azure Private DNS module using the following command:

```
Install-Module -Name Az.PrivateDns -force
```

3. Now, we need to create a new DNS zone using the following command. You will need to give it a name and point it to an existing RG:

```
$zone = New-AzPrivateDnsZone -Name demo.packt.com
-ResourceGroupName VNet_Demo_ResourceGroup
```

4. Lastly, we need to link the newly created DNS zone with a VNet using the following command. You will need to add your own RG name and VNet ID to link it to the correct VNet:

```
$link = New-AzPrivateDnsVirtualNetworkLink -ZoneName
demo.packt.com `

  -ResourceGroupName VNet_Demo_ResourceGroup -Name
"mylink" `

-VirtualNetworkId /subscriptions/xxx/resourceGroups/
VNet_Demo_ResourceGroup/providers/Microsoft.Network/
virtualNetworks/DemoVNet -EnableRegistration
```

5. Lastly, let's confirm that our DNS zone has been created successfully. To do this, use the following PowerShell command:

```
Get-AzPrivateDnsZone -ResourceGroupName VNet_Demo_
ResourceGroup
```

The output of the command is shown in the following screenshot:

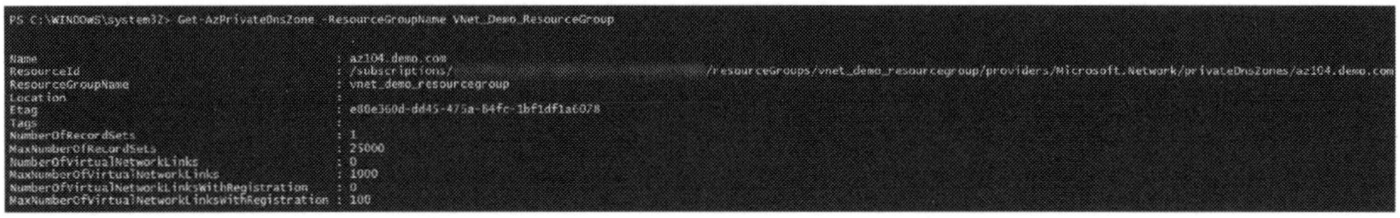

Figure 14.38 – Verifying that the private DNS zone has been created successfully

In this section, we had a look at what Azure DNS is and the difference between Azure DNS and Azure Private DNS. We also looked at how to configure a private DNS zone, link it to an existing VNet, and verify that it has been created successfully.

We encourage you to read up on Azure DNS further by using the following links:

- https://docs.microsoft.com/en-us/azure/dns/dns-overview
- https://docs.microsoft.com/en-us/azure/dns/private-dns-overview

Summary

In this chapter, we discussed how to create VNets including VNet peering, and how to configure private and public IP addresses and UDRs. We also had a look at subnetting in Azure and learned how to configure endpoints and private endpoints for VNets. Lastly, we looked at how Azure DNS works and configured a custom private DNS zone, linking it to an existing VNet via PowerShell.

Skills that students have gained after reading this chapter and following along with the hands-on demos include virtual networking, custom routing in Azure, securing resources via endpoints and private endpoints, and Azure DNS.

In the next chapter, we'll cover how to secure access to VNets.

15

Securing Access to Virtual Networks

This chapter focuses on securing access to virtual networks. You will learn how to create security rules and associate a **Network Security Group** (**NSG**) with a subnet or network interface. You will also learn how to effectively evaluate security rules and try a hands-on deployment on Azure Firewall and Azure Bastion. These are key skills to have as an Azure administrator and ensure you have good experience securing a network and deploying network security components.

In this chapter, we will cover the following main topics:

- Associating an NSG with a subnet
- Creating NSG rules
- Evaluating effective security rules
- Implementing Azure Firewall and Azure Bastion

Technical requirements

To follow along with the hands-on lessons, you will need access to the following:

- An Azure Active Directory as a global administrator. If you do not have access to one, students can enroll for a free account at `https://azure.microsoft.com/en-in/free/`.

- An Azure subscription is also required; you can either register with your own credit card or enroll for the free $200 one-off credit by using the following link: `https://azure.microsoft.com/en-us/free/`.

- PowerShell will be used for some of the lab sections. For more details on how to configure PowerShell, visit `https://docs.microsoft.com/en-us/powershell/azure/install-az-ps?view=azps-1.8.0`.

Associating an NSG with a subnet

When it comes to deploying resources on virtual networks within Azure, it is recommended to only allow the required traffic from a security point of view. One of the free solutions on the Azure platform to use for traffic filtering is called NSGs. NSG rules are evaluated by priority using the following five-tuple information:

- **Source**: This is where the traffic will be coming from, which can be set to the **any** option, an IP address or IP address range, a service tag, or an application security group.

- **Destination**: This will be the end destination receiving the traffic, which can be set to the **any** option, an IP address or IP address range, a service tag, or an application security group.

- **Source port**: This is the ports from where the traffic is originating, which can be a single port such as port 80 or multiple ports such as 80 and 443.

- **Destination port**: These are the ports that the traffic is destined for, which can be a single port such as port 80 or multiple ports such as 80 and 443.

- **Protocol**: The protocol can be set to **TCP, UDP, ICMP,** or any protocol.

Based on the preceding configuration, the NSG rule can be configured to either block or allow traffic.

> **Important Note**
> NSGs can be assigned on a subnet or at a network interface card level.

Let's look at how to create an NSG via the Azure portal and associate it with an existing subnet, using the following steps:

1. Navigate to the Azure portal by opening a web browser and visiting `https://portal.azure.com`.

2. In the left menu, select **Create a resource**, and in the search bar, type `network security group`, and then click **Create**:

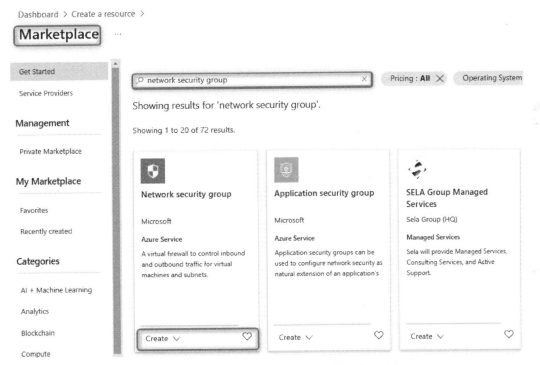

Figure 15.1 – Azure Marketplace filtered for the NSG

3. Next, select an existing subscription and resource group and give the NSG a name, such as `Prod-NSG`, and assign it to a region – in my case, I'm going to choose **East US**. Then, click on **Review + create**:

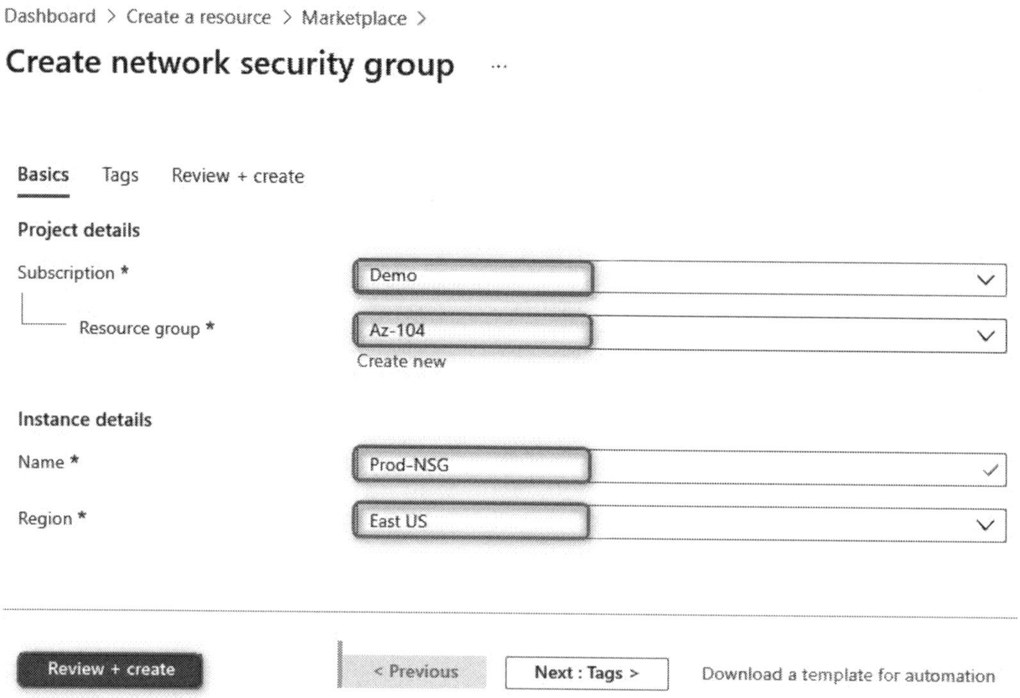

Dashboard > Create a resource > Marketplace >

Create network security group   ...

Basics   Tags   Review + create

Project details

Subscription *   Demo   ∨

└──── Resource group *   Az-104   ∨
                                        Create new

Instance details

Name *   Prod-NSG   ✓

Region *   East US   ∨

[Review + create]   [< Previous] [Next : Tags >]   Download a template for automation

Figure 15.2 – Creating an NSG

4. Once the validation has passed, click on **Create**. The resource will be created within a few minutes.

Now that we have successfully created our NSG, we are going to assign it to all resources on the subnet level for a specific **virtual network** (**VNet**). To do this, let's navigate to the newly created NSG overview page in Azure. This can be found under the **All resources** section.

5.   Under **Settings** on the **NSG** page, select the **Subnets** blade and click on + **Associate**:

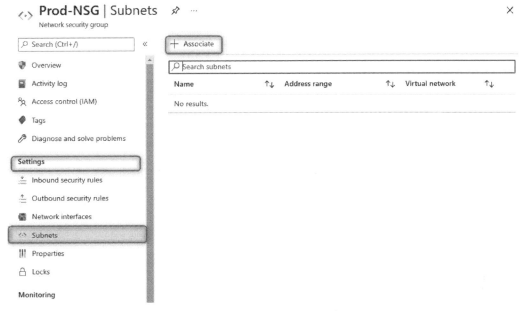

Figure 15.3 – The Subnets blade

6.   Next, select an existing VNet – in my case, this will be **Vnet-prod-US**. Select an existing subnet – in my case, this will be **prod-subnet**. Then, click on **Ok**.

In this demonstration, we covered what the purpose of NSGs is and how to create a new NSG via the Azure portal and assign it to an existing subnet.

In the next section, are going to have a look at how to configure NSG rules.

Creating NSG rules

Now that we have associated the NSG with its default rules with a subnet, we need to create a new NSG rule that will deny **Remote Desktop Protocol (RDP)** traffic from the internet to the entire VNet. In order to do this, we need to do the following:

1. Navigate to the Azure portal by opening a web browser and visiting `https://portal.azure.com/#home`.

2. In the left menu, select **All resources**, and in the search bar, type `network security group`. Select the NSG we created earlier – in my case, it will be **Prod-NSG**:

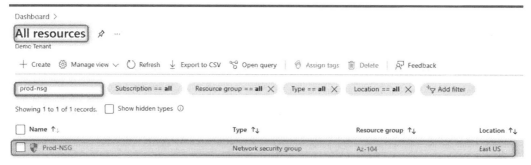

Figure 15.4 – Selecting the newly created NSG

3. Under the **Settings** pane, select **Inbound security rules** and click on **Add**:

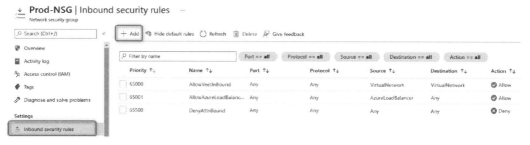

Figure 15.5 – Adding an inbound rule to the NSG

4. Next, under **Source**, select **Service Tag**, and under **Source service tag**, select **Internet** from the dropdown list. Next, leave **Source port ranges** with an asterisk sign. **Destination** will be the **VirtualNetwork** option from the dropdown list. **Service** will be **RDP** from the dropdown list. Enter the destination port range as `3389`. Select **TCP** as the protocol. Leave **Priority** at `100`. Choose the **Deny** action. Lastly, give the rule a name of `Deny-RDP` and click on **Add**:

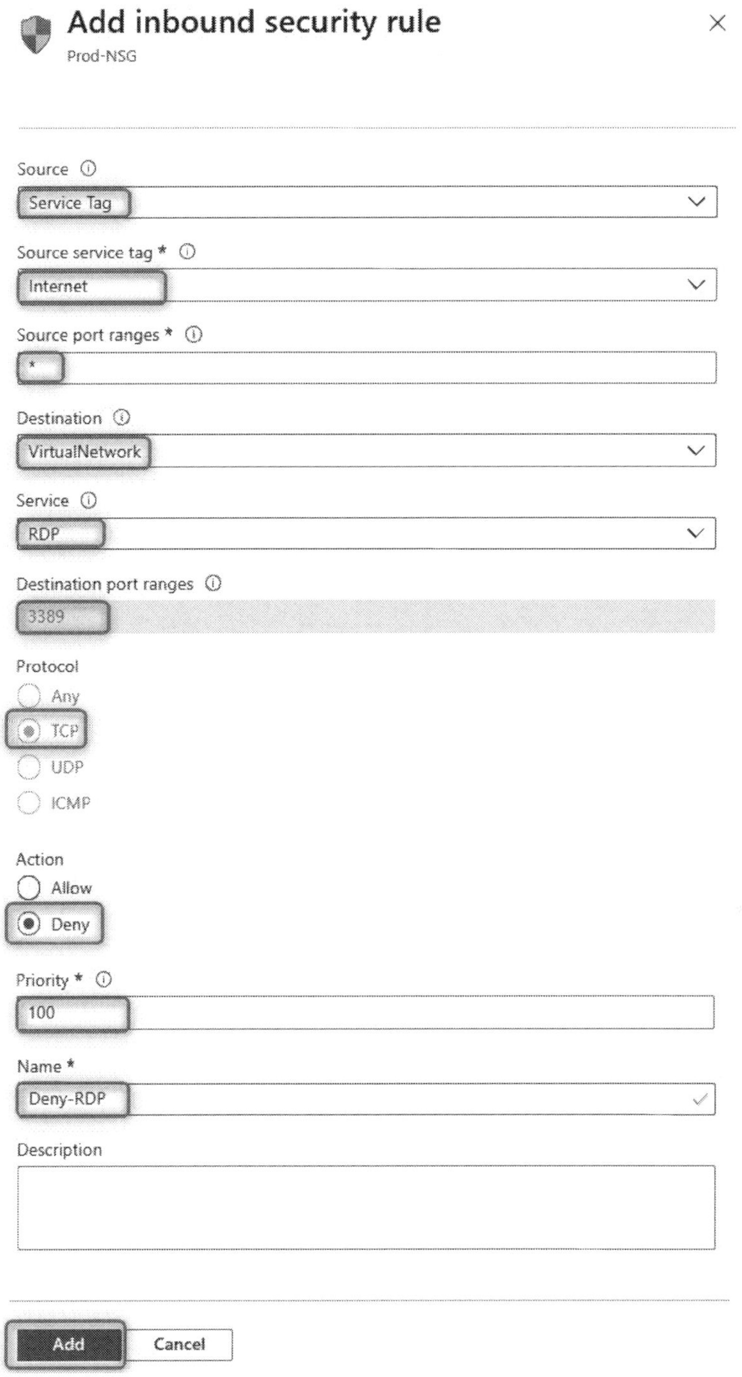

Add inbound security rule
Prod-NSG

✕

Source ⓘ

Service Tag ⌄

Source service tag * ⓘ

Internet ⌄

Source port ranges * ⓘ

*

Destination ⓘ

VirtualNetwork ⌄

Service ⓘ

RDP ⌄

Destination port ranges ⓘ

3389

Protocol

○ Any

⦿ TCP

○ UDP

○ ICMP

Action

○ Allow

⦿ Deny

Priority * ⓘ

100

Name *

Deny-RDP ✓

Description

Add   Cancel

Figure 15.6 – Configuring the inbound security rule

5. The final step is to verify that the RDP session is not allowed to any **virtual machine (VM)** within the subnet via the internet:

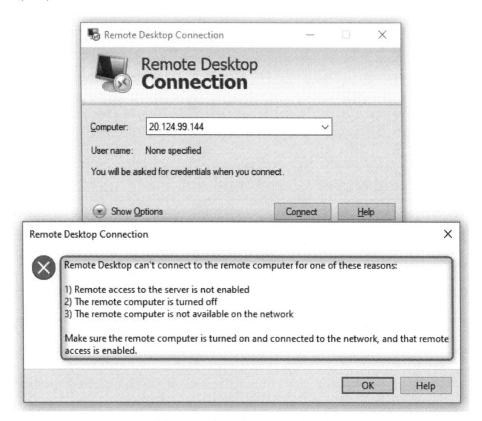

Figure 15.7 – Proof that our inbound security rule is denying RDP traffic

This concludes the demonstration of how to configure NSG rules. We also confirmed that our newly created rules are working as expected. We encourage students to further read up on NSGs by using the following links:

*   `https://docs.microsoft.com/en-us/azure/virtual-network/network-security-groups-overview`
*   `https://docs.microsoft.com/en-us/azure/virtual-network/tutorial-filter-network-traffic`

Next, we are going to look at how to evaluate effective NSG rules.

Evaluating effective security rules

When you create an NSG, there are some default inbound and outbound security rules created for you automatically. The default rules are low-priority rules. You can also add custom rules to them. You can create inbound and outbound security rules. NSG rules follow priority, with the lowest rule number taking preference over the next rule.

The following is a screenshot of NSG inbound rules that show two RDP rules – one to allow RDP and one to deny RDP. The RDP rule with the lowest priority takes preference, meaning that the *allow RDP rule* will take effect before the *deny RDP rule*:

Inbound port rules	Outbound port rules	Application security groups	Load balancing				

Network security group Prod-NSG (attached to subnet: prod-subnet)
Impacts 1 subnets, 0 network interfaces

Add inbound port rule

Priority	Name	Port	Protocol	Source	Destination	Action	
100	RDP	3389	TCP	105.244.170.205	10.10.10.4	✓ Allow	...
110	RDP_Deny	3389	TCP	105.244.170.205	10.10.10.4	✗ Deny	...
65000	AllowVnetInBound	Any	Any	VirtualNetwork	VirtualNetwork	✓ Allow	...
65001	AllowAzureLoadBalancerInBound	Any	Any	AzureLoadBalancer	Any	✓ Allow	...
65500	DenyAllInBound	Any	Any	Any	Any	✗ Deny	...

Figure 15.8 – The NSG inbound rules for RDP are allowed

If there are too many NSG rules to manually review or multiple NSGs associated with a resource and you are unsure of which rules are taking preference, it is a good idea to use a built-in tool in Azure called **Network Watcher** to check the flow of traffic by using the **IP flow verify** blade of the tool. More information can be found here: `https://docs.microsoft.com/en-us/azure/network-watcher/network-watcher-monitoring-overview`.

In this section, we had a look at NSG rules to understand how rules take preference and which advanced troubleshooting tools we can use in Azure to verify the flow of traffic.

Implementing Azure Firewall and Azure Bastion

Let's have a look at Azure Firewall and the different SKUs available and what functionality they have.

Azure Firewall

When it comes to networking in Azure, NSGs are considered a basic-level firewall. However, sometimes a solution is required that has more granular control over traffic, or a smarter firewall is required; this is where Azure Firewall shines.

Azure Firewall has three main policies that can be configured:

- **A Network Address Translation (NAT) rule**: This is used to translate the firewall's public IP address and port to a private IP address and port.

- **A network rule**: This has the same rules as NSGs but has additional features, such as being able to create rules based on **fully qualified domain names (FQDNs)** instead of just using IP addresses.

- **An application rule**: This is used to allow or deny traffic based on specific applications that are based on FQDNs.

The following diagram shows how rules in Azure Firewall are processed based on rule type:

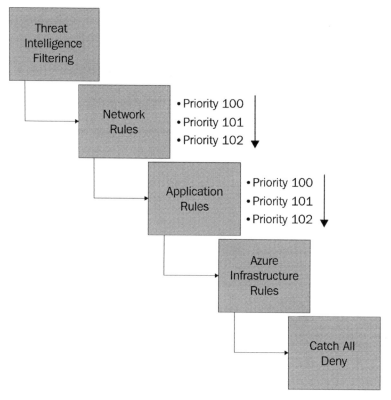

Figure 15.9 – Azure Firewall rule processing

It is important to understand rule processing within Azure Firewall, especially in troubleshooting scenarios.

> **Tip**
> Network rules are processed before application rules.

There are two SKUs for Azure Firewall:

- **Azure Firewall Standard**: This provides OSI layer three to OSI layer seven filtering, based on threat intelligence feeds directly from Microsoft. This enables Microsoft to feed Azure Firewall intelligence on known malicious IP addresses and domains to block these threats from accessing resources behind the firewall:

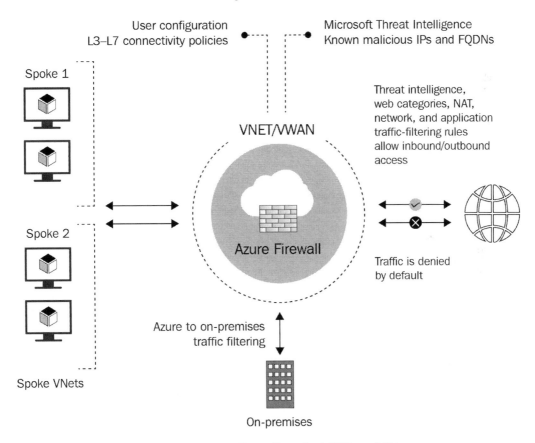

Figure 15.10 – Azure Firewall standard SKU capabilities

- **Azure Firewall Premium**: This provides advanced threat protection for organizations that are highly regulated, such as financial and healthcare institutions. This SKU supports **Transport Layer Security (TLS)** inspection of traffic to prevent malware and viruses from spreading across a network. It also supports URL filtering to include an entire URL and allow or deny a user access to websites by category, such as gambling sites and social media:

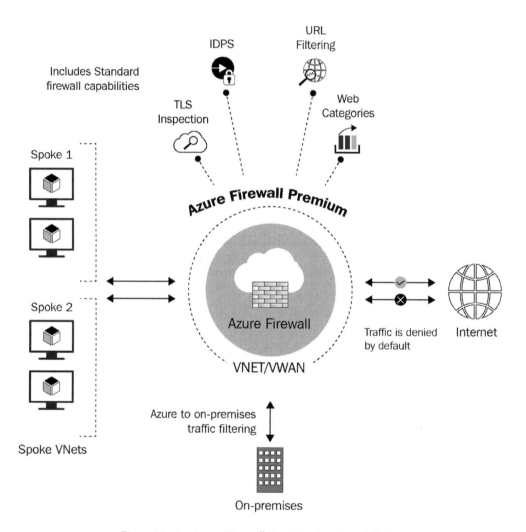

Figure 15.11 – Azure Firewall Premium SKU capabilities

The Azure Firewall Premium SKU offers the same features as the standard SKU and Premium features, such as TLS inspection and IDPS protection, to prevent the spread of malware and viruses across a network.

> **Note**
> Azure Firewall Manager can be used to centrally manage Azure firewalls across multiple subscriptions.

Azure Bastion

Traditionally, there were two main ways to connect to VMs in the cloud. The first was to assign a static public IP address and connect to them via the **Remote Desktop Protocol (RDP)** or **secure shell (SSH)**, but this was later replaced by removing the public IP address and using a **virtual private network (VPN)** to securely connect to the server via the RDP or SSH. The Azure Bastion service enables you to connect to a VM by using your browser and the Azure portal instead of using technologies such as VPN. Bastion is a **platform-as-a-service (PaaS)** that you provision inside the VNet in Azure, which provides secure connectivity on management ports such as the RDP and SSH. Here are some key benefits of using Azure Bastion:

- **The RDP and/or SSH directly in the Azure portal**: An RDP or SSH session via the browser.

- **Remote session via TLS**: Bastion uses an HTML5-based web client that is streamed to the device, connecting to it via TLS on port 443 for security purposes.

- **No public IP address required on a VM**: Bastion will open an RDP/SSH connection to the VM by using the private IP address, meaning no public IP address is required.

- **No additional firewall rules required**: There are no additional complex NSG rules required for this solution to work; only allow Bastion to access the required VMs.

- **Reduced attack surface**: VMs are better protected, as there are no public IP addresses assigned to them, which means external malicious users cannot port-scan the VM to detect weaknesses in the VM.

The following is a diagram that shows how Azure Bastion works:

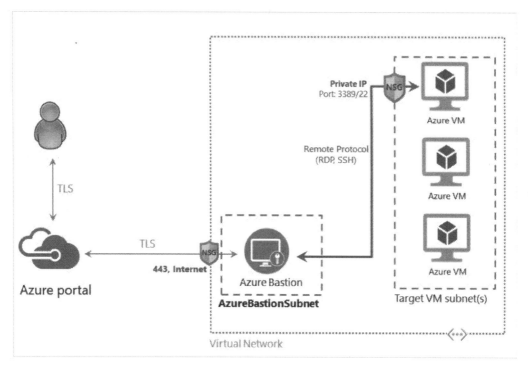

Figure 15.12 – How Azure Bastion works

Now that we have a better understanding of Azure Firewall and Azure Bastion, let's learn how to do the following via PowerShell:

- Create a new VNet with a VM.

- Deploy an Azure Firewall.

- Create a default route within the firewall.

- Configure an application rule to allow access to `www.google.com`.

- Configure a network rule to allow access to external **Domain Name System (DNS)** servers.

- Test the firewall rules.

To achieve the preceding objectives, follow these steps:

1. First, we need to connect to our Azure tenant by using the following PowerShell command:

   ```
   Connect-AzAccount
   ```

   The screenshot shows the output of the command:

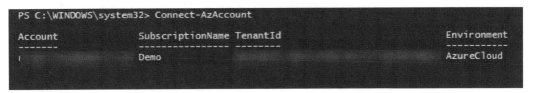

   Figure 15.13 – Connecting to the Azure tenant via PowerShell

2. If you have multiple subscriptions, you can use the following PowerShell command to select a specific subscription:

   ```
   Select-AzSubscription -SubscriptionId "your-
   subscription-id"
   ```

3. Now that we have selected our Azure tenant and subscription, let's go ahead and create a new **Resource Group** (**RG**):

   ```
   New-AzResourceGroup -Name Test-FW-RG -Location "East US"
   ```

   The screenshot shows the successful creation of the new RG:

```
PS C:\WINDOWS\system32> New-AzResourceGroup -Name Test-FW-RG -Location "East US"

ResourceGroupName : Test-FW-RG
Location          : eastus
ProvisioningState : Succeeded
Tags              :
ResourceId        : /subscriptions/c                              /resourceGroups/Test-FW-RG
```

Figure 15.14 – Creating the new RG

4. Next, we are going to create the VNet, which has three subnets — a bastion subnet, a firewall subnet, and the VM subnet:

   - $Bastionsub = New-AzVirtualNetworkSubnetConfig -Name AzureBastionSubnet -AddressPrefix 10.0.0.0/27

   - $FWsub = New-AzVirtualNetworkSubnetConfig -Name AzureFirewallSubnet -AddressPrefix 10.0.1.0/26

   - $VMSubnet = New-AzVirtualNetworkSubnetConfig -Name VMSubnet -AddressPrefix 10.0.2.0/24

- ```
  $testVnet = New-AzVirtualNetwork -Name Test-FW-VN
  -ResourceGroupName Test-FW-RG -Location "East US"
  -AddressPrefix 10.0.0.0/16 -Subnet $Bastionsub,
  $FWsub, $VMSubnet
  ```

Figure 15.15 – A newly created VNet with the three subnets

5. Next, we are going to create a public IP address for the Bastion service:

```
$publicip = New-AzPublicIpAddress -ResourceGroupName
Test-FW-RG -Location "East US" -Name Bastion-pip
-AllocationMethod static -Sku standard
```

The public IP address for Bastion is shown in the following screenshot:

Name ↑↓	Type ↑↓	Location ↑↓
Bastion-pip	Public IP address	East US
Test-FW-VN	Virtual network	East US

Figure 15.16 – A newly created public IP address for the Bastion service

6. Next, we are going to create the Bastion host:

```
New-AzBastion -ResourceGroupName Test-FW-RG -Name
Bastion-01 -PublicIpAddress $publicip -VirtualNetwork
$testVnet
```

The following screenshot shows the newly created Bastion service:

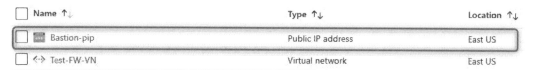

Figure 15.17 – Creating the Bastion service
```

7. Next, we are going to create the VM. You will be prompted to enter a username and password while running the script; please ensure that you remember this information:

```
#Create the NIC
$wsn = Get-AzVirtualNetworkSubnetConfig -Name  VMSubnet
-VirtualNetwork $testvnet
$NIC01 = New-AzNetworkInterface -Name VM01
-ResourceGroupName Test-FW-RG -Location "East us" -Subnet
$wsn

#Define the virtual machine
$VirtualMachine = New-AzVMConfig -VMName VM01 -VMSize
"Standard_DS2"
$VirtualMachine = Set-AzVMOperatingSystem -VM
$VirtualMachine -Windows -ComputerName VM01
-ProvisionVMAgent -EnableAutoUpdate
$VirtualMachine = Add-AzVMNetworkInterface -VM
$VirtualMachine -Id $NIC01.Id
$VirtualMachine = Set-AzVMSourceImage -VM $VirtualMachine
-PublisherName 'MicrosoftWindowsServer' -Offer
'WindowsServer' -Skus '2019-Datacenter' -Version latest

#Create the virtual machine
New-AzVM -ResourceGroupName Test-FW-RG -Location "East
US" -VM $VirtualMachine -Verbose
```

In this section of code, we have created the VM along with a password, as shown in the following screenshot. This information needs to be stored for use later:

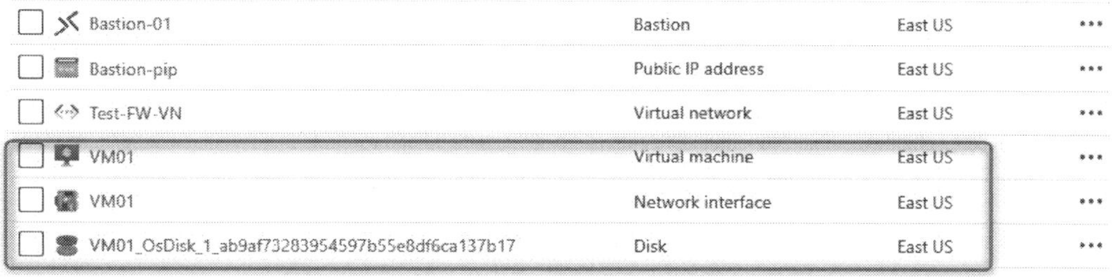

☐ ✕ Bastion-01	Bastion	East US	•••
☐ ▦ Bastion-pip	Public IP address	East US	•••
☐ ⟨·⟩ Test-FW-VN	Virtual network	East US	•••
☐ 🖥 VM01	Virtual machine	East US	•••
☐ 🖧 VM01	Network interface	East US	•••
☐ 🖴 VM01_OsDisk_1_ab9af73283954597b55e8df6ca137b17	Disk	East US	•••

Figure 15.18 – The created VM01 with its components

8. Next, we are going to deploy the firewall along with a public IP address:

```
# Get a Public IP for the firewall
$FWpip = New-AzPublicIpAddress -Name "fw-pip"
-ResourceGroupName Test-FW-RG `
   -Location "East US" -AllocationMethod Static -Sku
Standard
# Create the firewall
$Azfw = New-AzFirewall -Name Test-FW01 -ResourceGroupName
Test-FW-RG -Location "East US" -VirtualNetwork $testVnet
-PublicIpAddress $FWpip


#Save the firewall private IP address for future use


$AzfwPrivateIP = $Azfw.IpConfigurations.privateipaddress
$AzfwPrivateIP
```

The following screenshot displays the newly deployed firewall:

☐	Bastion-01	Bastion	East US
☐	Bastion-pip	Public IP address	East US
☐	fw-pip	Public IP address	East US
☐	Test-FW-VN	Virtual network	East US
☐	Test-FW01	Firewall	East US
☐	VM01	Virtual machine	East US
☐	VM01	Network interface	East US
☐	VM01_OsDisk_1_ab9af73283954597b55e8df6ca137b17	Disk	East US

Figure 15.19 – The Azure Firewall deployed

9. Next, we are going to configure a default route on the firewall along with a route table and associate the latter with our VMSubnet:

```
$routeTableDG = New-AzRouteTable `
  -Name Firewall-rt-table `
  -ResourceGroupName Test-FW-RG `
  -location "East US" `
  -DisableBgpRoutePropagation


#Create a route
 Add-AzRouteConfig `
```

```
    -Name "DG-Route" `
    -RouteTable $routeTableDG `
    -AddressPrefix 0.0.0.0/0 `
    -NextHopType "VirtualAppliance" `
    -NextHopIpAddress $AzfwPrivateIP `
  | Set-AzRouteTable


#Associate the route table to the subnet
Set-AzVirtualNetworkSubnetConfig `
    -VirtualNetwork $testVnet `
    -Name VMSubnet `
    -AddressPrefix 10.0.2.0/24 `
    -RouteTable $routeTableDG | Set-AzVirtualNetwork
```

In this section of code, we have created a new route table with a route named
DG-Route and associated it with the subnet.

The following screenshot displays the newly created route table:

☐	Bastion-01	Bastion	East US
☐	Bastion-pip	Public IP address	East US
☐	Firewall-rt-table	Route table	East US
☐	fw-pip	Public IP address	East US
☐	Test-FW-VN	Virtual network	East US
☐	Test-FW01	Firewall	East US
☐	VM01	Virtual machine	East US
☐	VM01	Network interface	East US
☐	VM01_OsDisk_1_ab9af73283954597b55e8df6ca137b17	Disk	East US

Figure 15.20 – The newly created route table

10. Next, we are going to create an application rule on the firewall to allow outbound
    access to www.google.com:

```
$AppRule1 = New-AzFirewallApplicationRule -Name Allow-
Google -SourceAddress 10.0.2.0/24 `
    -Protocol http, https -TargetFqdn www.google.com


$AppRuleCollection =
New-AzFirewallApplicationRuleCollection -Name App-Coll01
```

```
      -Priority 200 -ActionType Allow -Rule $AppRule1

$Azfw.ApplicationRuleCollections.Add($AppRuleCollection)


Set-AzFirewall -AzureFirewall $Azfw
```

In this section of code we have created a new Azure Firewall application rule to allow outbound access to Google.

The following screenshot displays the newly created Azure Firewall application rule:

Target FQDNs

name	Source type	Source	Protocol:Port	Target FQDNs
Allow-Google	IP address	10.0.2.0/24	Http:80,Https:443	www.google.com

Figure 15.21 – The application rule added to Azure Firewall

11. Next, we are going to configure a network rule on the firewall to allow outbound access to 8.8.8.8 on the port 53 UDP, which is for DNS resolution:

```
$NetRule1 = New-AzFirewallNetworkRule -Name "Allow-DNS"
-Protocol UDP -SourceAddress 10.0.2.0/24 `
    -DestinationAddress 8.8.8.8 -DestinationPort 53
$NetRuleCollection = New-AzFirewallNetworkRuleCollection
-Name RCNet01 -Priority 200 `
    -Rule $NetRule1 -ActionType "Allow"

$Azfw.NetworkRuleCollections.Add($NetRuleCollection)

Set-AzFirewall -AzureFirewall $Azfw
```

In this section of code, we have created an Azure Firewall application rule to allow outbound access to Google's DNS server, which is 8.8.8.8 for DNS resolution, as shown in the following screenshot:

IP Addresses

name	Protocol	Source type	Source	Destination type	Destination Addresses	Destination Ports
Allow-DNS	UDP	IP address	10.0.2.0/24	IP address	8.8.8.8	53
	0 selected ⌄	IP address ⌄	*, 192.168.10.1, 192.168.10.0/24, 19...	IP address ⌄	*, 192.168.10.1, 192.168.10.0/24, 1...	8080, 8080–8090, *

Figure 15.22 – Adding a firewall rule to allow outbound DNS traffic to 8.8.8.8

12. Finally, we are going to change the DNS server address for VM01 to 8.8.8.8 to align with the firewall rule for DNS:

```
$NIC01.DnsSettings.DnsServers.Add("8.8.8.8")
$NIC01 | Set-AzNetworkInterface
```

Now that we have completed all the required configurations, let's test and confirm the VM and firewall rules:

1. Navigate to the Azure portal by opening a web browser and visiting https://portal.azure.com.

2. Navigate to the new VM we created called **VM01**. On the **Overview** page, select **Connect** and choose **Bastion**:

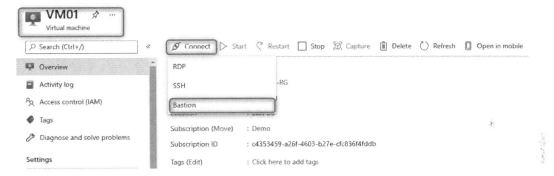

Figure 15.23 – Connect to the VM using Bastion

3. Next, the **Bastion** window is will appear, and you will need to enter the VM credentials you specified in *step 7* and then click on **Connect**:

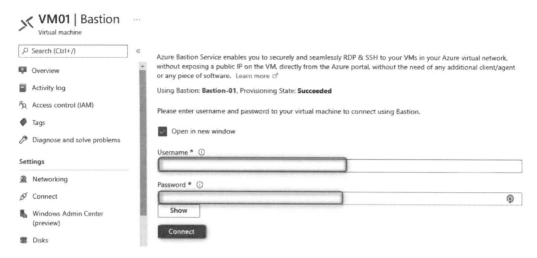

Figure 15.24 – Enter the credentials for the VM on the Bastion blade

4. On the VM, open up PowerShell and enter the following commands:

```
nslookup www.google.com
nslookup www.microsoft.com
```

Both commands should return answers, as the DNS queries are allowed through the firewall:

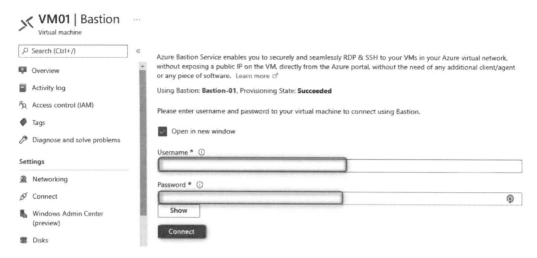

Figure 15.25 – Proof that the firewall DNS settings are working as expected

5. Next, we want to confirm that we are able to browse only to `www.google.com` and not any other sites. To do this, run the following command in PowerShell:

```
Invoke-WebRequest -Uri https://www.google.com
```

The preceding command will request the `www.google.com` website via the PowerShell **command-line interface (CLI)**:

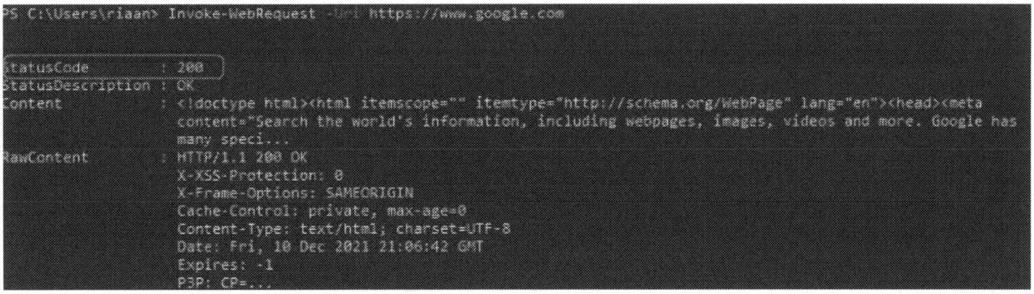

Figure 15.26 – The firewall allowing traffic to www.google.com

6. Finally, let's confirm that we are not able to visit any other FQDN, such as `www.microsoft.com`. In order to test this, run the following command in PowerShell:

```
Invoke-WebRequest -Uri https://www.microsoft.com
```

The screenshot confirms that we cannot resolve `www.microsoft.com` based on the Azure Firewall configuration rules, which is the expected behavior:

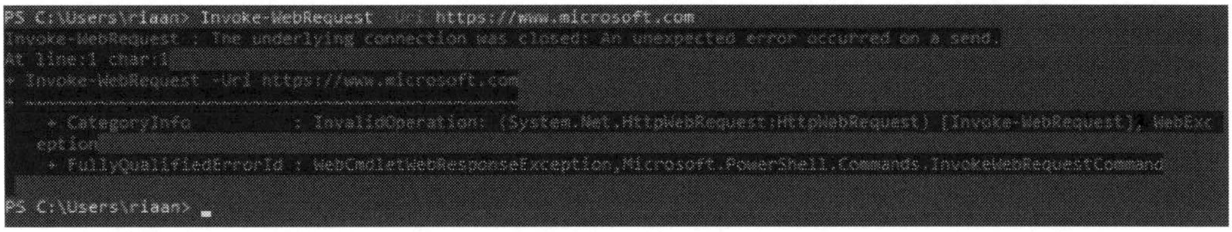

Figure 15.27 – Traffic is not allowed to www.microsoft.com as per our firewall configuration

To summarize this demo section, we have learned how to configure Azure Bastion along with an Azure firewall to allow DNS requests to `8.8.8.8` and only allow `www.google.com` from a browsing perspective and block all other sites.

We encourage you to further read up on Azure Bastion and Azure Firewall by using the following links:

- `https://docs.microsoft.com/en-us/azure/firewall/`
  `overview#:~:text=Azure%20Firewall%20is%20a%20`
  `cloud,availability%20and%20unrestricted%20cloud%20`
  `scalability.`

- https://docs.microsoft.com/en-us/azure/firewall/threat-intel

- https://docs.microsoft.com/en-us/azure/firewall/policy-rule-sets

- https://docs.microsoft.com/en-us/azure/bastion/bastion-overview#:~:text=Azure%20Bastion%20is%20a%20service,browser%20and%20the%20Azure%20portal.&text=Using%20Azure%20Bastion%20protects%20your,-secure%20access%20using%20RDP%2FSSH.

If you want to remove the resources created in this section to avoid further costs, you can run the following command in PowerShell:

```
Connect-AzAccount
Remove-AzResourceGroup -Name Test-FW-RG
```

The preceding PowerShell commands will remove the RG we created earlier along with all resources within it to ensure there will be no unforeseen costs incurred by the resources for this chapter.

This will help you save additional costs.

Summary

In this chapter, we discussed what NSGs are and how to use them to create new rules, as well as how to associate them with a subnet. We also discussed how to evaluate NSG rules based on priority. Lastly, we covered Azure Firewall and Azure Bastion, what they do, and how to configure them via a hands-on demo.

After reading this chapter, you should now know how to secure VNets via an NSG and secure resources by using Azure Bastion and Azure Firewall. In the next chapter, we'll cover how to configure load balancing by using Azure Application Gateway and internal and external load balancers, and how to troubleshoot load balancing.

16
Configuring Load Balancing

In the previous chapter, we covered network security and explored topics such as **network security groups (NSGs)**, firewalls, and Azure Bastion. This chapter focuses on **high availability (HA)** with reference to the relevant objectives of the AZ-104 exam, such as configuring an Azure Application Gateway and creating and configuring an internal and public load balancer. You will also learn how to create health probes for your load balancer and configure load balancing rules. The chapter will end with how to troubleshoot these load balancing services.

In this chapter, we are going to cover the following main topics:

- Azure load balancing services
- Azure Load Balancer
- Configuring an **internal load balancer (ILB)**
- Configuring a public load balancer
- Azure Application Gateway
- Configuring Azure Application Gateway
- Azure Front Door
- Configuring Azure Front Door

Technical requirements

To follow along with the hands-on material, you will need the following:

- Access to an Azure subscription with owner or contributor privileges. If you do not have access to one, you can enroll for a free account: `https://azure. microsoft.com/en-us/free/`.

- PowerShell *5.1* or later installed on a PC where labs can be practiced; note that many examples can only be followed from a PC.

- Installation of the AZ module, which can be performed by running the following in an administrative PowerShell session:

```
Set-ExecutionPolicy -ExecutionPolicy RemoteSigned -Scope
CurrentUser
```

You can also run the following:

```
Install-Module -Name Az -Scope CurrentUser -Repository
PSGallery -Force
```

Azure load balancing services

Azure offers several services for load balancing. Microsoft views these services as being separated by web-type workloads (HTTP(S)-type traffic) and by global and regional delivery.

Regional services

Regional services are designed to distribute traffic within Azure **virtual networks** (**VNets**) and services within a single region. Typically, these would be used for **virtual machines** (**VMs**) and containers.

Global services

Global services are designed to distribute traffic across different regions. This can also be used to extend services beyond the Azure cloud into other clouds or on-premises environments. They also include features for better system performance on a global scale by creating distributed workloads that can cater to specific regional requirements. Typically, these would be used for global web services that require local regional services and HA.

Load balancer service options

Azure provides two load balancer services catered to traffic that is not HTTP(S)-related, meaning that they are not intended for web-related workloads. These are frequently used to distribute traffic between VMs:

- Azure Load Balancer (regional service)
- Traffic Manager (global service)

In addition to the preceding services, there are currently two services that can be deployed to cater to web-based traffic, being HTTP(S) traffic, and are delivered as Layer 7 load balancers. These are Azure Application Gateway and Azure Front Door.

> **Top Tip**
>
> As of the time of writing, Azure has a cross-region load balancer in preview; you can read more about the service here: `https://docs.microsoft.com/en-us/azure/load-balancer/cross-region-overview`.

These services offer **Secure Sockets Layer** (**SSL**) offloading, path-based load balancing, and session affinity configuration settings. You can also choose to enable the web application firewall feature, which scans the traffic received by your applications and assesses this for anomalous behavior, particularly focused on web applications. The two services that can be used for web-based load balancing are as follows:

- Application Gateway (regional service)
- Azure Front Door (global service)

Next, we will discuss the features available in Application Gateway and Front Door, and also understand their purposes.

SSL offloading

SSL is the technology that enables encrypted communication between your browser and web application service. This has now been replaced by a new technology called **Transport Layer Security** (**TLS**). One of the benefits of both Application Gateway and Azure Front Door is that they provide SSL offloading or TLS termination that effectively transfers the decryption function to the load balancing service implemented. This provides several benefits to your application infrastructure, namely better performance and utilization of your backend services. This termination functionality also enables the load balancer to interrogate the traffic to provide more intelligent management features such as routing and header management.

Path-based load balancing

Both Azure Front Door and Application Gateway support URL path-based routing. The functionality provided by this feature enables you to split traffic based on your URL path. Traffic can be split and separated to route to different backend pools by matching your path-based rules. You may choose, for instance, to serve different content types through separate backend server pools; there could be several reasons for doing so, for instance, you may want to deliver images from a slower storage set as they are not required for instant consumption, whereas your videos may be designed for live streaming. The delivery of both these resource types requires different sets of resources and configurations; if you enabled path-based routing, you could look for the /image portion of your URL and route those to the image backend pool, likewise for your videos. This enables a much more controlled and dynamic management flow for your applications. The following diagram illustrates the splitting we discussed previously:

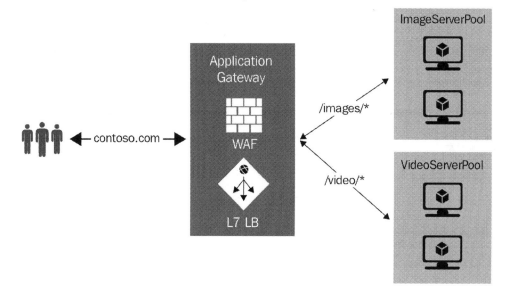

Figure 16.1 – URL path-based routing

As you can see from the preceding diagram, traffic is routed based on its source URL type. The conventions for this are defined relative to the root path on the server, with / representing the root. In the preceding diagram, should your website domain be `contoso.com`, the `/images/*` pattern would be the equivalent of `contoso.com/images/`. The wildcard represents any character after the path as part of the search term.

> **Top Tip**
>
> Note that the URL pattern cannot include # or ? as its character. Each pattern must start with a / character.

Session affinity

Session affinity is the ability to retain communications between the same source and destination systems for the life of the communication window established between the systems. This means if *user1* passes through some load balancing service to *server1*, all communication from *user1* to the central load-balanced service would flow directly to *server1* from the user. Without this, traffic would be balanced between servers and services, meaning that the second call from the user could be routed to *server2* or *serverx*. Enable this where session integrity is required by your applications.

Web application firewall

The **web application firewall** (**WAF**) is a specialized service that caters to protecting web-based traffic to protect from vulnerabilities and exploits. The service is based on the **Core Rule Set** (**CRS**) developed by the **Open Web Application Security Project** (**OWASP**). The service is easy to implement and requires no modification of your application code to be functional, and it works in line with your traffic. All alerts raised will be logged in the WAF log, which is integrated into Azure Monitor. You can customize rules based on your requirements and against several sites served by the Application Gateway.

> **Top Tip**
>
> You can protect up to 40 websites using the WAF service per Application Gateway instance.

There are several protections the service caters to, including the following:

- Protection against HTTP protocol violations and anomalies
- SQL injection attacks
- **Cross-site scripting (XSS)** attacks
- Geo traffic filtering (allow/block regions from accessing your applications)

The following diagram is an illustration of the WAF service in action:

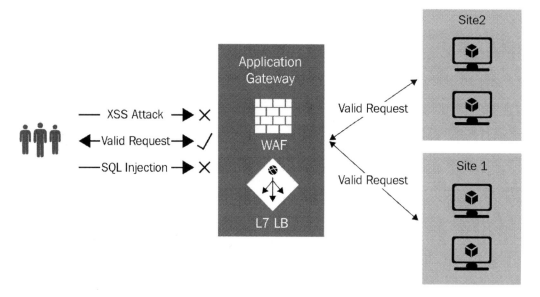

Figure 16.2 – URL path-based routing

Now that you understand more about the load balancing services available to you in Azure, we will explore each of these services in a bit more detail and explore the configuration of each of these.

Azure Load Balancer

Azure Load Balancer is a load balancer that operates at the transport layer (Layer 4 in the OSI network reference stack). Azure Load Balancer supports the **Transmission Control Protocol (TCP)** and **User Datagram Protocol (UDP)**, and it can be used to load-balance traffic to your applications and is generally used in scenarios where you would like to enable HA. The concept of HA refers to the ability of your applications or services to sustain some form of downtime; should you sustain a loss of a workload or node, your load balancer will redirect traffic to the remaining available and functional workloads or nodes. Load balancers provide scalability by sharing the load of the traffic among several responding servers, which also creates resiliency as traffic is not dependent on a single node to respond. Azure load balancers provide high throughput and low latency and can scale up to millions of flows. They support various inbound and outbound scenarios.

The Azure Load Balancer service can be used for the following:

- **Public load balancer**: Incoming internet traffic is load-balanced to VMs.
- **ILB**: Traffic can be load-balanced across VMs inside a virtual network. You can also use it in a hybrid scenario, where it reaches a load balancer inside an on-premises network.
- **Port forwarding**: You can forward traffic to specific ports on specific VMs using inbound **network address translation (NAT)** rules.
- **Outbound connectivity**: You can also provide outbound connectivity for VMs inside a virtual network using it on Azure Load Balancer as a public load balancer.

> **Top Tip**
> Whenever you hear a reference to HA or scalability, you should immediately start to question whether a load balancer should be implemented; in many scenarios, this will be one of the resources you will need in your toolset.

Now that you understand a bit about what load balancing is and, more specifically, what Azure Load Balancer is, we will explore some of the features and capabilities it provides.

Features and capabilities

Azure Load Balancer offers several features and capabilities as part of its service, such as load balancing, port forwarding, automatic reconfiguration, health probes, and outbound **source NAT (SNAT)** connections.

Load balancing

Traffic can be distributed from a frontend pool to a backend pool using rules. Azure Load Balancer uses a **five-tuple hash** by default, which is composed of the source IP address, source port, destination IP address, destination ports, and the IP protocol number to map flows to the available servers in the backend pool.

Port forwarding

Inbound NAT rules can be created to forward traffic from a specific port of the frontend IP address of the load balancer to a specific port of a backend instance inside an Azure VNet. Therefore, the same hash-based distribution is used as with load balancing. This can be used for the **Remote Desktop Protocol** (**RDP**) and **Secure Shell** (**SSH**) sessions to VMs inside the VNet. Multiple internal endpoints can be mapped to various ports on the same frontend IP address. The VMs can be remotely administered using the frontend IP address. This way, an additional jump box is not needed.

Automatic reconfiguration

The load balancer will automatically reconfigure itself when instances are scaled up or down. There is no need for additional operations on the load balancer when VMs are added or removed from the backend pool.

Health probes

Azure Load Balancer uses health probes to determine the health of the VMs in the backend pool. The load balancer will stop sending new connections to a VM instance when a probe fails to respond. There are different health probes provided for HTTP, HTTPS, and TCP endpoints.

Outbound connections (SNAT)

Outbound connections are automatically translated to the public frontend IP address of the load balancer. When used on ILBs, a rule must be configured to allow outbound internet access.

> **Top Tip**
> When you configure an HTTPS health probe, you will require a certificate to perform the probe assessment.

Now that you understand some of the features and capabilities of Azure load balancers, we will explore the different **stock keeping units** (**SKUs**) available in Azure and what they differ on.

Load Balancer SKUs

Azure Load Balancer comes with two different SKU options, Basic and Standard. They differ in price, features, and delivery of the service.

Basic

The Basic load balancer is free to use and has the following capabilities:

- **Backend pool size**: The Basic tier supports up to 100 instances inside a backend pool.
- **Health probes**: TCP and HTTP.
- **Outbound connections**: A single frontend is supported, which is selected at random when multiple frontends are configured. The default SNAT is used when there is only an ILB that is serving a VM, VM scale set, or availability set.
- **Diagnostics**: Support for Azure Log Analytics for a public load balancer only, backend pool health count, and SNAT exhaustion alert.
- **Default security**: Open by default; NSGs are optional.
- **Management operations**: 60-90+ seconds.

The Basic SKU has the following limitations on the service that the Standard SKU doesn't:

- **Availability zones**: Not available
- **Outbound rules**: Not available
- **HA ports**: Not available
- **TCP Reset on Idle**: Not available
- **Multiple frontends**: Not available
- **Service-level agreement** (**SLA**): Not available
- **Global VNet peering support**: Not supported
- **NAT Gateway support**: Not supported
- **Private link support**: Not supported
- **Cross-region load balancing**: Not supported

Now that you know about what the Basic SKU offers and doesn't offer, we will explore the Standard SKU offering.

Standard

The Standard tier of Azure Load Balancer carries a cost. The charge is based on the number of rules and the data that is associated with the resource and is processed, inbound and outbound. This SKU is designed to be secure by default and has the following capabilities:

- **Backend pool size**: The standard tier supports up to 1,000 instances inside a backend pool.

- **Health probes**: TCP, HTTP, and HTTPS.

- **Availability zones**: Support for zone-redundant and zonal frontends for inbound and outbound connections and cross-zone load balancing.

- **Outbound connections**: Multiple frontends can be used per load balancing rule opt-out. Pool-based outbound NAT can be explicitly defined using outbound rules. Outbound scenarios must be explicitly created to use outbound connectivity for the VM, VM scale set, or availability set. VNet service endpoints can be reached without defining outbound connectivity. Public IP addresses and **Platform as a Service** (**PaaS**) that are not available using VNet service endpoints must be reached with outbound connectivity.

- **Outbound rules**: Outbound NAT configuration needs to be defined using public IP addresses, public IP prefixes, or both. You can configure the outbound idle timeout as well as custom SNAT port allocation.

- **Diagnostics**: Azure Load Balancer has support for Azure Monitor, with features including health probe status, outbound connection health (SNAT successful and failed flows), multi-dimensional metrics, and active data-plane measurements.

- **HA ports**: Highly available ports for the ILB only.

- **Default Security**: These are secure by default. Unless internal load balancers are whitelisted by an NSG, the endpoints are closed to inbound flows by default. Public IP addresses and load balancer endpoints are secured as well.

- **TCP Reset on Idle**: This can be enabled on the idle timeout on any rule.

- **Multiple frontends**: For inbound and outbound connections.

- **Management operations**: < 30 seconds for most operations.

- **SLA**: 99.99% for a data path with two healthy VMs.

- **Global VNet peering support**: Supported for standard ILBs.

- **NAT Gateway support**: Supported for public load balancers and ILBs.

- **Private link support**: Supported only for standard ILBs.

- **Cross-region load balancing**: Supported for public load balancers.

As you will have seen, there are some distinct differences between the two types of load balancers. It's important to understand these differences prior to deploying any solution. One of the key items to look out for is the Standard SKU as you will need to explicitly define an NSG rule to allow traffic to flow through the load balancer. Also, remember that the basic SKU doesn't offer an SLA, which is critical to production environments and ensuring that you have conducted due diligence. Another important feature of the Standard SKU is the option to have multiple frontends, which enables you to control traffic to multiple firewalls and services and helps you better manage your traffic. Next, we will explore configuration.

Configuring an ILB

In this demonstration, we are going to create and configure a load balancer from the Azure portal. We are going to route internal traffic with a basic load balancer to spread incoming requests to multiple VMs. For this demonstration, we are going to create a load balancer, backend servers, and network resources at the Basic pricing tier.

Creating the VNet

First, we are going to create the VNet, backend servers, and a test VM. To do this, take the following steps:

1. Navigate to the Azure portal by opening `https://portal.azure.com`.

2. Create a new resource group for this exercise named `AZ104-InternalLoadBalancer`. Open the resource group once created, click **Overview** on the left menu, then click **Create**.

3. Type `virtual network` in the search bar and click **Virtual network**:

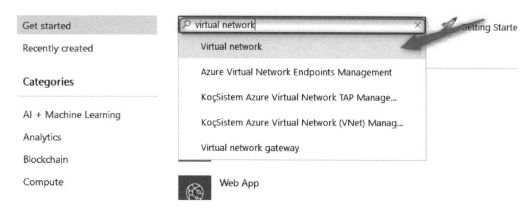

Figure 16.3 – Creating a virtual network

4. Click **Create**.

5. Enter the following values for the **Basics** tab, then click **Next : IP Addresses >**:

    - **Subscription**: Select a subscription

    - **Resource group**: `AZ104-InternalLoadBalancer`

    - **Name**: `PacktLBVnet`

    - **Region**: A region of your choice (choose the same region for all subsequent resources in this chapter)

6. Enter the following values for the **IP Addresses** tab, and click **Next : Security >**. Set **IPv4 address space** to `172.16.0.0/16`, set **Subnet name** to `PacktLBBackendSubnet`, and set **Subnet address range** to `172.16.0.0/24`. You can leave the default configuration for **NAT GATEWAY** and **Services**. Click **Add**.

7. Set the following options:

    - **Bastion Host**: Disable

    - **DDOS Protection Standard**: Disable

    - **Firewall**: Disable

8. Click **Review + create**. Click **Create**.

Now that the VNet is in place, you will now work on creating the VMs.

Creating the VMs

Please ensure that the AZ module is installed as per the *Technical requirements* section at the beginning of the chapter.

In the next demonstration, we are going to create three Windows Server VMs from PowerShell and place them in an Availability Set. To do so, you will perform the following steps:

Note: Change the parameters to suit your requirements.

```
# First connect your Azure account using your credentials
Connect-AzAccount

# Parameters
$ResourceGroup = "AZ104-InternalLoadBalancer"
$Location = "WestEurope"
$SubscriptionId = "xxxxxxx"
$AvailabilitySetName = "PacktLBAvailabilitySet"
$VirtualNetworkName = "PacktLBVnet"
$SubnetName = "PacktLBBackendSubnet"
$VMUserName = "Packtadmin"
$VMPassword = "P@55w0rd()"

# If necessary, select the right subscription as follows
Select-AzSubscription -SubscriptionId $SubscriptionId

# Create an Availability Set for the VMs
New-AzAvailabilitySet -Location "$Location" -Name
"$AvailabilitySetName" -ResourceGroupName "$ResourceGroup" -Sku
aligned -PlatformFaultDomainCount 2 -PlatformUpdateDomainCount
2
# Set up Your VM Admin Credentials
[securestring]$secStringPassword = ConvertTo-SecureString
$VMPassword -AsPlainText -Force
[pscredential]$cred = New-Object System.Management.Automation.
PSCredential ($VMUserName, $secStringPassword)
# Deploy two VMs Inside the Availability Set
for ($vmNum=1; $vmNum -le 3; $vmNum++){
    if ($vmNum -eq 3){$vmName = "PacktLBVMTest"} # Test VM
```

```
    else{$vmName = "PacktLBVM$vmNum"}
    New-AzVm -ResourceGroupName "$ResourceGroup" -Name
"$vmName" -Location "$Location" -VirtualNetworkName
"$VirtualNetworkName" -SubnetName "$SubnetName"
-SecurityGroupName "PacktNetworkSecurityGroup"
-PublicIpAddressName "$($vmName)PublicIpAddress"
-AvailabilitySetName "$AvailabilitySetName" -Credential $cred
-OpenPorts 3389 -Size "Standard_DS1_v2"
}
```

Now that your VMs are deployed, we will work on the load balancer next.

Creating the load balancer

Now, we can create the load balancer using the Azure portal as follows:

1. Navigate to the Azure portal by opening `https://portal.azure.com`.

2. Open the `AZ104-InternalLoadBalancer` resource group we created, click **Overview** on the left menu, then click **Create**.

3. Click **See more in Marketplace** next to **Popular products**:

Figure 16.4 – See more in Marketplace

4. Click **Networking** on the left **Categories** pane and click **Load Balancer** on the right blade screen. Then, click **Create**:

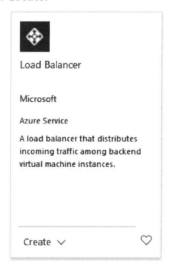

Figure 16.5 – Load Balancer

5. Enter `AZ104-InternalLoadBalancer` for **Resource group**, `PackLoadBalancer` for **Name**, **West Europe** for **Region**, set **SKU** to **Basic**, **Type** to **Internal**, and finally, **Tier** to **Regional**. Click **Next : Frontend IP configuration >**:

Create load balancer   ...

| Basics | Frontend IP configuration | Backend pools | Inbound rules | Outbound rules | Tags | Review + create |

Azure load balancer is a layer 4 load balancer that distributes incoming traffic among healthy virtual machine instances. Load balancers uses a hash-based distribution algorithm. By default, it uses a 5-tuple (source IP, source port, destination IP, destination port, protocol type) hash to map traffic to available servers. Load balancers can either be internet-facing where it is accessible via public IP addresses, or internal where it is only accessible from a virtual network. Azure load balancers also support Network Address Translation (NAT) to route traffic between public and private IP addresses. Learn more.

Project details

Subscription *   AzureTraining

└─── Resource group *   AZ104-InternalLoadBalancer
                                   Create new

Instance details

Name *   PackLoadBalancer

Region *   West Europe

SKU * ⓘ   ○ Standard
                                   ○ Gateway
                                   ◉ Basic

                                   ⓘ Microsoft recommends Standard SKU load balancer for production workloads.
                                   Learn more about pricing differences between Standard and Basic SKU ⧉

Type * ⓘ   ○ Public
                                   ◉ Internal

Tier *   ◉ Regional
                                   ○ Global

Review + create   < Previous   **Next : Frontend IP configuration >**   Download a template for automation ℞Give feedback

Figure 16.6 – Creating a load balancer

6. Click + **Add a frontend IP configuration**. Enter `PacktLBFEName` as **Name**, select **PackLBVnet** as **Virtual network**, and in **Subnet**, select **PacktLBBackendSubnet**. Set **Assignment** to **Dynamic**, and click **Add**:

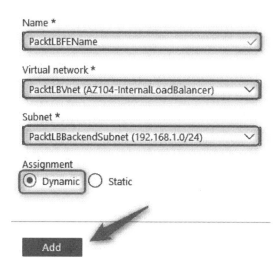

Figure 16.7 – Add a frontend IP configuration

7. Click **Next : Backend pools >**.

8. Click + **Add a backend pool**. Enter `PacktLBBackendPool` as **Name**, set **Associated to** as **Virtual machines**, **IP Version** as **IPv4**, and then click + **Add** under **Virtual machines**.

9. On the pop-up screen, select **PacktLBVM1** and **PacktLBVM2**, then click **Add**.

10. Click **Add** again:

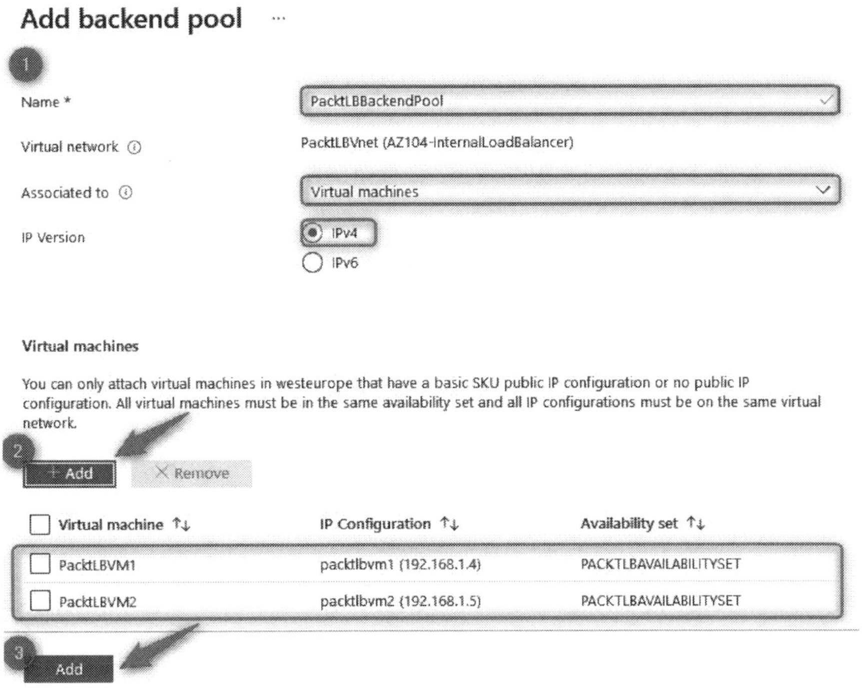

Figure 16.8 – Add a backend pool

11. Click **Review + create**. Click **Create**.

You now have the load balancer resource configured with a frontend IP address. You have also configured your backend pool in line with the deployment consisting of **PacktLBVM1** and **PacktLBVM2**. We now need a mechanism for load balancing traffic between our VMs and we need a method of detecting the health of our services on the VMs. Next, we'll configure the health probes for our load balancer before moving on to investigating rules to distribute the traffic to the VMs.

Creating the health probes

The next step is to create a health probe for the load balancer, which is used for the load balancer to monitor the status of the VM. The probe will dynamically add or remove VMs from the load balancer rotation, based on the response to the health checks that are performed by the health probe. To create a health probe, take the following steps:

1. Open your Load Balancer resource.

2. Under **Settings**, select **Health probes**, and then select **Add**:

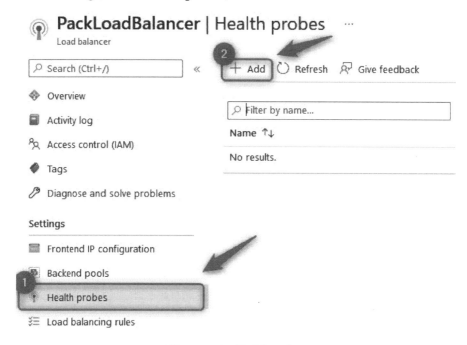

Figure 16.9 – Health probe

3. Enter `PacktHealthProbe` as **Name**, set **Protocol** to **HTTP**, set **Port** to `80`, **Path** to `/`, **Interval** to 5 (this is the number of seconds between probe attempts), **Unhealthy threshold** to 2 (this is the number of consecutive probe failures that occur before a VM is considered unhealthy), and click **Add**:

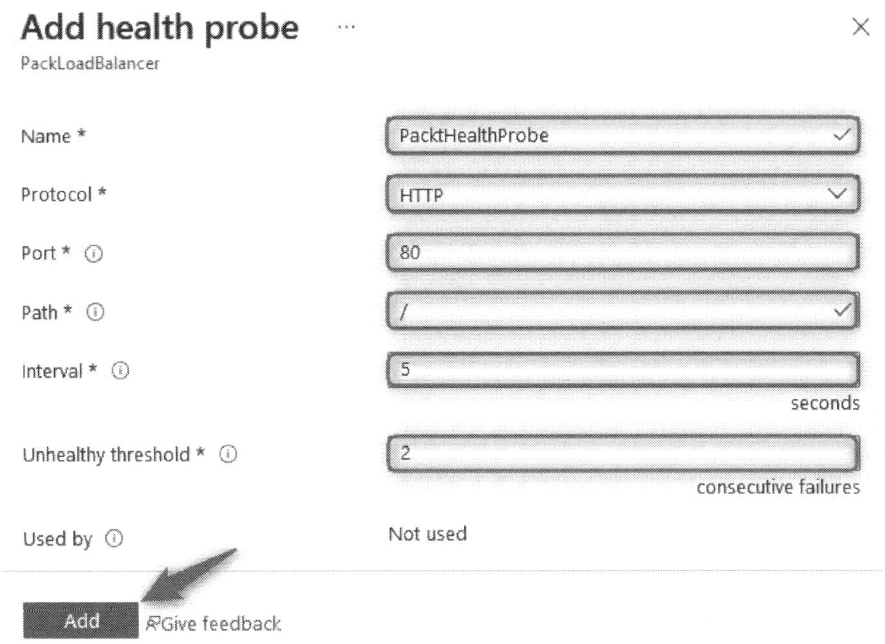

Figure 16.10 – Add health probe

Now that you have deployed your health probe for the load balancer, we will move on to creating your first load balancing rule.

Creating load balancing rules

Load balancing rules define how the traffic is distributed to the VMs inside the backend pool. When you create a new rule, you define the frontend IP configuration for incoming traffic, the backend IP pool that receives the traffic, and the required source and destination ports. The rule that we are going to create listens to port 80 at the frontend. The rule then sends the network traffic to the backend pool, also on port 80. To create the rule, take the following steps:

1. Open the Load Balancer resource.

2. Under **Settings**, select **Load balancing rules**, and then select **Add**:

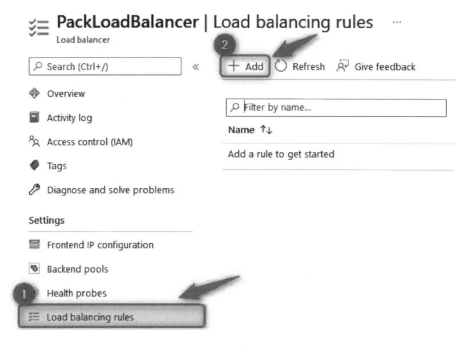

Figure 16.11 – Load balancing rules

3. Enter `PacktLoadBalancerRule` for **Name**, set **IP Version** as **IPv4**, select
    PacktLBFEName for **Frontend IP Address**, select **PackLBBackendPool** for
    Backend pool, set **Protocol** as **TCP**, **Port** as `80`, **Backend port** as `80`, select
    PacktHealthProbe (HTTP:80) for **Health probe**, set **Session persistence** as **None**,
    leave **Idle timeout (minutes)** as the default, and leave **Floating IP** as the default
    (normally **Disabled**). Click **Add**:

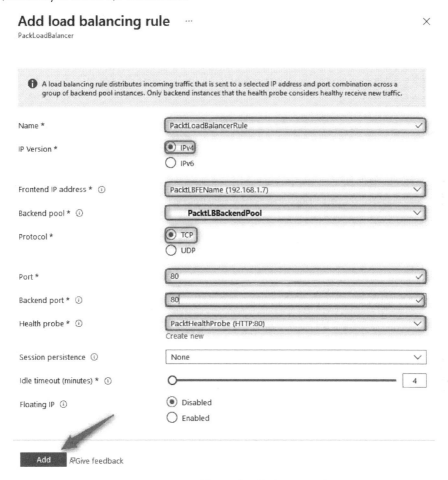

Figure 16.12 – Adding a load balancing rule

Now that your load balancer is all configured, you are ready to start testing it to confirm it
works as expected. Next, we will walk through how to go about testing your load balancer.

Testing the load balancer

To test the VMs properly, we are going to install **Internet Information Services (IIS)** on the `PacktLBVM1` and `PacktLBVM2` VMs using PowerShell. Then, we can use the `PacktLBVMTest` VM to test the load balancer by calling its private IP address. First, we need to obtain the private IP address of the load balancer. Take the following steps:

1. Open the Load Balancer resource.

2. Under **Settings**, select **Frontend IP configuration**, and copy the private IP address as follows:

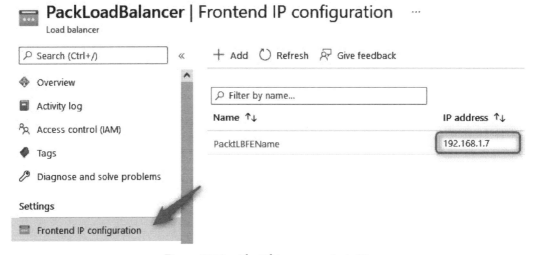

Figure 16.13 – Identifying your private IP

3. Now, we need to connect to the `PacktLBVM1` and `PacktLBVM2` VM using an RDP session on the public IPs and install IIS and a testing web page on it. Connect to both the VMs, open the PowerShell console, and paste and run the following PowerShell script:

```
# Install IIS
Install-WindowsFeature -name Web-Server
-IncludeManagementTools
# Remove default htm file
remove-item C:\inetpub\wwwroot\iisstart.htm
#Add custom htm file
Add-Content -Path "C:\inetpub\wwwroot\iisstart.htm" -Value
$("Hello World from " + $env:computername)
```

> **Top Tip**
>
> Instead of connecting to each VM and configuring IIS services, you can also use Azure Automation Workbook or Azure VM PowerShell Script Extension.

4. Next, connect to the `PacktLBVMTest` VM using RDP as well, open a browser session (such as Internet Explorer), and navigate to the private IP address of the load balancer obtained from *Step 2*. Refresh the browser a couple of times to see the load balancer distributing the requests over the two VMs, as the following screenshot shows:

Hello World from PacktLBVM1

Figure 16.14 – Testing the load balancer

You have now successfully deployed your first ILB within Azure, and you now understand how load balancing is used to distribute access to workloads as needed, as well as the service catering to HA requirements for inaccessible workloads. You have also learned that ILBs are for traffic that is internal or private to your VNets and restricted from public access, and public load balancers are used to load balance public-facing workloads. Next, we will explore the configuration of a public load balancer.

Configuring a public load balancer

In this section, we are going to create a public load balancer using the Azure **command-line interface** (**CLI**). You can copy the code snippets in Azure Cloud Shell, which is accessible from the Azure portal. The full script for creating the public load balancer can be downloaded from GitHub as well. Refer to the location specified in the *Technical requirements* section at the beginning of this chapter.

Creating the public load balancer

To create the public load balancer, a series of steps need to be taken. In the upcoming sections, we will create the public load balancer with all the necessary components:

1. Navigate to the Azure portal by opening `https://portal.azure.com`.

2. Click the Azure CLI icon at the top right of the Azure portal to open an Azure CLI instance:

Figure 16.15 – Opening the Azure CLI

3. If you have never used the CLI before, you will be required to set up storage for this; follow the prompts on the screen to configure your container on a storage account.

4. When asked for the environment, you can select PowerShell; if you decide you would like to use Bash, then enter the following, which will open PowerShell in the Bash terminal, and press *Enter*:

```
pwsh
```

> **Top Tip**
>
> You should note that when using PowerShell within Bash, you cannot define variables in the Linux Bash format.

5. You may reuse the resource group from the previous exercise, or should you wish to create a new one, you can run the command as follows, using `AZ104-PublicLoadBalancer` as an example resource group name:

```
# Create a resource group
az group create --name AZ104-PublicLoadBalancer --location
westeurope
```

> **Top Tip**
>
> Please note, when pasting into the CLI, you need to right-click and paste; you can't use keyboard shortcuts such as *Ctrl + V* or *Cmd + V*.

6. Next, we are going to configure a public IP address for the load balancer to access it from the internet. A standard load balancer only supports standard public IP addresses, as shown in the following code:

```
# Create a public IP address
az network public-ip create --resource-group AZ104-
PublicLoadBalancer --name PacktPublicIP --sku standard
```

7. Now, we are going to create the load balancer and the components, including a frontend IP pool, a backend IP pool, a health probe, and a load balancer rule. To create the load balancer, add the following code:

```
# Create the Load Balancer
az network lb create `
   --resource-group AZ104-PublicLoadBalancer `
   --name PacktPublicLoadBalancer `
   --sku standard `
   --public-ip-address PacktPublicIP `
   --frontend-ip-name PacktFrontEnd `
   --backend-pool-name PacktBackEndPool
```

> **Top Tip**
>
> The ` (*tilde*) symbol in your Azure CLI commands allows you to split your commands and run them on the next line for more readable code.

8. All VM instances are checked by the health probe to define whether they are healthy enough to send network traffic to them. VM instances that are unhealthy are removed from the load balancer until the probe check determines that they are healthy again. To create the health probe, add the following code:

```
#Create the health probe
az network lb probe create `
   --resource-group AZ104-PublicLoadBalancer `
   --lb-name PacktPublicLoadBalancer `
   --name PacktHealthProbe `
   --protocol tcp `
   --port 80
```

9. The load balancer rule defines the frontend IP configuration for the incoming traffic and the backend IP pool to receive the traffic, together with the required source and destination ports. To create the load balancing rule, run the code as follows:

```
#Create the Load Balancer rule
az network lb rule create `
   --resource-group AZ104-PublicLoadBalancer `
   --lb-name PacktPublicLoadBalancer `
   --name PacktHTTPRule `
   --protocol tcp `
   --frontend-port 80 `
   --backend-port 80 `
   --frontend-ip-name PacktFrontEnd `
   --backend-pool-name PacktBackEndPool `
   --probe-name PacktHealthProbe
```

Now that your load balancer is deployed, we are ready to move on to the deployment of the VNet, which we will look at next.

Creating the VNet and NSG

This section will deal with the creation of your VNet and NSG; run the following:

1. We now need to create the VNet to deploy the VMs too, with the following code:

```
#Create a virtual network
az network vnet create `
   --resource-group AZ104-PublicLoadBalancer `
   --location westeurope `
   --name PacktVnet `
   --subnet-name PacktSubnet
```

2. Next, we will create an NSG. It is a requirement for a standard load balancer that the VMs in the backend have NICs that are placed in an NSG. For standard IPs or resource SKUs in Azure, an NSG is what defines the traffic that is allowed or not. The default configuration for NSGs is to disallow all traffic (that is, the NSG is configured for whitelisting). We need to create the NSG to define the inbound connections to the VNet as follows:

```
az network nsg create `
   --resource-group AZ104-PublicLoadBalancer `
   --name PacktNetworkSecurityGroup
```

3. To allow inbound connections through port 80, create an NSG rule as follows:

```
#Create a Network Security Group rule
az network nsg rule create `
   --resource-group AZ104-PublicLoadBalancer `
   --nsg-name PacktNetworkSecurityGroup `
   --name PacktNetworkSecurityGroupRuleHTTP `
   --protocol tcp `
   --direction inbound `
   --source-address-prefix '*' `
   --source-port-range '*' `
   --destination-address-prefix '*' `
   --destination-port-range 80 `
   --access allow `
   --priority 200
```

4. We need to create two network interfaces and associate them with the NSG and the public IP address. To create the NICs, run the code as follows:

```
#Create NICs
for ($i = 1; $i -le 2; $i++){
   az network nic create `
      --resource-group AZ104-PublicLoadBalancer `
      --name PacktNic$i `
      --vnet-name PacktVnet `
      --subnet PacktSubnet `
      --network-security-group PacktNetworkSecurityGroup `
      --lb-name PacktPublicLoadBalancer `
```

```
        --lb-address-pools PacktBackEndPool
}
```

You now have your public load balancer deployed and you need to configure your backend servers. We will do this next.

Creating backend servers

Now, we need to set up the backend servers. We are going to create two VMs that are going to be used as backend servers for the load balancer. We are also going to install **NGINX** (which is an open source, high-performance HTTP server, and reverse proxy) on them to test the load balancer:

1. We are going to create two VMs with NGINX installed on them and create a `Hello World Node.js` app on the Linux VMs. For this, we need to create a file called `cloud-init.txt` and paste the configuration into it. The following `cloud-init` configuration installs all the required packages, then creates the Hello World app, and then starts the app. To create the `cloud-init.txt` file, paste the following line:

    ```
    nano cloud-init.txt
    ```

2. Paste in the following configuration code. The first part under `packages:` adds the packages:

    ```
    #cloud-config
    package_upgrade: true
    packages:
        - nginx
        - nodejs
        - npm
    ```

3. The next part sets up the server; paste this into the editor:

    ```
    write_files:
    - owner: www-data:www-data
    - path: /etc/nginx/sites-available/default
    content: |
    server {
        listen 80;
        location / {
    ```

```
        proxy_pass http://localhost:3000;
        proxy_http_version 1.1;
        proxy_set_header Upgrade $http_upgrade;
        proxy_set_header Connection keep-alive;
        proxy_set_header Host $host;
        proxy_cache_bypass $http_upgrade;
    }
}
```

4. The next part creates the app; paste this in the editor too:

```
- owner: azureuser:azureuser
- path: /home/azureuser/myapp/index.js
content: |
var express = require('express')
var app = express()
var os = require('os');
app.get('/', function (req, res) {
res.send('Hello World from host ' + os.hostname() + '!')
})
app.listen(3000, function () {
console.log('Hello world app listening on port 3000!')
})
```

5. And the final part that you paste will run the app:

```
runcmd:
    - service nginx restart
    - cd "/home/azureuser/myapp"
    - npm init
    - npm install express -y
    - nodejs index.js
```

6. With the preceding blocks of code, we have now created the `cloud-init.txt` file for our VMs. Save the file in the editor by pressing *Ctrl + X*. Press *Y* and *Enter* on your keyboard; this will save and exit the editor.

7. Now, we can continue with creating the two VMs and apply the configuration on them, as follows:

```
# Create two virtual machines
for ($i = 1; $i -le 2; $i++){
az vm create `
    --resource-group AZ104-PublicLoadBalancer `
    --name myVM$i `
    --nics PacktNic$i `
    --image UbuntuLTS `
    --generate-ssh-keys `
    --custom-data cloud-init.txt `
    --no-wait
}
```

Now that your backend servers are in place, they are ready to be used, so let's run through some testing next to confirm that all is operational as expected. Please give your servers about 5 to 10 minutes to provision before moving to the next step.

Testing the load balancer

To test the load balancer, we need to obtain its public IP address and paste this into a browser window. Wait for the VMs to be fully provisioned and running. You can check this in the Azure portal:

1. To obtain the public IP address, run the following code in the Azure CLI:

```
#Obtain public IP address
az network public-ip show `
    --resource-group AZ104-PublicLoadBalancer `
    --name PacktPublicIP `
    --query [ipAddress] `
    --output tsv
```

2. Paste the output of this line of code into your browser window, which can be on any computer, to see Azure Load Balancer in action:

Hello World from host myVM1!

Figure 16.16 – Testing the public load balancer

You have just successfully connected to your web application through the public load balancer. You should now feel confident working with public load balancers and understand the distinction between public load balancers and ILBs. Next, we will explore some basic troubleshooting you can perform on a load balancer.

Troubleshooting load balancing

At times, you may have problems with your deployed load balancing service, and you will be required to troubleshoot in order to ascertain the root cause of the issue and identify how to rectify the issues.

For this exercise, we will work with the resources you deployed in the previous chapter. Since these no longer exist, please redeploy in the same way, then do the following:

1. Navigate to your load balancer on the Azure portal. Under **Settings**, click **Health probes**.

2. Click on your health probe and change the port to 800 from 80. Click **Save**.

3. Navigate back to your test VM and connect to the IP address of your load balancer. Notice that you get an error message when connecting:

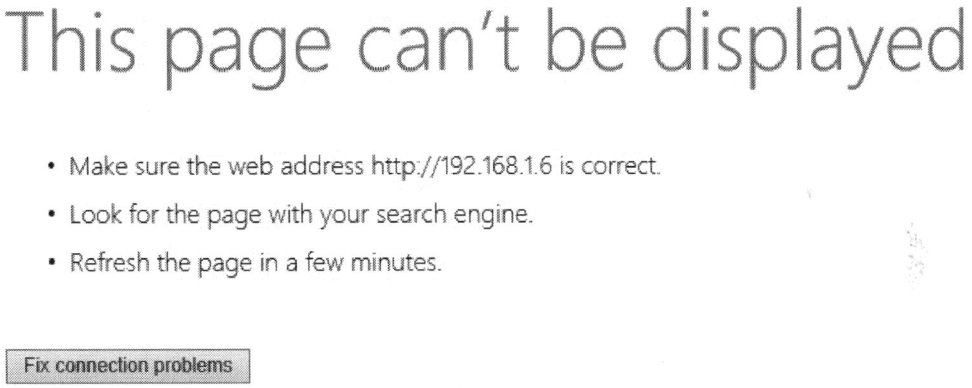

This page can't be displayed

- Make sure the web address http://192.168.1.6 is correct.

- Look for the page with your search engine.

- Refresh the page in a few minutes.

Fix connection problems

Figure 16.17 – Connection error

4. Change the probe port back to 80 and notice you now receive a success message:

Hello World from PacktLBVM1

Figure 16.18 – Connection success

5. Navigate to both your backend VMs and click **Networking** under **Settings**. Click **Add inbound port rule**.

6. Configure as follows and click **Add**:

    - **Source: Any**

    - **Source port ranges:** *

    - **Destination: Any**

    - **Service: Custom**

    - **Destination port ranges:** *

    - **Protocol: Any**

    - **Action: Deny**

    - **Priority: 1010**

    - **Name:** `Port_80_Block`

7. Attempt to connect to your load balancer again and notice you again receive an error message.

You have now seen some common problems around load balancing connection configuration that could occur, and you know where to look for that going forward. You should now feel comfortable troubleshooting load balancers. In the next section, we will explore an application gateway.

Azure Application Gateway

Azure Application Gateway is a load balancing service that operates as a Layer 7 load balancer, which means it's capable of interrogating the source request and directing its destination based on the path. Splitting destinations by path is a common function for web-based load balancing scenarios where resource delivery can be split into different pools and SKU types, which we discussed earlier in the chapter.

The main component to remember about this service is that it's designed for **regional** load balancing of **web-based** services. One of the features of the service is the ability to enable WAF features that are catered to protecting against exploits and vulnerabilities of your web application workloads. Another main benefit of the service is the ability to enable SSL offloading capabilities, which can improve the performance of your web services as the strain is removed from them and delivered by the application gateway directly.

The Application Gateway service offers several features such as:

- **Multiple-site hosting**: This enables several sites to be hosted behind your application gateway, up to a limit of 100 websites. Each of these can be associated with its own backend pool. Sites can be directed based on URL, such as `sitea.com` and `siteb.com`, as well as subdomains, such as `images.sitea.com` and `videos.sitea.com`.

- **Redirection**: You can enable the automatic redirection of HTTP-based traffic to HTTPS. Along with this, you have granular control that allows redirects to occur for the whole site, as well as for path-based redirection and applying HTTPS enforcement for only certain paths of your site. You also have the ability to redirect to any other site that may be external to your Azure sites.

- **Auto-scale**: The service has the ability to auto-scale depending on the requirements.

- **Zone-redundancy**: The service has zone-redundancy options available to it too, making the service more resilient.

- **Session affinity**: There are occasions where you require traffic to flow to the same server for a connection with a client. The service relies on cookies to provide session affinity.

- **WebSocket and HTTP/2 traffic**: Application Gateway has native support for the WebSocket and HTTP/2 protocols. Configuration is simple and you can choose to either enable or disable the feature as required.

- **Connection draining**: When you are planning for service outages or unplanned failures, you can enable a more graceful removal of services by disabling new requests to specified servers that are to be removed from a backend pool.

- **Custom error pages**: In the event of an error, you have the capability to deliver your own custom error pages that may contain your own branding and styles.

- **Rewrite HTTP headers and URLs**: You have the ability to rewrite HTTP headers, which allows you to pass additional information in your requests and responses between the client and server. This enables you to improve your security and governance posture within your application. When rewriting URLs, you can rewrite the hostname, path, and querying string for your request based on the conditions you configure.

> **Top Tip**
> The `Standard_v2` SKU of Application Gateway requires the use of a static **virtual IP** (**VIP**).

Now that you know about some of the capabilities and features available to the Application Gateway service, we will explore how to configure it.

Configuring Azure Application Gateway

You now have some information about what Azure Application Gateway is and what it does. You will now experience deploying one and seeing how it works.

Creating an Azure application gateway

To create an Azure application gateway, perform the following steps:

1. Navigate to the Azure portal by opening `https://portal.azure.com`.

2. Create a new resource group for this exercise named `AZ104-ApplicationGateway`.

3. Create a VNet with the following values:

    -   **Subscription**: Select a subscription

    -   **Resource group**: **AZ104-ApplicationGateway**

    -   **Name**: `ApplicationGatewayVNET`

    -   **Region**: A region of your choice (choose the same region for all subsequent resources in this chapter)

    -   **Address range**: `10.1.0.0/16`

    -   **Subnet name**: Default

    -   **Subnet Address range**: `10.1.0.0/24`

    -   **NAT GATEWAY**: Leave the default value

    -   **Services**: Leave the default value

4. Open the newly-created resource group, click **Overview** on the left menu, then click **Create**.

5. Type application gateway in the search bar and click **Application Gateway** in the pop-up dialog:

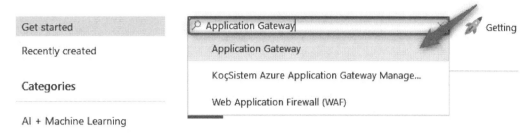

Figure 16.19 – Creating an application gateway

6. Click **Create**.

7. Enter the following values for the **Basics** tab, then click **Next : Frontends >**:

- **Subscription**: Select a subscription

- **Resource group**: **AZ104-ApplicationGateway**

- **Name**: ApplicationGateway

- **Region**: The same region as chosen for the preceding VNet

- **Tier**: **Standard V2**

- **Enable autoscaling**: **Yes**

- **Minimum instance count**: 0

- **Maximum instance count**: 2

- **Availability zone**: **None**

- **HTTP2**: **Disabled**

- **Virtual network**: Select the VNet you created previously

- **Subnet**: **default (10.1.0.0/24)**

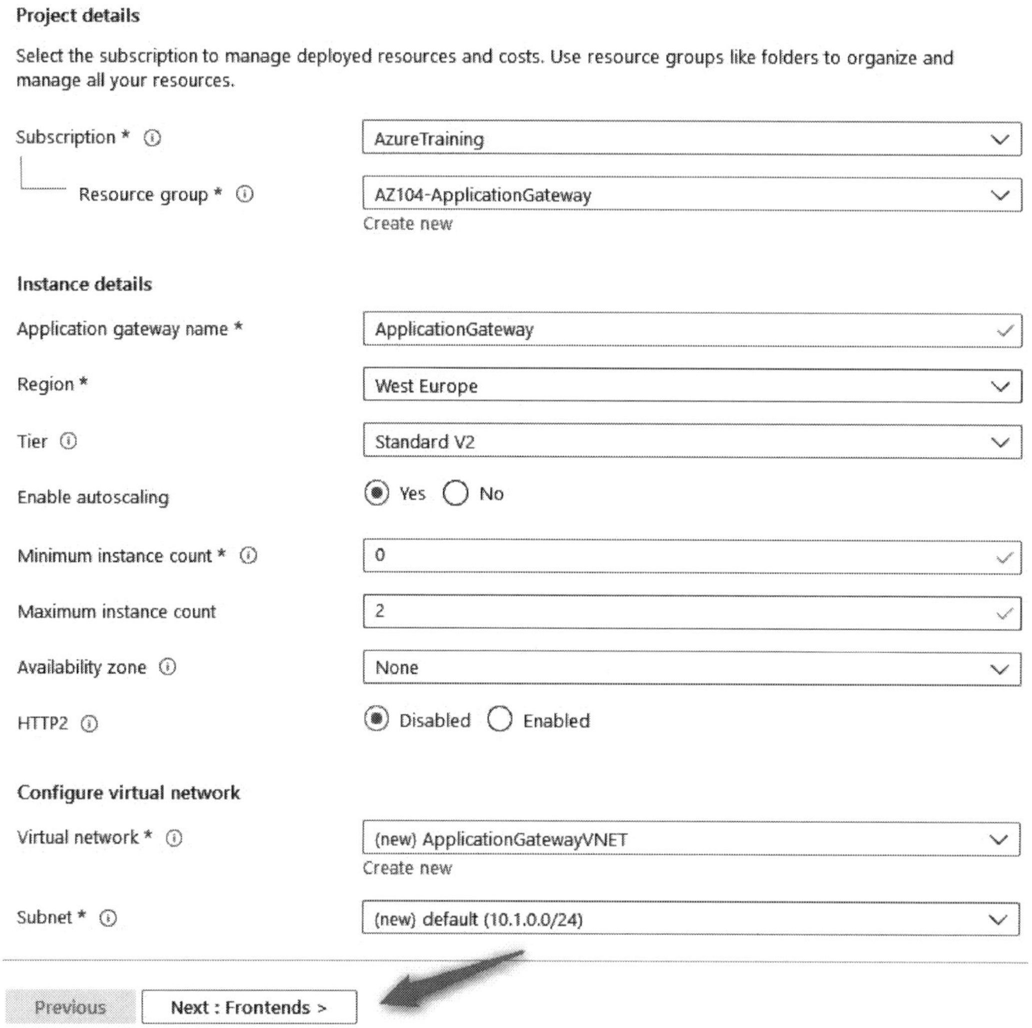

Project details

Select the subscription to manage deployed resources and costs. Use resource groups like folders to organize and manage all your resources.

Subscription * ⓘ	AzureTraining ⌄
Resource group * ⓘ	AZ104-ApplicationGateway ⌄
	Create new

Instance details

Application gateway name *	ApplicationGateway ✓
Region *	West Europe ⌄
Tier ⓘ	Standard V2 ⌄
Enable autoscaling	◉ Yes ◯ No
Minimum instance count * ⓘ	0 ✓
Maximum instance count	2 ✓
Availability zone ⓘ	None ⌄
HTTP2 ⓘ	◉ Disabled ◯ Enabled

Configure virtual network

Virtual network * ⓘ	(new) ApplicationGatewayVNET ⌄
	Create new
Subnet * ⓘ	(new) default (10.1.0.0/24) ⌄

[Previous] [Next : Frontends >]

Figure 16.20 – Application Gateway – Basics

8. Enter the following values for the **Basics** tab, then click **Next : Backends >**:

- **Frontend IP address type**: **Public**
- **Public IP address**: **Add new** (name this as something unique)

Figure 16.21 – Application Gateway – Frontends

9. Click **Add a backend pool**. In the pop-up blade, enter the following and click **Add**:

    - **Name**: `backendpool`

    - **Add backend pool without targets**: **Yes**

Figure 16.22 – Application Gateway – backend pool

10. Click **Next : Configuration >**.

11. Note that your configuration screen lists your frontend and backend pools. The routing rules are the magic connectors between these linking public IPs to your backend resources. Click **Add a routing rule**. In the pop-up blade, enter the following:

- **Rule name**: `webtraffic`

- **Listener name**: `webtraffic`

- **Frontend IP: Public**

- **Protocol: HTTP**

- **Port**: `80`

- **Listener type: Basic**

- **Error page url: No**

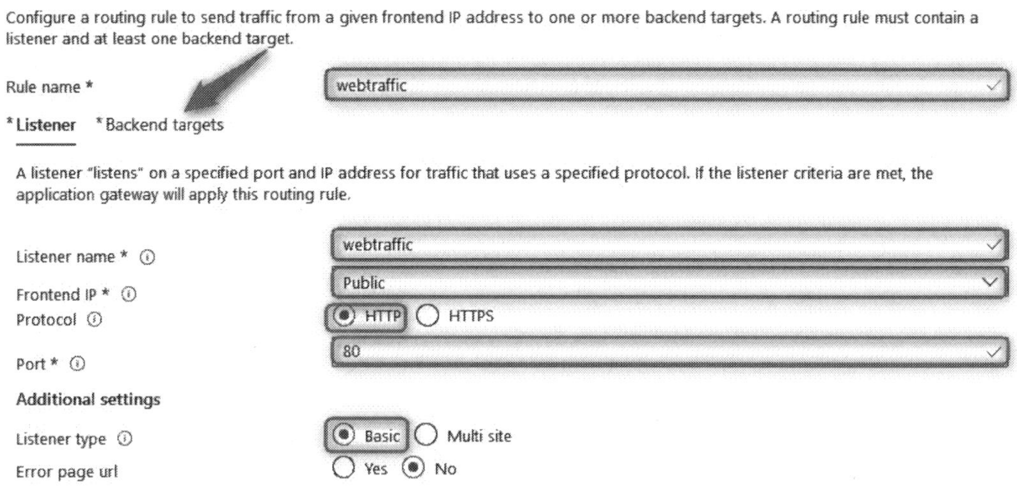

Configure a routing rule to send traffic from a given frontend IP address to one or more backend targets. A routing rule must contain a listener and at least one backend target.

Rule name *   webtraffic

*Listener   *Backend targets

A listener "listens" on a specified port and IP address for traffic that uses a specified protocol. If the listener criteria are met, the application gateway will apply this routing rule.

Listener name * ⓘ   webtraffic

Frontend IP * ⓘ   Public

Protocol ⓘ   ⦿ HTTP   ◯ HTTPS

Port * ⓘ   80

Additional settings

Listener type ⓘ   ⦿ Basic   ◯ Multi site

Error page url   ◯ Yes ⦿ No

Figure 16.23 – Application Gateway – Listener

The rule we are configuring will listen for HTTP traffic on port `80` through the public IP we created. The **Basic** listener type forwards all traffic from any frontend IP to a backend pool, the **Multisite** option will listen on the domain and redirect according to the specified prefix given for the routing rule. Click the **Backend targets** tab.

12. Enter the following and click **Add**:

- **Target type: Backend pool**.

- **Backend target**: Select **backendpool** in the dropdown.

- **HTTP settings**: **Add new**. Then, enter the following: **HTTP settings name** as `httpset1`, **Backend protocol** as HTTP, **Backend port** as 80, click **Yes** for **Override with new host name**, and select **Pick host name from backend target**. You can leave the rest as the defaults:

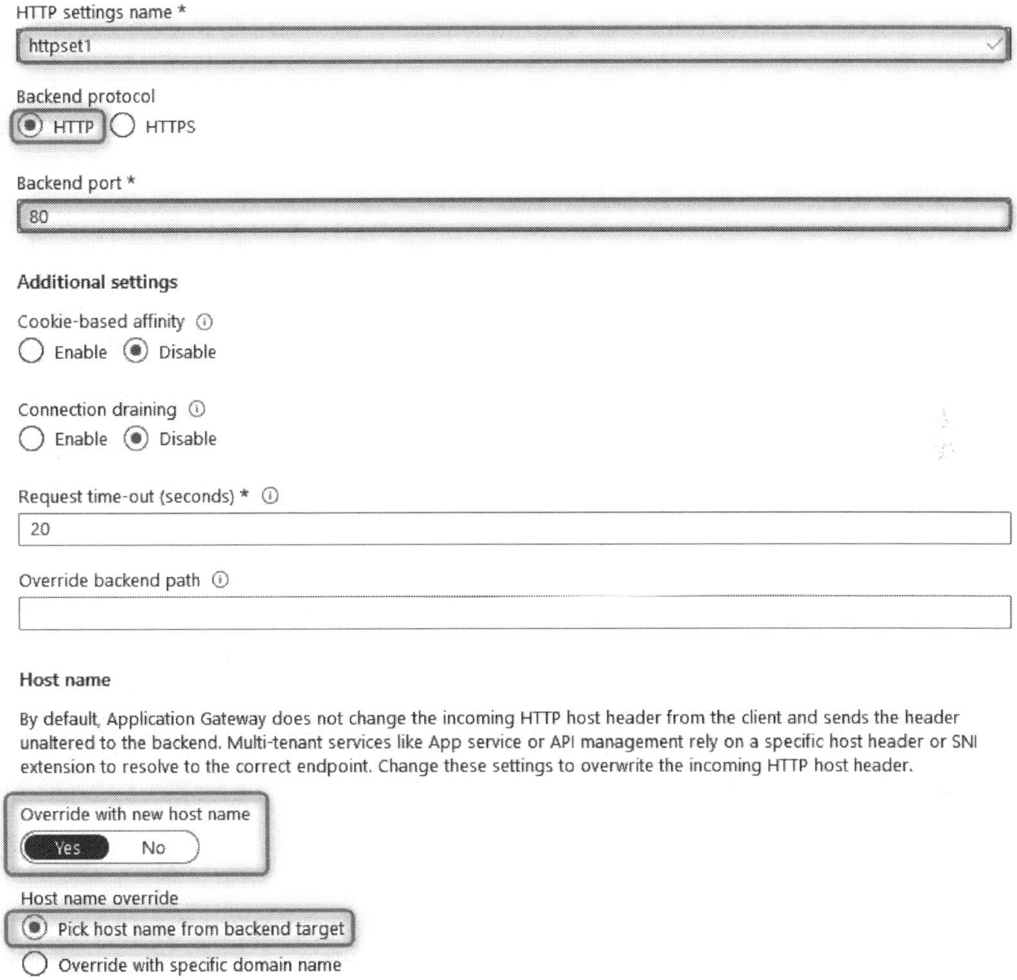

HTTP settings name *

httpset1

Backend protocol

(●) HTTP ( ) HTTPS

Backend port *

80

Additional settings

Cookie-based affinity ⓘ

( ) Enable (●) Disable

Connection draining ⓘ

( ) Enable (●) Disable

Request time-out (seconds) * ⓘ

20

Override backend path ⓘ

Host name

By default, Application Gateway does not change the incoming HTTP host header from the client and sends the header unaltered to the backend. Multi-tenant services like App service or API management rely on a specific host header or SNI extension to resolve to the correct endpoint. Change these settings to overwrite the incoming HTTP host header.

Override with new host name

(Yes   No)

Host name override

(●) Pick host name from backend target

( ) Override with specific domain name

Figure 16.24 – Application Gateway – HTTP settings

13. Click **Add**.

14. Click **Next : Tags** > and then **Next : Review + create** >. Click **Create**.

Now that your application gateway is deployed, you will need an application on the backend to test the service; we will deploy this next.

Deploying your web app

You will need at least one application on the backend of your application gateway for the public IP address you created to route through to the application. We will deploy that app now, following these steps:

1. Open the Azure CLI and select PowerShell, or open `pwsh` as you did in the public load balancer exercise.

2. Run the following command, replacing the name with a unique name you choose and the resource group with the one you created previously:

    ```
    New-AzWebApp -name "azwebapp12341234" -ResourceGroupName
    "AZ104-ApplicationGateway" -Location "westeurope"
    ```

3. Open your Application Gateway resource and click **Backend pools** on the left navigation menu under the **Settings** context. Click on your backend pool.

4. Dropdown the **Target type** selector and change to **IP address** or **FQDN**, and set **Target** to the web app you just created followed by `.azurewebsites.net` (for example, `azwebapp12341234.azurewebsites.net`). Click **Save**.

5. Click on **Overview** for your application gateway and note the frontend public IP address and paste it into your browser. Note that it fails.

6. Now, go to **Health probes** on the left menu under **Settings** and click **Add**.

7. Enter the following details and click **Test**. If a health probe has already been created, then skip to the note below the settings:

    *   **Name**: `httpprobe`

    *   **Protocol**: **HTTP**

    *   **Host**: The same FQN you used previously

    *   **Path**: /

    *   **HTTP settings**: **httpset1**

    *   All other settings leave as their default state

    If you discover that a health probe already exists, then please use the following settings. Adapt the hostname to what you have for your web app and use the preceding settings where necessary:

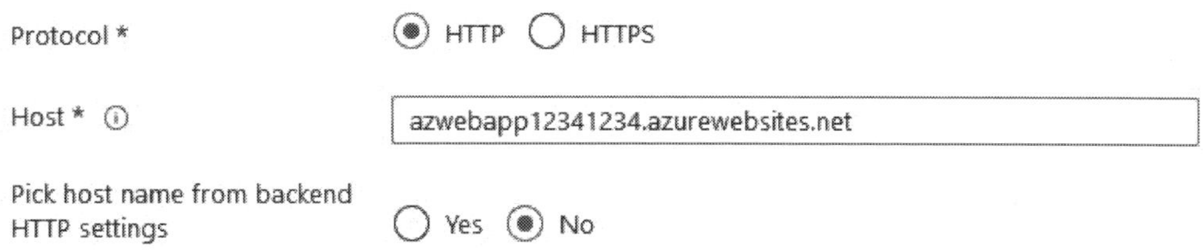

Protocol *	⦿ HTTP ◯ HTTPS
Host * ⓘ	azwebapp12341234.azurewebsites.net
Pick host name from backend HTTP settings	◯ Yes ⦿ No

Figure 16.25 – Application Gateway – health probe

8.   After a successful validation, click **Add**:

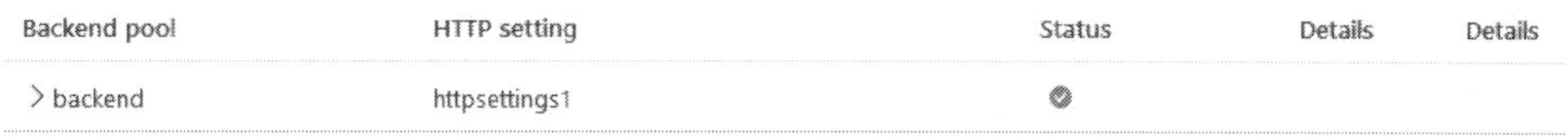

Backend pool	HTTP setting	Status	Details	Details
⟩ backend	httpsettings1	⊘		

Figure 16.26 – Application Gateway – health probe success test

You have just successfully configured your web app and added it to the application gateway. You are now ready to test it, which we will run through next.

Testing the application gateway

Now that your application gateway is configured, it is ready to test. To do this, perform the following steps:

1.   Paste the frontend public IP address from the previous part into your web browser. You should expect to see a web page of sorts; this will validate your connection.

2.   Navigate back to your web application and click on **Overview** in the left pane.

3.   Click **Stop** at the top of the page:

Figure 16.27 – Web app – Stop

4.   Note that when you navigate to the public IP of your application gateway, you get an error message as expected.

5.   Wait about 5 minutes and navigate back to your Application Gateway service and click on **Backend Health** under the **Monitoring** context.

6.   Note how you get an unhealthy message indicating an issue on the backend:

Server (backend pool)	Port (HTTP setting)	Status	Details
azwebapp12341234.azurewebsites.net (bac...	80 (httpset1)	● Unhealthy	Received invalid status code: 403 in the bac...

Figure 16.28 – Application Gateway – unhealthy backend

7.   Do not delete your resources, as these will be used in the next exercise.

Now that you have experienced deploying Azure Application Gateway and have seen the merits it brings to regional load balancing for services, as well as how to troubleshoot when issues occur, you should now feel comfortable working with application gateways. Next, we will explore how Azure Front Door works in the same space but at a global level.

Azure Front Door

Azure Front Door is a load balancing service that also operates as a Layer 7 load balancer much like Azure Application Gateway. The service is very similar except that it is designed for **global** delivery of services as opposed to **regional**. The service also has the ability to enable WAF services and is designed for web-based workloads. One of the great benefits of the Front Door service is its ability to offer different traffic-routing methods:

- **Latency**: This is designed for faster connections to your services by routing requests to the backends that have the lowest latency. This means that services located closer to where you are connecting from globally will be faster and, therefore, respond quicker.

- **Priority**: You can assume a primary delivery backend pool for your service with a backup (secondary) backend pool when the primary pool fails.

- **Weighted**: This option is for when you have several backend pools and want to distribute traffic in a weighted fashion by assigning requests to backend pools in a ratio type proportion.

- **Session affinity**: This is where the user of your service is required to connect to the same server.

Front Door offers several features (many similar to Application Gateway), such as the following:

- URL path-based routing
- Multiple website hosting
- Session affinity
- SSL offloading
- Health probes
- Custom domains
- WAF
- URL Redirect
- URL Rewrite
- IPv6 connectivity
- HTTP/2 Protocol

You now know how to deploy regional load balancing services in Azure. You also know and understand how Azure Front Door works at a global level for load balancing services. You should feel comfortable at this point with the concept of load balancing and understanding the various services available in Azure to serve this purpose. The next skill you will need to learn is how to troubleshoot these services, which we will explore in the next chapter.

Summary

In this chapter, we covered various load balancing services available to us on the Azure platform and how they bring HA to our workloads, both regionally and globally. We also explored how services such as Azure Application Gateway and Front Door enhance these services by analyzing application layer requests to split requests across service areas and resources. In the next chapter, we will explore monitoring and troubleshooting for networks in Azure in more detail.

17
Integrating On-Premises Networks with Azure

In the previous chapter, we covered load balancing services in Azure and explored the configuration of services such as Load Balancer and Application Gateway.

This chapter continues with this objective by covering how to integrate your on-premises network with an Azure virtual network. In this chapter, we are going to focus on **virtual private network** (**VPN**) connections from your on-premises environment to Azure. You will learn how to create an Azure VPN gateway, and you will learn how to configure a **Site-to-Site** (**S2S**) VPN using an on-premises server and Azure VPN Gateway. At the end of the chapter, we will explore Azure Virtual WAN and the capabilities this introduces.

In this chapter, we are going to cover the following main topics:

- Azure VPN Gateway
- Creating and configuring an Azure VPN gateway

- Creating and configuring Azure ExpressRoute
- Azure Virtual WAN
- Configuring Azure Virtual WAN

Technical requirements

To follow along with the hands-on material, you will need the following:

- Access to an Azure subscription with owner or contributor privileges. If you do not have access to one, you can enroll for a free account at `https://azure.microsoft.com/en-us/free/`.

Azure VPN Gateway

Azure VPN Gateway provides a secure gateway that can be used for sending encrypted traffic over the internet between an Azure virtual network and an on-premises location. This gateway can be used for sending encrypted traffic between different Azure virtual networks and the Microsoft networks as well.

For each virtual network, you can only have one VPN gateway. You can, however, create multiple connections to the same VPN gateway. When creating multiple connections, all the VPN tunnels will share the available gateway bandwidth.

A virtual network gateway is created with two or more **virtual machines** (**VMs**) that are deployed in a gateway subnet. This is a specific subnet that is created for the VPN connection. The VMs that are deployed in the gateway subnet are created at the same time as the virtual network gateway is created. The VMs are then configured to contain specific gateway services and routing tables to connect to the gateway in Azure. It is not possible to configure the gateway services and routing tables manually. All gateway **stock keeping unit** (**SKUs**) except for the Basic SKU include 128 **Point-to-Site** (**P2S**) connections in the price.

Azure VPN Gateway offers the following pricing tiers:

- **Basic**: This tier provides a maximum of 10 S2S/**virtual network** (**VNet**)-to-VNet tunnels (10 are included in the price) and a maximum of 128 P2S connections. The average bandwidth is 100 Mbps.
- **VpnGw1**: This tier provides a maximum of 30 S2S/VNet-to-VNet tunnels (10 are included in the price) and a maximum of 250 P2S connections. The average bandwidth is 650 Mbps.

- **VpnGw2**: This tier provides a maximum of 30 S2S/VNet-to-VNet tunnels (10 are included in the price) and a maximum of 500 P2S connections. The average bandwidth is 1 Gbps.

- **VpnGw3**: This tier provides a maximum of 30 S2S/VNet-to-VNet tunnels (10 are included in the price) and a maximum of 1,000 P2S connections. The average bandwidth is 1.25 Gbps.

- **VpnGw4**: This tier provides a maximum of 100 S2S/VNet-to-VNet tunnels (10 are included in the price) and a maximum of 5,000 P2S connections. The average bandwidth is 5 Gbps.

- **VpnGw5**: This tier provides a maximum of 100 S2S/VNet-to-VNet tunnels (10 are included in the price) and a maximum of 10,000 P2S connections. The average bandwidth is 10 Gbps.

There is also the option for an **availability zone** (**AZ**) variation of each Gateway SKU, except for Basic, denoted with a suffix of AZ, for example, VpnGw4AZ. They offer similar specifications and are as follows:

- **VpnGw1AZ**: This tier provides a maximum of 30 S2S/VNet-to-VNet tunnels (10 are included in the price) and a maximum of 128 P2S connections. The average bandwidth is 650 Mbps.

- **VpnGw2AZ**: This tier provides a maximum of 30 S2S/VNet-to-VNet tunnels (10 are included in the price) and a maximum of 128 P2S connections. The average bandwidth is 1 Gbps.

- **VpnGw3AZ**: This tier provides a maximum of 30 S2S/VNet-to-VNet tunnels (10 are included in the price) and a maximum of 128 P2S connections. The average bandwidth is 3 Gbps.

- **VpnGw4AZ**: This tier provides a maximum of 100 S2S/VNet-to-VNet tunnels (10 are included in the price) and a maximum of 128 P2S connections. The average bandwidth is 6 Gbps.

- **VpnGw5AZ**: This tier provides a maximum of 100 S2S/VNet-to-VNet tunnels (10 are included in the price) and a maximum of 128 P2S connections. The average bandwidth is 10 Gbps.

For better redundancy (high-availability) options, it is, of course, better to select the AZ variant, but understand that it costs significantly more than the standard SKU. This would be desirous for customers and workloads where constant connectivity is essential to operations and downtime would be costly to the client. Next, we will explore S2S VPN connections.

S2S VPN connections

An S2S VPN gateway connection is a connection over an IPsec/IKE (IKEv1 or IKEv2) VPN tunnel. These connections can be used for hybrid configurations and cross-premises configurations. It is designed to create a secure connection between a location and your virtual network over the internet. The location can be an office or even another VPN gateway, as an example. Once the S2S VPN connection is configured, you can connect every device from that location to Azure using the same VPN location.

An S2S connection requires a compatible VPN device located on-premises that has a public IP address assigned to it. It should not be located behind a NAT. S2S connections are designed to be persistent in nature and always on; this is not required, of course, but important to understand the intended design.

> **Top Tip**
>
> For more information about the compatible VPN devices, you can refer to the following documentation: https://docs.microsoft.com/en-us/azure/vpn-gateway/vpn-gateway-vpn-faq#s2s.

The following diagram shows an S2S VPN connection from an on-premises environment to Azure:

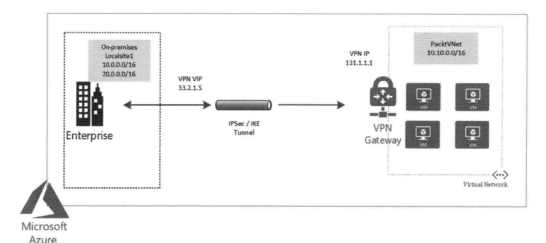

Figure 17.1 – S2S VPN tunnel

In the next section, we are going to look at multi-site VPNs.

Multi-site VPN connections

A multi-site VPN connection is a variation of the S2S connection. You use this type of connection for connecting to multiple on-premises sites from your virtual network gateway. It is required that multi-site connections use a route-based VPN type gateway. All connections through the gateway will share the available bandwidth. This is because each virtual network can only have one VPN gateway.

The following diagram shows a multi-site VPN connection from an on-premises environment to Azure:

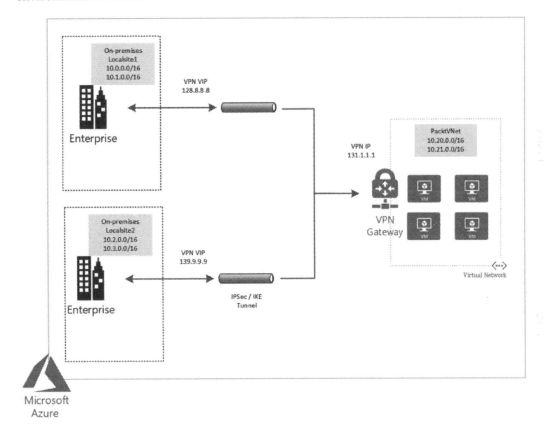

Figure 17.2 – Multi-site VPN tunnels

In the next section, we are going to look at the P2S VPN.

P2S VPN connections

A P2S VPN gateway connection is designed to create a secure connection between an individual client and your virtual network over the internet. It is established from the client's computer and is useful for people who are working from different locations, such as from their home or from a hotel. A PS2 VPN is also the best solution if you only have a few clients to connect to a virtual network.

A P2S connection does not require an on-premises, public-facing IP address as S2S VPN connections do. You are able to use P2S connections together with S2S connections over the same VPN gateway. You need to make sure that the configuration requirements for both connections are compatible so that you can use both connection types over the same gateway.

The following diagram shows a P2S VPN connection from an on-premises environment to Azure:

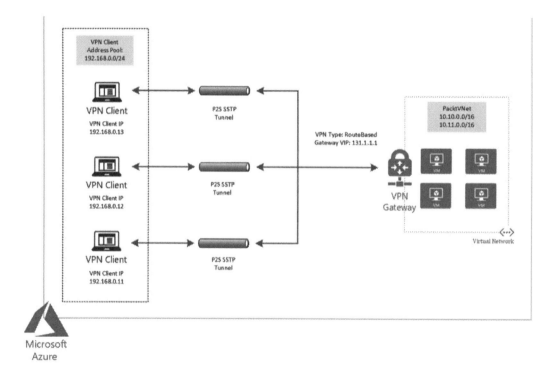

Figure 17.3 – P2S VPN tunnel

In the next section, we are going to look at ExpressRoute.

ExpressRoute

ExpressRoute offers a private connection that is facilitated by a connectivity provider. ExpressRoute connections don't go over the public internet, but they use a more reliable connection. These types of connections offer lower latencies, higher security, and faster speeds than connections that go over the internet. You can use it to extend your on-premises networks to Azure and Office 365. Connections can be made from an any-to-any (IP VPN) network, a virtual cross-connection at a co-location facility, and a point-to-point Ethernet network connection.

ExpressRoute uses a virtual network gateway, which is configured with a gateway type of ExpressRoute instead of a VPN. By default, the traffic is not encrypted, but you can create a solution that encrypts the traffic that goes over the ExpressRoute circuit.

The following diagram shows an ExpressRoute connection from an on-premises environment to Azure:

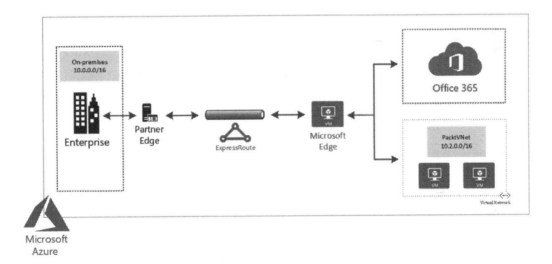

Figure 17.4 – ExpressRoute VPN tunnel

Now that we have looked at the different types of VPN connections you can configure, we are now going to create and configure an Azure VPN gateway.

Creating and configuring an Azure VPN gateway

In the upcoming sections, we are going to configure an Azure VPN gateway, configure an S2S VPN, and verify the connectivity between Azure and the on-premises environment.

We are going to use Windows Server 2019 with the **Routing and Remote Access Service (RRAS)** enabled to serve as the compatible VPN device that is installed on the on-premises environment.

Creating and configuring an Azure VPN gateway

To create a VPN gateway, you can perform the following steps to follow along in our example:

1. Create a new resource group named AZ104-VPNGateway.

2. Click **+ Create** on the **Overview** screen for the resource group.

3. Type vpn gateway in the search bar and press the *Enter/Return* key. Click **Virtual network gateway** from the options that are returned:

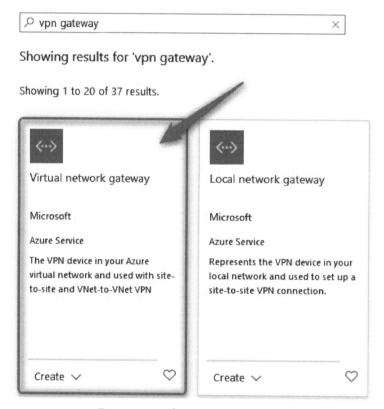

Figure 17.5 – Choosing VPN gateway

4. Click **Create**.

5. Enter the following and click **Review + create**:

    - **Subscription**: Select your Azure subscription.

    - **Name**: `az104gateway`.

    - **Region**: **West Europe** (or select what you prefer).

    - **Gateway type**: **VPN**.

    - **VPN type**: **Route-based**.

    - **SKU**: **Basic**.

    - **Generation**: **Generation1**.

    - **Virtual network**: Use an existing VNet or create a new one named `az104gatewayvnet`.

    - **Public IP address**: **Create new**.

    - **Public IP address name**: `az104gatewayip`.

    - **Public IP address SKU**: **Basic**.

    - **Assignment**: **Dynamic**.

    - **Enable active-active mode**: **Disabled**.

    - **Configure BGP**: **Disabled**.

6. The creation of the resource takes about 45 to 60 minutes so it's a good time to grab some coffee and reflect on your learnings so far.

You have now deployed a VPN gateway. Next, we will explore the creation of an S2S VPN connection using the Gateway service. First, we will need a VM to act as the VPN server.

VPN server deployment

To deploy your VPN server, you will need to perform the following steps:

1. Navigate to your VPN resource group.

2. Click **+ Create** on the **Overview** screen for the resource group.

3. Type `custom deployment` in the search bar and click **Template deployment (deploy using custom templates)** from the options that are returned:

Figure 17.6 – Custom deployment

4. Click **Create**.

5. Click **Build your own template in the editor**:

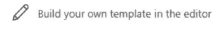

Figure 17.7 – Use your template

6. Paste the following and click **Save**:

```json
{
    "$schema": "https://schema.management.azure.com/
schemas/2019-04-01/deploymentTemplate.json#",
    "contentVersion": "1.0.0.0",
    "parameters": {
        "vmName": { "type": "string", "defaultValue":
"az104vpnserver" },
        "adminUsername": { "type": "string",
"defaultValue": "Packtadmin" },
        "adminPassword": { "type": "securestring",
"defaultValue": "P@55w0rd()" },
        "windowsOSVersion": { "type": "string",
"defaultValue": "2019-Datacenter" },
        "vmSize": { "type": "string", "defaultValue":
"Standard_D2s_v4" },
        "resourceTags": { "type": "object",
"defaultValue": { "Application": "AZ104 VPN Gateway" } },
        "vnetName": { "type": "string", "defaultValue":
"vpnvnet" },
        "subnetName": { "type": "string", "defaultValue":
"vnpsubnet" }
    },
    "functions": [],
    "variables": {
```

```
        "diagnosticsStorageAccountName":
"[concat(parameters('vmName'),'sa01')]",
        "nicName": "[concat(parameters('vmName'),'-
nic01')]",
        "nsgName": "[concat(parameters('vmName'),'-
nsg-01')]",
        "publicIPName":
"[concat(parameters('vmName'),'-ip-01')]"
    },
    "resources": [
        {
            "name":
"[toLower(variables('diagnosticsStorageAccountName'))]",
            "type": "Microsoft.Storage/storageAccounts",
            "apiVersion": "2021-04-01",
            "location": "[resourceGroup().location]",
            "tags": "[parameters('resourceTags')]",
            "sku": { "name": "Standard_LRS" },
            "kind": "Storage"
        },
        {
            "name": "[variables('publicIPName')]",
            "type": "Microsoft.Network/
publicIPAddresses",
            "apiVersion": "2020-11-01",
            "location": "[resourceGroup().location]",
            "tags": "[parameters('resourceTags')]",
            "properties": { "publicIPAllocationMethod":
"Dynamic", "dnsSettings": { "domainNameLabel":
"[toLower(parameters('vmName'))]" } }
        },
        {
            "name": "[variables('nsgName')]",
            "type": "Microsoft.Network/
networkSecurityGroups",
            "apiVersion": "2020-11-01",
            "location": "[resourceGroup().location]",
            "properties": {
```

```
                       "securityRules": [ {
                             "name": "nsgRule1",
                             "properties": { "description":
"description", "protocol": "Tcp", "sourcePortRange": "*",
"destinationPortRange": "3389", "sourceAddressPrefix":
"*", "destinationAddressPrefix": "*", "access": "Allow",
"priority": 100, "direction": "Inbound" }
                          } ]
                    }
              },
              {
                    "name": "[parameters('vnetName')]",
                    "type": "Microsoft.Network/virtualNetworks",
                    "apiVersion": "2020-11-01",
                    "location": "[resourceGroup().location]",
                    "dependsOn": [ "[resourceId('Microsoft.
Network/networkSecurityGroups', variables('nsgName'))]"
],
                    "tags": "[parameters('resourceTags')]",
                    "properties": {
                          "addressSpace": { "addressPrefixes": [
"99.0.0.0/24" ] },
                          "subnets": [ {
                                "name": "[parameters('subnetName')]",
"properties": { "addressPrefix": "99.0.0.0/24",
"networkSecurityGroup": { "id": "[resourceId('Microsoft.
Network/networkSecurityGroups', variables('nsgName'))]" }
}
                          } ]
                    }
              },
              {
                    "name": "[variables('nicName')]",
                    "type": "Microsoft.Network/
networkInterfaces",
                    "apiVersion": "2020-11-01",
                    "location": "[resourceGroup().location]",
                    "dependsOn": [ "[resourceId('Microsoft.
Network/publicIPAddresses', variables('publicIPName'))]",
```

```
"[resourceId('Microsoft.Network/virtualNetworks',
parameters('vnetName'))]" ],
            "tags": "[parameters('resourceTags')]",
            "properties": {
                "ipConfigurations": [
                    {
                        "name": "ipConfig1",
                        "properties": {
                            "privateIPAllocationMethod":
"Dynamic",
                            "publicIPAddress": { "id":
"[resourceId('Microsoft.Network/publicIPAddresses',
variables('publicIPName'))]" }, "subnet": { "id":
"[resourceId('Microsoft.Network/virtualNetworks/subnets',
parameters('vnetName'), parameters('subnetName'))]" }
                        }
                    }
                ]
            }
        },
        {
            "name": "[parameters('vmName')]",
            "type": "Microsoft.Compute/virtualMachines",
            "apiVersion": "2021-03-01",
            "location": "[resourceGroup().location]",
            "dependsOn": [
"[resourceId('Microsoft.Storage/storageAccounts',
toLower(variables('diagnosticsStorageAccountName')))]",
"[resourceId('Microsoft.Network/networkInterfaces',
variables('nicName'))]" ],
            "tags": "[parameters('resourceTags')]",
            "properties": {
                "hardwareProfile": { "vmSize":
"[parameters('vmSize')]" },
                "osProfile": { "computerName":
"[parameters('vmName')]", "adminUsername":
"[parameters('adminUsername')]", "adminPassword":
"[parameters('adminPassword')]" },
                "storageProfile": {
```

```
              "imageReference": { "publisher":
"MicrosoftWindowsServer", "offer": "WindowsServer",
"sku": "[parameters('windowsOSVersion')]", "version":
"latest" },

              "osDisk": { "name":
"[concat(parameters('vmName'),'osdisk')]", "caching":
"ReadWrite", "createOption": "FromImage" }
            },
              "networkProfile": { "networkInterfaces":
[ { "id": "[resourceId('Microsoft.Network/
networkInterfaces', variables('nicName'))]" } ] },
              "diagnosticsProfile": {
"bootDiagnostics": { "enabled": true,
"storageUri": "[reference(resourceId('Microsoft.
Storage/storageAccounts/',
variables('diagnosticsStorageAccountName'))).
primaryEndpoints.blob]" } }
            }
          }
      ]
}
```

7. Notice all your values are prepopulated; click **Review + create**.

8. Click **Create**.

9. Log in to your server using a **Remote Desktop Connection (RDC)**. Use the following credentials:

    - **Username**: Packtadmin

    - **Password**: P@55w0rd()

10. On the **Server Manager** window that appears, with the default being on the **Dashboard** menu, click **Add roles and features**:

Server Manager
Server Manager • Dashboard
Manage
Tools
View
Help
Dashboard
Local Server
All Servers
File and Storage Services
WELCOME TO SERVER MANAGER
QUICK START
WHAT'S NEW
LEARN MORE
1 Configure this local server
2 Add roles and features
3 Add other servers to manage
4 Create a server group
5 Connect this server to cloud services
Hide
ROLES AND SERVER GROUPS
Roles: 1 | Server groups: 1 | Servers total: 1
File and Storage Services 1
Manageability
Events
Performance
BPA results
Local Server 1
Manageability
Events
Services
Performance
BPA results
All Servers 1
Manageability
Events
Services
Performance
BPA results

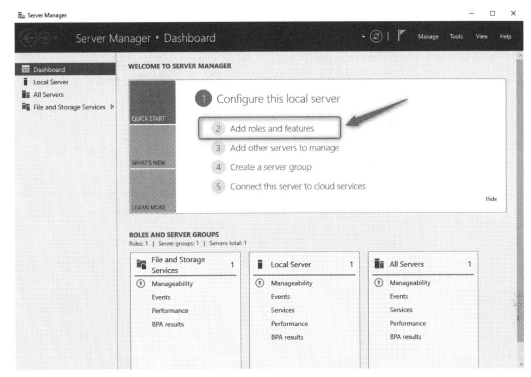

Figure 17.8 – Add roles and features

11. On the **Add roles and features** wizard, click **Next**.
12. Select **Role-based or feature-based installation**. Click **Next**.
13. Click **Next** again.
14. Select **Remote Access** and click **Next**:

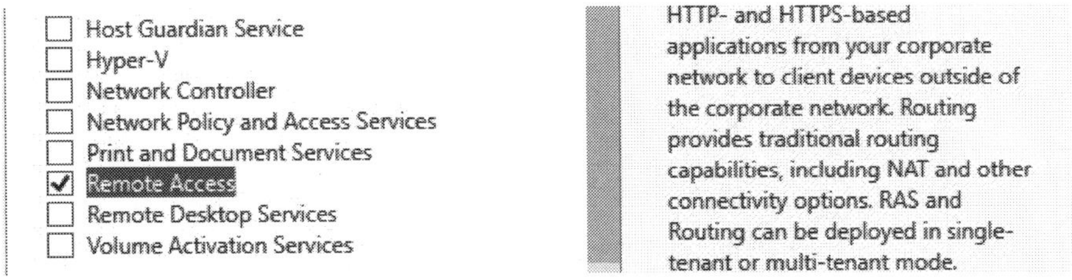

Host Guardian Service
Hyper-V
Network Controller
Network Policy and Access Services
Print and Document Services
Remote Access
Remote Desktop Services
Volume Activation Services
HTTP- and HTTPS-based applications from your corporate network to client devices outside of the corporate network. Routing provides traditional routing capabilities, including NAT and other connectivity options. RAS and Routing can be deployed in single-tenant or multi-tenant mode.

Figure 17.9 – Remote Access feature

15. For the **Features** and **Remote Access** pages, click **Next**.

16. For **Role Services**, select **Direct Access and VPN (RAS)**. Then, click **Add Features** on the pop-up window that appears. Click **Next**.

17. Click **Next** until you get to the confirmation screen and click **Install**.

18. Before closing the wizard, click **Open the Getting Started Wizard**:

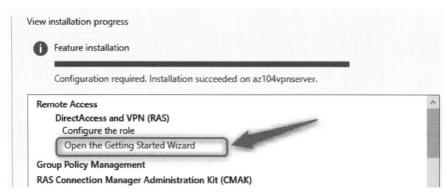

Figure 17.10 – Open the Getting Started Wizard

19. Click **Deploy VPN only**.

20. Right-click on the Start button and click **Computer Management**:

Figure 17.11 – Right-click on Start

21. Click on **Device Manager**, then click on **Action** on the top menu, and click **Add legacy hardware**:

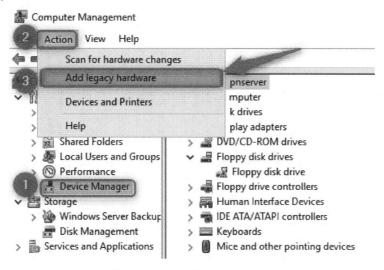

Figure 17.12 – Device Manager

22. On the wizard, click **Next**. Then click **Install the hardware that I manually select from a list (Advanced)** on the subsequent screen. Click **Next**:

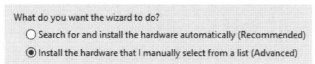

Figure 17.13 – Installing hardware

23. Scroll down to select **Network adapters** and click **Next**.

24. Select **Microsoft** under **Manufacturer**, and then **Microsoft KM-TEST Loopback Adapter** under **Model**:

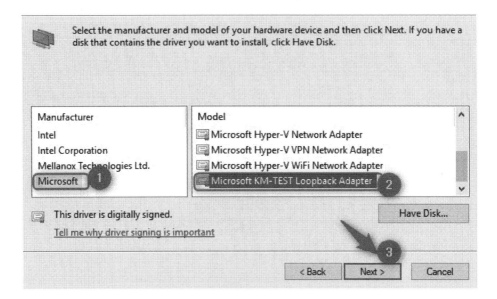

Figure 17.14 – Adding a loopback adapter

25. Click **Next**, then click **Finish** on the screens that follow. Close the **Computer Management** window.

26. On the **Routing and Remote Access** window, right-click on your server and click **Configure and Enable Routing and Remote Access** on the pop-up window:

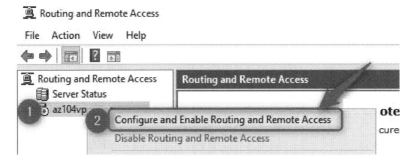

Figure 17.15 – Configure routing feature

27. On the next wizard, click **Next**. Select the **Virtual private network (VPN) access and NAT** option. Click **Next**:

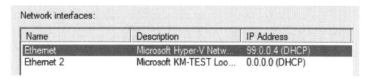

Figure 17.16 – VPN and NAT

28. Select the **Ethernet** interface (which will show the 99.0.0.0 range next to it). Click **Next**:

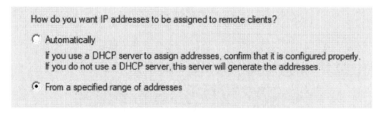

Figure 17.17 – Ethernet interface

29. For **IP Address Assignment**, select **From a specified range of addresses**. Click **Next**:

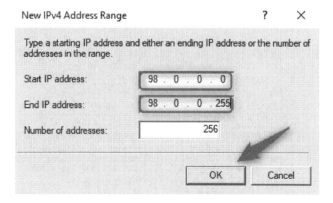

Figure 17.18 – IP Assignment on VPN

30. Click **New....** Specify as follows and click **OK**. Click **Next**:

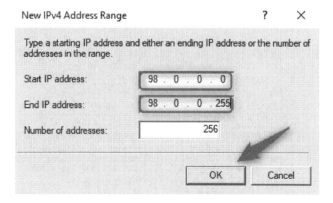

Figure 17.19 – New IPv4 range

31. Leave the next selection as **No** and click **Next**:

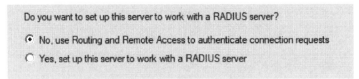

Figure 17.20 – RADIUS server configuration

32. Click **Finish**. You will get warned about your firewall and you will be required to open port 4500 and 500 UDP on both inbound and outbound on the server through the **Windows Defender Firewall with Advanced Security** window.

33. When the following screen pops up, click **OK**:

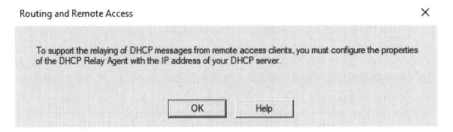

Figure 17.21 – DHCP option

34. Click the Start button and then **Windows Security**:

Figure 17.22 – Windows Security

35. Click **Firewall & network protection** on the left, then click **Advanced settings** on the right:

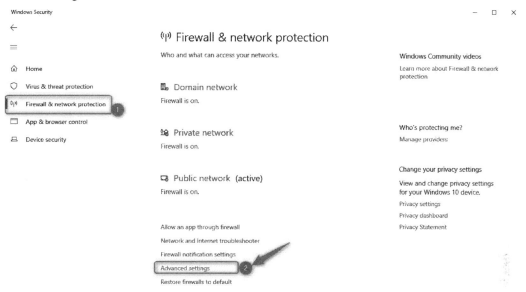

Figure 17.23 – Firewall and network protection

36. Click **Inbound Rules** on the left and then **New Rule...** on the right:

Figure 17.24 – New Inbound Rule

37. Select **Port** and click **Next**.

38. You can configure the rule as follows, and click **Next**:

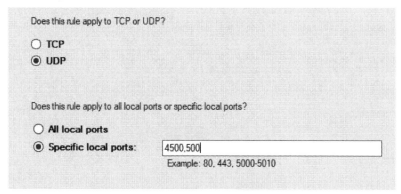

Figure 17.25 – UDP rule

39. Click **Allow the connection** and then click **Next**.

40. Click **Next** again, leaving **Domain**, **Private** and **Public** selected.

41. Enter **Name** as VPNGW-inbound. Click **Finish**.

42. Repeat the process for outbound, changing the name to VPNGW-outbound, and ensure that you select **Allow the connection**.

43. Navigate back to the **Routing and Remote Access** window. Right-click on **Network Interfaces** and click **New Demand-dial Interface…**:

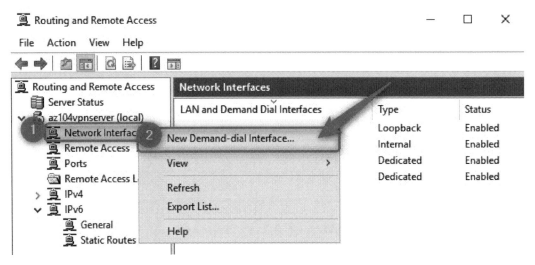

Figure 17.26 – New Demand-dial Interface

44. Click **Next**, then change the name to Azure VPN, and click **Next**.

45. Select **Connect using virtual private network (VPN)** and click **Next**.

46. Select **IKEv2** and click **Next**.

47. Enter the IP address of the VPN gateway from Azure. Click **Next** on this and the next screen.

48. Click **Add**, then enter the following and click **OK** (if your VNet associated with the VPN gateway is a /16 range, then your subnet is 255.255.0.0; if it is a /24 range, then it is 255.255.255.0). Click **Next**:

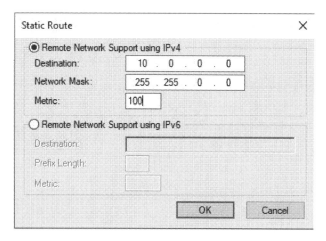

Figure 17.27 – Static route

49. Click **Next**, then **Finish**.

50. Right-click **Azure VPN** and click **Properties**.

51. Click the **Security** tab and then click **Use preshared key for authentication**. Generate a key you would like to use as a secret for the S2S connection, paste it into the **Key** field, and click **OK**:

Figure 17.28 – IKEv2 key

You have just configured your VPN server for the VPN gateway in Azure. Next, we will configure the Azure VPN Gateway side to establish an S2S connection.

S2S VPN Configuration

To configure an S2S VPN tunnel using Azure VPN Gateway, we will use a Windows server with RRAS features installed. This will work as the equivalent of an on-premises appliance that would typically run a persistent connection with the VPN gateway. An S2S tunnel is typically designed to be persistent:

1. Navigate to your VPN resource group.

2. Click + **Create** on the **Overview** screen for the resource group.

3. Type `local network gateway` in the search bar and press *Enter/Return*. Click **Virtual network gateway** from the options that are returned:

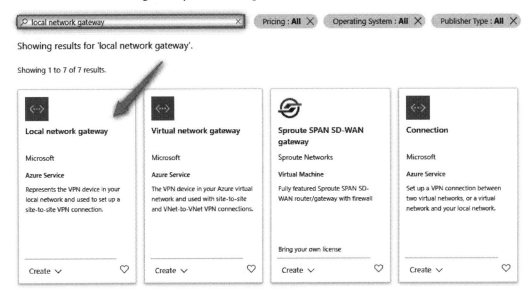

Figure 17.29 – Choosing Local network gateway

4. Click **Create**.

5. Enter the following and click **Review + create**:

   - **Subscription**: Select your Azure subscription.

   - **Resource Group**: `AZ104-VPNGateway`.

   - **Region**: **West Europe** (or select what you prefer).

   - **Name**: `VPNServer`.

- **Endpoint**: IP address.

- **IP address**: Enter the IP address of the VM you spun up in the previous exercise.

- **Address Space(s)**: `99.0.0.0/24`.

6. Click **Create**.

7. Navigate to the VPN gateway you deployed earlier in the chapter.

8. Click on **Connections** under the **Settings** context.

9. Enter the following and click **OK**:

- **Name**: `Azureto2019`.

- **Connection type: Site-to-site (IPsec)**.

- **Virtual network gateway**: The gateway you configured earlier.

- **Local network gateway**: Select the one you created in the previous steps.

- **Shared key**: Paste your key used in the previous exercise.

- **Use Azure Private IP Address**: Unselected.

- **IKE protocol: IKEv2**.

10. Now that you have configured the S2S components, go back to your VPN server and navigate to the **Routing and Remote Access** window.

11. Click **Network Interfaces** and right-click on your Azure VPN interface and click **Connect**. If all is configured correctly, you should successfully connect:

Figure 17.30 – RRAS VPN connection

Now that you have configured your Windows VPN server, we will test it in the next section.

Verify connectivity via the Azure portal

To verify connectivity, follow these steps:

1. Navigate to your VPN Gateway resource on the Azure portal.

2. Click **Connections** under the **Settings** context. Note the connection on the right-hand side of the screen; a status of **Connected** shows that the tunnel has been successfully established. If the view does not update, there is also a refresh button at the top of the page:

Name	↑↓	Status	↑↓	Connection type	↑↓	Peer	↑↓
AzureVPN		Connected		Site-to-site (IPsec)		VPNServer	•••

Figure 17.31 – S2S connected in Azure

In the next section, we will explore VNet to VNet connectivity.

VNet to VNet connections

Configuring a VNet-to-VNet connection is a simple way to connect VNets. Connecting a virtual network to another virtual network is similar to creating an S2S IPSec connection to an on-premises environment. Both the connection types use Azure VPN Gateway. The VPN gateway provides a secure tunnel IPsec/IKE and they communicate in the same way. The difference is in the way the local network gateway is configured.

When you create a VNet-to-VNet connection, the local network gateway address space is automatically created and populated. If you update the address space for one VNet, the other VNet automatically routes to the updated address space. This makes it faster and easier to create a VNet-to-VNet connection than an S2S connection.

> **Top Tip**
>
> To create a VNet-to-VNet connection from the Azure portal, you can refer to the following tutorial: `https://docs.microsoft.com/en-us/azure/vpn-gateway/vpn-gateway-howto-vnet-vnet-resource-manager-portal`.

Create and configure Azure ExpressRoute

In the following exercise, we will explore the creation of an ExpressRoute circuit. We will only emulate the deployment as it typically includes involvement from a provider with a corresponding circuit configuration at the edge to join Azure:

1. Create a resource group named AZ104-ExpressRoute in **West Europe**.

2. Click in the search bar at the top of the Azure screen and type express route, and then press *Enter/Return*. Click **ExpressRoute circuits** from the options that appear:

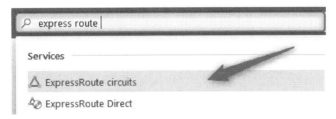

Figure 17.32 – Deploying an ExpressRoute circuit

3. Enter the following and click **Next : Configuration >**:

   - **Subscription**: Select your Azure subscription.

   - **Resource Group**: AZ104-ExpressRoute.

   - **Region**: **West Europe** (or select what you prefer).

   - **Name**: az104expressroute.

4. Depending on how you have procured your ExpressRoute circuit, this will determine what options you select next. Since this demonstration will not really be an ExpressRoute connection, we will configure it as follows and click **Review + create**:

   - **Port Type: Provider**.

   - **Create new or import from classic: Create new**.

   - **Provider**: Select a provider.

   - **Peering Location**: Select a location.

   - **Bandwidth: 200Mbps**.

   - **SKU: Standard**.

   - **Billing model: Metered**.

- **Allow classic operations: No.**

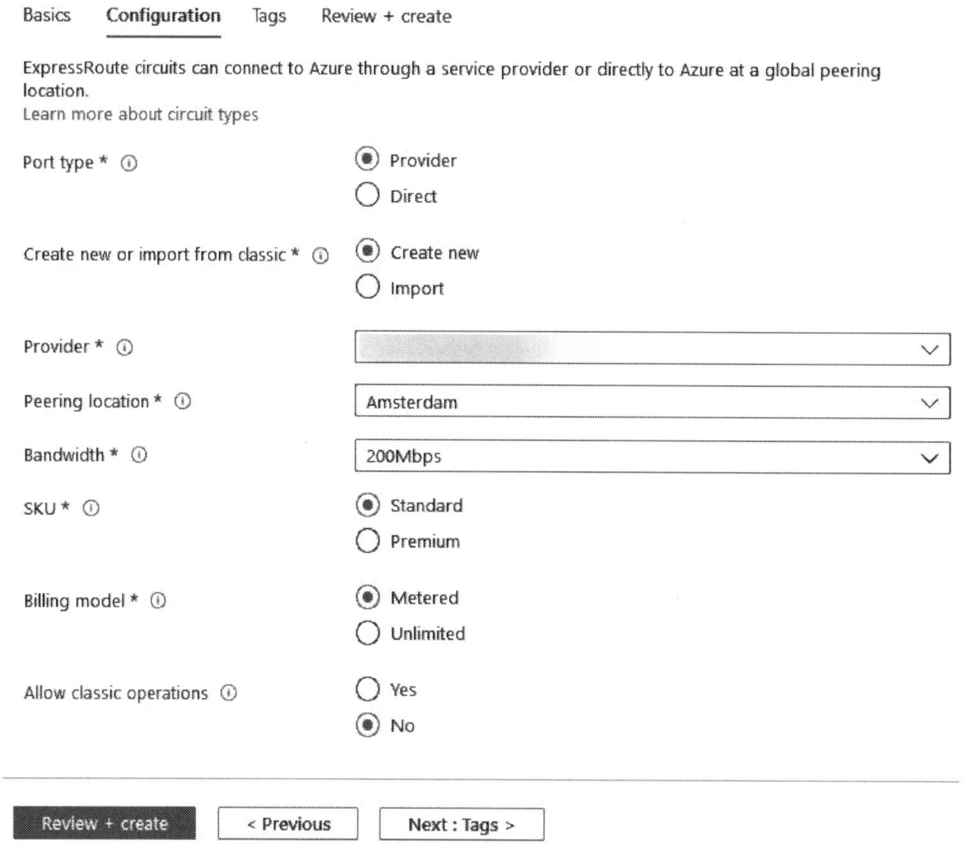

Basics   **Configuration**   Tags   Review + create

ExpressRoute circuits can connect to Azure through a service provider or directly to Azure at a global peering location.
Learn more about circuit types

Port type * ⓘ	⦿ Provider
	○ Direct
Create new or import from classic * ⓘ	⦿ Create new
	○ Import
Provider * ⓘ	[ ] ∨
Peering location * ⓘ	Amsterdam ∨
Bandwidth * ⓘ	200Mbps ∨
SKU * ⓘ	⦿ Standard
	○ Premium
Billing model * ⓘ	⦿ Metered
	○ Unlimited
Allow classic operations ⓘ	○ Yes
	⦿ No

[Review + create]   [< Previous]   [Next : Tags >]

Figure 17.33 – ExpressRoute configuration

5.   Click **Create**.

For the completion of setting up an ExpressRoute circuit connection, you will need to contact your ExpressRoute provider and confirm the circuit numbers as part of your deployment. You will provide them with the service key associated with the circuit you have deployed in Azure.

For additional reading and guidance on the deployment steps, you can read these articles:

- *ExpressRoute overview*: https://docs.microsoft.com/en-us/azure/expressroute/expressroute-introduction

- *Create and modify an ExpressRoute circuit*: https://docs.microsoft.com/en-us/azure/expressroute/expressroute-howto-circuit-portal-resource-manager

Now that you understand how to configure an ExpressRoute circuit, you can feel confident in starting the deployment in your organization. Next, we will explore Azure Virtual WAN.

Azure Virtual WAN

Azure Virtual WAN provides a mechanism for a managed hub-and-spoke network within Azure. It consolidates all your endpoint connection types into a single service that simplifies the management of your complex networks and enables transitive network functionality.

The following diagram shows an illustration of the various interconnections that may be employed in a typical environment:

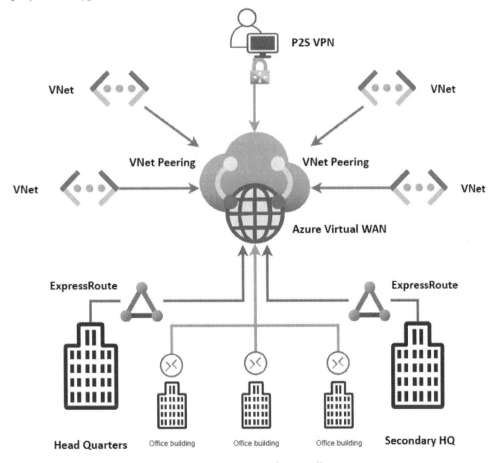

Figure 17.34 – Azure Virtual WAN illustration

As illustrated in the preceding diagram, you could have a variety of connection types, such as ExpressRoute, S2S connections, P2S connections, and even VNet peering. All the traffic flow configurations are managed through Azure Virtual WAN, which will also configure your transitive network flows, eliminating the need for an additional **Network Virtual Appliance (NVA)**. The deployment of Virtual WAN also allows for the deployment of a firewall in the solution, allowing you to secure traffic natively through your hub-and-spoke model.

There are two SKUs that you can purchase as part of the service:

- **Basic**: The following connections are supported:

  - S2S VPN connections

  - Branch-to-branch

  - Branch-to-VNet connections and VNet-to-branch

- **Standard**: The following connections are supported:

  - P2S connections

  - S2S connections

  - ExpressRoute (ExpressRoute to ExpressRoute connections are only supported through ExpressRoute Global Reach)

  - VNet-to-VNet connections (including Hub Transit)

  - VNet-to-Hub and Hub-to-VNet connections

  - Branch-to-branch

  - Branch-to-VNet connections and VNet-to-branch

  - Azure Firewall

  - NVA in a Virtual WAN

Effectively, the intention of Virtual WAN is to act as a head-end for your network being the primary routing service for all your interconnections required.

> **Top Tip**
> While you can upgrade from the Basic to Standard SKU, you cannot downgrade from Standard to Basic. This is important in deciding your direction for implementation and upgrading.

Now that you understand what Virtual WAN is, we will look at the deployment of the service next.

Configuring Azure Virtual WAN

In order to configure Azure Virtual WAN, you will need to perform the following steps:

1. Create a new resource group named AZ104-VirtualWAN.

2. Click + **Create** on the **Overview** screen for the resource group.

3. Click **Networking** on the left menu, then select **Virtual WAN** from the options on the right:

Figure 17.35 – Virtual WAN

4. Enter the following and then click **Review + create**:

    - **Subscription**: Select your Azure subscription.

    - **Resource group**: AZ104- VirtualWAN.

    - **Resource group location**: **West Europe** (or select what you prefer).

    - **Name**: az104virtualwan.

    - **SKU**: **Standard**.

5. Click **Create**.

6. Navigate to your Virtual WAN and click **Hubs** under the **Connectivity** context.

7. Click + **New Hub**.

8. Enter the following details and click **Next : Site to site >**:

    - **Region**: **West Europe** (or select what you prefer)

    - **Name**: vwanhub

    - **Hub private address space**: 110.0.0.0/24

9. Select **Yes** for **Do you want to create a Site to site (VPN gateway)?**, select **1 scale unit – 500 Mbps x 2**, and set **Routing preference** as **Microsoft network**:

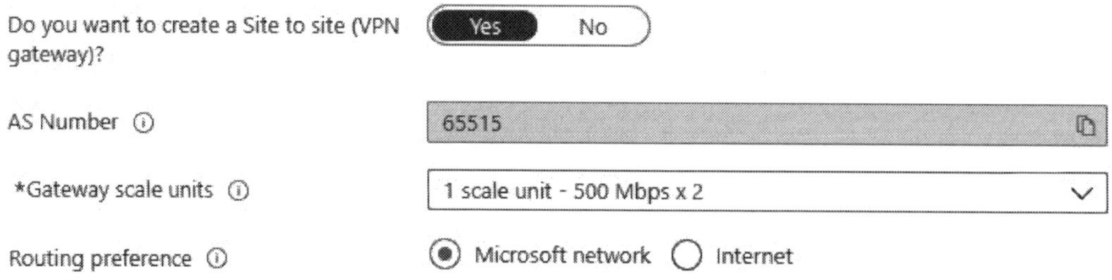

Do you want to create a Site to site (VPN gateway)?   `Yes`   No

AS Number ⓘ   `65515`

*Gateway scale units ⓘ   `1 scale unit - 500 Mbps x 2`   ⌄

Routing preference ⓘ   ⦿ Microsoft network   ◯ Internet

Figure 17.36 – Hub site

10. Click **Review + create**, then click **Create**.

Now that you have a Virtual WAN deployment, you will create a VPN site next.

Creating a VPN Site

In this exercise, you will create your first VPN site for the Virtual WAN:

1. Navigate to your Virtual WAN and click **VPN sites** under the **Connectivity** context.
2. Click **+ Create site**.
3. Enter the following details and click **Next : Links >**:

    • **Region**: **West Europe** (or select what you prefer)
    • **Name**: Windows_RRAS
    • **Device Vendor**: **Windows RRAS**
    • **Private address space**: 99.0.0.0/24

4. Enter the following details and click **Next : Review + create >**. Here, **Link Speed** refers to the speed in MBps of the line, and **Link IP address/FQDN** is your VPN server/NVA device that you are connecting to:

    • **Link Name**: rraslink
    • **Link Speed**: **50**

- **Link provider name**: `rras server`
- **Link IP address/FQDN**: Public IP of your VPN VM

5. Click **Create**.

Now that you have created your VPN site, you will need to connect this to the hub next.

Connecting your VPN site to the hub

Now that your site is configured, you will need to connect to your VPN connection using your VPN server:

1. Navigate to your Virtual WAN and click **Hubs** under the **Connectivity** context.
2. Click on your Virtual WAN from the options on the right.
3. In the **Virtual Hub** pane, click **VPN (Site to site)** under the **Connectivity** context.
4. Click **Clear all filters** to view your VPN site:

Figure 17.37 – Clear all filters

5. Select your VPN site and click **Connect VPN sites**:

Figure 17.38 – Associate VPN site

6. Fill in **Pre-shared key (PSK)** and leave all the other settings as default values. Click **Connect**:

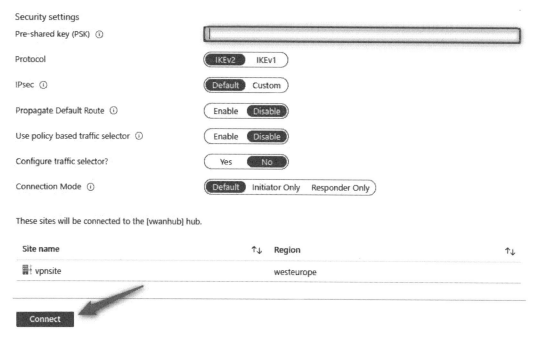

Figure 17.39 – S2S VPN configuration

7. You will see **Connection Provisioning status** stating **Succeeded**:

Figure 17.40 – Connection Provisioning status

Now you have a VPN connection, you will attempt to connect to this next.

Connect to your VPN site

Now that your site is connected to the hub, you can connect to this using your VPN server:

1. Log on to the server you provisioned for the *Creating and configuring an Azure VPN gateway* exercise. Navigate to **Routing and Remote Access** and create a new demand-dial interface.

2. Click **Next**, then change the name to Azure VWAN VPN, and click **Next**.

3. Select **Connect using virtual private network (VPN)** and click **Next**.

4. Select **IKEv2** and click **Next**.

5. Navigate to your Virtual WAN and click **Hubs** under the **Connectivity** context.

6. Navigate to your Virtual WAN and click **VPN (Site to site)** under **Connectivity**.

7. Click on the text next to **Gateway scale units**:

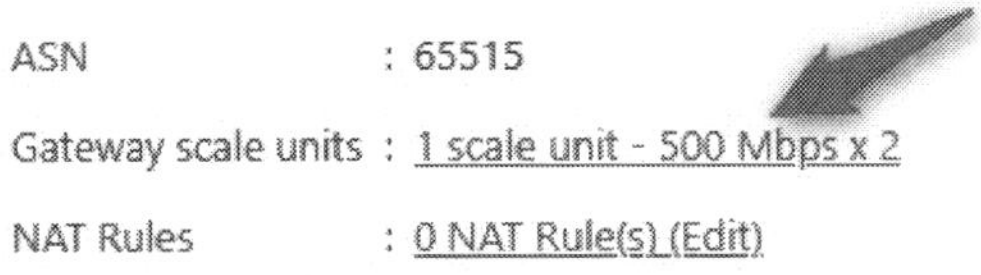

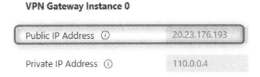

Figure 17.41 – Gateway scale units

8. Note the public IP address under **VPN Gateway Instance 0**:

VPN Gateway Instance 0

Public IP Address ⓘ   20.23.176.193

Private IP Address ⓘ   110.0.0.4

Figure 17.42 – Public IP Address

9. Enter this IP address of the VPN gateway from Azure in the **Demand-Dial Interface** wizard on the RRAS server. Click **Next** on this and the next screen.

10. Click **Add**, then enter the following and click **OK**. If your VNet associated with the VPN gateway is a /16 range, then your subnet is 255.255.0.0; if it is a /24 range, then it is 255.255.255.0. Click **Next**:

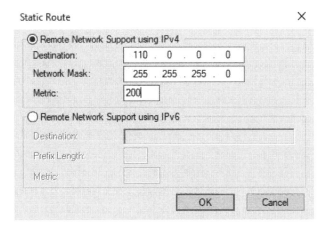

Figure 17.43 – Static route

11. Click **Next**, then **Finish**.

12. Click **Network Interfaces**, right-click **Azure VWAN VPN**, and click **Properties**.

13. Click the **Security** tab and then click **Use preshared key for authentication**. Use the key you generated earlier, paste it into the **Key** field, and click **OK**:

Figure 17.44 – IKEv2 key

14. Right-click on your **Azure VWAN VPN** interface and click **Connect**. If all is configured correctly, you should successfully connect:

Azure VWAN VPN   Demand-dial   Enabled   Connected

Figure 17.45 – RRAS VPN connection

You have now experienced connecting a S2S VPN using both Azure Virtual WAN and Azure VPN Gateway. You should feel confident in implementing the basic network structures you need within your Azure environments.

Summary

In this chapter, we covered various services for connecting on-premises networks to Azure, such as through Azure VPN Gateway and Azure Virtual WAN. You have learned about the various types of VPN connections available to you and the difference between each of them. You have also experienced the configuration of several of these. You should now feel comfortable in connecting your networks to Azure and what services to use. In the next chapter, we will explore monitoring and troubleshooting for networks in Azure in detail.

18
Monitoring and Troubleshooting Virtual Networking

This chapter focuses on monitoring and troubleshooting network connectivity. In this chapter, we are going to focus on how you can monitor your virtual networks using Network Watcher. You will learn how to manage your virtual network connectivity and how you can monitor and troubleshoot on-premises connectivity as well as use Network Watcher. We will end this chapter by covering how to troubleshoot external networking.

In this chapter, we are going to cover the following main topics:

- Network Watcher
- Configuring Network Watcher

Technical requirements

To follow along with the hands-on material, you will need the following:

- Access to an Azure subscription with owner or contributor privileges. If you do not have access to one, you can enroll for a free account at `https://azure.microsoft.com/en-us/free/`.

- PowerShell *5.1* or later installed on a PC from which labs can be practiced; note that many examples can only be followed on a PC.

- Installation of the `Az` module, which can be performed by running the following in an administrative PowerShell session:

```
Set-ExecutionPolicy -ExecutionPolicy RemoteSigned -Scope
CurrentUser
```

You can also run the following:

```
Install-Module -Name Az -Scope CurrentUser -Repository
PSGallery -Force
```

Network Watcher

Azure Network Watcher is a network monitoring solution that provides tools to diagnose, monitor, and view metrics and logging for resources in an Azure virtual network. This includes application gateway traffic, load balancers, and ExpressRoute circuits.

Azure Network Watcher offers the following capabilities:

- **Monitoring**
- **Network diagnostics**
- **Metrics**
- **Logs**
- **Tools for troubleshooting connection problems**

Network Watcher will be automatically enabled when a new virtual network is created or updated. There is no extra charge for enabling Network Watcher inside a subscription.

> **Top Tip**
>
> To make use of Network Watcher, you will require the appropriate **role-based access control** (**RBAC**) role permissions, such as Contributor, Owner, or Network Contributor.

Monitoring

Monitoring provides several tools that are useful for monitoring your network traffic as well as creating visibility of your Azure **Virtual Network** (**VNet**) resources and how they communicate with each other. The following figure depicts the tools available under the **Monitoring** context in the **Network Watcher** blade:

Figure 18.1 – Network Watcher, Monitoring

We describe each of these tools in more detail in the following subsections.

Topology

The **Topology** tool enables you to visually understand the interconnections between resources and how they are configured to communicate with each other within a VNet. This can be a great high-level overview of the VNet you are working with.

Connection monitor

This is a cloud-based hybrid network monitoring solution that can monitor the communication between **virtual machines** (**VMs**) and endpoints. An endpoint can be another VM, a URL, an IPv4 or IPv6 address, or a **fully qualified domain name** (**FQDN**). The network communication is monitored at regular intervals and information about latency, network topology changes, and the reachability between a VM and the endpoint is collected. If an endpoint becomes unreachable, Network Watcher will inform the user about the error. The reason for this can be a problem with the memory or CPU of a VM, a security rule for the VM, or the hop type of a custom route.

Network Performance Monitor

Network Performance Monitor (**NPM**) is a hybrid network monitoring solution. It can monitor network connectivity for on-premises and cloud networks, and between various points in your network infrastructure. It can detect issues such as routing errors and blackholing. The monitoring solution is stored inside Azure Log Analytics.

NPM can create alerts and notifications when network performance errors appear, and it can localize the source of the problem to a specific network device or segment.

It offers the following capabilities:

- **Performance monitor**: A performance monitor can monitor the network connectivity across cloud deployments and on-premises locations. It can also monitor connectivity between multiple data centers, branch offices, multi-tier applications, and microservices.

- **Service connectivity monitor**: You can identify the network bottlenecks inside the network infrastructure and detect the exact locations of the issues in the network. You can also monitor connectivity between users and services.

- **ExpressRoute monitor**: You can monitor the ExpressRoute connection between the on-premises locations and Azure.

Latency problems are also monitored. The connection monitor will provide the average, minimum, and maximum latency observed over time. The monitoring solution is capable of monitoring network performance between various points in the network infrastructure and it can generate alerts and notifications.

As of July 1, 2021, this has been considered a legacy service; you can no longer add new tests to an existing workspace, nor can you create new workspaces in NPM. You should now use the new Azure Connection Monitor instead and are advised to migrate any tests you had configured in NPM to Azure Connection Monitor.

Network diagnostic tools

There are several network diagnostic tools presented to you in Network Watcher. You can, for instance, diagnose network traffic filtering for VMs, determine the next hop of your traffic on route to an intended destination, or even identify why a VM is unable to communicate with other resources because of a security rule.

Using Azure Network Watcher, you can diagnose outbound connections from a VM. You can also diagnose problems with an Azure VNet gateway and connections, capture packets to and from a VM, view security rules for a network interface, and determine relative latencies between Azure regions and internet service providers.

The following tools are available as presented in the following screenshot:

Figure 18.2 – Network Watcher, network diagnostic tools

Let's look at them in more detail.

IP flow verify

An IP flow can verify and test the communication and inform you as to whether the connection has succeeded or failed. It is used to assess traffic flow to and from the internet and on-premises environments. An IP flow can tell you which security rule allowed or denied the connection and communication. To use **IP flow verify**, you specify a source (local) and destination (remote) IPv4 address and port. Along with this, you enter the corresponding packet information such as your protocol **transmission control protocol / user datagram protocol (TCP/UDP)** and direction of traffic flow (**Inbound/Outbound**):

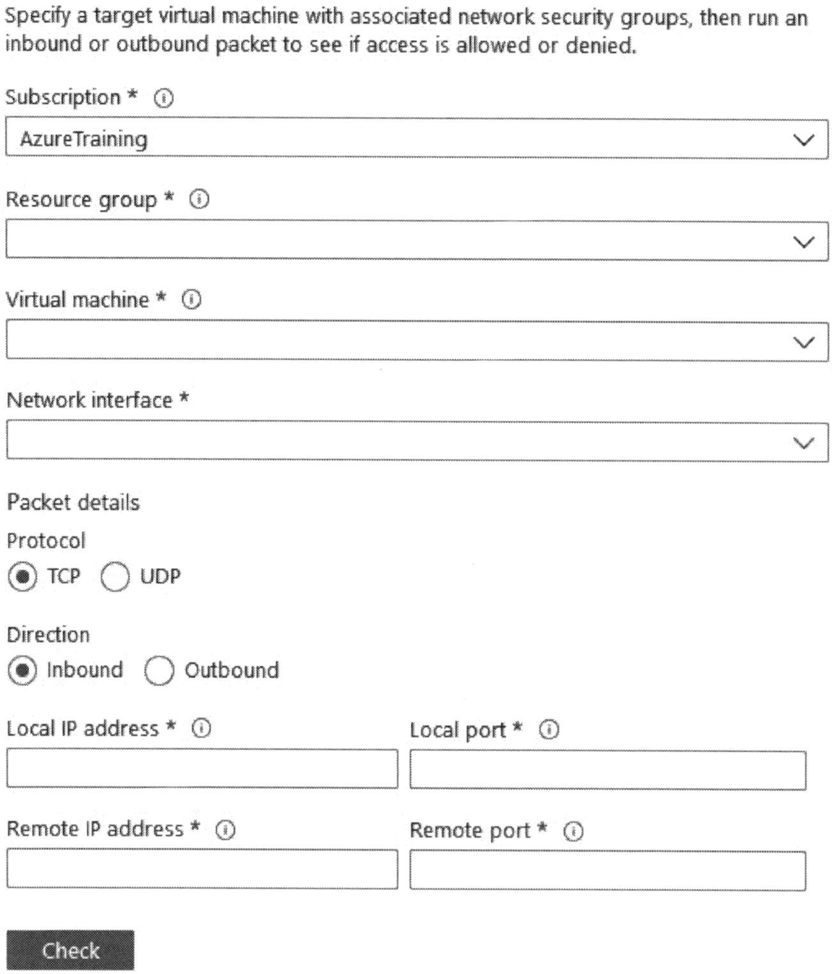

Specify a target virtual machine with associated network security groups, then run an inbound or outbound packet to see if access is allowed or denied.

Subscription * ⓘ

> AzureTraining   ∨

Resource group * ⓘ

>   ∨

Virtual machine * ⓘ

>   ∨

Network interface *

>   ∨

Packet details

Protocol

◉ TCP   ◯ UDP

Direction

◉ Inbound   ◯ Outbound

Local IP address * ⓘ   Local port * ⓘ

> _____   _____

Remote IP address * ⓘ   Remote port * ⓘ

> _____   _____

Check

Figure 18.3 – Network Watcher, IP flow verify

NSG diagnostic

This tool enables you to identify the net effect of applied **network security group** (**NSG**) rules that apply as well as identify all NSGs that will be used. The output will expose the end result *allow and deny* status for the identified flow. To run **NSG diagnostic**, you again specify your source and destination. The source can be an IPv4 address or a **Classless Inter-Domain Routing** (**CIDR**) range, or it can be a service tag, whereas the destination specified is an IP address only. You also choose your port for the destination, specify your traffic protocol (TCP/UDP/ **Internet Control Message Protocol** (**ICMP**)/All) and direction. The diagnostic supports VMs, network interfaces, VM scale set network interfaces, and application gateways.

Next hop

Network Watcher can also diagnose network routing problems from a VM. When a VNet is created, there are several default outbound routes created for that VNet as well. Outbound traffic from all resources that are deployed in a VNet is routed based on Azure's default routes. In cases where you want to override the default routing rules or create additional rules, **Next hop** can be used to test the communication between the different routes. When the communication fails, you can then change, add, or remove a route to resolve the problem.

Effective security rules

This is used to determine the overall effective security rules applied to your VM and will combine all relevant NSG rules together to display the net rule effect. This can be extremely helpful when assessing why your traffic is blocked and where you have several NSGs.

VPN troubleshoot

This is used when there are issues between your VNet gateways and connection endpoints that require troubleshooting. Multiple gateways and connections can be troubleshot at the same time.

Packet capture

The **packet capture** feature in Network Watcher allows you to capture packets for traffic related to your VM, being both inbound and outbound from the VM. The capture enables you to have more visibility of your network traffic, garnering key insights such as intrusion detection traffic, network statistics, and other network-related communications and traffic. This is enabled as a VM extension and relieves you of running your own VM-hosted packet capture utilities to achieve the same results.

Connection troubleshoot

This tool enables you to assess TCP connections between a VM and either a VM, URI, IPv4 address, or even FQDN. The aim of the tool is to reduce the time required in identifying connectivity issues and assist with determining the root cause.

Metrics

The **Metrics** category primarily contains usage and quota data as per the following category:

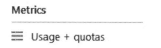

Figure 18.4 – Network Watcher, Metrics

Usage + quotas

This pane provides an easy mechanism to gain visibility of your usage against each quota, as well as providing the ability to request a quota increase for additional consumption of services:

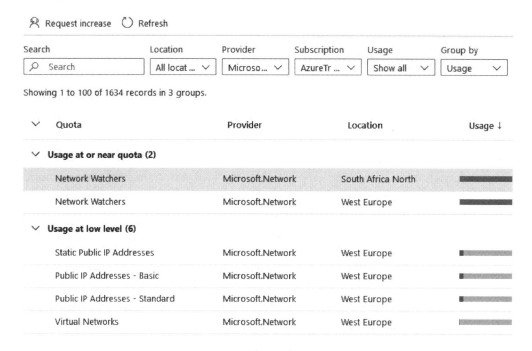

Figure 18.5 – Network Watcher, Usage + quotas

Next, we will explore what logs are and the types of logs we can collect.

Logs

Logs provide several logging tools that are useful for investigating usage and troubleshooting. These logs can be analyzed using several tools, such as the Traffic Analytics feature and Power BI:

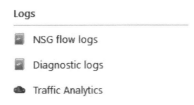

Figure 18.6 – Network Watcher, Logs

Next, we will explore the various log types found in the service.

NSG flow logs

NSGs are responsible for allowing or denying the inbound and outbound traffic to a network interface in the VM. The **NSG flow logs** feature can log the port, protocol, whether traffic is allowed or denied, and the source and IP address. The NSG flow logs feature is where you configure the logging of your flows.

Diagnostic logs

This pane allows you to configure the diagnostic logging settings for your resources; it will record NSG events and rule counts as NetworkSecurityGroupEvent and NetworkSecurityGroupRuleCounter. The logs can be stored in a variety of locations such as Log Analytics, Event Hubs, or an Azure storage account.

Traffic Analytics

Traffic Analytics can provide rich visualization of the data that is written to the NSG flow logs.

> **Top Tip**
> Network Watcher is a regional service, which means that you need to deploy it for each region that you require the service.

In the sections that follow, we are going to see Network Watcher in action.

Configuring Network Watcher

Now that you understand what Network Watcher is, we will explore in the following sections how to configure and use the various components available to the service.

Network resource monitoring

In this demonstration, we are going to monitor the network on VMs. For this demonstration, create three Windows Server 2016 data center VMs inside one VNet. We can use these VMs for monitoring. Before we are able to monitor the network using network resource monitoring, we need to install the Network Watcher agent on the three VMs. After that, we are going to inspect the network traffic.

Installing the Network Watcher agent

You will set up three VMs labeled `networkwatcher1`, `networkwatcher2`, and `networkwatcher3`. To install the Network Watcher agent on a VM in Azure, take the following steps:

1. Navigate to the Azure portal by opening `https://portal.azure.com/`.

2. Deploy a new resource group named `AZ104-NetworkWatcher` and a new VM deployed as follows:

   - **Subscription**: Select a subscription.

   - **Resource group**: `AZ104-NetworkWatcher`.

   - **Name**: `networkwatcher1`.

   - **Region**: A region of your choice (this must be the same for all subsequent resources in this chapter).

   - **Virtual Network: NetworkWatcherVnet**.

   - **Subnet Name: NetworkWatcherSubnet**.

   - **Network Security Group: NetworkWatcherSecurityGroup**.

   - **Open Ports: 3389**.

   - **Size: Standard DS1 v2**.

3. Once deployed, open the VM settings, and under **Settings**, select **Extensions +
    applications**, and then click the **Add** button:

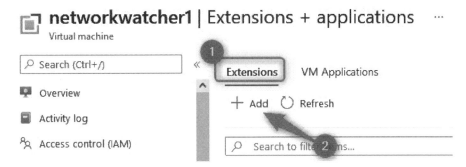

Figure 18.7 – Adding a VM extension

4. Type network watcher in the search box, click the **Network Watcher Agent for
    Windows** icon, and click **Next**:

Figure 18.8 – Adding the Network Watcher Agent for Windows extension

5. Click **Review + create** on the screen that follows, then click **Create**.

6. Repeat these steps for the other two VMs as well and install the agent on them.
    Increase the count associated with the VM name as mentioned at the beginning of
    this exercise.

Now that Network Watcher Agent for Windows is installed on all the VMs, we can enable
it for a specific region.

Enabling Network Watcher

To enable Network Watcher in a specific region, take the following steps:

1. Navigate to the Azure portal by opening `https://portal.azure.com/`.

2. Click the hamburger menu in the top-left corner of the Azure home screen. Select **All services**:

Figure 18.9 – Selecting All Services

3. Type `network watcher` in the search bar, then click **Network Watcher**:

Figure 18.10 – Selecting network watcher

4. On the Network Watcher **Overview** page, select the Network Watcher service with the **Subscription** and **Location** details that match the VM you deployed earlier. In my case, this is West Europe:

Figure 18.11 – Selecting your Network Watcher

> **Top Tip**
>
> Note that upon deploying your first VNet in an Azure region, Azure will automatically create the associated `NetworkWatcher_<region>` resource.

5. If Network Watcher is not already deployed for your region, click **+ Add** at the top of the screen. Select **Subscription** and **Region** and click **Add**:

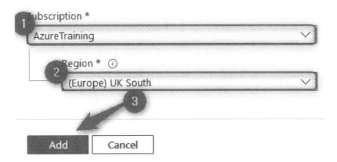

Figure 18.12 – Enabling a new Network Watcher region

Now that Network Watcher is enabled, we can actually start monitoring the network resources.

Monitoring network connectivity

Network monitoring can be used for monitoring connection reachability, latency, and network topology changes. To do this, you need to set up a Connection Monitor instance.

Take the following steps to set this up:

1. With the Network Watcher resource still open, in the left menu under **Monitoring**, select **Connection monitor**. Click **+ Create**.

2. We are going to use the monitor resource for testing the connectivity between VM1 and VM2. Therefore, enter the following values and click **Next: Test groups >>**:

   - **Connection Monitor Name**: VM1-VM2-Test.

   - **Subscription**: Select the subscription where the VMs are deployed.

   - **Region**: Select the region you chose for your VMs.

   - **Workspace configuration**: Leave the default option checked (this will create a new workspace for you):

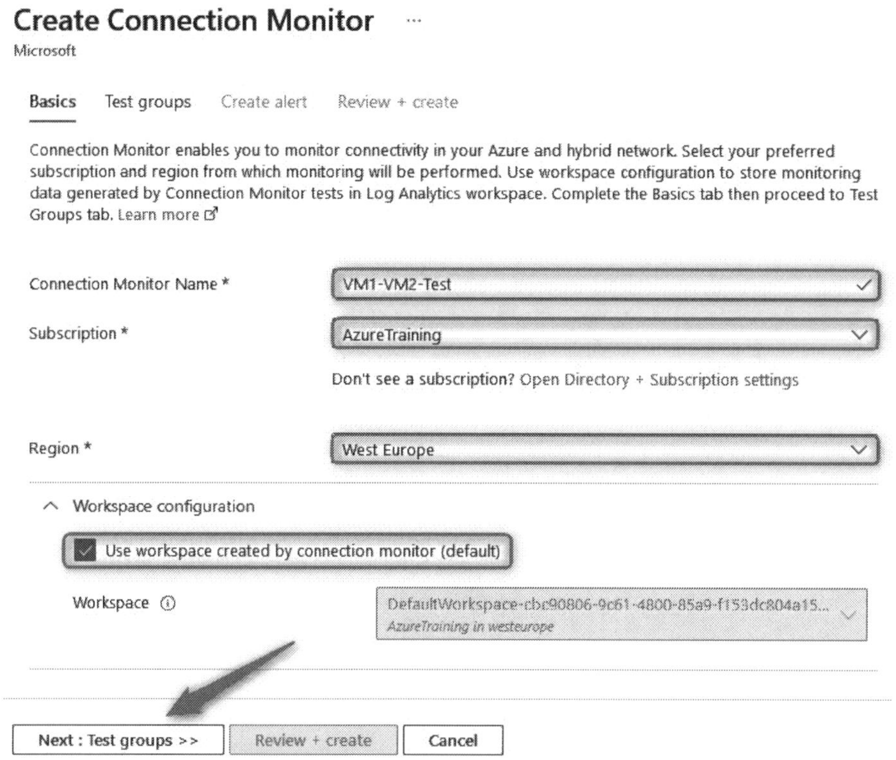

Figure 18.13 – Create Connection Monitor, Basics

3. Type VM1-VM2-Test in **Test group name** and click **Add sources**:

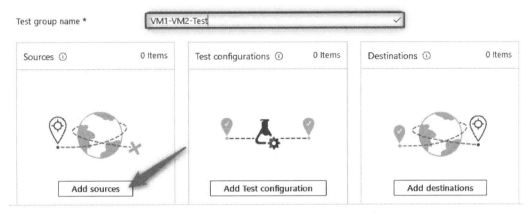

Figure 18.14 – Create Connection Monitor, Add sources

4. On the **Add Sources** blade, select your networkwatcher1 VM, then click **Add endpoints** at the bottom of the screen:

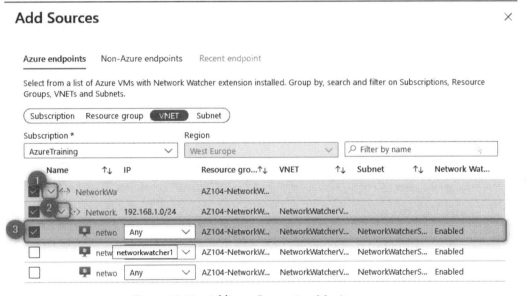

Figure 18.15 – Adding a Connection Monitor source

5.   Perform the same for **Add destinations**, this time selecting `networkwatcher2`. Click **Add endpoints** at the bottom of the screen:

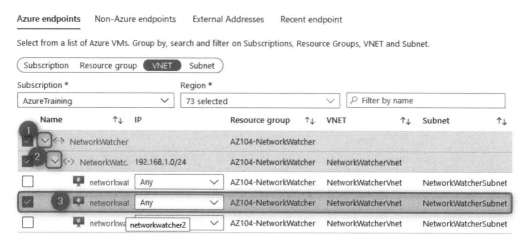

Figure 18.16 – Adding a Connection Monitor destination

6.   Click **Add Test configuration**, then enter the following into the blade. Click the **Add Test configuration** button at the bottom when done:

- **Test configuration name**: `VM1-VM2-Test-Config`.

- **Protocol**: TCP.

- **Destination Port**: `3389`.

- Check the **Listen on port** checkbox.

- **Test Frequency**: **Every 30 seconds**.

- **Checks failed (%)**: `5`.

- **Round trip time (ms)**: `100`.

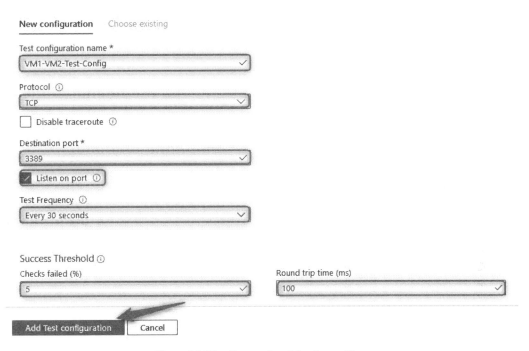

Add Test configuration ×

New configuration   Choose existing

Test configuration name *

| VM1-VM2-Test-Config |

Protocol ⓘ

| TCP |

☐ Disable traceroute ⓘ

Destination port *

| 3389 |

✓ Listen on port ⓘ

Test Frequency ⓘ

| Every 30 seconds |

Success Threshold ⓘ

Checks failed (%)

| 5 |

Round trip time (ms)

| 100 |

| Add Test configuration | | Cancel |

Figure 18.17 – Connection Monitor settings

7. Click **Add Test Group**.

8. Click **Next: Create alert >>**.

9. Note that you can create an alert by clicking the **Create alert** checkbox at the top of the screen. Click **Select action group** near the bottom of the page. You can create an action group by entering your email address and clicking **Create action group**, or by selecting an existing one. Click **Done**.

10. Click **Review + Create**, then click **Create**.

11. You will notice after a few minutes that the connection is good and gets a pass:

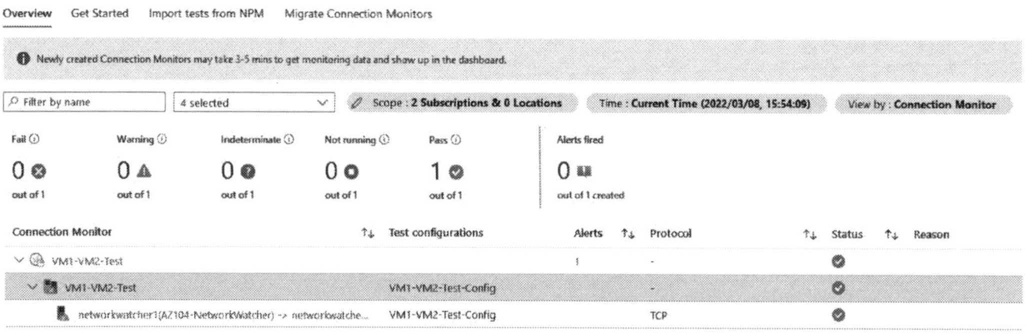

Figure 18.18 – Connection Monitor Overview

We are now able to monitor the network connectivity. In the next section, we are going to look at how to manage the connectivity.

Managing VNet connectivity

As you are now aware, you can manage your VNet connectivity from the Azure portal. In the upcoming section, we are going to look at the possibilities that the Azure portal has to offer to manage the VNet connectivity.

Network topology

The network topology section in the Azure portal displays an overview of the VNets inside an Azure subscription and a resource group. To view the network topology section, you have to take the following steps:

1. Navigate to the Azure portal by opening `https://portal.azure.com/`.

2. Click the hamburger menu in the top-left corner of the Azure home screen. Select **All services**.

3. Type `network watcher` in the search bar, and click **Network Watcher**.

4. Under the **Monitoring** context, select **Topology**.

5. Select the required details in **Subscription**, **Resource Group**, and, if relevant, **Virtual Network**, as shown in the following screenshot:

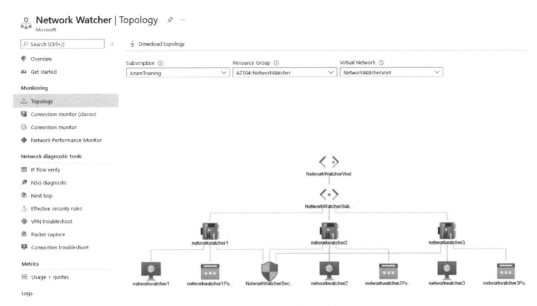

Figure 18.19 – Network Topology

> **Top Tip**
>
> Note that if you are not able to find your resource group in **Topology** under
> Network Watcher, you can also develop this by navigating to your VNet and
> selecting **Diagram** under the **Monitoring** context.

6. You can now drill down into all the components of the network, such as the VNet,
   Network interface card (**NIC**), VMs, and IP address, by clicking on the items in the
   topology. This will take you to the settings of the different resources.

7. You can download the topology as well, by clicking the **Download topology** button
   in the top menu:

Figure 18.20 – Downloading Network topology

Besides monitoring the networks in Azure, you can also monitor the on-premises
connectivity. We are going to look at this in the next section.

Monitoring on-premises connectivity

You can monitor your on-premises connectivity using Network Watcher as well. It offers two different features for this, NPM and VPN troubleshoot, which, just like the other features, are accessible from the Azure portal.

Configuring next hop

You can use the next hop feature to specify a source and destination IPv4 address. The communication between these addresses is then tested, and you will get informed about what type of next hop is used to route the traffic. When you experience a routing error or problem, you can add, change, or remove a route to resolve this.

> **Top Tip**
>
> If you don't see your resource group as one of the options in the drop-down selection, give it a few minutes and it should show up as an option. Another option you can try is to trigger a change on your VM such as changing the size.

To see this in action, you need to take the following steps:

1. Navigate to the Azure portal by opening `https://portal.azure.com/`.
2. Click the hamburger menu on the top-left corner of the Azure home screen. Select **All services**.
3. Type `network watcher` in the search bar, and click **Network Watcher**.
4. Under the **Network diagnostic tools** context, select **Next hop**.
5. In the settings blade, add the following values:

    - **Resource group**: `AZ104-NetworkWatcher`.
    - **Virtual machine**: `networkwatcher1`.
    - **Network interface**: This is selected automatically.
    - **Source IP address**: This is selected automatically as well.
    - **Destination IP address**: `13.107.21.200` (a Bing server IP address).

6. Select **Next hop**.
7. You will see the following result. In this case, there is no next hop because the connection is going straight to the internet, therefore, it shows **Next hop type** as **Internet**:

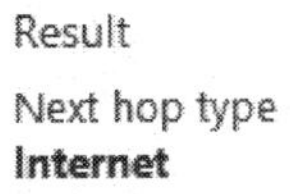

Result

Next hop type
Internet

Figure 18.21 – Next hop result

8. If you change the destination IP address to one of the IP addresses of the other VMs, which in my case is 192.168.1.5, you will see the following result:

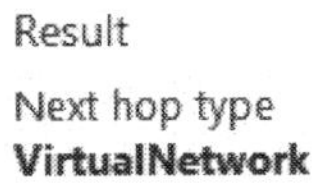

Result

Next hop type
VirtualNetwork

Figure 18.22 – Next hop result 2

You have just evaluated the next hop within the Azure network fabric and understand how your traffic will flow. You now know how to identify whether your traffic is flowing along the intended path to the destination. This tool will help you identify potential initial network flow issues in the future and save you time. In the next section, we are going to look at how to troubleshoot a VPN connection.

VPN troubleshoot

For the VPN troubleshoot demonstration, we are going to use the VPN connection that we created in the previous chapter.

You can diagnose the VPN connection by taking the following steps:

1. From the **Network Watcher** blade, select **VPN troubleshoot** from under **Network diagnostics tools**.

2. In the **VPN troubleshoot** blade, you can filter your VPN gateway choice by selecting the subscription, resource group, and location:

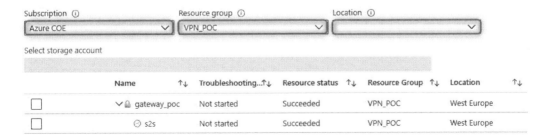

Figure 18.23 – VPN troubleshoot

3.   You can start the troubleshooting diagnostic by selecting the checkbox next to
     your corresponding gateway. You also need to select or create a storage account
     for storing the diagnostic information. After selecting the checkbox, you can start
     the troubleshooting process by clicking **Start troubleshooting** in the top menu, as
     shown in the following screenshot:

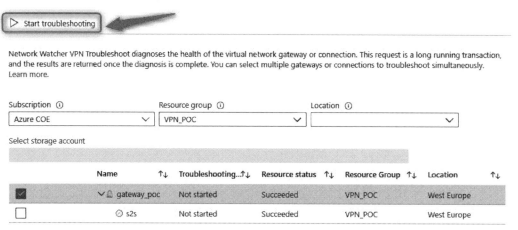

Figure 18.24 – VPN troubleshoot, Start troubleshooting

4.   This will start the troubleshooting process, and, in my case, the VPN connections
     seem healthy:

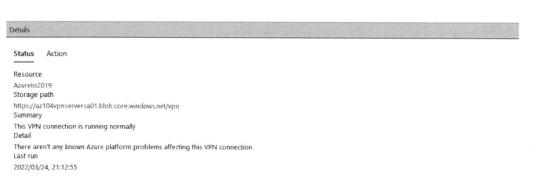

Figure 18.25 – VPN troubleshoot, troubleshooting

Should you have an issue, you can click on the **Action** tab to see the recommendations:

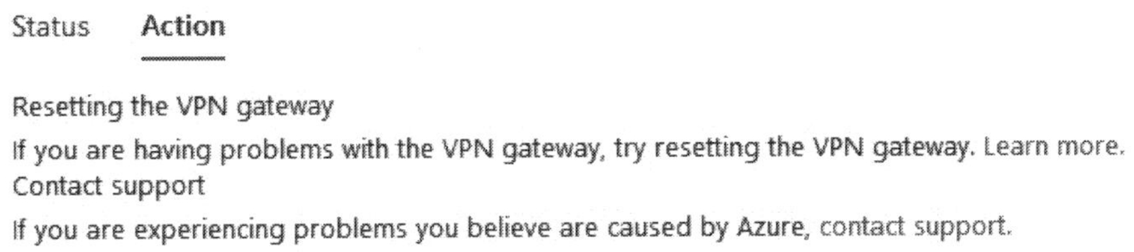

Status   **Action**

Resetting the VPN gateway
If you are having problems with the VPN gateway, try resetting the VPN gateway. Learn more.
Contact support
If you are experiencing problems you believe are caused by Azure, contact support.

Figure 18.26 – VPN troubleshoot, Action

You can manage external networking using Azure Network Watcher as well. We will cover this in the upcoming section.

Troubleshooting external networking

Azure Network Watcher offers three features to monitor and troubleshoot external networking. The features are **IP flow verify**, **Effective security rules**, and **Connection troubleshoot**, which are going to be covered in the next sections.

IP flow verify

With IP flow verify, you can detect whether a package is allowed or denied to or from a network interface of a VM. Included in the information are the protocol, the local and remote IP addresses, the direction, and the local and remote ports. When a packet is denied, the name of the routing rule that denies the packet is returned. You can use this to diagnose connectivity issues from or in the on-premises environment and to and from the internet. You can basically choose any source or IP address to verify the connectivity.

To run IP flow verify, you need to enable an instance of Network Watcher in the region where you plan to run the tool. This is similar to the demonstration covered in the *Enabling Network Watcher* section that appeared earlier in this chapter, where we enabled Network Watcher for a particular region.

Using IP flow verify

In this demonstration, we are going to use IP flow verify to test the connection between two of the VMs that we created in the first demonstration. To use IP flow verify, perform the following steps:

1. Inside the **Network Watcher** resource blade, under the **Network diagnostic tools** context, select **IP flow verify**.

2. On the settings page, add the following settings:

    - **Resource group**: AZ104-NetworkWatcher.

    - **Virtual machine**: networkwatcher1.

    - **Network interface**: This will be filled in automatically after selecting the VM.

    - **Protocol: TCP**

    - **Direction: Outbound**

    - **Local IP address**: This is filled in automatically as well.

    - **Local port**: 60000.

    - **Remote IP address**: 13.107.21.200 (a Bing server IP address).

    - **Remote port**: 80.

3. Click the **Check** button and notice the successful result.

4. The request is executed and the result it will return will be that access is allowed, because of the AllowInternetOutBound security rule, as shown in the following screenshot:

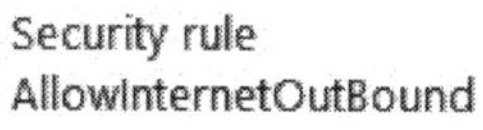

Security rule
AllowInternetOutBound

Figure 18.27 – AllowInternetOutBound

5. Repeat the actions up to *Step 3* again, and this time, make the following changes:

    - **Direction: Inbound**

6. This will result in the following, which is denied because of the DenyAllInBound rule:

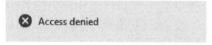

Security rule
DenyAllInBound

Figure 18.28 – DenyAllInBound

We've looked at how to use IP flow verify to test the connection between two of the VMs. In the next part, we are going to look at effective security rules.

Effective security rules

The effective security rules feature displays all the security rules that are applied to the network interface and the subnet where the network interface is. It then aggregates both. This will give you a complete overview of all the rules that are applied to a network interface, and it will give you the ability to change, add, or remove rules. You need to select the right subscription, the resource group, and the VM to get an overview of the applied security rules, as shown in the following screenshot:

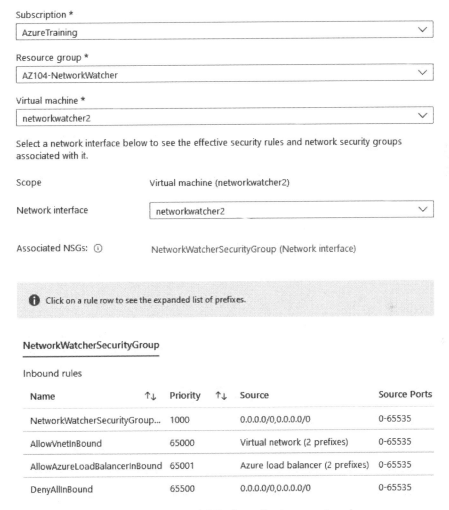

Figure 18.29 – Network Watcher, effective security rules

We've now seen an overview of the security rules that are applied to the network interface. In the next section, we are going to cover connection troubleshoot.

Connection troubleshoot

Azure Network Watcher connection troubleshoot enables you to troubleshoot network performance and connectivity issues in Azure. It provides visualization of the hop-by-hop path from source to destination, identifying issues that can potentially impact your network performance and connectivity.

Azure Network Watcher connection troubleshoot provides the following features and insights:

- A graphical topology view from your source to destination.
- It checks the connectivity between the source (VM) and the destination (VM, URI, FQDN, or IP) address.
- It offers hop-by-hop latency.
- It can identify configuration issues that are impacting reachability.
- It provides all possible hop-by-hop paths from the source to the destination.
- It checks latency (such as minimum, maximum, and average latency) between the source and destination.
- The number of packets dropped during the connection troubleshoot check.

> **Top Tip**
>
> Connection troubleshoot requires that the source VM has the `AzureNetworkWatcherExtension` VM extension installed. For installing the extension on a Windows VM, you can refer to `https://docs.microsoft.com/en-us/azure/virtual-machines/extensions/network-watcher-windows?toc=/azure/network-watcher/toc.json`, and for a Linux VM, you can refer to `https://docs.microsoft.com/en-us/azure/virtual-machines/extensions/network-watcher-linux?toc=%2Fazure%2Fnetwork-watcher%2Ftoc.json`.

To check network connectivity using connection troubleshoot, you have to take the following steps:

1. From the **Network Watcher** overview blade in the Azure portal, under the **Network diagnostic tools** context, select **Connection troubleshoot**.
2. Select your subscription and resource group.
3. Select **Virtual machine** in **Source type** and then select your VM.

4. For the **Destination** settings, select the **Specify manually** radio button, enter www.packt.com in **URI, FQDN or IP address**, set **Protocol** to **TCP**, and set **Destination port** to 80.

5. Click **Check**. The agent will automatically be installed on the source machine when you click the check button if it is not installed already.

6. Notice the success message:

Figure 18.30 – Reachable

7. Try the same, this time setting **Destination** to a VM and selecting another VM. Set **Destination port** to 22. Click **Check**.

8. Notice the failure message you receive:

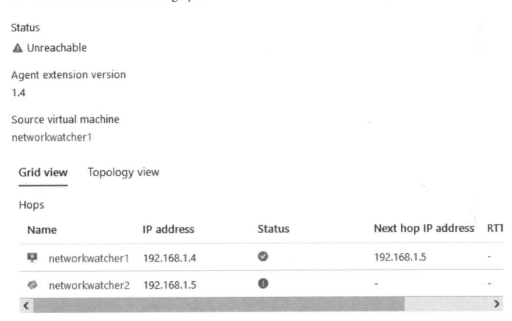

Figure 18.31 – Connection troubleshoot error

We have now checked an outbound connection from a VM using connection troubleshoot and seen both a success and failure message from the system.

Summary

In this chapter, we covered the fifth part of the *Configuring and Managing Virtual Networking* objective by covering how to monitor and troubleshoot your network traffic in Azure Network Watcher. We also covered how to monitor and troubleshoot on-premises and external network connectivity using Network Watcher. You should now feel confident in not only implementing network infrastructure components within Azure but also in the monitoring and management of those services. You should be comfortable in distinguishing the difference between the various services available in Azure, and comfortable in identifying which tools you should use to troubleshoot issues on your networks using Network Watcher.

In the next chapter, we will cover some labs, and you will get to test some of your new-found skills and become more confident in working with networks in Azure.

19
Practice Labs – Configuring and Managing Virtual Networking

In this chapter, we are going to get our hands dirty and look at how we can implement some of the things we learned around Azure networking, load balancing technologies, and practical management tips.

In this chapter, we are going to cover the following main topics:

- Virtual network subnetting lab
- Global peering interconnectivity lab

Technical requirements

The technical requirements before proceeding with this chapter are as follows:

- Access to an Azure subscription with global administrator and billing administrator privileges. If you do not have access to one, you can enroll for a free account: https://azure.microsoft.com/en-in/free/.

- PowerShell 3.6.1 or later versions installed on a PC from which labs can be practiced. Note that many examples can only be followed from a PC. Alternatively, you can also use https://shell.azure.com.

- Installation of the AZ module can be performed by running the following code in an administrative PowerShell session:

```
Set-ExecutionPolicy -ExecutionPolicy RemoteSigned -Scope
CurrentUser
Install-Module -Name Az -Scope CurrentUser -Repository
PSGallery -Force
```

- Download the following ZIP files and extract them somewhere easily accessible to you. If you have done this in previous labs, it is no longer required to perform this step. For assistance in downloading and extracting, we have the following steps for guidance.

> **Note**
> Even though the labs are on GitHub, no GitHub account is required to access the labs.

Downloading and extracting files for labs

Follow these steps to download and extract the files:

1. Navigate to the following URL and download the archive folder (.zip): https://github.com/MicrosoftLearning/AZ-104-MicrosoftAzureAdministrator/archive/master.zip.

2. Depending on the browser you are using, you will likely be presented with different versions of the following dialog. Click **Save File** and **OK** at the bottom of the screen:

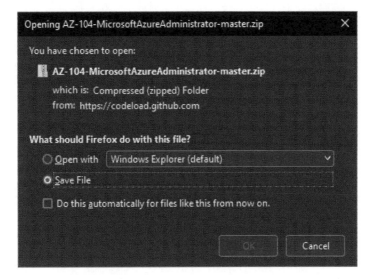

Figure 19.1 – Downloading files (ZIP)

3. Right-click the ZIP file you downloaded, and click **Extract All...** (on Windows systems):

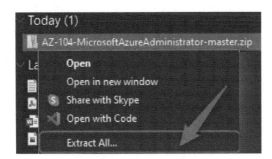

Figure 19.2 – Extract All (ZIP)

4. Navigate to your downloaded folder and follow instructions from the labs when needing files that will be in that folder.

You have downloaded all the files you need for the labs later in the chapter.

Virtual network subnetting lab

This lab will guide you through creating an Azure **virtual network** (**VNet**) with two subnets for implementing segmentation for your network. As part of the exercise, you will explore adding a **network security group** (**NSG**) to your deployment to enhance the security of the network. Finally, you will implement **domain name system** (**DNS**) for internal and external resolution.

Estimated time: 40 minutes

Lab method: PowerShell and the Azure portal

Lab scenario: In this lab, you play the role of an administrator who is looking to explore networking capabilities within Azure, including segmentation. As part of the exercise, you are looking to harden the security of your network to achieve your organization's security requirements by restricting traffic flow using NSGs. As part of your organization's requirements, you must implement DNS resolution services for internal and external queries. You need to ensure that the IP addresses allocated to your systems do not change. Your organization, Contoso, has several virtualized workloads, and you want to explore whether they can be run from Azure container instances using Docker images.

Visit the following link (**Lab URL**) to the official Microsoft learning GitHub labs, where you will be guided through each task step by step to achieve the preceding objective.

Lab objectives:

- **Task 1**: Create the VNet and two subnets
- **Task 2**: Deploy your VMs
- **Task 3**: Configure the **network interface card** (**NIC**) private and public IPs
- **Task 4**: Create your NSG and rules
- **Task 5**: Configure an internal DNS resolution
- **Task 6**: Configure an external DNS resolution

Lab URL: `https://microsoftlearning.github.io/AZ-104-`
`MicrosoftAzureAdministrator/Instructions/Labs/LAB_04-`
`Implement_Virtual_Networking.html`

Lab architecture diagram:

The following diagram illustrates the different steps involved in the exercise:

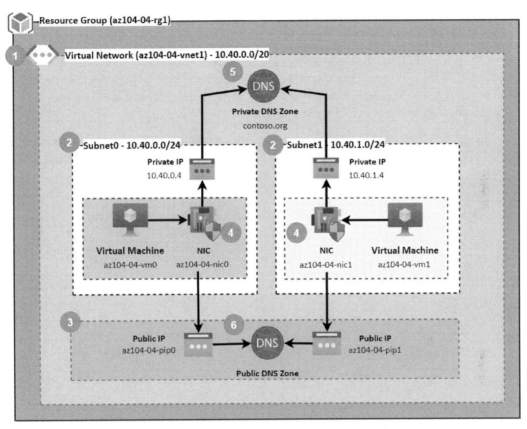

Figure 19.3 – Virtual network subnetting – architecture diagram

After working through this lab, you should have a good feel for how networks are implemented within Azure and how we handle both internal and external DNS resolutions for your networks. You have also experienced how VNets handle traffic between subnets within the same VNet. In the next lab, you will explore working with VNet peering and how this extends connectivity between VNets in Azure.

Global peering interconnectivity Lab

This lab will guide you through creating three VNets within Azure, two in one region and one in another. The purpose of this lab is to explore inter-site connectivity through VNet peering services and confirm that you can emulate on-premises network topologies through the logical networking options available to Azure.

Estimated time: 30 minutes

Lab method: PowerShell and the Azure portal

Lab scenario: In this lab, you play the role of an administrator who is looking to emulate existing work networks that have mesh WAN links across offices using Azure. You want to confirm that you can create VNet interconnectivity, that it can span both local and regional connections, and enable similar functionality to what you have today.

Visit the following link (**Lab URL**) to the official Microsoft learning GitHub labs, where you will be guided through each task step by step to achieve the preceding objective.

Lab objectives:

- **Task 1**: Provision your environment resources (resource group, VNets, and VMs)
- **Task 2**: Set up VNet peering
- **Task 3**: Test connectivity

Lab URL: `https://microsoftlearning.github.io/AZ-104-MicrosoftAzureAdministrator/Instructions/Labs/LAB_05-Implement_Intersite_Connectivity.html`

Lab architecture diagram:

The following diagram illustrates the different steps involved in the exercise:

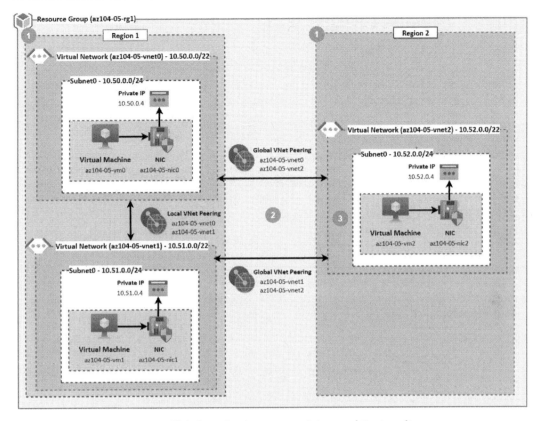

Figure 19.4 – Global peering interconnectivity – architecture diagram

After working through this lab, you should feel confident in routing traffic throughout Azure, both within the same region and across regions. You have hands-on experience working with global scale networking within Azure and should feel confident to emulate similar deployments in your daily role. The next lab will take this a step further and guide you through deploying multi-VNet infrastructure within Azure and using route tables to manage the traffic flow.

Traffic management lab

This lab will guide you through configuring a hub and spoke network topology, configuring route tables and **user-defined routes** (**UDRs**), and you will explore working with layer 4 and layer 7 load balancing solutions within Azure (particularly the Azure Load Balancer service and Application Gateway).

Estimated time: 60 minutes

Lab method: PowerShell and the Azure portal

Lab scenario: In this lab, you play the role of an administrator who is looking to extend upon the previous lab and confirm that traffic flow can be restricted to flowing through the hub network. You will use route tables with user-defined routes to implement the services and will validate it works as expected. Additionally, you are concerned about traffic distribution across both layer 4 and 7 load balances. You will be testing Azure Load Balancer and Application Gateway.

Visit the following link (**Lab URL**) to the official Microsoft learning GitHub labs, where you will be guided through each task step by step to achieve the preceding objective.

Lab objectives:

- **Task 1**: Provision your environment resources (resource group, VNets, and VMs)
- **Task 2**: Configure your network in a hub-and-spoke topology
- **Task 3**: Test VNet peering
- **Task 4**: Configure routing using UDRs
- **Task 5**: Deploy and configure load balancers
- **Task 6**: Deploy and configure Application Gateway

Lab URL: `https://microsoftlearning.github.io/AZ-104-MicrosoftAzureAdministrator/Instructions/Labs/LAB_06-Implement_Network_Traffic_Management.html`

Lab architecture diagram:

The following diagram illustrates the different steps involved in the exercise:

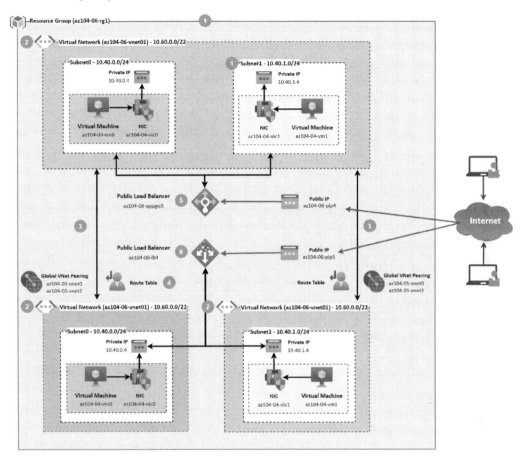

Figure 19.5 – Traffic management – architecture diagram

This lab requires eight vCPUs as the default configuration; this can be costly, and you may have a limit on the vCPU count. This can be raised but not if you are using a trial account. The demonstration will allow for single-core VMs too and you should be able to use the Standard_B1s SKU. This lab has helped you build the skills you need to deploy multi-VNet infrastructure within Azure and route traffic accordingly. You have also learned to implement load balancing services and explored how they enable you to create more resilient services.

Summary

In this chapter, we explored working with virtual networks on Azure and implementing security features such as NSGs as well as load balancers and Application Gateway. You went through a practical real-world type of scenario that you will likely encounter as an administrator. You should now feel confident in working with networks in Azure and being able to manage traffic flow effectively. It is best practice to remove unused resources to ensure that there are no unexpected costs, even though resources created in this lab do not incur additional costs.

In the next part of the book, we'll cover the monitoring of resources within Azure, leveraging Azure Monitor.

Part 5: Monitoring and Backing Up Azure Resources

This is the last part of the exam objectives, which focuses on monitoring and backing up Azure resources. This part accounts for 10-15% of the AZ-104 exam.

This part of the book comprises the following chapters:

- *Chapter 20, Monitoring Resources with Azure Monitor*
- *Chapter 21, Implementing Backup and Recovery Solutions*
- *Chapter 22, Practice Labs – Monitoring and Backing Up Azure Resources*

20
Monitoring Resources with Azure Monitor

In the previous chapter, we covered monitoring and troubleshooting network connectivity. In this chapter, we are going to focus on how you can monitor the rest of your Azure estate. We will explore the Azure Monitor service and explore the various components exposed through the service, such as metrics, alerts, Log Analytics, and Application Insights. You will gain hands-on experience working with several of the components of Monitor and become more confident in troubleshooting and monitoring your applications.

In this chapter, we are going to cover the following main topics:

- Azure Monitor
- Creating and analyzing metrics and alerts
- Querying Log Analytics
- Configuring Application Insights

Technical requirements

To follow along with the hands-on material, you will need the following:

- Access to an Azure subscription with owner or contributor privileges. If you do not have access to one, you can enroll for a free account: `https://azure.microsoft.com/en-us/free/`.

Azure Monitor

Azure Monitor is a monitoring solution in the Azure portal that delivers a comprehensive solution for collecting, analyzing, and acting on telemetry from cloud and on-premises environments. It can be used to monitor various aspects of your environments (for instance, the performance of applications) and identify issues affecting those applications and other resources that depend on them.

The data that is collected by Azure Monitor fits into two fundamental types – metrics and logs. Metrics describe an aspect of a system at a particular point in time and are displayed in numerical values. They are capable of supporting near real-time scenarios. Logs are different from metrics. They contain data that is organized into records, with different sets of properties for each type. Data such as events, traces, and performance data are stored as logs. They can then be combined for analytical purposes.

Azure Monitor supports data collection from a variety of Azure resources. Some of the metrics and logs that Azure Monitor provides are as follows:

- **Application monitoring data**: This will consist of data about the functionality and performance of the application and the written code, regardless of its platform.

- **Guest OS monitoring data**: This will consist of data about the OS on which your application is running. This can be running in any cloud or on-premises environment.

- **Azure resource monitoring data**: This will consist of data about the operation of an Azure resource.

- **Azure subscription monitoring data**: This will consist of data about the operation and management of an Azure subscription, as well as data about the health and operation of Azure itself.

- **Azure tenant monitoring data**: This will consist of data about the operation of tenant-level Azure services, such as Azure Active Directory.

Azure Monitor can collect data from several sources, as you can see from the following diagram:

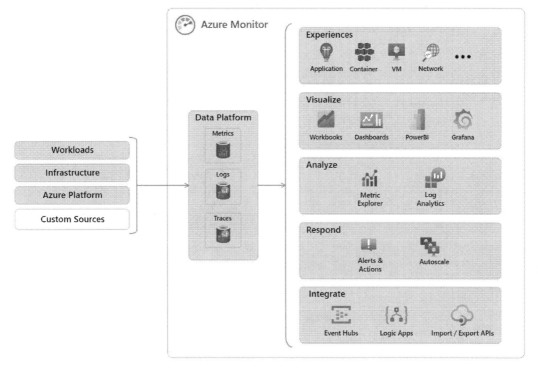

Figure 20.1 – Azure Monitor

As you can see from the diagram, its function is not limited to data collection and also becomes the central platform for the following:

- Gaining **insights** into your applications and resources
- Being able to **visualize** your environment and how it's performing
- Being able to **analyze** your data and environments
- Creating a mechanism to **respond** and take action against identified issues and triggers
- Allowing **automation** of your environment and creating an integration point between other tools and services that are not limited to Azure

We will now discuss the various functions contained within Azure Monitor.

The Activity log

The Activity log is used for tracking configuration changes within Azure, such as the deployment of resources to a resource group, or the modification of resources, such as adding tags. The following screenshot shows an example view of an Activity log:

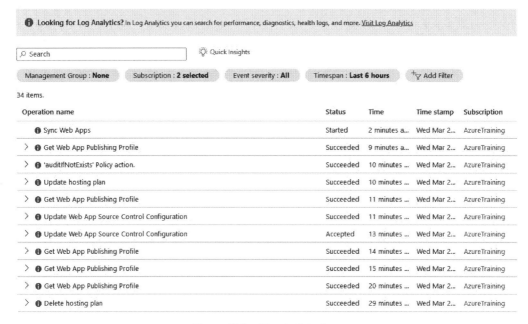

Figure 20.2 – The Activity log

As you can see, the Activity log displays several types of operations performed, such as the syncing of web apps and creating publishing profiles. You will note that the activity log contains **Operation name**, **Status**, **Time**, and **Subscription** details.

Next, we will explore what metrics are.

Metrics

Metrics describe an aspect of a system at a particular point in time and are displayed as numerical values. They are capable of supporting near real-time scenarios. Metric data can include CPU and memory performance data over time, disk throughput, **Input/Output Operations Per Second** (**IOPS**), and network performance.

Alerts

With alerts, Azure can proactively notify you when critical conditions occur in the Azure or on-premises environment. Alerts can also attempt to take corrective actions automatically. Alert rules that are based on metrics will provide near real-time alerting, based on the metric. Alerts that are created based on logs can merge data from different resources.

The alerts in Azure Monitor use action groups, which are unique sets of recipients and actions that can be shared across multiple rules. These action groups can use Webhooks to start external actions, based on the requirements that are set up for each alert. These external actions can then be picked up by different Azure resources, such as runbooks, functions, or logic apps. Webhooks can also be used for adding these alerts to external **IT Service Management** (**ITSM**) tools.

You can also set alerts for all the different Azure resources. Later in the chapter, we are going to create an alert. Next, we are going to explore what action groups are and the purpose they provide.

Action groups

Action groups are used for defining your notification preferences within Azure. These will be used for sending emails, SMSes, or even voice calls to alert you to something. These are consumed by a resource, such as an alert, that will initiate the notification.

These also provide the option to have an action triggered from the service, such as one of the following **action types**:

- Azure Automation Runbook
- Azure Function
- ITSM
- Logic App
- Secure Webhook
- Webhook

These actions make the service particularly powerful, as it can be used for environment automation, such as configuring a Logic App to notify users with particular configuration details and initiating a custom script against an application that initiates a workflow. The variation of possibilities is endless and enables you to perform significantly more powerful management tasks and flows. Your focus becomes more geared toward innovating and driving new solutions as opposed to remediation activities.

Insights

Monitor creates a view of relevant monitoring details specific to your resources and uses intelligence to extract value from collected data, such as performance, health, and availability data. These views are compartmentalized into resource-specific insight views, such as Application Insights, VM insights, and Container insights.

Application Insights

Application Insights is a telemetry tool used for monitoring and troubleshooting your applications using an instrumentation package (SDK). Your applications don't have to be hosted in Azure to make use of the service, but applications hosted in Azure can more easily consume the service through the click of a button that allows the service to be automatically configured as part of your application. Data collected in Application Insights can be consumed by several other complementary services such as alerts and PowerBI. This allows you to build valuable actionable solutions around your application data as well as create visibility into how your application performs and where problems can occur. Some of the items Application Insights looks for is how long a web request takes at various stages during your application delivery to a client:

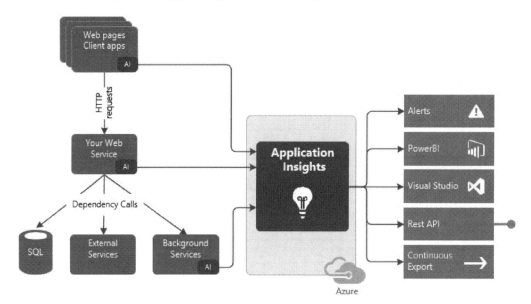

Figure 20.3 – An Application Insights overview

The service also has the ability to build an application map, showing components you need to be aware of as part of your service as well as allowing you to triage failures:

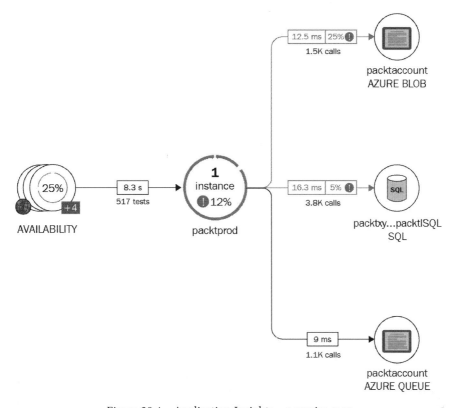

Figure 20.4 – Application Insights – a service map

As you can see, this service can prove invaluable to you and your organization by quickly garnering insights about your applications.

Log Analytics

Azure Log Analytics is a service that collects telemetry data from various Azure resources and on-premises resources. All that data is stored inside a Log Analytics workspace, which is based on Azure Data Explorer. It uses Kusto Query Language, which is also used by Azure Data Explorer to retrieve and analyze the data.

Analyzing this data can be done from Azure Monitor. All the analysis functionalities are integrated there. The term *Log Analytics* now primarily applies to the blade in the Azure portal where you can analyze metric data.

> **Top Tip**
>
> Azure Monitor now integrates the capabilities of Log Analytics and Application Insights into its service. You can also keep using Log Analytics and Application Insights independently.

Diagnostic settings

You can also configure diagnostic settings on different Azure resources. There are two types of diagnostic logs available in Azure Monitor:

- **Tenant logs**: These logs consist of all the tenant-level services that exist outside of an Azure subscription. An example of this is the Azure Active Directory logs.

- **Resource logs**: These logs consist of all the data from resources that are deployed inside an Azure subscription – for example, virtual machines, storage accounts, and network security groups.

The contents of these logs are different for every Azure resource. These logs differ from guest OS-level diagnostic logs. To collect OS-level logs, an agent needs to be installed on the virtual machine. The diagnostic logs don't require an agent to be installed; they can be accessed directly from the Azure portal.

The logs that can be accessed are stored inside a storage account and can be used for auditing or manual inspection purposes. You can specify the retention time in days by using the resource diagnostic settings. You can also stream the logs to event hubs to analyze them in PowerBI or insert them into a third-party service. These logs can also be analyzed with Azure Monitor, which doesn't require the logs to be stored in a storage account first. Azure Monitor provides the capability to address your log data based on a time period, which enables quick insights into historical and near real-time data views.

Now that we have some basic knowledge about Azure Monitor, we are going to look at the different areas where you can analyze data, alerts, and metrics across subscriptions.

Service Health

Service Health displays the Azure platform service health statistics; if there are currently any issues that are affecting your resources within your tenant, they will be reflected here. This space also contains service health history, as shown in the following screenshot:

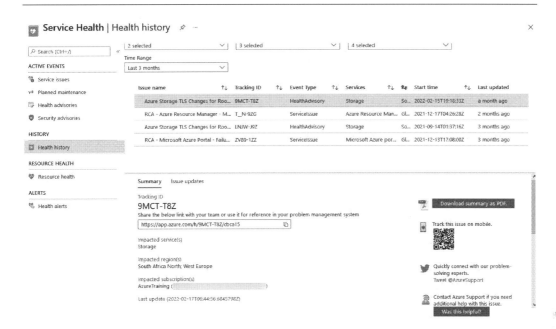

Figure 20.5 – Service Health

Note that there are different types of events highlighted for each entry, and the screenshot also identifies the status and services that are affected. Clicking an entry gives some details about the issue, as well as creating a downloadable PDF format in the bottom-right corner for a full description of each issue per entry.

Note that on the left pane under **ACTIVE EVENTS**, there are several categories:

- **Service issues**: This section notifies you of issues on the Azure platform that you need to be aware of and that may be impacting expected service delivery from the platform.

- **Planned maintenance**: This refers to platform maintenance that is planned and expected to be carried out; it will highlight the affected services as well as the planned work involved. All planned maintenance will contain dates so that your team can plan for outages and disruptions in services.

- **Health advisories**: All platform-related health advisories will appear here.

- **Security advisories**: Platform-related security advisories will show up here; note that these are not resource-related notifications but rather platform-related ones.

Next, we will explore the creation of metrics and alerts within Monitor.

Creating and analyzing metrics and alerts

There are several ways to consume and analyze alerts and metrics across Azure Monitor. You can consume this directly from the Monitor service as well as from the associated resource blade. In the upcoming sections, we will set up metrics and alerts and show you how to analyze them.

In order to follow along, you will need a resource to monitor metrics from; we will deploy a **virtual machine** (**VM**) to assist with this.

Creating a VM

For this exercise, you will be deploying a new VM to monitor against:

1. Navigate to the Azure portal by clicking on `https://portal.azure.com`.

2. Create a new resource group named `AZ104-Monitor`.

3. Create a new VM with the following attributes; you can also use the template from *Chapter 17*, *Integrating On-Premises Networks with Azure*, and modify the following as well as name the VNet and subnet:

   - **Subscription**: Select your Azure subscription.

   - **Resource Group**: `AZ104-Monitor`.

   - **Virtual machine name**: `MonitorServer`.

   - **Region**: `West Europe` (or select what you prefer).

   - **Image**: `Windows Server 2019 Datacenter - Gen 2`.

   - **Size**: `Standard_DS1_v2`.

   - **Username**: `packtadmin`.

   - **Password**: Select a password you want.

   - **Public inbound ports**: `RDP (3389)`.

   - **VNet name**: `monitorvnet`.

   - **Subnet name**: `monitorsubnet`.

Now that your VM is deployed, you can proceed to configure a metric monitor.

Creating a metric

To display the metrics for the various Azure resources in Azure Monitor, perform the following steps:

1. In the top search bar for Azure, type `Monitor` and click **Monitor** from the options that appear:

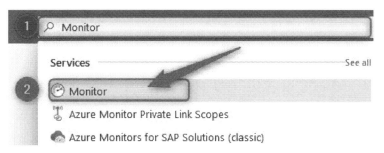

Figure 20.6 – Searching for Monitor

2. You will be presented with the following **Overview** screen:

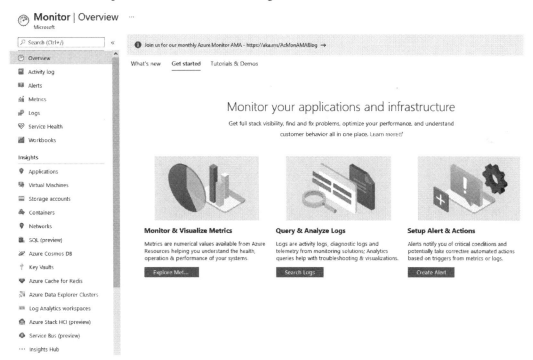

Figure 20.7 – Monitor | Overview

3. First, we're going to look at metrics. Therefore, on the left-hand menu, select **Metrics** or the **Explore Metrics** button from the **Overview** blade.

4. You will be prompted to select a scope; select your **Subscription**, **Resource group**, **Resource type**, and **Location** preferences, and click **Apply**. If you are following along, your details will be as follows:

    - **Subscription**: Select your Azure subscription.

    - **Resource Group**: AZ104-Monitor.

    - **Resource type**: Virtual machines.

    - **Region**: West Europe (or select what you prefer).

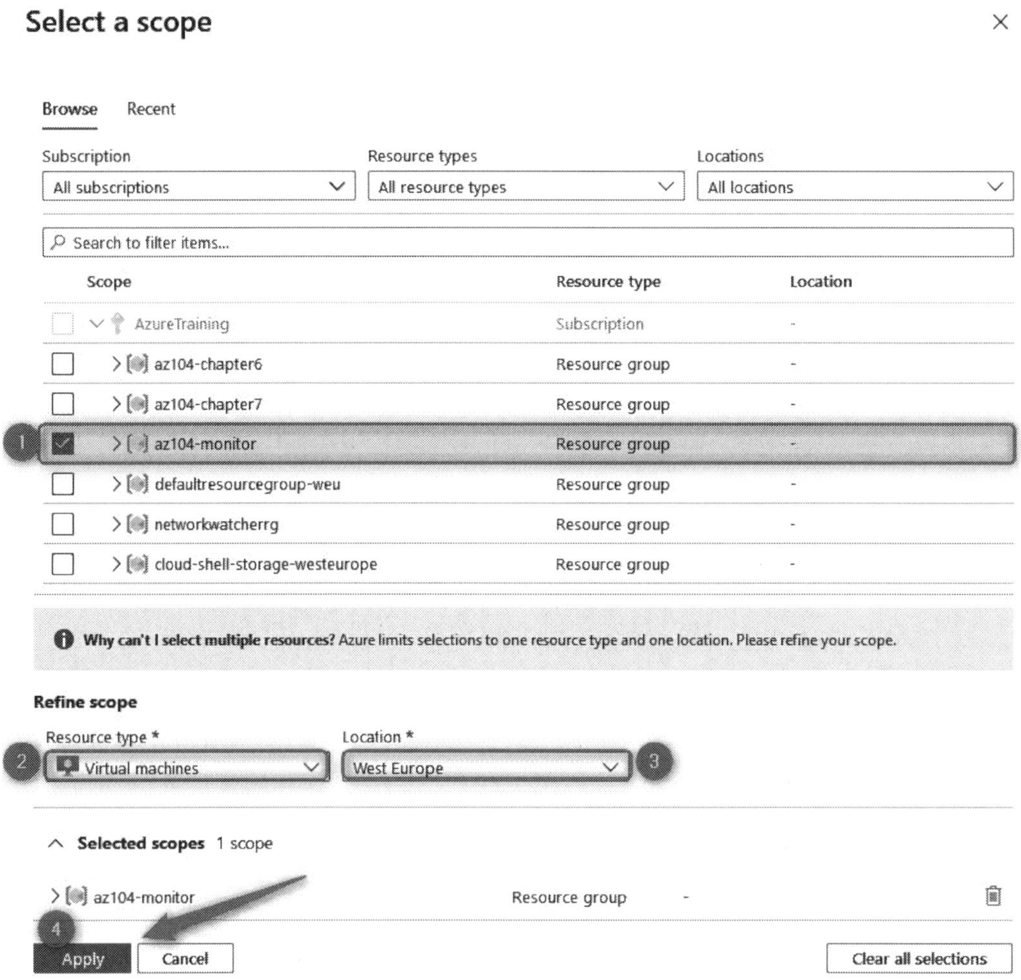

Figure 20.8 – Monitor – scope

5. On the **Scope** bar at the top of the screen, select **Percentage CPU** from the **Metric** dropdown and **Max** from the **Aggregation** dropdown:

Figure 20.9 – Monitor – selecting Metric and Aggregation

6. Since your VM hasn't been running for that long, we will change the time period that the chart is displaying for. Click the time bar in the top right of your **Metrics** blade and select **Last hour** from the **Time range** options, and then click **Apply**:

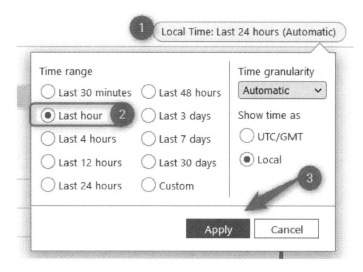

Figure 20.10 – Monitor – Changing the time period

7. Note how you can see your maximum CPU percentage usage over time. As a point of interest, you can load several charts to a single monitor page for instance, monitoring **Available Memory Bytes** on your VM:

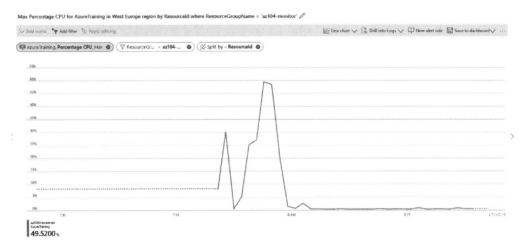

Figure 20.11 – Monitor – CPU usage over time

8. Let's look at adding another chart; click **+ New chart** at the top of the screen:

Figure 20.12 – New chart

9. Set the scope to be the same as before.

10. Azure monitors the available memory as opposed to memory usage, which can be calculated in reverse as total memory – available memory. The measure is more apt, as you can determine what percentage of memory is left before you trigger an alert that something is wrong on your VM, for instance. Select **Available Memory Bytes** from the **Metric** dropdown and **Max** from the **Aggregation** dropdown:

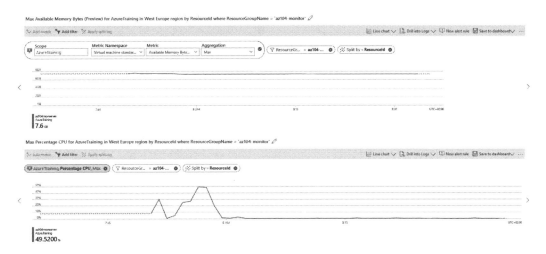

Figure 20.13 – Monitor – CPU usage over time

Top Tip

Take some time to look at the different metrics that you can choose from. This may be a part of the exam questions.

You have now experienced working with metrics and adding ones to different charts for monitoring in Azure. Next, we will create a dashboard with these charts. Keep your metrics screen open from this exercise from which to continue for the next exercise.

Creating a dashboard

Azure provides the capability of building dashboards and allows you to build some quick insights for your resources:

1. Using the charts from the previous exercise, click on the **Save to dashboard** dropdown and click **Pin to dashboard**:

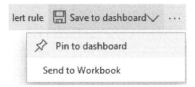

Figure 20.14 – Monitor – Pin to dashboard

2. Since we have not created a dashboard as yet, we will create a new one when saving. Click **Create new**, enter the following details, and click **Create and pin**:

    -   **Type**: **Private**

    -   **Dashboard name**: **MyFirstDashboard**

Figure 20.15 – Monitor – Pin to dashboard | Create new

3. Perform the **Pin to dashboard** action on the second chart, this time selecting **Existing** and choosing your dashboard from the previous step:

Figure 20.16 – Monitor – Pin to dashboard | Existing

4. Click the hamburger menu in the top left of the Azure portal:

Figure 20.17 – The hamburger menu

5. Click **Dashboard** from the menu:

Figure 20.18 – Dashboard

6. Click the dropdown at the top of the screen to select your dashboard, and select the one you created in the previous steps:

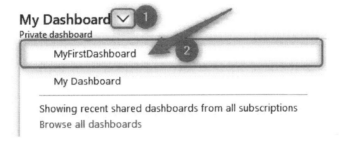

Figure 20.19 – Selecting your dashboard

7. Click **Edit** at the top of the screen to modify your dashboard view:

Figure 20.20 – Dashboard – Edit

8. Drag the two charts to be next to each other; each of these is called a tile. Note
    that you can attach several tiles to the dashboard. Once you are happy with the
    dashboard design, click **Save**:

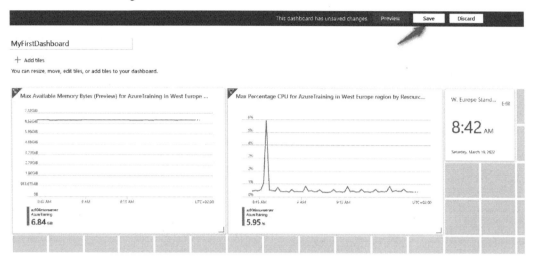

Figure 20.21 – Dashboard – customizing

> **Top Tip**
>
> Metrics are also available directly from the Azure resource blades. So, for
> instance, if you have a VM, go to the VM resource by selecting it. Then, in the
> left-hand menu, under **Monitoring**, you can select **Metrics**.

You now have your first dashboard set up and configured and have a convenient way to
dive into the relevant insights that you need across a resource or several resources and
metrics. In the next section, we're going to look at how to set up and analyze alerts in
Azure Monitor.

Creating an alert

To create an alert, perform the following steps:

1. Navigate to the **Monitor** blade.

2. From the left-hand menu, select **Alerts**. Click **+ Create** and then click **Alert rule**:

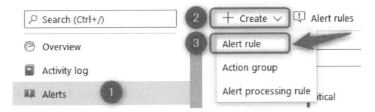

Figure 20.22 – Creating an alert

3. You will be prompted to select a resource on the right of the screen. Select the subscription where your VM from the previous exercises resides and select **Virtual machines** from the **Filter by resource type** dropdown. Select your VM from the list and then click **Done**:

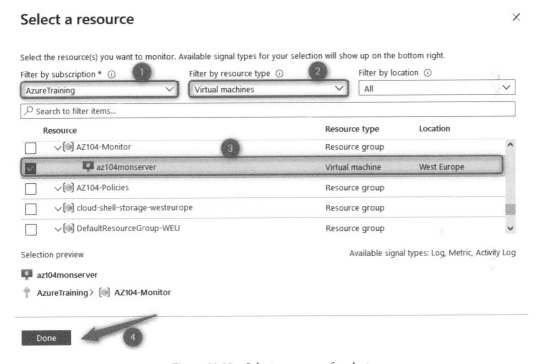

Figure 20.23 – Select a resource for alerts

4. Click **Next: Condition >**.

5. Now, you will configure the condition that will trigger the alert. On the right-hand side, you will be prompted to configure a signal, which is what alerts you to a condition being met and is the precursor to triggering the alert. Enter CPU in the search bar and select **Percentage CPU** from the options.

6. Configure **Alert logic** as follows and click **Done**:

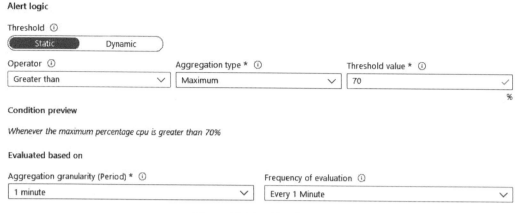

Figure 20.24 – Alert logic

7. Your condition has been configured to assess your CPU usage percentage when it exceeds 70% over a period of 1 minute. **Frequency of evaluation** is how long until it fires off an alert again (should an existing alert not still be active). Click **Next: Actions >**.

8. To receive an alert, you will need to have an action group configured, of which you currently have none. Click **+ Create action group**.

9. Configure the following settings and click **Next: Notifications >**:

    - **Subscription**: Select your Azure subscription.

    - **Resource group**: AZ104-Monitor.

    - **Action group name**: emailme.

    - **Display name**: emailme.

10. Select **Email/SMS message/Push/Voice** as **Notification type**. The right-hand screen will pop up with a prompt for details. Select the checkbox next to **Email** and enter your email address. Click **OK**.

11. Enter a name, such as `PersonalEmail`, and click **Next: Actions >**:

Figure 20.25 – The action group notification type

12. Note that you can configure several types of actions, such as firing off a logic app or function; this can be really powerful, especially where you need to adopt an automated remediation strategy.

13. Click **Review + create**. If you wish, you can click **Test action group** to get sent an example email to confirm that the action group is working as expected:

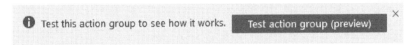

Figure 20.26 – Testing your action group

14. Click **Create**. Now that you have your action group, click **Next: Details >**.

15. Enter the following details.

   - **Subscription**: Select your Azure subscription.

   - **Resource group**: `AZ104-Monitor`.

   - **Severity**: **0 - Critical**.

   - **Alert rule name**: `CPU High`.

   - **Enable upon creation**: **Checked**.

   - **Automatically resolve alerts**: **Checked**.

16. Click **Review + create** and then click **Create**.

We have now created an alert and an action group that will alert a user via email when the CPU goes over 70% over a period of 1 minute. In the next section, we're going to configure diagnostic settings on resources.

Configuring diagnostic settings on resources

To enable the diagnostic settings for resources, perform the following steps:

1. Navigate to the VM you created previously.

2. Make sure that the VM is running, and in the left-hand menu, under **Monitoring**, select **Diagnostic settings**.

3. The **Diagnostic Settings** blade will open up. You will need to select a storage account where the metrics can be stored; if you don't have a storage account, you can create a new one.

4. Click on the **Enable guest-level monitoring** button to update the diagnostic settings for the VM.

5. When the settings are updated, you can go to **Metrics** in the **Monitoring** section for your VM on the left menu.

6. Change the metric namespace to **Guest (classic)**, and note that you have new metrics available from the **Metrics** dropdown after enabling diagnostic logging. You can analyze them in the same way that we did earlier in this chapter.

Now that you have configured diagnostic settings, we will explore triggering an alert from your VM to see how this works.

Triggering an alert

In this exercise, we will explore a method to push the CPU usage up high on our VM and then trigger the alert we configured previously:

1. Log on to your Monitor VM using **remote desktop protocol** (**RDP**).

2. Disable **IE Enhanced Security Configuration**. From **Server Manager**, you can click **Local Server** on the left-hand menu and then click **On** to change the setting:

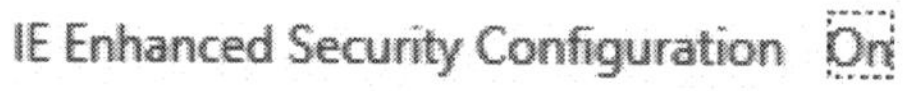

IE Enhanced Security Configuration   On

Figure 20.27 – IE Enhanced Security Configuration

3. Download FurMark: `https://www.guru3d.com/files-get/furmark-1-8-2,5.html`.

4. Install FurMark and launch it once complete.

5.   Click **CPU burner**:

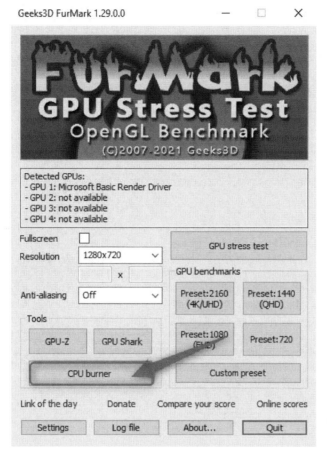

Figure 20.28 – FurMark

6.   Click **Start** to start running the tool and stress-testing the CPU on the VM:

Figure 20.29 – Running FurMark

7.   If you open **Task Manager**, note that the CPU is now sitting at 100%:

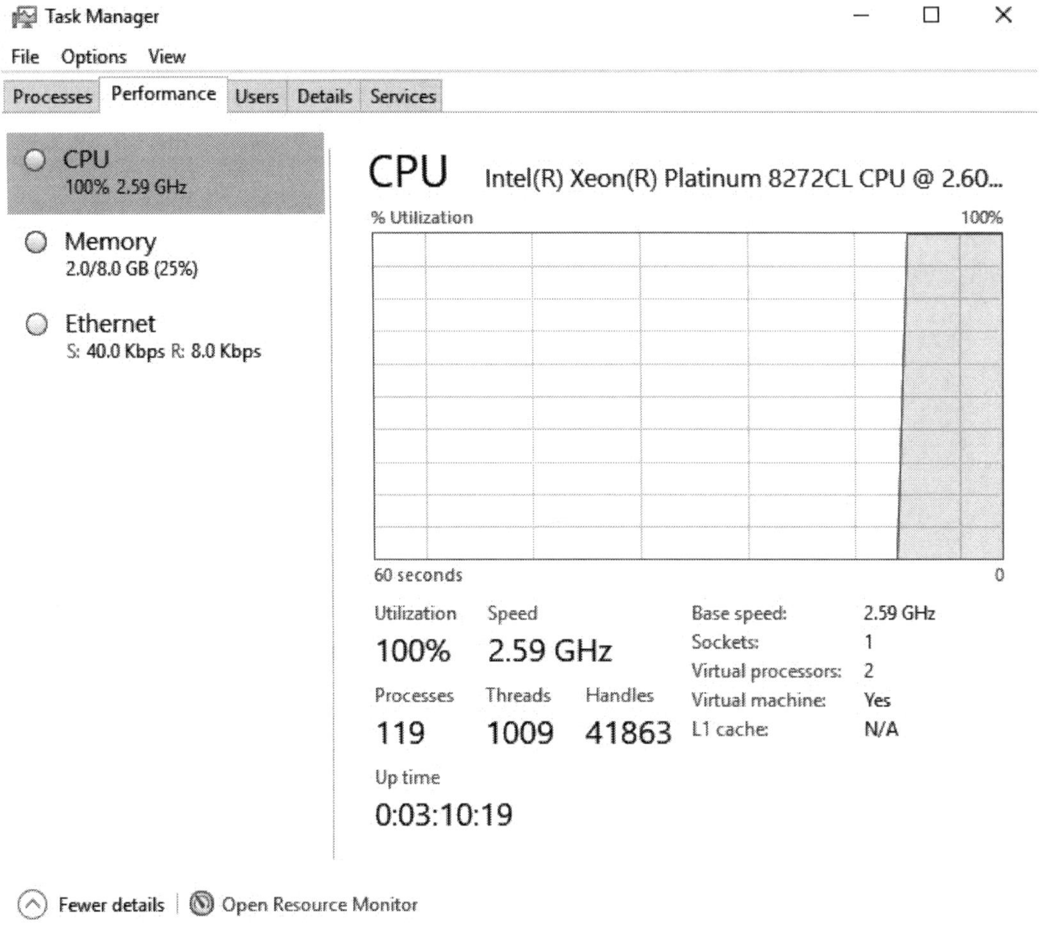

Figure 20.30 – Task Manager

8.   You will need to leave this running for a few minutes for Azure Monitor to register the detected CPU usage changes. Navigate to the dashboard you created earlier and note that the CPU is showing as 99.9%:

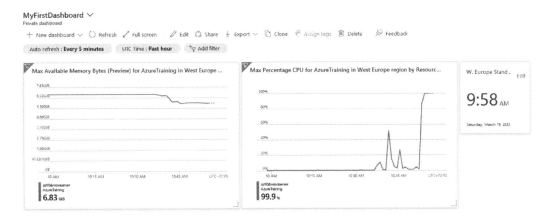

MyFirstDashboard ∨
Private dashboard

Figure 20.31 – Dashboard – showing high CPU usage

9. Check your email, as an alert should now be present to notify you of the detected issue.

You have successfully created some metric monitors in this section, explored how to add them to a dashboard, created an alert to be triggered should a metric anomaly be detected, and finally, explored what happens when an alert is triggered. You should now feel comfortable configuring metrics in Azure Monitor.

In the next section, we're going to look at the Azure Log Analytics service, which is now a part of Azure Monitor as well.

Querying Log Analytics

It can be useful to explore your logs in Log Analytics. Being able to query Log Analytics requires an understanding of **Kusto Query Language** (**KQL**). We will explore some basic queries in this exercise to understand how the system works.

Creating a Log Analytics workspace

Before we can display, monitor, and query logs from Azure Monitor, we need to create a Log Analytics workspace. For that, we must perform the following steps:

1. Navigate to the Azure portal by clicking on `https://portal.azure.com`.

2. Navigate to your **AZ104-Monitor** resource group.

3. Click **+ Create** to create a new resource.

4. Type log analytics in the search box and click **Log Analytics Workspace**:

Figure 20.32 – Log Analytics Workspace

5. Click **Create**.

6. Add the following values:

   • **Subscription**: Select your Azure subscription.

   • **Resource group**: AZ104-Monitor.

   • **Name**: az104loganalytics.

   • **Region**: West Europe (or select what you prefer).

7. Click **Review + create** and then **Create**.

Now that we have created a Log Analytics workspace, we can use it inside Azure Monitor to create some queries to retrieve data. We will do this in the next section.

Utilizing log search query functions

Azure Monitor is now integrated with the features and capabilities that Log Analytics offers. This also includes creating search queries across the different logs and metrics by using KQL.

To retrieve any type of data from Azure Monitor, a query is required. Whether you are configuring an alert rule, analyzing data in the Azure portal, retrieving data using the Azure Monitor Logs API, or being notified of a particular condition, a query is used.

The following list provides an overview of all the different ways queries can be consumed from Azure Monitor:

- **Portal**: From the Azure portal, an interactive analysis of log data can be performed. In there, you can create and edit queries and analyze the results in a variety of formats and visualizations.

- **Dashboards**: The results of a query can be pinned to a dashboard. This way, results can be visualized and shared with other users.

- **Workbooks**: By using Workbooks in Azure Monitor, you can create custom views of your data. This data is provided by queries as well.

- **Alerts**: Alert rules are also made up of queries.

- **Data export**: Exports of data configured for a storage account or Event Grid. Using M query, you can also export data to Excel or PowerBI, also created with queries. The query defines the data to export.

- **Azure Monitor Logs API**: The Azure Monitor Logs API allows any REST API client to retrieve log data from the workspace. The API request includes a query to retrieve the data.

- **PowerShell**: You can run a PowerShell script from a command line or an Azure Automation runbook that uses `Invoke-AzOperationalInsightsQuery` to retrieve log data from Azure Monitor. You need to create a query for this cmdlet to retrieve the data.

In the following section, we are going to create some queries to retrieve data from the logs in Azure Monitor.

Querying logs in Azure Monitor

To query logs in Azure Monitor, perform the following steps:

1. Navigate to the Azure portal by opening `https://portal.azure.com`.

2. In the top search bar for Azure, type `Monitor` and click **Monitor** from the options that appear. You will be directed to the **Overview** pane.

3. From the left menu, select **Logs**.

4. You may be presented with a tutorial popup screen, which you can close, or you can consume the content as you desire. All subsequent logins will present a query screen, allowing you to quickly perform common queries easily.

5. For this demo, we will use an environment Microsoft created to allow you to query data in a prepopulated system.

6. Navigate to `https://portal.azure.com/#blade/Microsoft_Azure_ Monitoring_Logs/DemoLogsBlade`, which is similar to your logs query space from *step 4*.

7. Note that the middle contains a screen that you can type in – this is where you create your queries, the bottom of which is the results area where your query results and graphics will be displayed. On the left pane, note several collapsed data menus; these represent data sources that can be queried from Log Analytics:

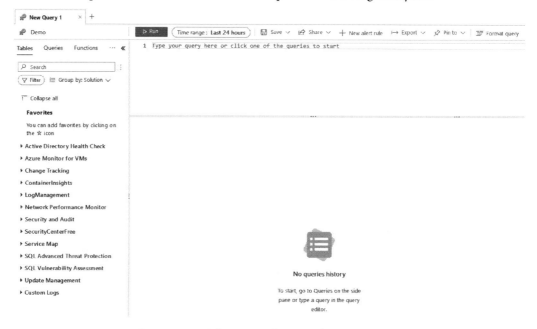

Figure 20.33 – The Log Analytics workspace – query

8. Select a data source – in this example, we will use **Azure Monitor for VMs**; click on this heading to open the underlying data source collections. Click on **InsightsMetrics** and then **Use in editor**:

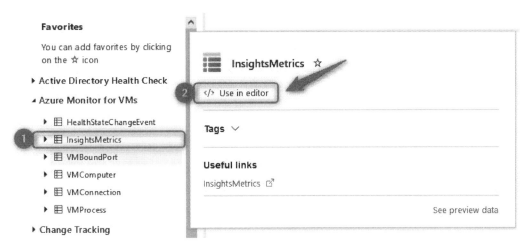

Figure 20.34 – The Log Analytics workspace – data source collections

9. Note that on your query pane, it has initiated a query that is labeled as your data source collection. For future queries, you can type the data source collection as opposed to selecting in this fashion.

10. Click the **Run** button to generate results that are stored in that table. Note that the data has headings that you can explore as you scroll through the results section. Some of the headings (columns) may be hidden from the result view:

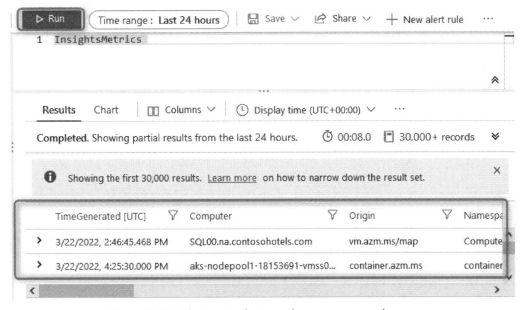

Figure 20.35 – The Log Analytics workspace – an example query

11. Open the collection source on the left pane to see the various data types associated with each row along with their heading name:

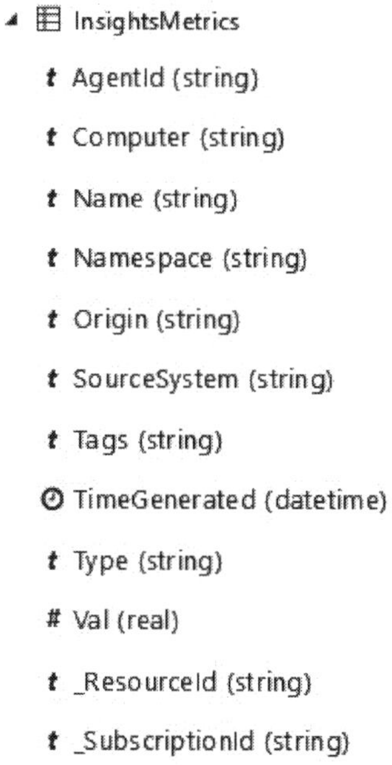

Figure 20.36 – The Log Analytics workspace – column types

12. Now that you know the headings, you may want to filter your data further and start to extract some relevant information – for instance, you can return an aggregated table with the computer(s) associated with the record(s) in your table by running the following command:

```
InsightsMetrics | summarize by Computer
```

The result of the command will be output similar to what is displayed in the following screenshot:

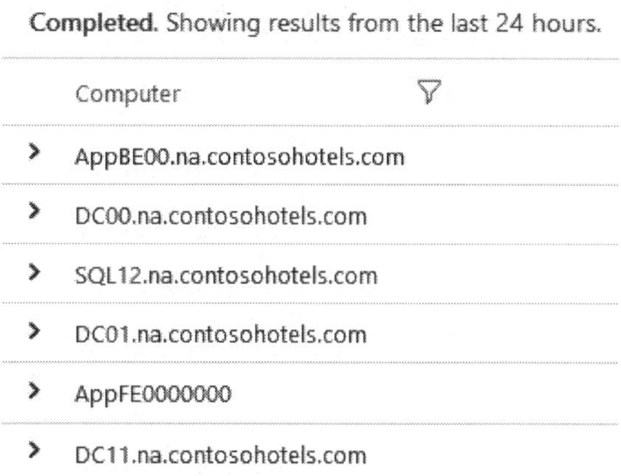

Figure 20.37 – The Log Analytics workspace – a summarize example

13. You can add a second column by modifying the query accordingly; this time, you will expect to see a computer name several times, as the unique returned value is a combination of the computer and the `TimeGenerated` column:

```
InsightsMetrics | summarize by Computer, TimeGenerated
```

14. Let's try a different query, such as the following, which will show the count of each type of alert detected:

```
Alert | summarize count() by AlertName
```

This will produce output similar to the following:

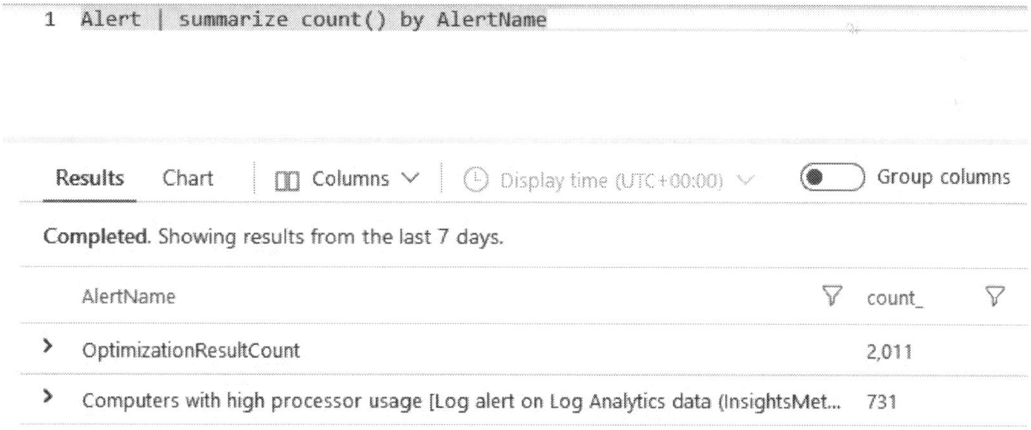

Figure 20.38 – The Log Analytics workspace – a summarize count example

15. Your default time range is 24 hours, as specified at the top of your query window next to the **Run** button. You can manually modify this by clicking the button and choosing an appropriate time range to query for, or you can modify your query directly:

Figure 20.39 – The Log Analytics workspace – time range

16. Let's modify the query:

```
Alert | where TimeGenerated > ago(2d) | summarize count()
by AlertName
```

17. You may want to visually understand this information and choose to display this in a bar chart – for example, if you were reporting on the count of each alert type you noticed in a week. You can do this with the following command:

```
Alert | where TimeGenerated > ago(7d) | summarize count()
by AlertName | render barchart
```

This will produce a visual output, defined as a bar chart, similar to the following:

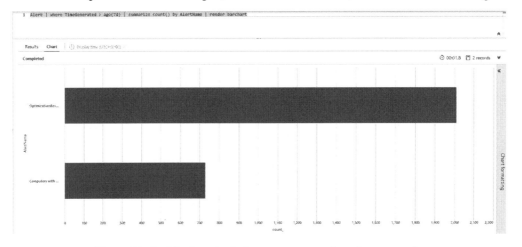

Figure 20.40 – The Log Analytics workspace – a bar chart example

18. You have many lines of data that can become difficult to sift and read through, so you may want to aggregate your results into something discernable, such as grouping results into predefined periods of time. We call this aggregating into **buckets/bins**. Modify the query accordingly to see the alert data collected into 1-day buckets, showing the number of alerts received per day for the last 7 days:

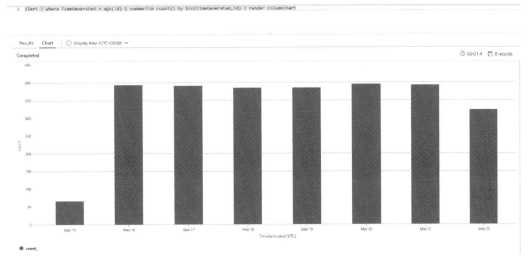

Figure 20.41 – The Log Analytics workspace – a binning example

You have just experienced some basic queries that you can perform in Log Analytics and can now understand the power behind what you can achieve using these queries. Remember that the result of these queries can be visualizations, notifications, and even automated actions as a result of data. You are encouraged to practice and learn more about this resource not just for the exam but also to enhance the way you deliver in your role for your organization and customers. You have now gained some valuable skills in navigating the basics of Log Analytics and should feel comfortable in understanding what a query is intended to do and predicting the outcome of queries, as well as being capable of building your own.

For some more examples, you can explore this URL: `https://docs.microsoft.com/en-us/azure/data-explorer/kusto/query/samples?pivots=azuredataexplorer`.

> **Top Tip**
>
> A detailed overview and tutorial on how to get started with KQL are beyond the scope of this book. If you want to find out more about this language, you can refer to `https://docs.microsoft.com/en-us/azure/data-explorer/kusto/query`.

Next, we will explore the configuration of Application Insights.

Configuring Application Insights

We will now deploy Application Insights. In this exercise, we will create a new web application service that we can associate with the Applications Insights resource and see the incoming data.

Creating your application

We will now deploy an application for monitoring; this application will be built from a GitHub repository and will take several minutes to provision after our code has run:

1. Navigate to the Azure portal by clicking on `https://portal.azure.com`.

2. Click the Azure CLI icon at the top right of the Azure portal to open an Azure CLI instance:

Figure 20.42 – Opening the Azure CLI

3. If you have never used the CLI before, you will be required to set up storage for this. Follow the prompts on screen to configure your container on a storage account.

4. When asked for the environment, you can select PowerShell. If you prefer to use **Bash**, then enter the following, which will open PowerShell in the Bash terminal, and press *Enter*:

    ```
    pwsh
    ```

5. Paste in the following and press *Enter*:

    ```
    # Parameters
    $ResourceGroup = "AZ104-Monitor"
    $Location = "WestEurope"
    $AppServicePlanName = "mylinuxappserviceplan10101"
    ```

```
$gitrepo="https://github.com/ColorlibHQ/AdminLTE.git"
$webappname="mywebapp$(Get-Random)"


# Create an App Service Plan for Linux
New-AzAppServicePlan -Name $AppServicePlanName -Tier
Free -Location $Location -Linux -ResourceGroupName
$ResourceGroup


# Create a Web App
New-AzWebApp -Name $WebAppName -ResourceGroupName
$ResourceGroup -Location $Location -AppServicePlan
$AppServicePlanName


# Modify the Web App to Dotnet
Set-AzWebApp -Name $WebAppName -ResourceGroupName
$ResourceGroup -AppServicePlan $AppServicePlanName
-NetFrameworkVersion 6


# Configure GitHub deployment from your GitHub repo and
deploy once.
$PropertiesObject = @{
    repoUrl = "$gitrepo";
    branch = "master";
    isManualIntegration = "true";
}
Set-AzResource -Properties $PropertiesObject
-ResourceGroupName $ResourceGroup -ResourceType
Microsoft.Web/sites/sourcecontrols -ResourceName
$WebAppName/web -ApiVersion 2015-08-01 -Force
```

Now that your application is ready, we will set up Application Insights.

Creating your Application Insights resource

You will now create your Application Insights resource using the following steps:

1. Navigate to your **AZ104-Monitor** resource group.

2. Click **+ Create**.

3. Type `application insights` into the search bar and click the **Application Insights** option that appears.

4. Click **Create**.

5. Enter the following details:

    - **Subscription**: Select your Azure subscription.

    - **Resource Group**: **AZ104-Monitor**.

    - **Name**: `az104monitorappinsights`.

    - **Region**: **West Europe** (or select what you prefer).

    - **Resource Mode**: **Workspace-based**.

    - **Subscription**: Select the Azure subscription for your Log Analytics workspace.

    - **Log Analytics Workspace**: Select the Log Analytics Workspace you created previously.

Figure 20.43 – Application Insights deployment

6. Click **Review + create**.

7. Click **Create**.

Now that you have your Application Insights resource ready, we will look at how to associate this with your web app next.

Associate your web app with Application Insights

Now that your Application Insights has been set up, you will need to link it to your application:

1. Navigate to the web app you created earlier.

2. Click on **Application Insights** under the **Settings** context.

3. Because the application is deployed in Azure, you can easily activate Application Insights for your web app with a few clicks. Click on **Turn on Application Insights**:

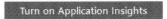

Enable Application Insights without redeploying your code

Turn on Application Insights

Figure 20.44 – Turn on Application Insights

4. Select **Enable**:

Figure 20.45 – Enable Application Insights

5. Then, click **Select existing resource**, select **az104monitorappinsights**, and click **Apply**:

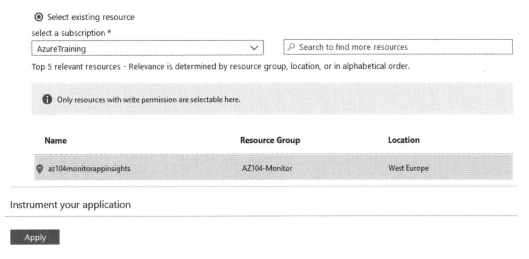

Figure 20.46 – Associating an application with Application Insights

6.   A prompt will appear, notifying you that your application will be restarted as an effect of applying the change. Click **Yes**:

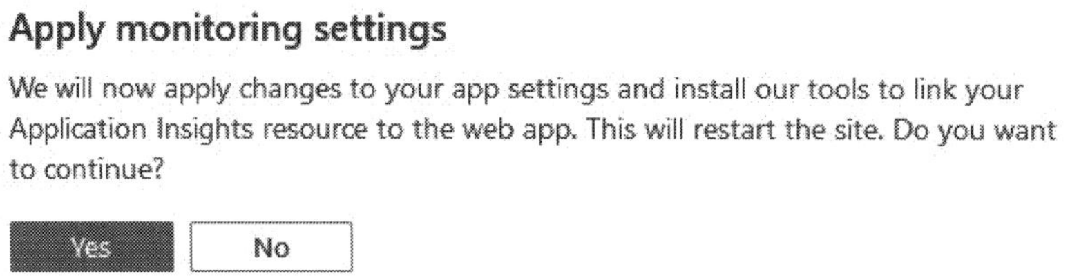

Apply monitoring settings

We will now apply changes to your app settings and install our tools to link your Application Insights resource to the web app. This will restart the site. Do you want to continue?

Yes   No

Figure 20.47 – Applying monitoring settings

You have now enabled Application Insights for your web app. Some applications do not support the automated integration method and will require a manual configuration of your code for Application Insights. You should now feel comfortable in deploying this service and enabling it for your Azure app services.

Summary

In this chapter, we have covered Azure Monitor. We have explored the various features of this service offering as well as investigated the configuration of some of the components. You have learned how to use metrics to monitor your Azure resources and alerts in order to get notified when certain things are happening with your Azure resources. We also used Azure Log Analytics and created queries so that we can get valuable data from the logs. You should now feel confident building and monitoring resources in Azure along with configuring alert notifications based on events that occur within your environment.

In the next chapter, we will cover backup and recovery. We will explore what services are offered within Azure and how to configure these to become confident in managing backup and recovery from within Azure.

21
Implementing Backup and Recovery Solutions

This chapter focuses on how to implement and configure backup and recovery solutions. This will involve learning how to deploy a **Recovery Services vault**, how to configure **backup policies**, how restore operations work, and how to perform site-to-site recovery via **Azure Site Recovery**. The last portion of this chapter will focus on how to configure backup reports. These skills are very important as they fall into **business as usual** (**BAU**) tasks for almost every organization and are a key skill to have going forward.

In this chapter, we will cover the following topics:

- Creating a Recovery Services vault
- Creating and configuring backup policies
- Performing backup and restore operations via Azure Backup
- Performing site-to-site recovery via Azure Site Recovery
- Configuring and reviewing backup reports

Technical requirements

To follow along with the hands-on sections of this chapter, you will need access to an Azure AD as a global administrator and have administrative privileges at the Subscription level – the Owner Role permission is preferred. If you do not have access to an Azure tenant, students can enroll for a free account at `https://azure.microsoft.com/en-in/free/`.

An Azure subscription is also required. You can either register with your credit card or enroll for the free $200 once-off credit by going to `https://azure.microsoft.com/en-us/free/`.

PowerShell will be used for some of the lab sections. For more details on how to configure PowerShell, go to `https://docs.microsoft.com/en-us/powershell/azure/install-az-ps?view=azps-1.8.0`.

Creating a Recovery Services vault

An Azure Recovery Services vault is a native service within Azure that stores data such as copies of data (backups), as well as configures VMs, servers, files, and more. An Recovery Services vault enables you to use the following:

- **Azure Backup**: Azure Backup is used to back up VMs, Azure File Shares, SQL servers, files and folders on-premises, Microsoft SharePoint, Microsoft Exchange, SAP HANA databases in Azure VMs, Azure Database for PostgreSQL servers, Azure Blobs, and Azure Managed Disks.

- **Site Recovery**: Site recovery is used for disaster recovery if resources become unavailable. This can be in a specific region within Azure or another data center located elsewhere, such as an on-premises environment.

Here are some of the benefits of using Recovery Services vaults:

- **Security**: Security is provided as part of the service to help protect cloud backups to ensure they can be safely recovered.

- **Hybrid**: Recovery Services vault enables Azure Backup to support cloud and on-premises workloads.

- **Permissions**: **Role-Based Access Control** (**RBAC**) permissions are supported to delegate the correct permissions to administrators or backup owners.

- **Soft Delete**: This is a feature that protects backups or backup data from being deleted by accident or maliciously. The data will be retained for 14 days after deletion to ensure there's no data loss.

Let's learn how to create a Recovery Services vault in our existing resource group (Az-104) via PowerShell:

1. First, we need to connect to our Azure tenant by using the `Connect-AzAccount` PowerShell command:

```
PS C:\WINDOWS\system32> Connect-AzAccount

Account              SubscriptionName TenantId                          Environment
-------              ---------------- --------                          -----------
                     Demo                                               AzureCloud
```

Figure 21.1 – Connecting to our Azure tenant via PowerShell

2. If you have multiple subscriptions, you can use the `Select-AzSubscription -SubscriptionId "your-subscription-id"` PowerShell command to select a specific subscription.

3. Now that we have selected our Azure tenant and subscription, let's go ahead and create a new Recovery Services Vault by using `New-AzRecoveryServicesVault -Name Az104RecoveryServicesVault -ResourceGroupName Az-104 -Location EastUS`:

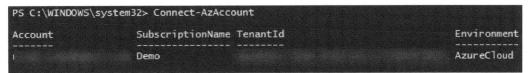

```
PS C:\Windows\system32> New-AzRecoveryServicesVault -Name Az104RecoveryServicesVault -ResourceGroupName Az-104 -Location EastUS

Name              : Az104RecoveryServicesVault
ID                : /subscriptions/                              /resourceGroups/Az-104/providers/Microsoft.RecoveryServices/vault
Type              : Microsoft.RecoveryServices/vaults
Location          : eastus
ResourceGroupName : Az-104
SubscriptionId    :
Properties        : Microsoft.Azure.Commands.RecoveryServices.ARSVaultProperties
Identity          :
```

Figure 21.2 – Recovery Service vault created via PowerShell

4. Next, we are going to set the redundancy level to georedundant storage:

```
$vault1 = Get-AzRecoveryServicesVault `
-Name Az104RecoveryServicesVault
Set-AzRecoveryServicesBackupProperty -Vault $vault1 `
-BackupStorageRedundancy GeoRedundant
```

5.   The next step is to confirm that the new vault has been created in the specified resource group within Azure:

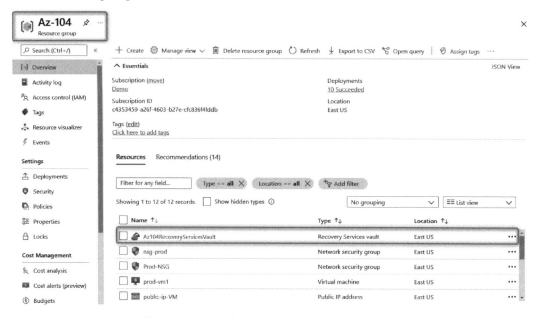

Figure 21.3 – Newly created Recovery Services vault

With that, we have successfully created a new Recovery Services vault within Azure via PowerShell. In the next section, we are going to take this a step further and discuss Azure Backup and how to configure a backup policy.

Creating and configuring backup policies

The Azure Backup service is used to back up resources and data in Azure. This can be used for cloud-only or hybrid scenarios, where you want to back up your on-premises VMs to Azure. Your on-premises backup solution can also be extended to the cloud in conjunction with Azure Backup. Azure Backup is capable of creating backups for VMs, files, folders, applications, workloads, system states, and volumes. Azure Backup consists of the following features and capabilities:

- **Back up on-premises resources to Azure**: Azure Backup offers short and long-term backup solutions. This can be a replacement for tape and off-site backups.

- **Back up Azure VMs**: Azure Backup offers independent and isolated backups. These backups are stored in a Recovery Services vault. This vault has built-in management for recovery points.

- **Automatic scaling**: You can get unlimited scale without maintenance overheads. Alerts can be set for delivering information about events.

- **Unlimited data transfer**: There is no limit to the amount of inbound and outbound traffic that can be transferred during the backup process. However, if you use the Azure import/export service to import large amounts of data, then a cost will be associated with inbound data.

- **Data encryption**: Data can be encrypted using an encryption passphrase. This is stored locally and is then needed to restore the data.

- **Short and long-term retention**: Recovery Services is where the backups are stored and provides short and long-term backups. Azure doesn't limit the time or length that data can be stored in a Recovery Services vault.

- **Multiple storage options**: Azure Backup offers two types of replication – **locally redundant storage** (**LRS**), where your data is replicated three times by creating three copies of the data within the same region, and **geo-redundant storage** (**GRS**), which is the default option, where the data is replicated to a secondary region.

You need to answer two questions when configuring a backup:

- Where is the workload running?

  - Is the workload running in Azure or somewhere else?

- What do you want to back up?

  - VMs, files and folders, SharePoint, Exchange, Hyper-V VMs, and so on.

Microsoft has added a new experience for administrators to create and manage backups called **Backup center**. With Backup center, you can view Recovery Service vaults, backup instances, and backup policies.

Now that we understand how Azure Backup works fundamentally, it is time to enroll a VM into Azure Backup and create a backup policy. Let's configure a backup policy for an Azure virtual machine that has been deployed to the same resource group (Az-104):

1. Navigate to the Azure portal by opening a web browser and going to `https://portal.azure.com`.

2. Browse to the relevant resource group (in the preceding section, I used Az-104) and select the Recovery Services vault (`Az104RecoveryServicesVault`):

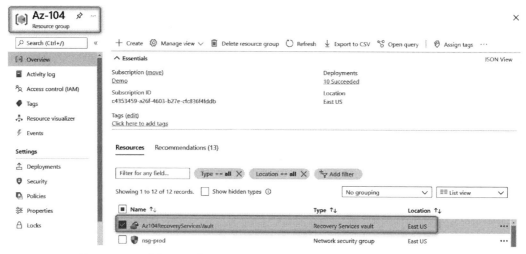

Figure 21.4 – Selecting the Recovery Services vault within the Azure portal

3. Next, select the **Backup** option:

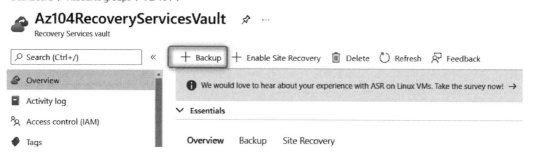

Figure 21.5 – Configuring Azure Backup

4. Next, select **Azure** as the workload type and choose **Virtual Machine**. Then, select **Backup**:

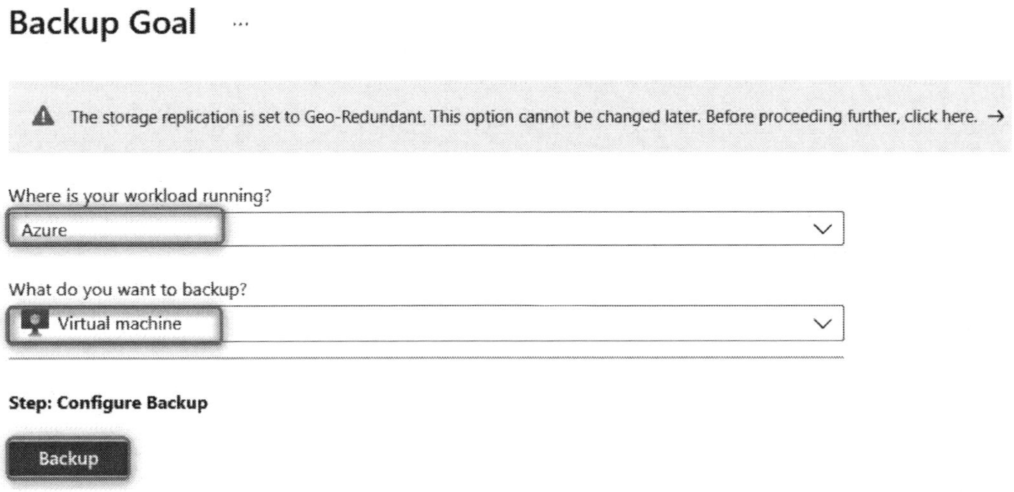

Backup Goal ...

> ⚠ The storage replication is set to Geo-Redundant. This option cannot be changed later. Before proceeding further, click here. →

Where is your workload running?

| Azure | ∨ |

What do you want to backup?

| 🖥 Virtual machine | ∨ |

Step: Configure Backup

[Backup]

Figure 21.6 – Selecting Azure Backup workloads

5. Instead of using the default backup policy, choose to **create a new policy** and provide the following details:

- **Policy name**: `AzureVMBackup`

- **Backup schedule**: `Daily`

- **Time**: `8:00 A.M.`

- **Timezone**: `(UTC) Coordinated Universal Time`

- **Instant Restore**: 2 days

- **Retention range**: 30 days

- Leave the rest of the settings as **Not Configured**:

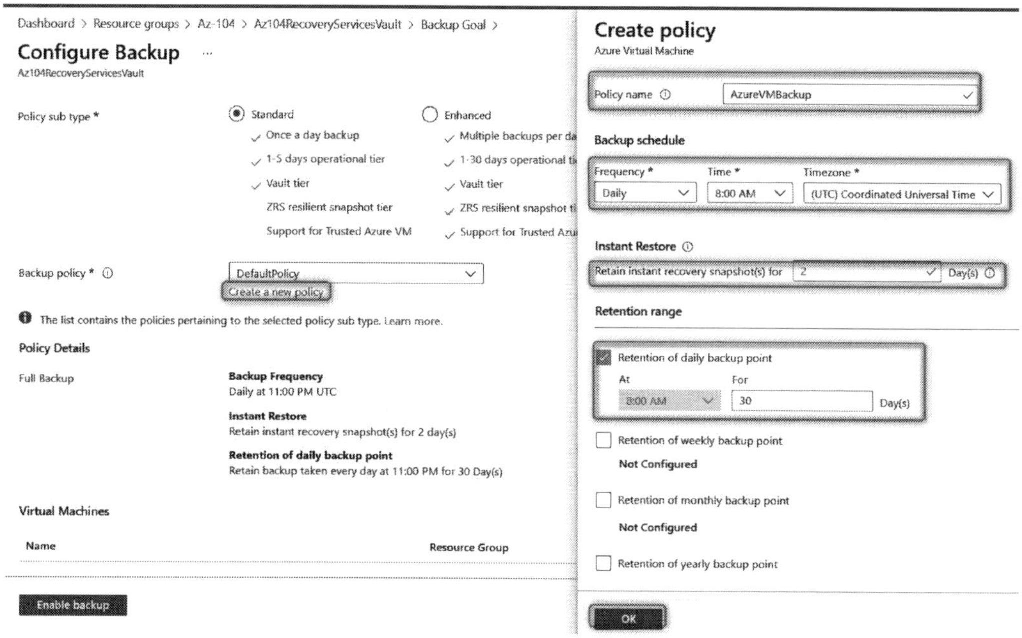

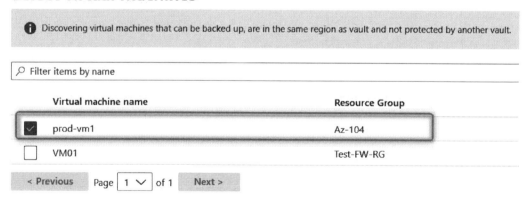

Figure 21.7 – Backup policy configuration

6. Under **Virtual Machines**, click on **Add** and select a virtual machine:

Select virtual machines

ⓘ Discovering virtual machines that can be backed up, are in the same region as vault and not protected by another vault.

○ Filter items by name

Virtual machine name	Resource Group
☑ prod-vm1	Az-104
☐ VM01	Test-FW-RG

< Previous   Page 1 ∨ of 1   Next >

Figure 21.8 – Selecting the VM related to the backup policy

7. Click on **Enable Backup**.

8. Once you're done, you will see that the VM has been enrolled in Azure Backup. After a while, the backup policy will trigger:

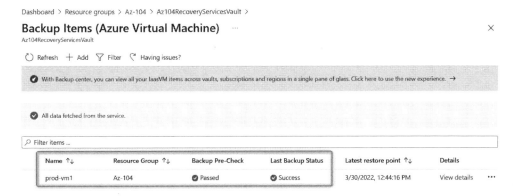

Figure 21.9 – Virtual machine successfully enrolled in Azure Backup

With that, we have successfully created an Azure Backup policy for virtual machines that will run daily and create a backup of the VM.

Performing backup and restore operations via Azure Backup

One of the most important parts of backup operations is to ensure that the resource gets backed up and can be restored. To test whether the resource was backed up correctly, you should test the backup by doing a restore.

Let's go ahead and use the Azure portal to trigger an on-demand backup:

1. Navigate to the Azure portal by opening a web browser and going to `https://portal.azure.com`.

2. In the top search bar, search for and select **Backup center**:

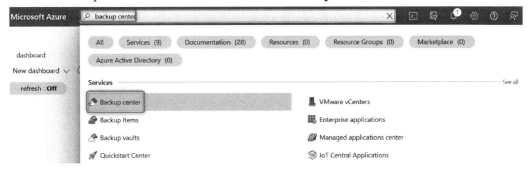

Figure 21.10 – Selecting Backup center

3. Under **Manage**, select **Backup instances** and choose your vault. In my case, this will be `Az104RecoveryServicesVault`:

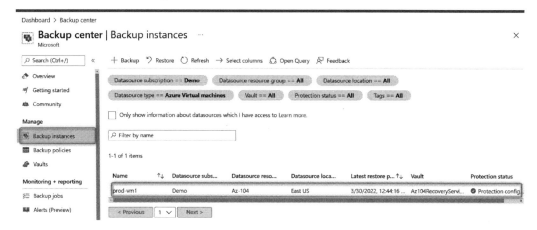

Figure 21.11 – Selecting your Recovery Services vault

4. Select **Backup Now**. This will kick off a backup immediately, regardless of any backup policy. It will ask you for how long you want to retain the backup and kick off the backup:

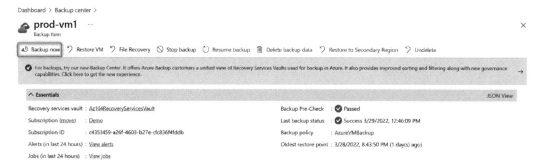

Figure 21.12 – Enabling Azure Backup

Now that we have created a backup of the VM, let's learn how to restore the backup via the Azure portal.

If you want to restore a backup via Backup center in the Azure portal, follow these steps:

1. Navigate to the Azure portal by opening a web browser and going to `https://portal.azure.com`.

2. In the top search bar, search for and select **Backup center**:

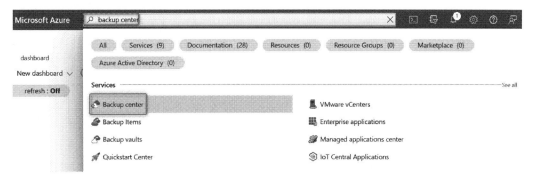

Figure 21.13 – Selecting Backup center via the Azure portal

3. Under **Manage**, select **Backup instances** and choose your vault. In my case, this will be `Az104RecoveryServicesVault`:

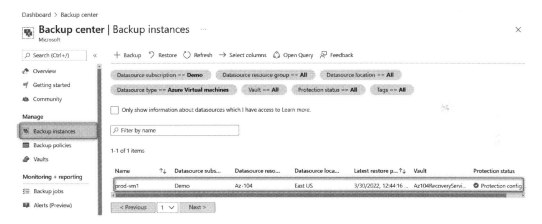

Figure 21.14 – Selecting the configured backup instance

4. Select **Restore VM**:

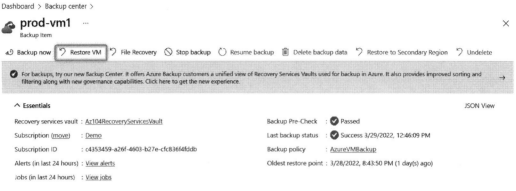

Figure 21.15 – Restoring a VM from a backup

5. You will be prompted to select a valid restore point:

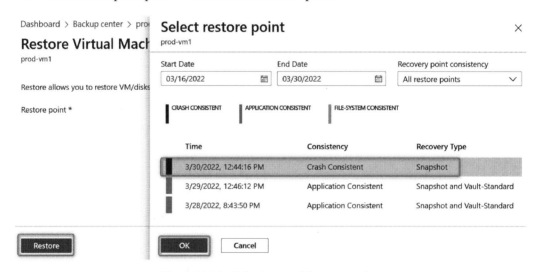

Figure 21.16 – Selecting a valid restore point

6. Next, under **Restore Configuration**, you need to choose if you want to replace the existing VM or create a new VM. In our case, we are going to select **Replace existing** and select a storage account for the staging location – we are going to use one of our existing storage accounts and click on **Restore**:

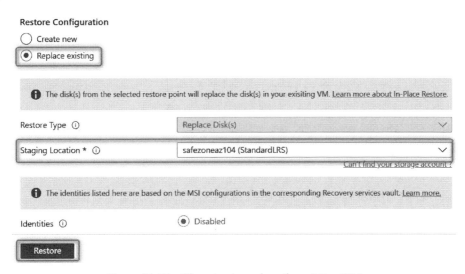

Figure 21.17 – Choosing to replace the existing VM

With that, we have successfully restored a VM via Backup center in the Azure portal.

I We encourage you to learn more by going to the following links regarding Azure Backup:

- https://docs.microsoft.com/en-us/azure/backup/backup-
  azure-vms-automation

- https://docs.microsoft.com/en-us/azure/backup/backup-
  center-overview

In this section, we learned how to perform backup and restore operations via Backup center in the Azure portal.

Performing site-to-site recovery via Azure Site Recovery

Azure Site Recovery is intended to be used as part of an organization's disaster recovery or business continuity plans, which it does by ensuring applications and workloads are accessible during outages. A simple example of Site Recovery would be to replicate a VM from the primary region to the secondary region. If the primary region goes offline, you can failover to the secondary region without issue.

> **Note**
> Azure Site Recovery can also be used to migrate on-premises VMs to Azure.

Let's go ahead and perform a site recovery:

1. Navigate to the Azure portal by opening a web browser and going to `https://portal.azure.com`. Select the Recovery Services vault we created in the *Creating a Recovery Services vault* section:

2. Click on **Enable Site Recovery**:

Figure 21.18 – Enable Site Recovery

3. Next, select **Enable replication** under **Azure virtual machines**. Here, set **Source location** to **East US**, **Azure virtual machine deployment model** to **Resource Manager**, **Source subscription** to **Demo** (select your subscription here), **Source resource group** to **Az-104**, and **Disaster recovery between availability zones** to **No**. Click **Next**:

Dashboard > Az104RecoveryServicesVault >

Enable replication ...

1 Source   (2) Virtual machines   (3) Replication settings

Source location * (i)	East US ∨
Azure virtual machine deployment model * (i)	Resource Manager ∨
Source subscription * (i)	Demo ∨
Source resource group * (i)	Az-104 ∨
Disaster Recovery between Availability Zones? * (i)	No ∨
Availability Zones (i)	Select ∨

Previous   Next

Figure 21.19 – Site recovery replication settings

4. Select your VM and make sure it has been started. In my case, this will be **prod-vm1**. Click **Next**:

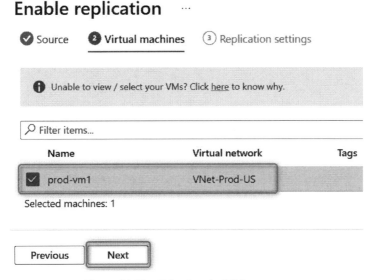

Figure 21.20 – Selecting the VM resource

5. Next, set **Target location** to **West US** and click **Enable replication**:

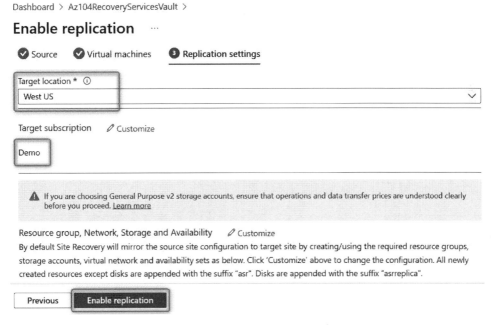

Figure 21.21 – Enabling site-to-site replication

6. Once you've done this, you will notice that a new resource group has been created with the suffix -asr. In my case, it is Az-104-asr, which has a virtual network and the OS disk of the VM we configured as part of the site recovery options.

7. To confirm that site recovery has been completed successfully, browse to Az104RecoveryServicesVault and select **Site Recovery Dashboard**. Here, you should see charts for **Replication health** and **Failover health**:

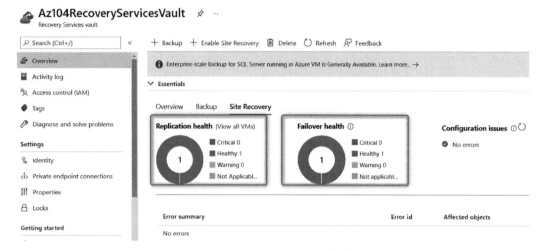

Figure 21.22 – Site-to-site recovery health status

8. Once the resources have been replicated, you can click on the **Failover** or **Test Failover** button to simulate or initiate an actual failover, respectively:

Figure 21.23 – Failover options

With that, we have configured Azure site recovery and know how to initiate a failover.

We encourage you to read up on Azure site recovery by going to the following links:

- `https://azure.microsoft.com/en-us/services/site-recovery/#overview`

- `https://docs.microsoft.com/en-us/azure/site-recovery/site-recovery-overview`

In this section, we learned how to perform failover operations via the Azure portal.

Configuring and reviewing backup reports

In the *Creating and configuring backup policies* section, we learned how to configure backups using Azure Backup. Now, we are going to learn how to configure backup reports to forecast cloud storage and auditing for backup and restore operations.

Let's go ahead and configure backup reports via Backup center in the Azure portal:

1. Navigate to the Azure portal by opening a web browser and going to `https://portal.azure.com`. Choose to **Create a new resource**.

2. Search for and select **Log Analytics Workspace (LAW)**:

Create a resource   ···

Figure 21.24 – Creating a Log Analytics Workspace (LAW)

3. After clicking on **Create**, configure the following settings and click **Review and create**:

   - **Subscription**: Demo (Select your subscription)

   - **Resource group**: Az-104

   - **Name**: BackupLAW

- **Region**: East US:

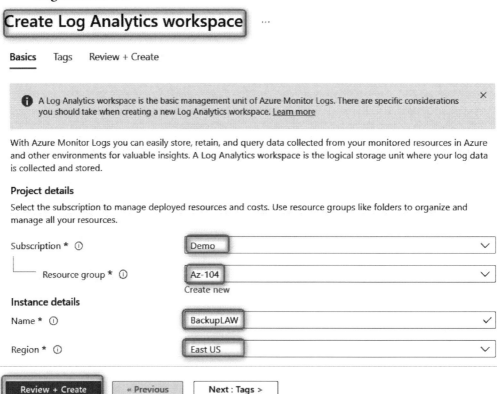

Figure 21.25 – Log Analytics Workspace configuration settings

4. Once your Log Analytics Workspace has been created successfully, search for and select **Backup center** within the Azure portal:

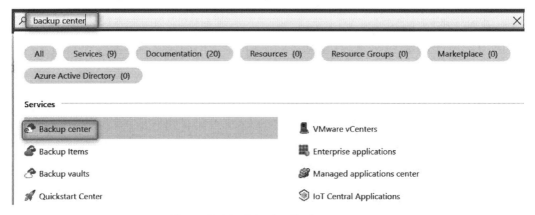

Figure 21.26 – Selecting Backup center

5. Next, select **Vaults** and select your vault that is used for backups. In my case, this is `Az104RecoveryServicesVault`.

6. Under **Monitoring**, select **Diagnostic settings** and select **Add diagnostic setting**:

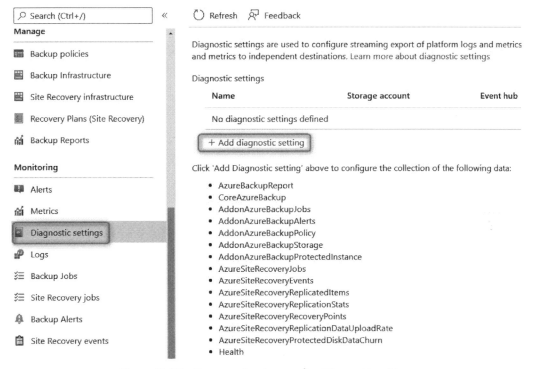

Figure 21.27 – Recovery Services vault – Diagnostic settings

7. Give the diagnostic setting a name, such as `VaultDiagnostics`, and select the following options:

- `CoreAzureBackup`

- `AddonAzureBackupJobs`

- `AddonAzureBackupAlerts`

- `AddonAzureABackupStorage`

- `AddonAzureBackupProtectedInstance`

- `Send to Log Analytics Workspace` and select the `BackupLAW` workspace we created earlier

8. Click on **Save**:

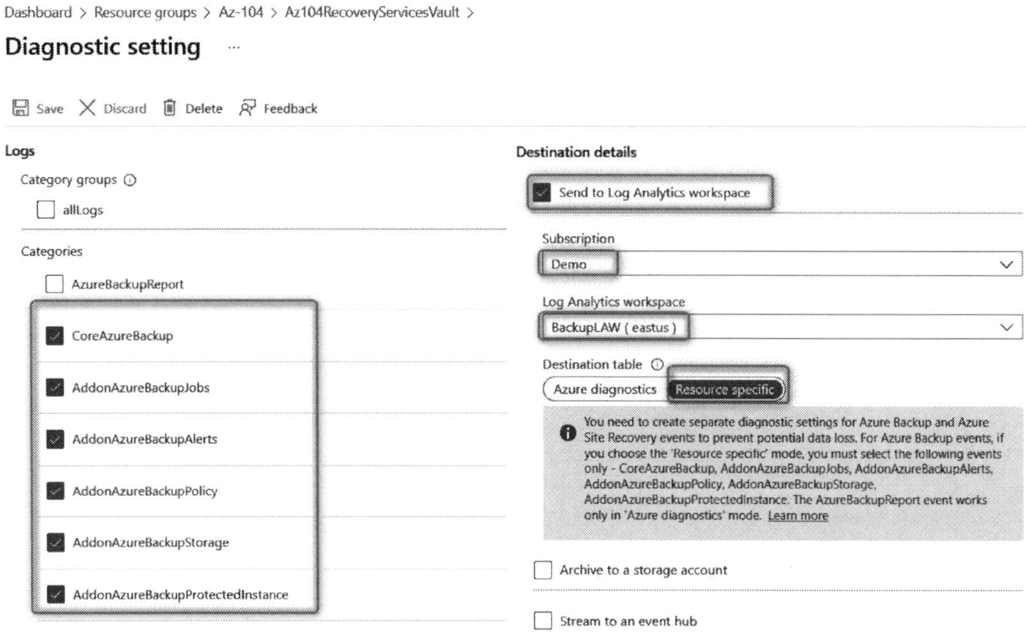

Figure 21.28 – Recovery Services vault – Diagnostic setting configuration

9. Under **Manage**, select **Backup reports**.

10. On the **Overview** page, select the subscription and newly created LAW (**BackupLAW**). It will pull all the backup data into the report.

With that, we have learned how to configure Azure Backup reports.

In this section, we learned how to create and configure backup reports via the Azure portal. We encourage you to read up on Azure Backup reports by going to the following links:

- `https://docs.microsoft.com/en-us/azure/backup/configure-reports`

- `https://docs.microsoft.com/en-us/azure/backup/backup-reports-email`

Summary

In this chapter, we discussed what Recovery Services vaults are and how to configure them, as well as what Azure Backup is and how it works, including how to configure a backup policy. We addressed how to perform backup and restore operations by using Azure Backup. We also addressed how to perform site-to-site recovery via the Azure portal and how to configure backup reports.

Now that you have read this chapter and followed along with the hands-on demos, you should be able to implement backups and recover them, as well as deploy Azure infrastructure.

In the next chapter, we'll learn how to configure a lab environment with Azure Backup and Azure site recovery while completing some hands-on examples.

22

Practice Labs – Monitoring and Backing Up Azure Resources

In this chapter, we are going to look at how we can get our hands dirty and implement some of the things we learned around Azure Backup, **Azure Site Recovery** (**ASR**), and practical management tips.

In this chapter, we are going to cover the following main topics:

- Azure Recovery Services Vault with **virtual machine** (**VM**) backup lab
- Azure Monitor lab

Technical requirements

The technical requirements for this chapter are as follows:

- Access to an Azure subscription with global administrator and billing administrator privileges. If you do not have access to one, you can enroll for a free account: `https://azure.microsoft.com/en-in/free/`.

- PowerShell 3.6.1 or later installed on a PC from which labs can be practiced. Note that many examples can only be followed from a PC. Alternatively, you can use `https://shell.azure.com`.

- Installation of the AZ module can be performed by running the following code in an administrative PowerShell session:

```
Set-ExecutionPolicy -ExecutionPolicy RemoteSigned -Scope
CurrentUser
Install-Module -Name Az -Scope CurrentUser -Repository
PSGallery -Force
```

- Download the following ZIP files and extract them somewhere that is easily accessible to you. If you have done this in previous labs, it is no longer required to perform this step. For assistance in downloading and extracting, we have the following steps for guidance.

> **Note**
>
> Even though the labs are on GitHub, no GitHub account is required to access the labs.

Downloading and extracting files for labs

Follow these steps to download and extract the files:

1. Navigate to the following URL and download the archive folder (`.zip`): `https://github.com/MicrosoftLearning/AZ-104-MicrosoftAzureAdministrator/archive/master.zip`.

2. Depending on the browser you are using, you will likely be presented with different versions of the following dialog. Click **Save File** and **OK** at the bottom of the screen:

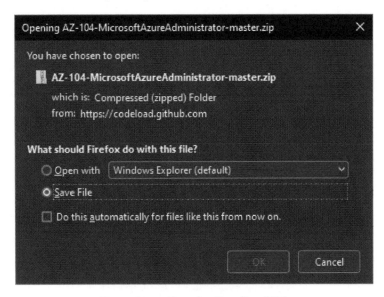

Figure 22.1 – Downloading files (ZIP)

3. Right-click on the ZIP file you downloaded, and click **Extract All...** (on Windows systems):

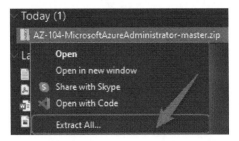

Figure 22.2 – Extract All (ZIP)

4. Navigate to your downloaded folder and follow the instructions from GitHub labs as these files that are required will be in that folder

You have downloaded all the files you need for performing the labs later in the chapter.

Azure Recovery Services Vault with VM backup lab

This lab will guide you through creating a VM and recovery vault in Azure. They will be separated across two resource groups and a backup policy implemented for the VM to the vault. You will be configuring file and folder backups as well as recovery of these back to your VM. In addition to this, you will recover a VM from a snapshot and explore the soft delete options inside of the Azure Recovery vault under Backup services.

Estimated time: 50 minutes

Lab method: PowerShell and the Azure portal

Lab scenario: In this lab, you play the role of an administrator who has been asked to assess Azure Recovery Services. You will need to assess its ability to backup and restore files. You will also assess its capability to restore VMs both using snapshots and the soft delete functionality.

Visit the following link (**Lab URL**) to the official Microsoft learning GitHub labs, where you will be guided through each task step by step to achieve the preceding objective.

Lab objectives:

 I. **Task 1**: Provision your environment resources (resource group, VNets, and VMs)

 II. **Task 2**: Set up your Azure Recovery Services vault

 III. **Task 3**: Configure the Recovery agent

 IV. **Task 4**: Configure file and folder backup

 V. **Task 5**: Recover files

 VI. **Task 6**: Recover files using snapshots

 VII. **Task 7**: Review the soft delete functionality

Lab URL: `https://microsoftlearning.github.io/AZ-104-MicrosoftAzureAdministrator/Instructions/Labs/LAB_10-Implement_Data_Protection.html`

Lab architecture diagram:

The following diagram illustrates the different steps involved in the exercise:

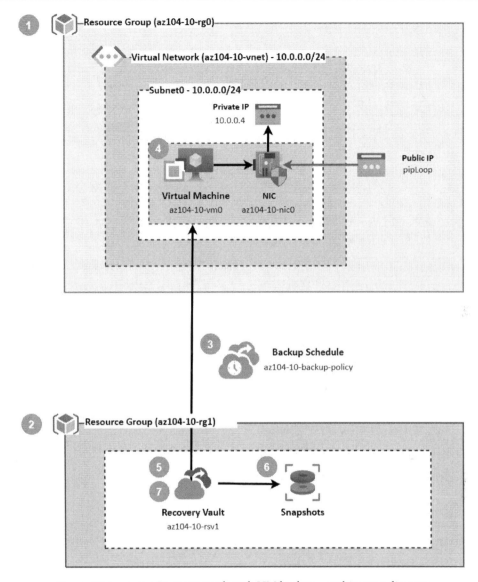

Figure 22.3 – Azure Recovery vault with VM backup – architecture diagram

You have now explored how to implement a Recovery vault within Azure and how to use this for your backup services on your VM, setting up a backup schedule, and even restoring the data. You have seen how easy it is to work with these services and should feel confident in employing this in your environments.

Azure Monitor lab

This lab will guide you through creating a VM and setting up Azure Monitor in Azure. You will configure diagnostic settings and export these to Log Analytics and review various mechanisms to analyze data about your environment.

Estimated time: 45 minutes

Lab method: PowerShell and the Azure portal

Lab scenario: In this lab, you play the role of an administrator who has been asked to provide analytical data regarding the performance and configuration of resources deployed within Azure. Your primary focus will be on VMs. You conclude that Azure Monitor may be able to fulfill your requirements and you look to assess the capabilities of Azure Monitor combined with Log Analytics to assist you in your mandate.

Visit the following link (**Lab URL**) to the official Microsoft learning GitHub labs, and you will be guided through each task step by step to achieve the preceding objective.

Lab objectives:

I. **Task 1**: Provision your environment resources (resource group, VNets, and VMs)

II. **Task 2**: Register the required resource providers for your subscription

III. **Task 3**: Set up Log Analytics

IV. **Task 4**: Evaluate default monitoring on VMs

V. **Task 5**: Configure VM diagnostics

VI. **Task 6**: Assess the functionality of Azure Monitor

VII. **Task 7**: Assess the functionality of Log Analytics

Lab URL: `https://microsoftlearning.github.io/AZ-104-MicrosoftAzureAdministrator/Instructions/Labs/LAB_11-Implement_Monitoring.html`

Lab architecture diagram:

The following diagram illustrates the different steps involved in the exercise:

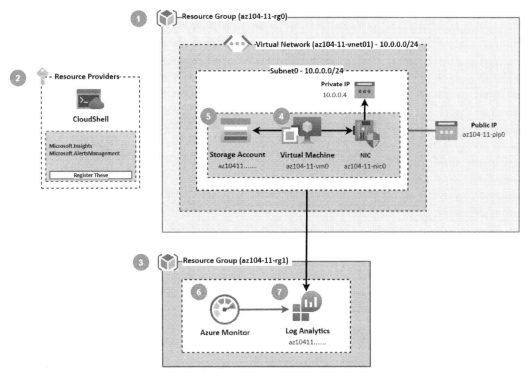

Figure 22.4 – Azure Monitor lab – architecture diagram

You have now explored how Azure Monitor can assist you in the operational monitoring of your systems and the various systems you can use to consume the metric data relating to the services you have. Working with these takes lots of practice and is something that you will use frequently in your role. Continue to practice and explore this to become an expert and explore third-party tools that can further extend the functionality you derive from having these metrics exposed to you.

It is best practice to remove unused resources to ensure that there are no unexpected costs, even though resources created in this lab do not incur additional costs.

Summary

In this chapter, we explored working with Azure Recovery vaults for implementing backups, testing the backup of files, and restoring these. You also explored Azure Monitor and the capabilities it presents to you. Now that you have hands-on experience working on both these services within Azure, you should feel confident in delivering Azure Site Recovery within your daily role and activities. Both services provide key administrative supporting services that are critical to all organizations, and it will be beneficial to practice these skills frequently.

In the next part of the book, we'll cover some mock questions and answers to prepare you for taking the AZ104 exam.

23
Mockup Test Questions and Answers

This chapter covers important practice questions that will prove helpful for preparing for the exam.

Managing Azure identities and governance (15-20%)

Let's go through some of the key questions related to Azure identities and governance that can help from an exam point of view:

1. You are the administrator for Contoso Airlines. You have an environment in your Azure subscription named `Contoso-Azure-Subscription`:

Resource	Resource Group	Region	Lock Type
Storage account	pre-production-1-rg	East-US	None
Virtual Machine Disk	pre-production-1-rg	East-US	None
Virtual Network	pre-production-2-rg	East-US	Read-Only
None	production-rg-1	West Europe	Delete-Lock
None	production-rg-2	South Africa North	None

Name	Role
ContosoAdmin1	Owner at the subscription level
ContosoAdmin2	Security Adminstrator at the subscription level
ContosoAdmin3	Network Contributor at the subscription level

Figure 23.1 – Contoso-Azure-Subscription resources

You plan to create a new virtual network in the `production-rg-2` resource group. Which of the following administrators would be able to add another subnet to the virtual network?

A. `ContosoAdmin1` only

B. `ContosoAdmin2` only

C. `ContosoAdmin3` only

D. `ContosoAdmin1` and `ContosoAdmin2` only

E. `ContosoAdmin2` and `ContosoAdmin3` only

F. `ContosoAdmin1` and `ContosoAdmin3` only

G. `ContosoAdmin1`, `ContosoAdmin2`, and `ContosoAdmin3`

2.   You are the administrator for Contoso Airlines. You have an environment in your Azure subscription named `Contoso-Azure-Subscription`:

Resource	Resource Group	Region	Lock Type
Storage account	pre-production-1-rg	East-US	None
Virtual Machine Disk	pre-production-1-rg	East-US	None
Virtual Network	pre-production-2-rg	East-US	Read-Only
None	production-rg-1	West Europe	Delete-Lock
None	production-rg-2	South Africa North	None

Name	Role
ContosoAdmin1	Owner at the subscription level
ContosoAdmin2	Security Adminstrator at the subscription level
ContosoAdmin3	Network Contributor at the subscription level

Figure 23.2 – Contoso-Azure-Subscription resources

You plan to create a new virtual network in the `production-rg-2` resource group. Which of the following administrators would be able to assign additional users to the virtual network?

A. `ContosoAdmin1` only

B. `ContosoAdmin2` only

C. `ContosoAdmin3` only

D. `ContosoAdmin1` and `ContosoAdmin2` only

E. `ContosoAdmin2` and `ContosoAdmin3` only

F. `ContosoAdmin1` and `ContosoAdmin3` only

G. `ContosoAdmin1`, `ContosoAdmin2`, and `ContosoAdmin3`

3. You are the administrator for Contoso Airlines. You have an environment in your Azure subscription named `Contoso-Azure-Subscription`. The management locks are set at the resource group level:

Resource	Resource Group	Region	Lock Type
Storage account	pre-production-1-rg	East-US	None
Virtual Machine Disk	pre-production-1-rg	East-US	None
Virtual Network	pre-production-2-rg	East-US	Read-Only
None	production-rg-1	West Europe	Delete-Lock
None	production-rg-2	South Africa North	None

Name	Role
ContosoAdmin1	Owner at the subscription level
ContosoAdmin2	Security Adminstrator at the subscription level
ContosoAdmin3	Network Contributor at the subscription level

Figure 23.3 – Contoso-Azure-Subscription resources

The company plans to move all the resources in the `pre-production-1-rg` resource group to the `pre-production-2-rg` resource group. True or False: *The move will be successful.*

A. True

B. False

4. You are the administrator for Contoso Airlines. You have an environment in your Azure subscription named `Contoso-Azure-Subscription`. The management locks are set at the resource group level:

Resource	Resource Group	Region	Lock Type
Storage account	pre-production-1-rg	East-US	None
Virtual Machine Disk	pre-production-1-rg	East-US	None
Virtual Network	pre-production-2-rg	East-US	Read-Only
None	production-rg-1	West Europe	Delete-Lock
None	production-rg-2	South Africa North	None

Name	Role
ContosoAdmin1	Owner at the subscription level
ContosoAdmin2	Security Adminstrator at the subscription level
ContosoAdmin3	Network Contributor at the subscription level

Figure 23.4 – Contoso-Azure-Subscription resources

The company plans to move the storage account in the `pre-production-1-rg` resource group to the `production-1-rg` resource group. True or False: *The move will be successful.*

A. True

B. False

The following set of questions is based on a scenario. There are multiple questions related to the same scenario. Please read the questions carefully.

You are the Azure administrator at Contoso Airlines. Contoso Airlines has a subscription named **Production** and three resource groups called **US**, **EU**, and **APAC**. You have been asked to create a custom **role-based access control (RBAC)** role based on the Virtual Machine Contributor role. This custom role must be assigned to the **EU** resource group.

Complete the following PowerShell script to achieve the required result:

```
$role =          SLOT 1          "          SLOT 2          "
$role.Id = $null
$role.Name = "VM Custom"
$role.Description = "Can monitor and restart virtual machines."
$role.Actions.Clear()
$role.Actions.Add("Microsoft.Storage/*/read")
$role.Actions.Add("Microsoft.Network/*/read")
$role.Actions.Add("Microsoft.Compute/*/read")
$role.Actions.Add("Microsoft.Compute/virtualMachines/start/action")
$role.Actions.Add("Microsoft.Compute/virtualMachines/restart/action")
$role.Actions.Add("Microsoft.Authorization/*/read")
$role.Actions.Add("Microsoft.ResourceHealth/availabilityStatuses/read")
$role.Actions.Add("Microsoft.Resources/subscriptions/resourceGroups/read")
$role.Actions.Add("Microsoft.Insights/alertRules/*")
$role.Actions.Add("Microsoft.Support/*")
$role.AssignableScopes.Clear()
$role.AssignableScopes.Add("/          SLOT 3          ")
          SLOT 4          -Role $role
```

Figure 23.5 – PowerShell script to create a custom RBAC

1. As per *Figure 23.5*, what should be in slot 1?

   A. `New-AZRoleDefinition`

   B. Az role definition

   C. `Set-AZRoleDefinition`

   D. `Get-AZRoleDefinition`

2. As per *Figure 23.5*, what should be in slot 2?

   A. Virtual Machine Contributor

   B. Virtual Machine Reader

   C. `Production/EU`

   D. `subscription/production/resourcegroups/EU`

3. As per *Figure 23.5*, what should be in slot 3?

    A. Virtual Machine Contributor

    B. Virtual Machine Reader

    C. Production/EU

    D. subscription/production/resourcegroups/EU

4. As per *Figure 23.5*, what should be in slot 4?

    A. New-AZRoleDefinition

    B. Az Role definition

    C. Set-AZRoleDefinition

    D. Get-AZRoleDefinition

5. As per *Figure 23.5*, what syntax should be present in slot 1?

    A. Microsoft.Authorization/*/read

    B. Microsoft.Authorization/read/

    C. Microsoft.Authorization/*

    D. Microsoft.Authorization/read/*

6. As per *Figure 23.5*, what syntax should be present in slot 2?

    A. Microsoft.Resources/subscriptions/ *

    B. Microsoft.Resources/subscriptions/resourcegroups/read

    C. Microsoft.Resources/subscriptions/resourcegroups/*

    D. Microsoft.Resources/subscriptions/read

7. As per *Figure 23.5*, what syntax should be present in slot 3?

    A. Microsoft.Support/*/*

    B. Microsoft.Support/*

    C. Microsoft.Support/read/*

    D. Microsoft.Support/write/*

Implement and manage storage (15-20%)

Let's go through some of the key questions related to implementing and managing storage in Azure that can help from an exam point of view.

The following set of questions is based on a scenario. There are multiple questions related to the same scenario. Please read the questions carefully.

You are the administrator for the ACME shipping company. You are in the process of creating a **Shared Access Signature (SAS)** for the storage account named **Shipping**:

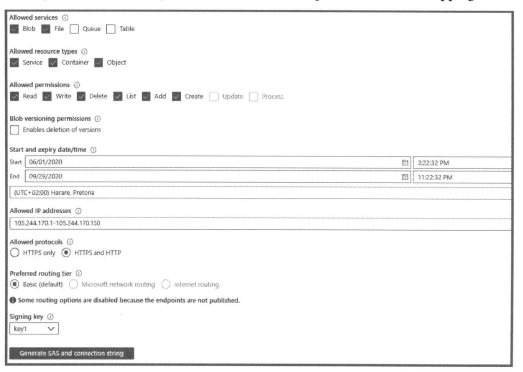

Figure 23.6 – SAS configuration

Based on the preceding screenshot, answer the following questions:

1. True or False: *The SAS that's been created is considered best practice.*

    A. True

    B. False

2. True or False: *If you connect via Storage Explorer from public IP* `105.244.170.39` *on September 29, 2020, at 11 P.M., you will be able to create a new blob container.*

   A. True

   B. False

3. True or False: *If you connect via Storage Explorer from public IP* `105.244.170.39` *on September 29, 2020, at 11 P.M., you will be able to create a new blob container.*

   A. True

   B. False

4. True or False: *If you connect via Storage Explorer from public IP* `105.244.170.39` *on September 30, 2020, at 11 A.M., you will be able to create table storage.*

   A. True

   B. False

5. True or False: *All Azure general-purpose V1 and V2 storage accounts are encrypted automatically.*

   A. True

   B. False

Deploy and manage Azure compute resources (20-25%)

Let's go through some of the key questions related to deploying and managing Azure compute resources that can help from an exam point of view:

1. You are the administrator for the ACME shipping company. You have been tasked with deploying an application in the production subscription. The application has the following requirements:

   - Protect against a single point of failure

   - Comply with a 99.99% **Service-Level Agreement (SLA)**

   Which of the following solutions will suffice?

   A. Deploy burstable virtual machines

   B. Deploy virtual machines in an availability set

C. Deploy virtual machines behind a single public IP address that resides on a next-generation firewall

D. Deploy virtual machines across availability zones

E. Deploy virtual machines that have public IPs assigned directly to each virtual machine

The following set of questions is based on a scenario. There are multiple questions related to the same scenario. Please read the questions carefully.

You are the administrator for Contoso Airlines. You decide to make your life easier by making use of PowerShell scripts to automate the installation of the IIS role on your Windows servers.

You need to complete the following script:

```
    SLOT 1        -ResourceGroupName "myResourceGroupAutomate"
-ExtensionName "IIS"
-VMName "myVM"
-Location "EastUS"
-   SLOT 2    Microsoft.Compute
-ExtensionType CustomScriptExtension
-TypeHandlerVersion 1.8
-   SLOT 3        '{"commandToExecute":"powershell Add-WindowsFeature Web-Server"}'
```

Figure 23.7 – PowerShell script to install the IIS role on Windows servers

Based on the preceding screenshot, answer the following questions:

2. As per the preceding screenshot, what command should be present in slot 1?

    A. `Get-AZVMExtension`

    B. `Set-AZVmExtension`

    C. `Set-AZVMAccessExtension`

    D. `New-AzVm`

3. As per the preceding screenshot, what command should be present in slot 2?

    A. `OS-Version`

    B. `VM-Type`

    C. `OS-Type`

    D. `Publisher-Type`

    E. `Publisher`

4. As per the preceding screenshot, what command should be present in slot 3?

   A. `New-Config`

   B. `New-AzDiskConfig`

   C. `String`

   D. `Setting`

   E. `SettingString`

5. You are the administrator for Contoso Airlines. You have been asked to add two additional network interface cards with static public IP addresses to a production virtual machine that is running in the East-US region. What do you need to do to make this change?

   A. Disassociate the current virtual network interface card

   B. Restart the virtual machine

   C. Disassociate the current public IP address on the virtual network interface card

   D. Shut down the virtual machine and associate the additional network interface cards with public IPs

   E. Remove the current Network Security Group

6. You are the administrator for Contoso Airlines. You have been asked to deploy an Azure Kubernetes cluster. The requirements are as follows:

   - The virtual network for the AKS cluster must allow outbound connectivity.

   - You have limited IP address space, so you need to ensure that the nodes get an IP address from the Azure VNet subnet. This should result in pods receiving IP addresses from a different address space.

   Which of the following solutions meets these requirements?

   A. Network Security Groups

   B. Kubenet

   C. Azure **Container Network Interface (CNI)**

   D. Azure Load Balancer

7. You are the administrator for Contoso Airlines. You have been asked to deploy an Azure Kubernetes cluster. The requirements are as follows:

   - The virtual network for the AKS cluster must allow outbound connectivity

   - Avoid managing **user-defined routes (UDRs)**

- Most of the pod communication is to resources outside of the cluster

- Pods must make use of the IP addressing from the subnet and be directly accessible

Which of the following solutions meets these requirements?

A. Network Security Groups

B. Kubenet

C. Azure CNI

D. Azure Load Balancer

8. You are the administrator for the ACME shipping company. You have been asked to deploy an international application to a set of four virtual machines. The application should have high availability to ensure that two virtual machines are always available in the event of a failure in one of the data centers.

You decide to deploy the virtual machines as part of three availability zones.

True or False: *This solution meets the requirements.*

A. True

B. False

9. You are the administrator for the ACME shipping company. You have been asked to deploy an international application to a set of four virtual machines. The application should have high availability to ensure that two virtual machines are always available in the event of a failure in one of the data centers.

You decide to deploy the virtual machines as part of an availability set.

True or False: *This solution meets the requirements.*

A. True

B. False

10. You are the administrator for the ACME shipping company. You have been asked to deploy an international application to a set of four virtual machines. The application should have high availability to ensure that two virtual machines are always available in the event of a failure in one of the data centers.

You decide to deploy the virtual machines with managed disks in an availability set.

True or False: *This solution meets the requirements.*

A. True

B. False

11. You are the administrator for the ACME shipping company. You have been asked to deploy an international application to a set of four virtual machines. The application should have high availability to ensure that two virtual machines are always available in the event of a failure in one of the data centers.

    You decide to deploy one virtual machine behind a load balancer.

    True or False: *This solution meets the requirements.*

    A. True

    B. False

12. True or False: *You can connect a network interface card to a virtual network that's been deployed to a different region.*

    A. True

    B. False

13. True or False: *When deploying a virtual machine with its network interface card to a virtual network, the virtual network and virtual machine must exist in the same region.*

    A. True

    B. False

The following set of questions is based on a scenario. There are multiple questions related to the same scenario. Please read the questions carefully.

You are the administrator for the ACME shipping company. You have been asked to create a script that will deploy 35 virtual machines to an availability set. The following are the requirements for the script:

- Maximize the availability of all VMs across the availability set in the event of a VM failure

- Maximize the availability of all VMs across the availability set in the event of underlying system updates

The following screenshot shows the script you need to complete:

```json
{
  "$schema": "https://schema.management.azure.com/schemas/2019-04-01/deploymentTemplate.json#",
  "contentVersion": "1.0.0.0",
  "parameters": {
    "location": {
      "type": "string",
      "defaultValue": "[resourceGroup().location]",
      "metadata": {
        "description": "Location for all resources."
      }
    }
  },
  "resources": [
    {
      "type": "Microsoft.Compute/availabilitySets",
      "name": "availabilitySet1",
      "apiVersion": "2020-06-01",
      "location": "[parameters('location')]",
      "properties": {
        "                      SLOT 1        ": 3,
        "                      SLOT 2        ": 20
      }
    }
  ]
}
```

Figure 23.8 – ARM template to deploy virtual machines to an availability set

14. As per the preceding screenshot, what parameter is required in slot 1?

    A. `PlatformFaultDomainCount`

    B. `FaultDomainCount`

    C. `PlatformUpdateCount`

    D. `UpdateCount`

15. As per the preceding screenshot, what parameter is required in slot 2?

    A. `PlatformFaultDomainCount`

    B. `FaultDomainCount`

    C. `PlatformUpdateCount`

    D. `UpdateCount`

16. You are the administrator for Contoso Airlines. You have been asked to deploy three web applications for the development team. You decide to make use of Azure web apps in different subscriptions. The following are the requirements for web app one:

    ▪ Support two instances

    ▪ Support a custom domain

    ▪ Use the most cost-effective solution

Based on these requirements, which of the following App Service tiers do you require for web app one?

A. Free

B. Basic

C. Standard

D. Premium

E. Isolated

17. You are the administrator for Contoso Airlines. You have been asked to deploy three web applications for the development team. You decide to make use of Azure web apps in different subscriptions. The following are the requirements for web app two:

- Support five instances

- 14 GB disk space

- Use the most cost-effective solution

Based on these requirements, which of the following App Service tiers do you require for web app two?

A. Free

B. Basic

C. Standard

D. Premium

E. Isolated

18. You are the administrator for Contoso Airlines. You have been asked to deploy three web applications for the development team. You decide to make use of Azure web apps in different subscriptions. The following are the requirements for web app three:

- Support 11 instances

- 35 GB disk space

- Use the most cost-effective solution

Based on these requirements, which of the following App Service tiers do you require for web app three?

A. Free

B. Basic

C. Standard

D. Premium

E. Isolated

Configure and manage virtual networking (25-30%)

Let's go through some of the key questions related to configuring and managing virtual networking in Azure that can help from an exam point of view:

1. You are the administrator for Contoso Airlines. You have been asked to deploy two virtual machines behind an Azure load balancer for traffic on port 443. All maintenance will take place via RDP and should be sent to a virtual machine named prod1 behind the load balancer.

   What do you need to do to achieve the preceding requirements?

   A. Create an inbound **Network Address Translation (NAT)** rule

   B. Add another VM

   C. Create an outbound NAT rule

   D. Create and attach an additional public IP to prod1

   E. None of the above

2. You are the administrator for Contoso Airlines. You have been asked to deploy two virtual machines behind an Azure load balancer for traffic on port 443. Here, successive requests from the same client IP need to be handled by the same virtual machine.

   Based on the preceding requirement, which of the following solutions is required when configuring the load balancer?

   A. Backend Port

   B. Backend Pool

   C. Health Probe

D. Session Persistence

E. Floating IP

3. True or False: *You can use Traffic Manager to inspect traffic between two virtual machines.*

   A. True

   B. False

4. True or False: *You can use Network Watcher to inspect traffic between two virtual machines.*

   A. True

   B. False

5. You need to limit outbound HTTPS traffic to specific **fully qualified domain names (FQDNs)**. Which of the following technologies supports this?

   A. **Network Security Groups (NSGs)**

   B. **Application Security Groups (ASGs)**

   C. Azure Firewall

   D. **Just-in-Time VM Access (JIT VM Access)**

The following set of questions is based on a scenario. There are multiple questions related to the same scenario. Please read the questions carefully.

You are the administrator for Contoso Airlines. You need to do the following:

- Create a new virtual network named `UdemyNetwork` with an address space of `10.50.0.0/16`:

  - The virtual network only requires one subnet with a range of `10.50.0.0/16`

- Create a new private DNS zone named `private.udemytest.local`

- Create a link for the virtual network with the newly created private DNS zone

You decide to make use of an Azure CLI script to automate the preceding requirements.

You need to complete the following script:

```
[SLOT 1] vnet [SLOT 2] \
--resource-group UdemyRG
--location "West Europe" \
--name UdemyNetwork \
--address-prefix 10.50.0.0/16 \
--subnet-name "prodsubnet" \
--subnet-prefixes 10.50.0.0/16

[SLOT 3] create --resource-group "UdemyRG" \
--name "private.udemytest.local"

[SLOT 4] vnet create --resource-group "UdemyRG" \
--name DNSLink \
[SLOT 5] private.Udemytest.local \
--virtual-network "UdemyNetwork" \
-e true
```

Figure 23.9 – Azure CLI script to deploy virtual network resources

6. Based on the preceding script, which parameter is required in slot 1?

    A. Az DNS

    B. Az network

    C. Az domain

    D. Az create

7. Based on the preceding script, which parameter is required in slot 2?

    A. New

    B. Update

    C. Create

    D. Amend

8. Based on the preceding script, which parameter is required in slot 3?

    A. Az network private-DNS zone

    B. Az network private-DNS link

    C. Az network public-DNS zone

    D. Az network public-DNS link

9. Based on the preceding script, which parameter is required in slot 4?

    A. `Az network private-DNS zone`

    B. `Az network private-DNS link`

    C. `Az network public-DNS zone`

    D. `Az network public-DNS link`

10. Based on the preceding script, which parameter is required in slot 5?

    A. `DNS zone`

    B. `Zone`

    C. `DNS link`

    D. `Link`

11. True or False: *You need an agent on a virtual machine to make use of Azure Bastion.*

    A. True

    B. False

Monitor and back up Azure resources (10-15%)

Let's go through some of the key questions related to monitoring and backing up Azure resources that can help from an exam point of view:

1. You are the administrator for Fabrikam Publishers. You are responsible for all Azure resource backups. You decide to create a new backup policy that should back up all VMs where SQL servers are running. This policy needs to be able to only back up the data that has changed since the full backup. Which of the following policy types should be used?

    A. Azure Virtual Machine policy -> Differential backup

    B. SQL Server in Azure VM -> Differential backup

    C. SQL Server in Azure VM -> Log backup

    D. Azure Virtual Machine policy -> Full backup

2. You are the administrator for the Contoso Hotel group. You have an Azure virtual machine called `Tax_Returns` that has Azure Backup enabled. The branch manager has accidentally deleted an important file and requested that you recover that file. Which recovery method will be the fastest without disrupting the current VM and does not require additional resources to be created?

    A. File Recovery

    B. Restore VM

    C. Restore VHD

    D. Azure Site Recovery Failover

3. You are the administrator for Fabrikam Publishers. You are responsible for monitoring a web application called `HotelApp` in the `Production` subscription. You need to be alerted when the web app stops and send an email to an existing action group called `AdminActionGroup`. Which of the following statements will correctly configure the alert target, target hierarchy, and alert criteria?

    A. `Alert Target = All App Services, Target Hierarchy = "Production" > "HotelApp", Alert criteria = "Stop web app"`

    B. `Alert Target = All App Services, Target Hierarchy = "Production" > "HotelApp", Alert criteria = "Start web app"`

    C. `Alert Target = All App Services, Target Hierarchy = "Production" > "HotelApp", Alert criteria = "Restart web app"`

    D. `Alert Target = All App Services, Target Hierarchy = "Production" > "HotelApp", Alert criteria = "All admin operations"`

4. You are the administrator for Stark Enterprises. You are responsible for all VMs in the `Production` resource group. You plan to configure Azure Backups for the VMs. Which of the following are required to enable Azure VM backups? Choose all that apply.

    A. Recovery Services Vault

    B. Backup Policy

    C. Resource Group

    D. Retention Range

5. You are the administrator for Fabrikam. Your organization has a web application with the following requirements:

    Requirement 1: Fabrikam developers need to be able to see when users use the application, from which browser or operating system, and what pages they are most interested in.

    Which of the following Application Insight features could be used for **Requirement 1**?

    A. Funnels

    B. Cohorts

    C. Impact

    D. User Flows

    E. Users, Sessions, and Events

    F. Retention

6. True or False: *Azure Log Analytics agents can only collect telemetry data for Windows and Linux virtual machines in Azure.*

    A. True

    B. False

Mockup test answers

The following are the answers to the mockup test questions.

Manage Azure identities and governance

1. **Answer**: The correct answer is ContosoAdmin1 and ContosoAdmin3 only as the owner has permissions for the resources that are created within the subscription. ContosoAdmin3 has the Network Contributor role, which allows them to make changes to the network. ContosoAdmin2 is incorrect as this role is used to view and update security permissions for Azure Security Center, not virtual networks.

    More information can be found at https://docs.microsoft.com/en-us/azure/role-based-access-control/built-in-roles.

2. **Answer**: The correct answer is `ContosoAdmin1` only as this is the only role that has RBAC permissions. The Network Contributor role is incorrect as no Contributor roles have permission to manage RBAC access. The Security Administrator role is incorrect as this is used to view and update security permissions for Azure Security Center, not virtual networks.

    More information can be found at `https://docs.microsoft.com/en-us/azure/role-based-access-control/built-in-roles`.

3. **Answer**: True. Even though there is a read-only resource lock on the destination resource group – that is, `pre-production-2-rg` – the move will still succeed. This is a *gotcha* question as it is important to understand how resource locks work. It is important to understand that when you're using read-only locks, you can't add or remove resources traditionally; however, you can still move resources to a resource group with a read-only resource lock.

    More information can be found at `https://docs.microsoft.com/en-us/azure/azure-resource-manager/management/lock-resources`.

4. **Answer**: True. You will be able to move the storage account to the `production-1-rg` resource group as the lock type is set to delete only, which means you can do the move. However, you won't be able to delete the storage account once it is in `production-1-rg` due to the lock type.

5. **Answer**: `Get-AZRoleDefinition` is correct as we need to base this custom RBAC role on the Virtual Machine Contributor role template. `New-AZRoleDefinition` is incorrect as this command is used to create the new custom RBAC role. Az role definition is incorrect as this is an Azure CLI command that is used to create a custom RBAC role; the requirement is to use PowerShell. `Set-AZRoleDefinition` is incorrect as this command is used to modify a custom RBAC role; however, we first need to use the `Get-AZRoleDefinition` command to retrieve the role before creating/updating a custom role.

    More information can be found at `https://docs.microsoft.com/en-us/azure/role-based-access-control/custom-roles-powershell`.

6. **Answer**: The correct answer is Virtual Machine Contributor as the requirement is to base this template on the Virtual Machine Contributor template. Virtual Machine Reader is incorrect as this is not the template we should use as per the requirements. `Production/EU` is incorrect as these are not valid parameters. `subscription/production/resourcegroups/EU` is incorrect as although these are valid parameters, they should be in the `Assignable Scopes` section of the template.

More information can be found at `https://docs.microsoft.com/ en-us/azure/role-based-access-control/custom-roles- powershell#create-a-custom-role`.

7. **Answer**: The correct answer is `subscription/production/ resourcegroups/EU` as this RBAC role should only be assignable under the Production subscription and only be available for the resources in the EU resource group. `Production/EU` is incorrect as the syntax does not include the words `subscriptions` and `resourcegroups`. Virtual Machine Operator and Virtual Machine Reader are both incorrect as these are Azure roles and cannot be used in the Assignable Scopes section.

    More information can be found at `https://docs.microsoft.com/ en-us/azure/role-based-access-control/custom-roles- powershell#create-a-custom-role`.

8. **Answer**: `New-AZRoleDefinition` is correct as this parameter is required to create the new custom RBAC role. `Set-Az-RoleDefinition` and `Get-AZRoleDefinition` are incorrect as these are used to update an existing custom RBAC role or retrieve an existing custom RBAC role, respectively. However, in this instance, we are creating a brand new custom RBAC role. The Az role definition is incorrect as this is an Azure CLI command and is used to create a custom RBAC role; the requirement is to use PowerShell.

    More information can be found at `https://docs.microsoft.com/ en-us/azure/role-based-access-control/custom-roles- powershell#create-a-custom-role` and `https://docs.microsoft. com/en-us/cli/azure/role/definition?view=azure-cli-latest`.

9. **Answer**: The correct syntax for JSON format is `Microsoft.Authorization/*/ read` as you would need permission to read roles and role assignments. All the other options are incorrect as this is the only correct syntax option.

10. **Answer**: The correct answer is `Microsoft.Resources/subscriptions/ resourcegroups/read` as you would need to have read permissions to view all the resources within the resource groups. All the other syntax options are incorrect:

```
{
  "assignableScopes": [
    "/"
  ],
  "description": "Lets you create and manage Support requests",
  "id": "/subscriptions/{subscriptionId}/providers/Microsoft.Authorization/roleDefinitions/cfd33db0-aaaa-ffff-eeee-cdbdf3b6ff2f",
  "name": "cfd33db0-aaaa-ffff-eeee-cdbdf3b6ff2f",
  "permissions": [
    {
      "actions": [
        "Microsoft.Authorization/*/read",
        "Microsoft.Resources/subscriptions/resourceGroups/read",
        "Microsoft.Support/*"
      ],
      "notActions": [],
      "dataActions": [],
      "notDataActions": []
    }
  ],
  "roleName": "Support Request Contributor",
  "roleType": "BuiltInRole",
  "type": "Microsoft.Authorization/roleDefinitions"
}
```

Figure 23.10 – ARM template with read permissions on the Resource Group level

More information can be found at `https://docs.microsoft.com/en-us/ azure/role-based-access-control/built-in-roles#management- -governance`.

11. **Answer**: The correct answer is `Microsoft.Support/*` as you would need permission to create and update support tickets. All the other syntax options are incorrect:

```
{
  "assignableScopes": [
    "/"
  ],
  "description": "Lets you create and manage Support requests",
  "id": "/subscriptions/{subscriptionId}/providers/Microsoft.Authorization/roleDefinitions/cfd33db0-aaaa-ffff-eeee-cdbdf3b6ff2f",
  "name": "cfd33db0-aaaa-ffff-eeee-cdbdf3b6ff2f",
  "permissions": [
    {
      "actions": [
        "Microsoft.Authorization/*/read",
        "Microsoft.Resources/subscriptions/resourceGroups/read",
        "Microsoft.Support/*"
      ],
      "notActions": [],
      "dataActions": [],
      "notDataActions": []
    }
  ],
  "roleName": "Support Request Contributor",
  "roleType": "BuiltInRole",
  "type": "Microsoft.Authorization/roleDefinitions"
}
```

Figure 23.11 – ARM template with the support permission set to all

More information can be found at `https://docs.microsoft.com/en-us/ azure/role-based-access-control/built-in-roles#databases`.

Implement and manage storage

1. **Answer**: False. As per the screenshot, the allowed protocols are set to HTTPS and HTTP. HTTP is not considered a secure protocol. As recommended by the Azure team, you should always make use of HTTPS instead.

More information can be found at `https://docs.microsoft.com/en-us/ azure/storage/common/storage-sas-overview#best-practices- when-using-sas`.

2. **Answer**: True. You will be able to connect as the following requirements have been met: allowed IP addresses, start and expiry dates, as well as allowed resource types and allowed permissions.

    More information can be found at `https://docs.microsoft.com/en-us/ azure/storage/common/storage-sas-overview#best-practices- when-using-sas`.

3. **Answer**: True. You will be able to connect as the following requirements have been met: allowed IP addresses, start and expiry dates, as well as allowed resource types and allowed permissions.

    More information can be found at `https://docs.microsoft.com/en-us/ azure/storage/common/storage-sas-overview#best-practices- when-using-sas`.

4. **Answer**: False. Table storage is not allowed. The date specified is also past the allowed expiry date.

    More information can be found at `https://docs.microsoft.com/en-us/ azure/storage/common/storage-sas-overview#best-practices- when-using-sas`.

5. **Answer**: True. All Azure Storage accounts are encrypted by default using **Storage Service Encryption (SSE)**.

    More information can be found at `https://docs.microsoft.com/en-us/ azure/storage/common/storage-account-overview`.

6. **Answer**: Deploying virtual machines across availability zones is correct as this will protect the application from a single point of failure and provide an SLA of 99.99%. Deploying burstable VMs is incorrect as this will not meet the availability requirements. Deploying virtual machines behind a single IP address on a next-generation firewall is a good idea from a security point of view, but it will not assist with high availability and single points of failure. Deploying virtual machines with public IPs directly assigned is incorrect as this will not protect a single point of failure or meet the SLA requirements. This is also a big risk from a security point of view and you would be advised against it.

    More information can be found at `https://docs.microsoft.com/en-us/ azure/availability-zones/az-overview#availability-zones`.

7. **Answer**: `Set-AZVMExtension` is correct as this configures the Windows **Desired State Configuration (DSC)** extension on a virtual machine in a resource group. `Get-AZVMExtension` is incorrect as this will retrieve the properties of a virtual machine extension that's been installed on the VM. `Set-AZVMAccessExtension` is incorrect as this will add the **Virtual Machine Access (VMAccess)** extension to a virtual machine. `New-AzVM` is incorrect as this will create a new virtual machine:

```
Set-AzVMExtension -ResourceGroupName "myResourceGroupAutomate" `
    -ExtensionName "IIS" `
    -VMName "myVM" `
    -Location "EastUS" `
    -Publisher Microsoft.Compute `
    -ExtensionType CustomScriptExtension `
    -TypeHandlerVersion 1.8 `
    -SettingString '{"commandToExecute":"powershell Add-WindowsFeature Web-Server"}'
```

Figure 23.12 – Configuring DSC via the Set-AzVMExtension command

More information can be found at `https://docs.microsoft.com/en-us/azure/virtual-machines/windows/tutorial-automate-vm-deployment`.

8. **Answer**: `Publisher` is correct as this command is used to specify the publisher's name. All the other options are incorrect:

```
Set-AzVMExtension -ResourceGroupName "myResourceGroupAutomate" `
    -ExtensionName "IIS" `
    -VMName "myVM" `
    -Location "EastUS" `
    -Publisher Microsoft.Compute `
    -ExtensionType CustomScriptExtension `
    -TypeHandlerVersion 1.8 `
    -SettingString '{"commandToExecute":"powershell Add-WindowsFeature Web-Server"}'
```

Figure 23.13 – The correct switch to use to specify the publisher

More information can be found at `https://docs.microsoft.com/en-us/azure/virtual-machines/windows/tutorial-automate-vm-deployment`.

9. **Answer**: `SettingString` is correct as this command is used to specify the PowerShell command to install the Web-server role on the virtual machine. All the other options are incorrect:

```
Set-AzVMExtension -ResourceGroupName "myResourceGroupAutomate" `
    -ExtensionName "IIS" `
    -VMName "myVM" `
    -Location "EastUS" `
    -Publisher Microsoft.Compute `
    -ExtensionType CustomScriptExtension `
    -TypeHandlerVersion 1.8 `
    -SettingString '{"commandToExecute":"powershell Add-WindowsFeature Web-Server"}'
```

Figure 23.14 – The correct switch to use install the Web-server role via PowerShell

More information can be found at `https://docs.microsoft.com/en-us/azure/virtual-machines/windows/tutorial-automate-vm-deployment#automate-iis-install`.

10. **Answer**: The correct answer is to shut down the virtual machine and add the network interface cards that are associated with the public IP addresses. Disassociating the current network interface card is incorrect as you need at least one interface card associated at all times. Restarting the VM is incorrect as this will not add the required IPs. Disassociating the current public IP address is incorrect as this might break your session with the VM and is not required to achieve the required outcome. Removing the current NSG is incorrect as it is not a requirement to add additional network interfaces and public IPs.

More information can be found at `https://docs.microsoft.com/en-us/azure/virtual-network/virtual-network-network-interface-vm#add-a-network-interface-to-an-existing-vm`.

11. **Answer**: Kubenet is correct as this meets the requirements, especially since the pods will receive an IP address from a logically different address space that utilizes **Network Address Translation (NAT)** to communicate with resources on the virtual network. NSG and Azure load balancers are incorrect as these will not meet the requirements. Azure CNI is incorrect as this should be used when the IP address space is not limited as the IP address spacing must be unique, which means it takes up more IP addresses as opposed to using NAT.

More information can be found at `https://docs.microsoft.com/en-us/azure/aks/configure-kubenet` and `https://docs.microsoft.com/en-us/azure/aks/configure-kubenet#overview-of-kubenet-networking-with-your-own-subnet`.

12. **Answer**: Azure CNI is correct as this solution allows pods to make use of the IP address from the subnets and is directly accessible. Kubenet is incorrect as it works by using Network Address Translation. NSG and Azure load balancers are not the correct solutions.

More information can be found at `https://docs.microsoft.com/en-us/azure/aks/configure-azure-cni`.

13. **Answer**: True. Availability zones can be used to protect against data center-level failures.

More information can be found at `https://docs.microsoft.com/en-us/azure/virtual-machines/manage-availability#use-availability-zones-to-protect-from-datacenter-level-failures`.

14. **Answer**: False. Availability sets cannot protect virtual machines from data center failures. However, availability sets can protect against the failure of one or more VMs within a single data center.

    More information can be found at `https://docs.microsoft.com/en-us/azure/virtual-machines/manage-availability#configure-multiple-virtual-machines-in-an-availability-set-for-redundancy`.

15. **Answer**: False. Even if you use managed disks with availability sets, this cannot protect against data center-level failures.

    More information can be found at `https://docs.microsoft.com/en-us/azure/virtual-machines/manage-availability#use-managed-disks-for-vms-in-an-availability-set`.

16. **Answer**: False. Even by having a load balancer handling the traffic, if only one VM has been deployed and if it goes offline, there will be no redundancy for the application.

    More information can be found at `https://docs.microsoft.com/en-us/azure/virtual-machines/manage-availability#combine-a-load-balancer-with-availability-zones-or-sets`.

17. **Answer**: False. You can only assign a network interface to a virtual network that exists in the same subscription and region as the network interface card.

    More information can be found at `https://docs.microsoft.com/en-us/azure/virtual-network/virtual-network-network-interface#create-a-network-interface`.

18. **Answer**: True. The VM, along with its network interface card and the virtual network, must reside in the same region.

    More information can be found at `https://docs.microsoft.com/en-us/azure/virtual-network/virtual-network-network-interface#create-a-network-interface`.

19. **Answer**: The correct parameter is `PlatformFaultDomainCount` as three is the maximum amount of fault domains you can have for ARM deployments.

    More information can be found at `https://docs.microsoft.com/en-us/azure/virtual-machines/manage-availability#configure-multiple-virtual-machines-in-an-availability-set-for-redundancy`.

20. **Answer**: The correct parameter is `PlatformUpdateCount`. The maximum update domain count is 20 for ARM deployments.

More information can be found at `https://docs.microsoft.com/en-us/azure/virtual-machines/manage-availability#configure-multiple-virtual-machines-in-an-availability-set-for-redundancy`.

21. **Answer**: The correct tier is Basic as it supports up to three instances with a custom domain and is the most cost-effective based on the requirements.

More information can be found at `https://azure.microsoft.com/en-us/pricing/details/app-service/linux/`.

22. **Answer**: The correct tier is Standard as it supports up to 10 instances and 50 GB of disk space. It is also the most cost-effective based on the requirements.

More information can be found at `https://azure.microsoft.com/en-us/pricing/details/app-service/linux/`.

23. **Answer**: The correct tier is Premium as it supports up to 30 instances in supported regions and 250 GB of disk space. It is also the most cost-effective based on the requirements.

Configure and manage virtual networking (30-35%)

1. **Answer**: The correct answer is to create an inbound NAT rule for prod1 as this will allow RDP traffic to be sent to the required VM via port forwarding. Creating an additional VM is incorrect as this is not required and won't achieve the required outcome. Creating an outbound NAT rule is incorrect as we need an inbound rule as the VM sits behind the load balancer. Creating and attaching another public IP to prod1 is incorrect as this will bypass the requirement to make use of the load balancer and will expose the VM, which is a security risk.

More information can be found at `https://docs.microsoft.com/en-us/azure/load-balancer/tutorial-load-balancer-port-forwarding-portal#create-an-inbound-nat-port-forwarding-rule`.

2. **Answer**: The correct answer is session persistence as this will allow you to select the distribution of traffic. There are three options for session persistence: none, client IP, and client IP and protocol. The backend port and backend pool are incorrect as this will not allow you to enable session persistence, but rather add a VM to the backend pool or port. The health probe is incorrect as this is used to monitor the health status of the application. Floating IP is incorrect as this is Azure's term for a portion of what is known as **Direct Server Return (DSR)**.

   More information can be found at `https://docs.microsoft.com/en-us/azure/load-balancer/load-balancer-distribution-mode#configure-source-ip-affinity-settings/`.

3. **Answer**: False. Traffic Manager cannot be used to inspect traffic between virtual machines. However, it does have built-in monitoring for endpoints.

   More information can be found at `https://docs.microsoft.com/en-us/azure/traffic-manager/traffic-manager-monitoring`.

4. **Answer**: True. You can make use of Network Watcher to capture the traffic of a virtual machine and inspect it using a tool such as Wireshark.

   More information can be found at `https://docs.microsoft.com/en-us/azure/network-watcher/network-watcher-packet-capture-manage-portal#before-you-begin`.

5. **Answer**: Azure Firewall is correct as it supports limiting outbound HTTPS traffic to a specified list of FQDNs, including wildcards. This feature does not require SSL termination. NSG is incorrect as it cannot filter outbound traffic by FQDNs; instead, it does so by using IPs or grouped IPs, such as the `Internet` tag. ASG is incorrect as this feature allows you to group VMs to make managing inbound and outbound traffic easier. JIT VM Access is incorrect as this is used to access Azure VMs remotely. JIT VM Access automatically creates NSG rules to allow temporary access to resources (VMs).

   More information can be found at `https://docs.microsoft.com/en-us/azure/firewall/overview`.

6. **Answer**: The correct answer is Az network as you need to specify the network you are going to create.

7. **Answer**: The correct answer is Create as you need to create the network since it does not exist. All the other options are incorrect based on the script.

8. **Answer**: The correct answer is `Az network private-DNS zone` as this command is used to specify the new DNS zone. All the other options are incorrect based on the following script:

```
az network vnet create \
--resource-group UdemyRG
--location "West Europe" \
--name UdemyNetwork \
--address-prefix 10.50.0.0/16 \
--subnet-name "prodsubnet" \
--subnet-prefixes 10.50.0.0/16

az network private-dns zone create --resource-group "UdemyRG" \
--name "private.udemytest.local"

az network private-dns link vnet create --resource-group "UdemyRG" \
--name DNSLink \
--zone private.Udemytest.local \
--virtual-network "UdemyNetwork" \
-e true
```

Figure 23.15 – The correct command to specify the new DNS zone

More information can be found at `https://docs.microsoft.com/en-us/azure/dns/private-dns-getstarted-cli#create-a-private-dns-zone`.

9. **Answer**: The correct answer is `Az network private-DNS link` as this command is used to link the virtual network to the DNS zone. All the other options are incorrect based on the script.

10. **Answer**: Zone is correct as you need to specify the DNS zone you want to link to the DNS link. All the other options are incorrect based on the following script:

```
az network vnet create \
--resource-group UdemyRG
--location "West Europe" \
--name UdemyNetwork \
--address-prefix 10.50.0.0/16 \
--subnet-name "prodsubnet" \
--subnet-prefixes 10.50.0.0/16

az network private-dns zone create --resource-group "UdemyRG" \
--name "private.udemytest.local"

az network private-dns link vnet create --resource-group "UdemyRG" \
--name DNSLink \
--zone private.Udemytest.local \
--virtual-network "UdemyNetwork" \
-e true
```

Figure 23.16 – The correct switch to specify the DNS zone and link it to the DNS link

More information can be found at `https://docs.microsoft.com/en-us/azure/dns/private-dns-getstarted-cli#create-a-private-dns-zone`.

11. **Answer**: False. You do not need to install an agent or any software on your browser or Azure virtual machine.

    More information can be found at `https://docs.microsoft.com/en-us/azure/bastion/bastion-faq`.

Monitor and back up Azure resources

1. **Answer**: SQL Server in Azure VM is correct as this supports differential backup, which is required to only backup the data that has changed since the last full backup. SQL Server in Azure Log backup is incorrect as this will focus on log backup instead of differential data backup. Azure VM full backup policy is incorrect as this does not meet the requirements of differential backup as well as SQL backup running inside the VM. Azure VM differential backup is incorrect as only full backups are possible, no differential backups for Azure VMs.

   More information can be found at `https://docs.microsoft.com/en-us/azure/azure-monitor/app/usage-segmentation`.

2. **Answer**: File recovery is correct. We can download the script to create an SMB link to browse and recover the file. Restore VM will not suffice as this will take some time and require additional resources to be created. Restore VHD will not suffice as this will require some time and resources to mount. Azure Site Recovery will not suffice as the deleted file will replicate to the other region. This is the distinct difference between backup and failover.

3. **Answer**: Alert target is where you choose the web application – in this case, this is `HotelApp`. Target hierarchy is where you select which subscription the web app is residing in. Alert criteria are what you want to monitor. This includes the trigger you want to be notified about, which in this case is when the web app stops.

4. **Answer**: When configuring an Azure VM backup for the first time, you will need to create or link an existing Recovery Services vault as this is where the backups will be managed. A backup policy is required as this contains information such as the frequency of backups, as well as their retention periods. A resource group is required as this service needs to be linked to a resource group. Retention range is incorrect as this forms part of the backup policy criteria.

5. **Answer**: Users, Session, and Events is the correct feature as this can be used to find out when people use a web app, what pages they are most interested in, where they are located, and what browsers and operating systems they use. The **Cohorts** feature is incorrect as this feature provides a set of users, sessions, events, or operations that have something in common and where you have to analyze a specific set of users or events repeatedly. The impact feature is incorrect as this is used to analyze how load times and other properties influence conversion rates. The retention feature is incorrect as this helps you analyze how many users return to your app and how often they perform particular tasks or achieve goals. The User flows feature is incorrect as this is used to visualize how users navigate between the pages and features on your site.

6. **Answer**: False. Log analytics can be used to collect telemetry data from Windows and Linux machines in any cloud and on-premises environments.

   More information can be found at `https://docs.microsoft.com/en-us/azure/azure-monitor/platform/log-analytics-agent`.

Index

Packt.com

Subscribe to our online digital library for full access to over 7,000 books and videos, as well as industry leading tools to help you plan your personal development and advance your career. For more information, please visit our website.

Why subscribe?

- Spend less time learning and more time coding with practical eBooks and Videos from over 4,000 industry professionals

- Improve your learning with Skill Plans built especially for you

- Get a free eBook or video every month

- Fully searchable for easy access to vital information

- Copy and paste, print, and bookmark content

Did you know that Packt offers eBook versions of every book published, with PDF and ePub files available? You can upgrade to the eBook version at packt.com and as a print book customer, you are entitled to a discount on the eBook copy. Get in touch with us at customercare@packtpub.com for more details.

At www.packt.com, you can also read a collection of free technical articles, sign up for a range of free newsletters, and receive exclusive discounts and offers on Packt books and eBooks.

Other Books You May Enjoy

If you enjoyed this book, you may be interested in these other books by Packt:

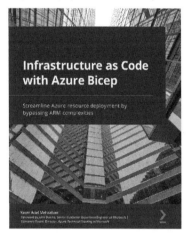

Infrastructure as Code with Azure Bicep

Yaser Adel Mehraban

ISBN: 978-1-80181-374-7

- Get started with Azure Bicep and install the necessary tools
- Understand the details of how to define resources with Bicep
- Use modules to create templates for different teams in your company
- Optimize templates using expressions, conditions, and loops
- Make customizable templates using parameters, variables, and functions
- Deploy templates locally or from Azure DevOps or GitHub
- Stay on top of your IaC with best practices and industry standards

Microsoft Azure Fundamentals Certification and Beyond

Steve Miles

ISBN: 978-1-80107-330-1

- Explore cloud computing with Azure cloud
- Gain an understanding of the core Azure architectural components
- Acquire knowledge of core services and management tools on Azure
- Get up and running with security concepts, security operations, and protection from threats
- Focus on identity, governance, privacy, and compliance features
- Understand Azure cost management, SLAs, and service life cycles

Packt is searching for authors like you

If you're interested in becoming an author for Packt, please visit `authors.packtpub.com` and apply today. We have worked with thousands of developers and tech professionals, just like you, to help them share their insight with the global tech community. You can make a general application, apply for a specific hot topic that we are recruiting an author for, or submit your own idea.

Share Your Thoughts

Now you've finished *Exam Ref AZ-104 Microsoft Azure Administrator Certification and Beyond*, we'd love to hear your thoughts! Scan the QR code below to go straight to the Amazon review page for this book and share your feedback or leave a review on the site that you purchased it from.

`https://packt.link/r/1-801-81954-8`

Your review is important to us and the tech community and will help us make sure we're delivering excellent quality content.

Made in the USA
Columbia, SC
10 October 2022

69252644R00424